FAMOUS
RUSSIAN
AIRCRAFT

TUPOLEV
Tu-95 & Tu-142

YEFIM GORDON
AND
DMITRIY KOMISSAROV

Tupolev Tu-95/Tu-142

strategic bomber

Yefim Gordon and Dmitriy Komissarov

First published in 2017 by
Hikoki Publications Ltd
1a Ringway Trading Est
Shadowmoss Rd
Manchester
M22 5LH
England

Email: enquiries@crecy.co.uk
www.crecy.co.uk

Layout by Polygon Press Ltd., Moscow
Colour profiles: Sergeu Ignat'yev and Viktor Mil'yachenko
Line drawings: Tupolev JSC, Pavel Mikhailov and Andrey Yurgenson

ISBN 9 781857 803785

Printed in Malta by Melita Press

Title page: All Russian Air Force Tu-95MSs with enough service life remaining are now being upgraded to carry Kh-101/Kh-102 cruise missiles externally.

Right: Russian Air Force Tu-95MS '20 Red'/RF-94122 *Doobna* taxies in after a training sortie. The Nos. 1 and 4 engines have been shut down already to save fuel.

Table of Contents

Acknowledgements

This book is illustrated with photos by Yefim Gordon, Sergey Aleksandrov, Vitaliy Alyab'yev, Vyacheslav Babayevskiy, Alex Beltyukov, Vyacheslav Bulochnikov, Vladislav Dmitrenko, Anton Dovbush, Viktor Drushlyakov, Aleksandr Dzhus, Mikhail Gribovskiy, Mike Gordon, Dmitriy Kazakov, Yevgeniy Kazyonnov, Aleksandr Khitrov, Dmitriy Komissarov, Sergey Komissarov, Sergey Krivchikov, Aleksandr Mishin, Dmitriy Pichugin, Oleg Podkladov, Sergey Popsuyevich, Dmitriy Ryazanov, Vadim Savitskiy, Sergey Sergeyev, Sergey Skrynnikov, Konstantin Tyurpeko, Sanat Gaba, as well as from the Russian State Archive of the Economy (RGAE), the Russian State Archive of Scientific & Technical Documents (RGANTD), the archives of the Tupolev JSC, the Beriyev TANTK, RSK MiG, the Mikhail M. Gromov Flight Research Institute (LII), the TASS News Agency, the RIA Novosti News Agency, the US Air Force, the US Navy, *Interavia* magazine, *Flight International*, *Jane's All the World's Aircraft*, the Russian Aviation Research Trust, the personal archives of Yefim Gordon, Sergey and Dmitriy Komissarov, and Konstantin Udalov.

The authors wish to express special thanks to Vladimir Rigmant, Sergey Komissarov, Mikhail Gribovskiy, Yevgeniy Kazyonnov and Andrey Sal'nikov, all of whom have unearthed valuable archive information and unique photos.
The authors have also made use of information from the following web sources: www.aviaforum.ru, www.airwar.ru, www.joebaugher.com, www.airforce.ru, www.life.ru, www.vesti.ru, www.russianplanes.net, www.arms-expo.ru, www.testpilot.ru, www.avsim.su, www.topwar.ru, www.indiastrategic.in, www.bmpd.livejournal.com, www.vpk-news.ru, www.armsdata.net, www.centrasia.ru, www.rbase.new-factoria.ru, www.asn24.ru., www.tvzvezda.ru, www.engine.aviaport.ru, www.npomash.ru, www.russianarms.ru, www.migavia.com, www.forumavia.ru, www.vologda18.ru, www.militaryparitet.com, www.aviaengeneer.ru, www.nuclear-poligon.ru, www.aviaspace.ru, www.dogswar.ru, www.ria.ru, www.vrn.kp.ru, www.fedpress.ru, www.modernarmy.ru,www.uacrussia.ru.

No prizes for guessing what type of aircraft this unit flies! 1006th TBAP personnel line up at Uzin AB in October 1989 to celebrate their winning the Soviet Air Force's socialist competition. Unit CO V. M. Maskayev is foremost.

Introduction

In 2009 a big book on the Tupolev Tu-95/Tu-142 aircraft family, which is known to the western world by the NATO reporting name *Bear*, was published in the well-known Famous Russian Aircraft series of monographs. This book was a success with the readers, not only because the subject was one of the true symbols of the Cold War – and one of the aircraft used most actively in the military stand-off between the Soviet Union and the West, but also because the *Bear* is still very much alive, soldiering on for 60 years now. Unlike some contemporary combat aircraft (and even some newer ones), which have vanished from the inventory and gone the way of all metal, the Tu-95 bomber and Tu-142 anti-submarine warfare aircraft are still around in considerable numbers; they remain an important asset of the modern Russian Air Force and Russian Naval Aviation respectively. Like its US counterpart, the Boeing B-52 Stratofortress, which has shown similar longevity, the Tu-95 – to be precise, its ultimate Tu-95MS variant – is being updated to allow it to fill its designated role adequately in the 21st century. The upgraded Tu-95MS has received the capability to carry new-generation long-range cruise missiles, including versions with conventional warheads.

Moreover, another important event has taken place since then. Even at the height of the Cold War, when the Soviet Union and the West were on the brink of armed conflict, the Tu-95 was never used in anger (unlike the B-52). At the end of 2015, however, the Tu-95 finally made its combat debut in the war against the common enemy of the East and the West alike – global terrorism, Russian Air Force *Bears* launching Kh-555 and Kh-101 cruise missiles at real-life targets – Islamic State (IS) terrorist infrastructure in Syria. This combat experience has made it possible to assess the efficacy of the updated aircraft and new Russian weapons used for the first time in the Syrian War and pinpoint their weaknesses that are to be addressed as soon as possible. This is invaluable for the refinement of a strategic strike system that looks set to serve on with the Russian Aerospace Force for a while yet.

It should be noted that this new edition of the Tu-95/Tu-142 monograph differs considerably from the previous one. Almost all chapters of the book have been thoroughly revised and expanded; this was made possible by the availability of new documentary material and previously unreleased photos. The chapters dealing with the many versions of the *Bear* include more detailed information on the updated Tu-95MS used in the strikes against IS targets and information on the Tu-116 special VIP transport which was omitted from the previous edition. Also, a number of errors which had found their way into the previous edition have now been corrected. The authors hope that many readers – aviation fans and professional researchers of Soviet/Russian aviation alike – will find the new book on the *Bear*'s history useful.

Russian Air Force (121st TBAP) Tu-95MSs on the flight line at Engels-2 AB in the 1990s, with an IL-62 staff transport and two Tu-134UBL crew trainers at the far end of the row.

A perfect upper view of a grey-painted Russian Air Force Tu-95MS illustrating the high wing aspect ratio. Note the weathered insignia; the red star on the port wing has faded to white.

A different Tu-95MS in the same colour scheme comes up from below, flying over thick overcast as it approaches an IL-78 tanker for a fuel top-up. The black circle on the rear fuselage top is the window of the MAIS astroinertial navigation system.

CHAPTER ONE

The forerunners

Assuming that the development and testing of nuclear weapons in the USA, which culminated in the atomic bombings of Hiroshima and Nagasaki on 6th and 9th August 1945 respectively, came as a complete surprise for the Soviet government would be wrong. True enough, the Soviet Union started actively pursuing its own nuclear programme after the Second World War, but as early as 1943 the Soviet government had taken the decision to launch an indigenous nuclear weapons programme. This decision had been prompted by the information furnished by Emil Julius Klaus Fuchs (better known simply as Klaus Fuchs), a German physicist involved in the Manhattan Project; he had contacted the Soviet military intelligence service and worked as an undercover agent successfully supplying information on the American nuclear programme until his arrest and imprisonment in 1950. Even at that early stage, when the Soviet Union and the USA

were still allies, the decision makers in Moscow had had the foresight to take measures aimed at achieving nuclear parity with the USA and discouraging a possible nuclear attack.

General scientific supervision of the Soviet nuclear effort was entrusted to the eminent physicist Dr. Igor' V. Kurchatov, who would later head the Nuclear Energy Institute (IAE – *Insti**toot ah**tomnoy **energh**ii*). Concurrently Lavrentiy P. Beria, who was best known as the dreaded chief of the People's Commissariat of Internal Affairs (i.e., police) but also supervised a number of high-priority weapons programmes, was placed in charge of the Soviet nuclear programme. Consequently the Soviet defence industry, a massive collection of facilities that had resulted from the Great Patriotic War (1941-45) – the part of the Second World War that started with the German invasion of the Soviet Union – was brought into the development consortium.

Still in USAAF markings, Boeing B-29-5-BW 42-6256 *Ramp Tramp* sits at Tsentrahl'naya-Ooglovaya airbase near Vladivostok in the Soviet Far East after force-landing there on 20th July 1944, with Soviet Naval Aviation/ Pacific Fleet pilots in the foreground.

B-29-15-BW 42-6358 obtained in the same way is seen at the same base prior to the ferry flight to Moscow, with typical local scenery in the background.

Unlimited funding was provided for research and production.

The objective of the programme was defined as follows: to create and test the first Soviet atomic bomb within the shortest possible time for the purpose of countering what was already being perceived as a major post-war threat from the West.

While development of the nuclear weapon was the main priority, of course, the Powers That Be were quick to realise that creating a suitable delivery vehicle for the bomb (once the latter had been successfully tested and was ready for production) was equally important. This meant a requirement for new heavy bombers with intercontinental range. The problem was that Soviet aircraft designers had no prior experience with such bombers because the Red Army Air Force's heavy bomber branch (then known as the ADD, *Aviahtsiya* **dahl'**nevo **dey**stviya – Long-Range Aviation), which had come into existence in 1942, had not been created from the outset with intercontinental strikes in mind. Its original mission objectives were considerably more modest, since the primary target at the time – Nazi Germany – was just a few hundred miles away.

In the immediate post-war years a reassessment of the operational requirements for long-range military aircraft led to a decision to place more emphasis on bomber development. In 1947 the heavy bomber branch operated a fleet of 1,839 aircraft; the most potent of these were Petlyakov Pe-8 four-engine bombers (originally called TB-7, *tyazholyy bombardirovshchik* – heavy bomber), of which the ADD had only 32 – the few that had survived the war. There also were a similar number of repaired ex-US Army Air Force Boeing B-17 Flying Fortresses and Consolidated B-24 Liberators. These had landed in Soviet-held territory as a result of navigation errors, or had been brought down by powerplant failures or enemy action and recovered by the Soviet troops; the ones which could be made airworthy were absorbed without much ado by the Soviet Air Force.

The bulk of the Soviet bomber fleet, however, consisted of a motley collection of outdated Ilyushin IL-4 (DB-3F) indigenous twin-engine medium bombers serving in the night bomber role, Lisunov Li-2

airliners/transports (a licence-built derivative of the Douglas DC-3, NATO reporting name *Cab*) outfitted as Li-2VP bombers (*voyennoye primeneniye* – military use) and North American B-25 Mitchell bombers supplied by the USA under the Lend-Lease Agreement during the Great Patriotic War. Neither of these types could fill the envisaged intercontinental bomber role. For one thing, these aircraft lacked the required range; for another, with their low speed and poor defensive armament they stood no chance when pitted against contemporary fighter forces.

The range requirement was perhaps the most important one. The Soviet Union was one of the world's largest countries in terms of land area (covering one-sixth of the world's land area, as the Russians were wont to say in those days), and the ability to fly non-stop from home bases to targets that could be thousands of miles away was crucial.

Soviet military commanders had no difficulty envisioning a scenario where USAAF intercontinental bombers – already extant in the form of the Boeing B-29 Stratofortress in the mid-1940s – could hold the Soviet Union hostage. It became apparent that the only way to counter this threat was to develop an indigenous long-range heavy bomber force with similar capabilities. A radius of action of 3,000-4,000 km (1,863-2,484 miles) was required to pose any kind of threat to the USA.

Apart from range, the future strategic bomber would also have to be reasonably fast (so as to complicate fighter intercepts), have an exceptional payload (considering that the first-generation nuclear weapon would be fairly crude and heavy), and have potent defensive armament.

However, we are jumping ahead of the story a bit. In 1944 two Soviet aeronautical design bureaux – OKB-156 headed by Chief Designer Andrey Nikolayevich Tupolev and OKB-482 headed by Chief Designer Vladimir Mikhaïlovich Myasishchev (the first iteration of the Myasishchev OKB) – were tasked with preliminary configuration studies that would eventually lead to full-scale development of a heavy bomber with intercontinental range. (OKB = **opytno-konstrooktorskoye byuro** – experimental design bureau; the number is a code allocated for security reasons.) The two bureaux were instructed to take due account of the success enjoyed in the Pacific Theatre of Operations (TO) by the B-29, which was devastatingly effective at the time; the Superfortress had already begun to wreak havoc on the Japanese mainland and was operating routinely from bases thousands of miles away, flying safely over wide expanses of ocean.

In 1944 the Myasishchev OKB prepared two project studies designated DVB-202 and DVB-302 (*dahl'niy vysotnyy bombardirovshchik* – long-range high-altitude bomber; sometimes referred to as 'aircraft 202' and 'aircraft 302' respectively). Both designs were four-engine bombers clearly inspired by the B-29; they shared the latter's general arrangement (and even such exterior details of the Superfortress as the extensively glazed parabolic nose and the landing gear design), differing primarily in having somewhat higher-set wings – almost shoulder-mounted instead of mid-set. The high-wing layout was chosen because the bomb bay was to accommodate a 5,000-kg (11,020-lb) bomb (incidentally, the Myasishchev designs had one bomb bay rather than two, as on the B-29). The two projects differed from each other mainly in the powerplant, the DVB-202 having Shvetsov M-72TK air-cooled 18-cylinder radials while the DVB-302 was to be powered by liquid-cooled V-12 engines – Mikulin AM-46 petrol engines or Charomskiy ACh-31 diesels.

Chief Designer Andrey N. Tupolev in his Major-General's uniform with government decorations, including the Gold Star Medal awarded with the Hero of Socialist Labour title.

The team which was responsible for copying the B-29. Left to right: B-4 chief project engineer Dmitriy S. Markov, OKB-156 chief structural strength engineer Aleksey M. Cheryomukhin, Chief Designer Andrey N. Tupolev, his deputy Aleksandr A. Arkhangel'skiy and general arrangement group chief Sergey M. Yeger.

An unserialled Tu-4 (c/n 220202) sits on a snow-covered hardstand in the course of trials. This aircraft was later serialled '7 Black', being the seventh Tu-4 off the Kazan' production line.

Concurrently, OKB-156 started work on the 'aircraft 64' four-engine bomber project. Though similar in size to the Pe-8 (which, incidentally, had started life in the Tupolev OKB as the ANT-42 when Vladimir M. Petlyakov was still Andrey N. Tupolev's aide), the new aircraft had almost twice the take-off weight. The '64' was a very heavy aircraft with an envisaged maximum bomb load close to 5,000 kg (11,020 lb), and range with this load was estimated to be between 3,000 and 4,000 km (1,863-2,484 miles). Unlike the B-29, the Tupolev bomber featured low-set wings, twin tails (in one of the project configurations) and liquid-cooled engines instead of air-cooled radials. Another distinctive feature was that the captain and co-pilot sat side by side under individual 'bug-eye' cockpit canopies (of the sort seen on the Douglas C-74 Globemaster transport and the

Douglas XB-42 Mixmaster bomber). The '64' was to feature very heavy defensive armament designed to much the same specifications as that of the Superfortress. In fact, in some instances this armament surpassed that of the B-29 in coverage and capability.

Though design of the '202', '302', and '64' progressed rapidly and with little difficulty, the exigencies of the on-going war prevented initiation of prototype construction. The difficulties lay not so much with technology, but rather with the scarcity of strategic materials.

Not surprisingly, the Soviet leaders Iosif V. Stalin managed to keep himself apprised of the events and advances in both indigenous and foreign aviation. Though not a specialist in the field, he was nevertheless sufficiently knowledgeable to ask prying and revealing

A brand-new Tu-4 awaiting delivery at Kazan'-Borisoglebskoye, the factory airfield of plant No.22.

questions of his subordinates and to make accurate assessments of hardware and strategies.

When it became clear that the Myasishchev and Tupolev teams had run into development problems with their new bomber projects, Stalin, along with the leaders of the national aviation industry and the Commander-in-Chief of the Soviet Air Force, made a decision to reverse-engineer the B-29 in order to save precious time and field a long-range bomber as soon as possible. The Superfortress, which had already earned considerable respect among Soviet aeronautical engineers and the Soviet military, was considered an ideal long-range bombing platform. Most importantly, it was determined that with the proper insights it might be possible to produce the aircraft in the Soviet Union, using the existing facilities and available personnel.

Fortuitously, three USAAF B-29s had made emergency landings in the Soviet Far East in July-November 1944 after suffering battle damage or technical problems during raids on Japan. These aircraft – a Boeing/Wichita-built B-29-5-BW serialled 42-6256 and two B-29-15-BWs serialled 42-6365 and 42-6358 – were immediately interned by the Soviet authorities because the Soviet Union was officially not at war with Japan at the time. (In April 1941, two months before the German aggression, the Soviet Union had signed a Pact of Neutrality with Japan valid for a five-year term. For four years the Soviet Union abided strictly by this pact. The reason was simple: virtually throughout the four-year Great Patriotic War the possibility of a Japanese aggression was a threat to be reckoned with. Should Japan invade the Soviet Far East as Nazi Germany wanted it to, this could place the USSR on the brink of total disaster – the nation would be unable to wage war on two fronts, at least in 1942-43. In April 1945 the USSR denounced this pact, declaring war on Japan and joining the action in the Far Eastern TO.) Within weeks of their arrival, the interned bombers (plus the wreckage of a fourth B-29 that had crashed in the Soviet Far East – a Boeing/Renton-built B-29A-1-BN serialled 42-93829) were moved to Moscow for detailed examination; one of the B-29s was completely disassembled there and all parts down to the last nut and bolt were studied and measured.

The American bomber was copied in a remarkably short time (only 20 months elapsed from the orders kicking off the reverse-engineering effort to the roll-out of the prototype in February 1947, and 23 months to the first flight on 21st May 1947) and hastily put into mass production under the designation B-4. (In fact, the designation B-4 denoted simply 'four-engined bomber' because Andrey N. Tupolev – who was not enthusiastic about copying someone else's design – did not want to assign a designation in the OKB's normal series to the B-29 copy.) Strictly speaking, there was no prototype as such because this first bomber was completed by the

aircraft factory in Kazan' to production standard and thus can be regarded as the first production machine.

Stalin had ordered that the B-29 be copied down to the smallest detail. Nevertheless, the B-4 (which was almost immediately redesignated Tu-4) was not a 100% carbon copy of the B-29. For one thing, it had different engines; copying the B-29's 2,200-hp Wright R-3350-23A Duplex Cyclones was pointless because a suitable Soviet engine existed – the Shvetsov ASh-73TK 18-cylinder radial rated at 2,400 hp for take-off and 2,000 hp for cruise flight (TK = **toor**bokom**pres**sor – turbosupercharger). This was effectively a 'cousin' of the R-3350 with a bigger displacement, having been evolved independently from the original licence-built Cyclone in the same manner. For another, the defensive armament was more potent, consisting of 20-mm (.78 calibre) cannons instead of 12.7-mm (.50 calibre) machine-guns. Finally, the identification friend-or-foe (IFF) transponder was different – which was quite natural.

Production of the Tu-4 (NATO reporting name *Bull*) continued until 1953 at three factories; different sources state total production as anything between 847 and 1,296 aircraft, which is far smaller than the B-29's production run of 3,943. The Tu-4 was mostly built in the conventional bomber version suitable for outfitting as a long-range reconnaissance aircraft. As a result of the successful Soviet nuclear weapons development programme, about 20 Tu-4s were modified to Tu-4A standard (**ah**tomnyy – nuclear; or, in this context, nuclear-capable) to carry the Soviet Union's first free-fall atomic bomb. These aircraft also served to carry out much of the atmospheric testing of Soviet nuclear weapons during the 1950s. The first Soviet production atomic bomb (the RDS-3 with a yield of 42 kilotons) was exploded at the Semipalatinsk Proving Ground in Kazakhstan on 18th October 1951 with extraordinary political and military repercussions across the globe. Production weapons were delivered to operational units within a few years of this event; as a result, extraordinary emphasis was placed on developing a suitable delivery vehicle.

On 14th September 1954 a Tu-4A dropped an RDS-3 bomb at the Totskoye Practice Range near Orenburg during Exercise *Snezhok* (Snowball) – the first Soviet all-arms exercise involving actual use of nuclear weapons. The purposes of the exercise were to test the effects of a nuclear blast on a fortified line of defence and on military materiel, to verify the scenario of an offensive by own forces in direct contact with the adversary without withdrawing them from the line of contact before the nuclear strike, and to teach the personnel (enlisted men and commanders alike) how to conduct offensive and defensive operations in a nuclear environment. The exercise involved a total of 45,000 servicemen, many of whom were exposed to nuclear contaminants.

During the early/mid-1950s the handful of Tu-4As were the only nuclear-capable aircraft in the Soviet Air Force's arsenal capable of striking at the US military bases positioned along the Soviet borders and around the Eastern Bloc at large.

As it was, the Tu-4 proved to be a turning point for the Soviet aircraft industry. Accessing the B-29 proved a major technological windfall and allowed the nation's aircraft design bureaux, most notably the Tupolev OKB, to shorten a normally lengthy learning curve into a matter of months, rather than years. This giant leap forward would prove the foundation of all future Soviet/Russian heavy bomber development and its fall-out would impact the history of the western world.

The target of greatest concern was, of course, the United States some 6,400 km (4,000 miles) distant. This was well beyond the range of the Tu-4A, particularly when it was carrying a heavy nuclear bomb. Only targets in Europe, North Africa, the Middle East, Japan and the Far East were within range.

Attempts to extend the Tu-4's range via in-flight refuelling (IFR) were modestly successful but little emphasis was placed on developing the technology. Only 52 Tu-4s were eventually modified to incorporate this capability: 26 were equipped as tankers and another 26 as receiver aircraft, utilising a wingtip-to-wingtip IFR system devised by Igor' I. Shelest and Viktor S. Vasyanin, two test pilots working at the Flight Test Institute (LII – *Lyotno-issledovatel'skiy institoot*). It was not until the advent of the Tupolev Tu-16 twin-turbojet medium bomber (NATO reporting name *Badger*) in the mid-1950s that IFR became relatively commonplace in the Soviet Air Force and the Soviet Naval Aviation.

Other studies at tackling the intercontinental range requirement included the option of one-way missions. How was this to be accomplished without recruiting suicidal crews? In the event of war, Tu-4s that were to attack the USA would be flown to their targets, drop the bomb (if they were lucky enough to penetrate the air defences) and the crew would then bail out over the Atlantic Ocean on the aircraft's abbreviated return leg. A waiting Soviet submarine would then pick them up and carry them home – hopefully to fly and fight another day.

Concurrently, early studies were undertaken envisaging the use of the Tu-4 as a stand-off weapons platform. Unmanned aerial vehicles launched by the Tu-4 would deliver nuclear warheads to the targets. Like IFR, the initial stand-off air-to-surface missile work of the early 1950s was only a preliminary step, and official interest in the concept was not strong enough initially to merit a more intensive effort.

Most of the ongoing emphasis on solving the range problem pursued the more conventional path of advanced bomber development. The objective was to develop an aircraft that could span, with payload, the distance between the Soviet Union and the USA and return – preferably without having to be refuelled.

Once the Tu-4 had successfully entered production, the Tupolev OKB began looking at more advanced versions to fill the role of stand-off missile carrier with intercontinental range. These studies resulted in the preliminary design (PD) projects tentatively designated 'aircraft 471', 'aircraft 473', 'aircraft 474', and 'aircraft 485'; in line with Tupolev OKB practice the first two digits indicated the year of origin and the third digit indicated the specific project within that year. All of these were spin-offs of the original Tu-4, differing primarily in having more engines to give greater overall horsepower, larger fuselages, longer wingspan and increased operating weights. For example, the '471' and '485' intercontinental bombers had six ASh-73TK radial engines, a wingspan increased to 56.0 m (183 ft 8$^{23}\!/\!_{32}$ in) and a normal operating weight increased to 86,207 kg (190,053 lb). Interestingly, information about these two projects somehow leaked through the infamous 'Iron Curtain' and appeared in the western aviation press. The mysterious 'Russian bomber' was referred to as the 'Tu-200' (a fictitious designation) and purported to be the Soviet counterpart of the Convair B-36 Peacemaker – the largest American bomber of the day.

Work on the new bomber project was divided into two stages. The first explored the various non-Tu-4 options that would permit non-stop intercontinental range – that is, flight over distances of 20,000 km (12,420 miles) or more. The second envisaged taking the basic Tu-4 and enlarging it into a design that would meet the range and payload specifications. Comparison charts utilising a variety of engine and airframe combinations were drawn to explore the various options.

The resulting studies showed that the specified 20,000-km range was not obtainable. Ranges of 15,000-16,000 km (9,315-9,936 miles) were, however, within the realm of possibility. In order to meet this specification, the aircraft would need to have a wing area of 300-340 m^2 (3,229-3,659 sq ft) and the take-off run at gross weight would be between 2,500 and 4,160 m (8,200-13,645 ft).

Second-generation studies included exploring options other than aircraft of immense size and weight with gazillions of engines. Instead, the designers concentrated on four-engine aircraft capable of performing the long-range heavy bomber function. These, in turn, served as a basis for future ultra-long-range designs that could be developed from the original aircraft without major modifications.

These diverse studies of different configurations utilising a variety of engine options led the design bureaux to conclude that the new aircraft should use the manufacturing and design experience gained with the Tu-4. It was therefore proposed that the new long-

Two more views of the Tu- 80 prototype illustrating the new stepped nose profile with a chin radome for the Rubidiy radar, the revised engine nacelles and the lateral sighting blisters. Note the bomber's pronounced nose-up attitude on the ground.

range bomber should be based on the Tu-4's circular-section fuselage of 2.9 m (9 ft 6³⁄₁₆ in) diameter mated to new wings of increased area (200 m², 2,153 sq ft) utilising a low-drag airfoil. Additionally, new and more powerful engines would replace the ASh-73TK radials. The aircraft would benefit from an increased fuel capacity, an increased bomb load, and improved aerodynamics.

The first aircraft to incorporate the proposed improvements to the Tu-4 was the 'aircraft 80', or Tu-80, which was developed in accordance with directive No.2052-804 issued by the Soviet Council of Ministers (i.e., government) on 12th June 1948. It represented an evolutionary development of the Tu-4 along the lines of Boeing's B-29 to B-50 transformation (in fact, it was the

Soviet response to the B-50), but the 'aircraft 80' was created to meet specific Soviet Air Force requirements. It was basically a drastically redesigned Tu-4 with greater overall dimensions, a normal take-off weight increased from 47,500-47,600 kg (104,720-104,940 lb) to 51,500 kg (113,540 lb) and significantly longer range. The new bomber eliminated many of the Tu-4's obvious failings while featuring improved aerodynamics and a more potent defensive armament.

Improved ASh-73TKFN radials were fitted, the FN denoting *for**see**rovannyy, s nepo**sred**stvennym **vprys**kom **top**liva* – uprated, with direct fuel injection. The ASh-73TKFN had an output of 2,720 hp (2,026 kW) at sea level and 2,360 hp (1,758 kW) at altitude; it was also more fuel-efficient than the basic ASh-73TK.

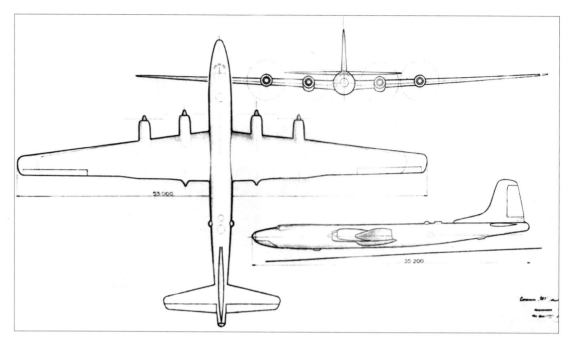

A provisional three-view drawing of the 'project 487' ultra-long-range bomber from the preliminary develop-ment project files. Note the stippled lines in the upper view showing an alternative version with shorter-span wings.

New, more efficient AV-16U four-blade variable-pitch propellers replacing the Tu-4's V3-A3 propellers were also developed to make better use of the available engine power. The engines were mounted in new nacelles with higher thrust lines, low-drag circular-section cowlings, and separate ventral oil cooler ducts instead of the Tu-4's chin-mounted oil coolers increasing the cross-section area. Additionally, the fuel capacity of the Tu-80 was increased by 15% over that of the Tu-4. This was accomplished by increasing the span of the wing centre section and improving the size and location of the fuel tanks in the wing torsion box.

The Tu-80, which was 3 m (9 ft 10 in) longer than its predecessor, featured more capacious bomb bays and revised crew accommodation as well – the designers positioned the majority of the crew in the forward section of the aircraft. The radio operator, for instance, was moved from the centre pressure cabin to the forward one. A conventional stepped windscreen replaced the Tu-4's curved nose glazing integrated into the fuselage contour, thus eliminating the thicket of glazing framework ahead of the pilots with many small transparencies that generated annoying internal reflections and distorted the view. Both the navigator and the bomb-aimer sat in the extreme nose where they enjoyed an excellent forward field of view. As on the predecessor, a pressurised communication crawlway passing above the tandem bomb bays permitted in-flight access to the centre pressure cabin.

A new, larger vertical tail (necessitated by the more powerful engines and increased wingspan) replaced the original Tu-4 design. The armament included modified Tu-4-style remote-controlled gun barbettes mounting 23-mm cannons, the dorsal and ventral ones being buried in the fuselage insofar as possible to reduce drag. A chin-mounted *Rubidiy* (Rubidium) ground mapping radar enclosed by a dielectric fairing was fitted to assist the bomb-aimer in locating targets, replacing the Tu-4's **Kobal't-M** (Cobalt) radar in a semi-retractable radome between the bomb bays. The Rubidiy was developed in 1949-52 under the guidance of V. S. Dekhtyaryov; it was based on the Kobal't-M, with the addition of a module integrating it with the optical bombsight.

Aerodynamically the Tu-80 was somewhat cleaner than the Tu-4. The fuselage of greater fineness ratio with the more pointed nose, the new engine nacelles with a smaller cross-section area and wetted area and the less draggy cannon and radar installations gave it a lift/drag ratio of 18 versus 17 for the Tu-4.

These structural, mechanical and aerodynamic improvements gave the Tu-80 a range of 8,200 km (5,092 miles). This was an increase of 30-35% over that of the Tu-4, which had a range of 5,000-5,600 km (3,105-3,479 miles).

Unfortunately for Tupolev, the Soviet Air Force decided these performance improvements were not enough to merit Tu-80 production. While the aircraft was under development, even higher performance targets had been set and thus more advanced designs had begun to come to fruition. The sole Tu-80 prototype made its first flight on 1st December 1949 and successfully completed manufacturer's flight tests but was quickly relegated to flight test work on behalf of forthcoming bombers of considerably higher capability. It ended its days as a gunnery target at a practice range.

In fact, work on the Tu-80's successor, the 'aircraft 85' (Tu-85, NATO reporting name *Barge*), proceeded in parallel with the earlier design, starting under the project name 'aircraft 487'; its development

The first prototype Tu-85 ('85/1') during initial flight tests.

Two more views of the '85/1'. The large dorsal supercharger fairings of the VD-4 engines incorporating the engine/intercooler air intakes are clearly visible. The stripes on the fin are photo calibration markings.

The second prototype Tu-85 ('85/2') seen during trials.

was officially ordered by the Soviet Council of Ministers directive No.3929-1608 dated 16th September 1949. The Tu-85 was a derivative of the Tu-80 with new wings of longer span (55.96 m versus 43.58 m; 183 ft 7⁹⁄₆₄ in versus 142 ft 11¾ in) and greater area (273.6 m²; 2,945 sq ft versus 1,862.16 sq ft), plus a new powerplant – four 4,000-hp Shvetsov ASh-2TK 28-cylinder four-row air-cooled radials or 4,300-hp (2,980-kW) Dobrynin M-253K (later renamed VD-4K) 24-cylinder water-cooled radials driving AV-44 four-blade propellers. The avionics and equipment were also updated, including an improved Rubidiy-M radar. When completed, the Tu-85 proved to be an even more capable weapons delivery platform. Utilising the technological advances generated under the Tu-80 programme, it became the forerunner to the radically different Tu-95 – the subject of this book.

The first prototype ('85/1') was completed in September 1950 and took to the air on 9th January 1951. Flight tests quickly verified Tupolev's performance predictions. The VD-4K engines powering the '85/1' proved more than sufficient to give the aircraft the speed and range required for its intercontinental mission. During one test flight the Tu-85 flew a 12,018-km (7,463-mile) mission and reached a maximum speed of 638 km/h (396 mph) at 10,000 m (32,810 ft).

The Tu-85 had a normal take-off weight of 90,880 kg (200,360 lb) and a maximum TOW of 98,180 kg (216,450 lb). The normal bomb load was 5,000 kg (11,020 lb), while the maximum bomb load over short ranges was 18,000 kg (39,670 lb). Once again, two separate bomb bays were provided fore and aft of the wing centre section torsion box. The largest single bomb that could be carried weighed 9,000 kg (19,840 lb), which was the largest conventional bomb then on the inventory.

The successful testing of the Tu-85 gave the Tupolev OKB and other entities involved the impression that their long-range bomber aspirations had been achieved. The aircraft met its range and payload requirements without difficulty. It was predicted that the Tu-85 could, if necessary, reach and bomb the US mainland with only modest effort. The second prototype (the '85/2') featuring various improvements based on the first machine's test results flew on 28th June 1951. Production plans were initiated and all three aircraft factories building the Tu-4 (No.18 in Kuibyshev, No.22 in Kazan' and No.23 in Moscow) were due to launch Tu-85 production.

Just as these plans were reaching fruition, however, intelligence reports of US anti-aircraft defences and progress in interceptor fighter development indicated that a bomber powered by reciprocating engines would have few chances of survival. All things considered, it was evident that with a maximum speed

of 620-650 km/h (385-403 mph) the Tu-85 was too slow for the strategic bombing mission in the post-Second World War environment. It would be a sitting duck for advanced radar-equipped transonic and supersonic interceptors, such as those then under development in the USA (the 'Century series'). The proposed ultra-long-range version of the Tu-85 with a further increased wing area and new radial engines – 4,000-hp Maslennikov M-51s, 6,000-hp Charomskiy M-35 diesels or 6,000-hp Yakovlev M-501 diesels – would be even slower due to the higher drag, with a maximum speed of 600-630 km/h (372-391 mph). Another projected version – the mixed-power 'aircraft 85A' with two 2,700-kgp (5,950-lbst) Klimov VK-1 centrifugal-flow turbojets in the rear ends of the inboard engine nacelles to act as boosters – would be faster but at the expense of shorter range.

Moreover, combat experience in the Korean War, which by 1952 was serving as a testing ground for the latest in US and Soviet aviation technology, added weight to this conclusion. The USAF's B-29 bombers, which had made a good showing in the Second World War when they were opposed by piston-engined fighters, proved vulnerable to North Korean Mikoyan/Gurevich MiG-15 *Fagot* jet fighters. This fact had not gone unnoticed by the major combatants. Although the USA had already curtailed the development of piston-engined bombers, the Korean War served to justify expeditious development of their jet-powered successors. Production of the enormous B-36, America's last intercontinental bomber to be primarily powered by reciprocating engines, was halted after fewer than 400 had been built. Concurrently, development of the all-turbojet Boeing B-47 Stratojet and Boeing B-52 Stratofortress was stepped up. In Europe, Great Britain began development of four-turbojet medium-range strategic bombers known as the 'V-bombers' – the Vickers Type 660 Valiant (which first flew in May 1951 and entered service with the Royal Air Force in January 1955), Avro 698 Vulcan (first flown in August 1952 and inducted in July 1956) and Handley Page HP.80 Victor (first flown in December 1952 and inducted in April 1958).

Assessing the development of bombers and air defence systems in the West, the Soviet military quickly revised their general operational requirement (GOR) for a strategic bomber. Like its immediate predecessor, the Tu-85 was cancelled after only two prototypes had been built, becoming the last of the kind – the world's last piston-engined heavy bomber to fly. Work on more advanced heavy bombers powered by either turboprop or turbojet engines were given highest priority. Of central importance was the fact that these advanced aircraft capable of high subsonic speeds would be able to carry the Soviet Union's rapidly growing stockpile of first-generation nuclear bombs.

CHAPTER TWO

The *Bear* is born: Design and testing

Vladimir M. Myasishchev's original design bureau (OKB-482) had been disbanded in 1946 on the pretext that it 'failed to yield tangible results' – not least because the aforementioned DVB-202 and DVB-302 projects had not materialised. In 1950, however, Myasishchev approached the Soviet government with an offer to create a strategic bomber having a maximum speed of up to 950 km/h (590 mph) and a range of more than 13,000 km (8,073 miles). Hence in 1951 a new design bureau, OKB-23, was established in Fili (a borough of Moscow) for this purpose, with Vladimir M. Myasishchev as Chief Designer.

The man providing initiative for this aircraft, which was to be powered by four turbojet engines, was Aleksandr A. Mikulin, Chief Designer of the OKB-300 engine design bureau. He offered the AMRD-03 axial-flow turbojet (AM for Aleksandr Mikulin and RD for

*reaktivnyy **dvig**atel'* – jet engine) which was under development since 1949. This engine, later redesignated AM-3 in production form, was the first Soviet high-powered turbojet, offering an estimated take-off thrust of 8,200 kgp (18,080 lbst), which was subsequently increased to an even more impressive 8,700 kgp (19,180 lbst). Shortly afterwards the proposal was given approval by the government; Myasishchev was instructed to proceed as rapidly as possible. The new bomber would have to be capable of carrying a 5,000-kg (11,020-lb) atomic bomb non-stop to the continental US and returning. A heavy defensive armament would offset any deficiencies in performance.

The future Myasishchev jet bomber, which would eventually become the M-4 (NATO reporting name *Bison-A*), utilised the best aerospace technology and engineering talent in the Soviet Union's vast

A large scale model of the '95' in TsAGI's T-101 wind tunnel. It is hard to judge the shape of the engine nacelles from this angle.

The Tupolev OKB's preliminary design section chief Boris M. Kondorskiy.

A provisional three-view drawing of the projected 'aircraft 489'. Note the single bomb bay, the contra-rotating propellers and the main gear fairings integrated with the inboard engine nacelles.

aerospace industry. Virtually unlimited funding was provided in the hope this would expedite development.

Andrey N. Tupolev, the patriarch of Soviet bomber design, knew about the initial project studies leading up to the M-4. Now Tupolev was known as a man who did not take kindly to competition. Not surprisingly, he was less than overjoyed at the prospect of Myasishchev, his former aide and disciple, stealing the limelight from him; the two now found themselves in bitter rivalry for the right to create a strategic high-speed bomber for the Soviet Air Force.

Back in the spring of 1948 OKB-156 – specifically its PD section under the direction of Boris M. Kondorskiy – initiated research on its own heavy and ultra-heavy transonic bomber designs. By then the Tupolev OKB had received a copy of a report titled *'Researching the Flight Performance of a Swept-Wing Heavy Jet Bomber'* that had been prepared by the Central Aero- and Hydrodynamics Institute named after Nikolay Ye. Zhukovskiy (TsAGI – *Tsentrahl'nyy aero- i ghidrodinamicheskiy institoot*). Building on captured German research into high aspect ratio swept wings, as well as on own research by TsAGI and the Tupolev OKB, the report examined large aircraft with an all-up weight ranging from 80,000 to 160,000 kg (from 176,370 to

352,730 lb) and with wing sweep angles of 25° to 35° at quarter-chord in considerable detail. Some 46 possible configurations were reviewed in the calculations, utilising up to eight 2,040-kgp (4,500-lbst) Klimov RD-45 centrifugal-flow turbojets (a Soviet copy of the British Rolls-Royce Nene I) or indigenous 3,000-kgp (6,610-lbst) Mikulin AM-TKRD-01 axial-flow turbojets providing an aggregate thrust of 12,000 to 24,000 kgp (26,455 to 52,910 lbst).

Using this research as the basis, additional theoretical and practical work by the Tupolev OKB and TsAGI paved the way for the development of 'aircraft 88' (the future Tu-16), which first flew on 27th April 1952.

The earlier Tu-85 also served as an expansion point for the Tupolev OKB's experience. Both aircraft led to the realisation that a take-off weight of some 150,000 kg (330,600 lb) and wings swept back 35° at quarter-chord, with an aspect ratio of 9, were required in order for a large bomber to fly the requisite range and achieve the desired speed-at-altitude while carrying a reasonable bomb load.

With early project studies of the Tu-16, the results obtained with the Tu-85, and all the world's previous experience of bomber design on hand, by 1950 the outlook of the future Tupolev high-speed intercontinental bomber began to crystallise. The chosen swept-wing configuration had been thoroughly studied by the engineers at TsAGI, who had declared it the best option for the new bomber. The internal layout of the fuselage was basically borrowed from the Tu-85 – it was deemed suitable when coupled with the new wing configuration (although this layout was yet to change, as you will see). As for the powerplant, Boris M. Kondorskiy and his team quickly narrowed the options to either turbojet or turboprop propulsion, though which of the two (or a combination thereof) was best remained undecided at this early stage. Calculations indicated that four turboprops in the 10,000- to 12,000-ehp (7,460- to 8,952-kW) class with a specific fuel consumption (SFC) of 0.25-0.3 kg/hp-hr (0.6-0.66 lb/hp-hr) would be necessary for the transonic speed and range performance targets to be achieved.

Actual work on the design aspects of the new bomber began with upgrade studies of the basic Tu-4 and Tu-85 to meet the Air Force's new specification. Various engine studies led the designers to examine the possibility of refitting the Tu-4 with four 5,163-ehp TV-2 turboprops (TV stands for **toor**bovinto**voy** [**dvig**atel'] – turboprop engine) developed by OKB-276 under Chief Designer Nikolay D. Kuznetsov and driving AV-41B four-bladed contra-rotating propellers of 4.2 m (13 ft 9 in) diameter (AV = *avtomaticheskiy [vozdooshnyy] vint* – 'automatic airscrew', i.e., variable-pitch propeller with automatic pitch control). Such a conversion would increase the maximum speed to 676 km/h (420 mph), the cruising speed to 580-600 km/h (360-372 mph) and

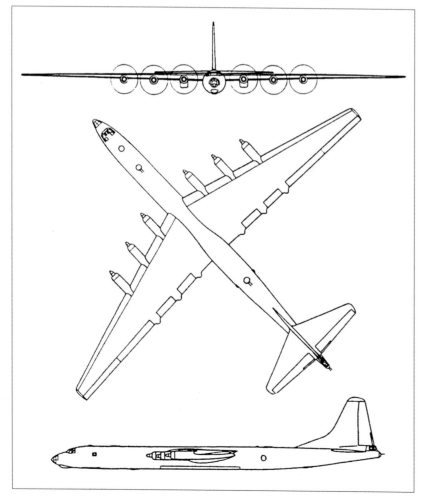

range to 6,900 km (4,285 miles). This project (known in-house as 'aircraft 94') became the basis for an attempt by Tupolev to undertake a fleet-wide major upgrade of the Tu-4 – which eventually never materialised, being considered not worthwhile because the performance increase was too small.

The second step in the proposed modernisation programme was an upgraded Tu-85 re-engined with either 6,250-ehp (4,596-kW) TV-2F (*forseerovannyy* – uprated) or 10,000-ehp (7,355-kW) Kuznetsov TV-10 turboprops; the maximum all-up weight was increased to 118,000 kg (260,150 lb) and 121,000 kg (266,760 lb) respectively, including 60,000 kg (132,280 lb) of fuel and 5,000 kg (11,020 lb) of bombs in both versions. In this case the estimated range was 16,000 km (9,936 miles) for the TV-2F powered version and 17,200 km (10,681 miles) for the TV-10 powered version; maximum speed was 700 km/h (435 mph) and 740 km/h (460 mph) respectively, while cruising speed was 620-640 km/h (385-397 mph) and 640-660 km/h (397-410 mph) respectively. The service ceiling was 12,000 m (39,370 ft) and 13,500 m (44,290 ft) respectively. However, again these figures (especially the speed) were seen as unimpressive and a decision was made to continue the design studies.

The next step involved a 'clean sheet of paper' bomber with a variety of wing configurations and engine options, including mixed powerplants. Five powerplant options were considered:
• four AM-3 turbojets;
• a combination of four TV-10 turboprops and two AM-3 turbojets;
• four TV-10 turboprops and two 5,000-kgp (11,020-lbst) TR-3A axial-flow turbojets (*toorbore'aktivnyy* [*dvigatel'*] – turbojet engine) developed by OKB-165 under Chief Designer Arkhip M. Lyul'ka;
• four Kuznetsov TV-4 turboprops (sometimes reported as TV-04) rated at 6,300 ehp for take-off and two AM-3 turbojets;
• four TV-10 turboprops.

As these studies progressed, the anticipated wing area was increased from 274 to 400 m² (from 2,949 to 4,305 sq ft) and the wing sweep angle varied from 0° to as much as 45°. Aspect ratios from 6.8 to 11.75 were explored.

A surviving desktop model of the pure jet version shows a rather unusual layout. The mid-set wings were swept back 45° and the wing centre section was positioned well forward so that the rear fuselage was inordinately long, giving the aircraft an uncannily dachshund-like appearance. The conventional tail unit with the horizontal tail positioned just above the fuselage was also sharply swept. The four AM-3 turbojets were arranged in staggered vertical pairs in conformal nacelles flanking the centre fuselage so that the lateral air intakes were positioned a short way ahead

of the wing leading edge (immediately aft of the flight deck); the air intakes had a semi-circular shape. The lower pair of engines were positioned below the wing roots to exhaust under the wings, while the upper pair were located farther aft (immediately aft of the wings' rear spar, as on the Tu-16). This dictated the use of the same curious design feature as on the Tu-16 – the upper engines' inlet ducts were very long and passed right through the wing torsion box, the root portions of the spars being designed as massive hollow frames. The upper engines were set at a small toe-in angle to stop the jet efflux from impinging on the fuselage skin. This was assisted by specially shaped nacelle/fuselage fairings (so-called 'active fillets' aft of the engine nozzles): the jet exhaust sucked away the air flowing around the wing roots and fuselage, at the same time directing the airflow in that zone. At that early stage there were still three pressure cabins (as on the Tu-85), the centre cabin being located just ahead of the vertical tail and featuring elliptical lateral blisters for

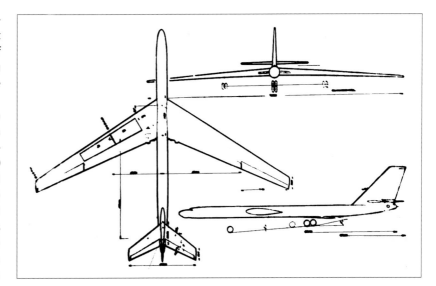

Top: A very schematic three-view of the competing Myasishchev 'M' project from the PD project documents. The engines are buried in the wing roots, as on the actual M-4. The nose unit of the bicycle gear had twin wheels at this early stage.

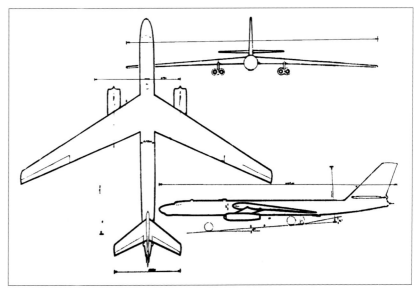

Above: Another three-view showing an alternative project version of the 'M' with the arranged in B-52 style pairs under the wings. The main gear unit also has twin wheels in this version.

observation and gun aiming. The blisters protruded only a little beyond the fuselage contour to minimise drag, and to provide the waist gunner with an acceptable field of view rearwards and downwards the fuselage sides had characteristic depressions or 'dimples' downstream of the blisters, giving an hourglass cross-section. The chin radome was shaped in such a way that its rear end was flush with the fuselage underside, making the nose look almost like the bow section of a flying boat's hull. The model gave no clear idea of the main landing gear design, but the wings were unencumbered by main gear fairings, which (together with the aircraft's proportions) suggested a bicycle landing gear.

Eventually the choice was narrowed to two basic versions of the preliminary design having a similar airframe; one was powered by four turbojet engines and the other by four turboprops. The slightly anhedral (2°30') wings were swept back 35° (to be precise, 34°59'37.3") up to rib 16 and 33°33' outboard of it. This was made possible by the fact that the outer portions utilised thinner airfoils which ensured an acceptably high cruise Mach number even at lower sweep; the airfoils were chosen in such a way as to ensure that the root portions stalled first, preserving lateral stability and roll control. The wings featured three pairs of boundary layer fences on the upper surface to limit spanwise flow, delaying tip stall and improving aileron efficiency; these fences (as well as the 35° wing sweep) would become typical of Tupolev aircraft. The trailing edge inboard of the ailerons was occupied by powerful flaps; these were positioned in the propeller wash on the turboprop version, which increased lift in take-off/landing mode appreciably (by up to 35%). The conventional tail unit had 40° sweepback on both vertical and horizontal tail surfaces, the latter featuring no dihedral.

The tricycle landing gear was patterned on that of the Tu-16 – all three units retracted aft, the main units featuring four-wheel bogies which somersaulted through 180° during retraction to lie back to front in elongated fairings extending beyond the wing trailing edge. The large clamshell doors in these fairings opened only when the gear was in transit, reducing drag. On the turboprop version the main gear fairings conveniently blended into the inboard engine nacelles to minimise cross-section area, the engines featuring bifurcated exhaust pipes. (Again, these fairings became a trademark feature of Tupolev aircraft designed in the 1950s and 1960s. The Tupolev OKB even took out a patent for this main gear design.) The nose unit had twin 1,100 x 330 mm (43.3 x 13 in) wheels while the mainwheel size was 1,500 x 500 mm (59.05 x 19.68 in); tyre pressure was 7 kg/cm² and 9 kg/cm² (100 psi and 128.5 psi) respectively.

The calculations indicated that the turboprop version with engines rated at 12,000-15,000 ehp (8,826-

11,032 kW) was the most suitable option for achieving a range in excess of 13,000 km (8,073 miles). In the configuration required to meet this range specification the aircraft's design take-off weight could be as high as 200 tons (440,900 lb). The estimated maximum speed at 10,000 m (32,810 ft) was about 800 km/h (496 mph). The take-off run was estimated as 1,500 m (4,920 ft).

By comparison, an aircraft of the same size and weight powered by four AM-3 turbojet engines with a take-off thrust of 9,000 kgp (19,840 lbst) offered a range of not more than 10,000 km (6,210 miles) and required a take-off run in excess of 2,000 m (6,560 ft). The only advantage of the jet-powered version was its higher maximum speed, which would be about 900 km/h (559 mph).

A final review of the various options and their performance estimates finally led Andrey N. Tupolev to give priority to range over maximum speed and select the turboprop version over the jet-powered one, even though the latter had won favour from the aircraft industry and the military (commonly referred to as 'the Customer'). The reasoning behind this decision was the high priority placed on range – the proposed heavy bomber had to reach its target by all means. The first-generation Soviet turbojet engines simply did not have the fuel efficiency needed to achieve this.

Not surprisingly, the Soviet Air Force (VVS – *Voyenno-voz**doosh**nyye **see**ly*) and the Ministry of Aircraft Industry (MAP – *Mini**ster**stvo aviatsi**on**noy pro**mysh**lennosti*), who were well aware of the progress the Myasishchev OKB was making with its M-4 jet bomber, contested Tupolev's decision. Quite simply, they regarded Myasishchev's and Tupolev's bomber projects as a belt-and-braces policy in case one of these proved to be stillborn. As far as the Air Force and MAP were concerned, the competing projects should have maximum commonality from a technology standpoint (including propulsion technology) so as to minimise technical risks. The debate dragged on for so long that eventually Iosif V. Stalin summoned Andrey N. Tupolev to the Kremlin for a meeting. Upon hearing Tupolev's arguments in favour of the turboprop powerplant Stalin, who had entrusted Myasishchev with the work on the jet bomber, chose to play safe and sanctioned the acceleration of initial development work on the Tupolev strategic bomber, with appropriate funding.

It should be noted that, according to the recollections of Leonid L. Kerber (one of Tupolev's closest aides who was responsible for the design of electrical, navigation and communications equipment), the General Designer recounted that meeting as follows:

'Stalin said: "Comrade Tupolev, do you think you can add more engines to one of your existing bombers so as to make it capable of reaching the USA, completing its objective and then returning to report on the results?" (Sic;

that last bit was probably Tupolev's rendition – this kind of solecism was certainly not typical of Stalin – *Auth*.)

I replied that installing additional engines would not be the biggest issue. The main problem was that indigenous engines were not fuel-efficient and would require a huge amount of fuel to fly such a mission. There was simply not enough room on board the aircraft to hold that much fuel.

"So you believe this is not possible?"

"That's right, Comrade Stalin. Exactly so" – I said.

Stalin was silent for a while. Then he walked up to his desk, opened a folder that was lying on it, looked through a few pages of the document inside, and then he spoke again.

"That's odd. Because here we have another aircraft designer who says this is possible, and he says he can do it." (The 'other designer' was of course Vladimir M. Myasishchev – *Auth*.)

Stalin closed the folder and dismissed me with a nod. I got it that he was very displeased.'

This meeting caused the Tupolev OKB to step up the work on the four-turboprop strategic bomber which was henceforth referred to in house as 'aircraft 95'. In those days 'no can do' was not accepted, especially in defence matters – even from the patriarch of Soviet aircraft design, as Tupolev had already learned (the hard way).

Meanwhile, the work on the turboprop engine intended for 'aircraft 95' was well under way at the Kuznetsov OKB in the city of Kuibyshev (now renamed back to Samara). The engine, which had started life as the TV-022 but was by then designated TV-2, had been evolved from the Junkers Jumo 022 experimental turboprop which had been captured by the Russians at the end of World War II. The Jumo 022 technology was quickly developed into full-scale hardware with the assistance of captive German propulsion engineers from Junkers AG who had been forcibly relocated to the Soviet Union to work at OKB-276.

A TV-022 prototype engine rated at 4,620 ehp (3,446 kW) successfully passed government bench tests in October 1950. The improved TV-2F version tested shortly afterwards delivered 6,250 ehp (4,596 kW). Concurrently OKB-276 started work on the TV-10 and TV-12 turboprops delivering 10,000 ehp (7,460 kW) and 12,000 ehp (8,952 kW) respectively, although the first of these remained in project form. At the time these were the world's most powerful turboprop engines by far.

Unfortunately the OKB-276 design team ran into major development problems with the big engines. It seemed certain that 18 to 24 months would be needed to overcome these problems, setting back the 'aircraft 95' programme considerably.

Because of the delays with engine development, Andrey N. Tupolev flew to Kuibyshev in order to have a talk with Nikolay D. Kuznetsov and review the TV-12

Chief Designer Nikolay D. Kuznetsov, head of the OKB-276 design bureau that created the engines powering the Tu-95.

turboprop's status. In the course of the meeting the two designers agreed that, in order to meet the bomber's development schedule it would be best to utilise the smaller TV-2F turboprops in a paired configuration as a stop-gap measure. As a result of this agreement

The Junkers Jumo 022 turboprop, the engine which served as the starting point in the development of the Kuznetsov TV-12 (NK-12).

Below: One of OKB-276's first own designs, the TV-2 turboprop.

The Kuznetsov 2TV-2F coupled turboprop engine. The common reduction gearbox and the air intake and drive shaft of the right-hand TV-2F are clearly visible.

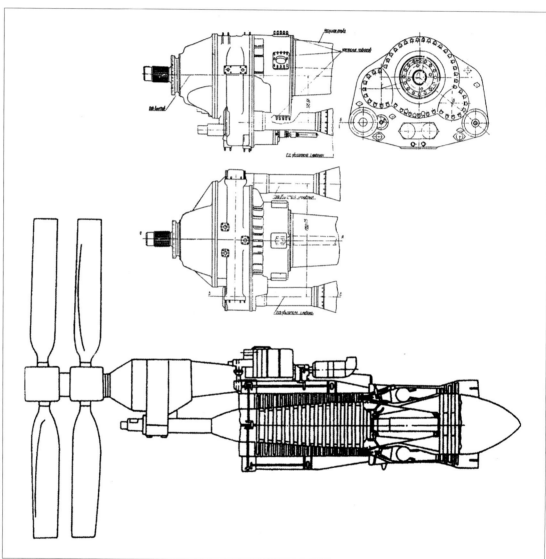

A schematic layout of the 2TV-2F and its common reduction gearbox and contra-rotating propellers.

OKB-276 quickly brought out a turboprop aptly designated 2TV-2F; it consisted of two TV-2F engines arranged side by side to drive a single propeller via a common reduction gearbox. This engineering solution was by no means unique; one might mention the wartime German Daimler-Benz DB 606 24-cylinder engine (a pair of DB 601 inverted-V 12-cylinder engine coupled to drive a common four-blade propeller) developed for the Heinkel He 177 Greif ('griffin' in German) heavy bomber, or the post-war Armstrong Siddeley Double Mamba turboprop created for the Fairey Gannet anti-submarine warfare aircraft of 1949 (two 'single Mambas' side by side driving four-blade contraprops via a common gearbox). The 2TV-2F had a take-off rating of 12,500 ehp at 7,650 rpm and a cruise rating of 6,500 ehp at 7,250 rpm with the aircraft cruising at 11,000 m (36,090 ft) and Mach 0.86; the SFC was 0.25 kg/hp-hr (0.6 lb/hp-hr) and 0.19 kg/hp-hr (0.42 lb/hp-hr) respectively. Dry weight less propeller was 3,780 kg (8,330 lb).

Development of the 2TV-2F's reduction gearbox proved to be a major undertaking in itself. At the time no aircraft-grade gearbox of comparable size, weight and power capacity had ever been built. The massive gearbox was connected to the TV-2F engines by extension shafts; its long conical rear fairing carried the engine accessories which were positioned above and between the engines.

Interestingly, one source claims that the coupled engines for the '95' were to consist of two 6,000-ehp Kuznetsov NK-6 turboprops side by side. In fact, however, the NK-6 was an afterburning turbofan, also known as the P-6 and rated at 21,500 kgp (47,400 lbst) – the world's most powerful engine in its class at the time, which remained in prototype form because the bombers it was to power did not materialise.

In parallel with the engine's on-going development, design of a propeller capable of efficiently absorbing the immense output of the 2TV-2F was undertaken. Preliminary calculations quickly showed that a propeller with a diameter of no less than 7 m (22 ft 11 in) would be required. This was unacceptable for at least two reasons. Firstly, such an enormous propeller was difficult to manufacture (the long blades needed to be sufficiently rigid); secondly, to provide adequate blade tip clearance it would require an inordinately tall landing

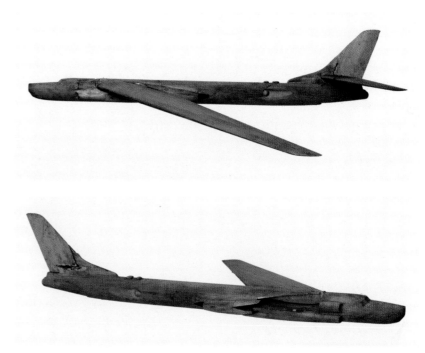

gear which would be both difficult to accommodate and very heavy.

In short order, it was decided that contra-rotating propellers would be best suited for the new engine. Though mechanically complicated and aerodynamically challenging, a design utilising contra-rotating propellers could be better accommodated by the propeller manufacturers and a propeller diameter of 5.6 m (18 ft 4½ in) would suffice, which meant the bomber's landing gear could be readily designed to meet more sensible height-above-the-ramp requirements.

This (unfortunately incomplete) wooden model shows a preliminary project version of 'aircraft 95' powered by four turbojet engines. The placement of the engines on the fuselage sides, with vertically paired air intakes, is unusual.

The same model after a full restoration, showing the aircraft's unusual proportions and high aspect ratio wings. Although the air intakes are directly above one another, the engines are not – the lower pair is ahead of the upper one and its nozzles are obscured by the wings. Note the recessed lateral observation blisters ahead of the tail.

A retouched picture from the advanced development project documents of the '95/1' with 2TV-2F turboprops, showing a desktop model with clouds added by the OKB artist.

A three-view drawing of the Tu-95's full-size mock-up, showing the aircraft's basic dimensions. Note the wide nacelles of the 2TV-2F coupled engines with a distinctive quasi-triangular cross-section.

swept wings were designed for transonic speeds, whereas calculations showed that the propellers' efficiency rating would decrease from 0.88 at Mach 0.64 to 0.78 at Mach 0.8, with an attendant reduction in altitude performance.

(OKB-120 later became known as the Stoopino Machinery Design Bureau (SKBM – **Stoo**pinskoye kon**strook**torskoye byu**ro** ma**shin**ostro**yen**iya), which was the Soviet Union's leading authority on propellers, auxiliary power units and some other items of aviation equipment. It is now called NPP Aero**sila** (na**ooch**no-proiz**vod**stvennoye predpri**ya**tiye – 'Aeropower' Research & Production Association).)

In due course a subscale version of the AV-60 was tested in one of TsAGI's wind tunnels. The propellers were driven by a liquid-cooled piston engine – apparently a wartime Klimov or Mikulin V-12 engine of unknown model – housed in a streamlined pod. Another version was tested in the T-107 transonic wind tunnel on an electrically powered rig. Later, the full-size version of the contraprops passed its tests on an outdoor rig.

On returning to Moscow after the meeting with Kuznetsov where the powerplant issue was resolved and making preliminary calculations of the bomber's parameters, Tupolev made another trip to the Kremlin. This time the meeting with Stalin was at Tupolev's initiative; he convinced the nation's leader that, now that a suitable engine was in the making, the 'aircraft 95' turboprop bomber project was worthy of continued support. At the end of the meeting Stalin warned

The OKB-120 design bureau supervised by Konstantin I. Zhdanov in the town of Rybinsk (the one in the south-east of the Moscow Region, not the one in the Yaroslavl' Region), took on the job, creating the advanced AV-60 contra-rotating propellers and their transmission assembly. One challenging aspect of the eight-blade design (two rows of four blades) was that, in combination with the new Kuznetsov engine, it had to provide an efficiency rating of 0.78 to 0.82 in order for the aircraft to meet its performance target. No previous engine/propeller combination had ever achieved such high numbers. The problem was that the bomber's

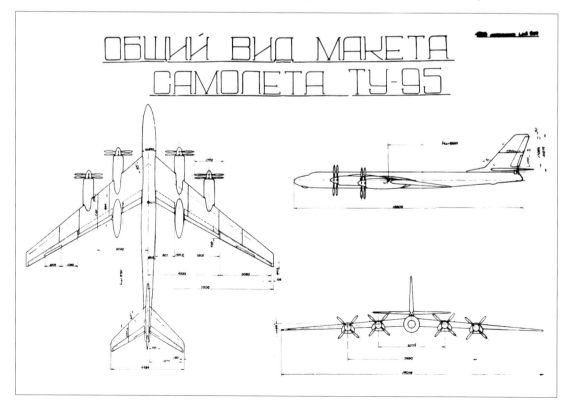

ОБЩИЙ ВИД МАКЕТА САМОЛЕТА ТУ-95

The design staff of the Tupolev OKB's general arrangements section in late 1951. Section chief Sergey M. Yeger is in the middle of the first row.

Tupolev that the strategic bomber programme was of paramount political importance and utmost care was needed to prevent sensitive information from leaking out. By the date of Stalin's approval, the work on the TV-2 turboprop at the Kuznetsov OKB had progressed to the point where prototype engines were delivering more than 5,000 ehp (3,730 kW) on a test bench.

Shortly afterwards, on 2nd April 1951, Andrey N. Tupolev sent a long letter to Stalin, apprising him of the strategic bomber programme's progress. In particular, he wrote:

'Since the day it was tasked with developing a high-speed long-range heavy bomber, our design bureau has been intensively exploring the subject. Now, after a good deal of persistent work, we are in a position to submit a specific proposal on the construction of such an aircraft.

The hardest part of the task […] was how to reconcile high speed with long range. Therefore the first phase of the work was to determine the maximum speed a swept-wing heavy aircraft can currently attain, regardless of the available power of its engines. Experience and large-scale research undertaken at TsAGI shows that, given the current state of the art in aerodynamics, it is possible to reach a maximum speed of 950-960 km/h [590-596 mph] at an altitude of 8,000 m [26,250 ft] and 885-900 km/h [549-559 mph] at 12,000 m [39,370 ft]. […] In our further research we endeavoured to come as close as possible to reaching these speeds. We looked into the possibility of using jet engines to achieve this, determining the influence of the aircraft's size, weight and engine power on its speed, flight altitude and range. […] We arrived at the conclusion that, although jet engines make it possible to create a fast

A similar photo of the same section's design staff taken a year later. Some characteristic attributes of the era are present, such as a red banner with the Soviet coat-of-arms and state motto ('Proletarians of all nations, unite!').

A display model of the Tu-95's competitor – the M-4 in its ultimate form with buried engines and four-wheel nose/main gear bogies.

aircraft, they also make it extremely hard to achieve a range in excess of 10,000-11,000 km [6,210-6,840 miles]; a unique aircraft of extremely large size and high gross weight would be required. […]

The emergence of indigenous turboprop engines developed by [Nikolay D.] Kuznetsov which have passed their state bench trials has created a realistic prospect of developing turboprop-powered long-range bombers in the Soviet Union. Calculations show that with such a powerplant a reasonably sized bomber – that is, with an all-up weight of not more than 130-160 tons [286,600-352,730 lb] – can have much longer range than a jet bomber, as much as 14,000-15,000 km [8,695-9,320 miles] or even 18,000 km [11,180 miles].

Turboprop engines offer both high speed and long range, whereas jet engines enable high speed but over

relatively short range. The reason is the turboprops' lower fuel consumption; the attached graph shows that a jet bomber will have a fuel burn of 8-9.5 kg/km [28.36-33.7 lb/mile] whereas a turboprop bomber of the same size and weight will have a fuel burn of 4-4.5 kg/km [14.19-15.96 lb/mile].

Calculations made by our design bureau and the turboprop engine design bureau headed by Comrade Kuznetsov show that a long-range four-engine bomber should be powered by engines rated at 12,000 ehp. Chief Designer Comrade Kuznetsov has proposed developing a 12,000-ehp turboprop which will be available for installation on the aircraft in the first quarter of 1953. We believe that a high-speed long-range heavy bomber should be developed around these engines, which should be the powerplant of the production version. However, to

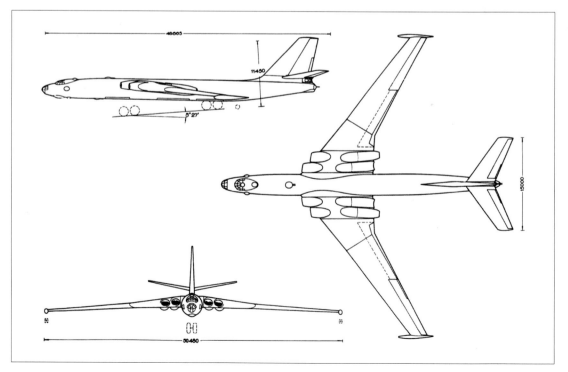

A three-view of the M-4, showing the bomber's dimensions. Note the strong nose-up ground angle (5°27') and the 'toe-in' of the four AM-3 turbojets.

Here, for comparison, is a desktop model of the original '95/1' powered by 2TV-2F engines; note the short forward fuselage and the shape of the engine air intakes. Regrettably no photos have survived of the actual '95/1' prototype.

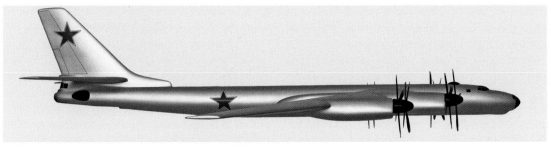

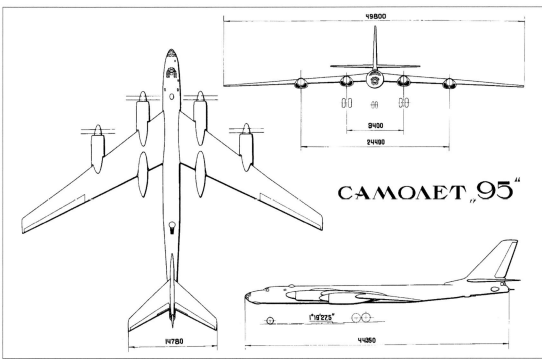

A drawing of the 2TV-2F powered '95' bomber from the ADP documents, showing how close the inboard engine nacelles were to the fuselage.

СAMOΛET „95"

save time it is advisable to use currently available engines and manufacture the first few aircraft with four coupled turboprops. These will be based on the TV-2 engine; [...] two such engines will drive a single propeller via common reduction gear, delivering a total of 12,000 ehp.'

One paragraph of the letter merits special attention. Tupolev wrote: *'We are confident that we are able to develop a long-range bomber with the required performance within a short time, since it is dimensionally similar to the "aircraft 85" bomber powered by four M-253K engines, which we have built and which is currently under test. This makes it possible to minimise the design schedule and prototype construction schedule, particularly if the crew accommodation in the front [pressure] cabin is taken as-is from "aircraft 85".* **Using the "85" as the basis makes it possible to borrow parts of the airframe structure** (our highlighting – Auth.) *and retain a huge number of equipment items supplied by subcontractors participating in the "aircraft 85" programme. We believe that such an aircraft can enter flight test next September.'*

On 11th July 1951 the Council of Ministers and the Communist Party Central Committee issued joint directive No.2396-1137, which was backed up by the appropriate MAP order No.654 that same day. In accordance with these documents OKB-156 was tasked with designing and building a long-range high-speed bomber in two versions. The first of these, with the provisional powerplant consisting of four 2TV-2F coupled turboprops, was to be ready for flight test by September 1952; the second version would have the definitive powerplant comprising four TV-12 single turboprops, and the second prototype manufactured in this configuration had to be ready for flight test by September 1953. Development of the TV-12 and the 2TV-2F was officially sanctioned by the same directive. Incidentally, the fact that the abovementioned MAP order was issued on the same day as the Council of Ministers directive speaks a lot for the importance attached to the project; as a rule, such MAP orders followed within a few days.

Another fact that testifies to the high priority of the project is that the issue of mass production was resolved within four days. On 15th November 1951 MAP's aircraft factory No.18 in Kuibyshev and its design office (OKB-18) were ordered to prepare for production of 'aircraft 95'. Tooling-up would be initiated during January 1952 and the necessary preparations for full-rate production were to be completed by 1st September 1952.

Meanwhile, the Myasishchev OKB and MMZ No.23 (*Moskovskiy mashinostroitel'nyy zavod* – Moscow Machinery Factory), where the design bureau resided, were preparing to launch production of the M-4. It was now well known (to *those who needed to know*, that is!) that the Myasishchev and Tupolev bombers would be competing with each other. In fact, the Soviet Air Force would be holding a fly-off to see which aircraft would be best able to accommodate its intercontinental heavy bomber requirement for the coming decades; this matter would be decided in the course of the two bombers' state acceptance (= certification) trials. The Soviet government (and, in particular, Stalin himself) believed that the tight development schedule, and the huge costs associated with developing two aircraft to fill the same role, were justified. The perceived threat of nuclear war with the USA provided the incentive necessary to expedite development.

Work on the advanced development project (ADP) of 'aircraft 95' began on 15th July 1951; it was performed by the OKB's technical projects department headed by Sergey M. Yeger. This work proceeded rapidly – in parallel with the actual manufacturing of the first prototype, which was built as engineering and manufacturing drawings were released. The actual design effort was led by Nikolay I. Bazenkov, one of Andrey N. Tupolev's closest associates. Creating the '95' was a monstrous effort that involved interacting with lots of subcontractors in the aircraft industry (such as the Kuznetsov OKB), the electronics industry etc., and Bazenkov was entrusted with co-ordinating this effort at OKB-156. He would later become the Tu-95's project chief and would also have similar responsibility for the Tu-114 *Rossiya* (Russia; NATO reporting name *Cleat*) long-haul airliner derived from the bomber, which lies outside the scope of this book.

It has been mentioned earlier that initially the Tu-85's fuselage layout was deemed suitable for the '95'. At the ADP stage, however, the fuselage's internal layout was considerably revised. For one thing, the straight-wing Tu-85 had the wing centre section placed amidships, with two bomb bays fore and aft of it. Conversely, on 'aircraft 95', which had swept wings, the centre section was moved forward along the fuselage, hence there was only one bomb bay aft of the wing torsion box, with fuel tankage fore and aft of it. The large bomb bay was conveniently located so that the bomb load was as close as possible to the centre of gravity (CG), and dropping the bomb(s) would not result in a strong CG shift.

For another, the separate waist gunner's station of the Tu-85 was found to be excessive; on the 'aircraft 95' the crew of eight was seated in two pressurised cabins instead of three. The front cabin (accessed via the nosewheel well) accommodated the captain and co-pilot side by side, the navigator/bomb-aimer ahead of and below the pilots, the aft-facing flight engineer aft of them, the forward-facing co-navigator and the dorsal gunner/radio operator (GRO) sitting under an observation blister. The co-navigator was known as a 'navigator/operator' (**shtoor**man-ope**rah**tor) or Nav/Op because he worked the aircraft systems but presumably could perform some navigation functions as well. in

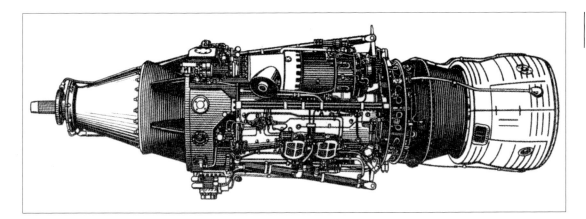

A drawing of the Kuznetsov NK-12 turboprop engine.

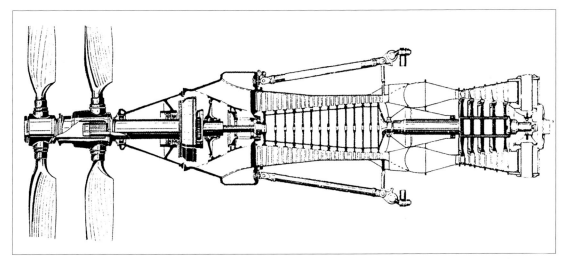

A schematic layout of the NK-12 showing the planetary reduction gearbox and the engine mount rods connecting the gearbox casing to the nacelle structure.

contrast, the 'proper' navigator in the extensively glazed extreme nose, which was accessed via a passage between the pilots' seats, was tautologically referred to as **shtoor**man-navi**gah**tor (both words mean 'navigator' in Russian). Normally he faced left, working with navigation instruments, except when he was using the optical bomb sight – then he faced forward.

The rear pressure cabin with a ventral access hatch was located at the aft extremity of the fuselage, accommodating two gunners, one of whom worked the ventral barbette and the other one the tail barbette. This latter gunner was titled defensive fire commander (koman**deer** ogne**vykh** oosta**nov**ok – lit. 'firing installations commander') because he had control over

An NK-12 (complete with engine mount rods) on a ground handling dolly. The slogan on the wall reads 'We will fulfil all the plans of the [Communist] Party!'.

Right: A ground rig for testing the contra-rotating propeller concept envisaged for the '95', with subscale propellers driven by a piston engine. Here it is mounted on a dolly for presentation purposes.

Far right: The same rig mounted in one of the wind tunnels at TsAGI.

Right and far right: Two views of the rig as the engine is run. Here the contraprops have been fitted with a spinner.

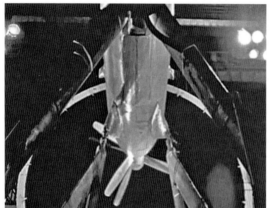

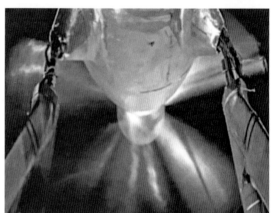

Here, for comparison, is the actual AV-60 propeller being tested on a special electrically powered rig in TsAGI's T-107 transonic wind tunnel.

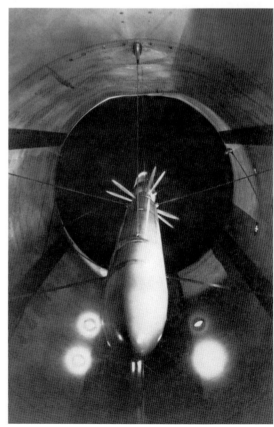

all three cannon barbettes. Hence the large elliptical observation/sighting blisters used by the gunner working the ventral barbette were located immediately ahead of the tail gunner's station glazing (below the horizontal tail). Placing two crewmen in the rear cabin improved combat co-ordination and boosted morale – the tail gunner was no longer 'alone out there'. The pressure cabins were protected from below and from behind by armour plate and, in the case of the tail gunner's station, by bulletproof glazing; the overall weight of the armour was 923 kg (2,034 lb).

The 'aircraft 95' was intended for attacking targets of strategic importance (such as military bases, seaports, defence industry facilities, political and administrative centres, and other similar entities) located deep within enemy territory that were otherwise inaccessible to other military aircraft. As a secondary role, the '95' was to fly naval missions, deploying anti-shipping mines and carrying out bombing and torpedo strikes against enemy shipping on remote oceanic TOs.

The bomb bay of the '95' was designed to accommodate a normal weapons load of 5,000 kg (11,020 lb) increasing to 15,000 kg (33,070 lb) in high gross weight configuration, although it was envisaged that as much as 18,000 kg (39,680 lb) of bombs could be carried in exceptional cases. The options included bombs of 250- to 9,000-kg (551- to 19,840-lb) calibre. Weapons options for the naval missions were AMD-500, AMD-1000, AMD-M, IGDM, Serpey, Lira and Desna naval mines, 45-36AVA wet-heater torpedoes, RAT-52 or A-2 rocket-propelled torpedoes.

(Note: AMD = *aviatsionnaya* **meena donnaya** – air-dropped bottom mine; IGDM = *indooktsionno-ghidrodinamicheskaya* **donnaya meena** – bottom mine with a combined induction/hydrodynamic

A different test rig with the AV-60 contraprops developed for the Tu-95. Note the protective grille behind the prop.

detector. *Desna* is the name of a river in European Russia; Lira (pronounced **lee**ra) means 'Lyre'. As for the nonsensical word *Serpey*, it is nothing more than an accidental anagram of the intended codename *Persey* (Perseus); quite simply, a typist had made an error when typing out the document clearing the weapon for service, and no-one had taken the responsibility to set her straight, believing that 'the Powers That Be know better'! 45-36AVA means 450-mm (17⁴⁵⁄₆₄ in) calibre, 1936 model, *[torpeda] aviatsionnaya, vysotnaya* – air-droppable torpedo for high-altitude attacks; RAT (later amended to RAT-52) = *re'aktivnaya aviatsionnaya torpeda* – jet-powered air-droppable torpedo, 1952 model.)

The second Tu-4LL engine testbed under the Tu-95 programme with a TV-12 turboprop in the No.3 nacelle. Note the air data boom on the nose and the fairing aft of the nosewheel well which houses a cine camera filming the propellers.

A 9,000-kg (19,840-lb) FAB-9000 M50 high-explosive bomb with a ballistic ring.

The RDS-4, the first Soviet operational nuclear bomb, was one of the Tu-95's weapons.

Normally all offensive weapons were to be carried internally; as per advanced development project, these included UAB-1600B, UB-2000F **Chai**ka (Seagull) and UB-5000F Kondor radio-controlled gliding bombs (*oopravlyayemaya [avia]bomba* – guided bomb). However, the ADP also envisaged external stores which were too bulky for internal carriage. These were the SNAB-3000 infrared-homing bomb (*samonavodyashchayasya aviabomba* – homing bomb), also known under the codename Krab (Crab), and the T-2 (aka 16Kh) first-generation cruise missile. The 16Kh, named *Priboy* (Surf), was the most advanced of several

Right and far right: Front and rear views of the RDS-4 nuclear bomb. Note the arming connector at the rear closed by a cover.

Below: The RDS-4 was much more compact than the globular RDS-3 visible in the background.

cruise missiles derived by Vladimir N. Chelomey's OKB-51 from the captured German Fieseler Fi 103 'buzz bomb' (better known as the V-1). However, none of these guided weapons would eventually be carried by 'aircraft 95'.

The guided and unguided conventional weapons (bombs, mines and torpedoes) were considered optional, since a thermonuclear device ('hydrogen bomb') was regarded as the primary weapon for the strategic bombing mission. Hence the bomb bay was heat-insulated and electrically heated, the temperature being maintained at +5-25°C (41-77°F) because nuclear weapons and their associated systems were sensitive to temperature fluctuations – if the nuke had a cold soak during high-altitude cruise, the chain reaction might not go ahead, with no explosion as a result.

The defensive armament consisted of six 23-mm (.90 calibre) cannons (apparently Nudelman/Rikhter NR-23 cannons at this early stage) in three remote-controlled powered installations – the Tu-85's five cannon barbettes were deemed excessive. Specifically, there was one pair with 300 rounds per gun (rpg) in a VT barbette (**verkh**naya too**rel'** – dorsal turret) ahead of the wings, another pair with 400 rpg in an NT barbette (**nizh**naya too**rel'** – ventral turret) aft of the wings and a third pair with 500 rpg in a DK tail turret (*distantsionno [oopravlyayemaya toorel'], kormovaya* – remote-controlled turret, rear). In fact, the capacity of the ammunition boxes was rather bigger – 1,000 rounds, 1,200 rounds and 2,000 rounds respectively. The dorsal and ventral barbettes had a 360° field of fire; they were positioned well aft of the wings and the dorsal one was designed to retract flush with the top of the fuselage when not in use, cutting drag. The defensive armament (specifically the barbettes, their remote control system and the optical sighting stations to which they were slaved) was developed by OKB-134 under Chief Designer Ivan I. Toropov, although the Tupolev OKB's armament department, or Section V (*vo'oruzheniye* – armament) headed by Aleksandr V. Nadashkevich obviously had a hand in the matter. (It may be mentioned that in the 1950s western aviation experts assumed the Tu-95's cannon armament to consist of seven cannons but they were wrong – unlike the Tu-16, there was no fixed forward-firing cannon in the nose.)

The ADP envisaged the following basic avionics and equipment. The '95' was to feature an AP-15 electric autopilot; navigation was assisted by two (main and back-up) ARK-5 Amur (a river in the Soviet Far East; pronounced like the French word *amour*) automatic direction finders, an SP-50 *Materik* (Continent) instrument landing system (ILS), a Meridian short-range radio navigation (SHORAN) system, RV-2 and RV-10 radio altimeters. (ARK = *avtomaticheskiy rahdiokompas* – ADF; SP = *[sistema] slepoy posahdki* – blind landing system; RV = **rah**diovysoto**mer** – radio altimeter.)

The communications equipment included two sets of 1RSB-70 communications radios (**rahdiostahnt**siya bombardi**rov**shchika – bomber-type radio), an RSIU-3 command link radio, an AVRA-45 emergency locator transmitter (avar**eey**naya **rah**diostahntsiya – emergency radio, 1945 model) and an SPU-10 intercom (samo**lyot**noye perego**vor**noye oo**stroy**stvo).

The '95' was to feature a Rubidiy-MM bomb-aiming/navigation radar in a chin radome, with a FARM add-on photographically recording the image on the radar display, and a PRS-1 *Argon* gun-laying radar (pri**tsel rah**diolokatsi**on**nyy strel**ko**vyy – radio gunsight) in the tail. The Rubidiy-MM (NATO codename *Short Horn*) was a further improved version of the Rubidiy-M. Like the PRS-1 (NATO codename *Bee Hind*), it had been first fitted to the second prototype Tu-85.

Electric power was provided by four 18-kilowatt GSR-18000 engine-driven generators, with 12SA-65 DC batteries (star**tyor**naya, aviatsi**on**naya [akkumu**lya**tornaya bata**rey**a] – aircraft-specific starter battery, capacity 65 A·h) as a back-up. The oxygen equipment included ten KP-24 breathing apparatus (kislo**rod**nyy pri**bor** – oxygen apparatus) – that is, with provision for two additional crew members – and eight KP-19 breathing apparatus, plus two KPZh-30 liquid oxygen converters (kislo**rod**nyy pri**bor zhid**kosnyy). The wing and tail unit leading edges, engine air intakes, flight deck windshield and navigator's station glazing were electrically de-iced, while the propeller blades had alcohol de-icing.

Photo equipment for planned reconnaissance, bomb damage assessment (BDA) and reconnoitring targets of opportunity comprised AFA-33/75 or AFA-33/100 daylight cameras (**a**ero**fot**oappa**raht** – aircraft camera) and NAFA-MK or NAFA-5S/50 cameras (noch**noy a**ero**fot**oappa**raht** – aircraft camera for night operations) for vertical photography, plus a KS-5S cine camera. The bomber was to be fitted with the PR-1 combined ELINT/ECM equipment (PR = po**mekh**ovoraz**ved**yvatel'naya [appara**too**ra]) and the SRO-2M IFF transponder (samo**lyot**nyy **rah**diolokatsi**on**nyy ot**vet**chik – aircraft-mounted radar responder) which was part of the then-new *Khrom-***Nik**el' (Chromium-Nickel) IFF system. Three LASM-49 inflatable dinghies (**lod**ka avar**eey**no-spa**sah**tel'naya, **ma**logaba**rit**naya – compact rescue dinghy, 1949 model) were provided in case of ditching.

Concurrently with the ADP design, in August 1951 the Soviet Air Force began drawing up the specific operational requirement (SOR) which the new bomber would have to meet. In accordance with the SOR and the aforementioned Council of Ministers directive, the aircraft was to have an operating range of up to 15,000 km (9,315 miles) with payload and a maximum range of 17,000-18,000 km (10,557-11,178 miles). Cruising speed was specified as 750-820 km/h (466-

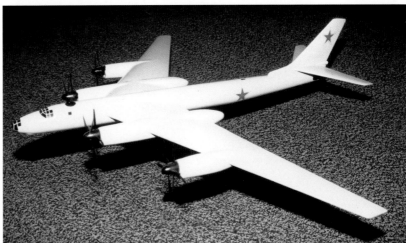

The model of the '95/1' with 2TV-2F engines.

509 mph) and maximum speed was expected to be 920-950 km/h (571-590 mph). The service ceiling was expected to be approximately 14,000 m (45,920 ft). The take-off run was estimated at 1,500-1,800 m (4,920-5,900 ft), depending on the weight.

After some revision the final performance estimates included a cruising speed of 750-800 km/h (466-497 mph) at an altitude of 10,000-14,000 m (32,810-45,920 ft). Maximum range now was estimated as 14,500-17,500 km (9,005-10,868 miles).

According to the technical projects department's assessments, the bomber's relatively high speed at altitude, combined with its heavy defensive armament,

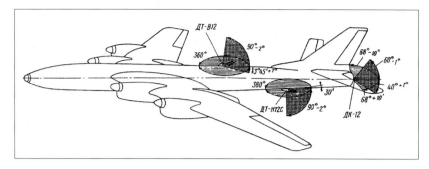

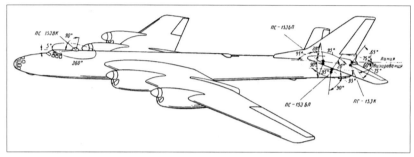

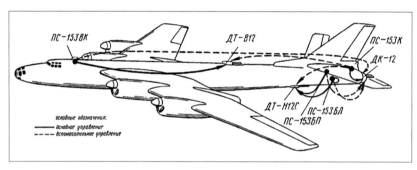

Top: A diagram showing the fields of fire of the DT-V12 dorsal turret, the DT-N12S ventral turret and the DK-12 tail turret.
Centre: The fields of view of the PS-153VK (dorsal), PS-153BL/PS-153BP (port/starboard) and PS-153K (rear) optical sights.
Above: A diagram showing how each sighting station controls the cannon turrets.

Below: The location of the defensive armament on the Tu-95.

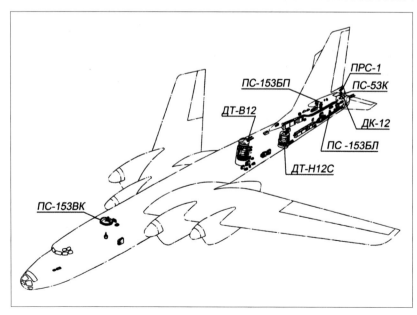

would make the '95' a difficult target for enemy fighters to intercept and attack. Additionally, the bomber's up-to-date navigation and communications suites gave it a high chance of success when operating singly or in a group, even in adverse weather and/or at night.

Though it had now been determined that the first prototype '95' would fly with 2TV-2F engines, it was decided that the second prototype would be powered by TV-12 engines. This engine was expected to have the same 12,500-ehp take-off rating (albeit at a higher speed of 8,300 rpm) and the same 6,500-ehp cruise rating in the same conditions as the 2TV-2F, but the SFC was rather lower – 0.225 kg/hp-hr (0.496 lb/hp-hr) and 0.164 kg/hp-hr (0.361 lb/hp-hr) respectively, and dry weight less propeller was 2,900 kg (6,390 lb). (Some sources assert the TV-12 had a maximum continuous rating of 12,000 ehp (8,952 kW) and a cruise power of 10,200 ehp (7,609 kW), all at sea level.)

Analysis of the powerplant options of 'aircraft 95' showed that, with a 9,000-kg (19,840-lb) bomb load, the 2TV-2F engined version would have an estimated combat radius of 6,000 km (3,726 miles) versus 7,500 km (4,658 miles) for the TV-12 engined version. This finalised the decision to proceed with the TV-12 and select this engine for the production bomber.

In-flight refuelling capability was envisaged for the '95' from the outset – initially in the form of the Shelest/Vasyanin wingtip-to-wingtip IFR system that had been tested on the Tu-4 and envisaged for the future Tu-16, which meant sister ships were to act as the tankers. This would turn the '95' into a true global strike system with the ability to fly missions in excess of 32,000 km (19,872 miles) if the aircraft was refuelled twice (on the outbound leg and on the return leg). With IFR, the '95' would be able to attack any point on the globe (except maybe parts of South America and the Antarctica) from Soviet territory and return to base without difficulty, which made the additional design effort seemingly worthwhile. Maximum range on internal fuel was estimated as 15,300 km (9,510 miles) and effective range with 5% fuel reserves as 13,500 km (8,390 miles). The take-off and landing run was estimated as 1,400-1,500 m (4,590-4,920 ft).

The '95' had no ejection seats – in an emergency the crew was supposed to bail out conventionally through the entry hatches. The reasoning behind this approach was that the aircraft would not operate in flight modes where ejection systems might be necessary – the cruising speed was fairly low. Also, dispensing with ejection seats gave a sizeable weight saving and (supposedly) enhanced crew comfort. (In fairness, this approach was nothing out of the ordinary at the time. Even on western strategic bombers of the day, only the pilots enjoyed the luxury of ejection seats, while the other crewmembers had to bail out in the old-fashioned way. Not until the advent of the Tu-16 were all

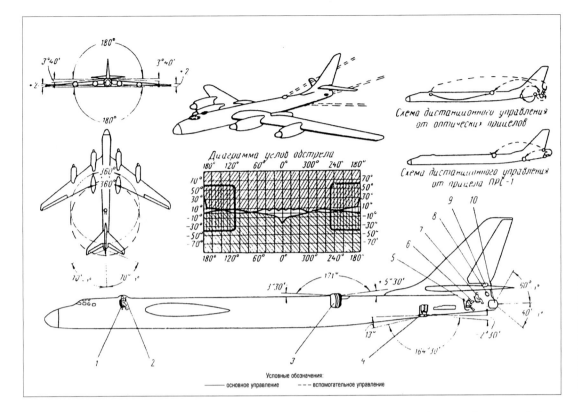

Диаграмма углов обстрела

Схема дистанционного управления от оптических прицелов

Схема дистанционного управления от прицела ПРС-1

Условные обозначения:
—— основное управление   – – – вспомогательное управление

Another drawing showing the cannon turrets (with their respective fields of fire) and the control thereof by means of the optical sights and (in the case of the tail turret) the PRS-1 gun laying radar.

crewmembers provided with ejection seats.) A curious feature of the '95' was that the flight deck floor incorporated a conveyor belt similar to the travelators found at many modern airports. It was hydraulically actuated, coming into action simultaneously with emergency extension of the nose gear unit and emergency opening of the entry hatch in the nosewheel well roof. The conveyor belt was powered by hydraulic accumulators, allowing it to run long enough for all crewmembers in the forward cabin to bail out even if all engines were dead and the engine-driven hydraulic pumps were out of action.

In order to expedite production entry the ADP stipulated that the '95' should have maximum parts and equipment commonality with the OKB's previous designs wherever appropriate. Indeed, the forward pressure cabin was taken virtually wholesale from the Tu-85, just like Andrey N. Tupolev had suggested in his letter to Stalin – the contours of the flight deck glazing, the long nose ahead of the stepped windscreen, the navigator's station glazing and the chin radome were identical. This saved money and speeded up development considerably, allowing the bomber to enter production and service at the earliest possible date.

Upon completion of the project work the ADP was submitted for review to the Air Technical Committee reporting to the Commander-in-Chief of the Soviet Air Force. On 31st October 1951 the Committee approved it. A month earlier, in September 1951, the OKB had started issuing the manufacturing drawings for

prototype construction; the complete set of these drawings took a full year to issue and, as mentioned earlier, actual prototype construction proceeded as the blueprints were released.

The tables on pages 38-39 show the ADP data of 'aircraft 95' as recorded in a so-called statistical file (*statkarta*) completed on 10th September 1951. Such files were filled out by MAP multiple times as an aircraft progressed from project to prototype to production hardware. Interestingly, at that early stage the aircraft did not yet have a proper 'Tu-something-or-other' designation – the file refers to it as the *Tu-4 2TV-2F "95"*. This designation may appear utterly misleading, as the aircraft was by no means a version of the Tu-4. The key to this puzzle is how to read it – it means 'Tupolev aircraft with no service designation, four 2TV-2F engines, manufacturer's designation 'Model 95'! This echoes pre-war Soviet aircraft designation practices when the number and type of engines was often included in the designation. For example, the Tupolev ANT-40 twin-engined bomber (better known as the SB, *skorosnoy bombardirovshchik* – fast bomber) had versions designated SB-2M-100 (with Klimov M-100 engines) and SB-2M-103 (with Klimov M-103 engines); as a result, the service designation was occasionally misinterpreted as 'SB-2'.

Construction of a full-size wooden mock-up of 'aircraft 95' commenced in August 1951 at MMZ No.156 'Opyt' (the prototype manufacturing facility at the Tupolev OKB's Moscow premises). Depending on the context, the word *opyt* translates as either 'experiment'

'Aircraft 95' advanced development project specifications	
Crew	8
Length overall	44.35 m (145 ft 6⅞ in)
Wing span	49.8 m (163 ft 4⅝ in)
Horizontal tail span	17.78 m (58 ft 4 in)
Height on ground	12.95 m (42 ft 5²⁷⁄₃₂ in)
Wing area	283 m² (3,046.19 sq ft)
Vertical tail area	38.63 m² (415.81 sq ft)
Horizontal tail area	54.49 m² (586.53 sq ft)
Powerplant	4 x 2TV-2F (coupled engines)
Engine power:	
take-off	12,500 hp
maximum continuous	12,000 hp (up to h = 6,000 m/19,685 ft)
nominal (cruise)	10,200 hp (V = 200 m/sec)
Propellers:	
model	AV-60 (contra-rotating)
no. of blades	4+4
diameter	5.8 m (19 ft 0¹⁄₃₂ in)
Fuel	Kerosene
All-up weight over the target:	
normal	105,000 kg (231,490 lb)
maximum	156,000 kg (343,920 lb)
Empty weight	66,760 kg (147,180 lb)
Payload:	
normal	38,240 kg (84,300 lb)
maximum	89,240 kg (196,740 lb)
Fuel load:	
normal	30,400 kg (67,020 lb)
maximum	81,800 kg (180,340 lb)
Bomb load:	
normal	5,000 kg (11,020 lb)
maximum	15,000 kg (33,070 lb)
exceptional	18,000 kg (39,680 lb)
Payload-to-weight ratio:	
normal payload	36.7%
maximum payload	57%
Power loading at sea level:	
normal weight	2.1 kg/hp (4.63 lb/hp)
maximum weight	3.12 kg/hp (6.88 lb/hp)

Maximum speed at normal TOW/maximum TOW: *	
at 8,000 m (26,250 ft)	912/890 km/h (566/552 mph)
at 9,000 m (29,530 ft)	940/900 km/h (583/559 mph)
at 10,000 m (32,810 ft)	908/850 km/h (564/528 mph)
Landing speed at normal weight/maximum weight	180/207 km/h (111/128 mph)
Climb time to 10,000 m, normal TOW/maximum TOW	11.0/26.0 minutes
Service ceiling over the target	13,000-13,500 m (42,650-44,290 ft)
Service ceiling at nominal power, normal TOW/maximum TOW	13,000/10,000 m (42,650/32,810 ft)
Maximum range	14,000-15,000 km (8,700-9,320 miles) [1]
Range:	
with 5,000 kg (11,020 lb) of bombs	14,580 km (9,060 miles) [2]
with 9,000 kg (19,840 lb) of bombs	13,750 km (8,540 miles) [3]
with 12,000 kg (26,455 lb) of bombs	13,250 km (8,230 miles) [4]
with 15,000 kg (33,070 lb) of bombs	12,650 km (7,860 miles) [5]
Endurance:	
with 5,000 kg of bombs	19 hours [2]
with 9,000 kg of bombs	18 hours [3]
with 12,000 kg of bombs	17.3 hours [4]
with 15,000 kg of bombs	16.5 hours [5]
Take-off run	1,500-1,800 m (4,920-5,910 ft)
Take-off distance to h=25 m (82 ft):	
with normal TOW	1,100 m (3,610 ft)
with maximum TOW	3,000 m (9,840 ft)
Landing run:	
landing weight 98,500 kg (217,160 lb), with bombs and 30% fuel	850 m (2,790 ft)
landing weight 76,000 kg (167,550 lb), with 10% fuel	660 m (2,165 ft)

Notes:

* Restricted by a dynamic pressure limit of 1,915 kg/m² (392 lb/sq ft) at altitudes up to 7,000 m (22,965 ft); at higher altitude the maximum permissible speed is Mach 0.86

1. With 5,000 kg (11,020 lb) of bombs, speed 750-820 km/h (465-509 mph).
2. All-up weight 156,000 kg (343,920 lb), fuel load 81,800 kg (180,340 lb), altitude 9,500-14,200 m (31,170-46,590 ft), speed 750-780 km/h (465-484 mph).
3. Fuel load 77,800 kg (171,520 lb), altitude 9,500-14,200 m.
4. Fuel load 74,800 kg (164,910 lb), altitude 9,500-14,200 m.
5. Fuel load 71,800 kg (158,290 lb), altitude 9,500-14,200 m.

or 'experience', both meanings being well and truly applicable. The mock-up was completed in late November; in the course of construction it was inspected three times by the Air Force's mock-up review commission (*maketnaya komissiya*), an expert panel whose task was to detect and eliminate any obvious errors at an early stage. This was an obligatory stage of the design process (similar to the so-called 'gates' of today) ensuring that any obvious errors were detected and eliminated before the first metal was cut, thereby avoiding waste of time and resources. The commission voiced considerable criticism, and many changes and improvements were incorporated as a result. In November the completed mock-up was examined again in detail by the commission and the following month the Soviet Air Force Commander-in-Chief Col.-

Gen. Pavel F. Zhigarev approved it for prototype construction.

'Aircraft 95/1' bomber prototype ('order 180-1')

In fact, however, MMZ No.156 had begun construction of the first prototype 'aircraft 95' as early as October 1951; thus, so many things were going on in parallel. The first prototype was known at the OKB as the '95/1' and referred to in MAP paperwork as *zakaz* 180-1 ('order 180-1'). Concurrently, a second airframe for static testing was laid down as well. Some sources, though, refer to the first prototype as 'order 176'.

(A linguistic comment must be made here. There are two related Russian words which are both translated into English as 'order'. In the above case, 'order' means not 'a verbal or written command from a superior', such as the aforementioned MAP orders (which corresponds to the word *pri**kaz***), but rather 'an order placed by a customer' (which corresponds to the word *za**kaz***). The degree of work involved in such orders varied from replacing a certain item of equipment to a complete refit into an entirely new version – or even construction from scratch, as in this case. For the sake of clarity, orders of the latter kind are hereinafter mentioned without a 'No.' – for example, 'order 881', the way they were listed in actual paperwork.)

Speaking of static tests and structural integrity – a critical aspect of the bomber's design – the Tupolev OKB's structural strength department headed by Aleksey M. Cheryomukhin was actively involved in the development effort from the start and shouldered an immense workload. This department was responsible for many critical aspects of airframe design, including the choice of the optimum engine location. In the meantime, aircraft factory No.18 was already gearing up to build the '95', and this meant not only design of the manufacturing jigs and tooling but the logistical aspects of production as well. This threw in additional complications for the structural strength department, since the on-going design changes necessary to ensure structural strength required the prototype's airframe to be modified repeatedly. This not only delayed completion and flight testing but also had a knock-on effect, disrupting production because these changes, in turn, had to be incorporated on the production line in Kuibyshev, with more delays as a result.

That was not all. Back when the B-29 was being copied, Cheryomukhin analysed the American bomber's airframe and concluded that the aircraft had been designed with substantially lower ultimate loads in mind than those prescribed by the Soviet structural strength standards (SSS) then in force. In other words, the SSS prescribed exceptionally large strength margins to accommodate projected loads – just to be on the safe side. As a result, aircraft designed to these standards ended up being overweight, which led to serious performance degradation. Hence, when 'aircraft 95' and the M-4 were being designed, the SSS and the methods of determining structural loads were reworked and approximated to those adopted in the USA. The combined efforts of TsAGI, OKB-156 and OKB-23 led to new insights into the structures and materials required for large swept wings. This technology was applied to the two bombers' wings; as a result, enormous weight savings were achieved without compromising structural integrity.

The avionics and electrical systems of the '95' bomber were quite advanced by the day's standards. For the first time in Soviet practice, aluminium wiring was used in the electric circuits which was much lighter than hitherto standard copper wires, and a lightweight

The ordnance options of 'aircraft 95' as per ADP specifications		
Type of ordnance	Maximum quantity	Total weight
1. Bombs		
FAB-250 M-46 *	36	9,000 kg (19,840 lb)
FAB-500 M-46	24	12,000 kg (26,455 lb)
BrAB-500	24	12,000 kg (26,455 lb)
FAB-1500 M-46	10	15,000 kg (33,070 lb)
FAB-1500 M-46	12 †	18,000 kg (39,680 lb) †
BrAB-1500 M-46	10	15,000 kg (33,070 lb)
FAB-3000 M-46	4	12,000 kg (26,455 lb)
BrAB-3000	4	12,000 kg (26,455 lb)
FAB-5000 M-46	2	10,000 kg (22,045 lb)
BrAB-6000	2	12,000 kg (26,455 lb)
FAB-9000 M-46	1	9,000 kg (19,840 lb)
UAB-1600B	4	6,400 kg (14,110 lb)
UB-2000F Chaika	4	8,000 kg (17,640 lb)
UB-5000F Kondor	2	10,000 kg (22,045 lb)
SNAB-3000 Krab ‡	4	12,000 kg (26,455 lb)
2. Naval mines		
AMD-500	16	8,000 kg (17,640 lb)
AMD-1000	6	6,000 kg (13,230 lb)
AMD-2M	12	13,200 kg (29,100 lb)
IGDM	12	13,200 kg (29,100 lb)
Serpey	6	8,700 kg (19,180 lb)
Desna	8	6,000 kg (13,230 lb)
Lira	8	7,600 kg (16,760 lb)
3. Torpedoes		
45-36AVA	8	9,320 kg (20,550 lb)
A-2 (RAT-52)	6	3,750 kg (8,270 lb)
4. Missiles		
T-2 (16Kh Priboy) ‡	2	5,240 kg (11,550 lb)

Notes:
* FAB = *foo**gahs**naya **a**via**bom**ba* – high-explosive bomb; BrAB = *brone**boy**naya **a**via**bom**ba* – armour-piercing bomb
† Exceptional cases
‡ External carriage

electrical de-icing system was incorporated; these features subsequently found wide use on new Soviet heavy aircraft. Additionally, a powerful self-contained starter system was developed for the TV-12 engine.

Control system technology also proved to be technologically challenging and sparked an argument between the Tupolev OKB and TsAGI. The institute had become a supporter of irreversible hydraulic actuators in flight control systems and insisted that they be used on the 'aircraft 95'. General Designer Andrey N. Tupolev, taking a more conservative approach, argued that the actuators had a poor reliability record and that using them would be premature – the 'good old' mechanical systems would suffice. This argument continued for a considerable time before Tupolev got his way – although special design measures had to be taken to reduce the control forces to an acceptable level by choosing proper aerodynamic compensation on the control surfaces. The resulting unboosted mechanical flight control system used on the '95', though requiring considerable strength on the part of its pilots, eventually proved highly dependable and trouble-free.

Tupolev's lack of faith in powered controls became almost legendary; one of his most famous quotes was *'The best hydraulic control actuator is the one that remains on the ground'* (i.e., is not installed on the aircraft). In fairness, this overly conservative approach once nearly resulted in the loss of a Tu-16 (which had similarly unboosted controls) when the pilots had to apply super-human efforts to recover from a spin. (Eventually reversible hydraulic actuators would be introduced in the production Tu-95's pitch and roll control circuits after all.)

In contrast, in continuing what it foresaw as the trend of future bomber design, the Myasishchev OKB did not hesitate to use irreversible hydraulic actuators on the M-4. Though this was a calculated risk mandated by the all-jet bomber's performance, the powered control system would prove to be a pain in the butt, with technical issues that took years to resolve.

Meanwhile, the 2TV-2F engine was cleared for flight tests by mid-1952. Eight Tu-4 bombers had been transferred from the Air Force to MAP's Flight Research Institute (LII – *Lyotno-issledovatel'skiy institoot*) located in the town of Zhukovskiy south of Moscow, in the early 1950s for conversion into engine testbeds; they had the common designation Tu-4LL (*letayushchaya laboratoriya* – lit. 'flying laboratory') but no two were identical. (Note: In Russian the term *letayushchaya laboratoriya* is used indiscriminately to denote any kind of testbed or research/survey aircraft.) Two of these aircraft were operated in the interests of the Tupolev OKB, including the fifth Moscow-built Tu-4 manufactured by MMZ No.23 (construction number 230501). In its third iteration this testbed had a 2TV-2F turboprop mounted in the No.3 (starboard inboard) position, replacing the standard ASh-73TK radial. The custom-made engine nacelle had the same design as on the '95/1' prototype, featuring a quasi-trapezoidal cross-section with a wide air intake below the propeller spinner. The original AV-60 contra-rotating propellers fitted to the 2TV-2F on the testbed had constant-chord blades with round tips but turned out to be unsatisfactory and were replaced by AV-60V propellers of the same 5.8 m diameter featuring tapered blades. In this configuration Tu-4LL c/n 230501 was referred to in paperwork as 'order 175LL' or 'aircraft 94/2'; this is not to be confused with the aforementioned 'aircraft 94' mid-life upgrade project for the Tu-4.

The '95/1' prototype powered by four 2TV-2F turboprops was finally completed by the autumn of 1952. Following a series of ground tests at MMZ No.156, it was disassembled and trucked piecemeal to the LII airfield in Zhukovskiy where the Tupolev OKB, like most of the Soviet aircraft design bureaux, had its flight test facility. The latter was known as ZhLiiDB (*Zhukovskaya lyotno-ispytahtel'naya i dovodochnaya bahza* – the Zhukovskiy Flight Test & Refinement Base). There the bomber was reassembled and, on 20th September 1952, submitted for manufacturer's flight tests.

Incidentally, getting the bomber there was not all that easy. The fuselage/inner wing/inboard nacelle assembly had to be towed on the aircraft's own landing gear (with all due precautions and security measures), as no low-loader trailers big enough for the job were available. However, when the intended route of the vehicle convoy from Moscow to Zhukovskiy was checked an unexpected complication arose – the final stretch of road from the Kuibyshev Highway to the airfield was narrower than the bomber's wheel track! The issue of widening this road was long overdue, Andrey N. Tupolev had long been promised it would be done, but, as a line from a song goes, 'promises made are promises broken'. However, Tupolev was not only a talented aircraft designer but also a brilliant organiser. Without hesitation he phoned the Soviet Minister of Defence Marshal Gheorgiy K. Zhookov.

'Gheorgiy Konstantinovich, here we have conjured up a weapon for you but we are unable to fire it' – he said.

'How so?'

'The road is not wide enough to take it to the proving ground.'

'Andrey Nikolayevich, I am not in the road construction business, you know.'

'That's true. But you do have engineer troops. I have been to that road to take a look at it, and methinks that they are able to do the road widening job in two or three months. Perhaps you can help with this?'

The wheels were set in motion. Soon the commander of the Soviet engineer troops and his retinue paid a visit to OKB-156. Andrey N. Tupolev showed them the huge bomber, then they all drove to Zhukovskiy to have a look at the road, and the military returned to Moscow to report on the matter. A week or two later the engineer troops personnel arrived, setting up field camps along the road, and the work began; the job was finished on schedule.

With memories of the past war still very vivid, it is no surprise that German words found their way into contemporary Russian slang. The reconstructed road was promptly dubbed 'Tupolewstraße' ('Tupolev Street' in German)! The name stuck, and the locals referred to this road as ***Toopolev-shtra**sse* for years afterwards. (Jokes aside, there is a *real* Tupolev Street in Zhukovskiy that runs along the north side of the LII airfield – but of

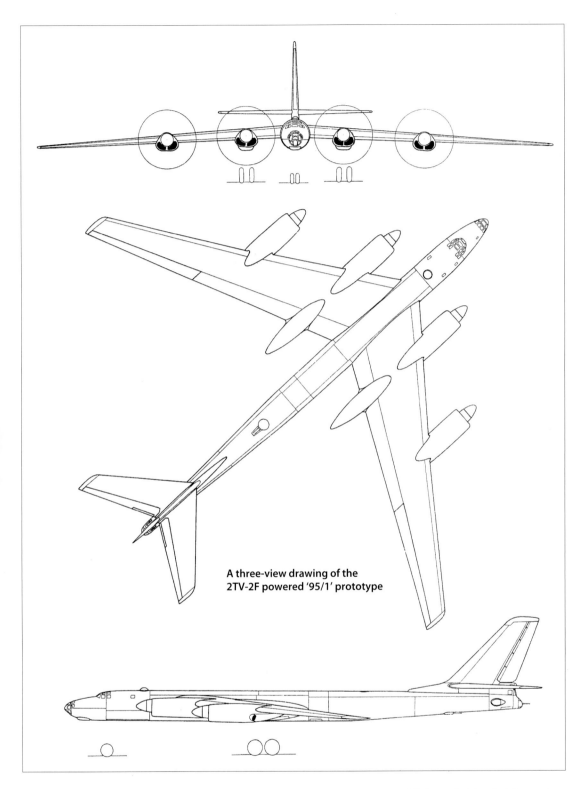

**A three-view drawing of the
2TV-2F powered '95/1' prototype**

course it was thus named after the General Designer's death in 1972.)

A hand-picked Tupolev OKB flight test crew was assigned to the new bomber. It was captained by project test pilot Maj. Aleksey D. Perelyot and included co-pilot Vyacheslav P. Marunov, flight engineer Aleksandr F. Chernov, navigator S. S. Kirichenko, radio operator Nikolay F. Mayorov, flight electrics engineer

I. Ye. Komissarov and flight technician L. I. Borzenkov. They started out by ground-running the engines and making low- and high-speed taxi runs.

While the crew (and the Tupolev OKB at large) was preparing for the bomber's maiden flight, the Ministry of State Security (MGB – *Ministerstvo gosudarstvennoy bezopahsnosti*, the forerunner of the notorious KGB) did its damnedest to preserve the secrecy surrounding the

The design staff of the Tupolev OKB involved in the creation of the Tu-95. First row, left to right: Kurt V. Minkner, Aleksandr A. Arkhangel'skiy, Andrey N. Tupolev, Nikolay I. Bazenkov and Dmitriy S. Markov. Second row, left to right: Aleksandr R. Bonin (hydraulics section), Aleksandr E. Sterlin (aerodynamics section), Sergey M. Yeger, Ivan S. Lebedev (cabin equipment team), Konstantin P. Sveshnikov (fuselage design team), Dmitriy A. Gorskiy (weapons section), Aleksey M. Cheryomukhin and Nikolay V. Kirsanov (crew rescue systems section).

highly classified programme. Special measures were developed and enforced to prevent leaks of sensitive information at the design bureau and its prototype manufacturing facility (MMZ No.156). In particular, all bars and eateries where alcohol could be consumed on the premises in the borough of Moscow where OKB-156 was located were closed (ostensibly for renovation) because a glass of vodka or a couple of beers could loosen the OKB employees' tongues, causing them to talk shop. The MGB also introduced severe control of the residential and farming area on the west bank of the Moskva River at Zhukovskiy from where it was easy to observe the runway (the then-active runway 08-26 which is now used as an aircraft parking ramp) and some of the hardstands at the LII airfield. Additionally, to prevent the prototype from being seen by the casual observer all work on it was undertaken before the traffic on the local roads and commuter trains of the Moscow-Kazan' Railway started moving.

On 12th November 1952 Aleksey D. Perelyot and his crew took the '95/1' prototype up on its first flight. On this occasion the bomber reached an altitude of just over 1,150 m (3,700 ft), remaining airborne for about 50 minutes.

Two more flights were made before the year was out. The fourth flight took place on 13th January 1953, and by mid-April the '95/1' had performed 16 flights, logging some 21 flight hours, with repairs and

modifications being made as appropriate after each flight. The 16th flight, which took place on 17th April, nearly ended in the loss of the aircraft when the automatic blade pitch control failed on all four propellers at once. Perelyot's superb piloting saved the day, however, and the prototype landed at Zhukovskiy without further damage. After this dramatic event the aircraft was grounded for almost a month while the Tupolev OKB and TsAGI put their collective heads together, trying to determine the cause of the failure. This was eventually traced to a material flaw and a solution developed, the OKB taking steps that would allow the prototype to fly again.

The actual figures for the prototype differed somewhat from those set out in the ADP (see table on page 38). Thus, empty weight was rather higher than anticipated – 79,212 kg (174,630 lb) net and 80,765 kg (178,060 lb) with test equipment fitted. The take-off weight during tests was 110,975 kg (244,660 lb); the fuel load had risen to 30,510 kg (67,260 lb) in normal TOW configuration and 90,000 kg (198,420 lb) in maximum TOW configuration. The dimensions were also slightly different, with a wing span marginally increased to 50.04 m (164 ft 2¾ in), a wing area of 283.7 m² (3,053.7 sq ft), a vertical tail area slightly reduced to 38.53 m² (414.73 sq ft) and a horizontal tail span reduced to 14.78 m (48 ft 5⁵⁄₆₄ in) – although the horizontal tail area was quoted as the same 54.49 m² (586.53 sq ft).

The time required to reach 10,000 m (32,810 ft) with an all-up weight of 108,000 kg (238,100 lb) was 18.5 minutes. Some of the equipment items were also different, such as the AV-60V propellers, the 12SAM-55 DC batteries (the M stands for mono**blochn**aya – monobloc, used attributively) and the RPDS radio.

The Soviet government and the Soviet Air Force Command closely monitored the flight test programme. The results of each test flight were reported all the way upstairs via MAP and the MGB. Additionally, Lt.-Col. Sergey D. Agavel'yan, the Air Force representative assigned to MMZ No.156, would promptly file reports on progress to the Air Force Commander-in-Chief, Col.-Gen. Pavel F. Zhigarev.

All the engineering and test personnel involved in the '95' programme were seriously overworked and stretched to the limit of their moral and physical abilities. Fatigue soon became a major problem; most members of the OKB's design and flight test teams were literally working around-the-clock, managing to grab just a few hours of sleep and spending all their time at the airfield, in the design office or at MAP meetings.

On 11th May 1953, disaster struck: the '95/1' crashed on its 17th flight. Andrey N. Tupolev happened to be at Zhukovskiy on the day of the accident and had monitored the flight from the control tower at Zhukovskiy, talking to the crew shortly after the take-off.

Initially the flight had proceeded normally. Suddenly, speaking in a remarkably calm – almost too calm – tone of voice, Aleksey D. Perelyot reported, *'I am in the vicinity of Noginsk* (a town in the Moscow Region north-east of Zhukovskiy – *Auth.*). *We have a fire in the No.3 engine. Vacate the runway. I will be coming straight in from the approach'* (i.e., without making the usual circuit of the field – *Auth.*). Two or three minutes later he radioed, *'We are unable to extinguish the fire. It is spreading; the engine nacelle and landing gear fairing are burning too. We are now approximately 40 km [24.8 miles] from the airfield.'* Another message was heard several minutes later: *'The engine has fallen off. The wing and main gear fairing are on fire. I have just ordered the crew to bail out. Watch for us.'* That was the last transmission from the crew.

Next thing, a phone call came in from the MGB office in Noginsk, informing that an aircraft had crashed in flames north-east of the town. On hearing this, Andrey N. Tupolev and Sergey D. Agavelyan jumped into a car and rushed off to Noginsk, followed in short order by the OKB's design staff and flight test personnel in several other automobiles. Upon arrival it turned out that the way to the crash site lay through sparsely wooded marshland impassable for any vehicle; someone managed to borrow a horse for Tupolev but the others were forced to trek through the marshland on foot. When they finally reached the scene, they were confronted by a horrifying sight – with several dozen tons of fuel remaining, the aircraft had exploded on impact, digging a huge crater 10 m (33 ft) deep with a fiercely burning fire. On the crater floor were the bomber's eight mainwheel tyres; like everything else inside, these were on fire, filling the air with smoke and the acrid stench of burning rubber. A second, smaller crater was located some way off where the detached No.3 engine had hit the ground.

As the enormity of the accident began to sink in, the men spread out and started searching the woods in the hope of finding survivors. They soon located the mangled remains of Perelyot and, shortly afterwards, the body of Kirichenko – the navigator had fallen to his death when his parachute did not open properly, wrapping itself around him. Next, peasants came running from a nearby village, reporting that five other men who had parachuted to safety were there.

The bottom line was that the prototype was destroyed and four of the eleven crew members on that fateful flight were dead – captain Aleksey D. Perelyot, navigator S. S. Kirichenko, flight engineer Aleksandr F. Chernov and A. M. Bol'shakov, a technician from the Special Equipment Research Institute (NISO – *Na***ooch***nyy insti***toot** *spetsi***ahl'***novo oboro***oo***daniya*) whose job was to measure vibration levels. The other seven – co-pilot Vyacheslav P. Marunov, radio operator Nikolay F. Mayorov, lead engineer N. V. Lashkevich, assistant lead engineer A. M. Ter-Akopyan, flight electrics engineer I. Ye. Komissarov, flight technician L. I. Borzenkov and Flight Research Institute engineer K. I. Vaiman – had survived. A Polikarpov S-2 biplane (the ambulance version of the U-2 *Mule* trainer/utility aircraft) arrived from Zhukovskiy to take Vaiman and Mayorov, who had suffered injuries, to hospital.

A special accident investigation board (AIB) chaired by the then Minister of Aircraft Industry Mikhail V. Khroonichev was appointed by the government to determine the cause of the crash. Various MGB subdivisions, the Air Force, the Soviet Armed Forces' General Staff, the Communist Party Central Committee, the Council of Ministers, and many other organisations participated in the investigation as well.

Nikolay F. Mayorov wrote in his post-accident report: *'Having taken off in the morning, we measured the fuel consumption as prescribed by the flight plan. During a final test with the engines at maximum power, when the aircraft was flying at 7,300 m [23,940 ft], a fire broke out in the No.3 engine. I had been watching the aircraft's behaviour through the dorsal observation blister. Hearing a loud pop, I saw a hole appear in the front part of the No.3 engine cowling and then noted an intense fire burning inside. I reported this to the captain. The engine was shut down immediately and [its] propellers were feathered. The fire suppression system was activated. Still, the fire kept on burning; as it did, parts of the aircraft began to fall off. We then realised that we would not be able to land normally.*

A three-view drawing of the NK-12 powered second prototype ('95/2') from the ADP drawings. Note the longer wing span and more evenly spaced engine nacelles giving a wider landing gear track.

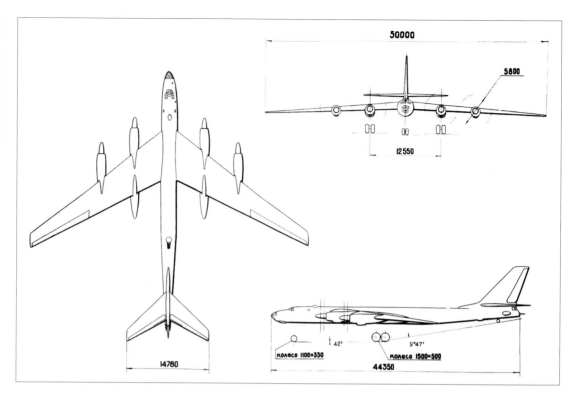

Below and bottom: Two drawings from the ADP documents showing the fuselage layout of the Tu-95. Note the fuel tanks ahead of the wings, in the wing torsion box and aft of the bomb bay.

Levelling out at an altitude of 5,000 m [16,400 ft], Perelyot directed the burning aircraft away from a heavily populated area and over a forest and immediately ordered all of us except flight engineer Chernov to bail out. I waited for a while. I remember looking inside the flight deck and seeing Perelyot, who was very composed. I realised that he intended to attempt an emergency landing. At an altitude of 3,000 m [9,840 ft] I jumped out. As I parachuted earthwards, I observed a huge fire erupt on the ground and a pillar of smoke start to rise.'

Lead engineer Nikolay V. Lashkevich later said he saw the burning No.3 engine fall off the aircraft as he descended by parachute. The propellers on the No.4 engine appeared to be fully feathered as well. Eventually the bomber rolled and entered a steep descending spiral, hitting the ground in a near-vertical dive.

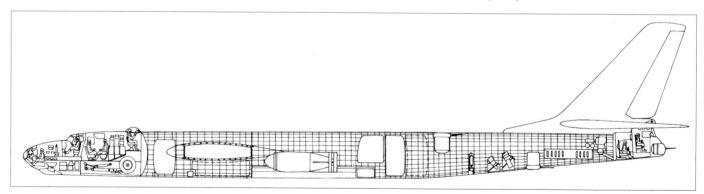

Perelyot and Chernov died in the resulting explosion; it was obvious they had tried to the last to save the aircraft. In 1955 Aleksey D. Perelyot was posthumously awarded the Hero of the Soviet Union title; two years later he was posthumously awarded the prestigious Lenin Prize. Kirichenko had successfully bailed out from the stricken bomber but was caught in the blast and heat of the ensuing explosion, which caused his parachute canopy to collapse. Bol'shakov, too, had egressed the aircraft but, apparently because of the psychological stress, had forgotten to put on his parachute and fell to his death; it was later reported that he was not familiar with the seat-pack type parachute and did not know how to use it.

As it often happens in a situation like this, while some people were trying to find out the reason of the crash, others were looking for a scapegoat. The first reaction of the Air Force was a decision to blame Engineer-Lt.-Col. Sergey D. Agavel'yan, the senior military representative at MMZ No.156, on the assumption that he had missed a critical defect which subsequently caused the crash. The submission for his formal indictment in a court-martial was prepared by an MGB officer assisting the Commander-in-Chief.

There was also an episode which speaks volumes about the atmosphere in the country at large (and in the Soviet aircraft industry in particular) in those days. The day after the crash Nikolay V. Lashkevich, who had also suffered injuries when bailing out and had a bandage on his head, was summoned to the Kremlin for a meeting with Lavrentiy P. Beria. The latter said: *'Help us get to the bottom of this. A strange team has gathered around Tupolev. Just look at their names – Yeger, Minkner, Kerber, Walther, Stoman… It's a regular German-Jewish nest.* (Implicit anti-Semitism was virtually government policy in the Soviet Union, and persons of Jewish descent were treated with suspicion – *Auth.*) *And mind you, there is not a single Communist Party member among the lot! Maybe that's where the key is? Maybe the crash is their handiwork? Now, you are an old-time Communist; I suggest that you take a closer look at these people. I wouldn't mind if you enlisted the help of a few other staunch Communists [in this matter], we will help you. And send us written reports if you find anything at all. I will invite you [to my office] again if necessary.'* Fortunately the 'offer' was not accepted – Lashkevich was disgusted by the idea of ratting on his colleagues.

As for the cause of the crash, the original hypothesis – which was supported and expounded on by the Air Force Main HQ's powerplant department and by the Kuznetsov OKB – seemed to explain everything in a very simple way. According to this hypothesis the engine bearer of the No.3 turboprop had failed, whereupon the engine had fallen off, severing the fuel lines and causing the disastrous fire. This theory was seemingly supported by recent accidents involving production Tu-4s where engine bearers had indeed failed. Thus the accident

could be attributed to poor manufacturing and engineering by the personnel of MMZ No.156. The latter were under the auspices of senior military representative Sergey D. Agavel'yan, who was accused of negligence. So was his counterpart at TsAGI, Engineer-Col. A. I. Solov'yov, who was responsible for checking the results of the engine bearer's static test programme, and he was also indicted accordingly.

The conclusion that structural failure of a defective engine bearer had caused the accident seemed to suit everybody in the Soviet aviation community just fine – even though it contradicted the actual facts: the No.3 engine had fallen off *after* the outbreak of the fire, not before it. It was officially declared as the cause by the propulsion section of the Soviet Air Force's Prototype Aircraft Construction Department (UOSAT – *Oopravleniye po opytnomu stroitel'stvu aviatsionnoy tekhniki*). The chief of this section, General Zaïkin, later drafted the Air Force C-in-C's order that would lead to the indictment of senior military representatives Agavel'yan and Solov'yov.

Top: A picture from the ADP documents showing the Tu-95 with TV-12 engines.

Above: A picture from the MAP statistical chart purportedly showing the second prototype (as the inscription indicates). In fact, however, it is a retouched photo of a desktop model – just like the top photo.

Having read the draft, the Air Force C-in-C Col.-Gen. Pavel F. Zhigarev realised the repercussions would not be limited to the two indicted officers, who would obviously receive the death sentence – other heads would roll as well. In his position, he was required to file daily reports to Stalin on the status of the 'aircraft 95'. In fact, everyone in the Soviet government kept a tab on the big bomber's development, including the MGB and Stalin's assistant, Minister of Internal Affairs Lavrentiy P. Beria. Zhigarev was aware that a lot of generals – including himself – could eventually find themselves as defendants in a court-martial; even though Stalin was dead, the times had not changed yet and there was a lot of power struggle going on. Assessing his options, Zhigarev summoned Agavel'yan and Solov'yov to his office and carefully listened to their accounts of how the engine bearers had been designed, developed and tested. Convinced of their innocence, he cancelled the indictment order and thus saved their lives.

Meanwhile, sessions of the AIB had been going on at the Ministry of Aircraft Industry for several days. Many of the board's members, as well as several engine design bureau heads, pointed the finger of blame at Tupolev. Some even went so far as to say that a former 'enemy of the people' should never have been trusted with building the strategic bomber. (Like many of his colleagues, Andrey N. Tupolev had been arrested on false charges as an 'enemy of the people' before the war and had done time in a prison design bureau under the auspices of the People's Commissariat of Internal Affairs, although his name was cleared afterwards.) With such *ad hominem* reasoning used against him, Tupolev wisely chose to keep silent; his deputies (Nikolay I. Bazenkov, Sergey M. Yeger, Kurt V. Minkner and others) answered the AIB's questions on his behalf.

Eventually, however, one of the soldiers tasked with excavating bits and pieces of wreckage at the crash site literally dug up crucial evidence, discovering a big chunk of a gear wheel from the No.3 2TV-2F engine's reduction gearbox. This was delivered to the Central Aero Engine Institute (TsIAM – *Tsentrahl'nyy institoot aviatsionnovo motorostroyeniya*) for detailed analysis. A renowned material strength expert, Robert S. Kinasoshvili, was asked to examine the fragment. He quickly determined by the structure of the metal that a fatigue failure had occurred because an improper choice of alloy. When the uncontained failure of the reduction gearbox occurred, oil from the gearbox was splashed onto the hot engines and ignited; because of the slipstream the fire then spread to the engine bearer, which failed when it was weakened by the flames.

Not surprisingly, members of the AIB refused to accept Kinasoshvili's conclusion that the gear had failed after only ten hours of operational service. Quite apart from any personal dislike they may have had for Tupolev, such a scenario certainly seemed unlikely. The

OKB-276 engine design bureau stuck rigidly to their claim that the gear had broken on impact with the ground and that the cause of the accident was faulty engine bearer design.

An AIB meeting specifically to address the engine manufacturers was called shortly thereafter. At this meeting, it was announced that documentary evidence from the quality control departments of the Kuznetsov OKB and experimental plant No.276 had surfaced pertaining to the testing of the 2TV-2F turboprop – in circumstances bordering on the supernatural. One day when Sergey D. Agavel'yan was walking down a corridor of the Tupolev OKB building he heard footsteps behind him, and gaining. When the other person caught up with him, he heard a muffled voice: *'You're looking in the wrong place! Look in Quality Control files 34 and 35.'* Not daring to see who it was, Agavel'yan walked on, but later reported the episode to Tupolev, who passed on the information to Minister of Aircraft Industry Mikhail V. Khroonichev. On hearing this, OKB-276 Chief Designer Nikolay D. Kuznetsov, who up to then had been nonchalant, suddenly turned pale and fainted. The files were brought up, revealing that reduction gear failures had occurred when the engine had logged only 30 and 40 hours of bench testing; fires had resulted on both occasions.

Now, in a remarkable *volte-face*, some members of the AIB turned their wrath on Kuznetsov, accusing him just as aggressively as they had Tupolev. Ironically, it was none other than Andrey N. Tupolev who saved Kuznetsov. Knowing the difficult situation with the bomber's powerplant, he stated that, while Kuznetsov should be disciplined for withholding this important information, more radical measures against him would harm the common cause. Tupolev felt Kuznetsov's design genius should not be wasted because of a single mistake; therefore, he openly stated that removing Kuznetsov from office would spell the end for OKB-276 – and, by extension, for the '95' bomber programme ('for want of a nail the shoe was lost' etc.). He asked the other engine design bureaux to assist in the refinement of the 2TV-2F turboprop. This task was of prime importance to the development of the '95' bomber, which was considered critical for achieving a strategic balance between the Soviet Union and the USA.

To be sure, 'Old Man Tupolev' was no angel (by many accounts), but you have to give him credit for sticking up for Kuznetsov at a time when Stalin's repressive machine was very much alive. In those days, in the Soviet Union expressing compassion or liberalism towards someone perceived as guilty – whether justly or not – was tantamount to a crime in itself. This was not lost on Kuznetsov, and the two designers became good friends and a great working tandem; the Kuznetsov OKB supplied the engines for many Tupolev designs.

Further investigation of the 2TV-2F engine indicated that the reduction gearbox had failed as a result of poor workmanship, not a fundamentally flawed design – the gear wheel in question had been manufactured with a departure from the prescribed technology. The person responsible – the real culprit – was identified and duly convicted. Today, the famous gear wheel is part of an exhibit at the factory in Samara where the mighty 2TV-2F turboprops were manufactured.

As a result of the '95/1' prototype's accident, the Soviet government took a more sensible approach to the problem and elected to assist OKB-276 in overcoming the failure. Structural strength standards were evolved for vital engine parts, such as the reduction gear. The development of these standards took considerable time and it was therefore decided that engine parts would be prioritised and analysed in the order of their importance.

On 15th October 1953 MAP issued order No.114 which was effectively the final report on the '95/1' bomber's accident: the intermediate gear of the 2TV-2F engine's reduction gearbox had failed as a result of insufficient strength and low resistance to fatigue. Secondary to this was the poor design of the fire extinguishing system in the engine nacelle. The major designers (Tupolev, Myasishchev, Kuznetsov and Mikulin) were ordered to provide proper accident-free flight testing of the '95' and M-4 aircraft. Tupolev, Kuznetsov and Aleksandr I. Makarevskiy (the then Director of TsAGI) declared that the TV-12 engine scheduled for the second prototype would have to be thoroughly tested on the ground before being mounted on the actual aircraft. Additionally, the complete aircraft would have to go through a new series of static and vibration tests.

Kuznetsov was also required to run the new TV-12 engine through a series of bench tests and then a series of flight tests on a Tu-4LL. Finally, all design bureaux involved with the new Soviet bomber programmes were to test their emergency fire extinguishing systems and prove they worked efficiently. Particular attention would be paid to the '95' and M-4 bombers.

'Aircraft 95/2' bomber prototype ('order 180-2')

While flight testing of the '95/1' had been in progress, MMZ No.156 had proceeded with the construction of the second prototype ('95/2', aka 'order 180-2'), which was powered by the intended TV-12 turboprops. Design work on this aircraft, referred to as the *dooblyor* (lit. 'back-up' or 'understudy'; the Soviet term for second prototypes used until the late 1960s), commenced in January 1952 and was finished within a month. This fast pace is surprising, since the difference from the '95/1' was not limited to the design of the engine nacelles and engine mounts. The TV-12s were to be housed in much cleaner circular-section nacelles with annular air intakes

around the propeller spinners and separate inlets for the oil coolers mounted well aft. Apart from that, the distance between the second prototype's inner engine nacelles (and hence the landing gear track as well) was increased from 9.4 m (30 ft 10¾ in) to 12.55 m (41 ft 2³⁄₃₂ in), requiring changes to the wing structure; the distance between the outer nacelles remained unchanged at 24.4 m (80 ft 0⅝ in). The nose-up ground angle was reduced from the first prototype's 1°19'27.5" to just 0°42'.

Construction of the '95/2' got under way in February 1952. Interestingly, the first prototype '95' had been 15% overweight. The second aircraft, benefiting from the learning curve of the first, came in at only 3% over the design empty weight. This was the result of better detail design and the use of refined, lighter structural materials, including the new V95 high-strength aluminium alloy.

The offensive weapons options were much the same as for the first prototype. External carriage of guided weapons was still envisaged but the 16Kh cruise missile no longer came into the picture. Instead, the '95/2' was to carry four RAMT-1400 **Shchooka** (Pike, the fish) stand-off anti-shipping missiles – the first of the kind in the Soviet Union. In the then-current Soviet terminology the weapon was known as a 'winged torpedo' (hence RAMT for *re'aktivnaya aviatsionnaya morskaya torpeda* – jet-propelled air-launched naval torpedo). Two guidance system versions were envisaged; the RAMT-1400A (Shchooka-A) missile had radio command line-of-sight guidance, using an optical sight, while the RAMT-1400B (Shchooka-B) was to have n inertial system for initial guidance and an active radar homing system for terminal guidance. However, the guided weapons were destined never to be fitted to the '95/2'.

The defensive armament was different from the first prototype. The 'aircraft 95/2' was fitted with six 23-mm Afanas'yev/Makarov TKB-495A cannons. This weapon was developed by the firearms design bureau in the city of Tula (hence TKB for *Tool'skoye konstrooktorskoye byuro* – Tula Design Bureau), and the long-barrel version (indicated by the A suffix) later entered production as the AM-23. The cannon barbettes were designated DT-V12 (*distantsionno [oopravlyayemaya] toorel', verkhnyaya* – remote-controlled turret, dorsal), DT-N12 (*distantsionno [oopravlyayemaya] toorel', nizhnyaya* – remote-controlled turret, ventral) and DK-12 (*distantsionno [oopravlyayemaya toorel'], kormovaya* – remote-controlled turret, rear). Other differences included changes to the de-icing system, which featured hot-air de-icing on the engine air intakes, command and communications radios of the same model (1RSB-70), and new LAS-5M rescue dinghies, of which there were two (the '5' indicates seating capacity).

Nikolay I. Bazenkov, the first project chief of the Tu-95.

Tupolev OKB Deputy Chief Designer Aleksandr A. Arkhangel'skiy.

Aleksandr V. Nadashkevich, the Tupolev OKB's leading weapons specialist, was responsible for the Tu-95's armament.

Sergey M. Yeger, a leading designer who supervised the construction of the first prototype ('95/1').

Aleksey M. Cheryomukhin, head of the Tupolev OKB's structural strength department.

Kurt V. Minkner, head of the Tupolev OKB's propulsion department.

Leonid L. Kerber, the Tupolev OKB's Deputy Chief Designer responsible for aircraft equipment.

Aleksey A. Tupolev, the Chief Designer's son, also participated in the Tu-95's development.

Airframe construction was completed in November 1952; however, nearly eighteen months would elapse before the '95/2' was cleared for its maiden flight. Though static tests consumed a large percentage of this time, Kuznetsov's extremely conservative approach to the engine and engine bearer design forced the bomber to sit idle for some six months until the first flight-cleared TV-12 engines were ready for delivery. This time the Kuznetsov OKB wanted to make absolutely certain there would be no repetition of the May 1953 tragedy.

Looking over Kuznetsov's shoulder was the Ministry of Aircraft Industry. Their supervision assured that the TV-12's improvements were properly accommodated and bench tests were held in full. In December 1953

MAP confirmed that the TV-12's performance met the specifications. In fact, the take-off and maximum continuous power exceeded the anticipated values by 2-3%, but so did the SFC. Certain engine parameters could only be determined in actual flight, but the designers felt confident the TV-12 would perform as promised.

On 12th December 1954 the TV-12 successfully completed its 100-hour government bench tests. That same year one more Moscow-built Tu-4, (the 146th production example, c/n 2303001) was urgently converted into a Tu-4LL for testing the TV-12 engine and its AV-60 contraprops (in a reference to the engine's intended application this job was known as 'order

180LL'). The massive engine was again installed in the No.3 position, the nacelle protruding far ahead of the wing leading edge so that the propellers' rotation plane was almost in line with the Tu-4's flight deck. A crew captained by Tupolev OKB test pilot Mikhail A. Nyukhtikov performed the flight tests.

Various engine improvements and miscellaneous engine-related delays impacted the first flight date of the second prototype '95'. Also, in the wake of the first prototype's crash the Kuibyshev factory No.18 was ordered to stop its preparations for production of the '95' and gear up to build the M-4; however, these orders were reversed when the TV-12 powered version did fly. Hence factory No.18 was instructed to build 15 such bombers in 1954-55 and deliver them to the Air Force, while engine factory No.24 (which, conveniently, was also located in Kuibyshev) was to launch production of the TV-12 turboprop. The latter had by then received the official designation NK-12 reflecting Nikolay Kuznetsov's initials.

As a belt-and-braces policy, the OKB-19 engine design bureau in Perm' headed by Chief Designer Pavel A. Solov'yov was now given the task of developing a new engine for the '95' bomber. This turboprop designated D-19 (D for *dvigatel'* – engine) would develop some 15,000 ehp (11,190 kW) for take-off and offer a cruise power of 12,300 ehp (9,175 kW). The SFC at maximum continuous power was to be 0.16 kg/hp-hr (0.35 lb/hp-hr). However, the D-19 never materialised, as subsequent developments rendered it unnecessary.

In December 1954 the '95/2' prototype finally received its TV-12 engines. At the beginning of January

1955, the aircraft was moved to ZhLIiDB in Zhukovskiy. On 21st January the second prototype was cleared for manufacturer's flight tests.

In accordance with a MAP order dated 28th July 1954 Mikhail A. Nyukhtikov was assigned to the '95/2' as project test pilot, with Ivan M. Sukhomlin as co-pilot; David I. Kantor was the engineer in charge. On 16th February 1955 the second prototype took to the air for the first time with Nyukhtikov and Sukhomlin at the controls; the flight went according to plan and was completed without incident.

In the spring of 1955 a Soviet government delegation headed by the nation's new leader Nikita S. Khrushchov and including Minister of Defence Marshal Gheorgiy K. Zhookov visited Zhukovskiy airfield, including the Tupolev OKB's flight test facility. Rumour has it that Andrey N. Tupolev resorted to a trick to get the delegation's attention; driving his personal car, he simulated a breakdown to block the road in front of the motorcade carrying Khrushchov and the others. When Khrushchov came out of his limousine and saw who it was, Tupolev started a conversation and enticed the delegation to visit his facility first. He invited Khrushchov to examine the flight deck of the '95/2', which Khrushchov did (and it was not easy for the rather corpulent Premier to climb through the entry hatch!). Tupolev took the opportunity to describe the bomber's development potential, and the trick worked – a month later the '95' was ordered into production.

Further testing consisted of another 67 flights, the aircraft logging a total of 168 flight hours. The final flight under the manufacturer's flight test programme took

Chairman of the USSR Supreme Soviet Nikolay M. Shvernik hands the Order of Lenin to Andrey N. Tupolev.

place on 8th January 1956, although the programme was not officially completed until 20th January.

67 of the 68 flights proceeded uneventfully. The only exception was a flight that took place in the summer of 1955. While the aircraft was on approach to Zhukovskiy after a test mission, flight engineer A. M. Ter-Akopyan reported by radio to the tower that the crew could not get the landing gear to extend.

Things on the ground got tense in a hurry. It would be virtually impossible to make a safe belly landing in the big bomber, and it appeared certain the aircraft would be wrecked if such a landing were attempted. While ground personnel discussed what to do, the bomber circled in the vicinity of Zhukovskiy to burn off fuel and reduce the landing weight. When Andrey N. Tupolev, his deputy Leonid L. Kerber and others from the OKB got word of the problem, they immediately left their offices in Moscow and drove straight to the airfield.

Kerber and his equipment specialists set up shop on the grass area next to the LII airfield's runway. With electrical system diagrams in place, they began looking for possible reasons for the electrohydraulic gear actuation system's failure. Tupolev nervously paced back and forth while Kerber studied his drawings. The aircraft had enough fuel remaining for four hours' flight.

It took Kerber two hours to make an assessment. At that point, he began radioing instructions to the crew. He ordered Ter-Akopyan to turn off all electrical power. As a result, for a while, the second prototype flew around Zhukovskiy without any radio contact. Finally, when the electrical systems were reactivated, a relay

switch that had been stuck was tripped and the landing gear immediately began to extend, and the bomber landed safely a few minutes later.

On 3rd July 1955 the aircraft was demonstrated publicly for the first time, making a low pass during the annual Air Fleet Day flypast at Moscow-Tushino airfield (now defunct) with four Mikoyan/Gurevich MiG-17 *Fresco-A* fighters as an escort. The sight and sound (a very distinctive rolling roar) of the big swept-wing turboprop bomber made a strong impression on the spectators, including the foreign military attachés who always attended such events. Soon the NATO's Air Standards Co-ordinating Committee (ASCC) assigned the reporting name 'Type 40' to the '95'; this was soon changed to *Bear* under the new coding system (in the 'B-for-bomber' category, the single-syllable name meaning a propeller-driven aircraft). The NK-12 engine, whose true designation was likewise unknown to the West, was referred to as 'Type K' until 1957; interestingly, Dipl.-Ing. Ferdinand Brandner, who was one of the aforementioned German engine specialists working in the Soviet Union until 1954 and had a hand in shaping the TV-12, provided the West with detailed information on this engine – but not the designation. For two years following the Tushino event, the western press assumed the aircraft to be a product of the OKB-240 design bureau headed by Sergey V. Il'yushin; hence the bomber was referred to as the IL-38 (which in fact is a four-turboprop anti-submarine warfare derivative of the IL-18 *Coot* medium-haul airliner).

Even after its Tupolev origins had been established, the correct designation remained unknown to the West,

Chief Designers Andrey
N. Tupolev and Vladimir
M. Myasishchev, the
principal designers of
Soviet heavy bombers.

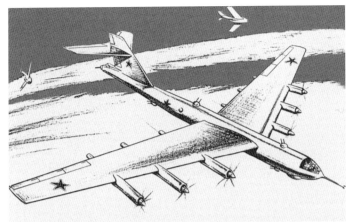

and the machine was erroneously called Tu-20. According to some sources, this misnomer arose because originally it had indeed been planned to assign the service designation Tu-20 to the new turboprop bomber, and this had somehow leaked to the West. Such provisional service designations were sometimes reused time and time again; the designation Tu-20 had previously been assigned to the 'aircraft 73' three-turbojet tactical bomber prototype of 1948, which evolved into the production twinjet Tu-14 *Bosun* ('aircraft 89'), and to the 'aircraft 79' reconnaissance version of 1949 based on the '73'. However, in the course of development so many documents with the '95' designation were issued and circulated by the OKB and government bureaucratic entities that it was deemed more convenient to leave the '95' designator alone – of which the western world had no notion. Western defence experts did, however, note that the Tu-95 designation was rather odd because Soviet heavy military aircraft normally received even-numbered designations, the odd-numbered ones being reserved for fighters. (As an aside, in the 1990s the designation Tu-20 was reused again – this time for a projected twin-turboprop business aircraft remarkably similar to the ill-starred Brazilian-Argentinean Embraer/FMA CBA-123 Vector biz-prop… which in the event never materialised. Talk about 'unlucky' designations!)

In the meantime, flight testing of the second prototype continued without let-up. The designers had

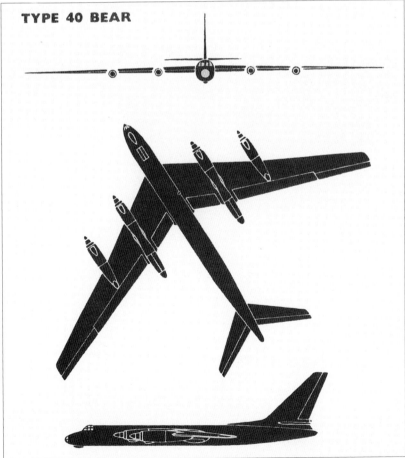

TYPE 40 BEAR

gone to great lengths to make the airframe as aerodynamically clean as possible; the airframe components were designed in such a way as to minimise harmful interference and hence drag. In cruise configuration at Mach 0.68 with a 4-5° angle of attack the aircraft had a lift/drag ratio of 17.5; this decreased to 8.3 with the flaps and landing gear down but increased again to 11.2 immediately before landing due to ground effect.

Maximum performance tests were initiated in September 1955; these including maximum range and payload missions. The first of these included a non-stop flight from Zhukovskiy to Khabarovsk in the Soviet Far East, then across to the Kamchatka Peninsula and then back to Zhukovskiy. It included dropping bombs on the Koora proving ground on Kamchatka. The flight covered a distance of 13,900 km (8,632 miles). The final

figure was 1,100 km (680 miles) less than the original specified range, but it was still sufficient to reach the North American continent, which was its specified target.

During the long range flight, the take-off weight of the '95/2' was 167,200 kg (368,600 lb). The fuel load was 84,440 kg (186,155 lb), Cruising speed was 750 km/h (466 mph), maximum speed was 880 km/h (546 mph), service ceiling was 12,150 m (39,850 ft) and the take-off run was 2,300 m (7,540 ft).

The following data on 'aircraft 95/2' is recorded in a MAP statistical file filled out on 27th September 1951 – well in advance of the machine's first flight, so the figures are provisional. The file refers to it as the 'Tu-4 2TV-12 ("95" No.2)' – i.e., Tupolev aircraft with no service designation powered by four TV-12s.

'Aircraft 95/2' specifications	
Crew	8
Length overall	46.17 m (151 ft 5²³⁄₃₂ in)
Wing span	50.04 m (164 ft 2⅞₄ in)
Horizontal tail span	14.78 m (48 ft 5⁵⁷⁄₆₄ in)
Height on ground	12.5 m (41 ft 0⅛ in)
Wing area	283.7 m² (3,053.72 sq ft)
Vertical tail area	38.53 m² (414.73 sq ft)
Horizontal tail area	54.49 m² (586.53 sq ft)
Powerplant	4 x TV-12
Engine power:	
take-off	12,500 hp
maximum continuous	12,000 hp (up to h = 6,000 m/19,685 ft)
nominal (cruise)	10,200 hp (h = 8,600 m/28,220 ft, V = 200 m/sec)
Propellers:	
model	AV-60 (contra-rotating)
no. of blades	4+4
diameter	5.8 m (19 ft 0¹⁄₂ in)
Fuel	Kerosene
All-up weight:	
normal	143,300 kg (315,920 lb)
maximum	156,000 kg (343,920 lb)
All-up weight over the target	107,000 kg (235,890 lb)
Empty weight	72,430 kg (159,680 lb)
Payload:	
normal	70,870 kg (156,240 lb)
maximum	83,570 kg (184,240 lb)
Fuel load:	
normal	63,500 kg (139,990 lb)
maximum	76,200 kg (167,990 lb)
Bomb load:	
normal	5,000 kg (11,020 lb)
maximum	15,000 kg (33,070 lb
CG range	17-25% mean aerodynamic chord
Wing loading:	
normal weight	505 kg/m² (103.5 lb/sq ft)
maximum weight	550 kg/m² (112.76 lb/sq ft)

Power loading at sea level:	
normal weight	2.86 kg/hp (6.31 lb/hp)
maximum weight	3.12 kg/hp (6.88 lb/hp)
Maximum speed at 107,000 kg AUW: *	
at 8,000 m (26,250 ft)	916 km/h (569 mph)
at 9,000 m (29,530 ft)	920-950 km/h (571-590 mph)
at 10,000 m (32,810 ft)	899 km/h (558 mph)
Landing speed	190-215 km/h (118-133 mph)
Rate of climb:	
at sea level	17 m/sec (3,345 ft/min)
at 5,000 m (16,400 ft)	16.4 m/sec (3,227 ft/min)
at 10,000 m	10.4 m/sec (2,046 ft/min)
Climb time:	
to 5,000 m	5.0 minutes
to 10,000 m	10.9 minutes
Service ceiling over the target	13,000-14,000 m (42,650-45,290 ft)
Service ceiling at nominal power	13,000-13,500 m (42,650-44,290 ft)
Range:	
with 5,000 kg (11,020 lb) of bombs	15,000 km (9,320 miles) [1]
	17,000-17,500 km (10,560-10,870 miles) [2]
with 9,000 kg (19,840 lb) of bombs	15,900-16,300 km (9,880-10,130 miles) [3]
with 12,000 kg (26,455 lb) of bombs	12,500-13,600 km (7,770-8,450 miles) [4]
Take-off run:	
with normal TOW	1,400-1,500 m (4,590-4,920 ft)
with maximum TOW	1,700-1,800 m (5,580-5,910 ft)
Take-off distance to h=25 m (82 ft):	
with normal TOW	2,500-2,700 m (8,200-8,860 ft)
with maximum TOW	3,300-3,500 m (10,830-11,480 ft)
Landing run (landing weight 90,000 kg/198,420 lb)	1,400-1,500 m (4,590-4,920 ft)
Landing distance from h=25 m	3,000-3,400 m (9,840-11,150 ft)

Notes:
* Restricted by a dynamic pressure limit of 1,915 kg/m² (392 lb/sq ft) at altitudes up to 7,000 m (22,965 ft); at higher altitude the maximum permissible speed is Mach 0.86
1. Normal TOW/normal fuel, speed 750-820 km/h (465-509 mph).
2. Maximum TOW/maximum fuel, altitude 9,000-14,000 m (29,5370-45,930 ft), speed 730-750 km/h (453-465 mph).
3. Fuel load 72,200 kg (159,170 lb), altitude 9,000-14,000 m.
4. Fuel load 69,200 kg (152,560 lb), altitude 9,500-14,200 m.

CHAPTER THREE

'First-generation' Air Force versions

Tu-95 strategic bomber (*izdeliye* V)

Even as the tests of the second prototype continued, the Kuibyshev aircraft factory No.18 launched low-rate initial production (LRIP) of the bomber, which had by then received the service designation Tu-95. The Mikoyan MiG-23 tactical fighter had an interim version between the initial MiG-23S *Flogger-A* and the MiG-23M *Flogger-B* that had no suffix letter to the designation, despite being the *second* version; it was popularly known as **dva**dtsat' **tre**tiy '*bez* **book**vy' (MiG-23 with no [suffix] letter, or *sans suffixe*), and by analogy the initial production version of the bomber is hereinafter called Tu-95 *sans suffixe*. At the OKB and the factory the aircraft had the in-house product code '*izdeliye* V' (the third letter of the Cyrillic alphabet). ('*Izdeliye* (product) such-and-such' was, and still is, a common way of coding Soviet/Russian military hardware items in paperwork for security reasons.)

By mid-1955 ten Tu-95s *sans suffixe* of the pre-production batch and the first production batch – five aircraft in each – were in various stages of assembly in Kuibyshev. These aircraft powered by NK-12 engines were considerably different from the '95/2' prototype, featuring a 2.72-m (8 ft 11 ⁵⁄₆₄ in) fuselage stretch, fully functional systems and a complete set of avionics and armament; this incurred a weight penalty, increasing empty weight by 5%. The production-standard bomber's maximum take-off weight was increased from the second prototype's 156,000 kg (343,920 lb) to 172,000 kg (379,190 lb) and the maximum fuel load from 76,200 to 80,730 kg (from 167,990 to 177,980 lb). With a 5,000-kg (11,020-lb) normal bomb load the aircraft had an effective range of 12,100 km (7,520 miles). Again, the production version was equipped with a Rubidiy-MM bomb-aiming/navigation radar in a flattened chin radome and a PRS-1 Argon

Front view of the first production Tu-95 (c/n 5800101).

gun-laying radar in a hemispherical radome above the tail gunner's station.

No information is available on the first flight dates of the first Kuibyshev-built Tu-95 (construction number 4800001). On 31st August 1955, however, two aircraft wearing the non-standard single-digit tactical codes '5 Black' (c/n 580003) and '6 Black' (c/n 5800101) – which were in fact sequential numbers allocated to Kuibyshev-built LRIP aircraft – were released by the factory. Both aircraft were used by the Tupolev OKB in a separate manufacturer's flight test programme that lasted from 1st October 1955 to 28th May 1956. Once this had been completed, on 31st May these two bombers and the second prototype were submitted for state acceptance trials to the Red Banner State Research Institute of the Air Force named after Valeriy P. Chkalov (GK NII VVS – *Gosudarstvennyy Krasnoznamyonnyy naoochno-issledovatel'skiy institoot Voyenno-vozdooshnykh sil*; the 'Red Banner' bit means the institute was awarded the Order of the Red Banner of Combat).

(Note 1: Until the mid-1950s Soviet military aircraft – notably fighters – had *serial numbers* in a three- or four-digit format; they were usually based on the aircraft's construction number – the last digit(s) of the production batch number plus the number of the aircraft in the batch, allowing more or less positive identification. In 1955, however, the VVS switched (probably for security reasons) to the system of two-digit *tactical codes* which is still in use today. Normally the code is simply the aircraft's number in the unit operating it, making positive identification impossible because several aircraft of the same type wear the same code. Three-digit tactical codes are rare and are usually worn either by fighters (or trainers) operated by the Air Force's flying schools or by development aircraft owned by the respective OKB; in the latter case they still tie in with the c/n, the fuselage number (line number) or the manufacturer's designation. On military transport aircraft, three-digit tactical codes were usually the last three of the former civil registration (many Soviet/Russian Air Force transports were, and still are, quasi-civilian). At the same time the Soviet Air Force's red pentastar insignia were deleted from the rear fuselage, remaining on the wings and vertical tail only.

Note 2: The c/ns of Kuibyshev-built Tu-95s originally had an all-numeric seven-digit format. For instance, c/n 4800002 means 1954 (the year when the aircraft was laid down, not the year when it was completed!), plant No.18 (as was often the case with Soviet aircraft c/ns, the first digit of the factory number was omitted to confuse hypothetical spies), Batch 000 (thus, provisions were made from the outset to build 100 batches or more), 02nd aircraft in the batch.

Curiously, due to a clerical error there were *two consecutive production batches numbered zero*: the abovementioned Batch 000 consisting of two aircraft

(c/ns 4800001 and 4800002) was followed by a 'very pre-production' Batch 00 comprising three aircraft with non-standard six-digit c/ns (580001 through 580003). Batches 1 and 2 had five aircraft each; from Batch 3 onwards there were mostly ten aircraft per batch. The c/n was originally stencilled on both sides of the forward fuselage and the vertical tail.)

The state acceptance trials went on for three months, being completed in August 1956. During the trials programme the '95/2' reached a maximum speed of 882 km/h (548 mph) and a service ceiling of 11,300 m (37,060 ft); its maximum range recorded at this stage was 15,040 km (9,340 miles). The two LRIP aircraft did not compare favourably because of their higher weight, showing shorter range and a lower service ceiling; in fact, their performance fell somewhat short of the figures stipulated by the Council of Ministers directive, which the customer (the Ministry of Defence) was understandably unhappy about. To remedy this, a decision was taken to boost the Tu-95's performance by installing uprated engines (see next entry).

The trials were not altogether without incident. The second pre-production Tu-95 (no tactical code, c/n 4800002), which was also used for test work, had the unenviable distinction of suffering two near-identical mishaps at the same location within a year. On 4th April 1955 this aircraft captained by Lieutenant Senior Grade Mikhail I. Mikhaïlov ran off the runway in a stiff crosswind when landing at Kuibyshev-Bezymyanka, the factory airfield of plant No.18, after its third flight, collapsing the port main gear unit and suffering damage to both port propellers and the port outer wing. The aircraft was repaired, but in April 1956 the scenario was repeated almost exactly, this time with Lt. Yuriy A. Dobrovol'skiy in the captain's seat – albeit for a different reason: the port main gear unit jammed halfway through retraction and would not extend fully on landing, with similar results. The aircraft was again repaired.

The Tu-95 *sans suffixe* remained in production until 1957. A total of 30 were built (up to and including c/n 7800406, which was released by the factory on 31st May 1957); these 30 Kuibyshev-built aircraft do not include c/n 6800402, which was completed as a Tu-116 VIP transport (see end of chapter).

Deliveries to the Long-Range Aviation (by then styled as DA – *Dahl'nyaya aviahtsiya*) commenced in April 1956. the first unit to equip with the new strategic bombers was the recently formed 409th TBAP (*tyazholyy bombardirovochnyy aviapolk* – Heavy Bomber Regiment) of the 106th TBAD (*tyazholaya bombardirovochnaya aviadiveeziya* – Heavy Bomber Division, roughly equivalent to a Bomb Group (Heavy) in the USAF), which was stationed at Uzin airbase (pronounced *Oozin*, aka Chepelevka AB) in the Kiev Region, central Ukraine. It deserves mention that the

Three more views of the first production Tu-95; the original tactical code '6 Black' indicates the sixth Kuibyshev-built example. Note the early-model 'towel rail' aerial on the nose.

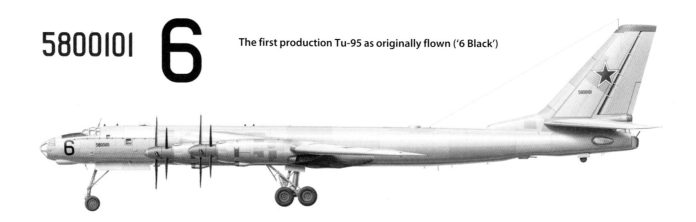

5800101 6

The first production Tu-95 as originally flown ('6 Black')

regiment's first commanding officer was Col. Nikolay N. Kharitonov, who left the unit in February 1958 to become a test pilot with the Tupolev OKB, eventually rising to chief test pilot. Induction of the new bomber proceeded quickly, and in the summer of 1956 several 409th TBAP Tu-95s *sans suffixe* participated in the Air Fleet Day flypast at Moscow-Tushino.

As for the two LRIP aircraft involved in the state acceptance trials, '5 Black' was subsequently delivered to a first-line unit of the DA, receiving the new and more conventional tactical code '56 Red'. In contrast, '6 Black' was retained by the Tupolev OKB and used for test and development work, becoming '46 Red'.

Initially it was suggested that the Air Force and the Tupolev OKB equip production Tu-95s with the wingtip-to-wingtip IFR system developed by LII test pilots Igor' I. Shelest and Viktor S. Vasyanin – the one used on the Tu-16Z *Badger-A* (Z = za***prahv***shchik – refuelling tanker) and various versions of the *Badger* equipped with a refuelling receptacle. The Tu-16Z featured a 37-m (121 ft 4⁴⁵⁄₆₄ in) hose stowed in a tube running the full length of the starboard wing's front spar and passing through the wing centre section. The hose had an outer diameter of 92 mm (3⅝ in) and an inner diameter of 76 mm (3 in), featuring steel fittings at both ends. It was deployed from the starboard wingtip by means of an LBZ-6A electric winch with a 85-m (278 ft 10 in) steel cable housed inside the starboard wing torsion box. An electropneumatic mechanism ejected the end of the hose from a wingtip-mounted guide tube protruding 1.8 m (5 ft 10⁵⁵⁄₆₄ in) beyond the trailing edge; this tube housed a stabilising drogue parachute at the end of the hose. A movable roller adjusted the tension of the winch cable; a cable cutter was provided, allowing the hose to be jettisoned in an emergency. The so-called main mechanism in the starboard wingtip hermetically connected a fitting at the front end of the hose to the tanker's fuel transfer line.

The refuelling technique was as follows. The receiver aircraft caught up with the tanker and assumed close echelon starboard formation. The hose was ejected from the tanker's starboard wingtip and extracted by the drogue parachute until it exited the wing completely and the Tu-16Z trailed the hose on a length of cable. The receiver aircraft deployed a special grapple on the outer side of the IFR receptacle. Moving closer, it placed the port wingtip over the hose so that the latter was inboard of the grapple, then moved to the right and the hose slid into the grapple. Now the tanker slowly rewound the cable until the fitting at the rear end activated a switch in the receptacle and automatically locked into position. When this had been done, the cable was rewound further until the front end of the hose re-entered the wingtip and locked into the tanker's main mechanism. Next, the receiver aircraft moved forward and the hose formed a U-shape, rotating the receptacle through 180° and activating another switch, whereupon fuel transfer could begin.

Therefore, in 1957 LII and the Tupolev OKB undertook a joint preliminary test programme to assess the possibility of refuelling the Tu-95 from the Tu-16Z; the two aircraft were captained by Tupolev OKB test pilot Aleksey P. Yakimov and Igor' I. Shelest respectively, with Yuriy G. Yefimov as engineer in charge. A number of test flights were undertaken from Zhukovskiy to check the technique of approaching the tanker and making contact. The Tu-95 ('46 Red', c/n 5800101) was not fitted with even a dummy receptacle; therefore the bomber merely rendezvoused with the tanker and acted out the refuelling procedure, superimposing the port wingtip on the hose and maintaining this formation long enough for a theoretical fuel transfer to take place. However, the Tu-95 was fitted with test equipment – a barograph, a speedograph, a gyrograph (pitch/yaw/roll rate recorder) and control surface motion sensors. The tanker was additionally fitted with AKS-2 cine cameras (appa***raht*** kino***syo***mochnyy) at the starboard wingtip and in the tail gunner/refuelling system operator's station.

Two flights were made at indicated airspeeds of 175-500 km/h (295-310 mph) and altitudes of 4,900 m (16,080 ft), 9,000 m (29,530 ft) and 10,000 m (32,810 ft);

Opposite page: Two aspects of Tu-95 c/n 5800101 after conversion as the Tu-95M prototype ('46 Red'). Note the T-shaped photo calibration markings and the number 4807 (meaning unknown) replacing the c/n.

The Tu-95M prototype ('46 Red', c/n 5800101)

Here, '46 Red' is shown during a test flight in 1957 to explore the possibility of wingtip-to-wingtip refuelling from a Tu-16Z tanker. The latter's fuel transfer hose with a stabilising parachute at the end appears extremely short in this view.

The port wingtip of Tu-95 '46 Red' is placed over the hose in a simulated contact.

Another view of Tu-95M '46 Red' seen from the starboard observation blister of the Tu-16Z tanker.

complicated than on a jet. When approaching the hose the Tu-95 rolled and yawed to the right because of the tanker's wake vortex but this was corrected by control inputs; Yakimov reported that the control forces required to maintain formation were quite high but these were expected to be lower on production Tu-95s.

On 28th April 1958, ruling No.26 on this issue was passed by the CofM Presidium's Commission on Defence Industry Matters (VPK – *Voyenno-promysh-lennaya komissiya*). However, it soon became obvious that a probe-and-drogue IFR system developed by OKB-918 under Semyon M. Alekseyev was better suited for the *Bear*; hence the Tupolev OKB used the latter system on some versions of the aircraft.

In due course the Tu-95s *sans suffixe* were refitted with more powerful NK-12M engines (see next entry). However, like the original NK-12s *sans suffixe*, these engines lacked automatic propeller feathering, and manual feathering did not always work reliably in an emergency. This became apparent as early as 24th December 1956 when the first operational loss of a Tu-95 occurred – the crew had tried in vain to feather the dead engine's propeller after a turbine failure. (According to some sources, this crash occurred on 16th March 1957; known accidents involving the type are listed in Appendix 2.) Not until the autofeathering feature was introduced on the NK-12MV engine (the V suffix probably denoted [*vozdooshnyy] vint* – propeller, since the new version worked with updated AV-60K props) and the surviving Tu-95s *sans suffixe* were refitted again, was this problem cured.

During the 1970s all surviving Tu-95s *sans suffixe* were updated with electronic countermeasures (ECM) systems, a new RBP-4 Rubidiy-MM2 navigation/attack radar – again codenamed *Short Horn* by NATO, since it fitted into the existing chin radome and the difference was not visible – and new navigation equipment. This allowed them to remain in first-line service into the early 1980s. The RBP-4 (*rahdiolokatsionnyy bombardi-rovochnyy pritsel* – radar bomb sight) was an advanced

the bomber's all-up weight was about 100,000 kg (220,450 lb). In these two flights eleven simulated contacts were made, the bomber's wing being placed on the fully deployed hose 10 cm to 3 m (3¹⁵⁄₁₆ in to 9 ft 10⁷⁄₆₄ in) from the wingtip. While the flights proved that a propeller-driven aircraft could use the wing-to-wing IFR technique, the propellers made it somewhat more

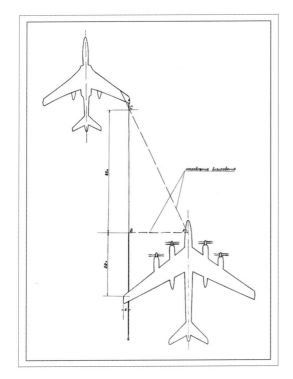

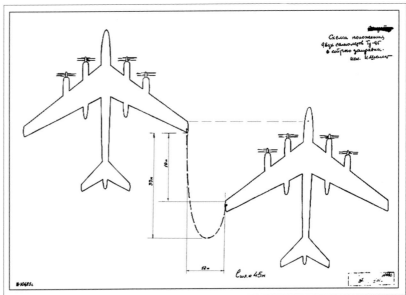

derivative of the Rubidiy-MM. It worked with an OPB-11R or OPB-11RM optical bombsight (*opticheskiy pritsel bombardirovochnyy*), which was linked to the radar and the autopilot. The radar could work in 360° search mode or scan a 45° sector whose axis could be directed incrementally within ±55° from the direction of flight. The RBP-4 could detect large targets, such as major industrial centres, at 150-180 km (93-111 miles) range and had a maximum targeting range of some

Top left: A drawing from the LII test report showing how the Tu-95 made contact with the tanker's hose. The hatched lines are the captain's lines of sight.

Top: A drawing from the same report showing how the Tu-95 could theoretically refuel from a sister ship equipped as a wing-to-wing tanker.

Above and above left: A Batch 000 Tu-95 (c/n 4800002) after coming to grief at Kuibyshev-Bezymyanka on 4th April 1955.

Left: '77 Red', a later pre-production Tu-95 from Batch 00 (c/n 580002), during a test flight.

Above: The final pre-production Tu-95, '56 Red' (formerly '5 Black', c/n 580003) depicted during the type's state acceptance trials.

Right: Another air-to-air shot of Tu-95 '56 Red'.

Right: The nine-man crew of '56 Red' receive a last-minute briefing before a flight.

Far right: The briefing is completed and the crew board the aircraft. Note the fairing on the nose gear door which is absent on other LRIP Tu-95s; this appears to be an antenna fairing rather than a bulge to accommodate a larger wheel.

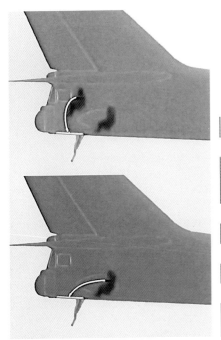

Right: This diagram from the Tu-95 flight manual's section on emergency procedures shows how the crew were to bail out in an emergency. First, the nose gear unit is extended pneumatically and the dorsal gunner dives through the entry hatch first. He is followed by the flight engineer, then the navigator/bomb-aimer, the co-pilot, the radio operator, and finally the captain.

Left: In the rear cabin the defensive fire commander bails out first, followed by the ventral gunner.

Below: Tu-95 '56 Red' was used for verifying the emergency escape system. Here the nose gear unit is extended independently, allowing the occupants of the forward cabin to bail out.

Centre left/bottom left: Two crewmen jump from the forward cabin. The main gear units remain retracted.

Centre right: A crewman dives head first through the entry hatch during the escape system test.

Bottom right: One of the rear gunners bails out, using the hydraulically actuated entry hatch door as a slipstream deflector.

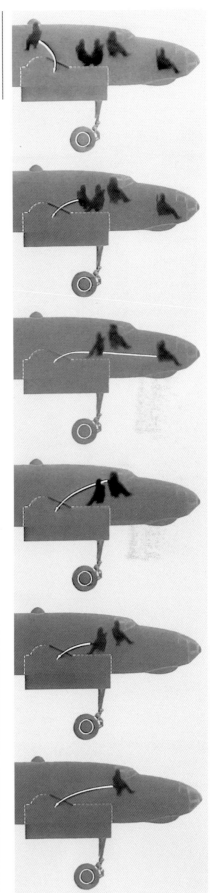

Right: Maintenance in progress on Tu-95 c/n 6800307 (note the jacks under the wing roots and rear fuselage). The navigator's station glazing was asymmetrical, with one extra pane on the starboard side.

Below: This view illustrates the *Bear*'s distinctive lines with a slender fuselage and high aspect ratio wings.

Bottom: '44 Red', an early Tu-95. The large tactical codes on the nose soon disappeared from the Tu-95s.

70 km (43.5 miles); it permitted bomb delivery from altitudes of 2,000-15,000 m (6,560-49,210 ft) at flight speeds of 300-1,250 km/h (186-776 mph). For better ECM resistance the radar worked in two selectable frequencies.

When further versions of the Tu-95 with obvious external differences became known in the West, the reporting name of the Tu-95 *sans suffixe* was amended to *Bear-A*.

Tu-95M strategic bomber (*izdeliye* VM)

The performance figures gleaned from the state acceptance trials were considerably lower than anticipated. Therefore the Tupolev OKB subjected the first production Tu-95 to a modification programme which ran from 20th August 1956 through 21st February 1957. By then the Kuznetsov OKB had developed a new version of the NK-12 turboprop uprated to 15,000 ehp for take-off and with an SFC

The final pre-production Tu-95 (c/n 580003)

580003 **56**

reduced from 0.225 to 0.21 kg/hp-hr (from 0.496 to 0.46 lb/hp-hr) at take-off power and from 0.165 to 0.158 kg/hp-hr (from 0.363 to 0.34 lb/hp-hr) at cruise power; these engines designated NK-12M (*modernizee*rovannyy – updated) were installed in Tu-95 '46 Red' (c/n 5800101) wearing the obscure number 4807 instead of the c/n. The maximum take-off weight was increased from 172,000 to 182,000 kg (from 379,190 to 401,230 lb) and the fuel load from 80,730 to 89,530 kg (from 177,980 to 197,370 lb). The resulting aircraft was designated Tu-95M (again standing for *modernizee*rovannyy) and had the product code *izdeliye* VM (that is, *izdeliye* V – *moderni***zee***rovannoye*).

The Tu-95M prototype underwent manufacturer's flight tests in September-October 1957, achieving a maximum speed of 905 km/h (562 mph) and a service ceiling of 12,150 m (39,850 ft). Maximum range proved to be 16,750 km (10,402 miles) and operational range was established as 13,000 km (8,073 miles).

Though these new figures were a considerable improvement over the performance of the first pre-production aircraft, they still did not meet the target stipulated by the original Council of Ministers directive. Regardless, it was decided to launch production of the Tu-95M immediately and add it to the Soviet Air Force inventory as rapidly as possible. This decision was given

The nose of the last Tu-95M built ('57 Red', c/n 8800605) as seen by the pilot of a NATO fighter. A strake aerial is fitted on the starboard side.

The white-painted undersides of the same aircraft. Note the colour division line on the engine nacelles and the exhaust-blackened main landing gear fairings.

Tu-95M '57 Red' (c/n 8800605)

8800605 **57**

even greater impetus when it turned out that the Tu-95's competitor, the Myasishchev M-4, had also failed to meet its stipulated range target of 12,000 km (7,460 miles), showing a range of only 9,500 km (5,900 miles) during manufacturer's tests in 1955.

Tu-95M production at factory No.18 began in 1957 and the numeration continued the Tu-95 *sans suffixe* sequence, the first production machine (c/n 7800407) being released by the factory on 31st October 1957. The new version remained in production until the end of 1958, the final aircraft (c/n 8800605) being manufactured on 31st December. The Tu-95M's production run was 19 aircraft – c/n 7800409 does not count, since this aircraft was again a Tu-116, but Batch 4 contained an extra airframe (c/n 7800411) used for static tests.

Thus, total Tu-95 *sans suffixe*/Tu-95M production (excluding the Moscow-built prototypes) was only 48 aircraft. Most sources say it was distributed over the years as follows: four aircraft in 1955, 23 aircraft in 1956, eight aircraft in 1957 and 14 aircraft in 1958; however, this adds up to 49 aircraft (which means that the Tu-95M static test airframe is included).

During the spring and autumn of 1958 Tu-95M c/n 7800410 (an in-service aircraft from the afore-mentioned 409th TBAP) underwent check-up tests at GK NII VVS to see if it met the specifications. A take-off weight of 182,000 kg (401,240 lb) was recorded, along with a weapons load of 5,955 kg (13,125 lb), which was the weight of a Soviet megaton-level nuclear bomb. With 4-5% fuel reserves remaining at the end of the mission, range was 13,200 km (8,197 miles). Maximum speed was 902 km/h (560 mph) and cruising speed was between 720 and 750 km/h (447-466 mph). These figures became the standard specifications for the Tu-95M and were used as a reference when new aircraft were being tested.

Outwardly the Tu-95M was almost identical to the Tu-95 *sans suffixe*, differing from the latter only in having small additional air scoops on top of the engine nacelles for cooling the generators. Hence both types had the same reporting name *Bear*, and subsequently *Bear-A*.

The Tu-95 went through many modernisation programmes, which allowed it to stay in service as a bomber for an extraordinary period of time. For example, at the request of the Long-Range Aviation Command a set of bomb cassettes was developed, enabling the Tu-95 to carry forty-five 250-kg (551-lb) conventional bombs, which allowed it to fulfil theatre-strategic and theatre-tactical missions in case of need; this modification came into being when the experience of the Arab-Israeli wars was analysed. The total bomb load in this configuration was 10,935 kg (24,110 lb) – about one-third of the maximum load carried by the Boeing B-52H (31,500 kg/70,000 lb).

The Tu-95 could carry 1946-model and 1954-model conventional bombs of 1,500 kg, 3,000 kg, 5,000 kg, 6,000 kg and 9,000 kg (3,305 lb, 6,610 lb, 11,020 lb, 13,230 lb and 19,840 lb) calibre on an MBD6-95 gantry-type bomb rack. The FAB-1500, FAB-3000 and FAB-5000 high-explosive bombs could also be suspended on BD5-95M racks; to maximise the number of FAB-1500s and FAB-3000s a pair of KD4-295 bomb cassettes could be installed. The *Bear-A* normally carried 500-kg (1,102-lb) HE bombs; later the range was augmented by 250-kg (551-lb) bombs, 100-kg (220-lb) and even 50-kg (110-lb) practice bombs. The PB-50 and -250 practice bombs were carried on the MBD6-95 rack and in KD3-695 bomb cassettes. (FAB = *foogahsnaya aviabomba* – HE bomb; PB = *prakticheskaya bomba*; BD = *bahlochnyy derzhahtel'* – beam-type rack; MBD = in this case, *mostovoy bahlochnyy derzhahtel'* – gantry-type rack; KD = *kassetnyy derzhahtel"* – bomb cassette.)

A Tu-95A takes off, showing the white-painted undersides. Note that the twin-wheel retractable tail bumper has been removed from this particular aircraft.

The first number after the letters in the bomb rack's designation denotes the weight class of munitions to be carried.)

Following the initial success of the first production version, the Tupolev OKB began exploring design options with the basic Tu-95 airframe. Though some of these studies resulted in one-off prototypes and others remained paper projects, most resulted in new versions adapting the *Bear* to new missions.

Tu-95A nuclear-capable strategic bomber (*izdeliye* V, 'order 180')

A version of the basic Tu-95 designated Tu-95A (*ah*tomnyy – atomic or nuclear; in this context, nuclear-capable) was developed and built to order specifically for delivering nuclear weapons, such as the 42-kiloton RDS-3 implosion-type atomic bomb (*izdeliye* 501-M,

codenamed 'Maria'), the 5-kiloton RDS-4 implosion-type bomb (*izdeliye* 244N, codenamed 'Tat'yana') – the first Soviet tactical nuke – and the 400-kiloton RDS-6S hydrogen bomb. (The RDS designator referring to Soviet nuclear charges stood for *re'aktivnyy dvigatel' spetsiahl'nyy* ('special reaction engine' or 'special jet engine') for security reasons. In later years the RDS acronym generated alternative explanations, such as *re'aktivnyy dvigatel' Stalina* ('Stalin's jet engine'), *Rosseeya delayet sama* ('Russia makes [the atomic bomb] on her own') etc.)

The Tu-95A differed from the baseline Tu-95 *sans suffixe* primarily in having a heat-insulated bomb bay equipped with an environmental control system which maintained the correct temperature throughout the aircraft's altitude envelope. This was necessary because nuclear munitions are sensitive to sub-zero temper-

Left and below left: A Tu-95A poised for take-off shows that the rudder and fin cap (but not the fin itself) were also painted white in the partial 'anti-flash' colour scheme.

atures and may malfunction after having had a cold soak at high altitude – the chain reaction might not go ahead, leading to non-detonation. Also, a special system performing the pre-release procedure (disengaging the multi-stage safety system, arming the detonator and activating the barometric sensors to explode the nuke at the preset altitude) and releasing the bomb was fitted.

Last but not least, the Tu-95A was provided with special protection from the effects of a nuclear explosion. Firstly, the gaps on the aircraft's exterior were sealed or minimised by riveting strips of metal to the perimeter of hatch covers, the edges of the bomb bay doors and wheel well doors. Secondly, glazed areas were blanked off from the inside before the bomb was dropped. Specifically, the navigator's station featured a sliding metal shutter on the optically flat lower pane and quick-fit metal blinds on the lateral panes. The flight deck side windows were closed by blinds made of a double layer of heavy fabric; the lower gunner's sighting blisters were closed by fixed flat blanks and multi-segment metal shutters whose shape matched the inside of the transparencies when closed, while the tail gunner's station glazing was also closed by multi-segment metal shutters. Thirdly, some equipment items and wiring bundles were encased in insulating materials. Finally, the aircraft received a so-called 'anti-flash' colour scheme, albeit a partial one – the undersurfaces, fuselage sides and rudder were given a coat of special high-gloss white paint to reflect the flash of the explosion as much as possible; the upper surfaces and the fin retained their natural metal finish. (By comparison, the British V-bombers initially wore a full 'anti-flash' colour scheme until grey/green camouflage was introduced in the 1970s.) In short, the changes were the same as those implemented on the Tu-16A *Badger-A* nuclear-capable bomber.

The Tu-95A was referred to in production as 'order 180'. Surprisingly, the OKB's product code did not change (*izdeliye* V), although logically it should have been *izdeliye* VA. By comparison, in the case of the Tu-16A the code was changed from *izdeliye* N to *izdeliye* NA.

Tu-95MA nuclear-capable strategic bomber (first use of designation; *izdeliye* VM, 'order 180')

A similar nuclear-capable version of the Tu-95M was brought out under the terms of the same 'order 180' as the Tu-95MA. It differed from the Tu-95A bomber only in the powerplant and the higher gross weight as described earlier. The designation Tu-95MA was later re-used for a one-off weapons testbed based on the Tu-95MS (see Chapter 5).

Again, the product code *izdeliye* VM did not change. Nor did the NATO reporting name change (*Bear-A*).

Tu-95U and Tu-95MU crew trainers ('95U', *izdeliye* VU)

During the 1970s the Tu-95 and Tu-95M bombers began to show their age. All feasible modifications and upgrades within the limits of the airframes' fatigue lives had been implemented, and it was finally decided to replace these aircraft in the bomber role with newer aircraft. Accordingly, many *Bear-As* were relegated to the training role where they served out the rest of their operational careers.

By the late 1980s virtually all remaining airworthy Tu-95s *sans suffixe* and Tu-95Ms had been modified as conversion/proficiency trainers designated Tu-95U (*oochebnyy* – for training) and known at the OKB as *izdeliye* VU. (Some sources, though, refer to the modified Tu-95Ms as Tu-95MU.) In accordance with its new role the aircraft had all offensive weapons systems removed (the defensive armament remained) and the bomb bay faired over; this had the effect of increasing the fuselage's structural stiffness, affecting the aircraft's handling. The Tu-95Us wore a distinctive red stripe around the aft fuselage to show that the aircraft had been withdrawn from first-line service and thus was not subject to arms limitation treaties.

The trainers were operated by the Long-Range Aviation's 43rd TsBP i PLS (*Tsentr boyevoy podgotovki i pereoochivaniya lyotnovo sostahva* – Combat Training & Aircrew Conversion Centre) at Dyagilevo AB in Ryazan', central Russia, which used them to introduce neophyte crews to the *Bear* and its unique flight characteristics. A few Tu-95Us survived long enough to see the demise of the Soviet Union, serving on until the early 1990s, whereupon the trainers finally ran out of service life and were scrapped.

Again, the trainer's NATO reporting name is *Bear-A*.

Tu-95 development aircraft with additional fuel tanks ('order 244')

In 1957-58 the Tupolev OKB worked on increasing the Tu-95's range and endurance. The Kuznetsov OKB was also called upon to develop a more powerful and fuel-efficient turboprop designated NK-20 which would help to meet the range performance goal. The requirement called for a take-off rating of 18,000-20,000 ehp (13,428-14,920 kW). The big idea was that with the new engines and certain airframe modifications providing increased fuel capacity, it might be possible to achieve ranges of up to 20,000 km (12,420 miles) without IFR.

As part of this effort, a single production Tu-95 was fitted with three additional fuel tanks (this job was known as 'order 244'). The No.5A tank was housed in the rear fuselage, while the Nos. 6A and 6B tanks were installed above the wing centre section torsion box. This increased the aircraft's estimated endurance at cruise power to 24 hours. The estimate proved fairly accurate; powered by NK-12M engines, the modified aircraft

A classic view of a Tu-95A from an intercepting NATO fighter.

stayed airborne for 23 hours 40 minutes during a test flight in 1958 to explore this capability.

However, the NK-20 engine never materialised and order 244 was cancelled. The fuel tank modification, though proven via the long distance flight, was not integrated into the production fleet. At a later date, extended range was achieved by introducing IFR capability on some versions of the Tu-95.

Tu-95V experimental hydrogen bomb carrier (Tu-95-202, 'order 242')

On 12th August 1953 the Soviet Union exploded its first thermonuclear device (hydrogen bomb) – the abovementioned RDS-6S – at the proving ground located 170 km (105 miles) west of Semipalatinsk, Kazakhstan, and known as the War Ministry's Practice

Range No.2 (UP-2 – *oochebnyy poligon*). Two years and three months later a thermonuclear device with a yield of 3 megatons – the RDS-37 (*izdeliye* 37D) two-stage H-bomb – was tested at the same location. For safety reasons the first version dropped by a Tu-16A on 22nd November 1955 was derated to 1.6 megatons; a 2.9-megaton version followed on 6th October 1957. The western world countered by stepping up its nuclear weapons development efforts substantially, with numerous nuclear devices being tested in the South Pacific and elsewhere. In effect, a race for maximum destructive power had begun, the only limiting factor being the size of the delivery aircraft's bomb bay.

In the autumn of 1954 the Soviet Union started work on an air-droppable thermonuclear weapon with a yield of no less than 100 megatons. The Tu-16A and the Tu-95

'74 Red', a Tu-95U trainer stripped of offensive armament, is seen here in the early 1990s. Note the coloured tips of the propeller spinners, a characteristic feature of Soviet military turboprop aircraft (probably meant for icing visualisation).

were contemplated as the delivery vehicle. It soon became evident that the Tu-95 was the only viable option for hauling such a behemoth – just as proposed from the outset by Academician Igor' V. Kurchatov (head of the Moscow-based Nuclear Energy Institute, the 'father of the Soviet atomic bomb') and Academician Yuliy B. Khariton, Chief Designer of the KB-11 design bureau within the Soviet Academy of Sciences' Laboratory No.2 specialising in nuclear weapons.

Initial design studies of a Tu-95 version able to carry the forthcoming 100-megaton H-bomb began in late 1954, immediately after the first discussions between Kurchatov and Andrey N. Tupolev. Deputy General Designer Aleksandr V. Nadashkevich, who (as mentioned earlier) headed the Tupolev OKB's Section V responsible for armament systems, became the new version's project chief.

Unlike all previous Soviet nuclear bombs, which had been developed by KB-11 situated in the town of Sarov (Gor'kiy Region), the three-stage 'superbomb' was created by NII-1011 established on 5th April 1955 within the framework of the Ministry of Medium Machinery (MSM – *Mini**ster**stvo **sred**nevo **mashin**ostro**yeniya**) which was responsible for all aspects of the Soviet nuclear programme. NII-1011 (now called the Russian Federal Nuclear Centre 'All-Russian Technical Physics Research Institute') was likewise tasked with developing nuclear weapons. It was located in Sokol township (Chelyabinsk Region); the place was codenamed Chelyabinsk-70 and is currently known as Snezhinsk ('Snow City'). The official designation of the new H-bomb was variously reported as AN602 or RN-202 (*izdeliye* 202). Contrary to the established Soviet tradition of using female given names as codenames for nuclear bombs, the 'superbomb' was codenamed '*Ivan*' – though it is occasionally called '*Vanya*' (the pet form of the name Ivan). The aircraft intended to carry it was designated Tu-95V, the suffix being variously explained as derived from the codename 'Vanya' or from *vodo**rod**naya **bom**ba* (hydrogen bomb). Some sources call it Tu-95-202, the designation being obviously derived from the bomb's product code. In paperwork the aircraft was referred to as 'order 242'.

Initially the designers at NII-1011 envisaged a bomb grossing at 40 tons (88,180 lb), but the Tupolev OKB said no. This weight amounted to 20% of the Tu-95's MTOW and would have impaired performance to an unacceptable degree – in fact, the bomber would have been unable to reach the test site, never mind the USA. Therefore, a smaller 'superbomb' was developed; while still packing a formidable 50-megaton punch, it had a gross weight of 20 tons (44,090 lb). This was a much more feasible figure for the Tupolev OKB engineering team, amounting to 12-15% of the Tu-95V's take-off weight.

The dimensions and weight of *izdeliye* 202 and its accommodation in the Tu-95's bomb bay were agreed upon during the first quarter of 1955, enabling the Tupolev OKB to begin detail design work. Preliminary calculations showed that the bomb could be housed entirely inside the bomb bay. Nevertheless, it was clear that the loads associated with carrying and releasing such a heavy single cargo item would necessitate a redesign and reinforcement of the fuselage structure; also, a purpose-built bomb rack and bomb release system would be required.

The designers chose to use a beam-type rack similar to the BD-206 rack developed for the Tu-95K missile strike aircraft (see below). The rack developed for the Tu-95V was designated BD7-95-242 (the first digit denoting weight class 7, the heaviest of all) or simply BD-242, in a reference to 'order 242'. It was attached to the hefty load-bearing beams forming the bomb bay sidewalls and featured three Der 5-6 electromechanical bomb shackles (*derzhahtel'*) rated at 9,000 kg (19,840 lb) each – two at the front and one at the rear. The only tricky moment associated with the design of the BD-242 was the installation of this rear bomb shackle, which had to be positioned at 90° to the fuselage axis because there were no centrally located load-bearing structural elements at the aft end of the bomb bay. Another challenge was the synchronisation of the bomb shackles, which had to open perfectly simultaneously. This problem was eventually solved and the bomb release system passed its bench tests without difficulty.

The bomb bay aperture was 1.78 m (5 ft 10²¹⁄₆₄ in) wide – same as on the standard bomber, but its length was increased to 7.15 m (23 ft 5½ in) long in order to accommodate the bulky bomb. Hence all fuselage fuel tanks except the No.1 tank, which was ahead of the wings, had to be deleted.

On 17th March 1956 the Council of Ministers issued directive No.357-228 officially tasking the Tupolev OKB with the development of the Tu-95V. The 12th production Tu-95 *sans suffixe* (c/n 5800302) manufactured on 25th April 1956 was delivered to the Tupolev OKB; in May-September 1956, concurrently with the development and testing of the bomb rack and release system, it was converted into the one-off Tu-95V prototype in the OKB's flight test facility hangar at Zhukovskiy. Following manufacturer's flight tests, the uncoded aircraft was delivered for testing to the Air Force's 71st Test Range at Bagerovo AB in the eastern part of the Crimea Peninsula, 14 km (8.7 miles) west of the city of Kerch. This outfit had overall responsibility for testing Soviet nuclear weapons; its head, Maj.-Gen. Viktor A. Chernorez, was a top-notch specialist who contributed immensely to equipping the Soviet Armed Forces with nuclear and thermonuclear weaponry. The testing of the Tu-95V at Bagerovo proceeded under the supervision of Engineer-Colonel Serafim M. Kulikov.

(Actually the designation '71st Test Range' was something of a misnomer because, in addition to an instrumented test range with a target for the bomb drops, the establishment included three Air Force units. The latter were the 35th OSBAP (ot**del**'nyy **smesh**annyy bombardi**rov**ochnyy avia**polk** – Independent (i.e., direct reporting) Composite Bomber Regiment) performing inert and live test drops, the 513th IAP (istre**bitel**'nyy avia**polk** – fighter regiment) providing protection, and the 647th SAPSO (**smesh**annyy avia**polk** spetsi**ahl**'novo obes**pech**eniya – Composite Special Support Air Regiment). This latter operated a mixed bag of utility, transport and reconnaissance aircraft, which varied over the years, and was tasked with air sampling in the wake of nuclear tests, aerial photography and transport/liaison duties. Only instrumented dummy versions of the bomb were dropped at Bagerovo; nobody in their right mind would test a live nuke in the Crimea which was, to use a common Soviet cliché, *the all-Union resort*!)

However, as the closing lines of a humorous Russian poem by Samuil Ya. Marshak go (concerning a puppy who ran away during a journey by rail and was substituted with a huge stray dog by the railway personnel, to the outrage of his lady owner): *'the dog may have grown during the journey!'* In the meantime the dog… sorry, the 'superbomb' had grown in weight to 24 tons (52,910 lb), or even 26 tons (57,320 lb). It was also bigger than the original mock-up, with a length of 8 m (26 ft 2³¹⁄₃₂ in) and a diameter of 2 m (6 ft 6⁴⁷⁄₆₄ in). In other words, the bomb was wider than the bomb bay and had to be carried in a semi-recessed position; hence the bomb bay doors had to be urgently redesigned to retract inward when the bomb was suspended (in similar manner to the Tu-95K) instead of opening outwards conventionally. (Some accounts say that the doors were simply removed.)

Hooking up the bomb was a task in itself. *Izdeliye* 202 was transported on a custom-made semitrailer of 40 tons (88,180 lb) capacity built by the Minsk Automobile Factory (MAZ) and towed by a stock YaAZ-210D 6x4 conventional tractor unit. This 'big rig' was too tall to fit under the Tu-95V if the latter was parked conventionally, therefore a special concrete-lined trench 1.4 m (4 ft 7 in) deep and 4.5 m (14 ft 9 in) wide had to be built; the articulated bomb transporter was backed into this trench, whereupon the aircraft was manoeuvred onto it from the other end, tail first. The loading procedure took more than two hours.

Moreover, the semi-external carriage rendered an environmentally controlled bomb bay impossible. Therefore the designers resolved the 'cold soak' problem by providing *izdeliye* 202 with a built-in heater; electric power for this was supplied via an umbilical cable. The latter also served for downloading the approved time delay and critical barometric altitude settings to the detonation mechanism, using a control panel in the flight deck.

The bomb was provided with an integral parachute retarding system giving the aircraft more time to get clear of the blast – a feature first used on the RDS-37. The system was developed by MAP's Paradropping Systems Research & Experimental Institute (NIEI PDS – Na**ooch**no-is**sled**ovatel'skiy eksperimen**tahl**'nyy insti**toot** para**shoot**no-de**sahnt**nykh sis**tem**) in Moscow. It weighed 800 kg (1,763 lb) and allowed the big bomb to descend from 10,500 m (34,450 ft) to the designated detonation altitude of 3,500 m (11,480 ft) in about 200 seconds. The testing of this system turned into a royal pain in the butt. The original version with a single canopy was unsatisfactory: the 1,600-m² (17,222 sq ft) parachute made of nylon fabric failed partially during the first drop. A four-canopy version of the same overall area was tried next, but this turned out to be even worse – due to poor synchronisation the 400-m² (4,305 sq ft) parachutes opened consecutively rather than simultaneously and were torn to shreds one by one, scattering fragments of nylon all over the place. In another case when the parachute retarding system failed completely, the bomb overshot the mark, sailing through the air until it landed in the Sea of Azov and sank. Adding offence to injury, all attempts to retrieve the bomb were unsuccessful, and eventually it was destroyed with explosives on the seabed.

The final version of the system reverted to a single-canopy layout but the parachute was appropriately modified for greater strength. The system had a multi-stage design: a 0.5-m² (5.38 sq ft) drogue parachute was deployed first, followed by a 5.5-m² (59.2 sq ft) second drogue parachute and then by three 42-m² (452 sq ft) parachutes which opened simultaneously to extract the 1,600-m² main canopy. The designers still had some reservations about the parachute retarding system's reliability; therefore a special safety feature was added to the bomb, precluding detonation if the bomb descended prematurely to the preset detonation altitude. This made sure the bomber would not be caught by the blast if the parachute failed to open.

Ballistic tests of dummy bombs and testing of the parachute retarding system were finally completed in 1959; the Tu-95V was now cleared to drop a live *izdeliye* 202 bomb. Yet, actual tests of the world's most powerful nuclear weapon were postponed for political reasons. Times of détente had come; Soviet Premier Nikita S. Khrushchov was due to visit the USA (this visit took place on 15th-27th September 1959), and it was deemed inappropriate for a massive weapon to be tested while the Soviet leader was on American soil. Hence the Tu-95V was delivered to Uzin AB. For more than two years it was used as a proficiency trainer by one of the resident DA units (the 409th TBAP) to avoid wasting the service lives of its regular Tu-95s, since the

Right and far right: A mock-up of the RDS-6S nuclear bomb. Note the brake petals incorporated into the stabiliser.

Top, above, right and above right: A mock-up of the *izdeliye* 202 hydrogen bomb. The hollow core of the stabiliser houses the parachute system.

Below: Another mock-up of the *izdeliye* 202 ('Vanya') bomb dropped on 30th October 1961. Note the nose aerials.

Below right: The complex parachute retarding system of the *izdeliye* 202 bomb.

The Tu-95V (c/n 5800302) with the *izdeliye* 202 thermonuclear bomb attached

5800302

specially configured bomb bay rendered it unusable for any other role.

In 1961, when the Cold War began to intensify again, the Tu-95V was 'returned to active duty'. First, the aircraft was flown to Kuibyshev-Bezymyanka for additional modifications at plant No.18, where it received a partial 'anti-flash' colour scheme, shutters for the flight deck/rear cabin transparencies and other protective features against the nuclear blast. In September 1961 the Tu-95V was ferried to Olen'ya AB, a bomber base near Olenegorsk (Murmansk Region) on the Kola Peninsula in the High North. This was because by then Soviet nuclear tests were no longer conducted in Semipalatinsk; since 1957 this was done at a new proving ground on the Novaya Zemlya ('New Land') archipelago located in the Arctic Ocean not far from the Kola Peninsula. (Previously it was mistakenly reported that the flight was made from Severomorsk-1 AB (known as Vayenga-1 AB until 1951), a Soviet Navy/North Fleet Air Arm base likewise located in the Murmansk Region.)

A crew captained by project test pilot Maj. Andrey Ye. Doornovtsev was assigned to the bomber. For starters they underwent additional instruction and training, flying practice sorties along the route to Novaya Zemlya they were to take. On 20th September the Tu-95V operated in a nuclear environment for the first time, flying chase for a Tu-16A captained by Lt.-Col. Vladimir F. Martynenko which dropped a bomb at the Novaya Zemlya proving ground. A similar mission was to take place on 2nd October 1961, but the Tu-95V suffered an engine failure halfway to Novaya Zemlya and returned to Olen'ya AB, leaving the Tu-16A to carry out the test alone.

On 6th October the roles were reversed – the Tu-95V made its first live drop of a thermonuclear bomb, with the same Tu-16A flying chase. This was not yet the *izdeliye* 202 'superbomb' but a smaller weapon. A 'dress rehearsal' took place several days later when the Tu-95V dropped a dummy version of the 'superbomb' at the Novaya Zemlya proving ground.

Finally, it was time for the real thing. The test was supervised by Nikolay I. Pavlov, head of MSM's 5th Main Directorate. On 30th October 1961 a live *izdeliye* 202 hydrogen bomb was hooked up to the Tu-95V, the bomber took off and headed east towards Novaya Zemlya. The crew consisted of captain Maj. Andrey Ye. Doornovtsev, co-pilot Capt. Mikhail K. Kondratenko, navigator Maj. Ivan N. Kleshch, Nav/Op Lt (SG) Anatoliy S. Bobikov, flight engineer Maj. Grigoriy M. Yevtushenko, radar operator Capt. Aleksandr F. Prokopenko, dorsal gunner (senior GRO) Lt (SG) Mikhail P. Mashkin, ventral gunner PFC Vasiliy Ya. Bolotov and tail gunner Capt. Vyacheslav M. Snetkov. Again, the same Tu-16A crewed by captain Lt.-Col. Vladimir F. Martynenko, co-pilot Lt (SG) Vladimir I. Mukhanov, navigator Maj. Semyon A. Grigoryuk, Nav/Op Maj. Vasiliy T. Muzlanov and GRO SSgt Mikhail Ye. Shumilov was flying chase. Its mission was to record the bomb drop and the explosion – and to tell the Tu-95V's crew when to release the bomb, should the *Bear*'s radar go unserviceable.

The two aircraft passed over Cape Kanin Nos on the Barents Sea coast in the Arkhangel'sk Region, then turned left and flew north-east over Rogachovo (a township and Soviet Air Force base in south-western Novaya Zemlya) and Pan'kova Zemlya Peninsula. Their designation was target area D-2 situated at Cape Sukhoy Nos ('Dry Nose') near Matochkin Shar, the narrow fjord separating the two islands of the archipelago – Severnyy (= Northern) and Yuzhnyy (= Southern). At 1130 hrs Moscow time the Tu-95V dropped the huge bomb; afterwards the crew reported that letting go such a heavy load made the aircraft pitch up perceptibly. As the bomb's parachute retarding system came into play, the aircraft made off towards Olen'ya AB at top speed.

The Tu-95V and the Tu-16A were respectively 40 km (24.85 miles) and 55 km (34.18 miles) away from ground zero (the hypocentre of the explosion) when the bomb detonated at 4,500 m (14,760 ft). Once the tremendous fireball had gone out, morphing into the tell-tale

Left row, top to bottom:

The crew of the Tu-95V reports readiness for the mission. Maj. Andrey Doornovtsev is nearest.

The mighty *izdeliye* 202 H-bomb is in place.

The Tu-95V starts its engines…

…and taxies out for take-off.

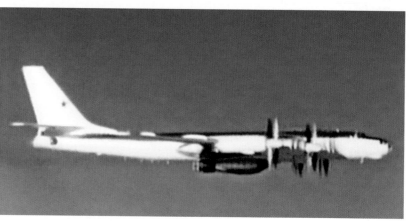

Right row, top to bottom:

The Tu-95V climbs away from Olen'ya AB.

The Tu-95V cruises towards Novaya Zemlya, with Maj. Vladimir Martynenko's Tu-16A flying chase.

Another view of the semi-exposed bomb at the moment of take-off.

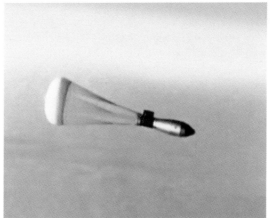

Far left: The *izdeliye* 202 bomb falls away; the first drogue parachute of the retarding system is already deployed.

Left: Here the main parachute has opened.

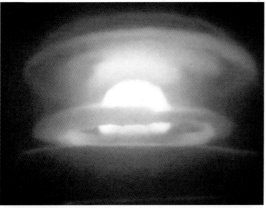

Left: Maj. Andrey Ye. Doornovtsev in the captain's seat of the Tu-95V

Far left: The first moments after the explosion. A huge fireball rises, surrounded by a so-called Wilson cloud…

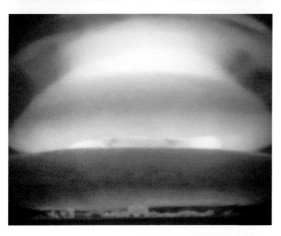

mushroom cloud, the crews disengaged the autopilots and braced for the blast wave. It caught up with the bombers at 115 km (71.46 miles) and 250 km (155 miles) respectively from ground zero; in fact, there were several consecutive blast waves but there was no danger of losing control. The Tu-95V's paintwork was scorched but otherwise the bomber suffered little damage. The strong atmospheric ionisation caused by the explosion interrupted radio communication for 40 minutes; unable to contact the crews, the men at the command post and at Olen'ya AB waited in uncertainty, fearing the worst, until communication was restored.

For safety reasons (including limitation of nuclear fallout and residual radiation) the yield of the *izdeliye* 202 tested on 30th October 1961 was limited to 50 megatons, half the originally envisaged figure. Even so, the blast was devastating; suffice it to say that, although this was an airburst, the blast wave bouncing off the ground generated a seismic shock wave which travelled around the globe three times! The blast wave also caused a good deal of collateral damage on the ground, from shattered windows to completely demolished buildings. The mushroom cloud could be observed from a distance of 800 km (496 miles) and peaked at 65 km (40.39 miles), rising past the stratosphere into the mesosphere; the cap of the mushroom cloud had a peak width of 95 km (59 miles) and its base was 40 km (25 miles) wide. Due to the lack of official information

…and develops into a multi-layer mushroom cloud.

The mushroom cloud rises above the layer of overcast. It peaked at an altitude of 65 km.

the blast was originally rumoured to be anywhere from 75 to 120 megatons (the latter figure apparently arose from leaked information that 'the actual yield had exceeded the design figure by 20%'). The feasibility of creating an H-bomb with a 100-megaton yield was reported to Nikita S. Khrushchov, who used this figure in a speech in front of the USSR's Supreme Soviet. In the event the 100-megaton version was never built, even though it was feasible – and thank goodness for that.

Continuing the series of codenames started with the first Soviet nuclear test, the 30th October 1961 test was codenamed 'Joe 111' by the US Central Intelligence Agency (in a rather disrespectful reference to Iosif V. Stalin). Later, someone mockingly dubbed the *izdeliye* 202 'Tsar Bomb', obviously by analogy with two famous tourist attractions in Moscow – the Tsar Bell (which never rang) and the Tsar Cannon (which never fired). The implication was unmistakable: the bomb was portrayed as something that is huge and impressive but there's just one little thing wrong with it – it doesn't work. This is unfair, because work it did; while *izdeliye* 202 was admittedly a technology demonstrator (or a 'can-do exercise', if you like), it was the most powerful weapon ever detonated in the history of mankind.

Predictably, the aircrews involved in the test received government awards; Andrey Ye. Doornovtsev was promoted to Lieutenant-Colonel and on 7th March 1962 was awarded the prestigious Hero of the Soviet Union (HSU) title. Equally predictably, the test caused strong condemnation in the western world and was one of the factors leading up to the Partial Test Ban Treaty (PTBT) now in force. This was signed in Moscow on 5th August 1963, banning nuclear weapon tests in the atmosphere, in outer space and under water.

Less than a year later the Tu-95V was used for another nuclear test at Novaya Zemlya; the weapon was a 20-megaton thermonuclear bomb having the same body as *izdeliye* 202. The same 'cast of characters' was involved: the Tu-95V was captained by Lt.-Col. Andrey Ye. Doornovtsev and the Tu-16A chase aircraft by Lt.-Col. Vladimir F. Martynenko. After two practice flights on 27th July and 2nd August the bomb was dropped at test area D-3 on 5th August. Again, it was released at 10,500 m (34,450 ft) but the detonation altitude was 3,500 m (11,480 ft); the bomb was dropped through thick overcast with a cloud top at 8,000 m (26,250 ft).

After the end of aerial nuclear tests the Tu-95V was withdrawn from use at Olen'ya AB. It did not fly again until the advent of the Tupolev Tu-144 *Charger* supersonic transport (SST), at which time it was put back into service as a freighter (!). After the fatal crash of the second production Tu-144 at the 1973 Paris Air Show on 3rd June 1973, the Tupolev OKB made changes to the Tu-144's structure and systems; as a result, the take-off weight increased, necessitating a new round of static

tests. The third Batch 5 aircraft (c/n 10053, or 05-3) was set aside for these tests, which were held in Novosibirsk at the Siberian Aviation Research Institute named after Sergey A. Chaplygin (SibNIA – *Sibeerskiy naoochno-issledovatel'skiy institoot aviahtsii*). The airliner's fuselage was delivered to Novosibirsk-Yel'tsovka airfield by a Soviet Air Force Antonov An-22 *Antey* (Antheus; NATO reporting name *Cock*) heavy transport, while the wing centre section was delivered by the Tu-95V which carried it under the fuselage. (Some sources, though, say Tu-144 c/n 10053 was subjected to fatigue testing by TsAGI in Zhukovskiy, logging about 5,000 cycles, and then was tested to destruction in the spring of 1979.)

Eventually the Tu-95V was transferred to another DA unit – the 1023rd TBAP based at Chagan AB near Semipalatinsk, which used it as a trainer until the aircraft was retired. According to another account, it was used as a ground instructional airframe until the mid-1980s. The aircraft was ultimately scrapped on site.

Tu-95R strategic reconnaissance aircraft (project)

In the late 1950s the Soviet Air Force asked the Tupolev OKB to develop a reconnaissance version of the Tu-95 as soon as possible to meet a pressing need for a long-range reconnaissance aircraft. A Council of Ministers directive issued on 20th May 1960 required the Tu-95R reconnaissance aircraft (*[samolyot-] razvedchik*) based on the Tu-95 *sans suffixe* to be available for check-up flight tests in the first quarter of 1961.

The Tupolev OKB began preliminary design work on how the mission equipment was to be arranged. In the meantime, however, the Tu-95M became available. Therefore developing a reconnaissance version of the initial bomber became pointless.

Tu-95MR strategic reconnaissance aircraft (Tu-95MR-2, *izdeliye* VR)

Using the Tu-95M as the basis, the Tupolev OKB developed the project further as the Tu-95MR (*modernizeerovannyy razvedchik* – updated reconnaissance aircraft) or *izdeliye* VR. The location of the mission equipment was identical to the stillborn Tu-95R. Also, as mentioned earlier, a probe-and-drogue IFR system was rapidly developed by OKB-918; accordingly, on 9th January 1962 the Council of Ministers issued a directive requiring this system to be incorporated on the Tu-95's reconnaissance version.

The pneumatically operated telescopic IFR probe was mounted above the navigator's station, and the fuel line conduit ran along the starboard side of the nose to the No.1 fuselage tank. Two retractable FPSh-5M probe illumination lights (*fara podsveta shtahngi*) were built into the upper side of the extreme nose, flanking the probe. Installation of the probe and the associated local

Tu-95MR '46 Red' displays the lateral and ventral ELINT blisters and the bulged camera bay doors. All camera ports are closed.

ДАЛЬНИЙ СТРАТЕГИЧЕСКИЙ САМОЛЁТ-РАЗВЕДЧИК Ту-95МР

НАЗНАЧЕНИЕ САМОЛЁТА Ту-95МР
ВЕДЕНИЕ РАЗВЕДКИ В ГЛУБОКОМ ТЫЛУ
ПРОТИВНИКА НА СУШЕ И НА МОРЕ
ДНЕМ И НОЧЬЮ

СОСТАВ СИСТЕМЫ
- ТРИ ВАРИАНТА СМЕННОГО ФОТООБО-
РУДОВАНИЯ ДЛЯ ЦЕЛЕЙ ДНЕВНОЙ И
НОЧНОЙ ФОТОРАЗВЕДКИ
- АППАРАТУРА РАДИОТЕХНИЧЕСКОЙ РАЗ-
ВЕДКИ СРС-1 (В ДИАПАЗОНАХ А Б В = ГД)
И „РОМБ-4" (лит А и Б)
- АППАРАТУРА РАДИОЛОКАЦИОННОЙ РАЗ-
ВЕДКИ „РУБИН-1Д"

МАКСИМАЛЬНАЯ СКОРОСТЬ		
НА ВЫСОТЕ 8 км	912	км/час
КРЕЙСЕРСКАЯ СКОРОСТЬ		
НА ВЫСОТЕ 10 км	750	км/час
ПРАКТИЧЕСКАЯ ДАЛЬНОСТЬ		
С 5% ОСТАТКОМ ТОПЛИВА		
ПРИ ПОСАДКЕ	15200	км
ПОТОЛОК	10-12	км
ДЛИНА РАЗБЕГА	2600	м
ВЗЛЕТНЫЙ ВЕС	1820	т

A drawing from the project documents showing the equipment fit and design performance of the Tu-95MR.

Here a Tu-95MR is shown with the camera windows of the vertical cameras in the bomb bay open.

A fine study of Tu-95MR c/n 7800506, the only example lacking IFR capability. Note the lateral ELINT blisters and the narrow transparency on the port side of the nose typical of the Tu-95MR.

structural reinforcement caused the rear row of the navigator's station glazing to be deleted; on the other hand, the Tu-95MR had an additional vertically disposed trapezoidal transparency on the port side of the nose which the standard bomber lacked. Additionally, while the *Bear-A* had gravity refuelling – a complex and time-consuming procedure, the Tu-95MR introduced single-point pressure refuelling. (Actually, 'single-point' is not entirely accurate, as there were two twin pressure refuelling connectors under the wing roots allowing several TZ-16 articulated fuel bowsers to be connected at a time.) The fuel system comprised 72 bag-type tanks.

The Tu-95MR was capable of both photo reconnaissance (PHOTINT) and electronic intelligence (ELINT); hence the crew included a reconnaissance systems operator with a workstation in the flight deck. An SRS-1AG general-purpose signals intelligence set (**stahn**tsiya razve**dk**i **svya**zi – SIGINT set) was fitted, with antennas in two teardrop-shaped dielectric fairings located ventrally at frames 13 (just aft of the nosewheel well) and 22. The SRS-1AG was provided with an FRU-1 photo recording device (**foto**reghist**ree**ruyushcheye oo**stroy**stvo) capturing the intercepted signals on film for later deciphering. The SRS-6 Romb-4A (Rhomboid, or Diamond) and SRS-7 Romb-4B SIGINT systems were

also fitted; their antennas were positioned in two elongated dielectric fairings on the rear fuselage sides between frames 65-72 (just ahead of the fin root fillet). Along with the IFR probe, the SIGINT fairings were the main recognition feature distinguishing the reconnaissance version from the bomber.

The extensive camera suite was mostly located on a special pallet in the bomb bay, with the exception of two oblique cameras between frames 67-70 with windows below the lateral ELINT blisters. Three alternative camera fits were possible:

• *Day option 1* comprised two fixed AFA-42/20 vertical cameras, four AFA-42/100 cameras in pairs on tilting mounts for two-strip vertical photography, an AFA-41/20 camera on a TAU mount (*topogra**fich**eskaya **a**ero**fot**ousta**nov**ka* – topographic aerial camera mount), a fixed AShchAFA-5 slot camera (*avtoma-**tich**eskiy shchele**voy a**ero**fot**oappa**raht***) for continuous shooting, and an AFA-42/100 oblique camera on a tilting mount.

• *Day option 2* comprised two AFA-40 vertical cameras and two AFA-42/20s (all rigidly installed on two trusses), an AFA-41/20 camera on a TAU mount, a fixed AShchAFA-5 slot camera and an AFA-42/100 oblique camera on a tilting mount.

• The *night option* comprised two NAFA-MK-75 cameras on a tilting mount in a common container, a fixed AShchAFA-5 camera and an AFA-42/100 oblique camera on a tilting mount. In this case the bomb bay also housed flare bombs or flash bombs on KD3-695 bomb cassettes.

The bomb bay was equipped with special fittings for the cameras and an environmental control system. The bomb bay doors were new – they were bulged perceptibly, protruding 90 mm (3³⁵⁄₆₄ in) beyond the fuselage contour because of the need to incorporate camera windows with electrically operated sliding shutters. The camera windows were located

Another view of a Tu-95MR in action showing the open camera ports.

asymmetrically: the port door had three of these (for the AFA-40, AFA-42/20 and AFA-42/100 cameras) while the starboard one had four (for the AFA-40, AFA-42/20, AFA-42/100 and AFA-41/20 cameras).

The chin radome was identical but instead of the usual Rubidiy-MM bomb-aiming radar it housed the newer *Rubin-1D* radar (Ruby; sometimes called R-1D for short). The latter was integrated with the PHOTINT suite and provided with a FARM-2A photo adapter for filming the image on the radarscope. The flare bomb cassette aft of the bomb bay was deleted and its bay doors were replaced by the aerial of the DISS-1 Doppler ground speed and drift sensor system (*doplerovskiy izmeritel' skorosti i snosa*). An ARK-U2 *Istok* (Source of a river) ADF was fitted; working with the R-802 command radio, it enabled accurate rendezvous with the tanker during in-flight refuelling. The electric system was modified, featuring 1-kVA PT-1000TsS three-phase AC converters (*preobrazovahtel' tryokhfahznyy*) to cater for the mission equipment.

The third production Tu-95M (c/n 7800410) was converted into the Tu-95MR prototype by the Kuibyshev aircraft factory, becoming the first *Bear* to feature IFR capability and single-point pressure refuelling. The conversion work was completed during the autumn of 1964. On 12th November Tu-95MR c/n 7800410 entered flight test; the results were satisfactory as far as both the reconnaissance equipment and the IFR system were concerned. As the latter system was tested, the Tu-95MR worked with a Myasishchev M-4-2 *Bison-A* single-point tanker. Three flights involving contacts with the tanker were made, including one at night; during this night flight the Tu-95MR received nearly 50 tons (110,200 lb) of fuel. All performance characteristics, with the exception of the longer endurance, remained unaffected as compared with the Tu-95M.

The trials were completed on 19th December 1964 and the aircraft was turned over to the Air Force, attaining initial operational capability. A further three Tu-95Ms (c/ns 7800501, 7800502 and 7800506) were upgraded to the reconnaissance configuration in the 1960s. Tu-95MR c/n 7800506 differed from the other three in lacking IFR capability. In paperwork the IFR-capable examples were referred to as Tu-95MR-2; in actual service, however, the reconnaissance version (with or without probe) was called Tu-95MR. The NATO reporting name was *Bear-E*.

Despite being Air Force aircraft, the Tu-95MRs operated over the seas and oceans, reconnoitring NATO carrier task forces; this is probably the reason why the MR suffix was sometimes erroneously deciphered as *morskoy razvedchik* (maritime reconnaissance aircraft). A common tactic for the *Bear-Es* was to operate in conjunction with a Tu-95K missile strike aircraft (see below). The latter detected maritime targets at long

range with its powerful radar, whereupon the Tu-95MR would overfly the target and do the photographing and electronic eavesdropping.

The four Tu-95MRs were operated quite intensively well into the late 1980s. Later they were converted into Tu-95U trainers, serving on in that role into the early 1990s when they were struck off charge and scrapped.

Tu-95 ECM aircraft prototype

At the end of the 1960s a single production Tu-95 was converted into an electronic countermeasures platform. The idea was that the specialised ECM version would be used for group protection, jamming the enemy's air defence (AD) radars while escorting a bomber formation. No separate designation has been reported for this aircraft.

The mission equipment was installed in the bomb bay, comprising SPS-22, SPS-33, SPS-44, SPS-55 and SPS-77 active jammers (*stahntsiya pomekhovykh signahlov* – lit. 'interference signal emitter'). The SPS-22, SPS-33, SPS-44 and SPS-55 were part of the *Buket* (Bouquet) family of jammers developed in the late 1950s; hence they were also known as the Buket-2 (or B-2 for short), Buket-3 (B-3), Buket-4 (B-4) and Buket-5 (B-5) respectively. They were able to jam several radars at a time, including multi-channel and tuneable radars. Each of the four sets covered a certain frequency band, working in a wavelength of 21.5-30 cm (B-2), 12.5-21.5 cm (B-3), 9.8-12.5 cm (B-4) and 8.6-9.8 cm (B-5). In turn, each of the four jammers had four transmitters working in different wavelengths (except the B-3, which had six), enabling it to cover the entire spectrum of wavelengths. The B-2, B-3, B-4 and B-5 sets each had their own range of reception channels (18, 45, 30 and 30 respectively) and the power output was 340-1,000 W, 500-100 W, 440-680 W and 400-860 W respectively. The weight was 854 kg (1,882 lb) for the B-2 set, 870 kg (1,918 lb) for the B-3 set, 722 kg (1,591 lb) for the B-4 set and 755 kg (1,664 lb) for the B-5.

In its day the Buket was the world's most powerful ECM suite, and contemporary electronic counter-countermeasures (ECCM) means were powerless against it. To maintain its function, the enemy radar could only change its operating frequency, but even then one of the four Buket systems would have it covered. Ground radars were jammed with full 360° coverage, and the Buket sets could function either automatically or semi-automatically. This obviated the need for an additional crewmember (the electronic warfare officer) – the jammers were operated by the Nav/Op from his workstation in the front pressure cabin. The SPS-77 jammer was optimised for low-altitude operations.

The aircraft remained a one-off – possibly because the ECM role was adequately filled by the Tu-16Ye *Badger-H* passive ECM aircraft and the Tu-16P *Badger-J* active ECM aircraft, which were built in quantity for the Long-Range Aviation. Incidentally, the Tu-16P was equipped with the same SPS-22, SPS-33, SPS-44, SPS-55 and SPS-77 jammers.

Tu-95DT ('aircraft 95DT') military transport aircraft (project)

A Council of Ministers directive issued on 12th August 1955 authorised the Tupolev OKB to commence work on a transport derivative of the Tu-95 that ultimately led to the Tu-114 long-haul airliner (which lies outside the scope of this book). Initially referred to as the Tu-95DT (*desahntno-trahnsportnyy* – paradrop/transport, used attributively), this was to be a military airlifter that would require only minimum modifications to the basic Tu-95 airframe. This concept was abandoned at an early stage in favour of a more radical option – the Tu-115 with a more capacious fuselage, which was based on the Tu-114 and thus likewise lies outside the scope of this book. (The Tu-115 was a stillborn project anyway.)

Tu-96 development aircraft ('aircraft 96', 'order 241')

The general trend in the post-war development of air defence systems (the advent of transonic interceptors, increasingly more capable ground-based AD radars and airborne fire control radars, etc.) dictated a need for high-performance bombers. Much emphasis was

placed on altitude performance, especially above the target where the bomber would run into the strongest opposition from enemy air defences – and strategic targets would be particularly well defended.

As mentioned earlier, the original Tu-95 had been designed for a service ceiling of 14,000-16,000 m (45,940-52,480 ft) but the Soviet military were not content with this. Hence, as early as the basic bomber's PD project stage, OKB-156 studied a high-altitude version that would offer a service ceiling of 16,000-17,000 m (52,480-55,760 ft). This aircraft had increased wing area and high-performance turboprop engines optimised for operation at extreme altitudes.

On 29th March 1952 the Council of Ministers issued directive No.1551-544 followed up by MAP order No.354 on 1st April. These documents required the Tupolev OKB to design and build an advanced Tu-95 derivative with improved high altitude performance. Bearing the in-house designation 'aircraft 96' (Tu-96), the new bomber was to be powered by four Kuznetsov TV-16 turboprops, then under development, and have a service ceiling over the target of 17,000 m with a 5,000-kg (11,020-lb) bomb load while cruising at 800-850 km/h (497-528 mph). Two prototypes were ordered; the first of these was required to commence its manufacturer's flight tests by July 1954 and be submitted for state acceptance trials by December 1954.

The same directive and MAP order required the Kuznetsov OKB to commence 100-hour bench testing of the TV-16 engine in May 1954 and have it available for flight testing in June 1954.

On 4th August 1952 the Soviet Air Force C-in-C endorsed the official specific operational requirement (SOR) for the 'aircraft 96'. The bomber was to have the following performance:

• Range with a 5,000-kg bomb load while cruising at 800-850 km/h was to be 9,000-10,000 km (5,589-6,210 miles) at a cruise altitude of 17,000 m, increasing to 10,500-11,000 km (6,521-6,831 miles) at 16,000 m and to 15,000 km (9,315 miles) at 15,000 m (49,210 ft). If additional fuel tanks were fitted, maximum range was to be 17,000-18,000 km (10,557-11,178 miles) at a cruise altitude of 14,000 m (45,920 ft).

• Maximum speed at an altitude of 8,000-9,000 m (26,250-29,520 ft) was to be 900-950 km/h (559-590 mph).

• The take-off run from a Class 1 airfield – this means a paved runway with a length of 3,250 m (10,660 ft) – was to be 1,500-1,800 m (4,920-5,900 ft).

• The normal bomb load was 5,000 kg, increasing to a maximum of 12,000 kg (26,455 lb) in high gross weight configuration at the expense of a reduced fuel load.

The defensive armament was largely unchanged, consisting of three powered turrets, each equipped with two 23-mm TKB-495A (i.e., AM-23) cannons. The

A desktop model of the Tu-96. The wings were to have a larger root chord (hence the main gear fairings protrude less beyond the trailing edge) and greater taper. The wing planform is inaccurate, with straight leading and trailing edges (compare this to the drawing on the opposite page).

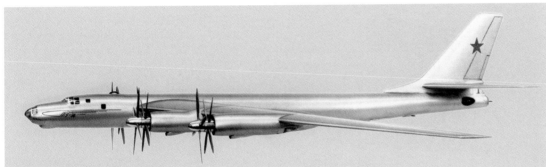

More views of the same model depicting the Tu-96. In side elevation or front view the difference from the Tu-95 is not obvious at all.

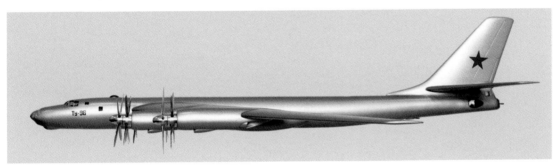

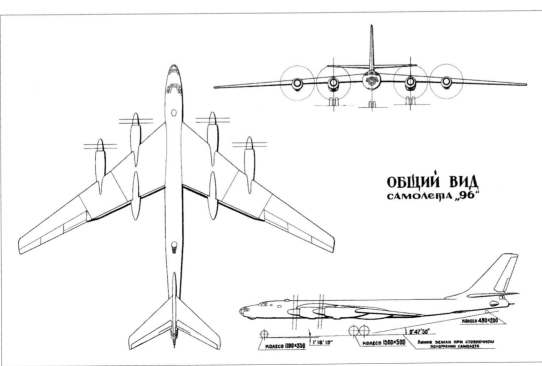

ОБЩИЙ ВИД
САМОЛЕТА „96"

КОЛЕСО 1100×330　　КОЛЕСО 1500×500　　КОЛЕСО 480×200

A three-view drawing of the 'aircraft 96' (Tu-96) bomber from the ADP documents. The increased-area wings were taken from the Tu-114 airliner and the planform differs from that on the model, featuring a kinked leading edge and a double-kinked trailing edge.

Opposite page: Two more views of the model of the Tu-96 bomber.

ammunition complement was 350 rpg for the dorsal turret (versus 300 rpg on the Tu-95), 400 rpg for the ventral turret and 500 rpg for the tail turret. The latter would be aimed by means of a new Ksenon (Xenon) gun-laying radar – although an early drawing from the 'aircraft 96' project documents showing the fuselage's internal layout clearly states the same PRS-1 Argon radar.

The aircraft featured the same Rubidiy-MM bomb aiming radar as on the basic Tu-95 bomber; incidentally, the crew was reduced to seven by eliminating the Nav/Op (radar operator) – his functions were performed by the navigator, who also used a PVB-1 or PS-50 bomb sight. There was also a Meridian long-range radio navigation (LORAN) system and an SP-50 Materik (Continent) instrument landing system. 'Aircraft 96' was equipped with RPDS and RPS long-range communication radios, a Khrom IFF interrogator and a Nikel' IFF transponder.

The TV-16 high-altitude turboprop was to have a 12,500-ehp take-off rating at 8,250 rpm, a maximum continuous rating of 12,000 ehp and a cruise rating of 6,500 ehp at 8,000 rpm (in Mach 0.7 cruise at an altitude of 14,000 m). The SFC at take-off power was estimated

'Aircraft 96' specifications

Crew	7
Length overall	46.167 m (151 ft 5¹⁵⁄₃₂ in)
Wing span	51.4 m (168 ft 7⅝ in)
Horizontal tail span	14.78 m (48 ft 5⁵⁄₆₄ in)
Height on ground	12.35 m (40 ft 6½ in)
Wing area	316.6 m² (3,407.58 sq ft)
Vertical tail area	38.53 m² (414.73 sq ft)
Horizontal tail area	54.49 m² (586.53 sq ft)
Wing sweep at quarter-chord:	
inboard	36°30'
outboard	33°22'
Vertical tail sweep	40°
Horizontal tail sweep	40°
Powerplant	4 x TV-16
Engine power:	
take-off	12,500 hp
maximum continuous	12,000 hp (up to h = 14,000 m/ 45,930 ft)
nominal (cruise)	10,200 hp (h = 14,000 m, V = 850 km/h / 528 mph)
Propellers:	
model	853A (contra-rotating)
no. of blades	4+4
diameter	6.25 m (20 ft 6⅟₁₆ in)
Fuel	kerosene
Empty weight	70,870 kg (156,240 lb)
All-up weight:	
normal	n.a.
maximum (range 15,000 km/9,320 miles)	140,000 kg (308,650 lb)
overload (range 18,000 km11,180 miles)	155,000 kg (341,720 lb)
All-up weight over the target	105,000 kg (231,490 lb)
Payload:	
normal	n.a.
maximum	69,130 kg (152,410 lb)
Fuel load:	
normal	n.a.
maximum	62,120 kg (136,950 lb)
overload (with extra tanks)	77,070 kg (169,910 lb)
Bomb load:	
normal	5,000 kg (11,020 lb)
maximum	12,000 kg (26,455 lb

CG range	17-25% MAC
Maximum speed:	
at sea level	525 km/h (326 mph) *
at 8,000 m (26,250 ft)	890 km/h (552 mph)
at 10,000 m (32,810 ft)	876 km/h (544 mph)
at 12,000 m (39,370 ft)	844 km/h (524 mph)
Landing speed	177 km/h (110 mph)
Rate of climb (AUW 105,000 kg):	
at sea level	18.6 m/sec (3,660 ft/min)
at 5,000 m (16,400 ft)	17.0 m/sec (3,345 ft/min)
at 10,000 m	15.4 m/sec (3,030 ft/min)
Climb time (AUW 105,000 kg):	
to 5,000 m	4.7 minutes
to 10,000 m	9.9 minutes
to 12,000 m	12.1 minutes
Service ceiling:	
AUW 105,000 kg	16,400 m (53,810 ft)
AUW 140,000 kg	14,600 m (47,900 ft)
Maximum range with 5,000 kg (11,020 lb) of bombs:	
AUW 115,000 kg (253,530 lb)	9,040 km (5,620 miles) [1]
AUW 140,000 kg	14,750 km (9,170 miles) [2]
	15,000 km (9,320 miles) [3]
AUW 155,000 kg	18,000 km (11,180 miles) [4]
Effective range with 5,000 kg of bombs:	
AUW 115,000 kg	8,270 km (5,140 miles) [1]
AUW 140,000 kg	13,430 km (8,350 miles) [2]
	13,600 km (8,450 miles) [3]
AUW 155,000 kg	16,200 km (10,070 miles) [4]
Take-off run:	
TOW 140,000 kg	1,090 m (3,580 ft)
TOW 155,000 kg	1,375 m (4,510 ft)
Take-off distance to h=25 m (82 ft):	
TOW 140,000 kg	3,000 m (9,840 ft)
TOW 155,000 kg	3,970 m (13,020 ft)
Landing run (landing weight 85,000 kg/187,390 lb)	850 m (2,790 ft)
Landing distance from h=25 m	1,730 m (5,680 ft)

Notes:

* Restricted by a dynamic pressure limit of 1,320 kg/m² (270 lb/sq ft) at altitudes up to 8,500 m (27,890 ft)

1. Fuel load 37,170 kg (81,950 lb), altitude 16,700 m (54,790 ft), speed 800 km/h (496 mph)

2. Fuel load 62,120 kg, altitude 16,000 m (52,490 ft), speed 800 km/h

3. Fuel load 62,120 kg, altitude 15,000 m (49,210 ft), speed 800 km/h

4. Fuel load 77,070 kg, altitude 15,000 m (49,210 ft), speed 800 km/h

as 0.24 kg/hp-hr (0.53 lb/hp-hr) and the cruise SFC as 0.135 kg/hp-hr (0.3 lb/hp-hr); actual bench tests, though, showed these values to be 0.225 kg/hp-hr (0.496 lb/hp-hr) and 0.165 kg/hp-hr (0.363 lb/hp-hr) respectively. The engine's dry weight was not to exceed 3,100 kg (6,830 lb); initial engine life was set at 100 hours.

The Kuibyshev engine factory No.24 was ordered to manufacture a development batch of sixteen TV-16s; six of these were to be delivered to the Tupolev OKB – two in late 1953 and four in early 1954. Concurrently OKB-120 headed by Konstantin I. Zhdanov was instructed to develop new contra-rotating propellers for the TV-16; these would have hollow steel blades rather than solid duralumin blades, as on the AV-60 propellers.

The data on 'aircraft 96' shown in the tables on these pages comes from a MAP statistical file filled out on 23rd December 1952 – well in advance of the machine's first flight, so the figures are provisional.

The advanced development project was completed in March 1953. According to the designers' estimates the bomber would have a take-off weight of 155 tons (341,710 lb), a maximum speed of 902 km/h (560 mph) and a cruising speed of up to 800 km/h (496 mph). Maximum effective range with 7% fuel reserves was estimated to be 16,200 km (10,060 miles), the absolute maximum range being 18,000 km (11,178 miles). Altitude over the target was estimated as 16,800 m (55,120 ft) at an all-up weight of 115,000 kg (253,530 lb).

Outwardly the Tu-96 differed from the Tu-95 in the wing planform. This was a case of 'reverse stan-dardisation' – the wings were taken straight from the Tu-114 airliner; hence the root chord was greater (the leading-edge and trailing-edge portions of the wing airfoil were extended). The inboard portions had slightly greater leading-edge sweep, creating a kink at the inner/outer wing manufacturing break, and flap chord was also increased, with a double trailing-edge kink at the flaps' outer ends, so that the main gear fairings

The ordnance options of 'aircraft 96' as per MAP statistical file		
Type of ordnance	**Maximum quantity**	**Total weight**
1. Bombs		
FAB-250 M-46	36	9,000 kg (19,840 lb)
FAB-500 M-46	24	12,000 kg (26,455 lb)
BrAB-500	24	12,000 kg (26,455 lb)
FAB-1000 (old model)	8	8,000 kg (17,640 lb)
FAB-2000 (old model)	6	12,000 kg (26,455 lb)
FAB-1500 M-46	8	12,000 kg (26,455 lb)
BrAB-1500 M-46	8	12,000 kg (26,455 lb)
FAB-3000 M-46	4	12,000 kg (26,455 lb)
BrAB-3000	4	12,000 kg (26,455 lb)
FAB-5000 M-46	2	10,000 kg (22,045 lb)
BrAB-6000	2	12,000 kg (26,455 lb)
FAB-9000 M-46	1	9,000 kg (19,840 lb)
UB-2000F Chaika *	4	8,000 kg (17,640 lb)
UB-5000F Kondor *	2	10,000 kg (22,045 lb)
SNAB-3000 Krab *	4	12,000 kg (26,455 lb)
2. Naval mines		
AMD-500	16	8,000 kg (17,640 lb)
AMD-1000	6	6,000 kg (13,230 lb)
AMD-2M	12	13,200 kg (29,100 lb)
IGDM	12	13,200 kg (29,100 lb)
Serpey	6	8,700 kg (19,180 lb)
Desna	8	6,000 kg (13,230 lb)
Lira	8	7,600 kg (16,760 lb)
3. Torpedoes		
45-36MAV	8	9,320 kg (20,550 lb)
RAT-52	6	3,750 kg (8,270 lb)
4. Missiles		
RAMT-1400 Shchooka *	4	6,400 kg (14,110 lb)

* External carriage

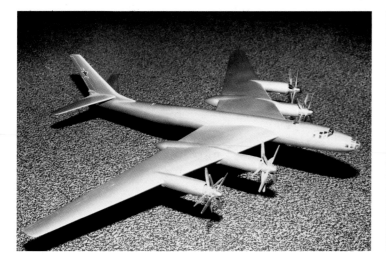

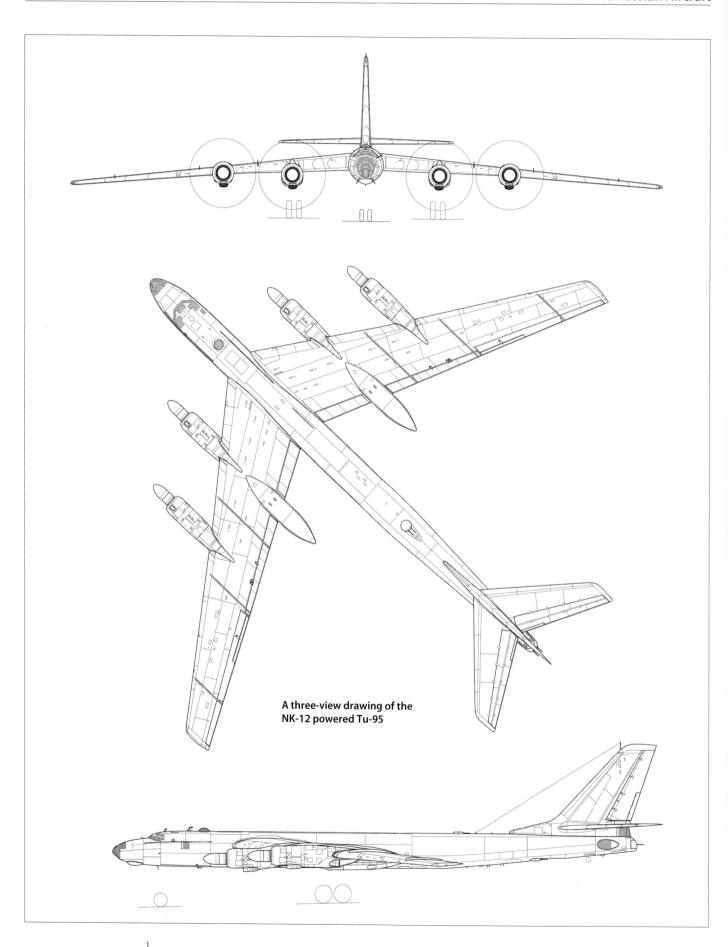

A three-view drawing of the
NK-12 powered Tu-95

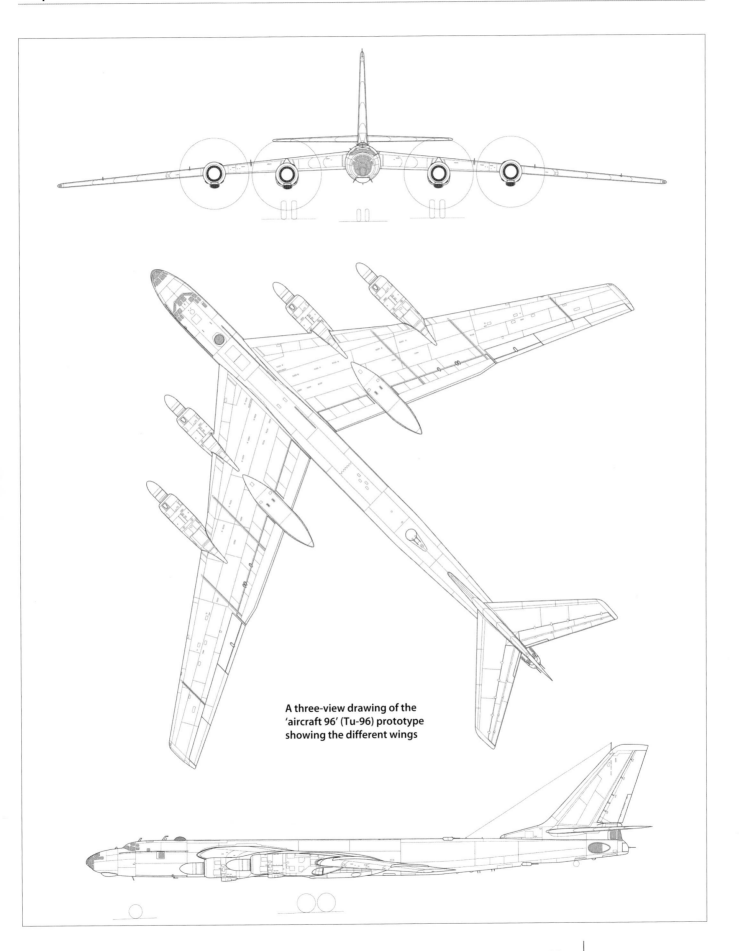

A three-view drawing of the
'aircraft 96' (Tu-96) prototype
showing the different wings

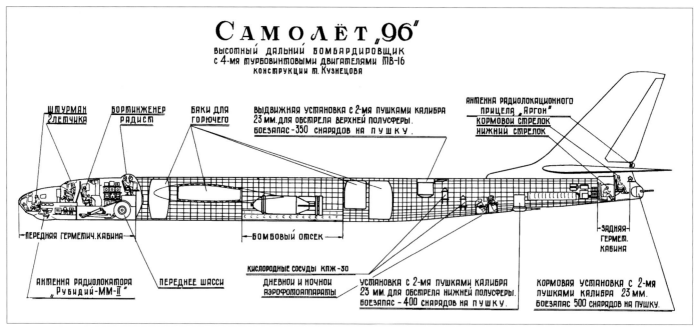

Самолёт „96"

высотный дальний бомбардировщик
с 4-мя турбовинтовыми двигателями ТВ-16
конструкции т. Кузнецова

ШТУРМАН
2 ЛЕТЧИКА

БОРТИНЖЕНЕР
РАДИСТ

БАКИ ДЛЯ
ГОРЮЧЕГО

ВЫДВИЖНАЯ УСТАНОВКА с 2-мя ПУШКАМИ КАЛИБРА
23 мм. ДЛЯ ОБСТРЕЛА ВЕРХНЕЙ ПОЛУСФЕРЫ.
БОЕЗАПАС—350 СНАРЯДОВ НА ПУШКУ.

АНТЕННА РАДИОЛОКАЦИОННОГО
ПРИЦЕЛА „АРГОН"
КОРМОВОЙ СТРЕЛОК
НИЖНИЙ СТРЕЛОК

ПЕРЕДНЯЯ ГЕРМЕТИЧ. КАБИНА

БОМБОВЫЙ ОТСЕК

ЗАДНЯЯ
ГЕРМЕТ.
КАБИНА

АНТЕННА РАДИОЛОКАТОРА
„РУБИДИЙ-ММ-II"

ПЕРЕДНЕЕ ШАССИ

КИСЛОРОДНЫЕ СОСУДЫ КПЖ-30
ДНЕВНОЙ И НОЧНОЙ
АЭРОФОТОАППАРАТЫ

УСТАНОВКА с 2-мя ПУШКАМИ КАЛИБРА
23 мм. ДЛЯ ОБСТРЕЛА НИЖНЕЙ ПОЛУСФЕРЫ.
БОЕЗАПАС — 400 СНАРЯДОВ НА ПУШКУ.

КОРМОВАЯ УСТАНОВКА с 2-мя
ПУШКАМИ КАЛИБРА 23 мм.
БОЕЗАПАС 500 СНАРЯДОВ НА ПУШКУ.

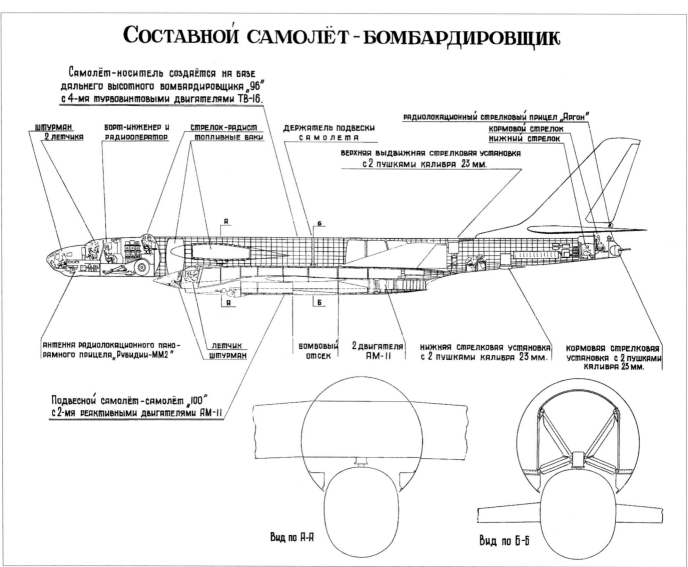

СОСТАВНОЙ САМОЛЁТ-БОМБАРДИРОВЩИК

Самолёт-носитель создаётся на базе
дальнего высотного бомбардировщика „96"
с 4-мя турбовинтовыми двигателями ТВ-16.

ШТУРМАН
2 ЛЕТЧИКА

БОРТ-ИНЖЕНЕР И
РАДИООПЕРАТОР

СТРЕЛОК-РАДИСТ
ТОПЛИВНЫЕ БАКИ

ДЕРЖАТЕЛЬ ПОДВЕСКИ
САМОЛЕТА

РАДИОЛОКАЦИОННЫЙ СТРЕЛКОВЫЙ ПРИЦЕЛ „АРГОН"
КОРМОВОЙ СТРЕЛОК
НИЖНИЙ СТРЕЛОК

ВЕРХНЯЯ ВЫДВИЖНАЯ СТРЕЛКОВАЯ УСТАНОВКА
с 2 ПУШКАМИ КАЛИБРА 23 мм.

АНТЕННА РАДИОЛОКАЦИОННОГО ПАНО-
РАМНОГО ПРИЦЕЛА „РУБИДИЙ-ММ2"

ЛЕТЧИК
ШТУРМАН

БОМБОВЫЙ
ОТСЕК

2 ДВИГАТЕЛЯ
АМ-11

НИЖНЯЯ СТРЕЛКОВАЯ УСТАНОВКА
с 2 ПУШКАМИ КАЛИБРА 23 мм.

КОРМОВАЯ СТРЕЛКОВАЯ
УСТАНОВКА с 2 ПУШКАМИ
КАЛИБРА 23 мм.

Подвесной самолёт-самолёт „100"
с 2-мя реактивными двигателями АМ-11.

Вид по А-А

Вид по Б-Б

Left: A drawing from the ADP document showing the internal layout of 'aircraft 96'.

Below left: A drawing showing 'aircraft 96' as a 'mother ship' for the projected Tupolev 'aircraft 100' (Tu-100) supersonic captive bomber.

Above: Head-on view of the Tu-96 prototype at Zhukovskiy.

Below and bottom: Two more aspects of '73 Red', the Tu-96 prototype. Note the photo calibration markings. The number 5836 is unrelated to the c/n.

protruded less beyond the trailing edge. Concurrently, wing span was increased to 51.4 m (168 ft 7⅜ in). As a result, wing area grew from the Tu-95's 283.7 m² (3,053.72 sq ft) to 316.6 m² (3,407 sq ft); total area including the portion inside the fuselage was 345.5 m² (3,718 sq ft). The wings had more effective multi-slotted flaps to improve field performance. A more subtle change was in the forward fuselage which incorporated a redesigned forward pressure cabin of greater volume to enhance crew comfort on long missions. The armour protection was similar to the Tu-95; the overall weight of the armour was 833 kg (1,836 lb).

Construction of the first prototype 'aircraft 96' commenced at the Kuibyshev factory No.18 in February 1953 (the aircraft was referred to in paperwork as 'order 241'). On 25th March that year the ADP was submitted for review to the Air Force. Unfortunately, just two months later the first prototype Tu-95 crashed, causing all work on 'aircraft 96' to be put on hold; first the cause of the crash had to be determined, and then the Tupolev and Kuznetsov OKBs concentrated on the second prototype Tu-95 and its TV-12 engine, which were given top priority. Delivery of the first TV-16 engines was postponed until December 1954, pushing delivery of the Tu-96 back until July 1955.

Presently the '95/2' was completed and entered flight test, allowing work on the Tu-96 to resume. The airframe (the c/n remains unknown) was finally ready in the early summer of 1956 – but not the engine. The experimental TV-16 turboprop, which was 'hotter' than the TV-12 (NK-12), turned out to be rather temperamental, repeatedly suffering failures during bench tests. Realising that the work was making slow progress and the TV-16 engine would not be available in time for the Tu-96's initial flight tests, Nikolay D. Kuznetsov and Andrey N. Tupolev agreed that NK-12 engines and AV-60 props would be fitted temporarily.

Coded '73 Red' and bearing the number 5836 (whose meaning is obscure) on the nose and tail instead of the c/n, the Tu-96 finally flew in April 1956 with the provisional powerplant. The test crew was captained by Ivan M. Sookhomlin and included co-pilot Aleksey P. Yakimov, navigator K. I. Malkhasyan and engineer in charge David I. Kantor. Subsequent testing also was undertaken using NK-12s, with a consequent reduction in performance, on the understanding that the TV-16s would be fitted when the new engine was cleared for flight. In the long run, however, this never happened.

As actually flown, the Tu-96 had an empty weight of 79,800 kg (175,930 lb) and a maximum TOW of 179,430 kg (395,580 lb), including 91,990 kg (202,800 lb) of fuel. Top speed was 880 km/h (546 mph) at 6,400 m (21,000 ft), 846 km/h (525 mph) at 10,000 m (32,810 ft) and 900-950 km/h (559-590 mph) at 8,000-9,000 m (26,250-29,530 ft). The service ceiling was only 12,400 m (40,680 ft); rate of climb was 14 m/sec (2,755 ft/min) at

2,000 m (6,560 ft), 14.6 m/sec (2,783 ft/min) at 6,000 m (19,685 ft) and 6 m/sec (708 ft/min) at 10,000 m, the aircraft reaching the latter altitude in 14.3 minutes. Maximum range was 15,000 km (9,315 miles).

In the meantime, however, at this early stage of the Tu-96's flight test programme the Soviet Air Force had a change of heart regarding the development and use of high-altitude strategic bombers. By the mid-1950s it had become clear that western fighters and surface-to-air missile (SAM) systems were achieving performance levels that would turn high-altitude bombers into vulnerable targets. Therefore, direct delivery of free-fall conventional bombs and nuclear weapons was no longer practicable. It was more likely that targets would be destroyed with stand-off weapons, such as air-to-surface missiles and rocket-boosted bombs.

The Tu-95 was considered ideally suited for this less demanding mission. Thus, it became apparent there no longer was any need for the more advanced but troubled '96' aircraft; hence Andrey N. Tupolev took the decision to concentrate on perfecting the production Tu-95 instead. On 28th March 1956 the Council of Ministers issued directive No.424-261, cancelling the Tu-96 programme.

The sole prototype was thus relegated to the test and development role. Later, it was concluded that, even with the slightly more powerful NK-12M engines, performance was unsatisfactory when compared to the jet-powered Tu-16. Eventually the Tu-96 was scrapped at Zhukovskiy in the late 1950s.

Tu-96 'mother ship' for 'aircraft 100' (Tu-100) bomber (project)

A study worthy of note at this point was the proposed use of the Tu-96 as a compound strategic strike system. As such, the Tu-96 would have served as a 'mother ship' for Tupolev's projected 'aircraft 100' (Tu-100) nuclear weapon transport. The latter would have been a supersonic aircraft with two alternative modes of operation – a manned 'parasite bomber' or a remote-controlled unmanned combat aerial vehicle (UCAV).

The Tu-100 was conceived as a rather compact aircraft with an oval-section fuselage, mid-set wings and conventional swept tail surfaces, the stabilisers with inset elevators being mid-set and the trapezoidal vertical tail having a very low aspect ratio. In one of the project configurations the moderately swept wings had constant leading-edge sweep and reduced trailing-edge sweep on the outer portions, resulting in a curious scimitar shape; another version had rhomboid wings with negative trailing-edge sweep. The powerplant initially consisted of two Mikulin AM-11M afterburning turbojets side by side in the rear fuselage rated at 5,500-6,000 kgp (12,130-13,230 lbst) each and breathing through a fixed-area chin intake. The payload – a single nuclear bomb weighing 1,250-1,500 kg (2,760-3,310 lb), such as the RDS-4 – was carried internally in a bay amidships. The crew of two was provided with ejection seats; the pilot sat under a teardrop canopy, the navigator/bomb-aimer sitting ahead of and below him in the extensively glazed and very pointed nose (the shape of the forward fuselage closely resembled the Vought F-8 Crusader fighter). To save space and weight the Tu-100 had a bicycle landing gear with a wheeled nose unit and a main skid located well aft. A bomb-aiming radar was located just aft of the nosewheel well in a teardrop radome.

Carrying the Tu-100 would require far-reaching changes to the Tu-96's centre/rear fuselage structure (including installation of a special beam-type rack) and the fuel system. The crew complement and defensive armament remained unchanged.

According to the designers' concept of the system, a Tu-96 would deliver the Tu-100 (carried semi-recessed in the bomb bay) to a point some 6,000-6,500 km (3,721-4,040 miles) from the base and 800-1,000 km (496-621 miles) from the target. The Tu-100 would then be launched to proceed on its mission, penetrating the enemy air defences at its maximum speed of 1,500 km/h (931 mph); it was expected to deliver a nuclear bomb and hopefully escape the blast, flying another 200-500 km (124-310 miles) at 1,000 km/h to land at the nearest base in home territory. Meanwhile, the Tu-96 was expected to return to base immediately in order to refuel and reload. Thus, the strike system's overall combat radius would be about 7,000-7,500 km (4,350-4,660 miles).

Development of the Tu-96 as a launch platform for the 'aircraft 100' went no further than the drawing board. Work was suspended when Tupolev began studying a more efficient configuration of the strike system that would involve the 'aircraft 108' (Tu-108), a supersonic design optimised to carry the '100', and an advanced version of the latter. The Tu-100 project was repeatedly modified; a late version was to feature identically rated but more fuel-efficient D-20 after-burning turbofans – the first of the kind in the Soviet Union – developed by OKB-19 under Chief Designer Pavel A. Solov'yov which would increase the maximum speed to 1,800 km/h (1,118 mph). However, neither aircraft was built.

'Aircraft 99' bomber (project)

The 'aircraft 99' bomber project can be mentioned here as a 'distant relative' of the original Tu-95. Due to concerns over the Kuznetsov OKB's ability to supply powerful and dependable turboprops, in 1953 the Tupolev OKB began studying alternative powerplants for the Tu-95 after the crash of the first prototype. The options included conventional turbojet engines and a new type of engines known as variable-discharge turbine (VDT) engines; the Russian term for the latter

was RVD (*re'aktivno-vintovoy dvigatel'* – lit. 'turbojet-propeller engine'). The purpose of this research was to determine the optimum aircraft characteristics utilising pure jet engines versus turboprops.

One of the VDT engine projects was developed by the newly established OKB-19 (then headed by Arkadiy D. Shvetsov) in Perm'; it was originally meant for the Tu-96 high-altitude high-speed strategic bomber. The engine's peculiarity lay in its ability to vary the ratio between shaft horsepower output and jet thrust, depending on the altitude. Thus, at 16,000 m (52,480 ft) – the design service ceiling of the Tu-96 – and a speed of 1,000 km/h (621 mph) the total thrust of one VDT engine was estimated to be about 5,000 kgp (11,020 lbst). This was split almost equally between propeller and exhaust thrust; propeller thrust was 2,600 kg (5,730 lb) with an efficiency of 0.8 and jet thrust was 2,400 kgp (5,290 lbst). During ascent to cruise altitude, power would remain relatively constant, though the propellers' efficiency would decay. In cruise mode, shaft horsepower remained constant at 12,000 shp up to 16,000 m (52,480 ft), decreasing above that level proportionally to the air pressure. Pure jet thrust, on the other hand, was expected to increase linearly from sea level to 16,000 m and then decay gradually. Thus, the total thrust of the VDT engine actually increased at the rated altitude.

Project studies of the 'aircraft 99' featured both buried engines and pylon-mounted engines. Some of the VDT configurations called for two to six engines. A version with four pylon-mounted engines proved to be the most efficient.

However, the complexity of the VDT engines led Tupolev to consider jet-powered alternatives. One configuration of 'aircraft 99' looked like a scaled-up Tu-16, featuring two 15,360-kgp (33,860-lbst) Dobrynin VD-5M non-afterburning turbojets with an SFC of 0.805 kg/kgp-hr flanking the centre fuselage aft of the wings' rear spar; the engines had air intake assemblies protruding beyond the wing leading edge, so that the inlet ducts passed through the wing torsion box which had cunningly designed spars with O-frames at the roots. Another had four 11,000-kgp (24,250-lbst) Dobrynin VD-7 turbojets with an SFC of 0.8 kg/kgp-hr in the wing roots in side-by-side pairs *à la* M-4, with flush air intakes in the wing leading edge resembling those of the British V-bombers.

'Aircraft 99' wing studies included configurations with areas varying from 300 to 450 m² (from 3,229 to 4,843 sq ft) and sweep angles varying from 45° to 55°. The take-off weights also varied, ranging from 150 to 250 tons (330,6907-551,150 lb). Wind tunnel tests in some of these configurations were conducted at TsAGI in Zhukovskiy.

Concurrently with this Tupolev project, however, the Myasishchev OKB moved ahead with an improved M-4 powered by four VD-7 turbojets instead of Mikulin

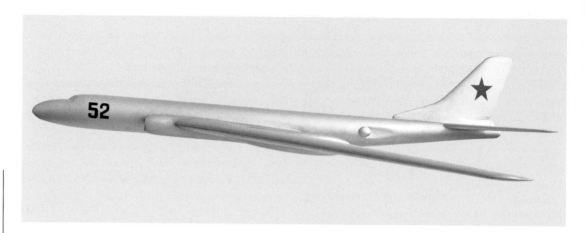

Three views of a model showing one of the version of the 'aircraft 99' project. With two VD-5F(M) turbojets, the aircraft looks like a scaled-up Tu-16, except for the location of the lateral observation blisters.

A different wooden model of the projected 'aircraft 99' bomber with four Dobrynin VD-7 turbojets arranged in pairs in the wing roots.

AM-3s. This new powerplant significantly improved the M-4's range to more than 13,000 km (8,073 miles). The new version of the *Bison* (known in house as the M-6) first flew in 1956, successfully passing its test programme and entering full-scale production in 1958 as the 3M *Bison-B* (aka 3MN, the N denoting *novyye dvigateli* – new engines). As a result, the Tupolev '99' bomber project became moot and was abandoned.

Tu-95K missile strike aircraft (*izdeliye* VK, 'order 206')

The rapid development of western anti-aircraft defence systems during the 1950s made it imperative that stand-off weapons and appropriate delivery vehicles be developed. Added to this, the new Soviet leader Nikita S. Khrushchov was famously enchanted by all sorts of missile systems, to the detriment of manned combat aircraft. Together, this meant that Soviet long-range bombers had to meet the new requirement (i.e., become less bomb-oriented and more missile strike-oriented) or be retired. This new capability permitted Soviet strategic aircraft to deliver weapons accurately on targets that otherwise were heavily defended.

Even in consideration of the new stand-off missile salient, the Tupolev OKB was well equipped to meet the new challenge. The Tu-95 was ideally suited in terms of range, payload and other parameters to carry a large air-launched weapon. This proved important when the Tu-95 was compared head-to-head with Myasishchev's M-4 and 3M bombers. Perhaps most importantly, the latter two had a bicycle landing gear and consequently a much smaller ground clearance than the Tu-95, which had a conventional tricycle gear. There was little question as to which aircraft was better suited as an air-to-surface missile platform.

On 11th March 1954 the Council of Ministers issued directive No.412-182 ordering development of the K-20 stand-off weapons system. (The K originally stood for *Kometa* (Comet) which was a generic codename of the Soviet air-launched cruise missile programme; later it came to denote *kompleks [vo'oruzheniya]* – integrated weapons system.) The K-20 (Kometa-20) was the first

Soviet strategic stand-off weapons system intended for use against stationary or low-mobility targets of importance, such as political and industrial centres, military bases and naval task forces. It consisted of the Kh-20 supersonic cruise missile (NATO codename AS-3 *Kangaroo*), the associated guidance system and a missile strike derivative of the Tu-95M strategic bomber designated Tu-95K (sometimes called Tu-95K-20).

The missile itself was developed in accordance with the same directive by the Mikoyan OKB's Section K (OKB-2-155) specialising in missiles; this was headed by Artyom I. Mikoyan's closest aide Mikhail I. Gurevich, while Aleksandr Ya. Bereznyak led the actual design effort. (Later, in 1967, OKB-2-155 became an organisationally separate enterprise named GMKB Raduga (*Gosudarstvennoye mashinostroitel'noye konstrooktorskoye byuro* – 'Rainbow' State-owned Machinery Design Bureau) and headed by Bereznyak. This entity created virtually all of the air-launched cruise missiles that saw service with the Soviet Air Force and the Soviet Naval Aviation.)

The Kh-20 drew heavily on the design of the Mikoyan OKB's unsuccessful I-7U interceptor whose development began in 1956. Like the I-7U, the missile had mid-set wings swept back 55° at quarter-chord,

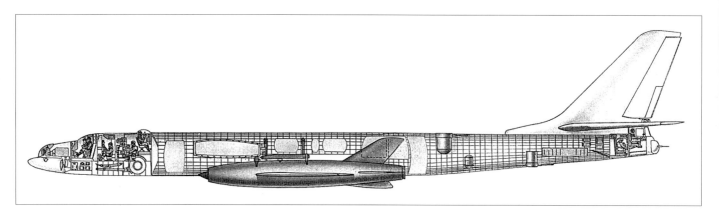

A drawing from the ADP documents showing the internal layout of the Tu-95K missile strike aircraft.

Two views of the Tu-95K with the Kh-20 missile from the ADP documents.

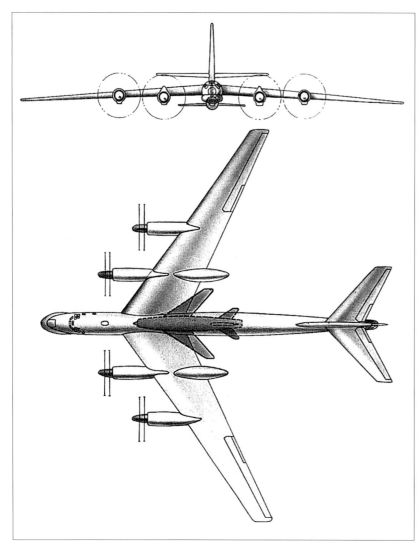

sharply swept conventional tail surfaces with all-movable stabilisers (stabilators) and a sharp-lipped axisymmetrical supersonic air intake in the extreme nose featuring a pointed centrebody (shock cone). The powerplant was also basically the same – a 9,810-kgp (21,630-lbst) Lyul'ka AL-7FK axial-flow afterburning turbojet (K = *korotkoresoorsnyy* – short-life) featuring a fixed-area supersonic Laval nozzle; this was to give the Kh-20 a speed of Mach 2. The missile carried an RDS-6S

thermonuclear warhead with a yield variously reported as 350 or 800 kilotons.

The Kh-20 had an overall length of 14.603 m (47 ft 10⁵⁄₆₄ in) less undernose pitot boom – or 15.415 m (50 ft 6⁵⁄₆₄ in) complete with pitot, a wing span of 9.03 m (29 ft 7½ in) and a launch weight of 11,600-11,800 kg (25,570-26,010 lb). This meant it was too bulky and heavy to be carried under the wings, as had been the case with previous missiles designed by OKB-2-155, and the Tu-95's turboprop powerplant with large-diameter propellers made underwing carriage impossible for such a large missile anyway. Therefore the Tu-95K was to carry the missile on the centreline, which restricted the offensive weapons load to just one missile. Until the moment of launch the Kh-20 was semi-recessed in the weapons bay, being suspended on a purpose-built retractable rack which lowered it into the slipstream prior to engine starting and release (this will be discussed later in the book).

The guidance system was developed by KB-1 headed by Vitaliy M. Shabanov within the Ministry of Defence Industry (MOP – *Ministerstvo oboronnoy promyshlennosti*) and comprised two subsystems. The Tu-95K was equipped with a purpose-built YaD navigation/attack radar (NATO codename *Crown Drum*) which also functioned as a weather radar; it had a search/target illumination channel and a missile guidance channel. (Curiously, the radar's designation was just like the Russian word *yad* meaning 'poison'.) The missile itself was fitted with a YaR active radar seeker for terminal guidance (its antenna was housed in the air intake centrebody), a YaK autopilot, and a mid-course guidance module picking up signals transmitted by the aircraft's radar and making altitude corrections.

Two launch modes were possible. In the so-called navigation mode, when there was no radar contact with the target, the Tu-95K's navigator either received the target co-ordinates from a target designator aircraft or calculated them and entered them into the range detection module of the missile's radar seeker, launching the missile from beyond the aircraft's own radar acquisition range (up to 600 km/372 miles). Once the Tu-95K was close enough to track the target with its

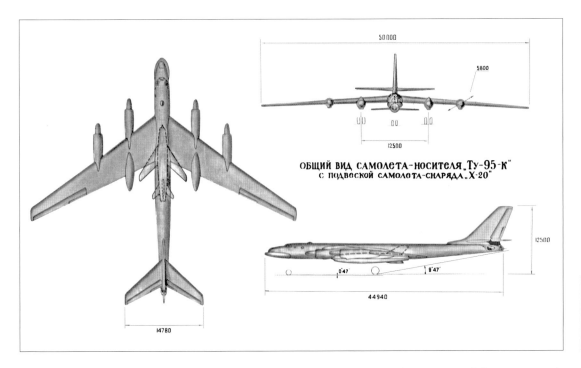

ОБЩИЙ ВИД САМОЛЕТА-НОСИТЕЛЯ „ТУ-95-К"
с подвеской самолета-снаряда „Х-20"

A three-view drawing of the Tu-95K (with Kh-20 missile attached) from the protocol of the mock-up review commission.

radar, it provided mid-course guidance to the missile. Alternatively, the navigator launched the missile after the radar had acquired the target; in the latter case the minimum distance to the target was shorter – up to 450 km (279 miles).

Depending on the flight level, the YaD radar had a detection range of 390-450 km (240-280 miles). Maximum missile launch range was 450-600 km (280-370 miles) in navigation mode and 370-430 km (230-270 miles) in radar tracking mode, again depending on the altitude. The Kh-20 was launched at 10,500-11,500 m (34,450-37,730 ft) – or, according to some sources, at any of four prescribed altitudes: 9, 10, 11 or 12 km (29,530; 32,810; 36,090 or 39,370 ft). The minimum launch distance was 150 km (93 miles); in this case the Tu-95K turned back immediately after the launch and there was no mid-course guidance.

The guidance technique was as follows. 46 seconds after release, when the Kh-20 was a safe distance ahead of the aircraft, the autopilot generated the so-called K1 command impulse, pulling up the missile into a climb. 221 seconds after release the autopilot generated the K2 command impulse, levelling off the missile at its cruise altitude of 15,000 m (49,210 ft). After the first 270 seconds of flight the missile caught the aircraft's radar beam, the K3 command impulse was transmitted and the mid-course guidance subsystem took over. The YaD radar determined the positions of the target and the missile relative to the aircraft, the target illumination channel working on a 10-cm wavelength and the missile guidance channel working on a 3-cm wavelength. On receiving the radar's signal, the YaR system generated a reply on a 2-cm wavelength with a certain delay; when this signal was picked up, the navigator could see the

A slightly different cutaway drawing from the same document showing the Tu-95K's crew positions, offensive and defensive armament.

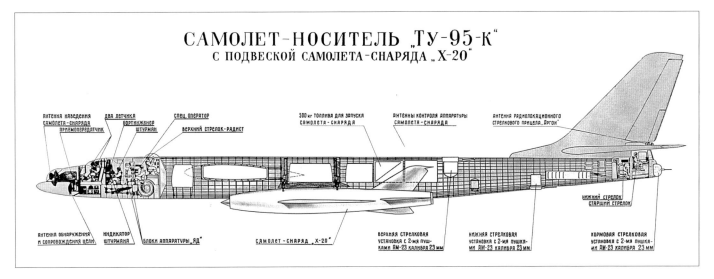

САМОЛЕТ-НОСИТЕЛЬ „ТУ-95-К"
с подвеской самолета-снаряда „Х-20"

СХЕМА УСТАНОВКИ АНТЕНН

Антенна обнаружения „ЯД1-1"

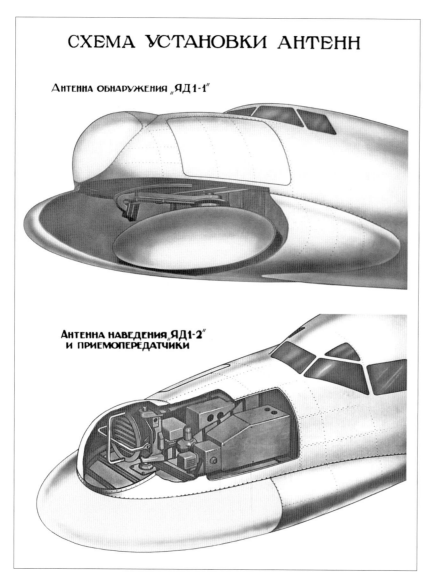

Антенна наведения „ЯД1-2"
и приемопередатчики

СХЕМА УГЛОВ ПОВОРОТА АНТЕНН

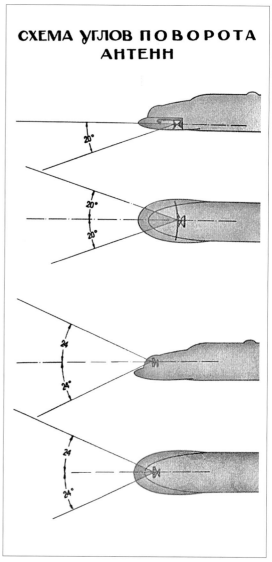

Above: Drawings from the same protocol showing the YaD radar's YaD1-1 search/target illumination antenna (top), YaD1-2 missile guidance antenna and radar set.

Above right: A diagram showing the scan angles of the radar's antennas.

Right: A drawing from the same document showing the BD-206 missile rack with its front and rear screw jacks, their supports, twin electric motors, angle drive gearboxes and drive shafts.

БАЛКА ПОДВЕСКИ САМОЛЕТА-СНАРЯДА „Х-20"

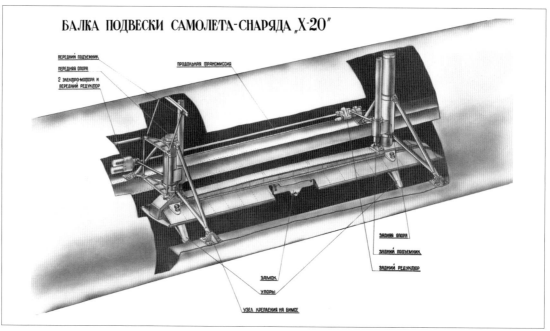

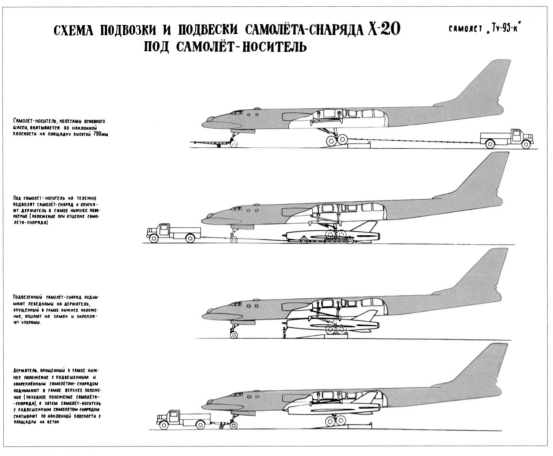

СХЕМА ПОДВОЗКИ И ПОДВЕСКИ САМОЛЁТА-СНАРЯДА Х-20 ПОД САМОЛЁТ-НОСИТЕЛЬ

Самолет „Ту-95-к"

A diagram from the same protocol showing the proposed missile loading sequence. The aircraft was to be towed onto two sloping ramps 700 mm high before the Kh-20 was wheeled in on a dolly. Once the missile had been hoisted up to the lowered pylon, hooked up and raised into cruise position, the bomber was towed off the ramps.

A drawing from the same document showing the attachment of the Kh-20 missile on the Tu-95K. Key:
1. Electric motors;
2. Support frame;
3. Screw jack; 4. Rear sway braces; 5. Missile rack; 6. Transverse bracing struts; 7. Front sway braces; 8. Fuel tank for missile engine starting.

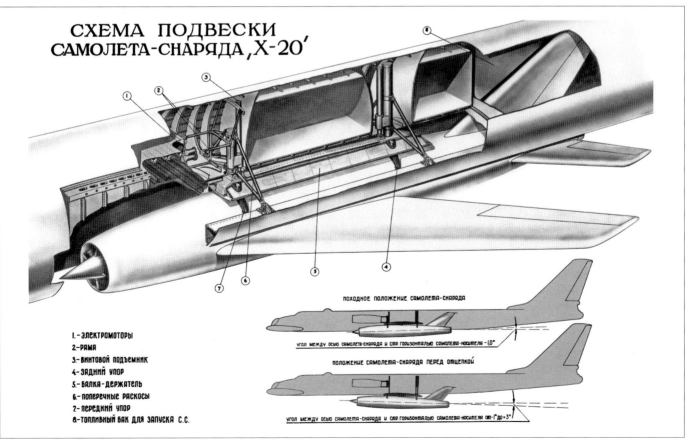

СХЕМА ПОДВЕСКИ САМОЛЕТА-СНАРЯДА „Х-20'

1.- ЭЛЕКТРОМОТОРЫ
2- РАМА
3.- ВИНТОВОЙ ПОДЪЕМНИК
4.- ЗАДНИЙ УПОР
5.- БАЛКА-ДЕРЖАТЕЛЬ
6.- ПОПЕРЕЧНЫЕ РАСКОСЫ
7.- ПЕРЕДНИЙ УПОР
8.- ТОПЛИВНЫЙ БАК ДЛЯ ЗАПУСКА С.С.

ПОХОДНОЕ ПОЛОЖЕНИЕ САМОЛЕТА-СНАРЯДА

УГОЛ МЕЖДУ ОСЬЮ САМОЛЕТА-СНАРЯДА И СТР. ГОРИЗОНТАЛЬЮ САМОЛЕТА-НОСИТЕЛЯ -1,0°

ПОЛОЖЕНИЕ САМОЛЕТА-СНАРЯДА ПЕРЕД ОТЦЕПКОЙ

УГОЛ МЕЖДУ ОСЬЮ САМОЛЕТА-СНАРЯДА И СТР. ГОРИЗОНТАЛЬЮ САМОЛЕТА-НОСИТЕЛЯ ОТ-1° ДО +3°

target and missile blips on his radarscope. If the missile had strayed from the desired track, he superimposed the missile marker on the target; the radar computed the missile's deviation angle and generated guidance commands so that the missile made a beeline towards the target. When this has been accomplished, the missile accelerated to maximum speed in level flight. The missile's flight level was maintained by a barometric altitude corrector linked to the YaK autopilot. When the Kh-20 came within 75 km (46.5 miles) of the target, the K4 command impulse was transmitted, switching the missile's guidance system to autonomous mode, whereupon the aircraft made a U-turn and headed for home. When the target was 16.5 km (10.25 miles) away the missile's engine was shut down and the guidance

Above: A wooden mock-up of the Tu-95K's nose showing the YaD radar's twin antennas.

Right: A diagram showing how the Kh-20 missile and the SM-20 aircraft are carried by the Tu-95K in cruise position (a) and pre-launch position (b). Oddly, the SM-20 is also called a missile here.

Opposite, top left: A wooden mock-up of the Tu-95K's centre fuselage showing the lowered BD-206 missile rack with sway braces extended.

Centre left: This picture shows the rack lowered onto a mock-up of the Kh-20 missile.

Below left: The BD-206 rack seen from behind.

Opposite, top right: A schematic mock-up of the Kh-20 attached to the BD-206 rack.

Centre right: A mock-up of the SM-20 aircraft in position with and without the retractable fairing closing the fighter's air intake.

Bottom right: This view shows the adapter required for hooking up the SM-20 to the rack.

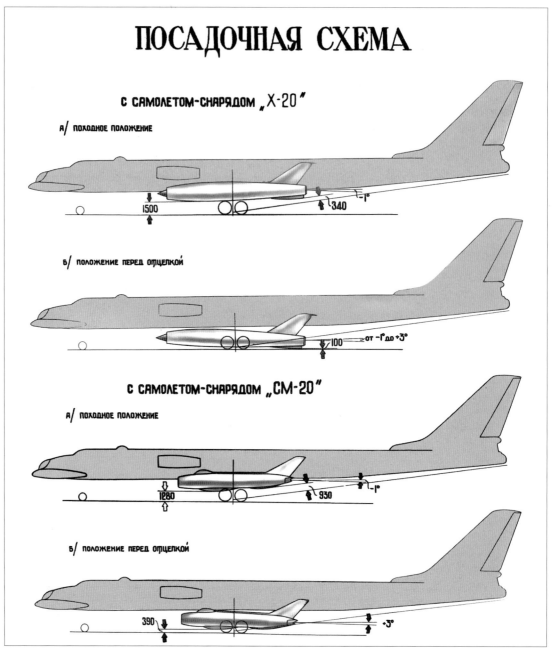

system put the missile into a 70° dive onto the target. The nuclear warhead was detonated at an altitude of 3,000-4,000 m (9,840-13,120 ft).

The Tu-95K's development was initiated in the spring of 1954, and General Designer Andrey N. Tupolev endorsed the ADP drawings on 26th October that year. Air Force C-in-C Air Chief Marshal Pavel F. Zhigarev approved the finalised SOR for the Tu-95K on 21st March 1955. Changes from the baseline bomber included the following:

• The YaD radar was installed in the redesigned fuselage nose, supplanting original bomber's glazed navigator's station and the Rubidiy-MM radar underneath it. Hence the navigator was relocated aft to a position behind the captain. The new radar was

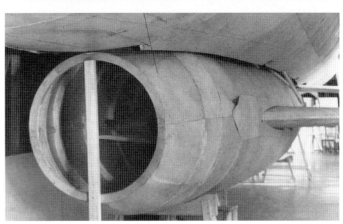

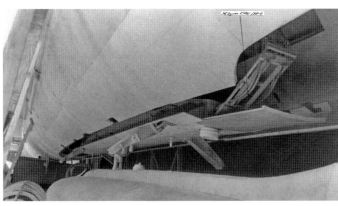

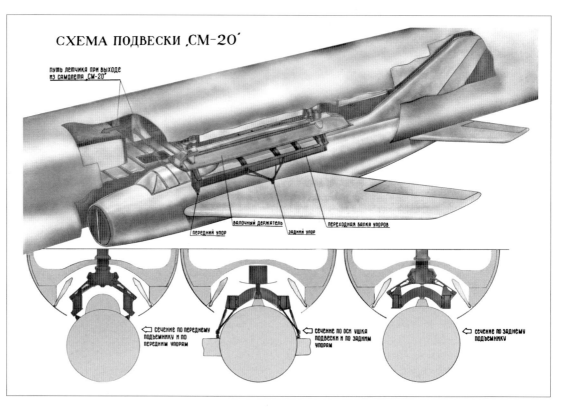

A drawing from the mock-up review commission's protocol showing the SM-20 aircraft suspended under the Tu-95K. The insets show cross-sections at the BD-206 rack's front screw jack, at the attachment lug and at the rear screw jack.

Below: Another view of the Tu-95K's centre fuselage mock-up with the SM-20 mock-up semi-recessed in the weapons bay.

Bottom: The same mock-up with the SM-20 lowered into pre-launch position; the adapter is specially marked. Note the Tu-95's fuselage frame numbers.

powerful but exceedingly bulky, with separate gyrostabilised antennas for the search/target illumination channel and the missile guidance channel. While the circular YaD1-2 antenna for the guidance channel fitted nicely inside the nose behind a bulged dielectric panel, the elliptical YaD1-1 antenna serving the search/target illumination channel required a huge radome of elliptical cross-section that was wider than the bomber's fuselage and was faired into the flight deck section. This 'duck bill' became the Tu-95K's main recognition feature. The search/target illumination antenna scanned through ±30° in azimuth and +3°30'/–12° in elevation, while the guidance antenna scanned through ±19° in azimuth and ±11°30' in elevation. A forward pressure bulkhead was added just ahead of the flight deck (at fuselage frame 3), and detachable panels were provided on the sides of the nose for maintenance access to the radar set and its supporting systems.

• The weapons bay (no longer a bomb bay, since bomb carriage was no longer possible) was greatly lengthened, commencing at frame 23 and terminating at frame 56 rather than frames 28 and 45 respectively on the bomber version. The flare bomb cassette aft of the original bomb bay was eliminated in so doing. Since the missile was carried semi-recessed in the fuselage to provide adequate ground clearance for take-off, a BD-206 missile rack was installed in the bay, being actuated by two vertical screw jacks attached by bracing struts to the fuselage longerons and frames 30 and 40; it interlocked with a lug on the missile's fuselage.

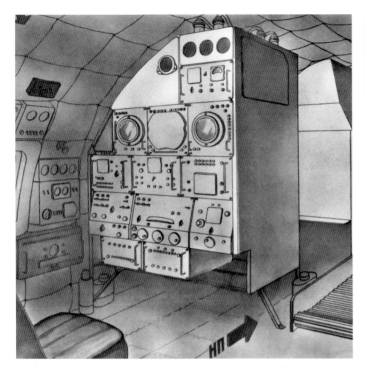

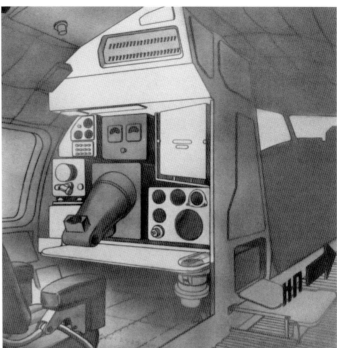

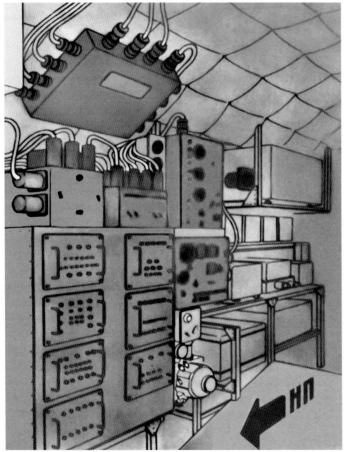

Top: A drawing from the mock-up review commission's protocol showing the Nav/Op's workstation of the Tu-95K. The arrow is marked 'NP' (*napravleniye polyota* – direction of flight).

Above: A drawing showing a weapons control system avionics rack.

Top: A drawing from the same protocol showing the navigator's workstation.

Above: A drawing showing a test equipment rack aft of the Nav/Op's workstation.

The flight deck of the Tu-95K's mock-up showing the test equipment indicators and circuit breakers. Note the ground steering handwheel on the captain's control yoke.

Two electric motors were installed on the starboard side near the front screw jack, transmitting torque to it and the rear screw jack via reduction gears and extension shafts. A cut-out for the missile's fin was provided at the top of frames 45-56. A retractable semi-parabolic fairing

was installed just ahead of the bay between frames 21-23, closing the missile's air intake during cruise to prevent the engine from windmilling. Prior to launch the fairing was retracted, the Kh-20 was lowered 950 mm (3 ft 1$\frac{13}{32}$ in) into the slipstream, its engine was

Right: A mock-up of the navigator's workstation, showing the radarscope sunblind with a periscopic viewing device and the special overhead control panel associated with the missile.

Far right: The same workstation without the radarscope sunblind.

The flight engineer's instrument panel in the Tu-95K' flight deck mock-up.

started and run up to cruise thrust, whereupon the missile was ready to go. In the semi-recessed position the missile had a 1° nose-down attitude with respect to the bomber's fuselage waterline; in the lowered position the angle could be from +1° to –1°. When no

missile was carried the bay was closed by three pairs of inward-opening pneumatically operated doors, the centre pair fitting around the BD-206 rack which was flush with the fuselage underside; the two pairs of sway braces folded flush to reduce drag.

• The fuselage fuel tanks were rearranged and their capacity was reduced. The No.2 tank was moved from under the wing centre section torsion box to a position above the weapons bay between frames 32-38; the No.3 tank was now between frames 42-45, the No.4 tank was moved to the No.3 tank's former position between frames 45-49, while the No.5 tank (which, like No.4, was divided into two halves) was at the No.4 tank's former position (frames 49-56). In addition to the regular fuel tanks in the fuselage and wings holding 90,400 kg (199,300 lb) of fuel, an auxiliary No.39 tank was installed in the weapons bay between frames 45-49 (between the halves of the No.4 tank) for starting the Kh-20's engine so as to avoid depleting the missile's fuel supply; unlike the other tanks, it was self-sealing. Engine starting could be done up to six times in a mission (in the event the launch was aborted).

• Changes were made to the electric system. In particular, three 4.5-kVA PO-4500 single-phase AC converters (*preobrazovahtel' odnofahznyy*) were installed to cater for the radar and other equipment.

Redesigning the centre fuselage to accommodate the missile and its launch systems proved to be quite a challenge; the enlarged weapons bay encroached on some key structural components which had to be altered (in particular, the longerons flanking the the weapons bay were reinforced). Additional work had to be undertaken to accommodate the redistribution of the aerodynamic loads. Scaled-strength models made of Plexiglas were built to study these changes. The resulting aeroelasticity issues led to the redesign of

The radar operator's (Nav/Op's) avionics rack in the Tu-95K' flight deck mock-up.

The U-shaped aerial of the Meridian SHORAN under the nose of the Tu-95K mock-up.

In 1955 a partial full-size wooden mock-up of the Tu-95K was built at MMZ No.156. It consisted of two sections – the forward fuselage (featuring the radomes and flight deck) and the centre fuselage with the weapons bay, including the BD-206 rack and parts of the fuel system. Schematic mock-ups of the Kh-20 missile, the Mikoyan SM-20 development aircraft (which will be discussed later in the book) and the special adapter for attaching the SM-20 were also manufactured.

The Air Force's mock-up review commission was appointed by Air Chief Marshal Zhigarev on 7th July 1955. Having examined the mock-up and studied the project materials on 7th-14 July, the commission noted in its protocol that:

'1. The flight performance of the Tu-95K missile strike aircraft submitted by MAP's OKB-156 to the mock-up review commission fails to meet the stipulations of the CofM directive No.412-182 of 11th March 1954 on the following counts:

- the combat radius is 6,250 km [3,880 miles] instead of the specified 6,500-6,700 km [4,040-4,160 miles];

- the aircraft's flight altitude at the moment of missile launch is 10,250 m [33,630 ft] instead of the specified 11,500-12,000 m [37,730-39,370 ft];

several major and minor structural components. Virtually all hydraulic, pneumatic and electrical lines in the area had to be redesigned and/or rerouted. This job was undertaken by a team headed by Iosif F. Nezval'.

The Tu-95K had a crew of nine: captain, co-pilot, flight engineer, navigator, electronic warfare officer (ELINT and ECM systems operator), Nav/Op (radar operator), dorsal gunner (senior GRO), ventral gunner (GRO) and tail gunner (defensive fire commander).

Specifications of the Tu-95K as per ADP documents	
Length overall	46.17 m (151 ft 5²³⁄₃₂ in)
Wing span	50.04 m (164 ft 2⁵⁄₆₄ in)
Aileron span	2 x 10.1 m (33 ft 1⁴⁄₆₄ in)
Flap span	2 x 12.95 m (42 ft 5²⁷⁄₃₂ in)
Mean aerodynamic chord	6.1 m (20 ft 0⁵⁄₃₂ in)
Horizontal tail span	14.78 m (48 ft 5⁵⁄₆₄ in)
Height on ground	12.5 m (41 ft 0⅛ in)
Landing gear track	12.55 m (41 ft 2⁵⁄₃₂ in)
Landing gear wheelbase	15.43 m (50 ft 7³¹⁄₆₄ in)
Wing area	283.7 m² (3,053.7 sq ft)
Horizontal tail area	54.49 m² (586.53 sq ft)
Elevator area (total)	13.59 m² (146.28 sq ft)
Elevator trim tab area (total)	1.38 m² (14.85 sq ft)
Vertical tail area	38.53 m² (414.73 sq ft)
Rudder area	8.95 m² (96.34 sq ft)
Rudder trim tab area	0.9 m² (9.69 sq ft)
Aileron area (total)	23.58 m² (253.81 sq ft)
Aileron trim tab area (total)	2.01 m² (21.64 sq ft)
Flap area (total)	45.5 m² (489.76 sq ft)
Empty weight	75,100 kg (165,570 lb)
Maximum take-off weight, including:	172,000 kg (379,200 lb)
crew	800 kg (1,763 lb)
cannon ammunition (2,400 rounds)	970 kg (2,138 lb)
Kh-20 missile	12,300 kg (27,120 lb)
missile engine starting fuel in tank No.39	500 kg (1,102 lb)
fuel in tanks Nos. 1-38	81,700 kg (180,120 lb)
engine oil	600 kg (1,322 lb)
All-up weight at the moment of missile launch	124,000 kg (273,370 lb)
Landing weight:	
normal (no missile and 19% fuel remaining)	85,000 kg (187,390 lb)
maximum	93,000 kg (205,030 lb) *

CG range	17-24% MAC
CG position immediately after take-off (gear up)	19.7% MAC
Wing loading at take-off weight	607 kg/m² (124.45 lb/sq ft)
Power loading	3.58 kg/hp (7.89 lb/hp)
Top speed at launch point/max continuous power:	
at 8,000 m (26,250 ft)	855 km/h (531 mph) †
at 10,000 m (32,810 ft)	835 km/h (518 mph) †
Effective range at 750 km/h (465 mph) IAS 13,000-13,400 km (8,080-8,330 miles) ‡	12,500 km (7,770 miles) †
Flight altitude at the moment of missile launch:	
before	10,250 m (33,630 ft) †
	11,500-12,000 m (37,730-39,370 ft) ‡
after	10,950 m (35,930 ft) †
	12,000-12,500 m (39,370-41,010 ft) ‡
Service ceiling in missile launch area:	
before launch	11,000 m (36,090 ft) †
after launch	11,800 m (38,710 ft) †
Ditto, with one engine shut down:	
before launch	9,000 m (29,530 ft) †
after launch	10,000 m (32,810 ft) †
Take-off run with a 172,000-kg TOW	2,250 m (7,380 ft) †
Take-off distance to h=25 m (82 ft)	6,200 m (20,340 ft) †
Approach speed with a 85,000-kg landing weight	197 km/h (122 mph) †
Landing run	1,200 m (3,940 ft) †

Notes:

* In exceptional cases the landing weight with the missile in place on paved runways may reach 102,500 kg (225,970 lb)

† Manufacturer's estimates with NK-12 engines and a 12,936-kg (28,519-lb) missile

‡ As per Council of Ministers directive with a 12,300-kg (27,120-lb) missile

The commission considers it necessary to demand that the Chief Designer of OKB-156 ensures compliance of the Tu-95K aircraft with the stipulations of the CofM directive.

2. The commission approves the Tu-95K mock-up submitted for review as the pattern for converting a Tu-95 aircraft into a launch platform for the K-20 weapons system, with the exception of the proposed technique of loading the Kh-20 [missile] which requires the aircraft to be rolled onto special sloping ramps. The commission considers it necessary to demand that OKB-156 should check the possibility of attaching the Kh-20 to the Tu-95K by means of jacks (i.e., the aircraft is jacked up – Auth.) and present the results to the Air Force by 1st September this year. Should this technique prove unsatisfactory, OKB-156 shall, jointly with the Air Force, review the drawings of the special ramps and work out a manufacturing schedule for these.

When the external load (i.e., missile – Auth.) is submitted for review, the OKB shall present materials confirming the possibility of using it during first-line operations (i.e., wind speed limits, apron loading limits, ambient temperature limits, the required means of transporting [the missile], the required number of maintenance personnel, the estimated time of arming and refueling the aircraft etc.). The OKB shall also present documents approved by MSM that the aircraft can be refuelled within 2-4 hours after the fully armed [missile] is attached.

OKB-156, MAP's OKB-155 and MOP's KB-1 shall eliminate the deficiencies noted and act on the commission's suggestions […].

3. The autonomous navigation equipment installed on the mock-up does not enable the aircraft to reach the designated missile launch point with the accuracy of ±10-15 km [±6.2-9.3 miles] specified by the CofM directive. Therefore the Minister of Aircraft Industry [Pyotr V. Dement'yev] is requested to accelerate development of an autonomous navigation system affording the required accuracy. […]

4. Materials confirming the safety of normal and emergency release of the Kh-20 [missile] at different altitudes and speeds (based on aerodynamic research, flight tests and TsAGI assessments) have not been presented for review. […]'

Two Tu-95s (c/ns 5800001 and 6800404) were converted into the unserialled Tu-95K prototypes by factory No.18; the job was known as 'order 206', probably reflecting the designation of the BD-206 missile rack. Modification work on the former aircraft lasted from 1st March through 31st October 1955; the first prototype made its first post-conversion flight on 1st January 1956, followed by the second aircraft in the summer of 1956. The prototypes differed from subsequent production Tu-95Ks in having test equipment, including data link aerials replacing the rear cannons and two cine cameras to capture the

separation sequence (an inward-looking camera in a teardrop fairing under the starboard wingtip and a forward-looking camera in a cylindrical pod just inboard of the No.3 engine).

Before flights with the Kh-20 could be ventured, a series of tests was held to verify the safety and viability of the missile's guidance system. To this end two MiG-19s *sans suffixe* (NATO reporting name *Farmer-A*) tactical fighters built by factory No.21 in Gor'kiy were transferred to the Mikoyan OKB from the Air Force and converted into avionics testbeds designated *izdeliye* SM-20. Perhaps it would be more accurate to call them missile emulators (this is exactly how they were referred to in Russian – *samolyot-imitahtor*, 'emulator aircraft') because they were to be carried aloft and launched by the Tu-95K, just like the real thing. Oddly, the mock-up review commission's protocol referred to the SM-20 as *samolyot-snaryad*, 'aircraft-type missile' (the Soviet term for cruise missiles used until 1960).

The fighters were lightened by removing the armament and some of the avionics – the **Oozel** (Knot) IFF transponder, SRD-1 gun ranging radar, MRP-48 marker beacon receiver, RV-2 radio altimeter, Sirena-2 radar warning receiver and NI-50IM navigation display. Instead, the missile's YaK autopilot was fitted, being partly housed in a large ventral teardrop fairing aft of the nose gear unit (other modules of the autopilot were located elsewhere). The missile's YaR terminal guidance radar seeker was not fitted to the testbeds.

A prominent square-section fuselage spine was added, featuring a hefty lug for the bomber's BD-206

Seen at Zhukovskiy in February 1956, '105 Red' (c/n N59210105) – the manned SM-20/1 (aka SM-20P) – shows off the prominent fuselage spine with the suspension lug amidships and the ventral teardrop fairing housing guidance system modules. No cannons were fitted.

A drawing from the ADP documents showing the purpose, composition and basic specifications of the Tu-95K-20 long-range weapons system, as well as the missile launch technique. The specs are: maximum combat radius 6,340-8,520 km (3,937-5,292 miles); the aircraft's top speed 860 km/h (534 mph); launch altitude 9-12 km (5.59-7.45 miles); circular error probable 4 km (2.48 miles); the missile's cruising speed 1,800-2,200 km/h (1,118-1,366 mph); missile cruise altitude 14.2-15.2 km (46,590-49,870 ft).

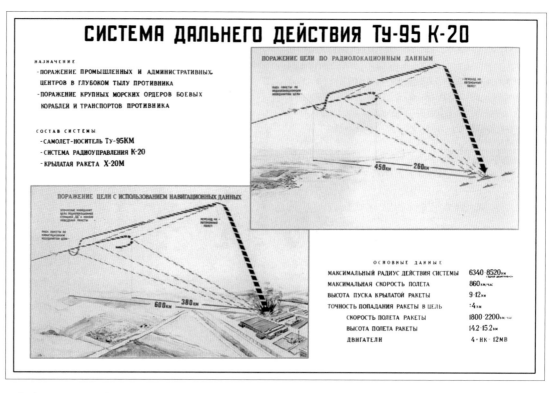

Below: A drawing showing how the Kh-20 first dips below the Tu-95K's flight level, then climbs above it and cruises at high altitude before diving onto the target.

Opposite page, top: Front view of the second prototype Tu-95K (c/n 6800404); note the camera pods under the starboard wing root and wingtip for recording missile launches.

Centre and bottom: Two more views of the same aircraft with a Kh-20 missile attached and the intake blank extended. Note the data link aerial in the tail turret.

rack; this necessitated a reduction in the capacity of the No.1 fuel tank. The SM-20's most unusual feature, however, was a modified tail unit combining the *Farmer-A*'s vertical tail (featuring a full-length rudder and small fin root fillet) with the higher-set stabilators of the later MiG-19S *Farmer-C*. Another non-standard feature was a whip aerial low on the starboard side of the nose.

Since the fighter's vertical tail was taller than the missile's and the horizontal tail was set higher, the SM-20 was hooked up to the bomber via a special adapter which increased the distance to the bomber's fuselage waterline by 300 mm (11¹¹⁄₁₆ in); this adapter could remain attached to either aircraft after separation. In spite of this, the ground clearance with the SM-20 in semi-recessed position was increased to 1 m (3 ft 3⅜ in). A special set of bomb bay doors was manufactured and

installed to fit around the SM-20's fuselage, whose contours differed from those of the missile.

The SM-20/1, which was completed in February 1956 and serialled '105 Red' (c/n N59210105), was an optionally piloted vehicle retaining the standard MiG-19's manual control system. Hence it was also known as the SM-20P (*peeloteeruyemyy* – manned or piloted). The idea was that once the aircraft had completed the simulated target run-in with guidance from the Tu-95K's radar, the human pilot would take over and fly the fighter back to base for a normal landing. The same technique had been used when the Mikoyan KS-1 (AS-1 *Kennel*) anti-shipping cruise missile was being tested, except that the demonstrator aircraft was the diminutive *izdeliye* K – a manned version of the KS-1 with a cockpit instead of the explosive charge and a retractable bicycle landing gear, which was carried

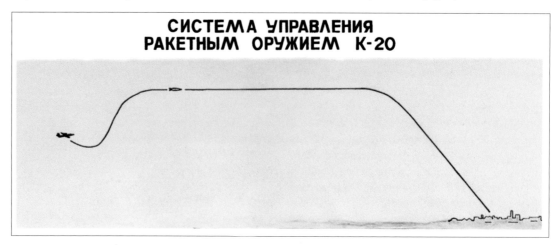

LII test pilot Sultan Amet-Khan who flew the SM-20/1 (SM-20P) during the tests of the Tu-95K.

and launched by the Tu-4K missile strike aircraft prototype. The SM-20P was equipped with an intercom so that the pilot could communicate with the bomber crew until the moment of launch. In an emergency the SM-20P could be released both by the Tu-9K's crew and by the fighter pilot. Should all release systems fail, the fighter pilot could open his cockpit canopy and climb into the bomber via a hatch in the front cabin's rear pressure dome measuring 0.65 x 0.7 m (2 ft 1¹⁹⁄₃₂ in x 2 ft 3³⁵⁄₆₄ in).

Conversely, the second aircraft completed in September 1956 – the SM-20/2 (c/n N59210425), which had its original serial '425 Red' removed for some reason – was remote-controlled, being guided back to base and landed in radio control mode after the target run-in.

Manufacturer's flight tests with the SM-20 began in the summer of 1956. Stages 1 and 2 of the tests proceeded in parallel between 4th August – 15th October (involving 13 missions flown by the first

prototype Tu-95K) and 15th August – 13th October (involving nine flights performed by the second prototype). Both prototypes took turns carrying the SM-20/1 but the fighter was not yet released by the bomber at this stage. The SM-20/1 (SM-20P) was flown by LII test pilot Sultan Amet-Khan and KB-1 test pilot Vasiliy G. Pavlov; A. I. V'yushkov was the engineer in charge. Incidentally, the Tu-95K that carried the SM-20P had three small windows on each side of the weapons bay to admit some light; the MiG pilot would otherwise have had to work in pitch darkness until the moment of release.

The SM-20P was hooked up to the Tu-95K with the pilot sitting in the cockpit. When the intake shutter fairing had been retracted and the SM-20 had been lowered into pre-launch position, the engines were not started until the bomber's pilot gave the OK via intercom when the altitude was right. After the SM-20P had been launched, heading towards the target

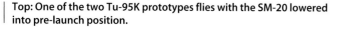

Top: One of the two Tu-95K prototypes flies with the SM-20 lowered into pre-launch position.

Below: The first prototype Tu-95K 'launches' the SM-20/1.

Above: Here the SM-20/1 is seen in semi-recessed position for cruise flight with the air intake blank extended. Note the windows admitting some light into the bomb bay for the benefit of the fighter's pilot.

Bottom: The unmanned (and uncoded) SM-20/2 is seen immediately after release. Note the sway braces of the BD-206 misssile rack.

'painted' by the Tu-95's radar, the pilot sat back and monitored the operation of the guidance system. When the system got a lock-on the pilot switched it off, steered away from the target and flew the aircraft back to base.

The SM-20P had trouble starting the engines at high altitude where the oxygen content was reduced, particularly after the engines had had a cold soak while the aircraft was on the pylon. Therefore, the aircraft was refitted with modified engines featuring a carburetted ignition system; eleven flights were made specifically to test this system.

The pilotless SM-20/2 joined in when disengagement and guidance tests began as stage 3 of the test programme, which spanned from mid-October 1956 through 24th January 1957. By the end of 1957 the two SM-20s had made 27 test flights involving conventional take-offs and 32 drops from the Tu-95K 'mother ships'. In October 1958 they were transferred to GK NII VVS in order to test the guidance system for ECM resistance. (It should be noted that ECM resistance was not one of the Kh-20 missile's strong points.) The SM-20/1 made nine flights at GK NII VVS, including seven drops from the Tu-95K.

After that, all tests involved flights with actual Kh-20 missiles and launches of same, involving the second prototype. These began on 6th June 1957 and ran through 29th July 1958. Jacking up the bomber or parking it on concrete ramps 700 mm (2 ft 3³⁵⁄₆₄ in) high under the main gear bogies to give it a 2°30' nose-down attitude and increase the ground clearance turned out to be unnecessary after all. Wheeling the Kh-20 missile in on its ground handling dolly was admittedly a tight squeeze – the clearance between the missile's fin and the bomber's belly was just 10 cm (3¹⁵⁄₁₆ in), but it did pass. After being wheeled into position the missile was lifted off the dolly by three BL-52 electric hoists (**bom**bovaya le**byod**ka – bomb hoists) and hooked up to the BD-206 rack; when it was raised into cruise position, its ground clearance was 0.65 m (2 ft 1¹⁹⁄₃₂ in).

The first launch of a Kh-20 took place on 17th March 1957. The missile fell short on range (250 km/155 miles instead of 400 km/248 miles) and altitude (12,500 m/ 41,010 ft instead of 15,000 m/49,210 ft) but accelerated to Mach 2.2 instead of the anticipated Mach 1.6, whereupon the AL-7FK engine failed. Problems with the AL-7FK persisted for a while but were eventually resolved.

Joint state acceptance trials of the K-20 weapons system began on 15th October 1958, lasting until 1st November 1959. The results were deemed satisfactory and the Tu-95K and the Kh-20 stand-off missile were recommended for production. By then, however, plant No.18 had already begun Tu-95K initial production in March 1958; the product code was *izdeliye* VK. The first production machines took part in the trials. The Kh-20 missile entered initial production at plant No.256 in

Doobna – the 'home factory' of OKB-2-155; later, production was transferred to machinery plant No.86 named after Gheorgi Dimitrov in Taganrog in southern Russia (Rostov Region). This factory (TMZD, *Taganrogskiy mashinostroitel'nyy zavod imeni Dimitrova*) would later be closely associated with the *Bear*, as recounted in Chapters 4 and 5.

The system was tested operationally against moving targets (decommissioned warships) in the Barents Sea. It was found that the Kh-20 missile could be effective against large ships as well as conventional

Top two photos: A Kh-20 missile on its ground handling dolly. The vertical tail was of necessity short. Note the slight wing anhedral.

Centre and above: The production version of the Kh-20 had faired bleed air outlets aft of the wing trailing edge.

The first production Tu-95K at Chkalovskaya AB during state acceptance trials. Like the prototypes, it had cine camera pods under the starboard wing root and starboard wingtip.

Side view of the same aircraft (c/n 8802004) with a Kh-20 missile in place

One of the Tu-95K prototypes sits parked on the grass after being struck off charge. The inboard camera pod is clearly visible.

(stationary) ground targets. The system received a favourable appraisal for dependability and ease of maintenance, support and operation.

On 9th September 1960 the Council of Ministers issued a directive officially including the K-20 weapons system (the Tu-95K and Kh-20 missile) into the operational inventory of the Soviet Air Force. The Tu-95K was the second version to be identified in the West and thus was allocated the reporting name *Bear-B*.

Tu-95K c/ns followed the same system but, inexplicably, production started with Batch 20; not only that but the first production machine (apparently coded '58 Red') was c/n 8802004! The last example laid down in 1959 (c/n 9802204) was relegated to static tests. In 1960 the c/ns switched to an eight-digit format – for example, a Tu-95K coded '68 Red' was c/n 60802301. Production continued until December 1961, the final machine being c/n 61802501; apart from the two prototypes, 47 new-build Tu-95Ks were manufactured (three in 1958, 17 in 1959, another 17 in 1960 and the final ten in 1961).

Later, 28 Tu-95Ks – 27 production aircraft and the second prototype – were updated to Tu-95KM standard (see below). The remaining 20 *Bear-Bs* stayed in service until the early 1980s. At the end of their service career some of them were modified for the training role and served as such into the early 1990s.

Tu-95KU crew trainer (*izdeliye* VKU)

The service entry of the Tu-95K eventually led to the need for a missile carrier trainer. Accordingly, the Tu-95KU (*izdeliye* VKU) was developed. The NATO reporting name was still *Bear-B*. In addition, several *Bear-B/Cs* were stripped of offensive armament and relegated to the crew training role during the late 1980s.

The Tu-95K was also to fill another training role, carrying the M-20 supersonic target drone derived

A Kh-20 missile attached to the lowered BD-206 rack of a Tu-95K prototype during trials.

A technician makes sure that everything is OK as the missile is attached to the rack.

A rear view of the same prototype, showing the telemetry aerials replacing the tail cannons.

A production Tu-95K (c/n 60802207) seen during check-up tests at GK NII VVS.

from the Kh-20 missile (M = *mishen'* – target) for training air defence crews. The M-20 was to simulate North American AGM-28 Hound Dog missiles launched by USAF B-52s. However, the project was abandoned as too costly; hence early-model Mikoyan/Gurevich MiG-21 *Fishbed* fighters converted into M-21 remote-controlled target drones were used in this capacity.

Tu-95K-10 missile strike aircraft/bomber (project)

In response to Council of Ministers directive No.710-338 issued on 2nd July 1958 the Tupolev OKB undertook a design study of a Tu-95K modification that would allow the aircraft to carry four K-10S (AS-2 *Kipper*) supersonic air-to-surface missiles under the wings. The K-10S, which had been developed by OKB-2-155 for the Soviet Navy's Tu-16K-10 *Badger-C* missile strike aircraft, had a mid-wing layout with a slender circular-section fuselage whose forward section tipped with a large ogival radome for the YeS-1 active radar seeker head incorporated a pressurised and heat-insulated bay housing the guidance system. Aft of this was the warhead bay followed by the fuel tank of steel construction, which was the main structural element absorbing all the loads. The wings swept back 55° at quarter-chord could fold upwards for ease of ground handling. The conventional tail surfaces consisted of stabilators with 55° leading-edge sweep and a fin-and-rudder assembly swept back 55°30' at quarter-chord; the vertical tail was detachable, and the tail surfaces were of cast magnesium alloy construction. The powerplant was a 3,250-kgp (7,160-lbst) Mikulin M-9FK axial-flow afterburning turbojet – a disposable single-mode version of the RD-9B powering the MiG-19 (again, K stood for *korotkoresoorsnyy* – short-life). It was installed in a conformal nacelle under the rear fuselage, breathing through a quasi-elliptical intake; the afterburner section extended beyond the tailcone, which mounted a mid-course guidance antenna.

The K-10S came with a choice of FK-10 or FK-1M conventional warheads, the latter model being designed for striking large vessels below the waterline, or a TK34 nuclear warhead. The missile was 9.75 m (31 ft 11⅞ in) long, with a wing span of 4.18 m (13 ft 8⁵⁄₁₆ in), a height of 2.27 m (7 ft 4³⁵⁄₆₄ in) and a body diameter of

1.0 m (3 ft 3⅜ in). The launch weight was 4,418-4,555 kg (9,740-10,040 lb), including 850-940 kg (1,870-2,070 lb) for the warhead.

The modification required the K-10U guidance system devised by a team led by S. F. Matveyevskiy for the missile to be integrated. This meant replacing the YaD radar with the *Badger-C*'s YeN navigation/attack radar working with the missile's YeS-2D mid-course guidance module picking up signals transmitted by the aircraft's radar and making altitude corrections, and the YeS-3A autopilot. The YeN was developed by the Leningrad-based OKB-283 of the Ministry of Electronics Industry (MRP – *Ministerstvo rahdioelektronnoy promyshlennosti*), an avionics house which later became LNPO **Len**inets (*Leningrahdskoye naoochno-proizvodstvennoye obyedineniye* – 'Leninist' Leningrad Scientific & Production Association) and then the Leninets Holding Co. It was likewise a twin-antenna radar with the search/target illumination channel antenna in a similar 'duck bill' radome and the guidance channel antenna in a neat teardrop-shaped chin radome. (In the above designations, N stands for *nositel'* – carrier [aircraft] or misssile platform and S for *snaryad* – missile.) The K-10 missile was smaller and lighter than the Kh-20; thus, it was presumed the Tu-95 would still be able to carry a free-fall nuclear bomb internally.

However, studies showed that the drag generated by the external stores would drastically impair the aircraft's flight performance and the project was cancelled before any metal was cut.

Tu-95KD development aircraft (*izdeliye* VKD)

The Tu-95K was the first production version of the *Bear* that demonstrated in practice the need for in-flight refuelling. The weight penalty and drag incurred by the missile and associated systems reduced the Tu-95K's range by nearly 2,000 km (1,242 miles) as compared to the *Bear-A*. To remedy this, on 2nd July 1958 the Council of Ministers issued directive No.710-338 tasking the Tupolev OKB with radically improving the K-20 weapons system's performance – especially range.

As already mentioned, in 1957 the wingtip-to-wingtip IFR system was considered for the Tu-95. On 28th April 1959 the VPK issued ruling No.37 requiring all Tu-95Ks to be thus equipped. However, it soon became obvious that the probe-and-drogue IFR system – dubbed **Kon**us (Cone) because of the conical drogue – was a better choice. The system was verified on the M-4 bomber working with Tu-16N *Badger-A* and M-4-2 single-point tankers. On 20th May 1960 the Council of Ministers issued directive No.527-213 requiring all Tu-95Ks to be fitted with the probe-and-drogue system. Flight testing was to be undertaken in 1961.

In May 1961 a production Tu-95K (c/n 9802103) was set aside at factory No.18 for modification with the

probe-and-drogue IFR system. This aircraft was meant to become the first Tu-95KD (*izdeliye* VKD), the D standing for **dahl'***niy* – long-range. Up to 50 tons (110,229 lb) of fuel could be transferred in a single sortie.

The Tu-95KD featured the following changes as compared to the Tu-95K:

• a telescopic IFR probe was mounted on top of the nose, just above the radar's YaD1-2 missile guidance antenna, with a prominent fuel line conduit running along the starboard side of the forward fuselage to the No.1 tank ahead of the wings;

• a fuel scavenging system was provided to empty the fuel left in the pipeline leading from the probe;

• a compressed air system was provided to operate the probe mechanism;

• a *Pritok* (Tributary of a river) secure radio link was provided, enabling the crews of the tanker and the receiver aircraft to communicate while maintaining radio silence.

Stage A of the Tu-95KD's joint state acceptance trials took place between 5th July and 8th September 1961. 18 flights were made, with a total duration of 38 hours. Stage B of the trials followed between 17th October 1961 and 30th January 1962, the aircraft logging 43 hours in 16 flights. An M-4-2 was the tanker in all cases.

The tests were successful and the aircraft was recommended for production. Still, the Tu-95KD remained a one-off because more changes were incorporated before the IFR-equipped version entered production as the Tu-95KM (see below).

Tu-95K/Tu-95KD with bomb dispensers

As already mentioned, the *Bear-B* was a dedicated missile platform. Not content with having a large proportion of its Tu-95 fleet unable to carry bombs, the Soviet Air Force asked the aircraft industry to think of a way to give the Tu-95K/Tu-95KD conventional bombing capability. To meet the request, a reusable bomb dispenser was developed by the Moscow-based

Another Tu-95K participating in the same parade ('11 Red') with a missile attached. Note the area-ruling of the inboard engine nacelles/main gear fairings.

60802207

Tu-95K c/n 60802207 with a dummy Kh-20 missile

Tu-95K '86 Red' was used in a test programme with two KMB free-fall bomb dispenser pods attached to the BD-206 missile rack.

The Kh-20 in red high-visibility test colours and in standard grey finish

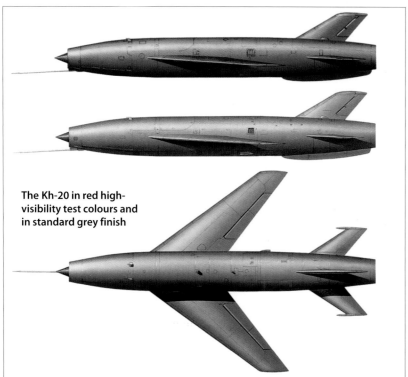

GSKB-47 (*Gosudarstvennoye soyooznoye konstrooktorskoye byuro* – State All-Union Design Bureau), which was the leading Soviet authority on aircraft bombs; the 'all-Union' bit indicates that the establishment had national importance. GSKB-47 is now called GNPP *Bazal't* (*Gosudarstvennoye naoochno-proizvodstvennoye predpriyahtiye* – 'Basalt' State-owned Research & Production Enterprise).

Designated KMB (*konteyner melkikh boyepripahsov* – 'small munitions container'), the bomb dispenser was a large pod resembling a modern air-launched cruise missile with the wings and pop-out jet engine stowed. The body having a roughly semi-elliptical cross-section had an ogival nose and a vertically cropped rear end featuring two low-set fins with strong dihedral; the fins were detachable. The pod's flattened underside incorporated clamshell doors for loading and dropping the bombs.

On the Tu-95K/Tu-95KD, two KMB bomb dispensers were installed side by side under the fuselage, being attached via a special adapter to the BD-206 pylon which was lowered flush with the closed missile bay doors. This required the fin on the inboard side of each pod to be removed. The same configuration was tested

Tu-95KM '22 Red' which was used by GK NII VVS in a test programme, with an inert Kh-20M0 attached

22

The Tu-95KD was also fitted experimentally with two KMB bomb dispensers attached to the BD-206 missile pylon. The IFR probe is clearly visible.

Below left: The centre fuselage of Tu-95K '86 Red' with the bomb dispensers and their mounting adaptor.

Below: Close-up of the KMB pods. Each pod has a single fin mounted on the outer side

concurrently on a Tu-22KD *Blinder-B* supersonic missile strike aircraft, which had a similar weapons bay design for carrying a single Kh-22 (NATO codename AS-4 *Kitchen*) ASM on a centreline BD-294-5F telescoping pylon. However, the KMB pod was destined not to enter production.

Tu-95KM missile strike aircraft (*izdeliye* VKM)

In 1962 the Kuibyshev aircraft factory launched production of an upgraded missile strike version designated Tu-95KM (*moderni**zee**rovannyy* – upgraded). Apart from having the IFR system tested on the Tu-95KD

Front view of a Tu-95KM (with a Kh-20M missile in place) running up the engines before a sortie.

Two views of Tu-95KM '22 Red' at GK NII VVS as it takes off and begins the landing gear retraction sequence.

A Tu-95KM has just launched a red-painted inert Kh-20M missile during trials at GK NII VVS. Note the ELINT blisters on the rear fuselage typical of this version.

prototype, these aircraft differed from the earlier Tu-95K in equipment fit as follows:

• A new PRS-4 Krypton gun-laying radar was fitted above the tail gunner's station. Unlike the hemispherical radome of the earlier PRS-1 Argon radar, the radome had an almost square section with very slightly bulged sides and rear end; this gave rise to the very appropriate NATO codename *Box Tail*.

• The SRS-4 Romb-4 SIGINT system was installed (its presence was revealed by the oblong dielectric blisters on the rear fuselage sides). Some sources suggest the Tu-95KM had an SRS-5 *Vishnya* (Cherry) communications intelligence (COMINT) set with a detection range of 300-350 km (186-217 miles).

• A new SPO-3 radar homing and warning system (*sistema preduprezhdeniya ob obloochenii* – 'irradiation warning system, i.e., RHAWS) was fitted instead of the earlier SPO-2.

• The flight/navigation suite was updated to include a KS-6D automatic heading reference system (*koorsovaya sistema* – AHRS or compass system), a DISS-1 Doppler ground speed and drift sensor system and the RSBN-2S Svod (Dome) short-range radio navigation system (*rahdiotekhnicheskaya sistema blizhney navigahtsii* – SHORAN). The RV-UM radio altimeter replaced the RV-2 and the ARK-11 automatic direction finder was fitted instead of the ARK-5.

• The communications suite was updated to feature a new RSB-70A radio and an RSIU-5 radio replacing the RSIU-4.

Concurrently, OKB-2-155 updated the Kh-20 missile. The new version intended for the Tu-95KM was designated Kh-20M (*modernizeerovannaya* – upgraded) and featured a new 3-megaton *izdeliye* 37D thermonuclear warhead. Range was improved to 380-600 km (236-372 miles) and service ceiling to 20 km (65,620 ft).

The upgraded weapons system comprising the Tu-95KM, the Kh-20M missile and its K-20 guidance system was designated Tu-95K-20. The weapons system's combat radius varied between 6,340 and

A Tu-95K-22 missile carrier with three Kh-22 missiles attached. The UKhO rear ECM fairing replacing the tail turret is clearly visible; the square-shaped side windows of the tail gunner's station are retained.

8,250 km (3,937-5,123 miles) and the launch point-to-target range was 450-600 km (270-372 miles). The Kh-20M definitely wasn't a 'fire and forget' weapon; the Nav/Op had to maintain guidance contact over most of the trajectory, which increased the missile's vulnerability to ECM and took the aircraft within 260-380 km (161-236 miles) of the target. Still, these figures were deemed palatable by the Air Force, considering the western state of the art in air defence systems in the early 1960s.

23 Tu-95KMs were built as such – ten in 1962, eight in 1963, four in 1964 and one in 1965. This version continued the Tu-95K's batch numbering sequence but introduced a new c/n system, the first new-build example being c/n 62M52502 – that is, year of manufacture 1962, *izdeliye* M5 (a product code for the Tu-95KM at the Kuibyshev factory), Batch 25, 02nd aircraft in the batch. Additionally, as noted earlier, 28 Tu-95Ks were upgraded to this standard, retaining their old c/ns. Thus, a total of 51 missile strike *Bears* received IFR capability. The total number of Tu-95K/Tu-95KD/Tu-95KM missile carriers completed was 71 (including the second prototype Tu-95K). The Tu-95KM's reporting name was *Bear-C*.

In due course the Tu-95KMs were retrofitted with a new *Toocha* (Storm cloud) weather/navigation radar. In the late 1960s several *Bear-Cs* were equipped with two RR8311-100 air sampling pods on pylons under the outer wings and a sensor pod above the starboard wing root for radiation reconnaissance (RINT) duties. This modification was made for exploring the results of above-ground nuclear testing, primarily Chinese ones. The RR8311-100 had been developed by the Yakovlev OKB for its Yak-25RRV *Mandrake* high-altitude RINT aircraft but then became a standard item in the VVS.

Tu-95K-22 missile strike aircraft (*izdeliye* VK-22 'Kama')

The rapid development of western air defences during the late 1960s and early 1970s meant that the Tu-95KM

had little chance of delivering its Kh-20 missile to the target. Hence on 13th February 1973 the Council of Ministers issued directive No.104-36 ordering the Tupolev OKB to undertake a further upgrade of the Tu-95KM. It involved integration of a new weapons system – the K-22 which meant adapting the *Bear-C* to carry the aforementioned Kh-22 *Boorya* (Storm) supersonic air-to-surface missile, which was lighter and faster than the Kh-20M and had autonomous guidance. The reconfigured aircraft was accordingly designated Tu-95K-22 (*izdeliye* VK-22) and the weapons system as a whole bore the designation K-95-22. This was the first version of the *Bear* developed under Nikolay V. Kirsanov, who had been appointed the Tu-95 family's new project chief after Nikolay I. Bazenkov's retirement in 1970.

The Kh-22 was developed by the aforementioned OKB-2-155 led by Aleksandr Ya. Bereznyak in accordance with a Council of Ministers directive dated 17th June 1958; it was also known as the D-2 (the D

This view shows clearly how up to three Kh-22 missiles could be carried by the Tu-95K-22. Note the egg-shaped ECM antenna pods.

Tu-95K-22 '31 Red' is depicted during check-up tests. The underwing BD-45K missile pylons and the Kh-22 missiles are evident here.

The same aircraft seen from the right, showing the rear pair of ECM antenna 'eggs' and the nose ECM thimble fairing above the radome. Here the former tail gunner's station is windowless, leaving only the ventral gunner's blisters.

probably stood for Doobna, a town in the Moscow Region where the design bureau was based). It was a supersonic (Mach 3) missile with low aspect ratio, mid-set delta wings with 75°35' leading-edge sweep and a cruciform tail unit (that is, upper and lower fins plus mid-set stabilators). The all-movable upper fin served for directional control while the lower fin folded for ground handling and carriage by the aircraft, deploying

after launch. The missile's airframe was designed to withstand considerable kinetic heating at high Mach numbers.

The powerplant was a Tumanskiy S5.33 (aka R201-300) twin-chamber liquid-propellant rocket motor developed by OKB-300 under Sergey K. Tumanskiy which was virtually a two-in-one motor (booster and sustainer). The motor ran on special TG-02

'95 Red', another *Bear-G*, with a full complement of missiles.

The Tu-95K-22 has two pairs of ECM antennas on the forward fuselage, and the starboard upper antenna is mounted right on top of the fuel line conduit from the IFR probe.

Starboard side view of '95 Red' illustrating all of the Tu-95K-22's front and rear ECM equipment fairings.

fuel (**top**livo ghipergo**lich**eskoye – hypergolic or self-igniting fuel), also known under the unclassified name *Samin* – an approximately 50/50 mixture of xylidine and triethylamine. The fuel was identical to the German Tonka-250 rocket fuel used in the Second World War; and indeed, some sources decipher TG as tro**fey**noye go**ryu**cheye – war booty propellant. The TG-02 fuel self-combusted when combined with AK-27I oxidiser – a 27% solution of nitrogen peroxide (amyl) in nitric acid (hence AK for **azot**naya kislo**ta**) with crystalline iodine added as a corrosion inhibitor (hence the I suffix). Both chambers were fed by turbopumps, had separate hydraulic systems for thrust and mixture control, separate pyrotechnic ignition and shutdown mechanisms but used the same fuel and oxidiser supply lines. Both chambers fired simultaneously during launch and the booster chamber was shut down later, the timing depending on the flight mode.

The missile's guidance system was designed by KB-1, which was by then within the framework of the State Committee for Electronic Equipment (GKRE – *Gosu**dar**stvennyy komi**tet** po **rah**dioelek**tron**ike*) and headed by Chief Designer Chizhov, and OKB-41 under Chief Designer Kolosov. (Note: In December 1957 several Soviet ministries were 'demoted' to State Committees due to changing policies during the Khrushchov era. The unlucky ones included MAP, which became the State Committee for Aviation Hardware (GKAT – *Gosu**dar**stvennyy komi**tet** po aviatsi**on**noy **tekh**nike*); MOP, which became the State Committee for Defence Technology (GKOT – *Gosu**dar**stvennyy komi**tet** po obo**ron**noy **tekh**nike*); and MRP, which became GKRE. In 1965, however, their names and status were restored after Nikita S. Khruschchov had been unseated and

replaced by Leonid I. Brezhnev as the Soviet leader in 1964. The former KB-1 is now the design office of the Almaz-Antey Air Defence Systems Corporation.)

The Kh-22 was developed in two versions – one for attacking small targets of importance with a high radar signature (such as large ships) and one for attacking large-area targets (carrier task forces, ship convoys, large ground targets etc.). The former (baseline) version designated Kh-22PG featured a PG active radar seeker head; the P in the designation referred to the guidance system's codename *Pla**net**a* (Planet), while G stood for *go**lov**ka [**sa**monave**den**iya]* – seeker head. The other version, designated Kh-22PSI, was equipped with a PSI self-contained navigation unit featuring a Doppler radar, a computer and a gyro. For stabilisation, pitch/roll control, and following the set course the Kh-22 featured an APK-22A autopilot with a hydraulic actuator; hydraulic power for this was provided by an electric pump. DC power was supplied by chemical batteries, with an electromechanical converter providing AC power for the equipment.

In the active radar homing version the Kh-22 could carry either a 950-kg (2,095-lb) conventional high-explosive/shaped-charge warhead (the so-called 'charge N') or a nuclear one ('charge M') with a yield ranging from 350 kilotons to 1 megaton. Only the nuclear warhead was fitted to the Kh-22PSI.

The basic specifications of the Kh-22 were as follows. The missile was 11.65 m (38 ft 2^{21}⁄$_{32}$ in) long, with a wing span of 3.0 m (9 ft 10^{7}⁄$_{64}$ in), and grossed at 4,200-4,500 kg (9,260-9,920 lb), including 950-1,000 kg (2,094-2,204 lb) for the warhead; the launch weight was also stated as 5,635-5,770 kg (12,420-12,770 lb). The launch altitude was 10,000-14,000 m (32,810-45,930 ft); after launch the missile climbed to a cruise altitude of 20,000-22,000 m (65,620-72,180 ft) from which it dived onto the target. Cruising speed was 2,700-3,000 km/h (1,677-1,863 mph); 'kill' range was 400-500 km (248-310 miles)

Below: Unlike the Tu-95K, the Tu-95K-22 could carry three KMB bomb dispenser pods. An example coded '98 Red' (?) was tested in this configuration.

Bottom: Close-up of the KMB pods under the Tu-95K-22. Note the extra ECM blisters.

Bottom right: Rear view of the pods; each pod is fitted with two stabilising fins.

A fine study of an in-service Tu-95K-22 ('06 Red') with three missiles.

Here the same aircraft is shown without missiles; the wing pylons are completely obscured by the inboard engines.

versus single targets and 500-600 km (310-372 miles) versus large-area targets, such as a carrier task force.

In cruise flight the missile was stabilised by the autopilot featuring an automatic altitude correction mechanism. Heading was determined by the guidance system. The PG radar of the active radar homing version tracked the target in the vertical and horizontal planes, providing inputs to the autopilot. When the radar scanner's vertical deflection reached a preset limit the autopilot put the missile into a 30° dive, the radar providing control inputs for terminal guidance. The conventional warhead detonated on impact, while the nuclear charge was detonated by a proximity fuse.

In the Kh-22PSI version, the aircraft detected the target, using its radar. Target co-ordinates were then downloaded to the missile's computer. After launch the PSI Doppler radar continuously determined the true speed, which was processed by the computer to calculate the distance covered by the missile; this was compared with the preset target range. At a preset distance from the target the autopilot initiated the terminal dive.

When used against large-area targets the Kh-22 had a 5-km (3-mile) circular error probable (CEP). At a later stage, range was to grow to 800-900 km (496-559 miles), providing the guidance system was upgraded.

The Kh-22 ASM had been originally developed for the Tu-22K, which carried a single missile on the

'06 Red' was one of the Soviet aircraft photographed for an album presented to NATO during a data exchange, hence the ruler providing scale.

117

Tu-95K-22 '52 Red' with RR8311-100 air sampling pods

centreline in a semi-recessed position. Hence, on learning of the Tu-95K-22's existence, western aviation experts initially assumed that the aircraft also carried only one missile. They were wrong: like the Tu-22M *Backfire* supersonic 'swing-wing' bomber/missile strike aircraft, the Tu-95K-22 carried up to three missiles.

The conversion included the following changes:

• The Tu-95K's BD-206 missile rack was replaced by a BD-45F centreline rack (F = *f'oozelyazhnyy* – fuselage-mounted) extended hydraulically to lower the missile clear of the fuselage prior to launch. Since the Kh-22 was smaller and shaped differently from the Kh-20, the weapons bay cut-out was reshaped to match the planform of the Kh-22's fuselage and was closed by three-section doors. While the centre and rear segments opened inwards as before, the front segments fitting around the missile's ogival nosecone had an ingenious design. The doors' insides were carefully shaped and their rotation axles were positioned inside the fuselage close to the centreline; when the doors rotated outwards, they slid inside the fuselage and the latter's underside at the front of the cut-out became concave instead of convex, accepting the missile's nose. The semi-parabolic retractable fairing closing the Kh-20's air intake was deleted as unnecessary.

• Two pylons with BD-45K missile racks (K = *kryl'yevoy* – wing-mounted) were installed inboard of the Nos. 2 and 3 engines, 1.9 m (6 ft 2⁵⁄₆₄ in) from the centreline, for carrying two more Kh-22s under the wing roots. The racks were quite long, and when the flaps were extended there was barely an inch of clearance between them and the racks' rear ends. Both types of racks were taken straight from the Tu-22M, hence the '45' in the designations. This is because the Tu-22M0 and Tu-22M1 prototypes (both codenamed *Backfire-A* by NATO) had the manufacturer's designations *izdeliye* 45-00 and *izdeliye* 45-01 respectively, the production Tu-22M2 *Backfire-B* was *izdeliye* 45-02 and the Tu-22M3 *Backfire-C* was *izdeliye* 45-03.

• The YaD twin-antenna radar was replaced with a PNA-B (NATO codename *Puff Ball*) target illumination/ground mapping radar developed by LNPO Leninets. This was an adaptation of the Tu-22M's PNA radar, itself an advanced derivative of the Tu-22K's PN radar (NATO *Down Beat*); the P again stood for the original guidance system's codename *Planeta*, while N stood for *nositel'* – [missile] carrier. The new radar had a single antenna which fitted nicely into the existing 'duck bill' radome; since the guidance channel antenna above it was deleted, the 'dog nose' upper radome being replaced by an identically shaped metal fairing.

• A comprehensive active ECM suite was fitted. A distinctive ogival tail fairing with flattened sides supplanted the DK-12 tail turret and the rear bullet-proof glazing of the tail gunner's station; hence the PRS-4 gun-laying radar was deleted. This fairing accommodated an SPS-151ZhK, SPS-152ZhK or SPS-153ZhK Siren'-MD (Lilac, pronounced *seeren'*) active jammer, the K probably denoting *kormovaya* – aft-mounted. The three jammers were interchangeable,

A red-painted Kh-22 test round and a production Kh-22 in natural metal finish.

differing in the range of frequencies covered. The fairing carried antennas and was vertically split, the halves opening like clamshell doors for maintenance access to the avionics which were mounted on a special truss-type bearer and cooled by air from special air scoops. This ECM fairing was also used on some versions of the Tu-16; hence it was called UKhO (*oonifitseerovannyy khvostovoy otsek* – standardised tail compartment), and the spelling of the Russian acronym coincided with the Russian word *ookho* (ear). Moreover, an SPS-151D,

SPS-152D or SPS-153D Siren'-D jammer was fitted, having a receiver antenna in a distinctive thimble-shaped fairing above the 'duck bill' radome and transmitter antennas in egg-shaped pods on short struts mounted low on the forward and rear fuselage sides to give 360° coverage.

• New missile pre-launch equipment called *Kama* (after a Russian river) was installed.

The first Tu-95KM earmarked for modification to the new standard (c/n 63M52608) was ferried to the

A Tu-95K-22 ('20 Red') takes off, carrying a single Kh-22PSI on the centreline. The Kh-22PSI has a distinctive metal nosecone with an inset dielectric panel for a Doppler radar instead of a full dielectric radome as on other versions of the missile.

A Tu-95K-22 minus external stores shows off its arrow-like shape.

This Tu-95KM carries RR8311-100 air sampling pods under the wings for radiation reconnaissance (RINT).

This publicity photo shows the final pre-flight briefing of the crew of a Tu-95KM configured for RINT duties. Note the chemical sensor pod above the starboard wing root.

A fine study of a Tu-95K-22 equipped with RR8311-100 air sampling pods.

Kuibyshev factory on 31st January 1973. Actual upgrade work commenced in June 1974 – some five months behind schedule because the required drawings and technical data did not become available until May 1974.

The Tu-95K-22 entered flight test on 30th October 1975. However, the first launch of a Kh-22 from a Tu-95K-22 did not take place until 1981. During the interim five-year period, the system passed through a painstaking test and debugging process; the missile itself was mostly tested on the Tu-22K.

Starting in 1981, a total of 42 Tu-95KMs were upgraded to the new standard at the Kuibyshev plant; some sources, however, claim that the conversions were performed by the Air Force's 148th ARZ (*aviaremontnyy zavod* – aircraft repair plant) in Belaya Tserkov' (Gayok AB) in accordance with a MAP/Air Force joint decision dated 20th April 1977. Following the Tu-95K-22's introduction into the inventory in 1987 it became an important weapons system in the Soviet Air Force. The NATO reporting name was *Bear-G*.

Just like the Tu-95KM, several Tu-95K-22s were equipped to carry RR8311-100 air sampling pods for monitoring nuclear tests – or possibly retained this modification from their pre-upgrade days. Also, a single *Bear-G* was fitted experimentally with three KMB bomb dispensers in an effort to give it conventional bombing capability. This time the pods were suspended from the existing pylons without any adapters, the missile bay doors remaining open; the pods were placed sufficiently far apart, which meant removing the inboard fins was not necessary. Once again, however, this installation was not used in service because the KMB dispenser remained experimental.

The type's service career proved to be brief; starting in the mid-1990s the Tu-95K-22s were progressively retired and scrapped at the Engels-6 aircraft storage and disposal facility in keeping with START-1 (Strategic Arms Reduction Treaty). Fortunately, a single example has been saved from the breaker's torch and is on display in the Long-Range Aviation Museum at Engels-2 AB together with other DA aircraft types.

Tu-95M-5 experimental missile strike aircraft (*izdeliye* VM-5 'Volga')

As early as 1960 the aforementioned OKB-2-155 started work on the KSR-5 supersonic air-to-surface missile; its development was officially sanctioned by Council of Ministers directive No.838-357 issued on 11th August 1962. Also known as the D-5, the KSR-5 resembled a scaled-down version of the Kh-22, to which it was similar both aerodynamically and structurally. It had a conventional mid-wing layout with delta wings having 75° leading-edge sweep and cruciform trapezoidal tail surfaces arranged in the vertical and horizontal planes; the tail unit consisted of stabilators, an all-movable dorsal fin and a fixed ventral fin which folded to port to facilitate ground handling, deploying after launch. The airframe was mostly made of aluminium alloys, with stainless steel used for the oxidiser tank. The circular-section fuselage was tipped by an ogival radome of glassfibre honeycomb construction. The powerplant was again a Tumanskiy S5.33 liquid-propellant rocket motor (aka R201-300).

The KSR-5 was 10.6 m (34 ft 9²¹⁄₆₄ in) long, with a wing span of 2.606 m (8 ft 6¹⁹⁄₃₂ in) and a body diameter of 0.92 m (3 ft 0⁷⁄₃₂ in). The launch weight varied from 3,850 to 3,930 kg (8,490-8,660 lb), including a 900-kg (1,980-lb) warhead; the latter could be a shaped-charge/high-explosive warhead ('version M') for use against a pinpoint target, such as a large surface ship, or a TK40-1 thermonuclear warhead ('version N') for use against a large target, such as a naval task force.

The KSR-5 was devised as a highly accurate 'fire-and-forget' missile for use against ground or maritime targets. The missile had a VS-K active radar seeker head, a BSU-7 autopilot (*bortovaya sistema oopravleniya* – on-

Nikolay V. Kirsanov, a leading designer at the Tupolev OKB, who suceeded Nikolay I. Bazenkov as the Tu-95's project chief.

The uncoded Tu-95M-5 sits on a snow-covered apron at Zhukovskiy with two KSR-5s under the wing roots. Note the thimble fairing of the SPS-141 jammer at the tip of the navigator's station glazing.

Four views of the Tu-95M-5 development aircraft, showing the location of the BD-352-11-5 missile pylons, the UKhO ECM fairing, the fuselage-mounted antennas similar to those of the Tu-95K-22 and the cine camera housing under the starboard wingtip.

board control system), a command link system for mid-course guidance, an altimeter and a speed sensor. The seeker head and the autopilot were also components of the Vzlyot (Take-off) guidance system. The VS-K acquired the target while the missile was still on the wing, using target information supplied by the aircraft's radar. In an ECM environment, the guidance system made use of the target co-ordinates stored in its memory; should the ECM become really severe and prolonged, the system switched to another operating frequency which hopefully was not yet jammed.

The KSR-5 was launched at an altitude of 9,000-11,000 m (29,530-36,090 ft) after the aircraft's radar had acquired the target and achieved a lock-on. The launch range was 200-240 km (124-149 miles). As the rocket motor fired three seconds after release and went to full thrust, the missile accelerated to 2,500-3,000 km/h (1,552-1,863 mph) and pulled up into a climb, cruising at an altitude of 22,500 m (73,820 ft) and receiving mid-course guidance from the aircraft. At a certain range from the target the radar seeker head achieved a lock-on; the missile still received course updates from the aircraft as required. When the target was 60 km (37.25 miles) away the missile entered a 30° dive; the aircraft was then free to manoeuvre at will or return to base. The radar seeker was turned off 1 km (0.62 miles) from the target. Detonation was performed by an impact fuse if a conventional warhead fitted or by a radio altimeter set for a predetermined altitude if a nuclear warhead was fitted.

Manufacturer's flight tests began in October 1964, followed by state acceptance trials in January-November 1968. Finally, on 12th November 1969 the KSR-5 was officially cleared for service with the Long Range Aviation and the Naval Aviation by Council of Ministers directive No.882-315 as part of the K-26 weapons system, with the Tu-16K-26, Tu-16KSR-2-5 and Tu-16KSR-2-5-11 (all three were known by the common NATO reporting name *Badger-G Mod*) as the missile platform. The system achieved IOC in 1970. The KSR-5 missile entered full-scale production at the Doobna Machinery Plant (DMZ – **Doob**nenskiy ma**shino**-stro**itel**'nyy za**vod**, formerly MAP plant No.256) in 1966, receiving the NATO codename AS-6A *Kingfish*.

Almost immediately the Tupolev OKB began exploring options of other missile platforms for the KSR-5. The same CofM directive No.104-36 issued on 13th February 1973 contained a decision to arm 33 Tu-95/Tu-95M bombers with the new missile as part of the K-95-26 weapons system. The latter utilised a different missile pre-launch system codenamed Volga (a Russian river); accordingly the *Bear-A* equipped for carrying the KSR-5 was designated Tu-95M-5 and had the in-house code *izdeliye* VM-5 'Volga'.

In October 1976 a production Tu-95M (no tactical code, c/n 8800601) was converted into the Tu-95M-5 prototype by plant No.18 in Kuibyshev. Like the *Badger-G Mod*, the aircraft carried two KSR-5 missiles on pylons with BD-352-11-5 missile racks; however, as distinct from the Tu-16, the pylons were located under the wing roots, as on the Tu-95K-22, and were of the same type. The racks were installed at a 3° nose-down angle and there was much greater clearance between the racks and the extended flaps as compared to the Tu-95K-22. A special subsystem was introduced for pressurising the missiles' avionics bays prior to launch. A modified Rubin-1KV radar (the same as on the *Badger-G Mod*) was fitted and an SPS-153 jammer was installed in a UKhO tail fairing supplanting the tail turret *à la* Tu-95K-22.

The Tu-95M-5 entered flight test in the autumn of 1976. The trials continued through May 1977 and were terminated when it became clear that the obsolete weapons platform offered no significant advantages over the Tu-16 armed with the KSR-5 missile. Hence the planned upgrade was not proceeded with and the Tu-95M-5 remained a one-off development aircraft (it would be wrong to regard it as a weapons testbed, since the missile had been tested much earlier). A year later the aircraft was modified again, becoming the Tu-95M-55 weapons testbed under the Tu-95MS programme (see Chapter 5).

Tu-95M-55 missile carrier/weapons testbed (*izdeliye* VM-021 'Doob')

In 1968-70 the leading Soviet integrator of avionics and aircraft weapons, the State Research Institute of Aircraft Systems (GosNII AS – *Gosu**dar**stvennyy na**ooch**no-is**sled**ovatel'skiy insti**toot** aviatsi**onn**ykh sis**tem**) – specifically, Section 5 headed by Vladimir I. Chervin – undertook the **E**kho (Echo) R&D programme which culminated in a proposal to develop reasonably simple and affordable long-range cruise missiles with nuclear warheads. Their small size and ability to fly nap-of-the-earth at ultra-low level (both of which made them hard to detect) allowed such missiles to penetrate enemy air defences effectively and hit the target with deadly accuracy.

This idea crystallised long before the USA had begun developing strategic cruise missiles, but the Soviet military leaders were not interested at the time, citing the missiles' 'low performance' as the reason. Serious research in this field at GosNII AS began only in 1975, a year after the Boeing Co. had started work on the AGM-86A Air-Launched Cruise Missile (ALCM). When this alarming news reached the Soviet leaders and the prospect of ALCMs being launched in large numbers by the USAF's strategic bombers loomed large, the go-ahead was given – and then the Soviet researchers had to work hard, trying to make up for time lost.

Serious research in the field of aircraft weapons was conducted at the Tupolev OKB under the leadership of Dmitriy A Gorskiy with the participation of

I. I. Tret'yakov, V. S. Demchenko, A. S. Smirnov and the personnel under their command. The Tupolev OKB and MKB Raduga (the latter was by then headed by Igor' S. Seleznyov) submitted a joint proposal for a low-level subsonic cruise missile with a nuclear warhead to be used against ground targets and surface ships with a low radar signature. Designated Kh-55, the missile was to have a correlation navigation system and a terrain-following feature helping it to avoid detection and interception. It was to be developed in standard-range and extended-range versions, the latter being designated Kh-55SM (*strategicheskaya, modifitseerovannaya* – strategic, modified). At first the MAP and Air Force top brass chose not to go ahead with the strategic version; however, they changed their minds in 1976 when it became known that Boeing was speedily developing the AGM-86B (ALCM-B) strategic cruise missile having more than twice the range of the original version.

In late October 1975 MAP issued an order initiating development work on the Kh-55 cruise missile. Development of the missile was officially sanctioned by a Council of Ministers directive issued on 8th December 1976, by which time the design work at MKB Raduga was well advanced.

The Kh-55 missile changed appreciably in the course of development. The first project version had a long pointed nose, an untapered rear end (which gave no indication of the propulsion type – jet engine or rocket motor) and an almost full-length dorsal conduit; the fuselage cross-section was circular, except where the wings were attached at approximately one-third of the length. The missile had a low-wing layout with high aspect ratio constant-chord wings having about 35° leading-edge sweep when deployed and tips cropped parallel to the fuselage axis. The tail unit comprised a short fixed fin and much longer all-movable stabilisers in an inverted-V arrangement, all three having a trapezoidal shape with no trailing-edge sweep. In pre-launch configuration the wings and tail surfaces were folded, the wing panels being positioned above one another, to enable carriage on a rotary launcher.

The second version, known in house as *izdeliye* 120, still had a low-wing layout but the wings had a lower aspect ratio, less sweepback and rounded tips; they were repositioned aft, being located amidships. The fuselage nose had a blunter ogival shape and the conduit was gone. For a while MKB Raduga contemplated a propfan engine with contra-rotating pusher propellers located aft of the tail surfaces but eventually opted for a small turbofan engine whose high fuel efficiency afforded the required range. The close-cowled engine was stowed inside the rear fuselage in pre-launch configuration and swung down on a pantographic mechanism immediately before release, the clamshell doors of the engine bay closing around

the engine pylon; aft of the engine bay the fuselage tapered off to a cropped cone. The tail unit was also revised, the sideways-folding fin being slightly larger and the stabilisers slightly smaller than before. The airframe was carefully shaped to minimise its radar cross-section.

Three engine makers – MNPO *Soyooz* (*Moskovskoye naoochno-proizvodstvennoye obyedineniye* – 'Union' Moscow Scientific & Production Association), the Omsk Engine Design Bureau (OMKB – *Omskoye motorno-konstrooktorskoye byuro*) and NPO Trood ('Labour' Scientific & Production Association, the Kuznetsov OKB) – offered disposable turbofan designs for the Kh-55. MKB Raduga picked the R95-300 developed by MNPO Soyooz under the guidance of Oleg N. Favorskiy. Initially rated at 300-350 kgp (660-770 lbst), this engine with a bypass ratio of 2.0 had a two-stage fan (low-pressure compressor), a seven-stage high-pressure compressor, an annular combustion chamber, a two-stage turbine, an aft-mounted cartridge starter, a built-in generator and a self-contained lubrication system. The R95-300 had full authority digital engine controls (FADEC). The engine was 0.85 m (2 ft 9$^{15}\!/_{32}$ in) long, with a diameter of 0.315 m (1 ft 0$^{13}\!/_{32}$ in), and weighed 95 kg (209 lb). It ran on ordinary T-1 or TS-1 jet fuel or specially formulated T-10 grade synthetic fuel (decilin), with an SFC of 0.785 kg/kgp·hr. Some sources call this engine RDK-300 (*re'aktivnyy dvigatel' korotkoresoorsnyy* – short-life jet engine). (The R95-300 turbofan is not to be confused with the 4,100-kgp (9,040-lbst) Gavrilov R95Sh non-afterburning turbojet developed for the Sukhoi Su-25 *Frogfoot* attack aircraft.)

Soon, however, MKB Raduga was asked to adapt the Kh-55 for naval use in addition to air launch because the KS-122 ground-launched/sea-launched cruise missile being developed by the *Novator* (Innovationist) OKB was facing serious delays. (The KS-122 eventually entered service as the RK-55 or *izdeliye* 3K12 *Rel'yef* (Terrain profile), receiving the NATO codename SSC-X-4 *Slingshot*.) As a result, the Kh-55's airframe was considerably redesigned. The definitive version, still known as *izdeliye* 120, had the fuselage diameter reduced from 0.77 to 0.514 m (from 2 ft 6$^{5}\!/_{16}$ in to 1 ft 8$^{15}\!/_{64}$ in) and the fuselage cross-section was made circular throughout in order to enable launch from a 533-mm (20$^{63}\!/_{64}$ in) torpedo tube. Hence the missile now had a mid-wing layout; the wings, which had the same shape with rounded tips, were now unswept, folding aft into a slit in the fuselage. The nose had a parabolic shape, the rear fuselage was again gently tapered; the tail surfaces were now all of the same size and the stabiliser anhedral was reduced.

The fuselage was mostly of aluminium/magnesium alloy construction and built in three sections. Section 1 featured a large dielectric radome enclosing some of the navigation/guidance system avionics. The front end of Section 2 (the centre fuselage) was a heat-insulated warhead bay, followed by a fuel tank incorporating the wing stowage bay. The wings, which were one-piece glassfibre reinforced plastic (GRP) structures lacking control surfaces, were stowed above one another to save space, making the missile look lop-sided when they were deployed by a pyrotechnical actuator with a synchronisation mechanism preventing asymmetrical deployment; the slits for the wings were closed by spring-loaded doors to ensure a smooth airflow. Further aft was the engine bay flanked by more fuel tanks; it featured ventral clamshell doors which closed again around the engine pylon when the engine was lowered into position. Section 3 (the rear fuselage) accommodated the BSU-55 automated flight control system and the self-contained tail surface actuators. It terminated in a tailcone which consisted of a spring-loaded telescopic rod and a set of concentric rings held together by fabric strips; the tailcone was collapsed in pre-launch configuration to save space, extending at the moment of launch to reduce drag and improve control efficiency. The all-movable fin and stabilators made of GRP had a double-jointed 'snap-action' design to make sure they were completely within the fuselage diameter when folded; they were similarly deployed by pyrotechnical actuators, the segments being held in position by locks.

Apart from the fuselage diameter, the final version of the Kh-55 was dimensionally unchanged, with a length of 5.88 m (19 ft 3½ in) and a wing span of 3.1 m (10 ft 2 in). The missile had a launch weight of 1,185 kg (2,610 lb), including a 410-kg (904-lb) warhead; some sources state the launch weight as 1,300 kg (2,870 lb). After being launched at 200-10,000 m (660-32,810 ft) and 540-1,050 km/h (335-652 mph) the missile would descend to 40-110 m (130-360 ft) and follow a pre-programmed route to the target, making use of the terrain-following feature. Cruising speed was 720-830 km/h (447-515 mph) or Mach 0.8; maximum range was 2,500 km (1,552 miles).

The compact thermonuclear warhead with a yield of 200 kilotons was specially developed for the Kh-55 by the Moscow-based All-Union Automatic Systems Research Institute named after Nikolay L. Dookhov (VNIIA – *Vsesoyooznyy naoochno-issledovatel'skiy institoot avtomahtiki*), a division of MSM, under the guidance of Arkadiy A. Brish. The missile had an inertial navigation system with mid-course correction based on correlation with the digital map downloaded into the missile's computer. The map-making software was specially developed for the Kh-55.

The Kh-55SM strategic version differed in having a marginally greater length of 6.04 m (19 ft 9⁵¹⁄₆₄ in) and conformal tanks of complex shape mounted low on the forward fuselage sides, which increased maximum fuselage width to the original 0.77 m and gave a quasi-

triangular cross-section. The launch weight rose to 1,465 kg (3,230 lb), although some sources quote a figure of 1,700 kg (3,750 lb); maximum range was 3,000 km (1,863 miles). The baseline Kh-55 received the NATO codename AS-15A *Kent-A*, the Kh-55SM being the AS-15B *Kent-B*.

On 19th July 1977 the Council of Ministers issued directive No.1021 which was followed up by MAP order No.271 that same day. Apart from specifying additional requirements for the Kh-55, these documents concerned the missile's delivery vehicle which was to be developed in 1977-79 (it eventually emerged as the Tu-95MS). Among other things, the MAP order stipulated that the Tu-95M-5 development aircraft (which was sitting idle by then) be converted into a weapons testbed for the Kh-55. Accordingly the aircraft was redesignated Tu-95M-55; the in-house code was *izdeliye* VM-021 – possibly as a reference to CofM directive No.1021.

Oddly, the abovementioned MAP order was worded as follows: *'For the purpose of broadening the scope of development work on the Kh-55 strategic cruise missile developed in accordance with Council of Ministers directive No.1021 of 19.07.1977 (sic – Auth.) the CofM Presidium's Commission on Defence Industry Matters has issued ruling No.153 of 22.06.1977 (! – sic – Auth.) which contains the following items:*

"1. To accept the MoD's and MAP's proposal of conducting the following work in 1977-79:

a) arming the Tu-95MS aircraft, which is being developed as a derivative of the Tu-142M, with Kh-55 missiles;

b) conducting the manufacturer's flight tests of the Kh-55 and the initial stage of its state acceptance trials on the Tu-95M-5 aircraft equipped with a single-round missile ejector rack appropriate for such tests, with the subsequent completion of these trials on the Tu-95MS".' The careless wording of the document made it sound as though the VPK was referring in the said ruling to a directive which did not exist yet!

The conversion, which was again performed by the Kuibyshev factory No.18 (or, according to some sources, at the OKB's flight test facility in Zhukovskiy) and took more than a year (from July 1977 to July 1978), involved removing the existing wing root pylons with the BD-352-11-5 missile racks, the Volga pre-launch system and all ECM gear (the DK-12 tail turret was reinstated). Only a single missile pylon was envisaged initially, but as the work progressed the designers decided to create two options for internal missile carriage – the single pylon and a six-round electro-hydraulic rotary launcher. The latter was designated MAPU-6-514 (*mnogopozitsionnoye aviatsionnoye pooskovoye oostroystvo* – multi-position aircraft-mounted launcher, six-round, model 514?) for a while but later redesignated MKU-6-5 (*mnogopozitsionnoye katapool'tnoye oostroystvo* –

The Tu-95M prototype was converted into the Tu-95N 'mother ship' for the Tsybin RSR reconnaissance aircraft.

The Tu-95N is seen here at the Soviet Air Force Museum in Monino in the mid-1960s; the tactical code '46 Red' has been removed.

This view of the Tu-95N shows the recess in the belly to accommodate the RSR and the camera fairing under the starboard wingtip to record the separation.

'multi-position ejector device', i.e., weapons rack, six-round, model 5). The No.2 fuselage fuel tank was removed to make room for the DISS-7 Doppler speed and drift sensor system and the MIS-7 inertial navigation system (*malogabaritnaya inertsiahl'naya sistema* – compact INS). A new APP-95 Doob (Oak) pre-launch system (*apparatoora podgotovki pooska*) was fitted, as were rotary launcher controls and test instrumentation recording the launch parameters. Appropriate changes were made to the electric system and the air conditioning/pressurisation system.

The Tu-95M-55 made its first flight on 31st July 1978. During the three and a half years that followed it logged 656 hours in 107 test flights, dropping many engineless dummy Kh-55 missiles and performing ten actual launches of instrumented prototype missiles; seven of these were credited as successful. The results of these tests proved instrumental in finalising the design both of the missile and the proposed production version of the Tu-95MS.

Tragically, on 28th January 1982 the testbed crashed at the LII airfield in Zhukovskiy while taking off for its 108th test flight. Due to the negligence of the ground services the Tu-95M-55 had not been properly de-iced; besides, it was overloaded, being 30,000 kg (66,140 lb) above the MTOW, and the CG was too far aft, rendering the aircraft unstable. Immediately after becoming airborne the Tu-95M-55 pitched up abruptly, stalled and hit the ground with strong left bank. The crew of ten – captain Nikolay Ye. Kool'chitskiy, co-pilot Viktor I. Shkatov, navigator Aleksandr S. Shevtsov, Nav/Op Aleksandr I. Nikolaïchev, radio operator Igor' N. Gorstkin, flight engineer Aleksandr A. Zhilin, test engineer Valeriy E. Serman, electrics engineer Vitaliy Ya. Ampleyev, flight technician Khaidar I. Sungatulin and flight technician Konstantin P. Makarov – died on the spot. (As an aside, Kool'chitskiy and Gorstkin had already had a close call in a test flight on 22nd October 1976, being forced to eject from a Tu-22M2 which had disintegrated in mid-air at maximum G load. This time fate caught up with them.)

Tu-95N 'mother ship' for Tsybin RS aircraft (Tu-95RS, 'order 236')

In 1955 the OKB-256 design bureau headed by Pavel V. Tsybin initiated work on a supersonic strategic reconnaissance/strike system based on a supersonic aircraft provisionally designated RS. The designation stood for *re'ak**tiv**nyy samo**lyot*** (jet aircraft, as simple as that), although some sources decipher RS as *re**kord** sko**rosti*** (speed record). The aircraft came in three versions – a manned bomber carrying a single *izde-liye* 244N thermonuclear bomb, a manned recon-naissance aircraft called RSR (*re'ak**tiv**nyy samo**lyot**-raz**ved**chik*; alternatively referred to as 2RS) and a cruise missile called RSS (*re'ak**tiv**nyy samo**lyot**-sna**ryad***, aka S-30) with a nuclear warhead in lieu of a cockpit.

The RS had a circular-section fuselage of high fineness ratio with a pointed nose, sharply swept mid-set trapezoidal wings of low aspect ratio and a short trapezoidal vertical tail. Powered by two wingtip-mounted 4,500-kgp (9,920-lbst) RD-013 ramjet engines designed by OKB-670 under Mikhail M. Bondaryuk, the RS was expected to attain cruising speeds in excess of 3,000 km/h (1,863 mph) or Mach 2.82. However, it had a design range of not more than 7,500 km (4,660 miles); therefore it was to be carried aloft by a modified bomber, semi-recessed in its bomb bay. The RS would be released at a range of up to 4,000 km (2,490 miles) from the base, using liquid-propellant rocket boosters to accelerate it enough for the cruise ramjets to be ignited; the combined strike system's overall range was to be 12,500-13,500 km (7,763-8,384 miles).

The initial project version of the RS bomber had a tail-first layout with trapezoidal canards and was to carry the bomb in a very unusual way – the weapon was provided with delta wings of 3 m (9 ft 10¾ in) span with endplate fins and rudders and was inserted into a hole

Above: The bomb bay was almost entirely faired over before the Tu-95N came to Monino.

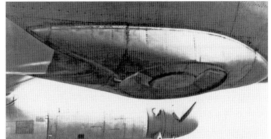

Left: The mysterious device immediately ahead of the Tu-95N's bomb bay.

in the tailcone; it looked as if the RS was giving birth to a baby aeroplane tail first. The bomb increased the aircraft's overall length from 27.5 m (90 ft 2⁴³⁄₆₄ in) to 30 m (98 ft 5⁷⁄₆₄ in); it was to be released 50 km (31 miles) from the target to glide towards it. A later version of the RS switched to a conventional layout, carrying the bomb (this time in normal wingless form) in a semi-recessed position amidships.

When the Council of Ministers issued directive No.1974-776 on 30th July 1955, ordering initial development of the RS, Tupolev was tasked with developing the 'mother ship'. The Tu-95 was the only possible option. The new configuration was designated Tu-95N ([*samo**lyot**-] no**sit**el'* – carrier aircraft or launch platform), aka Tu-95RS. During the second half of 1956, preliminary studies of the conversion were made jointly with the Tsybin OKB; this work proceeded under the supervision of designer Iosif F Nezval' at the Tupolev

Close-up of the cine camera fairing under the Tu-95N's starboard wingtip.

The Tu-95N still resides at what is now the Central Russian Air Force Museum. It has been given a new coat of silver paint in the meantime.

OKB's Zhukovskiy facility and was later transferred to the bureau's facility in Tomilino (a suburb of Moscow).

Suspending the long and heavy RS – the machine would gross at 30,000-40,000 kg (66,140-88,180 lb) – beneath the Tu-95 called for major modifications to the fuselage structure. The bomb bay was lengthened and fitted with a hefty beam-type rack for the parasite bomber, and the bay doors were modified. A circular device of unknown purpose in a flattened fairing was installed ahead of the bomb bay. All defensive armament was deleted. A cine camera was installed in a teardrop fairing under the starboard wingtip to capture the separation sequence. The new features were checked first on a full-size mock-up at MMZ No.156.

At the end of the summer of 1957 the Tupolev OKB started issuing the working drawings for the Tu-95N conversion to factory No.18. Rather than take an operational Tu-95 transferred from the Air Force as envisaged by the CofM directive, the OKB allocated the Tu-95M prototype ('46 Red', c/n 5800101) for this modification, which was known as 'order 236'. The conversion was completed in 1958 and the Tu-95N was flown from Kuibyshev-Bezymyanka to Zhukovskiy where the flight test programme was to be held.

Meanwhile, the Tsybin OKB built a subscale demonstrator of the RS designated NM-1 (*natoornaya model'* – proof-of-concept vehicle) for the initial flight tests. Shortly afterwards, however, the Council of Ministers took the decision to stop all work on the RS system. There were at least two factors behind this decision. Firstly, the R-7 intercontinental ballistic missile (ICBM) developed by OKB-1 under Sergey P. Korolyov had entered test, the first launch taking place on 21st August 1957; this led to a curtailment of the work on manned bombers, including the RS. Secondly, Andrey N. Tupolev was reportedly not on friendly terms with Pavel V. Tsybin and is said to have used his influence at MAP to get the RS project shut down.

Thus, the Tu-95N never made a single flight with the RS. OKB-256 persisted with the RSR (2RS) reconnaissance aircraft for a while, developing the 3RS version able to take off conventionally from a paved runway, but eventually the project was terminated and the almost complete full-size RSR prototype was scrapped. The Tu-95N 'mother ship' sat at Tupolev's flight test facility until the mid-1960s; later, it was flown to Monino airfield and donated to the Soviet Air Force Museum (now the Central Russian Air Force Museum) in Monino near Moscow where it remains on display to this day. Incidentally, the bomb bay was almost faired over before the aircraft went to the museum, and its 'mother ship' role is not immediately apparent.

Tu-95S missile strike aircraft (project)

As mentioned above, the Tsybin RSS (S-30) strategic air-launched cruise missile was also to be carried by the Tu-95. Thus on 31st July 1958 the Council of Ministers issued directive No.867-408, tasking OKB-256 and Tupolev's OKB-156 with developing a new airborne strike system designated Tu-95S-30. The directive stipulated the following performance figures:
- overall combat radius, 8,500-9,000 km (5,280-5,590 miles);
- missile launch range, 3,500-4,000 km (2,174-2,485 miles);
- the aircraft's cruising speed with missile attached, 700-800 km/h (435-496 mph);
- service ceiling with the missile attached, 11,000-12,000 m (36,090-39,370 ft);
- the missile's cruising speed, Mach 2.5-2.7;
- the missile's cruise altitude, 18,000-24,000 m (59,060-78,740 ft).

The Tu-95S missile carrier was to have IFR capability. The Tupolev OKB was required to submit the ADP of the Tu-95S-30 system in the second quarter of 1959, and the prototype was to enter flight test in the first half of 1961.

In addition to the Tsybin missile, the Tupolev OKB considered using the Tu-95 as a launch platform for a similar missile designed in-house (the 'aircraft 113'), which had been under development since May 1955. The 'aircraft 113' had the same layout with two wingtip-mounted engines but these were afterburning turbofans (Klimov VK-11s or Solov'yov D-20s), not ramjets; also, the wings and the conventional tail surfaces were swept, not trapezoidal (i.e., with positive trailing-edge sweep). The missile had a fuselage fineness ratio of 14.9 and wings swept back 60° at quarter-chord with an aspect ratio of 1.53. The circular-section fuselage had an ogival nose housing a radar seeker head, followed by a 3,700-kg (8,160-lb) nuclear warhead, fuel tanks and a control system bay. Fuel was also carried in the wing torsion box, and the fuel load was 18,000 kg (39,680 lb), amounting to 60% of the launch weight, which was 30,700 kg (67,680 lb). The 'aircraft 113' was to be 23 m (75 ft 5³¾₄ in) long, with a wing span of 8 m (26 ft 2¹½₂ in) and a wing area of 42 m² (452 sq ft). It was designed to cruise at 11,000-12,000 m (36,090-39,370 ft) and Mach 2.5, attaining a range of 3,000-4,000 km (1,863-2,490 miles).

However, development problems arising in the course of the project work (not least with the missile), led the Soviet military to reconsider the system's practicality. The successful development and production of ground-launched ICBMs soon rendered the issue moot; in February 1960 all work on the Tu-95S-30 system was abandoned.

Tu-95 'mother ship' for '130' (Tu-130) hypersonic aircraft (project)

Another project envisaging the use of the Tu-95 in the 'mother ship' role arose in connection with several studies undertaken by the Tupolev OKB during the late 1950s and early 1960s with a view to developing hypersonic aerial vehicles. In particular, the *Bear* was to serve as a launch vehicle for the experimental 'aircraft 130' (Tu-130, the first project to be thus designated). This was to be the prototype of the gliding final stage of an unmanned strike system designated DP – a tailless craft with a conical fuselage, extremely sharply swept delta wings and a short vertical tail. (The designation Tu-130 was reused in the 1990s for a twin-turboprop transport aircraft project similar to the CASA CN-235.)

Tu-95 'mother ship' for '136' (Tu-136) Zvezda hypersonic aircraft (project)

A similar project undertaken at the same time was the 'aircraft 136' (Tu-136, also the first project thus designated) manned aerospaceplane – also known as *Zvezda* (Star). This was to have a tail-first layout with extremely sharply swept wings and canards of cropped-delta planform, plus dorsal and ventral fins with inset rudders; the wing area was 38 m² (409 sq ft). The '136'

was expected to be placed into orbit by a UR-200 rocket as the first stage and two jettisonable rocket boosters under the wings. The orbital stage powered by a 3,000-kgp (6,610-lbst) liquid-propellant rocket motor was to have a structural weight of 2,500 kg (5,510 lb) and an all-up weight of 7,500-9,000 kg (16,530-19,840 lb), including 2,500-3,000 kg of fuel and oxidiser plus 2,300-3,600 kg (5,070-7,940 lb) of equipment. After de-orbiting and re-entry the '136' was to glide to a preset altitude; then the cockpit section would be jettisoned, whereupon it and the rest of the airframe would descend by parachute separately for recovery.

As a first step, however, the 'aircraft 136' was to be air-launched by a modified Tu-95 for investigating the hypersonic flight mode and verifying the landing technique. Two configurations were envisaged. The '136/1' would have a maximum speed of 1,000 km/h (621 mph), a flight altitude of up to 10,000 m (32,810 ft) and a landing speed of 300 km/h (186 mph). The '136/2' would be fitted with a huge booster stage increasing the maximum speed to 12,000 km/h (7,453 mph) and the maximum altitude to 100 km (62.1 miles).

Again, the aerospaceplane remained unbuilt. The designation Tu-136 was also reused in the 1990s for a twin-turboprop transport project – likewise unbuilt.

Tu-95K 'mother ship' for '139' (Tu-139) hypersonic aircraft (project)

One more hypersonic aircraft project which the Tupolev OKB was working on at the time was the 'aircraft 139' (Tu-139 – once again the first project thus designated). This was a more conventionally laid out aircraft which was remarkably similar in appearance to the North American X-15 hypersonic research aircraft which was under development since 1955 and first flew in June 1959. The '139' was to have a maximum speed in excess of 8,000 km/h (4,960 mph), a flight altitude of up to 200 km (124 miles) and a landing speed of 300 km/h (186 mph).

Once again the Tu-95 (specifically, the Tu-95K) was proposed as the 'mother ship' for the 'aircraft 139'. Of course the latter was carried semi-recessed in the specially modified weapons bay; in contrast, NASA's Boeing NB-52A/NB-52B that served as the 'mother ship' for the X-15 utilised a special pylon under the starboard wing. After release and rocket motor ignition the '139' pulled up into a climb, accelerating to 8,280 km/h (5,142 mph) by the time the rocket motor was shut down at an altitude of 60 km (37.2 miles). From this point the aircraft followed a ballistic trajectory, decelerating to 5,850 km/h (3,633 mph) at the apogee, which was 350 km (217 miles) from the launch point, and then accelerating again to 8,280 km/h at re-entry, which was 630 km (391 miles) from the launch point. After that, the '139' followed a flat descent trajectory, decelerating and landing.

A drawing from the project documents showing the Tu-95K as a 'mother ship' for the projected Tu-139 rocket-powered aerospace-plane. Note the Tu-139's flight profile at the bottom.

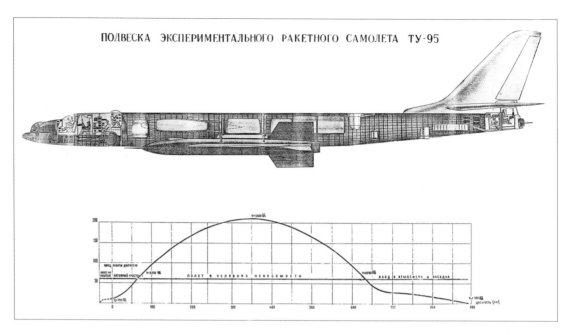

ПОДВЕСКА ЭКСПЕРИМЕНТАЛЬНОГО РАКЕТНОГО САМОЛЕТА ТУ-95

This drawing shows how the Voron reconnaissance drone and it solid-fuel rocket booster were to be attached to the Tu-95K before take-off.

The Tu-130, Tu-136 and Tu-139 programmes were terminated following the success of the R-7 rocket. Originally designed as an ICBM, the R-7 evolved into a capable space launch vehicle (SLV) for nearly all Soviet manned spacecraft, including the *Vostok* (East) and *Voskhod* (Sunrise) series; it continues in this role to this day with the Soyuz spacecraft series. In the late 1960s, however, the Mikoyan OKB's *Spiral'* aerospaceplane

project led to the modification of a Tu-95 as a 'mother ship' (see below). The designation Tu-139 was reused for a production supersonic reconnaissance UAV.

Tu-95K 'mother ship' for Voron (DSBR) reconnaissance drone (project)

In 1968 or 1969 the Soviet Union received a valuable gift from the North Vietnamese authorities – a USAF

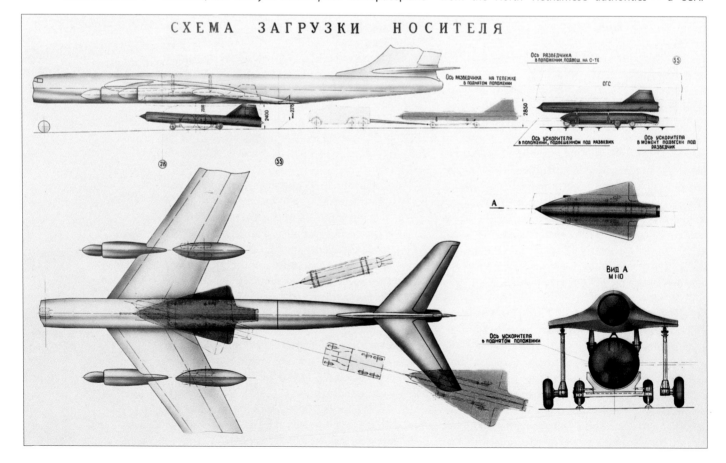

СХЕМА ЗАГРУЗКИ НОСИТЕЛЯ

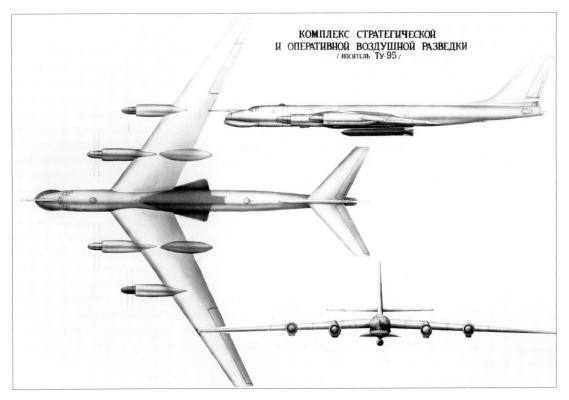

КОМПЛЕКС СТРАТЕГИЧЕСКОЙ
И ОПЕРАТИВНОЙ ВОЗДУШНОЙ РАЗВЕДКИ
/ носитель Ту-95 /

A three-view drawing from the project documents showing the Tu-95KM adapted to carry Tupolev's Voron hypersonic reconnaissance drone.

This drawing shows the design of the rack used for carrying the Voron drone and the latter's position in cruise and pre-launch modes.

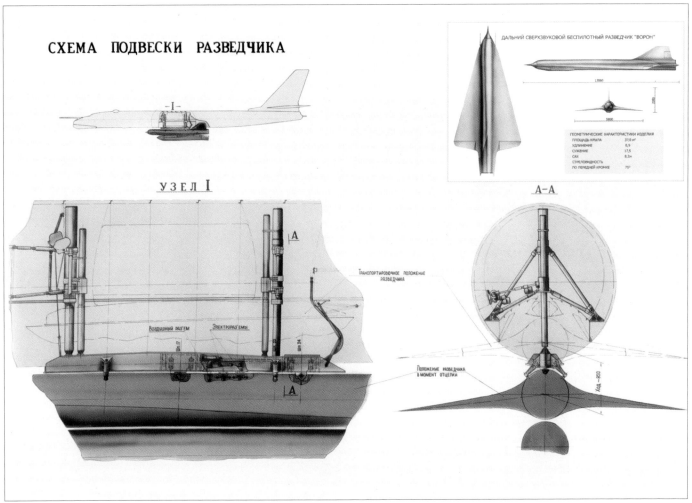

СХЕМА ПОДВЕСКИ РАЗВЕДЧИКА

ДАЛЬНИЙ СВЕРХЗВУКОВОЙ БЕСПИЛОТНЫЙ РАЗВЕДЧИК "ВОРОН"

УЗЕЛ I

A—A

The Mikoyan '105.11' lifting-body vehicle was hooked up to the modified Tu-95KM via a special adapter.

Test pilot Aviard G. Fastovets climbs into the '105.11' before the latter is lifted into the bomber's belly for a test flight.

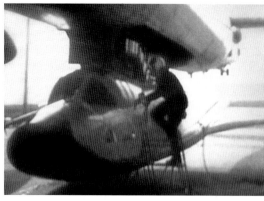

Tu-95KM c/n 63M52607 taxies out with the '105.11' suspended under its belly.

The '105.11' is lowered into the slipstream before separation.

The demonstrator flies under its own power after being released. Note the open air intake of the RD36-35 turbojet at the base of the fin.

Lockheed D-21 (GTD-21B) ramjet-powered Mach 3 reconnaissance drone which had crashed in Vietnam during the Vietnam War. It was subjected to detailed analysis with the participation of the leading MAP, MRP and defence industry enterprises, including the Tupolev OKB. On 19th March 1971 the VPK issued ruling No.57 prescribing the Tupolev OKB to develop a Soviet analogue of the D-21, making use of indigenous structural materials, engines and equipment.

In 1971 the Tupolev OKB brought out the project of such a reconnaissance drone called **Voron** (Raven) or DSBR (**dahl'niy samolyot bespilotnoy razvedki** – long-range unmanned reconnaissance aircraft; no numeric OKB designation is known. The Voron was intended for reconnoitring heavily defended areas that were too dangerous for manned reconnaissance aircraft. As one might imagine, it was extremely similar in appearance to the D-21 – right down to the two pitot booms flanking the circular air intake with its cshock cone. The main external difference lay in the shape of the wings which were close to a pure delta planform with 75° leading-edge sweep, whereas those of the D-21 had large curved leading edge root extensions similar in shape to the nose chines of the Lockheed SR-71 Blackbird Mach 3 spyplane. The provisional name Voron very probably derived from the fact that the D-21 was flat black overall, being covered with a special heat-dissipating paint – and so was the DSBR.

As was the case with the American drone, the cameras and their film cassettes were to be housed in a special capsule which was ejected and retrieved after the drone had passed over the target. (Incidentally, this technology was nothing new to the Tupolev OKB. On the Tu-123 **Yastreb** (Hawk) supersonic reconnaissance drone built in quantity for the Soviet Air Force the entire forward fuselage housing the cameras was jettisoned and parachuted to safety over territory controlled by friendly troops.)

The Voron had a 1,350-kgp (2,975-lbst) Bondaryuk RD-012 supersonic ramjet; it was to be accelerated to ramjet ignition speed by a massive solid-propellant rocket booster attached to the underside and delivering an awesome 47,500 kgp (104,720 lbst). Dry weight was estimated as 3,450 kg (7,605 lb) and own launch weight as 6,300 kg (13,890 lb), increasing to 14,120 kg (31,130 lb) with the rocket booster; some Tupolev OKB documents give the launch weight less booster as 6,000-7,000 kg (13,230-15,430 lb). Overall length was 13.06 m (42 ft 10¹¹⁄₆₄ in), wing span was 5.8 m (19 ft 0¹¹⁄₃₂ in) and height (less booster) was 2.08 m (6 ft 9⁵⁷⁄₆₄ in); wing area was 37.0 m² (397.85 sq ft). The drone was designed to cruise at 3,500-3,800 km/h (2,170-2,360 mph) and an altitude of 23,000-27,000 m (75,460-88,580 ft); maximum range was 4,600 km (2,855 miles).

Now, the Voron was to be carried by the Tu-160M – a precursor of the actual Tu-160 designed in 1969-70

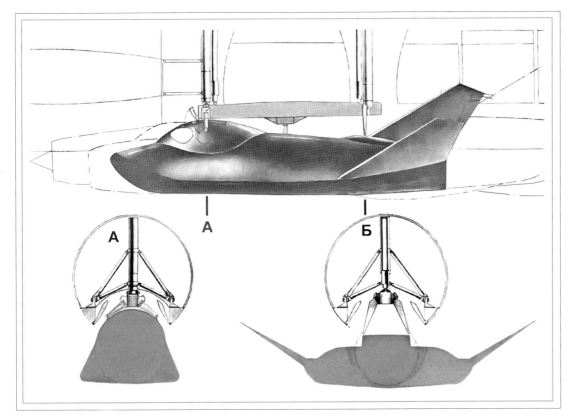

This drawing shows how the '105.11' was suspended in the Tu-95KM's bomb bay. The hatched lines show the Kh-20 missile and the SM-20 test aircraft to give a comparison of the size.

and resembling a modified Tu-144 SST. However, the Tupolev OKB also studied the possibility of using a modified Tu-95K as a 'mother ship' – apparently for test purposes.

Attaching the drone to the Tu-95K would be a complex procedure. The Voron sitting on its ground handling dolly would be 2.85 m (9 ft 4¹³⁄₆₄ in) high, whereas the Tu-95K's ground clearance was only 2.4 m (7 ft 10³⁄₆₄ in). Therefore the dolly was designed to tilt the drone, lowering its rear end so that the fin was 2.275 m (7 ft 5⁵⁄₆ in) above the ground. Once the Voron had been hooked up and lifted into semi-recessed position, a second dolly carrying the rocket booster was wheeled in and the booster was attached, whereupon the drone was ready for take-off. However, the Voron apparently never hatched.

Tu-95 Vostok spacecraft locator aircraft

On 22nd September 1960 GKAT issued an order requiring the Tupolev OKB and factory No.18 to modify two Tu-95 bombers for search and rescue missions as part of the Soviet manned spaceflight programme. These aircraft were to be equipped with a Pritok direction finding system to facilitate locating the big re-entry capsules of the then-current Vostok spacecraft and directing recovery teams towards them.

The Tu-95 modification programme was completed during November 1960 and the two aircraft entered service shortly thereafter. Unfortunately their identities are unknown.

Tu-95KM 'mother ship' for Mikoyan '105.11' aircraft

On 30th July 1965 MAP issued an order requiring the Mikoyan OKB to participate in the development of the abovementioned Spiral' aerospaceplane that would fulfil its mission in outer space and return to Earth, landing in aeroplane fashion. The design effort proceeded under the overall supervision of Gleb Ye. Lozino-Lozinskiy. The system was known as Project 105-205; it was a three-stage system comprising a reusable single-seat aerospaceplane developed by the Mikoyan OKB (*izdeliye* 105) as the third stage, a rocket booster as the second stage and a hypersonic suborbital launch aircraft developed by the Tupolev OKB (*izdeliye* 205) as the first stage.

The *izdeliye* 105 had a tailless delta layout and utilised a blended wing/body (BWB) design with a lifting body whose upturned nose was shaped like a wooden clog. The low-set wings had strong dihedral; the single vertical tail was small and highly swept. The retractable landing gear consisted of four units with metal skids. The curved main struts were located ahead of the wings, retracting upward and outward so that the skids lay flat against the fuselage sides, while the short rear struts were located at the aft extremity of the fuselage. At low speeds the aircraft was powered by a 2,000-kgp (4,410-lbst) Kolesov RD36-35K non-afterburning turbojet housed in the rear fuselage; the air intake was located at the base of the fin and closed by a special flap when the engine was shut down. In this flight mode the aircraft would be controlled by means of ordinary ailerons and a rudder. In orbit and in the upper reaches of the atmosphere/at hypersonic speeds, control was exercised by means of liquid-fuel rocket thrusters grouped in two clusters, each comprising three 16-kgp (35.27-lbst) units and five 1-kgp (2.2-lbst) units. For manoeuvring in orbit and de-orbiting the aerospaceplane was to have a liquid-fuel rocket motor with a 1,500-kgp (3,310-lbst) main chamber and two 40-kgp (88-lbst) auxiliary chambers.

In 1966 the Mikoyan OKB decided to build a technology demonstrator – a version of *izdeliye* 105 powered solely by a turbojet. Designated *izdeliye* 105.11, it would be used for subsonic flight tests in the atmosphere; the demonstrator would be carried aloft by a specially modified Tu-95KM.

Construction of the demonstrator began in 1968. In 1970 the Mikoyan OKB transferred the manufacturing process from MMZ No.155 (the OKB's prototype manufacturing facility in Moscow) to plant No.207 in Doobna, which completed the *izdeliye* 105.11 prototype (c/n 7510511101 – that is, factory code 75, *izdeliye* 105.11, Batch 1, 01st aircraft) in 1974. In 1975 the vehicle was delivered to GNIKI VVS in Akhtoobinsk where preparations for flight tests began. Although intended for air launch, the 105.11 could take off under its own power; to facilitate this, during the initial flight tests the skids on the main gear units were temporarily replaced with wheels. On 11th October 1976 it made the first real flight at the hands of Mikoyan OKB test pilot Aviard G. Fastovets.

Meanwhile, the Kuibyshev aircraft factory No.18 began converting a Tu-95KM transferred from the Soviet Air Force (c/n 63M52607) into the 'mother ship'. The missile bay was appropriately modified and a special access door was provided in the pressure dome of the forward pressure cabin, permitting the pilot of the '105.11' to climb into the cockpit in flight.

Captive flights beneath the modified Tu-95KM began in 1977. The programme reached an important milestone on 27th October that year when the 105.11 was released for the first time at 5,000 m (16,400 ft) with the engine running, flying safely back to base; again, Fastovets was at the controls in this flight. Eight such launches were made at this stage; next, the wheels on the main gear units were replaced with skids again for the second stage of the tests.

Performance and handling tests of the 105.11 involving air launches went on for a year. The final launch in September 1978 ended in a minor landing accident in which the 105.11 suffered some damage and was not repaired. By the time the tests ended the NPO *Molniya* ('Lightning' Scientific & Production Association) agency headed by Gleb Ye. Lozino-Lozinskiy had been established; it became the leader of the Soviet aerospaceplane development effort.

Yet, back in 1976 the Soviet Union had embarked on the development of an altogether different reusable space system – the Buran (Snowstorm, pronounced *boorahn*) space shuttle and the associated *Energiya* (Energy) SLV. By 1979 all work on the Spiral' system and the *izdeliye* 105 had been halted; yet the experience gained in the design process came in handy when creating the unique Buran/Energiya system. The 105.11 demonstrator eventually ended up in the Soviet Air Force Museum in Monino. The Tu-95KM 'mother ship' was not so lucky – it was scrapped.

Tu-95LL engine testbed

When the need arose in the mid-1950s for a flying testbed for verifying new powerful jet engines, the Tu-95 was a natural choice. It was large enough to accommodate the test instrumentation, test engineers and relevant mechanical systems; also, the stalky undercarriage allowed even the bulkiest engines to be installed under the bomber's belly without any trouble.

Accordingly, on 29th July 1957 the Ministry of Aircraft Industry ordered the Tupolev OKB to convert the second prototype Tu-95 into a testbed for the Kuznetsov NK-6 afterburning turbofan rated at 20,000 kgp (44,090 lbst) in full afterburner. This engine was initially regarded as the powerplant for the Tu-105 supersonic bomber prototype (the immediate precursor of the Tu-22) and several other bomber projects which did not materialise, including the Tu-106, Tu-108 and Tu-135.

Conversion of the '95/2' was performed at factory No.18 in 1957-58. Designated Tu-95LL (*letayushchaya laboratoriya* – flying laboratory), it was ready to fly during 1958.

The development engine was mounted in a special nacelle that was suspended from a hydraulically actuated trapeze mechanism installed in the bomb bay. The circular-section nacelle tapering towards the ends was built in three sections, featuring 32 frames and four longerons (two upper and two lower) to which the development engine was attached. The upper side of the centre section incorporated an armour plate to protect the aircraft from runaway blade fragments if the engine suffered an uncontained failure. A circular cover closed the engine's air intake to prevent windmilling when shut down; it retracted forward into a fairing ahead of the bomb bay before the nacelle was lowered clear of the fuselage for engine starting. This was done to avoid any influence of the boundary layer on engine operation (and to prevent the jet exhaust from damaging the fuselage skin). In an emergency the engine could be jettisoned; all connectors would be automatically severed by a pyrotechnical guillotine to facilitate separation of the nacelle from the bomber.

An automated fuel system was provided; fuel for test engine came from the Tu-95LL's normal fuel tanks.

The experimental engine had dual controls which could be operated either by the pilot from the centre control pedestal or by the test engineer from a special control panel. The test instrumentation suite measured 172 parameters at 371 control points.

The NK-6 was beset by serious problems and never reached production status, the Tu-105 and the Tu-105A (Tu-22) being powered by Dobrynin VD-7 afterburning turbojets instead. However, the ill-fated NK-6 was just one of six new engines to be tested on the Tu-95LL. Later, this aircraft was used for testing and refining the NK-144 (*izdeliye* F) afterburning turbofan for the Tu-144 SST with a take-off (maximum afterburner) rating of 17,500 kgp (38,580 lbst), a minimum-afterburner cruise rating of 3,970 kgp (8,750 lbst) and a non-afterburning cruise rating of 3,000 kgp (6,610 lbst), the NK-144A (*izdeliye* FA) uprated to 20,000 kgp (44,090 lbst) in full afterburner and 5,000 kgp (11,020 lbst) in minimum-afterburner cruise mode for the production Tu-144, the NK-144-22 for the Tu-22M0 and the NK-22 (*izdeliye* FM) rated at 22,000 kgp (48,500 lbst) in full afterburner for the Tu-22M1 and Tu-22M2.

The Tu-95LL remained in service with LII for some fifteen years until it was written off as time-expired. After that, its mission was filled by similarly converted Tu-142 and Tu-142M ASW aircraft (see Tu-142LL).

Tu-95LAL nuclear research aircraft ('order 247')

In the mid-1950s both the Soviet Union and the USA were seriously considering the possibility of developing nuclear-powered aircraft – an effort prompted, no doubt, by the encouraging experience with nuclear powerplants on surface ships, such as icebreakers. In the USSR such powerplants were developed by the Nuclear Energy Institute headed by Academician Igor' V. Kurchatov (IAE – *Insti**toot ah**tomnoy energhiĭ*; now known as the Kurchatov Institute). When the scope of work was widened to include nuclear powerplants for aircraft, this effort was supervised by Academician Aleksandr P. Aleksandrov.

On 12th August 1955 the Council of Ministers issued directive No.1561-868 ordering development of nuclear-powered aircraft. The Tupolev and Myasishchev OKBs took on the job, since nuclear powerplants were obviously only suitable for heavy aircraft. Work on such engines commenced at OKB-276 headed by Nikolay D. Kuznetsov and OKB-165 headed by Arkhip M. Lyul'ka; nuclear ramjets, turbojets and turbofans were explored. Reactors with air cooling and intermediate liquid metal cooling were designed; thermal and fast nuclear reactors were studied in great detail. Much attention was paid to the problems associated with exposure of humans to radiation and to developing radiation shields that were effective, yet compact and lightweight enough for aircraft.

The Tupolev OKB also jumped on the nuclear bandwagon, proposing a twenty-year R&D programme that would lead to the development of a nuclear-powered military aircraft. Both subsonic and supersonic designs were explored. Preliminary calculations showed that converting the Tu-95 to nuclear power would require a 100,000-kilowatt reactor with radiation shielding weighing 47 tons (103,620 lb); the total take-off power of the nuclear turboprops would be 55,000 hp and the take-off weight would be 136,000 kg (299,830 lb).

However, before the OKB had time to even assess the scope of work, intelligence reports started coming in from the USA in December 1955 about the Convair NB-36H Crusader research aircraft equipped with a small nuclear reactor. (This testbed, a heavily modified B-36 bomber, made 47 test flights between 17th September 1955 and 28th March 1957.) Academician Nikolay N. Ponomaryov-Stepnoy, who was a young IAE employee in the mid-1950s, recalled that Kurchatov once phoned Vladimir I. Merkin, one of his closest aides, telling him that he had been told of an aircraft flying in the USA with a reactor on board. *'[Kurchatov] said that he was going out to watch a play at the theatre but that by the end of the play he needed to have information on whether such a project was feasible. Merkin called us up for a meeting – or rather a brainstorming session. We concluded that such an aircraft does exist; it carries a reactor but its engines run on ordinary [aviation] fuel. In flight, research is undertaken on the dissipation of the*

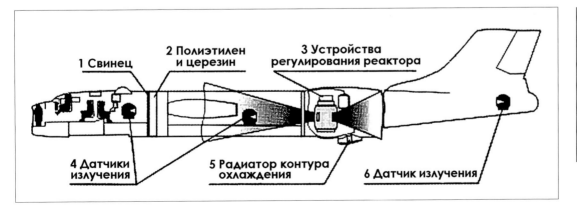

1 Свинец   2 Полиэтилен и церезин   3 Устройства регулирования реактора

4 Датчики излучения   5 Радиатор контура охлаждения   6 Датчик излучения

A diagram showing the special features of the Tu-95LAL nuclear research aircraft: the radiation shield with lead (1) and poly-ethylene/ceresin compound (2) layers, the reactor controls (3), the radiation sensors (4 and 6), and the reactor's coolant radiator (5).

A model showing the Tu-95LAL's centre fuselage structure and the reactor mounting pallet lowered onto a dolly for maintenance.

nuclear radiation – the issue that is so important for us; designing the radiation shielding on a nuclear-powered aircraft is impossible without conducting such research. Merkin drove to the theatre, where he apprised Kurchatov of our conclusions. After this, Kurchatov suggested to Tupolev that the latter conduct similar experiments.'

Below: A drawing of the Tu-95LAL's crew section from the ADP documents.

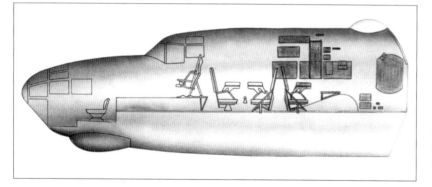

Right: An overall view of the Tu-95LAL.

Opposite page, above: A drawing from the ADP documents showing the VVRL-100 reactor with its radiation shielding and water cooling system. The right-hand side of the drawing shows the ground test rig on which the placement of the reactor and the radiation sensors was checked.

Opposite page, below: A cutaway drawing of the Tu-95LAL showing the windows in the reactor shield for exploring radiation reflection patterns.

On 28th March 1956 the Council of Ministers issued a directive ordering the Tupolev OKB to initiate preliminary design of a nuclear research aircraft based on the Tu-95 bomber.

For starters, Andrey N. Tupolev organised a course in Nuclear Physics 101 for the OKB's design staff. He invited some of the leading Soviet experts in this field – Aleksandr P. Aleksandrov, Vladimir I. Merkin, Aleksandr I. Leypoonskiy and others – to visit the OKB, delivering lectures on the basics of nuclear processes, the design of nuclear reactors and their radiation shielding, the requirements applied to structural materials, to the aircraft's control system etc. Pretty soon the lectures turned into heated discussions on how to reconcile the nuclear hardware with aircraft design requirements and restrictions. At first the scientists said the reactor and its ancillary systems would require a volume comparable to a small house. Yet the designers at OKB-156 managed to pack the reactor and all that goes with it into a remarkably small space while meeting the radiation shielding requirements. When the issue was brought up again at one of the seminars, Tupolev said: *'We don't cart houses around in aeroplanes'* and presented the OKB's reactor arrangement. The scientists were surprised at how compact it was and, after studying it carefully, agreed to it.

The main purposes which the nuclear research aircraft designated Tu-95LAL (*letayushchaya ahtomnaya laboratoriya* – flying atomic laboratory) would serve were defined in the course of the seminars. They included studying the effects of radiation on the airframe and equipment, as well as on the aircrew and ground personnel; checking the efficacy of the compact radiation shielding; exploring the reflection of gamma

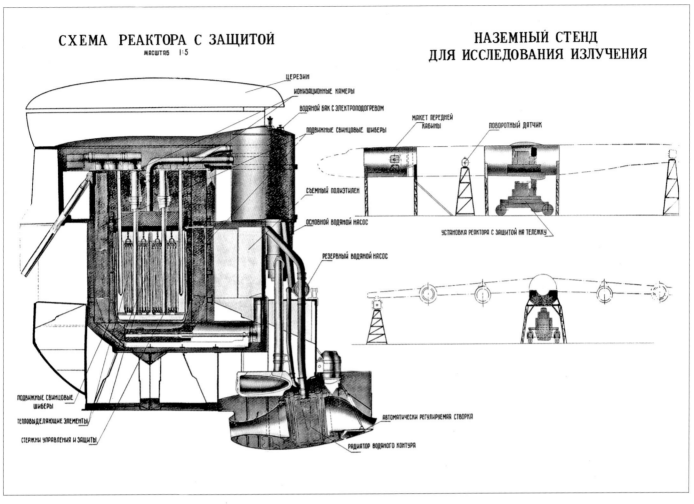

СХЕМА РЕАКТОРА С ЗАЩИТОЙ
МАСШТАБ 1:5

ЦЕРЕЗИН
ИОНИЗАЦИОННЫЕ КАМЕРЫ
ВОДЯНОЙ БАК С ЭЛЕКТРОПОДОГРЕВОМ
ПОДВИЖНЫЕ СВИНЦОВЫЕ ШИБЕРЫ
СЪЕМНЫЙ ПОЛИЭТИЛЕН
ОСНОВНОЙ ВОДЯНОЙ НАСОС
РЕЗЕРВНЫЙ ВОДЯНОЙ НАСОС
ПОДВИЖНЫЕ СВИНЦОВЫЕ ШИБЕРЫ
ТЕПЛОВЫДЕЛЯЮЩИЕ ЭЛЕМЕНТЫ
СТЕРЖНИ УПРАВЛЕНИЯ И ЗАЩИТЫ
АВТОМАТИЧЕСКИ РЕГУЛИРУЕМАЯ СТВОРКА
РАДИАТОР ВОДЯНОГО КОНТУРА

НАЗЕМНЫЙ СТЕНД
ДЛЯ ИССЛЕДОВАНИЯ ИЗЛУЧЕНИЯ

МАКЕТ ПЕРЕДНЕЙ КАБИНЫ
ПОВОРОТНЫЙ ДАТЧИК
УСТАНОВКА РЕАКТОРА С ЗАЩИТОЙ НА ТЕЛЕЖКУ

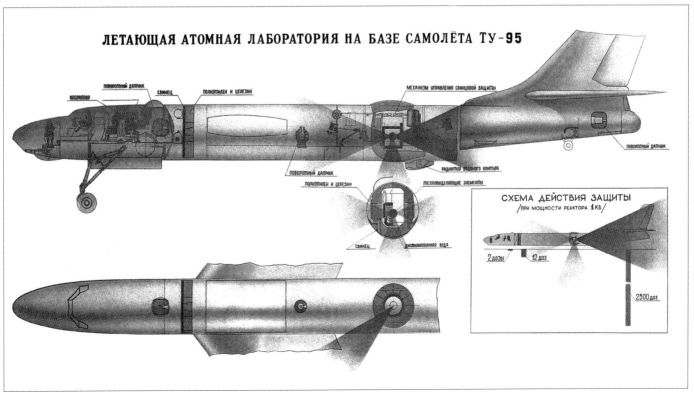

ЛЕТАЮЩАЯ АТОМНАЯ ЛАБОРАТОРИЯ НА БАЗЕ САМОЛЁТА ТУ-95

ОПЕРАТОР
ПОВОРОТНЫЙ ДАТЧИК
СВИНЕЦ
ПОЛИЭТИЛЕН И ЦЕРЕЗИН
МЕХАНИЗМ УПРАВЛЕНИЯ СВИНЦОВОЙ ЗАЩИТЫ
ПОВОРОТНЫЙ ДАТЧИК
ПОВОРОТНЫЙ ДАТЧИК
ПОЛИЭТИЛЕН И ЦЕРЕЗИН
РАДИАТОР ВОДЯНОГО КОНТУРА
ТЕПЛОВЫДЕЛЯЮЩИЕ ЭЛЕМЕНТЫ
СВИНЕЦ
ДИСТИЛЛИРОВАННАЯ ВОДА

СХЕМА ДЕЙСТВИЯ ЗАЩИТЫ
/ПРИ МОЩНОСТИ РЕАКТОРА 1 КВ/
2 ДОЗЫ
12 ДОЗ
2500 ДОЗ

The ground test rig built to check the placement of the nuclear reactor and its ancillary systems on the aircraft. The tests were held in Semipalatinsk.

rays and neutron rays from the atmosphere at varying altitudes, and evolving operational procedures for nuclear powerplants.

Speaking of radiation shielding, the Tu-95LAL incorporated the Tupolev OKB's know-how. The rival Myasishchev OKB used radiation shielding in the form of

a spherical capsule having equal-thickness walls, whereas the Tupolev OKB devised a variable-thickness shield, which saved weight. The reactor's shielding was thickest at the front (the side facing the crew), while the other walls were thinner. As for the forward pressure cabin where all the crew would be (the rear cabin was unmanned), the shielding at the sides and front was only just thick enough to absorb the radiation reflected from the atmosphere and coming from outside. One of the goals of the flight experiment was to measure the levels of this reflected radiation.

Many departments of the Tupolev OKB were involved in the work on adapting the Tu-95 for the nuclear research role, since the changes concerned not

The Tu-95LAL nuclear research aircraft as an instructional air-frame at Irkutsk fol-lowing retirement.

This view of the Tu-95LAL shows the ventral air scoop for the reactor's water radiator, the dorsal fairing above the reactor and the underwing radiation sensor pods.

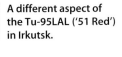

A different aspect of the Tu-95LAL ('51 Red') in Irkutsk.

The forward fuselage of the Tu-95LAL.

Above: Close-up of the Tu-95LAL's centre fuselage where the reactor was housed. Note the fairings enclosing the reactor and the water radiator's airflow adjustment flap.

Below right: The starboard wing of the Tu-95LAL with the starboard radiation sensor pod.

Below: The revolving rear radiation sensor visible through the observation blisters of the rear pressure cabin, which was unmanned.

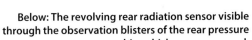

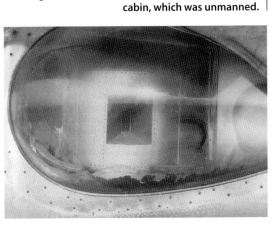

The Tu-95LAL in the process of being scrapped. The reactor pallet has been dropped on the tarmac, damaging the protective coating (fragments of it can be seen on the ground).

Opposite page: Two drawings from the ADP documents of the projected Tu-119 propulsion technology testbed which was to feature NK-14A nuclear turboprops in the Nos. 2 and 3 positions; note the piping from the reactor to the NK-14As.

created a structure that was both strong and highly resistant to the effects of radiation.

First of all, the Tomilino branch built a test rig consisting of two parts – a mock-up of the bomber's centre fuselage housing the reactor (with shielding) and a mock-up of the front pressure cabin, with radiation sensors arrayed around them. In 1958 this rig was completed and delivered to Semipalatinsk – specifically a test establishment nicknamed *Polovinka* (The Half) at a nearby airfield – for mating with the reactor. Shortly afterwards, the first airworthy Soviet nuclear reactor designated VVRL-100 was completed and declared ready for shipping, also to Semipalatinsk. (VVR means **vod**o-vodyanoy re'**ak**tor – pressurised water reactor in which water serves as the coolant in the primary (core) and secondary cooling loops, while the figures denote a power output of 100 megawatt.) The reactor ran for the first time in an underground nuclear facility in June 1959 and was then cleared for the proposed flight test programme.

A production Tu-95M coded '51 Red' (c/n 7800408) was transferred from the 1023rd TBAP for conversion by plant No.18 as the Tu-95LAL research aircraft, which was referred to as 'order 247'. All armament was deleted. The flight crew and researchers sat in the forward pressure cabin. Aft of this was the radiation shield between the crew and the reactor – a 5-cm (1^{63}⁄₆₄ in) bulkhead made of lead, followed by a 20-cm (7 ⅞ in) layer of special compound (a mixture of polyethylene and ceresin with boron carbide added).

The reactor was located at the aft end of the bomb bay. It was too tall to fit completely inside the fuselage cross-section, so a quite large humpbacked dorsal fairing was added immediately aft of the wings. The reactor was mounted on a special pallet which could be winched down for maintenance by mechanical hoists and wheeled away on a dolly, complete with water cooling jacket and the water/air heat exchanger. The latter was enclosed by a large ventral fairing further aft with an air scoop (similar to the air conditioning system heat exchanger fairing of the Tu-114). Water was forced through the cooling system by an ETsN100 electric centrifugal pump (*elek**trich**eskiy tsentro**bezh**nyy na**sos**) at 1,900 litres (418 Imp gal) per minute; overall water capacity was 540 litres (118.8 Imp gal). The reactor's control system was connected to a test engineer's control panel positioned in the crew compartment just aft of the flight deck.

The reactor's own shield consisted of a 5-mm (0^{13}⁄₆₄ in) layer of polyethylene with 3% boron added to contain neutron radiation and 13 lead blocks to contain gamma radiation; the overall effect was to reduce exposure levels in the crew cabin by a factor of 1,000-1,500. The lead blocks could be moved in flight by electric drives controlled by the test engineer to provide apertures up to 45° x 30° and let out swaths of radiation

only the airframe but many of the aircraft's systems as well. The main workload was shouldered by the general arrangement section (Sergey M. Yeger, Grigoriy I. Zal'tsman, Viktor P. Sakharov *et al*.) and the propulsion section (Kurt V. Minckner, Vladimir M. Vool, Aleksandr P. Balooyev, Boris S. Ivanov, N. P. Leonov *et al*.). Grigoriy A. Ozerov was the Tu-95LAL's project chief, while General Designer Andrey N. Tupolev exercised overall supervision of the programme.

The structural redesign was undertaken by the OKB's Tomilino branch headed by Iosif F. Nezval', a highly experienced Tupolev principal. The bomber's centre fuselage (the bomb bay area) was redesigned to accommodate the reactor and its support structure. Completely new materials were utilised for the latter, requiring the mastery of totally new manufacturing techniques. Working in close co-operation with chemical industry experts, the Tupolev OKB's non-metal technology department under Abram S. Faïnshtein

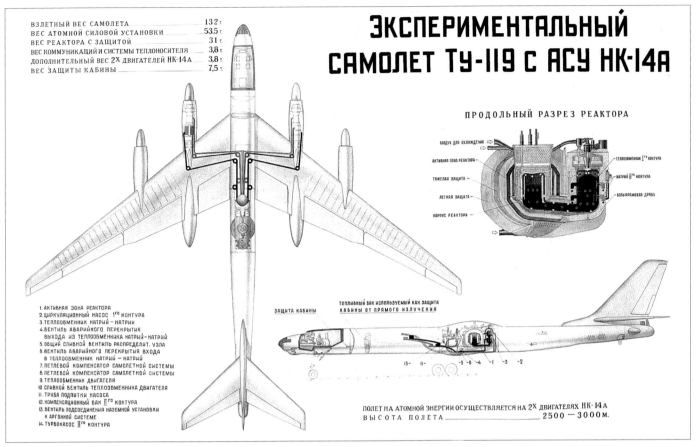

ВЗЛЕТНЫЙ ВЕС САМОЛЕТА — 132 т.
ВЕС АТОМНОЙ СИЛОВОЙ УСТАНОВКИ — 53,5 т.
ВЕС РЕАКТОРА С ЗАЩИТОЙ — 31 т.
ВЕС КОММУНИКАЦИЙ И СИСТЕМЫ ТЕПЛОНОСИТЕЛЯ — 3,8 т.
ДОПОЛНИТЕЛЬНЫЙ ВЕС 2ˣ ДВИГАТЕЛЕЙ НК-14А — 3,8 т.
ВЕС ЗАЩИТЫ КАБИНЫ — 7,5 т.

ЭКСПЕРИМЕНТАЛЬНЫЙ САМОЛЕТ Ту-119 с АСУ НК-14А

ПРОДОЛЬНЫЙ РАЗРЕЗ РЕАКТОРА

ВОЗДУХ ДЛЯ ОХЛАЖДЕНИЯ
АКТИВНАЯ ЗОНА РЕАКТОРА
ТЯЖЕЛАЯ ЗАЩИТА
ЛЕГКАЯ ЗАЩИТА
КОРПУС РЕАКТОРА
ТЕПЛООБМЕННИК Iᵍᵒ КОНТУРА
НАТРИЙ IIᵍᵒ КОНТУРА
ВОЛЬФРАМОВАЯ ДРОБЬ

1. АКТИВНАЯ ЗОНА РЕАКТОРА
2. ЦИРКУЛЯЦИОННЫЙ НАСОС 1ᵍᵒ КОНТУРА
3. ТЕПЛООБМЕННИК НАТРИЙ-НАТРИЙ
4. ВЕНТИЛЬ АВАРИЙНОГО ПЕРЕКРЫТИЯ ВЫХОДА ИЗ ТЕПЛООБМЕННИКА НАТРИЙ–НАТРИЙ
5. ОБЩИЙ СЛИВНОЙ ВЕНТИЛЬ РАСПРЕДЕЛИТ. УЗЛА
6. ВЕНТИЛЬ АВАРИЙНОГО ПЕРЕКРЫТИЯ ВХОДА В ТЕПЛООБМЕННИК НАТРИЙ – НАТРИЙ
7. ПЕТЛЕВОЙ КОМПЕНСАТОР САМОЛЕТНОЙ СИСТЕМЫ
8. ПЕТЛЕВОЙ КОМПЕНСАТОР САМОЛЕТНОЙ СИСТЕМЫ
9. ТЕПЛООБМЕННИК ДВИГАТЕЛЯ
10. СЛИВНОЙ ВЕНТИЛЬ ТЕПЛООБМЕННИКА ДВИГАТЕЛЯ
11. ТРУБА ПОДПИТКИ НАСОСА
12. КОМПЕНСАЦИОННЫЙ БАК IIᵍᵒ КОНТУРА
13. ВЕНТИЛЬ ПОДСОЕДИНЕНИЯ НАЗЕМНОЙ УСТАНОВКИ К АРГОННОЙ СИСТЕМЕ
14. ТУРБОНАСОС IIᵍᵒ КОНТУРА

ЗАЩИТА КАБИНЫ

ТОПЛИВНЫЙ БАК ИСПОЛЬЗУЕМЫЙ КАК ЗАЩИТА КАБИНЫ ОТ ПРЯМОГО ИЗЛУЧЕНИЯ

ПОЛЕТ НА АТОМНОЙ ЭНЕРГИИ ОСУЩЕСТВЛЯЕТСЯ НА 2ˣ ДВИГАТЕЛЯХ НК-14А
ВЫСОТА ПОЛЕТА — 2500 — 3000 м.

ЭКСПЕРИМЕНТАЛЬНЫЙ САМОЛЕТ Ту-119 с АСУ НК-14А

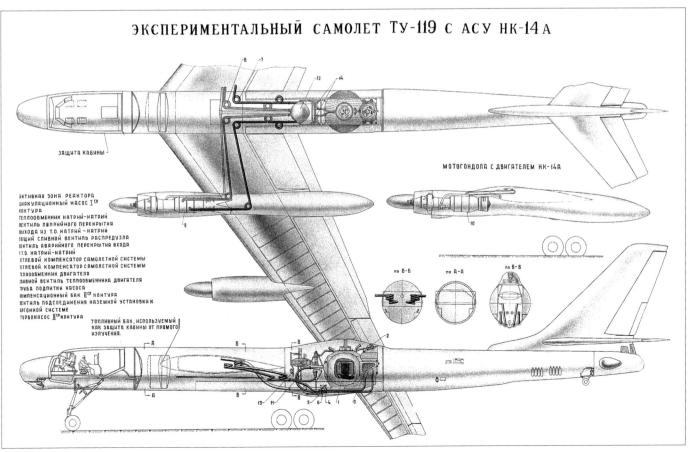

ЗАЩИТА КАБИНЫ

МОТОГОНДОЛА С ДВИГАТЕЛЕМ НК-14А

АКТИВНАЯ ЗОНА РЕАКТОРА
ЦИРКУЛЯЦИОННЫЙ НАСОС Iᵍᵒ КОНТУРА
ТЕПЛООБМЕННИК НАТРИЙ-НАТРИЙ
ВЕНТИЛЬ АВАРИЙНОГО ПЕРЕКРЫТИЯ ВЫХОДА ИЗ Т.О. НАТРИЙ-НАТРИЙ
ОБЩИЙ СЛИВНОЙ ВЕНТИЛЬ РАСПРЕДУЗЛА
ВЕНТИЛЬ АВАРИЙНОГО ПЕРЕКРЫТИЯ ВХОДА I Т.О. НАТРИЙ-НАТРИЙ
ПЕТЛЕВОЙ КОМПЕНСАТОР САМОЛЕТНОЙ СИСТЕМЫ
ПЕТЛЕВОЙ КОМПЕНСАТОР САМОЛЕТНОЙ СИСТЕМЫ
ТЕПЛООБМЕННИК ДВИГАТЕЛЯ
СЛИВНОЙ ВЕНТИЛЬ ТЕПЛООБМЕННИКА ДВИГАТЕЛЯ
ТРУБА ПОДПИТКИ НАСОСА
КОМПЕНСАЦИОННЫЙ БАК IIᵍᵒ КОНТУРА
ВЕНТИЛЬ ПОДСОЕДИНЕНИЯ НАЗЕМНОЙ УСТАНОВКИ К АРГОННОЙ СИСТЕМЕ
ТУРБОНАСОС IIᵍᵒ КОНТУРА

ТОПЛИВНЫЙ БАК, ИСПОЛЬЗУЕМЫЙ КАК ЗАЩИТА КАБИНЫ ОТ ПРЯМОГО ИЗЛУЧЕНИЯ

по Б-Б   по Д-Д   по В-В

A rather schematic desktop model of the proposed Tu-119 nuclear research aircraft.

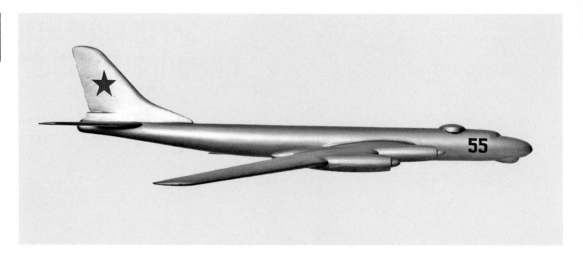

Another view of the Tu-119 model, showing the fairing over the reactor. The latter is placed directly aft of the flight deck, as distinct from the drawings on the previous page.

for the purpose of exploring radiation reflection patterns.

A radiation level sensor was installed at the front of the bomb bay in close proximity to the reactor. Another sensor was installed in the front pressure cabin just ahead of the radiation shield and a third in the rear cabin, looking out through the lateral observation blisters; two more sensors were mounted in distinctive teardrop-shaped pods under the outer wing panels adhering directly to the wing undersurface (these pods have previously been mistaken for the reactor's coolant tanks). All five sensors could revolve, scanning the space around them. There was also a small blister fairing on the starboard side of the fin near the top, probably housing a cine camera.

The extensive conversion took all of 1959 and 1960. In early 1961 the aircraft was flown to Zhukovskiy, and Minister of Aircraft Industry Pyotr V. Dement'yev came to see it, accompanied by Tupolev. The latter explained the design of the radiation shielding to the minister, stressing that *'the thing has to be absolutely tight, with not even the tiniest crack, or else the neutrons will escape'*. *'So what if they do?'* – Dement'yev said. Naughty 'Old Man Tupolev' was true to form: *'Supposing you go out on the airfield on a frosty day and your fly is open – what then? Your balls will freeze!'* The minister laughed: *'I get it.'*

Following initial flight tests to determine the effect of the new fairings on the aircraft's aerodynamics, the Tu-95LAL had the VVRL-100 reactor installed. From May to August 1961 the aircraft flew 34 test missions with the reactor both 'hot' (operational) and 'cold' (shut down). The flights were made by test pilots Mikhail A. Nyukhtikov, Yevgeniy A. Goryunov, Mikhail A. Zhila and others; engineer in charge Nikolay N. Ponomaryov-Stepnoy and camera operator V. Mordashev were also aboard.

The Tu-95LAL had a TOW of 145,000 kg (319,660 lb) and a landing weight of 110,000 kg (242,500 lb). The

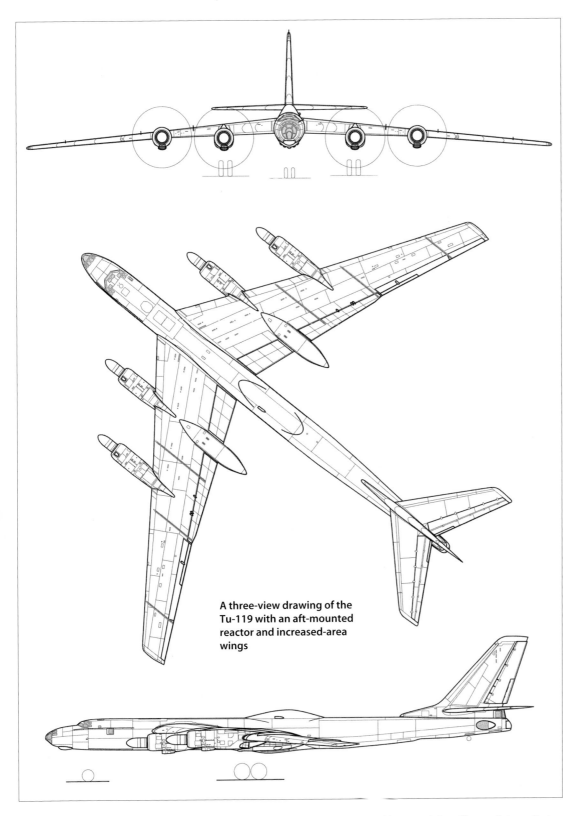

A three-view drawing of the Tu-119 with an aft-mounted reactor and increased-area wings

complete nuclear powerplant weighed 33,900 kg (74,735 lb), including radiation shield and support systems; the detachable pallet with the reactor weighed 14,500 kg (31,970 lb). Range was 4,700 km (2,919 miles) and cruising speed 750-800 km/h (465-496 mph). Normal endurance was 6.4 hours.

The tests quickly proved the efficacy of the radiation shielding. Exposure rates for the crew were extremely low; this gave rise to confidence in the ability of humans to work in close proximity to nuclear reactors.

However, the viability of the nuclear-powered aircraft concept was questionable from an economic standpoint. When it was concluded that the entire national budget for two years would be consumed by the project (!), the Powers That Be decided to terminate the effort and pursue other avenues of bomber development.

Other issues contributing to the programme's demise included the unwieldy nature of the radiation protection systems and the fact the USA had terminated its Aircraft Nuclear Program in 1961 (thus eliminating it as a technology threat). The Tu-95LAL was retired, languishing at Sary-Shagan airfield near Semipalatinsk for several years. Later it was flown to Irkutsk to become a ground instructional airframe at the Irkutsk Military Aviation Technical School (IVATU – *Irkootskoye voyennoye aviatsionno-tekhnicheskoye oochilishche*). Sadly, this unique aircraft was scrapped in the 1990s because people seeking a quick profit were unable to recognise its historical value or didn't care.

Interestingly, the test rig built for the Tu-95LAL outlived the aircraft and was used for radiation experiments for a long time afterwards.

Tu-119 ('aircraft 119') nuclear research aircraft (project)

Encouraged by the initial results obtained with the Tu-95LAL testbed, the Tupolev OKB began the next phase of the effort to create a nuclear-powered aircraft. The '119' (Tu-119) research aircraft was to be powered by Kuznetsov NK-14A nuclear turboprops and a 120-MW reactor. The NK-14A engine was based on the NK-12 in which the combustion chanber was replaced

by a heat exchanger in the reactor's secondary cooling loop. Actual design was scheduled to begin in 1965. In 1974 (!), two experimental NK-14A engines would be installed in a modified Tu-95 that would serve as the '119' testbed.

The location of the reactor in the former bomb bay was the same as on the Tu-95LAL (although one Tupolev OKB desktop model shows the '119' with the reactor just aft of the flight deck). Liquid metal (sodium) was used as the coolant. The pipelines from the reactor passed through the fuselage to the wing centre section and then out to the two NK-14A engines in the Nos. 2 and 3 positions. The Nos. 1 and 4 engines would be standard NK-12M turboprops running on jet fuel from integral tanks in the outer wings.

The Tu-119 was to have a take-off weight of 132 tons (291,000 lb). The nuclear powerplant weighed 53.5 tons (117,945 lb); this included 31 tons (68,340 lb) for the shielded reactor, 3.8 tons (8,380 lb) for the piping, another 3,8 tons of added weight for the NK-14As (as compared to NK-12s) and 7.5 tons (16,530 lb) for the crew cabin shielding, leaving 7.4 tons (16,310 lb) unaccounted for. During tests the Tu-119 was to fly at 2,500-3,000 m (8,200-9,840 ft) on the power of the nuclear turboprops alone.

With the cancellation of the Soviet nuclear-powered bomber programme, Tu-119 development was halted at the PD stage. Like its US equivalent, the Convair X-6 (initially based on the mixed-power B-36D Peacemaker and later on its XB-60 swept-wing, pure-jet derivative), it never reached the hardware stage.

This drawing shows how a further testbed based on the Tu-95 with a nuclear-powered turbo-jet was to have looked.

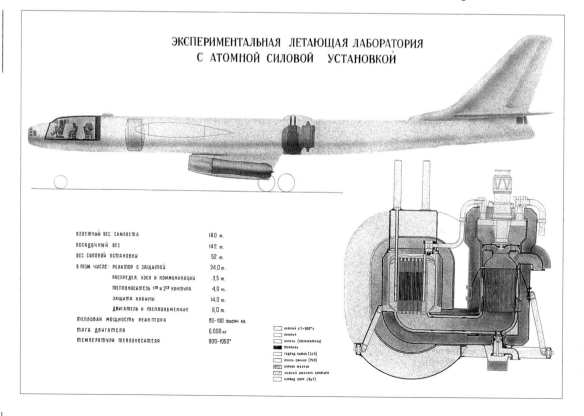

Tu-95 nuclear turbojet testbed (project)

A Tupolev OKB drawing shows a proposed propulsion testbed based on the Tu-95 featuring a reactor in the same position as the Tu-95LAL but having a 6,000-kgp (13,230-lbst) nuclear turbojet engine installed in a non-retractable nacelle under the centre fuselage at a strong nose-up angle. The aircraft was to have a take-off weight of 160,000 kg (352,740 lb) and a maximum landing weight of 142,000 kg (313,060 lb), including 52,000 kg (114,640 lb) for the nuclear powerplant. The latter included 24,000 kg (52,910 lb) for the reactor itself and its shielding, 6,000 kg (13,230 lb) for the nuclear turbojet, 14,000 kg (30,860 lb) for the crew cabin radiation shield and 4,000 kg (8,820 lb) of coolant in the primary and secondary cooling loops.

Tu-116 ('aircraft 116', Tu-114D – first use of designation) VIP transport

It is a known fact that the Tupolev OKB quickly evolved the Tu-16 twin-turbojet bomber into the Tu-104 *Camel* medium-haul airliner – the world's first jet airliner in sustained commercial service; the two aircraft differed largely only in the fuselage design, sharing the wings, tail surfaces, landing gear and powerplant. When the Tu-95 bomber came into being, the scenario was almost repeated – as early as May 1955 the OKB started work on its commercial derivative, the aforementioned Tu-114 long-haul airliner possessing transcontinental range. It shared the tail surfaces, landing gear and powerplant of the Tu-95 but had a new fuselage of much bigger diameter – 6.2 m (20 ft 4³⁄₃₂ in) permitting six-abreast single-aisle seating – and wings of greater area. This changed the aircraft's proportions completely, resulting in a very elegant airliner. The Tu-114 first flew on 15th November 1957 and, after rigorous testing, the aircraft entered service with Aeroflot Soviet Airlines in 1961.

Strictly speaking, the Tu-114 lies outside the scope of this book – in fact, it could merit a book in its own right. However, the airliner had a very unusual 'brother'. Almost concurrently with the development of the Tu-114 the Tupolev OKB was given the assignment of converting two production Tu-95 bombers into long-range VIP transports for top government officials with their retinue and security escorts. A requirement for such an aircraft arose with the opening of the 'Khrushchov thaw' and the resulting short-lived improvement in East-West relations. Piston-engined Ilyushin IL-14S *Crate* VIP transports were no longer adequate for the job, looking distinctly uncool (the USSR was a superpower, after all, and matters of prestige had to be considered). Similarly, the use of warships, such as the Type 68*bis* cruiser SNS *Sverdlov* which had taken a Soviet delegation to Portsmouth for the coronation of Queen Elizabeth II in 1953, seemed definitely inappropriate in the new conditions, running contrary to the Soviet Union's attempts to project a

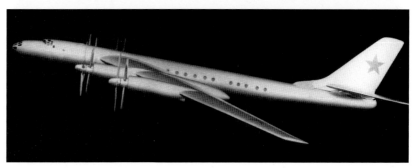

Top and above: A desktop model of the Tu-116 VIP aircraft, showing the slim fuselage with cabin windows.

Below: The Tu-116 had the same wing area as the basic Tu-95/Tu-95M.

A three-view drawing of the Tu-116 from the ADP documents.

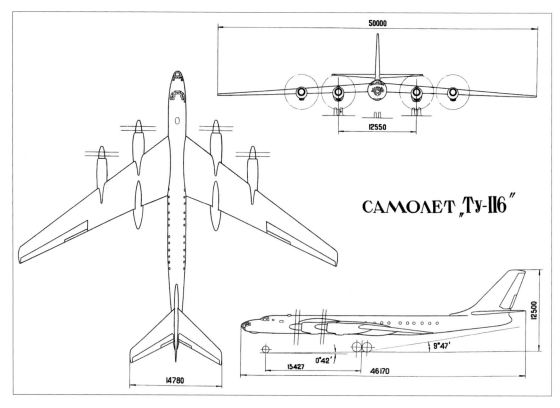

This drawing from the project documents shows the Tu-116's interior layout and crew accommodation.

more peaceful image. Now, development and testing of the Tu-114 was surely going to take time but the Soviet government was unwilling to wait for it and ordered a long-range VIP transport derivative of the *Bear-A* as a stop-gap measure.

The VIP transport received the in-house designation 'aircraft 116' and the official designation Tu-116. one of the two aircraft was intended for Nikita S. Khrushchov as head of state (First Secretary of the Communist Party of the Soviet Union), the other for Nikolay I. Bulganin as

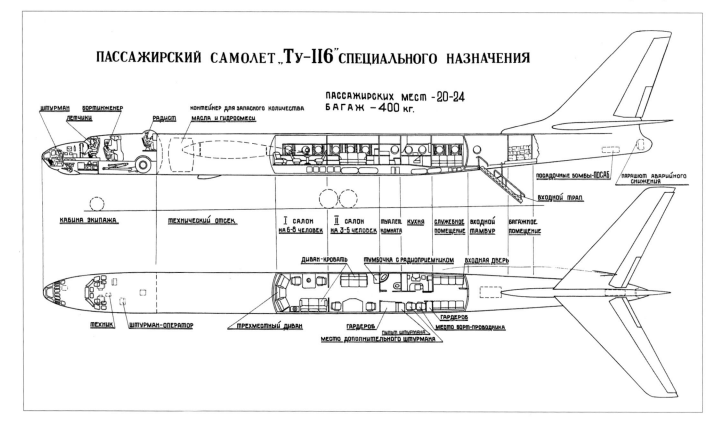

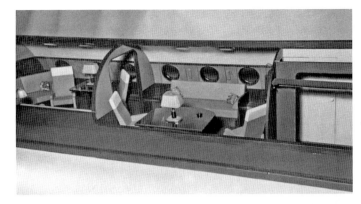
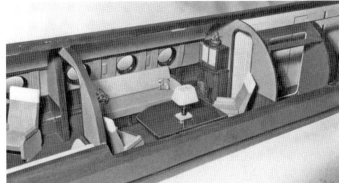
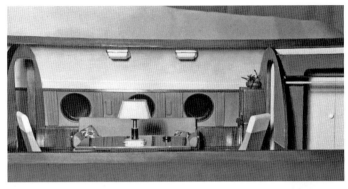
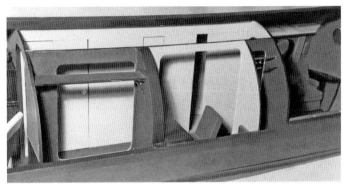
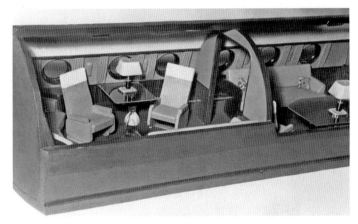
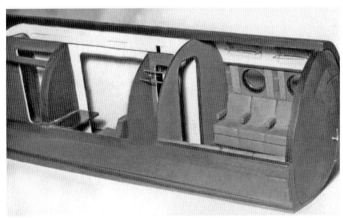

The photos on this page show a large cutaway model showing the Tu-116's interior. The upper two pictures show the No.2 (centre) VIP cabin; the other two pictures in this row show the No.1 (forward) VIP cabin with a curved sofa at the front.

Top to bottom: The No.2 VIP cabin; the service compartment with the navigator/informer's station and the galley; the rear cabin for the retinue with two three-seat sofas facing each other; and another view of the No.1 VIP cabin.

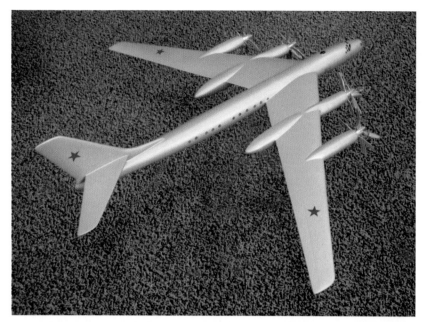

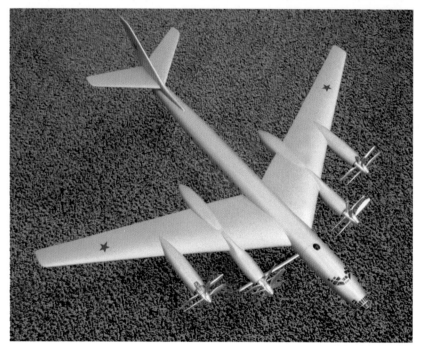

Two more views of the Tu-116 model illustrating the retention of the bomber's proportions and wing planform, as well as the cabin windows.

comfort non-stop over distances of 7,500-8,000 km (4,660-4,970 miles). The aircraft were originally to be presented for testing in September 1956, but on 28th March 1956 the Council of Ministers followed up with another directive postponing the deadline, knowing that the Tupolev OKB and the Kuibyshev aircraft factory were heavily burdened with higher-priority defence programmes.

According to the ADP, which was presented for review to the Air Force in April 1956 and approved in October 1956, in normal configuration the Tu-116 (Tu-114D) was to carry 20-24 passengers and 400 kg (880 lb) of luggage. If the main passenger was a top-ranking government official, the aircraft was to carry 10-12 armed security agents, plus service personnel – a flight attendant, a cook and so-called 'informer navigator' (**shtoor**man-infor**mah**tor). The latter was, for all practical purposes, an entertainer informing the VIPs what the aircraft was flying over at the moment.

Structurally the new aircraft was almost identical to the Tu-95, except that the bomb bay doors and the rear pressurised cabin with lateral blisters and rear glazing were eliminated; instead, fuselage section F5 was manufactured as a 'solid' tailcone. The space from the rear wing spar almost to the fin root fillet was occupied by a pressurised cabin with front and rear pressure domes; the cabin volume was 70.5 m³ (2,489.68 cu ft). Access to the cabin was via a ventral hatch at the rear closed by integral powered airstairs. The airstairs were no vain precaution, considering that the Tu-116 had a tall landing gear and the VIPs would not like to end up in the embarrassing situation when they would be unable to deplane because the available airstairs at a civil airport were too short! (Interestingly, the integral ventral airstairs had been considered for the real Tu-114 but ultimately rejected. It would be 20 years before such a feature would be incorporated on a Soviet large airliner – the 350-seat Ilyushin IL-86 *Camber* medium-haul widebody.)

All armament was removed. Well, actually the Tu-116 did carry bombs… the tailcone incorporated a ventral bay with POSAB flare bombs (*po**sah**dochnaya osveti**tel**'no-sig**nahl**'naya **a**via**bom**ba* – 'landing illumination and signal bomb') to be used for landing at night if the runway lighting was inoperative. The tailcone also housed a brake parachute facilitating emergency descent in the event of decompression.

The fuselage fuel tanks were also deleted – all fuel was carried in the wings in 66 bladder tanks. Total fuel capacity was 77,800 litres (17,116 Imp gal), which was enough for a maximum range of 11,190 km (6,950 miles) – or, according to some sources, 11,900 km (7,390 miles). The place of the former No.1 fuselage tank ahead of the front spar was occupied by reserve tanks for engine oil and hydraulic fluid. Again, this was no vain precaution – early-production Tu-95s were notoriously prone to

Chairman of the Soviet Council of Ministers. In the popular press of the day the two aircraft were referred to as the Tu-114D – the first aircraft to bear this designation, which was actually a cover story to avoid revealing the true designation. In this case the D suffix stood for *diploma**tich**eskiy* (diplomatic), not ***dahl**'niy* (long-range) – as distinct from the *second* Tu-114D, an extended-range intercontinentalversion of the real Tu-114 airliner, where the D indeed stood for ***dahl**'niy*.

On 12th August 1955 the Council of Ministers issued directive No.1496-835 ordering the Tupolev OKB to develop the bomber-to-biz-prop conversion, while factory No.18 was ordered to complete two production Tu-95s as VIP transports able to carry 20 passengers in

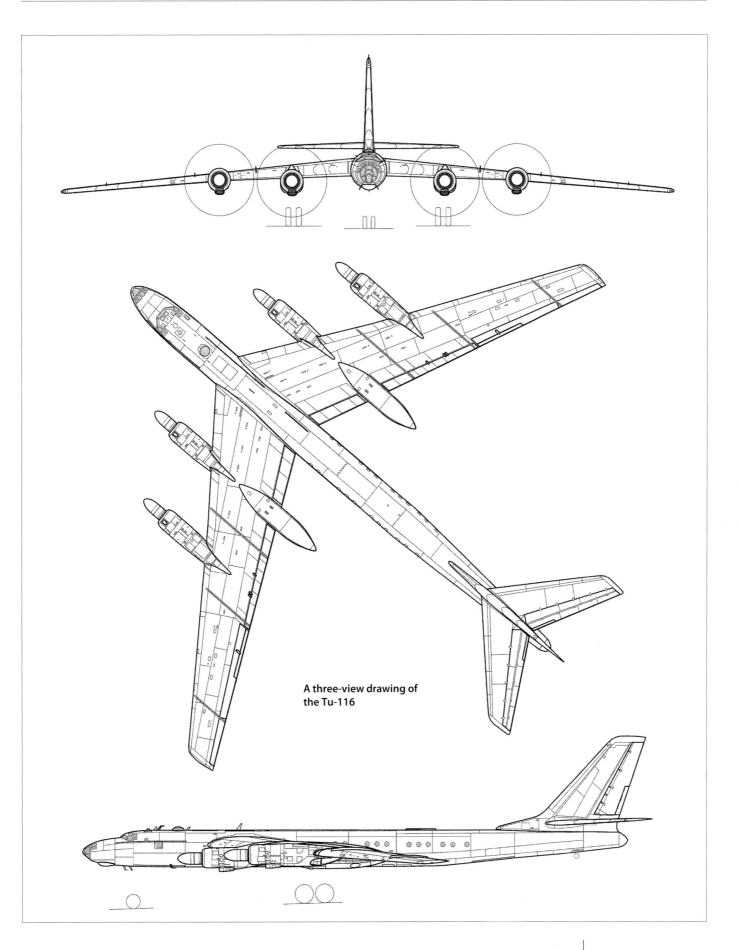

A three-view drawing of
the Tu-116

Top, centre and above:
The first of two Tu-116
VIP transports in its
original military guise as
'7801 Blue, showing the
civil-style 'lightning
bolt' cheatline and 'Tu'
logo on the nose.

Right: Here Tu-116
'7801 Blue' is shown
with the integral
airstairs deployed.

Far left: The navigator-informer's workstation on the port side.

Left: The passage through the service compartment into the No.1 VIP cabin.

Below left: A view forward from the retinue's cabin along the aisle through the service compartment and the No.2 VIP cabin into the No.1 VIP cabin.

Below: The service compartment, looking aft through the retinue's cabin, with the rear pressure dome and entry door at the end. Note the escape hatch in the roof (in case of a belly landing or ditching).

hydraulic leaks and their NK-12 turboprops had a prodigious appetite for oil. On a long-range VIP aircraft, reliability was a prime concern.

The avionics included the Rubidiy-MM radar (used as a navigation/weather radar), a **Gheliy** (Helium) communications radio with an RPS receiver, a 1-RSB-70 command radio with a US-8 receiver, three sets of RSIU-4P radios for added reliability, a duplicated ARK-5 ADF, RV-17 (high-range) and RV-2 (low-range) radio altimeters, and an SP-50 Materik ILS.

151

Left and above left: The No.1 VIP cabin with a curved sofa at the front (along the forward pressure dome) and a second sofa plus club-two seating. Note the telephone on the table.

Above, below and below left: The No.2 VIP cabin, looking aft. Note the radio near the doorway – the passengers have to listen to the news en route! The VIP cabins had carpeted floors.

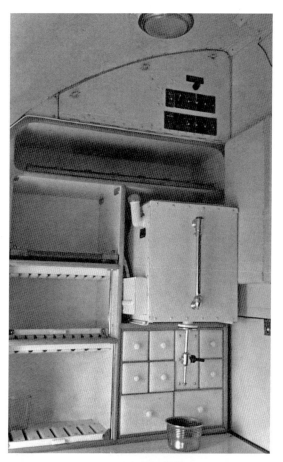

Left and far left: The galley on the starboard side, looking aft. These views show the storage spaces and the water heater above the table.

Far left: The lavatory located ahead of the galley. The wash basin is seen here…

Left: …and the toilet bowl.

Right: The starboard side seats, table and phone for the 'main passengers' in the forward cabin.

Far right: Club-two seating to port in the centre cabin, which boasted a larger table.

Right: The rearmost cabin had two facing banks of three seats along the walls for the retinue or bodyguards.

Far right: The inward-opening pressure door in the rear bulkhead. The entry vestibule and the carry-on baggage stowage area aft of the airstairs were unpressurised.

The front pressure cabin was identical to the Tu-95's, accommodating the captain, co-pilot, navigator, flight engineer, Nav/Op (working the weather radar) and radio operator. A seat was provided for a back-up navigator in case of flights along international airways.

During the Great Patriotic War, Soviet bombers were occasionally used for urgent VIP missions, carrying Soviet statesmen in very Spartan conditions (such as People's Commissar of Foreign Affairs Vyacheslav M. Molotov's flight to the USA in a Petlyakov Pe-8 in May 1942 to sign the Lend-Lease Agreement). The Tu-116 was very different – it offered all the requisite creature comforts. The cabin had 12 circular windows of 40 cm (1 ft 3¾ in) diameter on each side (6+3+2+1); these were stock Tu-104 units. Baggage shelves were installed in the windowless section aft of the entry hatch. The interior was provided with wall trim, carpets and

Close-up of the integral airstairs providing access to the passenger cabin; note the hydraulic actuating ram.

The second Tu-116 in its original guise as '7802 Blue'.

Another aspect of the same aircraft showing the tactical code.

The GK NII VVS flight crew that flew the Tu-116 during state acceptance trials.
Top: co-pilot Viktor S. Kipelkin

Top right: captain V. K. Bobrikov prepares to grab the throttles.

Above: Navigator Nikolay S. Zatsepa working with navigation charts.

Above right: Navigator Vladimir S. Pasportnikov uses the celestial compass.

Below: The first Tu-116 in flight, now sporting the civil registration CCCP-76462 and a Soviet flag instead of the red star.

elegant lighting. The pressurised cabin was divided by partitions into four compartments. The rearmost one had a pair of four-seat sofas along the walls for the retinue. Next came the service compartment with the galley and toilet to starboard; opposite the galley were two tandem seats for the flight attendant and a reserve navigator, while across from the toilet was a curtained-off cubicle for the 'informer navigator'. An emergency exit was provided in the roof of this compartment. Next came the No.2 VIP cabin with a three-seat couch to starboard (which could be folded out as a bed) and club-two seating with a table to port. Finally, at the front end was the No.1 VIP cabin seating six to eight, with a couch to port, club-two seating to starboard and a curved sofa for three at the front. The cabin was equipped with a Mir (the word can be translated from Russian as either 'world' or 'peace') radio and a pneumatic tube transport system allowing the passengers to communicate with the crew without yelling. Safety was also given due consideration – two LAS-5 rescue dinghies and two SP-012 inflatable life rafts (*spasahtel'nyy plot*) were provided for overwater flights.

The first Tu-116 (c/n 6800402) was rebuilt from an unfinished Tu-95 *sans suffixe*, originally wearing Air

Left and below left:
Tu-116 '7802 Blue' a few
seconds after becoming
airborne.

Below: CCCP-76462
begins the landing gear
retraction sequence on
take-off.

The crew of the Tu-116 lined up after a long-distance record-breaking flight. Actually there are three crews who took turns flying the aircraft. Note the flight crew access ladder and the extended passenger airstairs.

Force markings and the non-standard four-digit serial '7801 Blue'. It first flew on 23rd April 1957, undergoing manufacturer's flight tests until 4th October 1957. The second aircraft, originally '7802 Blue', was rebuilt from a Tu-95M (c/n 7800409); it was released by the factory on 3rd June 1957 and was submitted for monitored state trials in March 1958. The trials at GK NII VVS were carried out by test pilots V. K. Bobrikov and Viktor S. Kipelkin, test navigators Nikolay S. Zatsepa and Vladimir S.

Pasportnikov and radio operator V. S. Popov. Test pilot Ivan K. Vedernikov also took part in the trials which included a non-stop flight from Chkalovskaya to Irkutsk and back covering an overall distance of 8,600 km (5,340 miles). Upon landing the Tu-116 had enough fuel left for another 1,500-2,000 km (931-1,242 miles). The average speed was 800 km/h (496 mph).

On 28th June – 1st July 1958 Tu-116 '7802 Blue' made an ultra-long-range flight covering a distance of

OKB-156 General Designer Andrey N. Tupolev (centre) and Minister of Aircraft Industry Pyotr V. Dement'yev congratulate the crew on the success of the long-distance mission.

One of the Tu-116s after being transferred to the Air Force. Note the 'Excellent aircraft' maintenance award badge applied to the nose.

34,000 km (21,130 miles) with three intermediate stops, following a route close to the borders of the Soviet Union. The first leg of the journey took the aircraft from Moscow via Amderma, Tiksi and Cape Taigonos in the High North to Vladivostok in the Far East; the aircraft was crewed by V. K. Bobrikov, Viktor S. Kipelkin, Nikolay S. Zatsepa, Vladimir S. Pasportnikov and V. S. Popov. During the second leg the Tu-116 flew from Vladivostok to Tashkent in the south via Petropavlovsk-Kamchatskiy; the crew comprised N. G. Zhukovskiy, A. V. Smirnov, N. T. Teplov, I. V. Agayev and A. I. Moiseyev. The third leg was from Tashkent to Minsk in the west via Stalinabad, Frunze, Alma-Ata, Omsk, Dixon Island, Moscow, Leningrad, Tallinn, Riga and Vilnius. The crew comprised Ye. F. Danilov, A. V. Sorokin, N. S. Dyomkin, R. Kh. Abdeyev, Ye. A. Rozhin, I. V. Bystrov

An Air Force crew poses with the Tu-116 in the 1970s.

and F. N. Romanov. The final leg was from Minsk via Kiev, Kishinyov, Kerch, Tbilisi, Yerevan, Baku, Ashkhabad, Rostov and Voronezh back to Moscow.

Other ultra-long-range flights followed. At the same time test pilot Nikolay N. Kharitonov made a non-stop flight in the first Tu-116 from Moscow to Lake Baikal and back at an average speed of 740 km/h (459 mph). These flights and the results of the state trials confirmed the Tu-116's high degree of reliability with a performance matching that of the Tu-95.

A while later the Tu-116s were placed on the civil register. According to the Soviet system of 1958 which is still used today, the first two digits of the five-digit civil registration are a sort of code helping air traffic controllers to identify the type by its reggie and avoid placing unreasonable demands on the crew. The Tu-114s were registered in the 764xx block; in line with the Tu-114D cover story the first and second Tu-116s were registered as CCCP-76462 and CCCP-76463 respectively. Moreover, they even gained a colour scheme similar to that of the Tu-114 prototype, CCCP-Л5611 (i.e., SSSR-L5611) – but not of the production Tu-114s. In September 1958 the Tu-116 made its first flight abroad when one of the aircraft paid a visit to Prague-Ruzyne airport.

Nonetheless, despite favourable reports, the Tu-116 was not accepted as a VIP transport by the Soviet government flight due to the lack of automatic propeller feathering – a failing it shared with the Tu-95 and Tu-95M powered by NK-12 and NK-12M engines. With the advent of the NK-12MV, this problem was solved, but too late. By that time the Tu-114 offering a greater level of comfort had become available and was more suitable as a government VIP transport.

CCCP-76462 is seen immediately after retracting the landing gear on take-off.

Here the same Tu-116 is shown after being repainted in Aeroflot's 1973-style fleetwide standard livery. Note the registration repeated on the nose gear doors, Tu-114 style.

Tu-116 CCCP-76462 is on display in the Civil Air Fleet Museum in Ul'yanovsk (Barata-yevka airfield).

Another view of the Tu-116 in the museum in company with a Tu-144, a Tu-134AK, an IL-14 and a Yak-40, among other things.

The two Tu-116 were delivered to Long-Range Aviation regiments equipped with the Tu-95, transporting personnel during redeployments to forward operating locations. CCCP-76462, which was presently repainted in Aeroflot's 1973-style fleetwide standard livery, served with the 409th TBAP based at Uzin in the Ukraine until retired. Later it was donated to the Civil Air Fleet Museum at Ul'yanovsk, where it remains to this day as a unique exhibit. CCCP-76463 served with the 1023rd TBAP at Chagan AB in Kazakhstan until the early 1990s; it was then withdrawn from use and finally scrapped.

Tu-95 AWACS aircraft (Tu-126 'Ozero', project)

As part of the effort to neutralise the threat posed by US strategic bombers capable of striking across the North Pole, in 1958 the Tupolev OKB was tasked with developing an airborne early warning and control system (AWACS) aircraft for the Air Defence (PVO –

Specifications of the Tu-116	
Length overall	46.17 m (151 ft 5²³⁄₃₂ in)
Wing span	50.04 m (164 ft 2⁵⁄₆₄ in)
Horizontal tail span	14.78 m (48 ft 5⁵⁄₆₄ in)
Height on ground	12.5 m (41 ft 0⅛ in)
Wing area	283.7 m² (3,053.72 sq ft)
Vertical tail area	38.53 m² (414.73 sq ft)
Horizontal tail area	54.49 m² (586.53 sq ft)
Powerplant	4 x TV-12
Take-off weight:	
normal	124,000 kg (273,370 lb)
maximum	143,000 kg (315,260 lb)
Maximum speed at 6,300 m (20,670 ft)	870 km/h (540 mph)
Service ceiling	10,000-12,000 m (32,810-39,370 ft)
Effective range	8,000 km (4,960 miles)
Crew	7

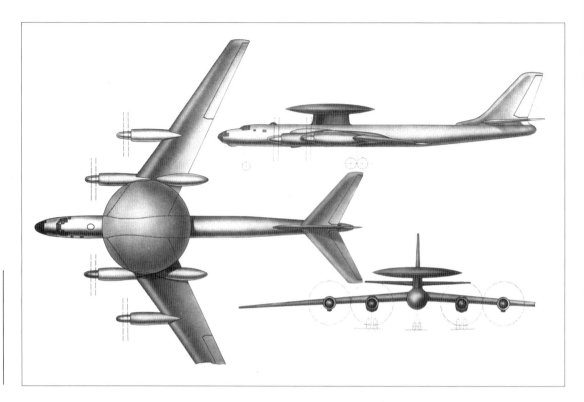

A provisional three-view drawing of the Tu-126 as originally conceived – a derivative of the Tu-95's airframe with an Ozero radar in a rotodome placed well forward. The *real* Tu-126 ended up being rather different!

Protivovoz**doosh**naya obo**ro**na). Designated Tu-126, this aircraft was to work in conjunction with the Tupolev Tu-128 *Fiddler* twin-turbojet long-range interceptor as part of the national air defence system. Both aircraft were developed in accordance with Council of Ministers directive No.608-293 of 4th July 1958 and GKAT order No.211 of 17th July. These documents stipulated the following performance for the AWACS aircraft: an endurance of 10-12 hours, a service ceiling of 8,000-12,000 m (26,250-39,370 ft) and a data transmission range of 2,000 km (1,242 miles). The search radar was to be capable of detecting a fighter-sized target (such as the Mikoyan/Gurevich MiG-17 *Fresco*) at 100 km (62.1 miles), a tactical bomber-sized target (such as the Ilyushin IL-28 *Beagle*) at 200 km (124 miles) and a heavy bomber-sized target (such as the Myasishchev 3M *Bison-B*) at 300 km (186 miles).

The task of developing the mission avionics suite was assigned to GKRE's NII-17, GKAT's OKB-373, NII-25 and GKRE's NII-101. (The Moscow-based NII-17, an establishment responsible for radar development, is now the Instrument Engineering Research Institute named after Viktor V. Tikhomirov (NIIP – N**a**oo**ch**no-is**sled**ovatel'skiy insti**toot** pri**bor**ostro**yen**iya). OKB-373 in Omsk is now the Central Design Bureau of Automatic Equipment (TsKBA – Tsen**trahl**'noye kon**strook**torskoye byu**ro** avto**mah**tiki). The Moscow-based NII-101 responsible for automatic control systems for the PVO is now the Automatic Equipment Research Institute named after Academician Vladimir S. Semenikhin (NIIAA – N**a**oo**ch**no-is**sled**ovatel'skiy insti**toot** avtoma**tich**eskoy appara**too**ry).) The Tupolev OKB, as the airframer and systems integrator, had overall responsibility for the project. The Air Force C-in-C Air Marshal Konstantin A. Vershinin endorsed the SOR for the Tu-126 AWACS on 9th April 1958; the PVO C-in-C Marshal Sergey S. Biryuzov did the same on 2nd September 1958.

Initially the Tu-95 or Tu-96 bomber – or possibly the Tu-116 – was contemplated as the basis for the Tu-126. The project, which was codenamed **Ozero** (lake), involved fitting the bomber with a powerful 360° search radar of the same name whose antenna was to be housed in a revolving lentil-shaped fairing called a rotodome above the fuselage. The rotodome was exceedingly large (its edges were in line with the inboard engines' propeller axes) and was carried on a singe wide-chord centreline pylon above the wing centre section; it was mostly of metal construction, with only a small dielectric section. All armament was deleted, the bomb bay was faired over to increase structural stiffness, and the rear pressure cabin was replaced by a Tu-116 style tailcone.

However, as things turned out it was deemed more expedient to design the first Soviet AWACS as a derivative of the Tu-114 whose capacious fuselage offered more room for the mission avionics and the mission crew. In its ultimate form the Tu-126 (NATO reporting name *Moss*) was based on the Tu-114's airframe and equipped with a *Liana* (Creeper; NATO *Flat Jack*) radar developed by NII-17 in a similar rotodome mounted well aft (hence it is sometimes called Tu-126 'Liana'). However, once again the real Tu-126 lies outside the scope of this book.

CHAPTER FOUR

The naval versions

Tu-95RTs maritime reconnaissance/OTH targeting aircraft (*izdeliye* VTs)

On 17th August 1956 the Council of Ministers issued directive No.1149-592 requiring MAP's OKB-52 based in the town of Reutov just east of Moscow and headed by Vladimir N. Chelomey, one of the Soviet Union's most prominent rocket engineers, to develop a supersonic sea-launched anti-shipping cruise missile for the Soviet Navy. Actually the directive concerned two missiles but these were two versions of the same design; the P-6 (aka 4K88, NATO reporting name SS-N-3C *Shaddock*) was optimised for missile-carrying submarines, while the P-35 (aka 4K44, SS-N-3A *Shaddock*) was to be launched by surface ships. Both models were derivatives of the earlier P-5 missile (aka 4K34, again codenamed SS-N-3C) from which they differed in having a radar seeker head for terminal guidance. The turbojet-powered

Mach 1.3 missile was tube-launched (which, in the case of the P-6, required the submarine to surface) and carried a conventional shaped-charge armour-piercing warhead or a 20-kiloton nuclear warhead.

The first launch of a P-35 took place on 21st October 1959; the P-6 followed suit two months later, on 23rd December 1959. Eventually the P-35 became the principal armament of the Soviet Navy's Type 58 (*Groznyy* class; NATO reporting name *Kynda* class) missile cruisers and Type 1134 (*Admiral Zozoolya* class; NATO *Kresta I* class) missile cruisers, while the P-6 was deployed on Type 651 (NATO *Juliett* class) diesel-electric missile submarines and Type 675 (NATO *Echo II* class) nuclear-powered missile submarines.

The P-6 and P-35 were controlled by an autopilot during the initial high-altitude stage of the trajectory, flying at 7,000 m (22,965 ft), with radio command course correction from a missile guidance operator

A fine study of 392nd ODRAP Tu-95RTs '17 Black' seen in 1983. The radomes were green on some aircraft and grey on others.

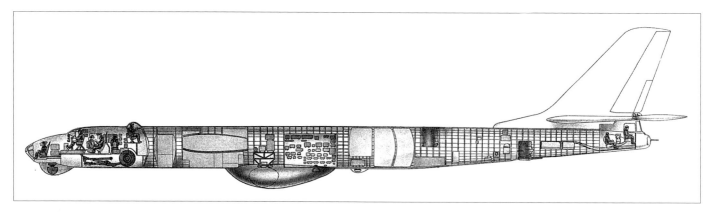

aboard the ship (who followed the missile's course on his radarscope) if the missile strayed from the desired track. About 40 km (25 miles) from the target the radar seeker head came into play, scanning the sea below and transmitting the picture via data link to the guidance operator's workstation. The guidance operator then selected a target among those 'seen' by the missile and transmitted a lock-on command, whereupon the missile singled out this target and switched to homing mode, descending to 100 m (330 ft).

This is where a complication arose. The P-6 and P-35 had a maximum launch range of about 400 km (248 miles); this was beyond the capabilities of the ships' guidance systems which could only 'see' as far as the radar horizon (this was especially the case with the submarines' missile guidance system codenamed *Argument*). The solution was obvious – an aircraft or helicopter performing the mid-course guidance or over-the-horizon (OTH) targeting mission. The Tu-16 was initially considered for this role but it was soon apparent that the Tu-95 was a better choice thanks to

its longer range and endurance (especially with IFR), which would also allow it to perform long-range maritime reconnaissance.

Hence on 21st July 1959 the Council of Ministers issued directive No.835-375 calling for the development of an OTH targeting/reconnaissance version of the *Bear*. Designated Tu-95RTs (*razvedchik-tsele'ookazahtel'* – reconnaissance/target designator [aircraft]), this was to become a key component of the world's first long-range maritime reconnaissance/strike system. The aircraft was to work not only with the cruisers armed with P-35 missiles and the submarines armed with P-6 missiles but also, in case of need, with *Redoot* (Redoubt, or Fort) mobile coastal defence missile systems based on the P-35B (*beregovoy* – shore-based) version of the missile.

A specialised targeting/reconnaissance system designated *Oospekh-U* (Success-U) with airborne and shipboard components was developed for the Tu-95RTs by the Kiev-based GSKB-483 under Chief Designer Ivan V. Kudryavtsev – the man who had been responsible for the development of the PRS-1 gun ranging radar in Omsk. The system was built around a powerful 360° search radar designated Oospekh-U1A, which could detect a destroyer-sized ship from at least 250 km (155 miles) range when flying at 10,000-12,000 m (32,810-39,370 ft). In targeting mode the radar was controlled by the radar operators only; in navigation/weather mode it could be controlled by the navigator as well. The radar featured built-in test equipment (BITE). The Oospekh-U system also included a data link system relaying guidance signals from the submarine or cruiser to the missile, as well as *Akoola-S* (Shark) HF burst communication equipment comprising a *Kristall* (Crystal) transmitter, a Rool'-M (Steering wheel) receiver and an *Arfa* (Harp) antenna/feeder system ensuring secure information exchange with the submarine or cruiser. The system made it possible to determine the target co-ordinates relative to the shipboard or shore-based command post and the parameters of the target's motion, which were then fed to the missile launch controls. Thus, the Soviet designers achieved a 'world's first' by creating a system ensuring real-time target data exchange between a missile and a submarine or surface

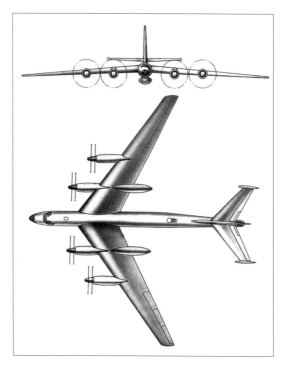

ship, enabling ships' crews to assess the tactical situation more accurately and choose the best targets for the missile strike.

On receiving launch orders the submarine would rise to periscope depth in order to establish radio contact with the Tu-95RTs. The radar data received from the aircraft was displayed on the guidance officer's screen, and the sub's commander would analyse the situation and pick a target. The target's bearing and range would then be determined and entered into the sub's missile control computer. The latter would analyse target lock-on and 'kill' probability, whereupon the commander would make the ultimate decision. If the decision was yes, the submarine would surface and the missile launch tubes would be tilted into position to fire. The P-6 missiles could be launched singly or up to four at a time (the stern tubes fired first so that the missiles launched from the bow tubes would not ingest the smoke from the previously departing missiles' solid-fuel rocket boosters, which might cause the turbojet sustainer to flame out). Each missile was guided as described above; if a group of enemy ships was attacked in a missile salvo, each ship was targeted by a separate guidance operator.

The Oospekh-U1A radar had sufficient detection range in targeting mode to allow the P-6/P-35 missile to be launched from maximum range. This, coupled with the Bear's long range, allowed the Tu-95RTs to designate targets up to 7,000 km (4,350 miles) away. The aircraft's mission capabilities included radar observation, electronic surveillance, and photo recon-

naissance of surface targets. It would provide this information to friendly surface vessels and submarines; besides, it could provide weather data to surface combatants.

In accordance with the Council of Ministers directive the Tupolev OKB was given two years to develop the Tu-95RTs; this would include integration of the radar and associated target designation systems. Hence completion of the prototype was originally scheduled for mid-1961. However, in March 1960 MAP issued resolution No. KA 20/948 shifting the completion deadline to the first quarter of the year and requiring plant No.18 to equip a production Tu-95M bomber with the envisaged mission avionics. Hence, to save time, an operational Tu-95M ('60 Red', c/n 8800510) was transferred to the OKB from the 409th TBAP at Uzin for conversion instead of building the Tu-95RTs prototype from scratch.

The Tu-95RTs differed from the *Bear-A* as follows:
• The bomb bay was transformed into an avionics bay housing the airborne components of the Oospekh-U system; its doors were faired over and the revolving antenna of the Oospekh-U1A radar was installed in their place. This antenna was enclosed by a huge teardrop radome, hence the radar was aptly codenamed *Big Bulge* by NATO.

• The articulated guidance antenna of the Oospekh-U system transmitting the amplified guidance signals to the missile was installed in a deep chin fairing replacing the Rubidiy-MM radar of the bomber version. Oddly, some western publications referred to this fairing as 'a

This diagram from the ADP documents shows the purposes, basic performance and typical mission profile of the Tu-95RTs.

Short Horn radar' – even though its shape was obviously different from that of the Rubidiy-MM or the Rubin-1. Other western publications used the 'more appropriate' description *Mushroom*, which in fact was equally incongruous because NATO codenames for Soviet radars invariably consisted of two words, not one. If one assumes this 'mushroom' to be a reference to *Toad Stool*, this codename was applied to the RBP-2 and ROZ-1 weather/navigation radars, both of which had a shallower radome. Anyway, the antenna under the Tu-95RTs's nose was not a radar at all.

• The aerials of the Arfa antenna/feeder system were mounted in distinctive cigar-shaped fairings at the tips of the horizontal tail.

• The flare bomb cassette in the rear fuselage used for night bombing sorties was deleted and replaced by an SRS-4 *Kvadraht-2* (Square, in the geometrical meaning) detailed SIGINT set whose antennas were enclosed by a small teardrop fairing mounted in place of the flare bomb bay doors. This system turned out to be inefficient and was later removed. The ELINT suite also

included an SRS-5 Vishnya COMINT set and an SRS-4A Romb-4 general-purpose SIGINT set (with the same elongated dielectric fairings on the rear fuselage sides as on the Tu-95MR and Tu-95KM) and a US-8 receiver. For PHOTINT duties the Tu-95RTs was equipped with an AFA-42/100 oblique camera in the rear fuselage.

The avionics of the Tu-95RTs also included an AP-15R autopilot, a DISS-1 Doppler speed/drift sensor system, an RSBN-2 SHORAN, a KS-6D AHRS, a TsSV-1MK airspeed/altitude reference unit (*tsentrahl' skorosti i vysoty*), a BTs-63 celestial compass and a Put'-1B (Way) navigation system. A TsNVU-I central navigation computer (*tsentrahl'noye navigatsionno-vychislitel'-noye oostroystvo*; the 'I' is an upper-case letter, not a Roman numeral) was installed. Working with the AHRS, the celestial compass and the Put'-1B system, it enabled navigation along a pre-programmed route with waypoints. Depending on the mode (primary or auxiliary), it determined the aircraft's grid co-ordinates with an error margin of 2.3-3.5% or 2.7-5.35% of the distance travelled and computed the polar co-ordinates. Depending on the distance to the next waypoint (10-200 km/6.2-124 miles or 200-1,200 km/124-745 miles), these were computed with an error margin of 2.7 km (1.68 miles) or 23 km (14.29 miles) respectively, and the heading changes were computed with a 2° error margin. Together with the radar the TsNVU-I deter-mined the co-ordinates of large surface targets, and radar data were used for making navigational corrections, using landmarks with known co-ordinates.

The Tu-95RTs had a crew of 11. Apart from the captain, co-pilot, navigator, flight engineer, radio operator/dorsal gunner, ventral gunner (who also performed certain ELINT functions) and tail gunner, the crew included main and back-up radar operators, the chief ELINT equipment operator and the operator of the Akula-S communications system.

In the autumn of 1962 the Tu-95RTs prototype was cleared for testing, with V. I. Bogdanov as engineer in charge. In its maiden flight the aircraft was captained by Tupolev OKB chief test pilot Ivan K. Vedernikov; the crew also included co-pilot Boris M. Timoshok, navigator Andrey M. Silenko, radio operator I. Mayorov, radar operator M. Vyshinskiy, ELINT equipment operator Shcherbakov and Akula-S communications system operator L. Serdyukov. Apparently there was no manufacturer's flight test programme as such; Stage A of the joint state acceptance trials programme commenced on 21st September 1962 and was completed on 4th June 1963, the aircraft logging a total of 107 hours 37 minutes in 23 flights. The test flights were made from the factory airfield (Kuibyshev-Bezymyanka), the LII airfield in Zhukovskiy and the DA bases in Belaya Tserkov' (Gayok AB) and Uzin (Chepelevka AB) in the Ukraine. At this stage the aircraft's empty weight was recorded as 82,438 kg

The Tu-95RTs prototype ('60 Red') at GK NII VVS during a military hardware display for the top government officials. The style of the c/n (8800510) and the absence of the IFR probe reveal the aircraft's origins as a converted Tu-95M bomber.

The Tu-95RTs prototype   8800510   60

(181,744 lb), with the CG at 19.9% MAC. During the trials the Tu-95RTs prototype attained a maximum speed of Mach 0.872 at 10,000-10,500 m (32,810-34,450 ft) and 674 km/h (418 mph) IAS at 5,000 m (16,400 ft); no vibration was apparent at these speeds and the aircraft handled normally.

In the course of Stage A the Oospekh-U suite worked up a total of 316 hours' operating time (230 hours on the ground and 86 hours in flight). When the mission avionics were being tested, the aircraft worked with a ground-based mobile receiver station, as well as with the North Fleet's Type 57*bis* (*Gnevnyy* class; NATO *Krupny* class) destroyer SNS *Derzkiy* (Cheeky; SNS = Soviet Navy ship) sailing in the Barents Sea. Soviet Navy Type 56 (*Spokoynyy* class; NATO *Kotlin* class) destroyers acted as practice targets; within a single 360° sweep of

Two production examples of the Tu-95RTs. The production model featured IFR capability and did not wear the c/n visibly.

Two views of a Tu-95RTs coded '18' from an AVMF test report. Note the 'Excellent aircraft' badge.

The accommodation of the crew. 1. Captain; 2. Co-pilot; 3. Navigator; 4. Jump seat; 5. Radar operator; 6. Flight engineer; 7. ELINT officer; 8. Gunner/radio operator; 9. Special comms operator; 10. Ventral gunner; 11. Tail gunner.

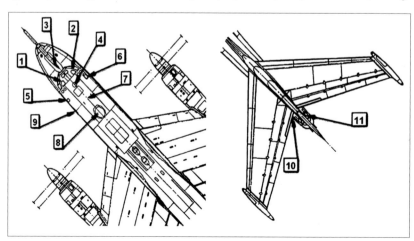

bodies of water (for example, the Kremenchug Reservoir or Lake El'ton in the Volgograd Region of Russia) were detected at 400-420 km (248-261 miles) range. At an altitude of 10,000-11,000 m (32,810-36,090 ft), minimum reliable communications range was 18-29 km (11.18-18 miles) and maximum reliable communications range was again 400-420 km.

Since the Tu-95RTs was equipped with a powerful radar and other sources of high-frequency radiation, the designers were concerned about its harmful effect on the crew. Hence HF radiation levels were measured at the crew's workstations; the strongest radiation of 3-6 mW/cm^2 was recorded at the navigator's station in the glazed nose, but even that was below the safe limit of 10 mW/cm^2.

The Stage A trials report, which was signed by OKB-156 General Designer Andrey N. Tupolev on 22nd July 1963, by GSKB-483 Chief Designer Ivan V. Kudryavtsev on 24th July and by Air Force representative Col. Sergey D. Agavel'yan on 30th July, said that *'the pitch and roll stability and control characteristics of the Tu-95RTs are almost identical to those of the Tu-95MV'* (sic – Auth.) and that *'the avionics suite of the Oospekh-U system enables detection of surface targets and transmission of target information to shore-based and shipboard receivers; the target co-ordinate determination accuracy […] meets the specifications'*. The pilots' appraisal of the aircraft was generally positive.

However, Stage A revealed a number of short-comings; the report contained four pages of comments on these. The biggest problem was poor electro-magnetic compatibility of the system's components (noise signals also travelled in the aircraft's electrical system when some components were switched on). A few other problems may be mentioned. In particular, the SKN-3 ventilated waterproof flight suits designed to protect the crew from hypothermia in the event of ditching or bailing out over water turned out to be unsatisfactory, being bulky and hampering the crewmen's movements, and the MSK-3 suits (*morskoy spasahtel'nyy kostyum* – maritime rescue suit), which were later used by Tu-95RTs crews in service, were not yet available. If the mission avionics were operated on the ground for more than an hour, the temperature in the avionics bay exceeded the ambient air temperature by 10-15°C (18-27°F); in hot weather with ambient temperatures of 30-35°C (86-95°F) this could cause damage to the avionics unless a mobile air handling unit was connected to cool them. This problem did not appear in flight even if the on-board cooling system was switched off.

The Oospekh-U1A radar also drew a lot of criticism. Firstly, the legibility of the radar imagery (especially to certain scales) left something to be desired; moreover, the radar imagery became distorted when the aircraft entered a sustained turn with 10-15° bank because the

the radar scanner, maximum detection range with 60% probability was 220 km (136 miles), increasing to 300-320 km (186-198 miles) with less probability. It should be noted that the target ships were setting up active ECM, trying to jam the aircraft's radar.

The Oospekh-U1A radar was also tested against highly reflective ground targets (such as the dam of the Kremenchug Hydroelectric Power Station on the Dnepr River and a railway bridge across the Dnepr near Cherkassy, both in the Ukraine), determining their co-ordinates with a range error of not more than 1.7 km (1.06 miles). Targets such as large cities (Moscow, Kiev, Khar'kov, Dnepropetrovsk, Dneprodzerzhinsk) or large

Left and below left:
Tu-95RTs '20 Black', a
392nd ODRAP aircraft, in
the snow at Kipelovo AB.

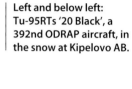

Three-quarters rear view
of a Tu-95RTs, showing
the angular radome of
the PRS-4 gun ranging
radar.

TsGV-10 vertical gyro (*tsentrahl'naya gheerovertikahl'*) toppled, and the gyro required five to seven minutes to restore its functionality after returning to straight and level flight. Secondly, the cathode-ray tube (CRT) of the radarscope (IKO, *indikahtor kroogovoy obstanovki* – '360° situation indicator') had an excessively short retention (i.e., viewing) time of only three to five seconds; as a result, the target blips disappeared from the radarscope before the radar antenna had time to do a full 360° scan, which required ten seconds in targeting mode and six seconds in navigation mode. The IKO featured a cursor which could be superimposed on a target of interest (or a landmark) by means of a joystick, but doing this was difficult, especially at short range (up to 40 km/24.8 miles), because the cursor moved too fast. Thirdly, at up to 140 km (87 miles) range the radar echo

'38 Black', a standard Tu-95RTs, lines up for take-off at Kipelovo.

was weakened by background clutter. Fourth, the navigator found the radar inconvenient to use because it required frequent tuning of the radarscope and switching between modes, which was tiresome. Finally, the radome incurred sizeable losses of the radar signal power, reducing target detection range; the design had to be revised before the Tu-95RTs entered production.

Frequent failures of the DISS-1 system occurred in the course of the trials. The available ground test equipment turned out to be inadequate for pre-flight checks of this system's serviceability. The Akoola-S communications system enabled two-way communication with SNS *Derzkiy* and shore command posts at up to 2,000 km (1,242 miles) range but, again, was not

Tu-95RTs '17 Black' (seen here on test at GANITs VMF) was modified with an SPS-151 jammer in an UKhO fairing replacing the tail turret.

Right and far right: Close-ups of the ogival UKhO fairing housing the SPS-151 jammer. The tailcone carries antenna fairings and is vertically split for maintenance access to the equipment inside.

A production Tu-95RTs in a winter setting. The No.3 propeller spinner on this particular aircraft is darker than the others.

Three-quarters front view of the same aircraft ('25 Black'). The joint line of the Oospekh-U1A radar's radome is at maximum width, the narrow top section of the fairing being made of metal.

Tu-95RTs '38' at the AVMF test centre (GANITs VMF) at Kirovskoye AB near Feodosiya. Note the light-coloured chin radome of the command link antenna.

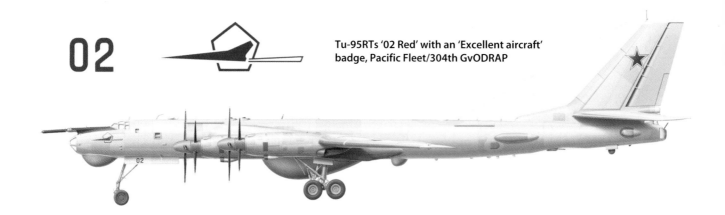

Tu-95RTs '02 Red' with an 'Excellent aircraft'
badge, Pacific Fleet/304th GvODRAP

Right and above right:
Soviet colour photos of
the Tu-95RTs are rare.
These views of '39
Black', a North Fleet
machine, were taken by
the Tupolev OKB for a
data file.

Below right: A side view
of the same aircraft,
showing the differently
coloured radomes and
the tandem BTs-63 star
trackers above the wing
centre section.

reliable enough. Criticism was also directed at the ergonomics of the crew's workstations (instruments party obscured by the controls, insufficient lighting etc.). Finally, the report pointed out that a lot of preparatory work as regards both crew and hardware was required for long missions, especially at night; errors in programming the TsNVU-I computer caused the aircraft to stray off course.

These problems were not easily resolved, necessitating additional test flights and causing delays, and Stage B of the state acceptance trials was not initiated until May 1964. It was completed in December 1964, involving 22 flights with a total time of 212 hours 57 minutes. Problems continued to surface with the complex electrical systems, but these were cured by the time the trials programme had been completed. During Stage B, the aircraft flew out to its maximum range and tracked real targets while transmitting data

to Soviet Navy ships. The trials showed that the system worked as required over long ranges and permitted accurate targeting of surface ships.

As early as 1963, before Stage B had even begun, the Kuibyshev aircraft factory launched production of the Tu-95RTs under the in-house product code '*izdeliye* VTs'. The production run amounted to 52 examples (three aircraft in 1963, four in 1964, ten aircraft a year in 1965-68 and the final five aircraft in 1969). The new-build machines had a separate construction number system quite different from that of the bombers; for example, a North Fleet Tu-95RTs coded '26 Black' was c/n 66MRTs310 – i.e., year of manufacture 1966 (again, the year when the aircraft was laid down, not when it was completed!), 'MRTs' is a version designator, Batch 3, 10th aircraft in the batch. Batch 0 had three aircraft, Batch 1 had seven (so that the two batches would add up to ten!); Batches 2 through 5 consisted of ten aircraft each, and the final Batch 6 had only two aircraft.

The production machines differed from the prototype in having IFR capability as standard, being equipped with the same refuelling probe as the Tu-95MR and the Tu-95KD/Tu-95KM. Apparently there were other changes to the targeting/reconnaissance system as a whole.

In August 1964 (as per Tupolev OKB sources; Soviet Navy sources state 1963!) the Tu-95RTs attained IOC with the Soviet Naval Aviation. On 30th May 1966 the Council of Ministers issued directive No.411-126 officially including the aircraft into the AVMF inventory. The Tu-95RTs soon became a familiar sight over international waters, receiving the NATO reporting name *Bear-D* and the nickname 'Eastern Express'. The type was used operationally until the late 1980s. Later, it served as a basis for the development of the Tu-142 anti-submarine warfare/maritime patrol aircraft described below.

A single North Fleet Tu-95RTs coded '31 Black' (c/n 67MRTs401) was retrofitted experimentally with an SPS-151 jammer in a UKhO tail fairing replacing the DK-12 tail turret and the PRS-1 gun ranging radar. At

Basic specifications of the Tu-95RTs	
Length overall	46.9 m (153 ft 10²⁹⁄₆₄ in)
Wing span	50.04 m (164 ft 2³⁄₆₄ in)
Height on ground	12.5 m (41 ft 0⅛ in)
Wing area	283.7 m² (3,053.7 sq ft)
Effective range:	
on internal fuel	14,000 km (8,700 miles) *
with one fuel top-up	17,000 km (10,560 miles)
Endurance:	
on internal fuel	21 hours *
with one fuel top-up	25 hours
Maximum speed	885-910 km/h (549-565 mph)
Cruising speed	680-770 km/h (422-478 mph)
Cruise altitude halfway through the mission	10,400 m (34,120 ft)
Detection range for a destroyer-sized surface target	250-300 km (155-186 miles)
Radar imagery transmission range	350-400 km (217-248 miles)
Maximum surface-to-surface missile guidance range	600-700 km (372-435 miles) †
ELINT systems' maximum detection range	500-550 km (310-341 miles)

Notes:
* Some sources state 14,600 km (9,070 miles) and 22 hours
† This figure is purely theoretical because the P-6 and P-35 had a range of only 400 km or so

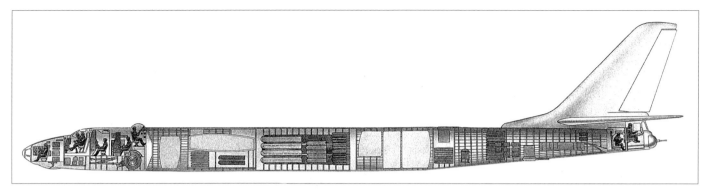

The internal layout of the Tu-95PLO, with sonobuoys and torpedoes but no 360° search radar.

least one *Bear-D* was equipped with RR8311-100 air sampling pods and a small cylindrical radiation sensor pod on top of the starboard wing root for RINT duties.

Tu-95PLO ASW aircraft (project)

In 1960 the US Navy began deploying submarine-launched ballistic missiles (SLBMs) whose capabilities – particularly range – were growing rapidly. The initial Lockheed UGM-27 Polaris A-1 had a range of 2,000-2,600 km (1,242-1,620 miles) but the Polaris A-3 version of 1964 improved this to 4,630 km (2,880 miles). The successor to the Polaris – the Lockheed UGM-73 Poseidon C-3 fielded in 1971 – had marginally shorter range (4,600 km/2,860 miles) but carried a bigger warload and introduced multiple independently targetable re-entry vehicles. In turn, the Poseidon's successor, the Lockheed UGM-96 Trident I (aka Trident C-4) of 1979, had a range of 7,400 km (4,600 miles), which was increased to 12,000 km (7,460 miles) in the Lockheed UGM-113A Trident II (Trident D-5) of 1988.

To neutralise this emerging new threat, the Soviet Navy needed a dedicated long-range anti-submarine

A drawing of the Tu-95PLO from the project documents. The aircraft was to be strictly a weapons platform, the search radar was to be carried by a modified An-22 at that stage.

warfare (ASW) aircraft capable of intercepting and destroying NATO's ballistic missile submarines before they got close enough to the Soviet coasts to launch their SLBMs. The Tupolev OKB was one of several Soviet aircraft design bureaux to take on the task in the early 1960s, initially proposing a straightforward adaptation of the Tu-95M designated Tu-95PLO (*protivolodochnaya oborona* – ASW).

The Tu-95PLO was not conceived as a stand-alone combat aircraft – it was to be part of an integrated airborne ASW system designated Tu-142 (!), a 'hunter-killer' pair. The existing weapons bay aft of the wings (between fuselage frames 28-45) was augmented by a smaller second payload bay closed by clamshell doors below the wing centre section torsion box (frames 19-28) which was reserved for sonobuoys. The aircraft was to have a weapons load of up to 9,000 kg (19,840 lb); several ordnance options were envisaged. In the search configuration the Tu-95PLO was to carry anything between 120 and 552 omnidirectional sonobuoys, depending on their model and size/weight. In the attack configuration the aircraft was armed with a choice of two to six homing anti-submarine torpedoes, or up to ten 384-kg (846-lb) PLAB-500-380 depth charges (*protivolodochnaya aviabomba* – anti-submarine bomb), or a single 5F48 Skal'p (Scalp) nuclear depth charge with a 1-kiloton yield, or four to ten RM-1 rocket-propelled naval mines (*re'aktivno-vsplyvayushchaya meena* – rocket-propelled ascending mine) or UDM versatile bottom mines (*ooniversahl'naya donnaya meena*). The 5F48, the first Soviet weapon in this category, was created by the All-Union Technical Physics Institute (VNIITF – *Vsesoyooznyy naoochno-issledovatel'skiy institoot tekhnicheskoy fiziki*, formerly the aforementioned NII-1011) under Chief Designer Aleksandr D. Zakharenkov. It weighed 1,600 kg (3,530 lb) less parachute retarding system and was to be detonated at a depth of 200 or 400 m (660 or 1,310 ft) by a timer 20.4 or 44 seconds after splashdown. A drawing from the project documents shows the Tu-95 carrying a mix of sonobuoys and torpedoes.

The Tu-95PLO was dimensionally identical to the baseline bomber, with a length of 46.2 m (151 ft 6$^{29}/_{32}$ in), a wing span of 50.04 m (164 ft 2$^{5}/_{64}$ in) and a height on ground of 12.5 m (41 ft 0⅛ in). With a normal take-off weight of 160,000 kg (352,740 lb) the aircraft was to have a range of 12,000 km (7,460 miles) and a take-off run of 1,500 m (4,920 ft) on paved runways or 1,850-2,400 m (6,070-7,870 ft) if operating from unpaved runways with a bearing strength of 6-8 kg/cm² (1.23-1.64 lb/sq in). On-station loiter time with a 9,000-kg ordnance load was to be 3.5-4 hours at a distance of 4,000 km (2,490 miles) from the base or 7-7.5 hours at a distance of 2,000 km (1,242 miles) from the base. In high gross weight configuration the TOW rose to 182,000 kg (401,240 lb) and the range to 15,000 km (9,320 miles); in this case operation was possible from paved runways only, with a take-off run of 1,950-2,100 m (6,400-6,890 ft). On-station loiter time with the same payload was increased to 6.5-7 hours at a distance of 4,000 km from the base or 10-10.5 hours at a distance of 2,000 km from the base. In both cases the maximum speed was 880 km/h (546 mph) and the loitering speed 450 km/h (279 mph).

However, the Tu-95PLO was strictly a 'killer' aircraft lacking such items as a powerful search radar (being equipped with only the standard Rubidiy-MM radar under the nose), a magnetic anomaly detector (MAD) and a thermal imager for detecting a submarine's heat wake. All of these systems were to be carried by a second ('hunter') aircraft based on the An-22 heavy transport, which had a similar powerplant of four NK-12MA turboprops, a capacious cargo hold and a payload of 60,000 kg (132,280 lb). This division of roles was caused by the size and weight of the then-current

Soviet avionics. (The concept was similar to the US Navy's Grumman AF-2 Guardian shipboard ASW aircraft where the radar-equipped but unarmed AF-2W was the 'hunter' and the armed AF-2S was the 'killer'.) Hence the Soviet military lost interest in this particular project, but the idea of an ASW version was developed further to become the Tu-142 described below.

Tu-142 maritime patrol/ASW aircraft ('aircraft 142', *izdeliye* VP/early version)

Later, when the Soviet electronics industry created mission avionics that were sufficiently compact and lightweight to allow a single aircraft to combine the 'hunter' and 'killer' roles in an ASW system, the idea of the 'anti-submarine *Bear*' got second wind. According to the Tupolev OKB's proposal (which the military accepted), the new long-range ASW aircraft was to be based on the Tu-95RTs. On 28th February 1963 the Council of Ministers issued directive No.246-86 requiring the OKB to develop and build such an aircraft; the prototype was to be submitted for trials in early 1966. The appropriate specific operational requirement (SOR) endorsed by the VVS Commander-in-Chief and AVMF Commander were issued to the OKB on 20th April 1963; the ADP was approved on 9th October 1963, and the mock-up review commission convened on 19th November that year.

The changes to the basic Tu-95's design were extensive enough to warrant an entirely new designation, 'aircraft 142' (Tu-142); the in-house

A diagram showing the role, performance, equipment and weapons of the Tu-142 ASW aircraft and illustrating its operational tactics.

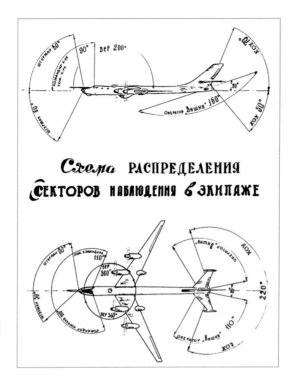

This diagram shows the fields of view afforded to the Tu-142's crew members.

difference was that the IL-38's TsVM-264 computer (*tsifrovaya vychislitel'naya mashina* – digital processor) was replaced by a TsVM-263 unit.

The STS was built around a 360° search radar likewise designated Berkut. As on the Tu-95RTs, the radar antenna was enclosed by a teardrop radome but the latter was somewhat smaller and was located further forward (below the wing centre section rather than aft of it) in order to make room for a capacious weapons bay. A second, smaller bay closed by clamshell doors was located aft of that; it was reserved for sonobuoys. More will be said about the avionics later.

Secondly, the mission equipment added weight and drag, which would cause a deterioration of performance – first and foremost range. Hence, to offset this, by comparison with previous versions of the *Bear* the Tu-142 had a radically reworked wing design. The wing airfoils were altered by curving the leading-edge section downward, wing camber was introduced and wing area was increased 2.5% to 295 m² (3,172 sq ft). Double-slotted flaps were used instead of Fowler flaps. The tail unit was also revised, making allowance for the lower take-off and landing speeds – variable-incidence stabilisers were introduced and increased-area rudder and elevators borrowed from the Tu-114 were used (elevator area was increased 14%). Also, the rudder travel limits were increased from ±15° to ±20°.

Third, now that we mention the wings, the fuel system was reworked. To make room for the mission avionics and the sonobuoy bay, the forward fuselage tank had to be deleted and the capacity of the rear fuselage tanks was reduced. To compensate for this, the Tu-142 featured integral tanks in the wing torsion box instead of the Tu-95's numerous fuel cells (bladder tanks). Only three bladder tanks remained – two in the wing centre section and one in the rear fuselage.

Fourth, the SOR contained a highly unorthodox clause included at the insistence of the AVMF top

product code was *izdeliye* VP, the P standing for *protivolodochnyy* (anti-submarine). Firstly, the aircraft had a Berkut-95 (Golden Eagle) search and targeting suite (STS) developed by the Leningrad-based NII-131, one of the Soviet Union's leading avionics houses. (After Khrushchov's removal from power in 1964 this establishment became VNIIRES (*Vsesoyooznyy naoochno-issledovatel'skiy institoot rahdioelektronnykh sistem* – All-Union Electronic Systems Research Institute) in the MRP system in 1965, subsequently becoming part of LNPO Leninets.) The STS was based on the Berkut suite created for the Ilyushin IL-38 *May* maritime patrol/ASW aircraft; as the '-95' suffix implies, the system incorporated changes to make it suitable for the Tu-95 with its different flight performance. The main

'12', an early-production Tu-142 ASW aircraft (*izdeliye* VP) with 12-wheel main gear bogies and a Gagara thermal imager in a chin fairing, at the GANITs VMF test centre in Feodosiya. Note the 'Excellent aircraft' badge.

command. In keeping with the then-current trend the Tu-142 was to be capable of operating from unpaved runways with a bearing strength of 6 kg/cm² (1.23 lb/sq in) in case the normal bases were destroyed by enemy action. To meet this requirement (absurd, in Andrey N. Tupolev's opinion) the OKB undertook an extensive redesign of the landing gear. Instead of the usual four-wheel bogies the main units featured huge 12-wheel bogies having a complex design with an articulated beam and three rows of four wheels with low-pressure tyres; the latter were smaller than hitherto, measuring 1,100 x 330 mm (43.3 x 13 in). This necessitated a redesign of the main gear fairings which were widened considerably and flattened, featuring a more pointed tip in side elevation; as a result, flap area was reduced. The 12-wheel main gear bogies became a distinctive feature of early-production Tu-142s, earning them the nickname *Sorokonozhka* (Centipede). The nose gear unit was also revised, featuring larger 1,140 x 375 mm (44.88 x 14.76 in) low-pressure tyres, which required the nosewheel well doors to be bulged at the rear.

Fifth, GU-54A irreversible hydraulic actuators were installed at last in the pitch, roll and yaw control channels to reduce the pilot workload. Accordingly the control system included artificial-feel mechanisms and electric trim mechanisms, as well as a KA-142 system (**kompleks avtomah**tov – automatic devices suite) enhancing stability and control in manual mode.

Sixth, the NK-12MV engines were fitted with new AV-60P propellers of increased diameter (5.8 m, 19 ft 0¹⁄₃₂ in) to improve the field performance. As compared to the AV-60K, propeller thrust was increased from 10,150 to 11,150 kgp (from 22,380 to 24,580 lbst).

Now, let's take a closer look at the Berkut-95 search and targeting suite. The Berkut radar had a variable directional pattern that was selected by the operator; it was stabilised in the bank and pitch planes to minimise the effect of the aircraft's manoeuvres on the radar's performance. The radar provided a link between the aircraft and the dropped sonobuoys, determining the latter's position with the help of the buoys' built-in beacons; it was also used for engaging targets with a high radar signature.

The Berkut-95 suite also included the SPIU device (*samolyotnoye preeyomo-indikah*tornoye *oostroystvo* – aircraft-mounted receiver/indicator, or ARI) processing and displaying the incoming signals generated by the sonobuoys, the TsVM-263 computer with an input/output panel, the PGK geographical co-ordinates input/display panel (*panel' gheografich*eskikh ko'or-*dinaht*), the pitot pressure input panel etc.

The TsVM-263 – occasionally called **Pla**mya-263 (Flame) – was a product of the Leningrad-based *Elektro-avtoma*tika (Electric Automatic Devices) OKB. It was a slightly modified version of the IL-38's TsVM-264 computer (the difference was in the software). Working together with the other avionics and equipment, the computer enabled the Tu-142 to manoeuvre as required by the navigational and tactical tasks. It also determined the submarine's location based on data supplied by the sonobuoys, processed the radar data, controlled the radar, operated the weapons bay doors and released the sonobuoys and weapons, keeping track of how many of these were left.

The TsVM-263 was a specialised single-address control computer using a binary code. All of the algorithms used for performing specific tasks were recorded on the computer's hard drive (read-only memory). This made sure that the system operated identically in flight and during ground checks, and also made it possible to restore system operation after glitches that could affect the contents of the buffer (random access memory). The computer's running speed was fairly low at 62,000 short operations per second; the ROM capacity was 8,192 registers.

Interaction between the computer and the radar was provided by an interface module converting the computer's commands into a suitable format for the antenna's actuators. The computer linked the STS with the airspeed, heading and altitude sensors, the vertical gyro, the navigation/flight suite and the armament. The STS fed inputs to the AP-5 autopilot, the Put-4 and Put'-3 navigation systems and the weapons control panels.

In the nose, the large dielectric fairing of the Oospekh system's data link antenna gave way to a shallower teardrop fairing, only the front half of which was dielectric; this housed a *Gagara-1* (Loon) thermal imager meant for detecting the heat wake of a submerged submarine. Additionally, a new Lira (Lyre) antenna/feeder system was used, with aerials in cigar-shaped fairings at the stabiliser tips which were smaller than those of the Arfa system fitted to the Tu-95RTs.

The new avionics were not limited to the Berkut-95 STS. A tailor-made PNS-142 flight/navigation suite (*peelotazhno-navigatsionnaya sistema*) was developed – a sophisticated and accurate system integrated with the targeting hardware in order to enable use of the ASW weapons, of which more will be said later. The aircraft was to be fitted with Kvadrat-2 and Koob-3 ELINT sets. Furthermore, the OKB and the MoD considered the option of equipping the Tu-142 with a system called **Pol**yus (Pole, in the geographical sense) which was to detect SLBM launches, pinpointing the launch co-ordinates, and attack the submarines with cruise missiles at up to 250 km (155 miles) range.

The Berkut-95 STS worked only in conjunction with other avionics supplying data which was fed into the computer or directly to the SPIU receiver/indicator device. The computer fed commands to the AP-5 autopilot and the weapons/sonobuoy release systems.

Together with the other mission equipment, the STS enabled the following:

A Tu-142 with 12-wheel main gear bogies during tests at GANITs VMF (the Naval Aviation Test & Research Centre) in Feodosiya.

• automated flight along a predesignated route;

• tactical manoeuvring in semi-automatic mode (when locating, tracking and destroying hostile submarines) or automatic mode (when fulfilling certain other missions);

• searching for submerged submarines by means of sonobuoys;

• computation of targeting data and accurate weapons delivery.

The Berkut-95 performed the following functions: setting up sonobuoys and monitoring their signals, detection of submerged submarines, determining their current co-ordinates and motion parameters (heading, travel depth and speed), and computation of targeting data for surface targets with a high radar signature or submerged targets. The suite was linked with the airspeed sensor, altimeter, compass and vertical gyro. It worked at flight levels of 500-2,000 m (1,640-6,560 ft) and airspeeds of 350-700 km/h (217-434 mph) within a combat radius of 5,000 km (3,105 miles) in sea states up to 4 on the Beaufort scale. Subs travelling at up to 35 kts and depths down to 400 m (1,310 ft) could be detected.

The Berkut-95 was designed to work with three types of sonobuoys – RGB-1 non-directional passive buoys (*rahdioghidroakusticheskiy booy* – radio hydraacoustic buoy), RGB-2 passive buoys and RGB-3 active/passive buoys. In practice, however, the latter type was not carried because it was expensive and unreliable. No magnetic anomaly detector was provided yet.

As compared to the IL-38's version of the suite, the number of automatically computed and performed tactical tasks was reduced to nine: flying to the search area, setting up a straight barrier of sonobuoys, monitoring such a barrier, offset dropping of RGB-2 buoys, setting up a circular barrier of sonobuoys, flying in parallel tacks, dropping bombs or torpedoes as directed by RGB-2 buoys, and dropping bombs as directed by the RGB-1 buoys' transponders.

The ARI picked up the signals emitted by the sonobuoys, processing them and feeding them to the computer. Information about submarines detected by the RGB-1 buoys was processed by the ARI's channel 1; information about submarines detected by the RGB-2 and RGB-3 buoys was visualised on two identical displays. The Channel 1 display was of a different type, featuring a grid which, in the absence of incoming radio signals, split the screen into 24 luminous squares, each one corresponding to a specific buoy. The display's electronic beam was controlled and the ARI's channels were switched by a built-in processor. When the ARI detected a signal from an RGB-1, the image on the screen was transformed into a vertical strip. Concurrently the device dwelled on the specific buoy, scanning it for two, five, six or ten seconds. Then the sonar operators listened to the buoy's signal to ascertain the nature of the target. Since the STS did not have any technical features facilitating the task of discerning the sounds of a submarine from the usual noises of the sea, success depended largely on the operators' experience and ability to identify the presence of a sub. If a credible contact with the target was established, the crew began the prescribed procedure of pinpointing, identifying and, if necessary, attacking the sub.

The signals emitted by RGB-2 buoys were picked up by two receivers, being visualised on the two identical displays and interpreted by two operators. The target bearing was determined by means of an electronic or mechanical sight.

When working with RGB-3s, the sonar operator manually cycled through the buoy's operating frequencies, watching the responses on the screen. A coded radio transmission switched the buoy from

Three views of Tu-142 (*izdeliye* VP) '44 Black' with 12-wheel main gear bogies at Kuibyshev-Bezymyanka, the factory airfield of plant No.18. The chin fairing houses a Gagara thermal imager.

passive mode to active mode (the RGB-3 began emitting signals which were reflected from the sub and then detected by the buoy). At the same time the rotating sweep diagram on the screen changed to a spiral scan diagram with a target 'blip' and a circular range diagram. Once the buoy had achieved a lock-on, the target bearing and range were entered into the central computer. When working with RGB-2 and RGB-3 buoys, the STS kept monitoring the RGB-1 buoys dropped earlier. A special ARK-UB direction finder integrated with the ARI was used to guide the aircraft towards the buoy which had 'sounded the alarm'.

The three types of sonobuoys optimised for operation with the Berkut-95 STS differed in size, weight, and operating modes. Yet, all of them had a basically similar design featuring a cylindrical body housing the mechanical components, a hydrophone, a data transmitter, a transponder, a parachute system, a battery pack and an automatic scuttling device. The buoys were carried in cassettes holding 22 units each.

The RGB-1 was the least specialised variety – a passive non-directional (that is, 'listen-only') buoy unable to give a bearing on the source of the detected noise). It was used for initial detection of submarines, for tracking the moving sub and, occasionally, as a reference point for aiming the weapons. The RGB-1 had three operating modes: receive/transmit, marker and standby (with three auto-activation settings to choose from). The three auto-activation settings (a feature of the buoy's amplifier) were meant to prevent false activation of the buoy by abnormally high background noise levels in rough seas. The amplifier activated the

data transmitter when the perceived noise level exceeded a certain limit selected prior to the flight.

The RGB-1's continuous operation time was three hours in standby mode and 45 minutes in marker mode. The aircraft could pick up the signals emitted by the buoy within a range of 40-50 km (24.8-31 miles). In the course of state acceptance trials held on the Black Sea, RGB-1s with the medium auto-activation setting detected a diesel-electric submarine travelling at 6-8 kts (11.2-14.8 km/h) in sea state 1-2 at a distance of 1,500-2,000 km (931-1,242 miles). In the Barents Sea the detection range turned out to be 1.5-2 times greater.

To stop the buoys from interfering with each other, each RGB-1 had its own transmitter frequency and its unique transponder code corresponding to its number in the set. The RGB-1 weighed 14 kg (30.86 lb); the cost in 1970 prices was 3,200 Soviet roubles.

The RGB-2 was a passive directional buoy; it was able to provide a magnetic bearing for the submarine with respect to the buoy, which the TsVM-263 computer then used to calculate a bearing with respect to the aircraft. When the buoy splashed down and activated, its hydrophone system having a 15° 'field of view' revolved at 8 rpm, driven by an electric motor via worm gear. The acoustic signals generated by submarines were picked up, transformed into electric signals of 0.2-0.3 seconds' duration, amplified and transmitted to the aircraft in frequency modulation mode.

The RGB-2 had a single operating mode. Its transmitter and transponder were basically similar to those of the RGB-1, with minor changes necessitated by the transmission of slightly different signals in larger

Routine maintenance of an early-model Tu-142 'centipede' with a Gagara thermal imager. The white objects on top of the fuselage in line with the propeller blades are not aerials but the tails of two An-12 transports parked in the background.

quantities. Detection range was similar to that of the RGB-1; continuous operation time was 40-45 minutes. The RGB-2 weighed 40 kg (88 lb) and was loaded in sets of ten; the cost in 1970 prices was 4,600 roubles.

The RGB-3 passive/active buoy was capable of determining both bearing and range (and hence the submarine's exact location). In fact, it was a self-contained sonar which was far more complex than the other two types of buoys. In addition to the receiver, the extendable lower portion of the buoy incorporated a hydroacoustic transmitter (pulse generator) and a transmitting antenna sending an audible signal through the water.

A peculiarity of the RGB-3 was that the buoy operated in passive (noise direction finding) mode after splashdown. The receiving antenna rotated much faster than that of the RGB-2, doing 3,000 rpm. Upon receiving a coded command from the aircraft the buoy switched to active mode – the pulse generator came into play, and the echo reflected from the target was picked up; the bearing and range data was transmitted to the aircraft as a 25-Hz signal. The active mode was particularly useful when the submarine switched to silent running mode and noise direction finding became inefficient. The Tu-142 was meant to carry four RGB-3s, each with its own code command frequency.

The RGB-3 weighed 185 kg (407 lb). Detection range was 2 km (1.24 miles) in active mode and 1-1.5 km (0.62-0.93 miles) in passive mode; continuous operation time in active mode was five minutes.

One of the weaknesses of the Berkut-95 suite's architecture was that certain important functions (reversing the radar scanner drive in 120° or 150° sector scan mode, tilting the radar scanner in the vertical plane, forming the sighting 'crosshairs', remotely switching the RGB-3 sonobuoys from active to passive mode and back) were entrusted to the central computer whose reliability turned out to be lower than predicted. Another disadvantage was created by the radar itself, namely the strong drag generated by the radome.

The Tu-142's envisaged offensive armament included AT-1 (AT-1M) and AT-2 (AT-2M) homing anti-submarine torpedoes, APR-1 **Ya**streb (Hawk) and APR-2 Or**lan** (Sea Eagle) anti-submarine missiles and free-fall anti-submarine bombs (depth charges) – both conventional and nuclear ones. The AT-1 was controlled in two planes by an acoustic homing system (hence the AT for akoos**tich**eskaya tor**ped**a); it could engage submarines travelling at depths up to 200 m (650 ft) and speeds up to 28 kts.

The AT-2 torpedo was originally developed for the IL-38. It had a complex retarding system with two 0.6-m² (6.45 sq ft) drogue parachutes and a 5.4-m² (58 sq ft) main brake parachute. After splashdown the AT-2 commenced target search, moving in a left-hand descending spiral with a radius of 60-70 m (200-230 ft)

at 23 kts (42.5 km/h), with a turn rate of 10-11 deg/sec. The torpedo's homing system worked in active/passive homing cycles, the active mode taking up some 35% of the time. If a target was detected and the target's own noise exceeded the level of the echo received in active guidance mode, the torpedo switched to passive mode. If the echo was stronger than the target's own noise, the system remained in active mode, guiding the torpedo all the way in. At the terminal guidance phase the torpedo accelerated to 40 kts (74 km/h). If target lock-on was lost at this point, the torpedo resumed the search sequence. A hydrodynamic detonator set off the warhead if the torpedo came within 18-12 m (59-39 ft) of the surface.

The improved AT-2M introduced a hydraulic system replacing the pneumatic system, a 10-20 kg (22-44 lb) increase in warhead weight and a disposable electric battery. The AT-2M could engage submarines travelling at up to 400 m (1,310 ft) depth; maximum range was 7 km (4.35 miles). Jumping ahead of the story, it may be noted that production of the basic AT-1 ended in 1970, making the AT-2 (AT-2M) the Tu-142's primary weapon.

The APR-1 (aviatsi**onn**aya protivo**lod**ochnaya ra**ket**a – air-launched anti-submarine missile) was fielded in mid-1971. The technique used with this weapon was to launch three missiles in quick succession. Upon splashdown the missiles commenced target search, one moving in a left-hand circulation, another in a right-hand circulation and the third in a straight line. As in the case of the AT-2 torpedo, the guidance system worked in cycles (active/passive homing). When target lock-on was achieved the missile increased power, accelerating to 60 kts (111 km/h) in six or seven seconds, and covered a distance of 1,000-1,200 m (0.62-0.75 miles). Again, maximum target depth was 400 m.

The APR-2 missile was added to the Tu-142's weapons range in 1981. After splashdown the APR-2 commenced target search, moving in a power-off descending spiral with a turn rate of 20 deg/sec. If no

An early-production Tu-142 leaves contrails across the sky. Note the main gear fairings and portions of the wing underside blackened by the engine exhaust.

target was detected, at a certain depth the rocket motor was ignited and the missile commenced a circulation in the horizontal plane. If the target was then detected the homing system guided the missile all the way in.

Defensive armament was reduced to a single DK-12 tail barbette with two AM-23 cannons. The other two barbettes were deleted because the mission avionics left no room for the dorsal barbette and its sighting station, and the likelihood of an engagement with fighters was considered small anyway. An SPS-100 *Rezeda-A* (Mignonette) active jammer was fitted by way of compensation.

It was suggested that the Tu-142 be equipped with several systems appropriate for its requires performance and mission objectives. One of them was a boundary layer control system (blown flaps) meant to improve field performance; yet, this idea was eventually dropped as too complex and costly. Another suggestion that was rejected called for a new crew escape system with ejection seats. Thus, in an emergency the Tu-142's crew would still have to bail out conventionally.

Considering the capabilities of the Tupolev OKB, the general belief was that the Tu-142 would not take long to design and the prototype would commence tests in late 1964. However, the aircraft had a long gestation period. First, the Council of Ministers issued directive No.358-218 on 30th April 1965 setting the deadline at the fourth quarter of 1966 and the LRIP batch at nine aircraft. Then a new CofM directive followed on 28th November 1967, moving the deadline to the second quarter of 1968.

In January 1968 the State commission monitoring the programme's status convened for yet another session. Mildly berating the OKB for slow progress, it set

a new deadline – the third quarter of 1968. And even that had to be moved to the first quarter of 1969.

It was not before 1968 that the first prototype Tu-142 (c/n 4200 – that is, [Tu-1]42, batch 0, aircraft 0) was completed at the Kuibyshev plant No.18 and ready for flight tests. The uncoded aircraft took to the air on 18th July 1968, captained by Ivan K. Vedernikov.

At an early design stage it was found necessary to lengthen the Tu-142's forward fuselage by at least 1.5 m (4 ft 11¾ in) to accommodate the mission equipment while making the flight deck spacious enough. Also, by then the type's progenitor, the Tu-95, had accumulated quite a lot of operational experience and the designers were aware of its bugs. The cramped flight deck was the main source of annoyance. Thus, a 1.7 m (5 ft 6¹⁵⁄₁₆ in) cylindrical 'plug' was inserted ahead of the wings.

The uncoded second prototype (c/n 4201) entered flight test on 3rd September 1968. It was the first to have this fuselage stretch, which was incorporated on all subsequent Tu-142s, and the Gagara-1 thermal imager but it did not yet have a full equipment fit. The first Tu-142 with a full equipment suite as specified by the 1967 MAP/Air Force decision was c/n 4202, which joined the test programme on 31st October 1968.

The three prototypes successfully completed the manufacturer's flight test programme and were involved in the state acceptance trials (by the end of 1969 the first two machines had made 42 and 27 flights respectively). The trials were mostly concerned with the mission equipment and armament. By 10th March 1970 the first prototype had logged 198 hours in 60 flights.

The Tu-142 had its share of failures during flight tests – including some rather curious ones like several occasions when the tubeless tyres came off the wheel rims on take-off or landing. This led to some claims to the plants which had produced the substandard tyres. Stage A of the state acceptance trials was completed in June 1970; trials and debugging of the Berkut radar were delayed until August.

On 22nd June 1969 the North Fleet Air Arm started picking personnel for a long-range ASW regiment operating Tu-142s. The first group started conversion training in Nikolayev on the Black Sea on 4th March 1970, and was ready to fly about three months later. However, the second group did not begin training until December 1971, so it was a long time before the unit was finally operational (see Chapter 8).

Deliveries to the Naval Air Arm began in 1970, the Tu-142 attaining IOC with the North Fleet. Keeping an eye on the movements of nuclear submarines in the world's oceans proved the highest priority during initial operational trials. When they were completed successfully, the aircraft was cleared for actual operational use. Accordingly, on 14th December 1972 the Council of Ministers passed a directive declaring the Tu-142 equipped with the Berkut-95 radar operational

Basic specifications of the Tu-142	
Take-off weight:	
normal	165,000 kg (363,760 lb)
maximum	182,000 kg (401,240 lb)
Ordnance load	9,000 kg (19,840 lb)
Maximum speed	900 km/h (559 mph)
Cruising speed (loitering at 1,000 m/3,280 ft)	450 km/h (279 mph)
Effective range on internal fuel:	
TOW 165,000 kg	12,000 km (7,460 miles)
TOW 182,000 kg	14,100 km (8,760 miles)
Effective range with one fuel top-up at 2,000 km (1,242 miles) from base	16,100 km (10,000 miles)
Take-off run with normal TOW:	
paved runway	1,400 m (4,590 ft)
unpaved runway	2,000 m (6,650 ft)
On-station loiter time (TOW 182,000 kg):	
at 2,000 km from base	10.2/12.3 hours *
at 3,000 km (1,864 miles) from base	8.1/10.2 hours *
at 4,000 km (2,490 miles) from base	6.1/8.2 hours *
at 5,000 km (3,105 miles) from base	4.1/6.2 hours *

* On internal fuel/with one fuel top-up at 2,000 km from base

The flight line at a Pacific Fleet base showing a curious mix of early-production Tu-142s *sans suffixe* (*izdeliye* VP or *Bear-F*) and Tu-142Ms (*izdeliye* VPM or *Bear-F Mod 2*).

with the Soviet Navy. The NATO reporting name of the initial version was *Bear-F*.

By the time work on the Tu-142's STS got under way full details of the Berkut radar and its capabilities were not yet available, but some of its shortcomings were already known. Still, these were not eliminated straight away and had to be dealt with later during flight tests.

Tu-142 avionics testbed

As part of the effort to develop the improved Tu-142MK (see below), the second prototype was fitted with the newly developed MMS-106 *Ladoga* magnetic anomaly detector named after Lake Ladoga in the Leningrad Region (a lake which is famous for the Road of Life – a supply route to the German-besieged Leningrad set up during the Great Patriotic War). The MMS-106 acted as a secondary source of information about submerged targets. It consisted of a magnetic anomaly sensor, an orientation module, a measurement channel and supporting systems, including two electronic filters, one of which cancelled out the influence of the aircraft's own magnetic field. For want of a better option the

A Tu-142 crew walk along the flight line past a late-production Tu-142M with four-wheel main gear bogies, a raised flight deck roof and no chin fairing for the Gagara-1 thermal imager.

The uncoded second prototype Tu-142 became a testbed for the MMS-106 Ladoga magnetic anomaly detector. The MAD was mounted at the top of the fin on a suitably extended fin cap.

ferromagnetic sensor mounted on a long boom (the MAD 'stinger') and enclosed by a dielectric fairing was installed atop the fin, pointing aft – probably the worst possible location since large static charges are accumulated here. There was really no other way of installing it, since the aft extremity of the fuselage – the preferred location for the MAD 'stinger' on ASW aircraft – was occupied by the gunner's station. A taller fin cap was fitted to accomplish this.

The still-uncoded Tu-142 c/n 4201 underwent tests in this configuration. Upon completion of the trials the aircraft was placed in storage. Eventually it became an exhibit at the Lugansk Aviation Museum established in 1996 at Lugansk-Ostraya Mogila AB (the name of the base translates as 'pointed barrow') with the MAD 'stinger' still in place. This is the sole surviving Tu-142 with the original 12-wheel main gear bogies.

Tu-142 maritime patrol/ASW aircraft (*izdeliye* VP/late version)

Early operational experience with the Tu-142 revealed a number of shortcomings. Flight performance was unsatisfactory – particularly range. With a 165,000-kg (363,760-lb) normal take-off weight the Tu-142 had a

The same aircraft currently resides in the Air Museum in Lugansk, the Ukraine, as the sole surviving 'centipede'. The KSR-2 anti-shipping cruise missile in the foreground has nothing to do with the Tu-142, being a weapon of several versions of the Tu-16.

range of only 8,250 km (5,124 miles) instead of the required 12,000 km (7,453 miles); at the 182,000-kg (401,230-lb) MTOW it was 9,860 km (6,124 miles) instead of 14,000 km (8,695 miles). By comparison, the Tu-95RTs had a range of 13,500 km (8,385 miles). This led the OKB to embark on an urgent effort to improve the type's performance – first and foremost by cutting weight.

As mentioned earlier, the SOR for the Tu-142 included a soft-field capability requirement leading to the incorporation of 12-wheel main gear bogies. A disconcerted Andrey N. Tupolev wrote to Minister of Defence Marshal Rodion Ya. Malinovskiy, arguing that operating such an aircraft from dirt strips was pointless. On 6th October 1970 the minister wrote back, stating his agreement, and the Soviet Navy dropped the controversial requirement. Hence late-production Tu-142s *sans suffixe* were fitted with lighter four-wheel main gear bogies in much slimmer fairings (identical to those of the Tu-114 airliner), and flap area was increased accordingly. Concurrently the Tu-142 reverted to the AV-60K propellers because the AV-60Ps gave disappointing field performance. Unfortunately, there is no knowing how much money went down the drain because of all these conversions and reconversions.

A crew rest area was provided on Tu-142 c/n 4211. From c/n 4231 onwards the Gagara-1 thermal imager, which proved to be totally inadequate, was deleted (hence the chin fairing vanished), the Rezeda-A jammer and the Kvadrat-2 SIGINT set were also removed. This, together with the new landing gear, cut empty weight by 3,685 kg (8,120 lb). The results were not entirely encouraging; take-off performance fell short of the requirements, the take-off run being 2,150-2,300 m (7,050-7,545 ft) rather than the stipulated 1,800-2,000 m (5,905-6,560 ft). On the other hand, range was improved and was now quite close to the target figure.

Only six Tu-42s (c/ns 4231 to 4241) were built in this configuration. Oddly, the late-production version had no separate service designation or product code. The NATO codename, however, was changed to *Bear-F Mod 1*.

Service entry was hampered by slow deliveries. The AVMF was to receive 36 Tu-142s during 1972 but only 12 were actually delivered (all with the original 12-wheel main gear bogies). This was due to delays in testing and production. The culprit was the Ministry of Aircraft Industry which, without consulting the AVMF, had decided to move Tu-142 production from the Kuibyshev aircraft factory to the Taganrog machinery plant No.86 named after Gheorgi Dimitrov (TMZD – *Taganrogskiy mashinostroitel'nyy zavod imeni Dimitrova*), where a branch office of the Tupolev OKB had been set up on 15th October 1971 pursuant to MAP order No.303. This move was caused by two reasons; the Kuibyshev factory had been chosen to build the new Tu-154 *Careless* three-turbofan medium-haul airliner, whereas TMZD would be standing idle when

production of the Beriyev Be-12 *Chaika* (Seagull; NATO codename *Mail*) ASW amphibian ended in 1973 as planned. The technical documentation was transferred from Kuibyshev to Taganrog not long afterwards and production at TMZD was initiated.

However, TMZD had no experience of building heavy landplanes, being traditionally associated with Gheorgiy M. Beriyev's flying boats. Nor did the factory airfield, Taganrog-Yoozhnyy (= southern), have a runway long enough for the Tu-142. This necessitated both retraining of the personnel and reconstruction of the plant with its partly obsolete equipment (TMZD had many machine tools dating back to the 1930s). This was a massive task which required considerable time to accomplish; yet, the engineering staff at Taganrog coped with it admirably. Moreover, rather than just turn out Tu-142s as per OKB drawings, they introduced numerous improvements – particularly in the flight deck, easing the pilot workload considerably.

In total, the Kuibyshev aircraft factory No.18 built 18 Tu-142s over a five-year period (two in 1968, five each in 1969, 1970 and 1971, and one during 1972) before turning production over to TMZD. Production was mostly in batches of five at both factories.

Tu-142 (modified) ASW aircraft (project)

In 1969 the Tupolev OKB was working on a version of the Tu-142 with a new *Korshun-K* (kite, the bird) STS designed by LNPO Leninets, a *Pingvin* (Penguin) thermal imager, a *Visla* towed (!) MAD (named after the Wisła River in Poland) and an updated PNS-142M flight/navigation suite. Though not built in this form, the project paved the way for the Tu-142MK (see below).

Tu-142M maritime patrol/ASW aircraft (*izdeliye* VPM, 'Tu-142')

The final Tu-142 produced at the Kuibyshev factory in 1972 (c/n 4242) became the *etalon* (pattern aircraft) for the production aircraft built by TMZD in Taganrog. This aircraft had an additional 0.3-m (1-ft) forward fuselage stretch and a redesigned flight deck which was widened 0.18 m (7⅟₆₄ in) and featured a raised roof to increase headroom and improve downward visibility by 1°30'. The crew seats were fitted with reclining backs for greater comfort. The cramped flight deck had been a constant source of complaints from *Bear* pilots.

The control system was revised by adding geared tabs to the elevators, using a revised AP-15R3 autopilot and a control yoke travel limiter which was linked to the AUASP-142 alpha, side-slip and G load limiter (*avtomaht oogla atahki, skol'zheniya i peregroozki*). An NPK-142M flight/navigation suite was fitted. Its main subsystem included TsVM-10TS-42 and TsVM-10-15-42 processors and a MAIS compact astroinertial system (*malogabaritnaya astroinertsiahl'naya sistema*) whose star tracker window was on top of the rear fuselage; the

acronym coincided with the Russian word *maïs* (maize). The back-up subsystem had its own VNPK-154 processor and included a DISS-7 Doppler sensor system and a Roomb-7 (Compass point) inertial AHRS.

The IFR probe was angled slightly downwards; this was supposed to facilitate contact with the tanker's drogue, compensating the aircraft's nose-up attitude. The main gear units had four-wheel bogies. The mission equipment was similar to that of Tu-142 c/n 4231.

Curiously, the Taganrog factory chose to continue the batch numbering from Kuibyshev production rather than start its own sequence. However, a new seven-digit system was introduced (certainly by the KGB to make life harder for hypothetical spies). For example, Taganrog-built Tu-142M '17 Red' was c/n 3600501; the first digit means year of manufacture 1973, the second refers to TMZD (plant No.86) and the remaining five digits do not signify anything at all – the idea is to

conceal the batch number and the number of the aircraft in the batch so that the c/n would not reveal how many have been built. The first two digits of these 'famous last five', as they are often called, change independently from the final three.

Additionally, aircraft with c/ns under the new system have fuselage numbers (f/ns) or line numbers; security is all very well but the manufacturer has to keep track of production, after all. Typically of Soviet aircraft, the f/n is not just a sequential line number (as in the case of Boeing and Douglas aircraft) but consists of a batch number and the number of the aircraft in the batch; thus, the c/n under the Kuibyshev system became the f/n in Taganrog. For example, Tu-142M c/n 3600501 is f/n 4245 (i.e., [Tu-1]42, Batch 4, fifth and final aircraft in the batch). The c/n is found on a metal plate riveted to the front bulkhead of the nosewheel well.

In order to distinguish Taganrog-built *Bear-Fs* from Kuibyshev-built ones (from which they differed anyway), the new machines were given the OKB designation Tu-142M (*modernizeerovannyy* – updated) and the in-house product code *izdeliye* VPM which was also used by the factory. Curiously, the abovementioned aircraft (f/n 4245) was the first Taganrog-built Tu-142M because the machines with f/ns 4243 and 4244 were set aside to become prototypes of the Tu-142MK (see below). Actually, the latter version was planned from the outset but took a while to develop, so the Tu-142M with the revised airframe but with the old Berkut-95 STS was an interim version.

Throughout most of 1973 the Taganrog factory geared up to produce the Tu-142M as per the Kuibyshev-built *etalon*. Production finally got under way during 1974 when the first two aircraft were completed; seven Tu-142Ms were built in 1975, seven more in 1976 and six in 1977. Somewhat surprisingly, the AVMF did not adopt the new identifier and in service the aircraft was still referred to simply as Tu-142. The Tu-142M's NATO reporting name was *Bear-F Mod 2*.

Tu-142MP development aircraft

In 1976 a single Tu-142M (f/n 4262) was outfitted experimentally with a new *Atlantida* (Atlantis) STS – an upgraded version of the Berkut-95. The STS featured new software making it possible to use APR-2 anti-submarine missiles and AT-3 (UMGT-1) torpedoes; a new defensive avionics suite was also installed. Designated Tu-142MP (the meaning of the suffix is unknown), the aircraft was tested but the planned fleetwide upgrade programme never went ahead.

Tu-142M weapons testbed

In 1977 a single Tu-142M served as a testbed for the Orlan (Sea Eagle) weapons system based on the Yastreb (Hawk) anti-submarine missile – apparently this name applied to the APR-1 anti-submarine missile.

Previous page, above:
A Tu-142M (*izdeliye* VPM)
with the weapons
bay doors open seen
over the ocean on
1st August 1986.

Previous page, below:
The same aircraft a few
minutes earlier; the doors
of the smaller rear bay
housing sonobuoys are
open. The absence of the
dorsal cannon barbette
is quite apparent.

Tu-142MK ASW aircraft (*izdeliye* VPMK, 'Tu-142M')

Over the years the effectiveness of ASW aircraft suffered seriously as a result of the progress made by submarine designers in making submarines quieter. Acoustic sonobuoys were becoming increasingly less effective in detecting these craft, meaning that a mission avionics suite based on new principles was required.

Research by ASW experts indicated that sonobuoys with a 2-10 Hz noise reception band were needed to hunt down modern submarines. Noises in this range are generated because of fluctuating cavitation on the submarine's propeller blades, for example, when the blades pass the elevators and rudders. Protruding structures on the submarine's hull generate vortices which disturb the water flow through the propeller disc, causing thrust pulsations. Such pulsations are common to all submarines, including those with five-, six-, or seven-bladed low-speed propellers; occasionally, flow departure from propeller blades gen-erates vortex noise with frequencies of up to 100 Hz. Contemporary Soviet sonobuoys, however, could only detect noise in the 3 to 10 kHz band.

In contrast, western SAR aircraft were equipped with low-frequency sonobuoys from 1960. Besides, they utilised so-called explosive sound sources (ESS) of varying power, shape, and sound spectrum generating sound waves for detecting submarines in deep waters.

In 1961-62 the Soviet Union conducted R&D in using ESS for locating submarines; the two research programmes were codenamed 'NIR' (*naoochno-issledovatel'skiye raboty* – research, as simple as that) and Yel' (Spruce). In 1965 a new programme code-named Udar (Blow; pronounced *oodahr*) was launched; work began on operational sonobuoy systems utilising ESS which were to be integrated with the Berkut search radar installed on the IL-38 and Tu-142.

It soon became clear that the Tu-142 could not carry the new system without major modifications and upgrades to the STS. Moreover, the existing TsVM-263 computer could not cope and would have to be replaced with a more capable *Orbita* (Orbit) digital computer developed by OKB Elektroavtomatika. This and development delays with other hardware (the ESS launchers were not ready, nor was the launch technique developed) caused the Udar programme to be put on hold. However, data obtained during this effort were put to good use when designing a new STS for the Tu-142. Development of an upgraded Tu-142 with a new STS called Korshun-K was initiated by a Council of Ministers directive issued as early as 14th January 1969; the SOR was endorsed by the Air Force's Deputy C-in-C (Armaments) on 20th March that year.

Usually research and development work on Soviet aircraft and their systems, even the most basic ones, proceeded under tight security wraps. Therefore the

meeting at Kipelovo AB in May 1970, which was attended by high-ranking AVMF officers, MAP representatives and the personnel of the resident Tu-142 unit was something of a sensation. Of course, the information revealed at the meeting was scarce, but it was good enough for the aircrews who were sick and tired of the Berkut radar's limitations and hoped that something new would come soon to replace it. However, as a Russian saying goes, 'you have to wait three years for what's been promised'. Not just three but *nine* years would elapse before the new aircraft attained IOC with the North Fleet Air Arm, with loads of bugs still to be ironed out.

When Tu-142 production was transferred to Taganrog it was decided to install the Korshun-K STS designed by LNPO Leninets on all subsequent Tu-142s. The new version received the manufacturer's designation Tu-142MK (*izdeliye* VPMK), the K standing for Korshun.

Despite the suite's relatively high level of automation, the crew was enlarged to eleven: captain, co-pilot, navigator, radar operator, combat navigator (who co-ordinated the crew's actions during ASW tasks), two sonar systems operators, communications officer, flight engineer, ECM/ESM suite operator and gunner (the latter two sat in the rear pressure cabin). It was obviously possible to eliminate at least one crewman and save approximately 1,500 kg (3,310 lb) of weight by deleting the gun barbette and associated equipment.

The new STS was designed to work in the sonic and infrasonic ranges. It included a radar subsystem, a data processing subsystem (which controlled the release of sonobuoys and weapons, among other things), a *Kaïra-P* (Great auk) sonar subsystem and a tactical information display subsystem (TIDS).

The new Korshun 360° search radar, which was put through its paces on the SL-18P avionics testbed operated by LNPO Leninets – a converted IL-18D airliner registered CCCP-75411 (c/n 187009205). Apart from scanning the sea and detecting surface targets (for example, submarines' periscopes could be detected at 20-25 km/12.4-15.5 miles range), the radar could communicate with some of the sonobuoys at 25-30 km (15.5-18.6 miles) range by sending coded signals.

The data processing subsystem based on the Argon-15 computer processed inputs from the control panel and data coming in from all components of the Korshun-K STS. It continuously kept track of the aircraft's position, sonobuoy splashdown positions, monitored submarine movements, traded information with other aircraft via data link, provided control inputs to the autopilot in automatic or semi-automatic flight during tactical manoeuvres, and launched the weapons.

The Kaïra-P sonar subsystem comprised two sets of equipment with separate operator workstations; hence the STS as a whole is sometimes referred to as '2Korshun-K' (or 2KN-K), the last letter referring to Kaïra.

The first prototype Tu-142MK (f/n 4243). Note the MMS-106 MAD on top of the fin and the cine camera fairing under the starboard wingtip for recording weapon/sonobuoy drops.

In the first prototype's original configuration the MAD boom was perfectly horizontal. Note the absence of cannons in the tail turret.

Each workstation featured two KR-4 CRT displays; one of them showed data from four sonobuoys at a time (in the form of echograms, spectrograms and target bearings), while the other could show information from the TIDS or back up the image from the other workstation. The Kaïra-P communicated with the sonobuoys on 56 channels, and communication range at an altitude of 1,500 m (4,920 ft) was 80 km (49 miles).

The TIDS eliminated the main weakness of all prior ASW systems – the lack of tactical situation displays enabling the crew to make better decisions. It used a preset range of commands stored in the computer's hard drive. The TIDS could operate in display mode or data processing mode. The four TIDS screens at the captain's, navigator's and sonar operators' workstations showed the tactical situation in the form of special symbols with two-digit codes for threat classification, vectors and circles. This included the aircraft's position and speed vector, sonobuoy drop positions, headings for directional buoys, positions of detected subs and up to six other parameters. The TIDS automatically switched from display mode to data processing mode, operating as a single-address digital computer.

To facilitate working with images and increase data presentation speed the combat navigator was provided with an optical 'pointer' (light pencil) projecting a big cruciform cursor on the display. If he pointed it at any place on the display and pressed certain keys on his keyboard a 'go-to' function was activated, guiding the aircraft automatically to the cursor position.

The Tu-142MK was also equipped with the MMS-106 Ladoga MAD (which, oddly, was not part of the STS), the NPK-VPMK flight/navigation suite (an updated version of the NPK-142M), the *Strela-142M* (Arrow-142M) communications suite, the **Nerchinsk** (a town in Siberia) specialised sonar set and the *Sayany* (a mountain ridge in Russia) defensive weapons system (NATO codename *Ground Bounce*). The comms suite included two R-857G radios, two R-832M radios and an R-866 radio, as well as scramblers and descramblers.

While being compatible with the Berkut-95 suite's sonobuoys, the Korshun-K worked with four new sonobuoys (RGB-75, RGB-15, RGB-25 and RGB-55A). The first two were used for primary detection of submarines and the other two for pinpointing them and monitoring their movements. However, the RGB-15 could also be used jointly with ESS for pinpointing the target.

The RGB-75 buoy picked up acoustic signals (low-frequency audible and infrasonic bands) generated by submarines, transforming them into electric signals and transmitting them to the aircraft for further processing. The buoy was 1,214 mm (3ft 11⁵⁄₆₄ in) long and weighed 9.5 kg (20.94 lb); the Tu-142M carries 24 of them. The buoy operates continuously after splashdown.

The RGB-15 buoy picked up acoustic signals (low-frequency audible and infrasonic bands) generated by submarines, as well as signals generated by explosive sound sources, transforming them into electric signals and transmitting them to the aircraft. The buoy's receiver had a 2 Hz – 5 kHz waveband. In active mode (when working with ESS) the distance from buoy to aircraft was determined by the radar's distance measuring channel, using data link; however, the buoy had no self-contained beacon.

In operating condition, the RGB-15's hydrophone was a cylinder of 80 mm (3¾ in) diameter and 1,400 mm (4 ft 6 in) long weighing 9.5 kg (20.28 lb). It incorporated six receivers and could be submerged 20, 150 or 400m (65; 490; and 1,310 ft); maximum operating time was 2 hours. The Tu-142MK carried 16 RGB-15s.

If the RGB-15 was used separately the noises picked up by the buoy were transmitted to the aircraft where the sonar operators analysed them, using a KR-P graphic equaliser which showed frequencies of 2-6 Hz; frequencies up to 5 kHz were analysed through headphones. While the buoy's capabilities in the visual waveband analysis mode were somewhat inferior to those of the RGB-75, the audio analysis offered some advantages in noise classification.

If used with ESS the RGB-15 picked up and transmitted both the primary signal (when the ESS detonated) and the echo reflected from the target. Detection range was 10-15km (6.25-9.3 miles) or more. Sometimes this combination worked as a primary search means in the active mode, especially when searching for low-noise submarines.

RGB-25 passive directional buoys were used to detect audio-frequency signals emitted by subs and determining their position; the signal was then processed and transmitted to the aircraft. The buoy's antenna was a collapsible three-dimensional framework composed of five separate grids joined by cylindrical hinges; the three inner grids carried 34 acoustic receivers. The antenna weighed 7 kg (15.5 lb). It was powered by an electric motor and rotated at 6 to 12 rpm, scanning the sea around the buoy.

When a submarine came into range the RGB-25 picked up the noise, amplified it and converted it into radio signals before transmitting them to the aircraft. A compass was used to determine the current heading the acoustic system was pointed at. The buoy's position and distance from the aircraft was calculated using the radar's DME channel. The RGB-25 was submerged 20 or 150 m (64 or 479 ft), remaining operational for about 40 minutes; target headings were determined with an error margin of 3°. The Tu-142MK carried ten such buoys weighing 45 kg (99.2 lb) each.

The RGB-55A was likewise a directional sonobuoy; however, it was an active buoy de-signed to send signals allowing the buoy's position to be determined. It also allowed the sonar operator to determine the radial component of the submarine's speed.

Aleksandr B. Kosarev, the Tu-142's project chief.

Opposite page: One of the first two prototypes at Zhukovskiy during trials. The MAD stinger, which was originally horizontal, has been angled upwards a little; this configuration was adopted for production.

The buoy's hydroacoustic transmitter was triggered by a special command from the aircraft, sending an audible signal through the water. The echo reflected from the target was then transmitted to the aircraft. This allowed the operator to determine signal return time and the Doppler frequency shift, calculating the target range and speed. Thus, just two or three buoys allowed the crew to pinpoint the sub and determine its speed and heading. If no acoustic signal was transmitted, the RGB-55A worked as a passive non-directional buoy.

RGB-55As were delivered in sets of 16. The Tu-142MK carried up to 15 such buoys with four different acoustic signal frequencies, depending on the mission. The buoy weighed 55 kg (121.25 lb) and operated at depths of 20-200 m (65-660 ft) for up to an hour; minimum detection range was 5 km (3 miles). The length of the acoustic signal was variable. All sonobuoys were scuttled automatically when their operation time expired.

It should be noted that the RGB-15 could be used jointly with explosive sound sources for pinpointing targets. Three types of ESS were used with RGB-15 sonobuoys in active mode. These were the MGAB-OZ, MGAB-LZ and MGAB-SZ free-fall HE bombs (*malogabaritnaya aviabomba* – literally 'compact bomb') with different charges (OZ = *odinochnyy zaryad* – single charge; LZ = *leeneynyy zaryad* – linear charge; and

Above: Sergey M. Golovin, who was Director of the Taganrog plant No.86 in the early years of Tu-142 production (up to 1978).

Opposite page: Three views of a different Tu-142MK prototype at Taganrog-Yoozhnyy. Note the engine nacelles partially painted white; the machines shown previously were natural metal all over. The cannons are fitted in this case.

Below: Russian Navy Tu-142M '66 Black' refurbished by the NARP plant at Nikolayev, the Ukraine, creates a small sandstorm as it taxies in after a check-up flight. The Nos. 1 and 4 engines are shut down already.

Tu-142MKs in the final
assembly shop in
Taganrog in 1991.

SZ = *speerahl'nyy zaryad* – spiral charge). All three models of ESS can be set to detonate at a depth of 25, 150 or 400m (82, 492 or 1,312 ft).

Since the Korshun-K suite worked with active buoys and ESS used for detecting submarines in deep waters, knowing the speed of sound propagation in the water at varying depths helped, since it differs in different parts of the world ocean. This is where the Nerchinsk system came in handy, working with the Kaïra-P sonar; it comprised two special buoys, a special *Istra* receiver (named after a town in the Moscow Region) and a deciphering/recording unit.

The Tu-142MK's offensive armament comprised bombs, AT-2M torpedoes and nuclear depth charges. All ordnance was released automatically, triggered by the tactical computer. In an emergency, the captain or combat navigator could jettison all ordnance, setting it for detonation or non-detonation. The weapons system hardware included bomb, torpedo and sonobuoy racks, NKBP-7 night-capable collimator bombsight (*nochnoy kollimahtornyy bombovyy pritsel*) and release controls, detonator controls and bomb/torpedo hoists. The defensive armament was limited to two AM-23 cannons.

Development work on the Tu-142MK and its systems followed the worst Soviet traditions of procrastination. The full-scale mock-up was completed a year behind schedule, and flight tests began in 1975 rather than in 1972 as originally planned. As already mentioned, the first two Taganrog-built Tu-142s (f/ns 4243 and 4244), both having no tactical codes, were retrofitted with this equipment in 1975 as the

Tu-142MK prototypes. The first of these successfully completed its maiden flight on 4th November 1975, captained by Ivan K. Vedernikov. That same year they were joined by a third Tu-142MK prototype (f/n 4264).

The Tu-142MK was the first version of the *Bear* to feature a magnetic anomaly detector. The MMS-106 'stinger' projecting aft from the fin tip became the main recognition feature of this version. On the first prototype the 'stinger' was originally horizontal; later it was angled slightly upward. The prototypes were all fitted with a cine camera in a teardrop-shaped fairing under the starboard wingtip to capture weapon and sonobuoy drops during trials.

The three prototypes took part in Stage A of the state acceptance trials which continued until 23rd October 1977, involving 236 flights with a total time of 869 hrs 18 min. The first aircraft was used to evaluate the radar and verify its ability to handle complex tasks, operating from Feodosiya on the Crimea Peninsula where the Navy's State Aviation Researchg Centre (GANITs VMF – *Gosudarstvennyy aviatsionnyy naoochno-issledovatel'skiy tsentr Voyenno-morskovo flota*) was located. The second Tu-142MK was based at Zhukovskiy, serving for performance testing. The third prototype was used to verify the MAD, ESS launchers and other equipment, operating from various airbases, including Sleezevo AB on the Kamchatka Peninsula.

The preliminary results were disappointing – performance fell utterly short of the requirements. In fact, only seven of the SOR's 31 items were complied with, and those were relatively unimportant ones. Nevertheless, a go-ahead was given for full-scale

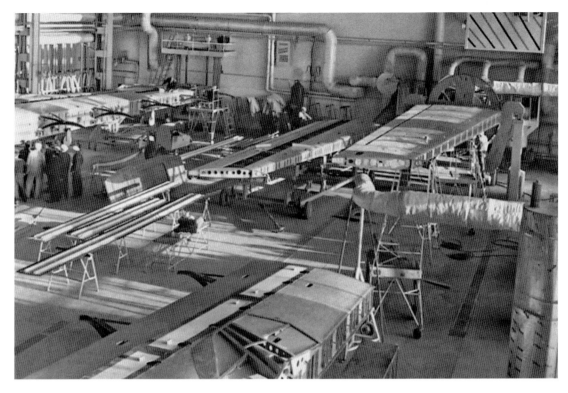

The Tu-142MK horizontal tail build-up area at the Taganrog plant.

production. This premature decision was bound to cause problems – and promptly did.

Stage B of the trials began on 22nd April 1978, lasting until 27th October; the three prototypes made a total of 136 test flights during this period. Deliveries to the AVMF began in 1979, even though the aircraft was beset by teething troubles. The new avionics suite and ASW equipment proved extremely unreliable as soon as

the Tu-142MK entered service (it was cleared for service by a Council of Ministers directive issued on 19th November 1980 and the Minister of Defence's order dated 6th December 1980). Besides, tests showed that the Korshun-K STS had little growth potential and was becoming obsolete even that early stage. Hence in July 1979 – more than a year before the Tu-142MK entered service – the VPK ruled that the STS needed upgrading.

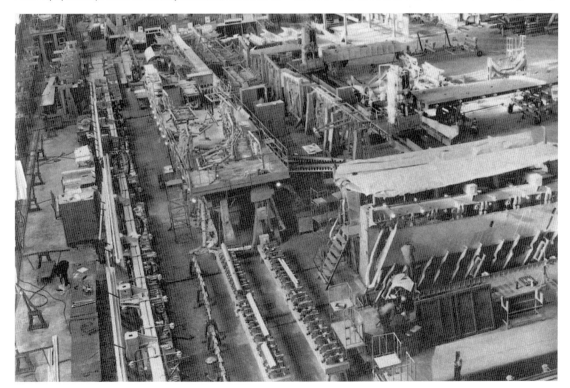

Tu-142MK airframe components being manufactured at TANTK.

The fuselage section build-up area at TANTK. A completed Tu-142MK forward fuselage is visible on the left.

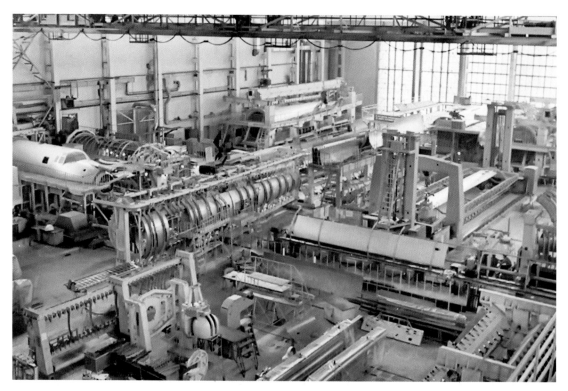

Tail unit components being assembled at the Taganrog plant in the 1980s. A slogan urging the workers to build communism still graces the shop wall.

The fuselage assembly jigs. The slogan on the wall reading 'We shall fulfil the state's five-year economic plan ahead of schedule!' again shows the picture was taken in Soviet times.

Another view of the fuselage section build-up and fuselage assembly shop in the 1980s. The slogan on the wall reads 'Glory to the Communist Party of the Soviet Union!', while a smaller placard on the assembly jig says that every worker should possess knowledge of economics.

The main flight data of the Tu-142MK, including field performance, were quite similar to those of the Tu-142. The fuel load was increased by 3,000 kg (6,610 lb); yet, this did not improve range or endurance because of the increase in all-up weight and the added drag caused by various new fairings. Thus, range on internal fuel was 12,000 km (7,500 miles) at a 185-ton (407,850-lb) MTOW; one fuel top-up increased it by 2,000 km (1,242 miles).

The Tu-142MK superseded the Tu-142M (*izdeliye* VPM) on the Taganrog production line during 1978. Eight Tu-142MKs were built in 1978, eight more in 1979 and nine in 1980. It should be noted that the batch numbering sequence ran uninterrupted from the start, and Tu-142MK production began with the last aircraft of

Batch 8 (f/n 4285). The Tu-142MK utilised the same seven-digit c/n system but had a separate sequence of the 'famous last five'.

Curiously, as with the Tu-142M, once again the Soviet Navy elected to use a different designation from the one used by the manufacturer. Thus, the Tu-142MKs equipped with the new Korshun-K STS were referred to as Tu-142Ms in service (not to be confused with the real Tu-142M preceding it). The Tu-142MK's NATO codename was *Bear-F Mod 3*.

A typical ASW sortie looked as follows. After reaching the search area the aircraft scanned it with the radar and then dropped RGB-75 sonobuoys (the most widely used type). If the buoys detected the presence of a submarine, more accurate data on the target's position could be required before tracking commenced. To this end, RGB-1 buoys (used with the Berkut-95 STS) or RGB-15s would be dropped.

RGB-15s could also be used in conjunction with ESS, or RGB-55As could be used in active mode (which is the least advisable and least common technique). These are non-stealthy methods, and the chances of detection are reduced. Tracking was done by placing straight or curved 'barriers' (strings of sonobuoys) along the anticipated directions of the submarine's travel; RGB-15s and RGB-55As could be used for this.

Depending on the objective received by the crew the aircraft could either attack the sub immediately after discovering it or track it for a while to see if it was getting too close to friendly ships.

The Tu-142MK's initial service period was disappointing – the avionics suite and sonobuoys turned out to be extremely unreliable. Operational experience revealed both weaknesses of the equipment and flaws in the design philosophy: much time was needed to process data supplied by the sonobuoys, the operator had to compare 'equaliser graphs' manually since there was no provision for this to be done automatically, the directional buoys had huge sidelobes etc.

The MAD represented the most difficult equipment to perfect. Its sensitivity was much lower than required, and this was not helped by its unfortunate location. The flight manual said the crew had to switch off four of the aircraft's eight generators, the hydraulic pump and some electronic equipment items to operate the MAD.

Early operational experience with the Tu-142 did not allow the AVMF to assess its capabilities fully, simply because the sonobuoys intended for it were not used for almost two years. The reason defies belief – the buoys were so classified that operational units never saw a whiff of them! After the buoys were finally declassified, for the next four years no one could tell for sure if the signal received was a real submarine or a false alarm because the data recorders used for debriefing were far from perfect. Finally, in 1985 some Tu-142s were fitted with the new Uzor-5V (Ornament; pronounced *oozor*)

magnetic data recorder: the situation became more or less clear, and the designers of the earlier inefficient equipment faced some serious claims.

Aircrews found conversion to the new STS difficult since the new system was very different in ideology from its predecessors. Though it's not recorded officially, logic suggested that the combat navigator should be in control in the search area since he has more tactical information than anyone else, while the pilot would be responsible for flight safety and for getting the mission accomplished. To speed up conversion training, representatives of research institutes and test navigators would fly training sorties with regular crews. Ironically, it often turned out that service navigators who had clocked much time on the Tu-142 were more expert than the test navigators who were supposed to be the best of the best.

Tu-142MK-E export ASW aircraft (Tu-142ME, *izdeliye* VPMK-E)

In the 1980s eight Tu-142MKs were delivered to the Indian Navy which was the sole export customer for the Tu-95/-142 family. Designated Tu-142MK-E or *izdeliye* VPMK-E (**eksportnyy** – export, used attributively),

Opposite page,
top to bottom:
A standard Indian Navy
Tu-142MK-E makes a
low flypast
at Taganrog.

Tu-142MK-E IN317
departs on a check flight
after being refurbished
by the Beriyev TANTK.

IN312, another Indian
Navy Tu-142MK-E,
taxies at Taganrog. The
small radome under the
nose reveals an upgrade
by Israel Aircraft
Industries.

This page, top: Stripped
to bare metal, an Indian
Navy Tu-142MK-E taxies
at Taganrog.

Above: The same
aircraft takes off on
the first post-overhaul
check flight.

Another shot of Israeli-upgraded Tu-142MK-E IN312 flying at Taganrog-Yoozhnyy.

they differed from the standard *Bear-F Mod 3s* in having a slightly downgraded mission equipment suite and lacking the lateral observation blisters in the rear pressure cabin, which were replaced by maintenance access hatches in similar manner to the Tu-95MS (see next chapter) and the Tu-142MZ. All stencilling and labelling was in English.

Curiously, some sources refer to these aircraft as Tu-142ME, thereby creating confusion with a proposed

upgrade programme (see below). The actual upgrade of these aircraft is described in Chapter 9.

Tu-142MZ ASW aircraft (*izdeliye* VPMZ)

In the mid-1980s the Tupolev OKB began another upgrade programme in order to enhance the Tu-142M's ability to track down modern 'quiet' nuclear-powered submarines. This was in accordance with VPK ruling No.208 which, in turn, was triggered by a Council of

Tu-142MKE IN314 is turned over to the owner after a post-repair test flight at Taganrog performed jointly by an Indian Navy crew and a Russian MoD test crew.

Top: Head-on view of the Tu-142MZ prototype parked at Zhukovskiy.

Centre and above: Two more views showing the Tu-142MZ's chin fairing and the aerials of the Sayany ECM/ESM suite under the gunner's station.

Left: Rear view of the Tu-142MZ prototype.

A publicity photo of a Tu-142MZ on the runway.

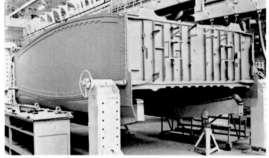

A Tu-142MZ centre section torsion box being assembled in Taganrog.

Ministers directive dated 4th January 1977. Both documents required the Tu-142M's capabilities to be significantly improved.

The aircraft featured a Korshun-N STS (occasionally called '2Korshun-N' or 2KN-N), the last N denoting the new *Nashatyr'-Nefrit* (Ammonia-Jade) ASW suite. The latter included the *Zarech'ye* sonar system with greater computing capability replacing the Kaïra-P; the name Zarech'ye, literally 'area beyond the river', denotes a borough in central Moscow beyond the Moskva River.

One of the mechanical shops at the Taganrog factory in the 1980s.

An almost complete Tu-142MZ amid a thicket of work platforms in the final assembly shop at TANTK. Note the annular centre portions of the engine nacelles awaiting installation and the red ballast in the No.2 nacelle for maintaining the CG position.

Three Tu-142MZs take shape at Taganrog.

TANTK plant department and service chiefs pose with a Tu-142MK.

Naval aircraft are rarely seen at the Russian Air Force's 929th State Flight Test Centre – but here we have a Tu-142MZ parked at Vladimirovka AB in Akhtoobinsk in the 1990s.

The Zarech'ye system was developed in keeping with a Council of Ministers directive issued on 4th January 1977 and a VPK resolution passed on 17th July 1979. Hence the new version was designated Tu-142MZ (*izdeliye* VPMZ), the Z standing for Zarech'ye; some sources quote the product code as *izdeliye* VPMKZ. Since the Cyrillic letter Z is identical to the numeral 3, the aircraft was sometimes erroneously referred to as 'Tu-142M3'. The Nashatyr'-Nefrit suite and the Zarech'ye system were designed to meet joint Air Force/Navy operational requirements dated 2nd October 1977 for the former suite and 22nd January 1980 for the latter one, as well as the amendments to the Tu-142MK's SOR approved by the Air Force's Deputy C-in-C (Armament) on 12th March 1985.

Besides RGB-1A and RGB-2 buoys, the Tu-142MZ could carry RGB-16, RGB-26 and RGB-36 buoys developed for the Nashatyr'-Nefrit suite. The RGB-16 passive broadband sonobuoy had been developed as a replacement for the RGB-15 and the RGB-75 as a result of a test programme held in 1984. It operated within a range of 2 Hz to 5 kHz; the level of internally generated noise was reduced somewhat and the number of possible transmission frequencies was increased from 24 on the older models to 64.

The RGB-26 low sonic range passive directional buoy replaced the less-than-successful RGB-25 model. Finally, the RGB-36 was an active buoy determining the target's bearing, range and radial speed.

The changes introduced by the Zarech'ye system allowed the STS to process a larger scope of more detailed information provided by the new sonobuoys. The system was able to work with eight RGB-16 buoys at a time, processing infrasonic and low sonic range signals while determining the target bearing. The number of data reception channels was increased to 108; the system's ECM resistance was improved. The STS included a new A-311 ADF compatible with new and old buoys alike; a test mode was added, allowing the ASW mission to be 'test run' on the ground.

The new equipment doubled the Tu-142's efficiency as an ASW platform, permitting search for submarines at up to sea state five while cutting sonobuoy expenditure by 50%. New weapons were also used: provisions were made for carrying UPLAB practice bombs (*oochebnaya*

The same uncoded Tu-142MZ sharing the apron with a Tu-22M3 bomber. The long conduit on the port side of the fuselage encloses wiring, unlike the one to starboard, which houses a fuel line.

protivolodochnaya aviabomba), and the old AT-2M torpedoes were replaced with AT-3 (UMGT-1) torpedoes and APR-2 missiles.

The Tu-142MZ was powered by improved NK-12MP engines. Additionally, changes were made to other systems, including the equipment cooling system.

Outwardly the Tu-142MZ could be readily identified by the shallow chin fairing enclosing several antennas and by a small thimble radome at the end of the glazed nose. Like the aerials under the gunner's station (identical to those of the Tu-95MS), they served the Sayany ECM suite. Other shared features with the

Another view of the same aircraft, showing the matt grey areas on the sides of the nose which are characteristic of the Tu-142MZ. The red signal light on the nose gear strut warns the ground personnel to stay away when the Korshun radar is switched on for a ground check.

Tu-95MS were the UKU-9K-502-I turret mounting two 23-mm Gryazev/Shipunov GSh-23L twin-barrel cannons (instead of the usual DK-12 turret with AM-23 cannons) and the absence of the lateral sighting blisters in the rear pressure cabin.

The additional equipment installed on the Tu-142MZ doubled the aircraft's efficiency as compared to the Tu-142MK while reducing the expenditure of sonobuoys 50%. The aircraft could detect submarines travelling at depths down to 800 m (2,620 ft) in rough seas (up to sea state 5).

According to the abovementioned VPK ruling the initial flight tests of the Tu-142MZ were to begin in the second quarter of 1982. However, as it so often happens, the development and test schedule kept slipping, and additional changes were introduced in the meantime. In particular, the designers added the abovementioned Sayany ECM system and proposed integrating the Kh-35 subsonic anti-shipping missile developed by MKB Raduga. Yet the Naval Aviation command objected strongly to having this weapon aboard the Tu-142MZ.

The prototype, a converted Tu-142MK (reported as f/n 42172), entered flight tests in early 1985. Stage A of the joint state acceptance trials began in April that year minus ASW missiles and the ECM suite; 49 test flights were envisaged initially but by the time Stage A ended the prototype had made 71 flights totalling 310 hours. In the course of the trials programme the prototype searched for nuclear-powered submarines in the Black Sea, Barents Sea and the Sea of Okhotsk, showing excellent results as compared to production-standard Tu-142MKs. The Air Force Deputy C-in-C endorsed the trials report in August 1986. Generally the results were good (the search for low-noise subs was twice as effective), except that the RGB-26 buoys obstinately would not provide a target bearing. The manufacturers were given a chance to rectify this.

Stage B of the State acceptance trials began on 13th November 1987, lasting until 30th November 1988. The final report stated that combat efficiency was improved of 2-2.5 times as compared to the Tu-142MK, sonobuoy expenditure was reduced by a similar factor and 'kill' probability using torpedoes was improved 20%. That same year the new model supplanted the Tu-142M on the Taganrog production line, becoming the *Bear*'s ultimate production version; again, the c/ns followed System 2 but the Tu-142MZ had a separate sequence of the 'famous last five' digits. The NATO reporting name was *Bear-F Mod 4*.

The Tu-142MZ was formally included into the AVMF inventory in 1993. The final example was built in 1994, putting an end to the long production of the *Bear* family. By then the former TMZD had been merged with the Beriyev OKB, or Taganrog Aviation Scientific & Technical complex named after Gheorghiy M. Beriyev, or Beriyev TANTK (*Taganrogskiy aviatsionnyy naoochno-tekhnich-*

eskiy kompleks); found itself in the unlikely position of building someone else's aircraft.

Tu-142MZ-C (Tu-142MZ-K) cargo aircraft (project)

As part of the *konversiya* policy (adaptation of defence industry enterprises and military equipment for civilian needs) that was popular with the Russian political leadership in the early 1990s, the Tupolev OKB and the TANTK proposed using a handful of company-owned Tu-142MZs as transport aircraft for carrying fuel and other cargoes. The *Bear-F*'s range enabled it to make non-stop flights to any location in Russia and othe CIS republics. The ASW equipment would be removed to create a bay accommodating up to 17,000 kg (37,480 lb) of cargo; the maximum TOW would be 185,049 kg (407,848 lb).

The proposed cargo version was designated Tu-142MZ-K (*kommercheskiy* – commercial) and offered to Aeroflot Russian International Airlines. In the Tupolev PLC 's English-language advertising materials it was called Tu-142MZ-C.

Range on internal fuel with the maximum payload and 7,000-kg (15,430-lb) fuel reserves was advertised as 9,150 km (5,718 miles), or 10,000 km (6,210 miles) if the payload was reduced to 10 tons (22,045 lb). Cruising speed was to be 740 km/h (462.5 mph); cruise altitude was 7,800-10,600m (25,590-36,190ft) and maximum endurance was 12.6 hours. The take-off run with a full payload was to be 2,540 m (8,330 ft).

Tu-142MR 'Oryol' communications relay aircraft (*izdeliye* VPMR, *izdeliye* MR)

This special mission aircraft was not entirely a Tupolev product, being developed by the Beriyev TANTK (then headed by Aleksey K. Konstantinov) pursuant to a Council of Ministers directive issued in 1972. The Tu-142MR (*izdeliye* VPMR or *izdeliye* MR) was a 'doomsday' aircraft maintaining communications between submerged Type 667A (NATO *Yankee* class) nuclear-powered ballistic missile submarines and shore-based or airborne command posts in the event of a nuclear attack, hence the R suffix (for *[samolyot-]retranslyator* – communications relay aircraft). It filled the same role as the Ilyushin IL-82 (a much-modified IL-76MD *Candid-B* transport) and the US Navy's Boeing E-6A Hermes, designated TACAMO (TAke Charge And Move Out). The aircraft was fitted with the *Oryol* (Eagle) mission equipment suite, and this name was sometimes applied to the aircraft itself.

Though based on the Tu-142MK's airframe, the Tu-142MR differed a lot from other *Bear-F* versions. Its most obvious identification feature was a large ventral canoe fairing supplanting the search radar. This enclosed a trailing wire aerial (TWA) drum arranged lengthwise and driven by a GM-40 hydraulic motor

Above and below: Another photoshoot of the Tu-142MR prototype at Taganrog-Yoozhnyy. In a head-on view, the aircraft's special role is not obvious at all.

Opposite page: More aspects of the machine. Despite commencing 42…, the numbers on the placards are inventory numbers for a photo album, not the f/ns – this is one and the same aircraft.

This aspect of the Tu-142MR prototype shows the satellite communication antenna blister aft of the wing trailing edge.

Tu-142MR '15 Black', North Fleet, 73rd OAE, Kipelovo AB; note the different shade of grey

Final assembly shop No.6 at TANTK, with a Tu-142MR in the foreground

(**ghid**romo**tor**). The TWA was a 7.5-mm (0¹⁹⁄₆₄ in) copper-coated steel cable 7,680 m (25,200 ft) or, according to some sources, 8,000 m (26,250 ft) long. It was fitted with a stabilising drogue, taking 37 minutes to deploy fully and 48 minutes to rewind. A pyrotechnically operated guillotine was provided to cut the cable, should the antenna fail to rewind. Another distinctive feature was a prominent forward-facing bullet fairing atop the fin housing a communications aerial. A dorsal dielectric teardrop fairing amidships enclosed a satellite communications or satellite navigation antenna. Not so obvious were the three turbo generators providing power for the mission equipment.

The prototype was converted from Tu-142MK f/n 4263 built in 1976, retaining the usual glazed nose. A deep chin fairing similar to that of early Tu-142 *sans suffixe* housed a Groza-134VR (Thunderstorm) weather radar. The aircraft first flew in July 1976, undergoing state acceptance trials until December 1980; these were held in Taganrog, Feodosiya and at Kipelovo AB.

New-build production aircraft (15 in all) had an upgraded equipment suite and differed outwardly by having the weather radar relocated to a large thimble radome supplanting the nose glazing (flanked by ECM antenna blisters). The radar's former location was occupied by a shallow Tu-142MZ-style chin fairing and

The production version of the Tu-142MR had the weather radar in a thimble radome supplanting the navigator's station glazing. Here '15 Black', a grey-painted North Fleet/76th OPLAP DD example, taxies at Kipelovo AB.

TANTK mechanical and assembly shop chiefs and foremen pose with an almost complete Tu-142MR.

Right and below: The one-off Tu-142MRTs maritime reconnaissance/OTH targeting aircraft, showing the Tu-95MS style 'duck bill' nose.

Three-quarters rear view of the Tu-142MRTs prototype at Taganrog. The aircraft was mostly unpainted, having the greenish colour of electrochemically coated duralumin.

Another aspect of the Tu-142MRTs, showing the large radome.

Below: Here the aircraft is jacked up for a nosewheel change.

Bottom: This view illustrates best the radome and ventral ELINT fairings of the Tu-142MRTs.

antennas under the gunner's station à la Tu-95MS, all serving the Sayany-RT ECM/ESM system.

Production Tu-142MRs introduced an altogether different 13-digit c/n system. Thus, the prototype was reportedly c/n 8058014401005; 805 is a code for the factory (TMZD), 801 is an in-house product code for the Tu-142MR, 44 means the quarter and year of manufacture (October-December 1984) and 01005 is the 'famous last five'. Curiously, one of the radar-nosed production machines had a lower c/n than the prototype (8058014401002).

The prototype (now coded '11 Black') was not updated to full production standard and was delivered to the AVMF in as-was (glass-nosed) condition. The Tu-142MR's NATO reporting name is *Bear-J*.

Tu-142MRTs maritime reconnaissance /OTH targeting aircraft (*izdeliye* 342Ts)

In the early 1980s the Tupolev OKB initiated an R&D programme codenamed ***Mor'e*** (Sea), which was – very appropriately – part of a broader-scope programme codenamed Okean (Ocean, pronounced *okiahn*). Its purpose was to develop a new-generation maritime reconnaissance/OTH targeting aircraft as a successor to the Tu-95RTs, since the *Bear-Ds* would run out of service life at the end of the decade. Unsurprisingly, the Tu-142MK – the then-current production version of the *Bear* – served as the basis. Hence the aircraft, which was initially known as the Tu-95MRTs, was quickly redesignated Tu-142MRTs (*modernizeerovannyy razvedchik-tseleookazahtel'* – updated reconnaissance

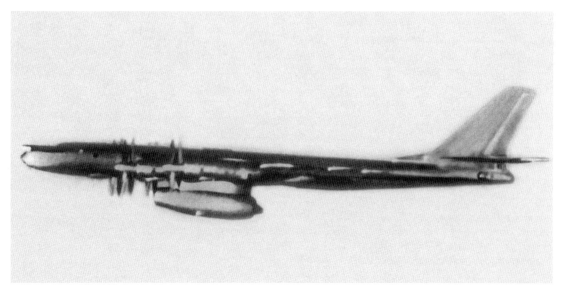

target designator aircraft). It was reportedly equipped with the upgraded Oospekh-1AV targeting system.

Moreover, whereas the Stage 1 Tu-142MRTs developed in 1984 was purely a reconnaissance/OTH targeting aircraft, Stage 2 was to add maritime strike capability by integrating Raduga Kh-32 supersonic anti-shipping missiles, two of which were to be carried under the wing roots on BD-45K pylons in the same manner as on the Tu-95K-22. The Kh-32 was an updated version of the Kh-22N (AS-4C) featuring an improved rocket motor and an improved guidance system; the N denotes *nizkovysotnaya* – low-altitude, indicating the possibility of launch at 1,000-8,000 m/3,280-26,250 ft). MKB Raduga had offered the Kh-32 (originally for the Tu-22M3) as a way of overcoming the old Kh-22's chief handicap – its short range of a few hundred kilometres making over-the-horizon attacks all but impossible because the Kh-22's seeker head could not find the target. Now while the Kh-22 cruised at 22,000 m (72,180 ft) on the way to the target, the Kh-32 was to climb almost to outer space (44,000 m/144,360 ft), then 'look beyond the horizon', detecting the target at 600-1,000 km (372-621 miles) range. The new missile also had a 'smarter' seeker head capable of classifying the targets and selecting the priority target (an aircraft carrier or a cruiser). Also, the Kh-32 had a much higher terminal velocity, which made it almost impossible to intercept. (Tests of the Kh-32 were eventually completed successfully in the late 1990s.)

The design work lasted ten years. In 1994 the Taganrog factory finally built the Tu-142MRTs prototype, using design documents supplied by what was by then the Tupolev ANTK (now the Tupolev PLC). Outwardly, for all practical purposes, the aircraft looked like a Tu-95MS missile strike aircraft with that distinctive 'duck bill' nose radome (presumably accommodating the missile data link antenna in this case) and the same rear fuselage and tail treatment (with equally distinctive ECM antennas below the gunner's station and at the top of the fin trailing edge and no lateral observation blisters) but with some features of the Tu-95RTs added – namely the huge ventral teardrop radome supplanting the weapons bay doors and the teardrop-shaped ELINT antenna fairing aft of it. This ELINT blister was located farther aft than on the Tu-95RTs and followed by a shallower second blister below the fin root fillet; the *Bear-D*'s lateral ELINT blisters were absent, as were the Arfa system's antenna fairings at the stabiliser tips.

Despite its *Bear-H* looks, the Tu-142MRTs prototype had a seven-digit c/n suggesting 1990 production with the 'famous last five' in the Tu-142MZ sequence (0604387), not a 13-digit c/n typical of the Tu-95MS (which had not been produced at Taganrog after 1984). Thus, we may assume that the machine was based on a *Bear-F Mod 4* airframe with some structural assemblies

Top and above: The second Tu-142LL (c/n 4243); the four-wheel main gear bogies and the raised flight deck roof are clearly visible.

Below: The first Tu-142LL on final approach to Zhukovskiy.
Centre and bottom: The first Tu-142LL takes off, showing the 12-wheel main gear bogies. The NK-32 development engine is semi-recessed in the bomb bay.

215

borrowed from the Tu-95MS. On the other hand, the aircraft reportedly had the product code *izdeliye* 342Ts identifying it as a derivative of the Tu-95MS (which had been provisionally designated Tu-342).

Just as the prototype was built, however, a change in the Russian MoD's concept of the system led to a review of the requirements and eventually prompted the decision to cancel the Tu-142MRTs programme; the next-generation reconnaissance/OTH targeting aircraft was now to be based on the Tupolev Tu-204 or Tu-214 twin-turbofan medium-haul airliner. Such an aircraft has not been built to date, and indeed some sources suggest the MoD is now in favour of a satellite-based system. The sole Tu-142MRTs never entered flight test, languishing at Taganrog-Yoozhnyy airfield and being progressively cannibalised for spares to keep other *Bears* airworthy until it was eventually scrapped.

Left and far left: Tu-142LL c/n 4243 at Zhukovskiy parked over a special trench with a jet blast deflector pipe. This allows the development engine to be run on the ground.

Opposite, centre: Close-up of the development engine pod on the second Tu-142LL. Note the shutter closing the air intake; it retracts into a fairing before the development engine is lowered and started up.

The second Tu-142LL was retrofitted with a weather radar in a chin radome. The IFR probe and the MAD 'stinger' were removed, leaving only stubs.

The Tu-142LL's crew at Zhukovskiy on 3rd May 1990 after setting a time-to-height record. Left to right: navigator V. Sedov, test engineer S. Solov'yuk, observer M. Geykhman, radio operator Yu. Ponomaryov, flight engineer A. Kovalenko, test engineer A. Bondarenko, V. Merkoolov, D. Bogdanov, co-pilot A. Atryukhin, captain V. Van'shin and test engineer S. Mokrousov.

The crew of the Tu-142LL pose with their mount at Zhukovskiy.

This photo taken in the early 1990s shows the Tu-142LL parked in front of a jet blast deflector at Zhukovskiy in company with another Tu-142.

Another view of Tu-142LL c/n 4243 parked over the blast deflector trench.

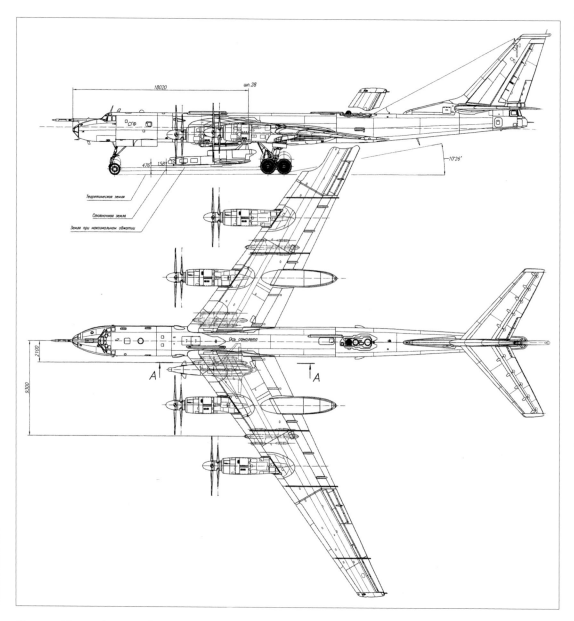

A drawing illustrating a projected conversion of a Tu-142MK as a 'mother ship' for the Tu-300 unmanned combat aerial vehicle.

Tu-142LL engine testbed

Two aircraft bore this designation. When the Tu-95LL engine testbed ran out of service life, the need for a replacement arose. Hence in the early 1970s the first prototype Tu-142 (c/n 4200) was converted into an engine testbed designated Tu-142LL for testing new large turbojet engines. Stripped of all ASW gear and armament, the aircraft was fitted with appropriate test equipment and the development engine mounting trapeze which had been removed from the hulk of the Tu-95LL.

The first Tu-142LL (the 'Centipede') was used to test three large jet engines. These were the Kuznetsov NK-25 three-spool afterburning turbofan rated at 14,300 kgp (31,525 lbst) at full military power and 25,000 kgp (55,110 lbst) in full afterburner for the Tu-22M3 bomber/missile strike aircraft, the Kolesov RD36-51A single-spool non-afterburning turbojet rated at

20,000 kgp (49,020 lbst) for take-off, 5,000 kgp (11,020 lbst) at maximum cruise power and 3,000 kgp (6,610 lbst) at minimum cruise power for the Tu-144D SST (*dahl'niy* – long-range) and the Kuznetsov NK-32 three-spool afterburning turbofan rated at 14,000 kgp (30,860 lbst) dry and 25,000 kgp (55,115 lbst) reheat for the Tu-160. The chin fairing of the Gagara thermal imager was originally retained but subsequently removed as unnecessary, resulting in a Tu-142M-style nose contour. The aircraft was used until the mid-1980s when it, too, was written off as time-expired.

The second *Bear-F* modified for the engine testbed role was the first prototype Tu-142MK (c/n 4243); the tactical code '043 Black' was reportedly assigned but not worn visibly. Again, all military equipment was removed. Interestingly, this aircraft reversed the sequence with the first Tu-142LL by having a chin-mounted ROZ-1 *Lotsiya* (Navigational directions, NATO

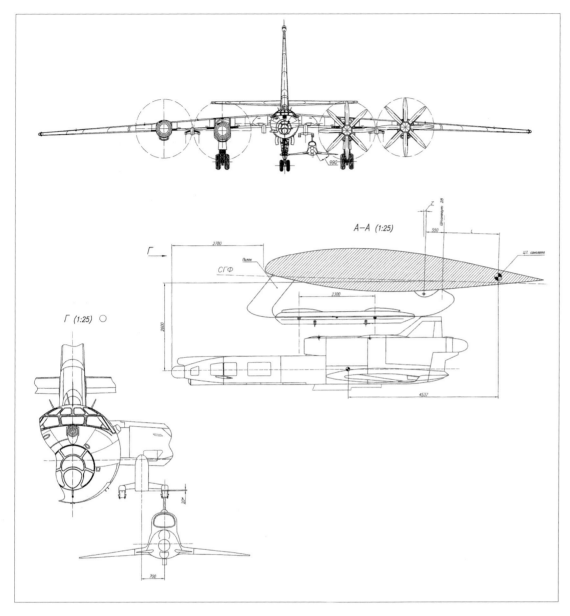

Front view of the projected 'mother ship' testbed with the UCAV suspended and details of the pylon.

Toad Stool) weather/navigation radar added (ROZ = **rah**diolo**kah**tor ob**zo**ra zem**lee** – ground mapping radar). This was enclosed by a small teardrop radome similar to that of the Tu-134 *Crusty* airliner (which had the same radar).

Tu-142LL c/n 4243 first flew in the late summer of 1986, captained by Tupolev OKB tst pilot Aleksandr A. Artyukhin. This aircraft, too, was fitted with an NK-32 development engine and made several flights to check the engine's surge limits, among other things.

On 3rd May 1990 the second Tu-142LL set several time-to-height and sustained altitude records in its class. The aircraft was captained by Valeriy F. Van'shin, with Aleksandr A. Artyukhin as co-pilot, V. M. Donskov and V. N. Sedov as navigators and Yuriy V. Ponomaryov as radio operator. The combined thrust of the four turboprops and the NK-32 was such that on the first attempt the aircraft kept pitching up during the climb,

almost trying to loop the loop, even though the pilots pushed the control yokes forward with all their might, and there was a distinct danger of losing control. Tu-142LL c/n 4243 sat at Zhukovskiy until the mid-1990s but was eventually struck off charge and scrapped.

Tu-142LL 'mother ship' for the Tu-300 UCAV (project)

In 1983 the Tupolev OKB, which had considerable experience in the field of unmanned aerial vehicles, began development of an unmanned combat aerial vehicle (UCAV) designated 'aircraft 300' (Tu-300) and named Korshun-U (the U suffix stood for *oo***dar**nyy – strike, used attributively). Like the preceding Tu-141/VR-2 Strizh (Swift, the bird) and Tu-143/VR-3 Reys (Flight) reconnaissance UAVs, the Tu-300 UCAV had a low-wing, tail-first layout with anhedral cropped-delta wings and small cropped-delta canards. A turbojet engine was buried in the rear fuselage, breathing through a dorsal air intake with an S-duct; the small trapezoidal vertical tail sat on top of the air intake trunk which also housed a parachute recovery system. However, the fuselage was much wider and deeper, reportedly incorporating an internal weapons bay; the warload could also be carried externally on a centreline pylon. The fuselage nose housed two thimble radomes above one another, with a transparent cupola enclosing an optoelectronic sighting system below them.

Despite being displayed publicly at several MAKS airshows in Zhukovskiy, the Tu-300 remains an enigma. Next to no detailed information is available on the UCAV – even the engine type and thrust remain undisclosed. However, unconfirmed reports say the Tu-300 has an all-up weight of 3,000 kg (6,610 lb), a cruising speed of 950 km/h (590 mph), a minimum operating altitude of 50 m (164 ft), a service ceiling of 6,000 m (19,685 ft) and a range of 200-300 km (124-186 miles). The UCAV was to be armed with both air-to-surface and air-to-air weapons; when fitted with appropriate avionics it could operate as a flying data relay station, loitering for up to two hours.

Flight tests began in 1991; the Tu-300 was launched from a sloping ramp with the assistance of two solid-fuel rocket boosters fitted under the wing roots. However, there is evidence that the Tupolev OKB also explored an air launch option for the UCAV and intended to convert a Tu-142 into a 'mother ship' for this purpose. An available detailed drawing shows what looks like a Tu-142MK with the radar and MAD removed. Instead of carrying the Tu-300 in a semi-recessed position in the weapons bay (with appropriately modified doors), the aircraft was to have two pylons under the wing roots, the port one mounting an adapter with two side-by-side ejector racks; the arrangement was remarkably similar to that of the Tu-95MS-16 (see Chapter 5). The Tu-300 was to be carried on the outer ejector rack, and there was barely enough room for its vertical tail beneath the *Bear*'s wing.

Apparently the 'mother ship' remained unbuilt – there is no evidence that it actually existed. The reason is simple – the Tu-300 programme was put on ice in the 1990s due to lack of funds. In 2007, however, the Tupolev JSC stated that it was dusting off the UCAV idea and that the Tu-300 design might be developed further.

Tu-142RTsD reconnaissance/strike aircraft (project)

In the 1980s, the Tupolev OKB considered expanding the Tu-142's range of missions by giving it anti-surface warfare (ASuW) capability for the first time. The aircraft was to become part of the *Drakon-1* (Dragon) long-range maritime reconnaissance/target designator system – a more advanced successor to the Oospekh-U. hence the Tu-142M adapted to the new role was

designated Tu-142RTsD; RTs denoted *razvedchik-tseleookazahtel'* (reconnaissance/target designator aircraft), while the D stood for Drakon.

The Tu-142RTsD was to be armed with a pair of Kh-22 missiles, carrying them under the wing roots on BD-45K pylons like the Tu-95K-22. Thus, apart from performing PHOTINT/ELINT and target designation over ranges of 1,100-1,400 km (680-870 miles), it would be capable of striking at surface targets of opportunity. However, the design work was making slow progress due to insufficient funding and the project was finally shelved in the late 1980s.

Tu-146 ASW/ASuW aircraft (project)

Also in the 1980s, the Tupolev OKB considered up-arming the Tu-142 with two brand-new air-to-surface missiles developed by OKB-455, aka the *Zvezda* (Star) OKB – the supersonic Kh-31 *Taïfoon* (Typhoon; NATO AS-17 *Krypton*) and the subsonic Kh-35 Uran (pronounced *oorahn*, meaning either 'Uranus' or 'uranium'; NATO AS-20 *Kayak*). Both missiles were to be integrated in anti-shipping and anti-radar versions.

Development of the Kh-31 had begun in 1975 – initially in the Kh-31P anti-radar version (*izdeliye* 77P; the suffix denoted *passivnoye samonavedeniye* – passive [radar] homing). The Kh-31A active radar homing anti-shipping missile (*izdeliye* 77A, for *aktivnoye samonavedeniye*) followed in 1978. The missile utilised a conventional layout with trapezoidal cruciform wings and aft-mounted all-movable cruciform rudders set at 45° to the vertical; the wings were shorter than the rudders. The forward body section housed the radar seeker head enclosed by an ogival radome, followed by the warhead and the powerplant. The latter comprised a solid-fuel ramjet sustainer occupying the rear one-third of the missile's body and a solid-fuel booster which fitted into the ramjet nozzle like a plug, being ejected after burnout. The ramjet had four small circular air intakes with shock cones located in the same planes as the wings and rudders; the air intake trunks blended into the housings of the control servos to form prominent fairings carrying the wings and rudders. When the missile was on the pylon the intakes were closed by conical plugs with off-centre tips which were whisked away by the slipstream as the booster fired, and the result was a very distinctive appearance. This layout reduced the missile's cross-section area and hence drag, while the use of a ramjet dramatically improved the missile's thrust/weight ratio.

The Kh-31 was 4.557 m (14 ft 11$^{13}/_{32}$ in) long less booster (or 4.7 m/15 ft 5$^{3}/_{64}$ in long, including booster), with a body diameter of 0.36 m (1 ft 2$^{1}/_{64}$ in), a wing span of 0.94 m (3 ft 1 in) and a rudder span of 1.1 m (3 ft 7$^{3}/_{32}$ in). The launch weight was 690 kg (1,520 lb), including 90 kg (198 lb) for the high-explosive warhead. The missile was carried on an AKU-58 ejector rack (*aviatsionnoye katapool'tnoye oostroystvo* – 'aircraft-mounted catapult device') ensuring safe separation and could be launched at up to 70 km (43 miles) range from an altitude of 50-15,000 m (160-49,210 ft).

Prior to launch the target co-ordinates provided by the aircraft's weapons control system were entered into the missile's inertial navigation system. When the booster fired, the Kh-31 climbed to 10,000 m (32,810 ft), accelerating to Mach 1.8 by the time the booster burned out and was ejected; then the sustainer ignited, taking the missile to Mach 3.1 (some sources say Mach 4.5!). At the terminal guidance phase the missile descended to 250-300 m (820-980 ft) and the radar seeker head located the target and achieved a lock-on. The missile entered flight test in 1982 and successfully passed its state acceptance trials in 1987-1990.

As for the Kh-35, development began in 1977 when the specifications were drawn up; the programme was officially sanctioned by a Council of Ministers directive issued on 16th April 1984 (or, according to some sources, 16th March 1983). Again, the missile had a conventional layout, featuring folding cruciform cropped-delta wings and trapezoidal rudders set at 45° to the vertical. The air-launched version was powered solely by a small turbofan buried in the rear fuselage and breathing through an oval-section ventral air intake (ground-launched and sea-launched versions had a solid-fuel rocket booster as well). The missile had an HE/fragmentation/incendiary warhead and a combined guidance system comprising an INS and an active radar homing system that came into play at the terminal guidance phase; the ARGS-35 active radar seeker head (*aktivnaya rahdiolokatsionnaya golovka samonavedeniya*) was virtually jam-proof, making the system immune to enemy ECM

The Kh-35 was 3.75 m (12 ft 3⅝ in) long, with a wing span of 1.3 m (4 ft 3³⁄₁₆ in) and a body diameter of 0.42 m (1 ft 4¹⁷⁄₃₂ in). The air-launched variety – conveniently using the same type of ejector rack (AKU-58) – had a launch weight of 480 kg (1,060 lb), including 145 kg (320 lb) for the warhead. Maximum 'kill' range was 130 km (80 miles); the missile was launched at altitudes up to 5,000 m (16,400 ft) and cruised at Mach 0.8-0.85, descending to 3-4 m (9-13 ft) at the terminal guidance phase.

In March 1984 the VPK issued a ruling requiring the Tupolev OKB to conduct an R&D programme for the purpose of integrating the Kh-31 and Kh-35 ASMs on the Tu-142. The customer (the Soviet MoD) also wanted the OKB to integrate the Sayany ECM system. Moreover, when India ordered its eight Tu-142MK-Es it expressed a wish that they be armed with missiles for ASuW duties.

Even before the VPK ruling, in February 1984, the Tupolev OKB's PD projects section started work on a project that was sufficiently different from the basic Tu-142M to warrant a separate designation, 'aircraft 146' (Tu-146). The project was completed in October 1984, envisaging an aircraft capable of ASW/ASuW operations up to 4,500 km (2,800 miles) from base; in addition to attacking submarines and surface ships with a displacement of up to 5,000 tonnes, the Tu-146 was to set up minefields and attack surface targets (including ground targets) with bombs if necessary.

In ASW configuration the Tu-146 was to carry sonobuoys, explosive sound sources, anti-submarine rockets or torpedoes, depth charges – and eight Kh-35 ASMs externally under the wings. In ASuW configuration the warload consisted of free-fall bombs and eight Kh-35 missiles (the Kh-31 was not considered). The flight performance was to match that of the Tu-142. In order to accommodate the equipment and weapons and improve the crew's working conditions the OKB considered giving the Tu-146 a new fuselage of larger diameter – possibly even as large as that of the Tu-114.

The Tu-146 met a favourable response from the Soviet MoD, but that's all there was – the PD project was not taken further. A possible reason is in-house competition from an all-new and much more capable ASW aircraft – the Tu-202 developed under an R&D programme codenamed Argon. This was to be a low-wing swept-wing aircraft with a large-diameter fuselage powered by four turbofan engines whose type was to be decided (the 12,000-kgp/26,455-lbst Solov'yov D-30KP two-spool turbofan was considered initially). However the Tu-202 did not materialise either.

Tu-142MN upgraded ASW aircraft (project)

At the turn of the century the Tupolev PLC proposed an upgrade programme for the Russian Navy's Tu-142M fleet. The reason for this was the change in priorities in anti-submarine warfare. The long range of current SLBMs means that missile submarines no longer need to venture far from their own shores to attack the adversary – in some cases an attack may even be launched from within their own territorial waters. This makes it utterly unrealistic to hunt down and destroy such a submarine with aviation assets; consequently, 'hunter' submarines become the main weapon against hostile subs, while ASW aircraft are assigned the mission of protecting friendly submarines from attack.

The new version of the *Bear-F* was designated Tu-142MN, the N suffix referring to a new *Novella* (Novel) STS developed by the Leninets Holding Co. The suite comprised a search radar, an optoelectronic sensor system, a sonar system, an ELINT system and an MAD. The aircraft was to be armed with eight anti-shipping missiles carried in pairs on underwing pylons; these were to be Kh-35U subsonic missiles or an air-launched version of the NPO Mashinostroyeniya 3M55 *Yakhont* (an archaic word meaning 'Emerald'; NATO SS-N-26 *Strobile*) supersonic ramjet-powered missile.

However, the programme was put on hold, the Russian Navy attaching higher priority to upgrading the IL-38.

Tu-142ME (Tu-142ME (1), Tu-142MSD) upgraded export ASW aircraft (project)

With a view to upgrading the Indian Navy's eight Tu-142MK-Es the Tupolev PLC proposed a mid-life update (MLU) programme. Designated Tu-142ME (also rendered as Tu-142M-E – or as Tu-142ME (1) to differentiate it from the Tu-142ME (2) described below), the upgraded aircraft was to have a service life extension, new avionics and new weapons. In addition to its primary role the Tu-142ME was to be capable of:

• ASuW and destruction of ground targets;
• setting up of minefields and mine barriers;
• detection of low-flying aircraft (in other words, a limited airborne early warning role);
• SIGINT;
• detection of maritime targets by means of a thermal imaging/low light level TV system;
• detection of dangerous weather phenomena (storm fronts and the like);
• monitoring and surveillance of offshore structures, such as oil rigs;
• maritime pollution control (detection and monitoring of oil slicks and the like);
• fishery control in littoral areas;
• monitoring and defence of territorial waters (the 200-mile economic exclusion zone) and pinpointing the co-ordinates of intruding vessels.

The upgrade envisaged replacing the Korshun-K STS with a *Morskoy zmey* (Sea Dragon) STS – the export version of the Novella suite, the same model as fitted to

An artist's impression of the upgraded Tu-142ME (Tu-142MSD) with a chin-mounted weather radar and six BrahMos-A supersonic anti-shipping missiles on underwing pylons.

A model showing the upgraded Tu-142ME (Tu-142MSD) with a load of eight Kh-35E subsonic anti-shipping missiles on underwing pylons.

the upgraded IL-38SD operated by the Indian Navy, with appropriate changes to adapt it to the Tu-142M. Hence, by analogy with the IL-38SD, the proposed upgrade was occasionally referred to as the Tu-142MSD in the press. As compared with the existing suite, the Sea Dragon offered higher efficiency, being designed with a modern avionics architecture. It enabled the following:

• detection, tracking and destruction of submarines;

• detection, tracking and destruction of surface ships;

• detection of low-flying aircraft;

• maritime surveillance;

• SIGINT of shipboard and shore-based emitters;

• location of crews in distress at sea.

The Tu-142ME's flight/navigation suite was to be upgraded as follows:

• the TsVM-10TS-42 and TsVM-10-15-42 processors were to be replaced with TsVM-90-600 processors;

• the DISS-7 Doppler speed/drift sensor and the ShO-17 Doppler sensor were to be replaced with the ShO-1SMA system;

• the L14MA astroinertial navigation system was to be replaced with the N-202 system;

• the L-21 flight/navigation suite control system was to be replaced with the KAPUI built-in test/control/display system;

• the standard altimeters calibrated in metric units (metres) were to be replaced with altimeters calibrated in Imperial units (feet);

• a coded altimeter was to be installed for reporting the altitude automatically when the aircraft was questioned by an IFF interrogator;

• a back-up artificial horizon was to be installed on the co-pilot's instrument panel to enhance flight safety;

• an additional satellite navigation system was to be installed, providing substantially more accurate data for navigation and targeting (including missile arming and launch). The proposed SNS-2 system (*spootnikovaya navigatsionnaya sistema*) makes it possible to determine the aircraft's exact position, speed and heading, using the American GPS satellite network, the Russian GLONASS satellite network, or both.

Indian-made avionics could also be integrated at the customer's request. Finally, the aircraft was to be powered by improved NK-12MPT engines driving AV-60T propellers having the same 5.6 m (18 ft 4½ in) diameter but broader-chord blades with a different airfoil. They are more efficient than the standard AV-60Ks, increasing take-off thrust by 15%, but are unfortunately heavier, weighing 1,350 kg (2,980 lb) versus 1,190 kg (2,620 lb), hence the T suffix denoting *tyazholyy* (heavy).

A drawing illustrating the principal features of the Tu-142ME (Tu-142MSD) MLU programme.

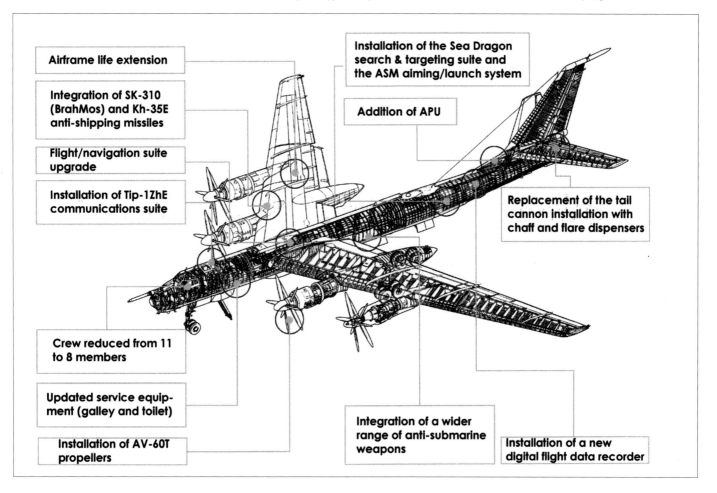

Airframe life extension

Integration of SK-310 (BrahMos) and Kh-35E anti-shipping missiles

Flight/navigation suite upgrade

Installation of Tip-1ZhE communications suite

Installation of the Sea Dragon search & targeting suite and the ASM aiming/launch system

Addition of APU

Replacement of the tail cannon installation with chaff and flare dispensers

Crew reduced from 11 to 8 members

Updated service equipment (galley and toilet)

Installation of AV-60T propellers

Integration of a wider range of anti-submarine weapons

Installation of a new digital flight data recorder

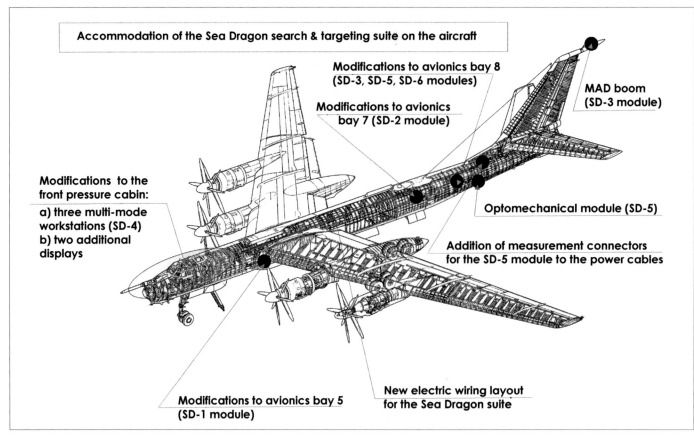

Accommodation of the Sea Dragon search & targeting suite on the aircraft

Modifications to avionics bay 8
(SD-3, SD-5, SD-6 modules)

Modifications to avionics
bay 7 (SD-2 module)

MAD boom
(SD-3 module)

Modifications to the
front pressure cabin:
a) three multi-mode
workstations (SD-4)
b) two additional
displays

Optomechanical module (SD-5)

Addition of measurement connectors
for the SD-5 module to the power cables

Modifications to avionics bay 5
(SD-1 module)

New electric wiring layout
for the Sea Dragon suite

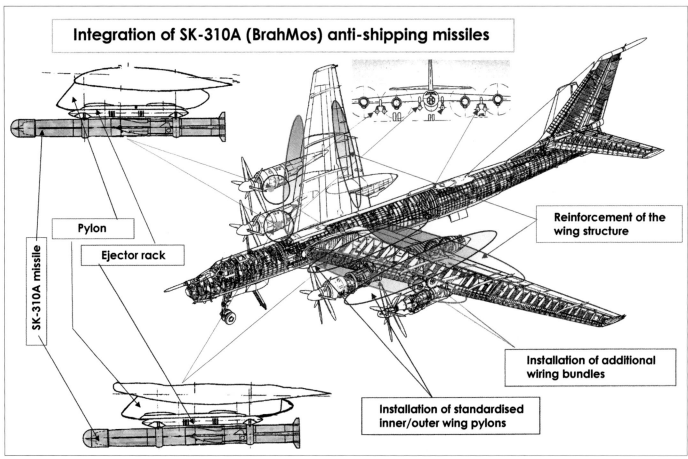

Integration of SK-310A (BrahMos) anti-shipping missiles

Pylon

Ejector rack

SK-310A missile

Reinforcement of the
wing structure

Installation of additional
wiring bundles

Installation of standardised
inner/outer wing pylons

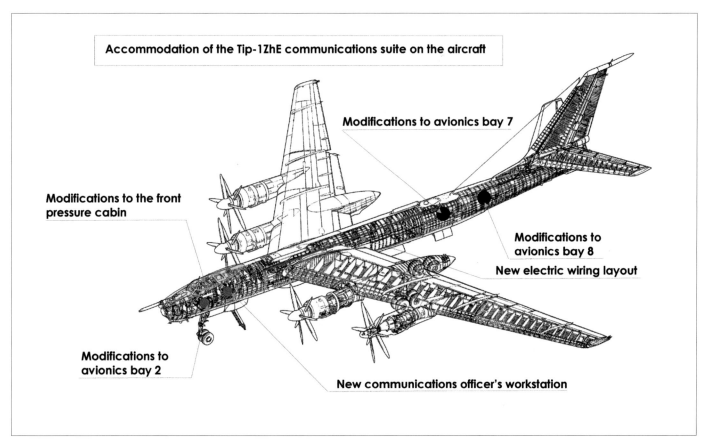

Accommodation of the Tip-1ZhE communications suite on the aircraft

Modifications to avionics bay 7

Modifications to the front pressure cabin

Modifications to avionics bay 8

New electric wiring layout

Modifications to avionics bay 2

New communications officer's workstation

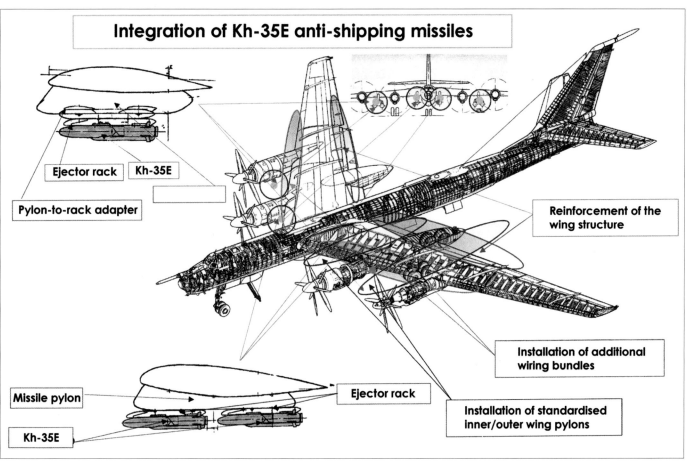

Integration of Kh-35E anti-shipping missiles

Ejector rack   Kh-35E

Pylon-to-rack adapter

Reinforcement of the wing structure

Installation of additional wiring bundles

Missile pylon

Ejector rack

Kh-35E

Installation of standardised inner/outer wing pylons

A model of the Tu-142MSD carrying eight Kh-35E missiles.

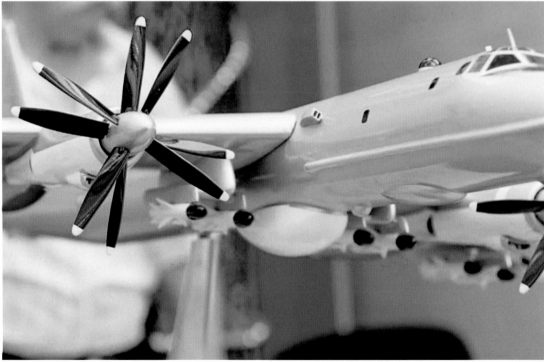

Close-up of the paired wing pylons for carrying Kh-35Es. The pylons are basically the same as on the upgraded Tu-95MS (see next chapter), except for the missile ejector racks.

Some outdated equipment items that were standard for the Tu-142M (Tu-142MK-E), namely the A-722-04 long-range radio navigation system, the RKA-M radio/celestial course corrector and the Roomb-1B navigational attitude & heading reference system (AHRS), were to be removed. A specialised weather radar was to be added under the nose, enabling the crew to detect dangerous weather phenomena and navigate by means of landmarks.

The Tu-142ME was also to feature a new-generation Type 1ZhE communications suite utilising state-of-the-art microprocessor technology, and the communications officer's workstation was to be redesigned completely. The suite provided voice link and automatic coded radio communication with ground control and 'friendly' ships and aircraft. It ensured:

• two-way voice communication in the metre, decimetre and decametre wavebands;

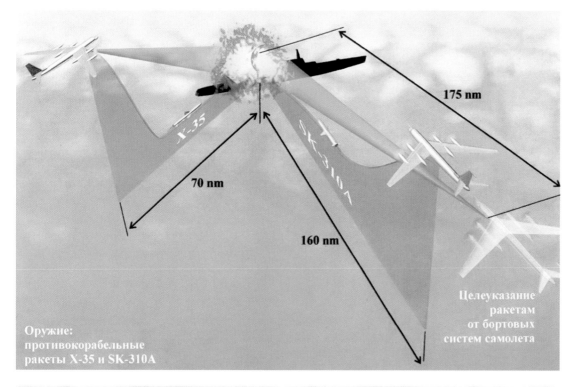

Оружие:
противокорабельные
ракеты X-35 и SK-310A

X-35

SK-310A

175 nm

70 nm

160 nm

Целеуказание
ракетам
от бортовых
систем самолета

A drawing from the
Tupolev PLC advertising
materials illustrating the
launch range of Kh-35E
and SK-310A BrahMos
missiles from the
Tu-142MSD (Tu-142MM-E)
when operating in ASuW
mode.

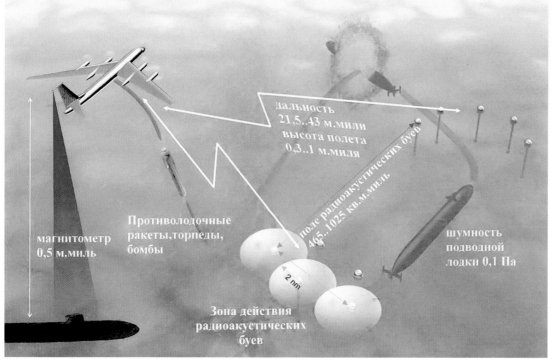

дальность
21,5..43 м.мили
высота полета
0,3..1 м.миля

поле радиоакустических буев
465..1025 кв.м.миль

магнитометр
0,5 м.миль

Противолодочные
ракеты,торпеды,
бомбы

шумность
подводной
лодки 0,1 Па

2 nm

Зона действия
радиоакустических
буев

This drawing shows the
detection range of the
Tu-142MSD's ASW
systems and weapons
when seeking and
attacking submarines.

• two-way data link;

• redundancy of voice link and coded radio communication channels;

• automatic sending of distress signals on all channels;

• standby mode for reception of emergency beacons in the metre and decimetre wavebands;

• recording of radio communications;

• audio reproduction of incoming standard messages;

• audio warning (voice alert) of dangerous flight modes and emergencies;

• security of voice and coded communications (scrambling and descrambling);

• automated control of the suite's components;

• automatic serviceability monitoring of the suite's components (health and usage monitoring).

The aircraft's combat efficiency was to be enhanced considerably by integrating new-

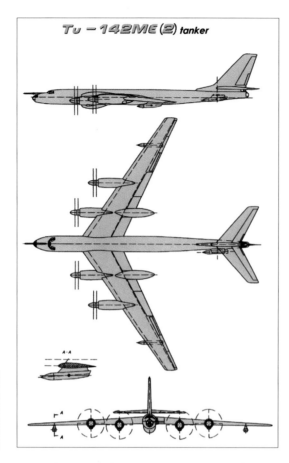

A three-view drawing of the proposed Tu-142ME (2) three-point tanker showing the location of the hose drum units.

launch weight of 2,500 kg (5,510 lb), including a 200-kg (440-lb) conventional warhead.

To enable this, four missile pylons were to be installed 2.1 m (6 ft 1⁵⁄₆₄ in) and 9.3 m (30 ft 6⁵⁄₆₄ in) from the centreline, with appropriate local reinforcement of the wing structure and installation of appropriate wiring. The maximum number of missiles was to be eight Kh-35Es (two per pylon, carried in tandem on the inboard pylons and side-by-side on the outboard ones) or six SK-310As – two on the inboard pylons and four in side-by-side pairs on the outboard pylons. With Kh-35E and SK-310 missiles, attacks against surface ship would be possible at 129.5 km (and 80 miles) and 296 km (184 miles) respectively.

The new anti-submarine weapons were intended for engaging submarines which are motionless or travelling at various depths. They included:

• the APR-3E new-generation anti-submarine missile, three of which were to be carried. The 525-kg (1,157-b) missile has a 45-kg (99-lb) warhead and is capable of hitting submarines travelling at speeds up to 80 km/h (43.2 kts) and depths up to 800 m (2,620 ft);

• the UMGT-1ME anti-submarine torpedo (again, three were to be carried). The 725-kg (1,600-b) missile has a 60-kg (132-lb) warhead and a 'kill' depth of 20-550 m (65-1,800 ft);

• the S-3V guided anti-submarine bomb, of which 14 were to be carried. The 94-kg (207-b) weapon contains 19 kg (42 lb) of explosive and can engage submarines travelling at depths up to 600 m (1,970 ft);

• MDM-3 Mod. 1 anti-shipping mines (12) and MDM-2 Mod. 1 anti-shipping mines (six).

For the purpose of carrying anti-shipping missiles the Tu-142ME was to be equipped with the following items:

• the abovementioned pylons (standardised for various missiles);

• ejector racks;

• a missile hoisting system;

generation anti-submarine weapons, anti-shipping missiles and naval mines. Two types of ASMs were proposed – the Russian Kh-35E and the SK-310A, an air-launched version of the BrahMos ASM (a derivative of the 3M55 co-developed by India and Russia; BrahMos is a portmanteau of the names of two rivers – Brahmaputra and Moskva). The SK-310A is an active radar homing supersonic missile with a solid-fuel rocket booster and a ramjet sustainer featuring a nose air intake with a shock cone that is closed by a parabolic cover until the moment of launch. It has a

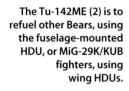

The Tu-142ME (2) is to refuel other Bears, using the fuselage-mounted HDU, or MiG-29K/KUB fighters, using wing HDUs.

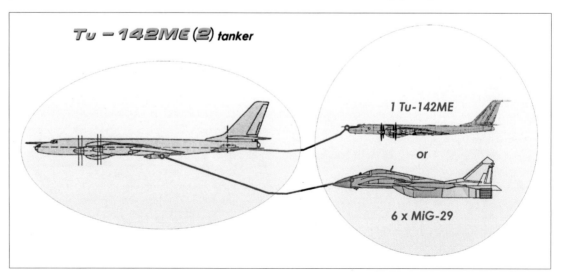

• a missile pre-launch and launch control system (SUPPR – *sistema oopravleniya podgotovkoy i pooskom raket*);

• control and display units at the crew workstations.

The upgrade also included measures aimed at extending the service life of the airframe and aircraft systems. However, the Russian upgrade was never implemented because the partners failed to agree on the financial terms, and India resorted to Israeli assistance instead (see Chapter 9).

Tu-142ME (2) refuelling tanker (project)

In parallel with the Tu-142ME, the Tupolev PLC offered an in-flight refuelling tanker version of the *Bear-F Mod 3* to the Indian Navy. The aircraft was designated Tu-142ME (2), oddly echoing the designations of Soviet/Russian DA tankers from the Myasishchev stable – the M-4-2 *Bison-A* and the 3MS-2/3MN-2 *Bison-B*. This designation was chosen because the Z suffix, which would have been appropriate for a refuelling tanker (*zaprahvshchik*), was already allocated to the Tu-142MZ where it had an altogether different meaning.

Like the IL-78, the aircraft was to be a three-point tanker with podded hose drum units arranged in the same fashion – two under the outer wings in line with the ailerons' centre sections and one on the port side of the rear fuselage on an L-shaped pylon. (Actually, just like on the IL-78M *Midas-B*, all three HDUs were carried on identical pylons, the centre pylon being attached to an airfoil-section horizontal adapter projecting from the fuselage so that the middle of the pod was in line with the stabiliser leading edge. The HDUs were installed in a slightly nose-down attitude.) Additional fuel tanks were suspended in the weapons bay, and of course appropriate local structural reinforcement was made and appropriate piping and wiring was installed. The gunner's station featured an additional control panel allowing the gunner to act as the refuelling systems operator (RSO). The search radar was retained, suggesting the aircraft could be reconfigured back for the ASW role if necessary.

The HDUs could be either Russian-made NPP Zvezda UPAZ-1As as fitted to the standard IL-78/IL-78M or British-made Flight Refuelling Ltd. Mk 32s as fitted to the Indian Air Force's IL-78MKI tankers. The UPAZ-1A (*oonifitseerovannyy podvesnoy agregaht zaprahvki* – 'standardised suspended refuelling unit' because it could be carried by tactical aircraft as well) had a 26-m (85 ft 3 in) hose and a flexible 'basket' drogue. The hose drum was powered by a ram air turbine (RAT) with an intake scoop on the port side which was normally closed. A second air intake in the nose closed by a translating cone was for an RAT driving a generator for the electric transfer pump. Normal delivery rate was 1,000 litres (220 Imp gal) per minute, increasing to 2,200 litres (484 Imp gal) in case of need.

The Tu-142ME (2) was intended for supporting the operations of both regular ASW-configured Tu-142MEs and the Indian Navy's new conventional take-off and landing shipboard fighters – Mikoyan MiG-29K single-seaters (*izdeliye 9.41*; K = *korabel'nyy* – shipboard) and MiG-29KUB two-seaters (*izdeliye 9.47*; KUB = *korabel'nyy oochebno-boyevoy* – shipboard combat trainer) which had been ordered on 20th January 2004 to equip the carrier wing of the new carrier INS *Vikramaditya*. During joint service operations they could also work with other types equipped with IFR probes (such as the Indian Air Force's Sukhoi Su-30MKI *Flanker-E* multi-role heavy fighters). According to estimates, the aircraft would be capable of transferring 30 tons (66,140 lb) of fuel within a 2,000-km (1,242-mile) combat radius and refuelling one Tu-142MK-E or six MiG-29K/KUBs in a single sortie. The project was not proceeded with.

Tu-142MRE communications relay aircraft (project)

Another version offered to the Indian Navy was the Tu-142MRE (*retranslyator eksportnyy* – export communications relay aircraft), an export version of the *Bear-J*. It was intended to fill the need for a link between shore-based command centres and the Indian Navy's nuclear-powered submarines.

A model of the Tu-142MRE showing no visible differences from the production Tu-142MR was displayed at the Hydro Aviation Show 2008 in Ghelendjik (Krasnodar Territory) on the Russian Black Sea coast in September 2008. The accompanying data placard advertised the following performance figures: maximum take-off weight 184,000 kg (405,640 lb); range 12,000 km (7,456 miles) on internal fuel or 13,300 km (8,264 miles)

A display model of the Tu-142MRE export communications relay aircraft.

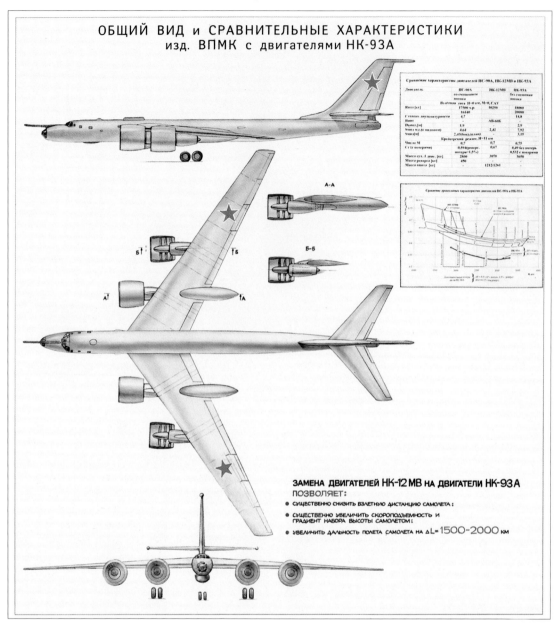

ОБЩИЙ ВИД и СРАВНИТЕЛЬНЫЕ ХАРАКТЕРИСТИКИ
изд. ВПМК с двигателями НК-93А

ЗАМЕНА ДВИГАТЕЛЕЙ НК-12 МВ НА ДВИГАТЕЛИ НК-93 А
ПОЗВОЛЯЕТ:
● СУЩЕСТВЕННО СНИЗИТЬ ВЗЛЕТНУЮ ДИСТАНЦИЮ САМОЛЕТА ;
● СУЩЕСТВЕННО УВЕЛИЧИТЬ СКОРОПОДЪЕМНОСТЬ И
   ГРАДИЕНТ НАБОРА ВЫСОТЫ САМОЛЕТОМ ;
● УВЕЛИЧИТЬ ДАЛЬНОСТЬ ПОЛЕТА САМОЛЕТА НА ΔL=1500-2000 км

A drawing from the project documents showing a proposed refit of the Tu-142MK-E with NK-93A shrouded propfans.

with one fuel top-up; loitering altitude with the TWA deployed 7,500-9,000 m (24,600-29,530 ft); speed with the TWA deployed 550-600 km/h (341-372 mph).

Even then, the issue of where to source the aircraft if India placed an order was a difficult one, considering that the *Bear-J* was no longer in production. The number of Tu-142MRs being small as it is, the Russian Navy would not be happy to part with any of these strategically important aircraft – and India would require at least two. The only option was seemingly to refurbish and convert a pair of Tu-142Ms from storage stocks. However, the project did not go ahead.

Tu-142MK upgraded ASW aircraft with NK-93A propfans (project)

In 1988 the Kuznetsov OKB (SNTK Trood) started work on a new type of engine – the NK-92 contra-rotating

integrated shrouded propfan (CRISP) rated at 18,000 kgp (39,680 lbst) for take-off and 3,200 kgp (7,050 lbst) for cruise. This was envisaged for various heavy aircraft, such as the projected Ilyushin IL-106 four-engined heavy military transport and the IL-90-200 twin-engined widebody long-haul airliner. The NK-92 was a three-spool engine; the core featured a seven-stage low-pressure compressor, an eight-stage high-pressure compressor, a multi-burner annular combustion chamber and single-stage HP and LP turbines. Downstream of these was a three-stage power turbine driving an SKBM (NPP Aerosila) SV-92 propfan of 2.9 m (9 ft 6¹¹⁄₆₄ in) diameter with an RSV-92 speed governor. The SV-92 had variable-pitch scimitar-shaped blades of composite construction – eight on the front row turning anti-clockwise when seen from the front and ten on the rear row turning clockwise; the power

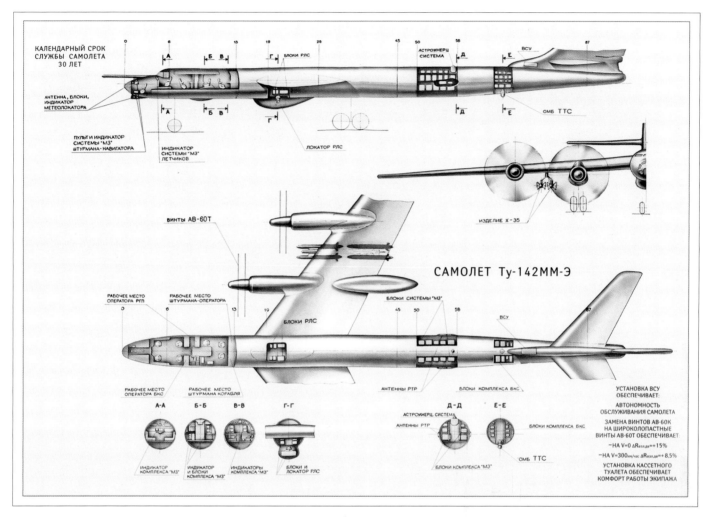

САМОЛЕТ Ту-142ММ-Э

was distributed 40/60 between the front and rear rows. The propfan gearbox was enclosed by a bullet-shaped spinner and the propfan itself had a shroud attached to the engine nacelle by radial struts and carrying a detachable cowl. The SFC was 0.23 kg/kgp-hr at take-off power and 0.49 kg/kgp-hr at cruise power. The engine pressure ratio was 28.85 at take-off power and 37.0 at cruise power and the turbine temperature was 1,520°K. The engine was 5.972 m (19 ft 7⁷⁄₆₄ in) long and weighed 3,650 kg (8,050 lb). The NK-92 had full authority digital engine control (FADEC).

In the 1990s the Tupolev ANTK contemplated the possibility of re-engining the Tu-142MK with a more refined version of the Kuznetsov CRISP designated NK-93A; the effort was headed by B. A. Gribanov. The existing engine nacelles were deleted and replaced by horizontal pylons, the inboard ones blending with the main gear fairings. The NK-93As were attached to these pylons so that the tops of the nacelles were almost level with the wing undersurface and the propfan shrouds were just ahead of the wing leading edge. The outer engines had standard single nozzles with conical centrebodies, while the inner ones were fitted with bifurcated jetpipes. According to the designers'

estimates, substituting the NK-12MV engines with NK-93As would increase the Tu-142MK's range by 1,500-2,000 km (931-1,242 miles), shorten the take-off run considerably and offer a significant improvement in rate of climb.

However, as an old Russian soldier song goes, 'On the map there were no hitches; /Alas! forgotten were the ditches /That we would have to cross.' Development of the NK-92/NK-93 proved to be rather protracted. The first prototype engine ran on a bench in 1989, but for various reasons (including the engine's failure to meet the project specifications and, according to some sources, opposition to the project within the industry) it was not until 2006 that a prototype engine was installed on one of LII's IL-76LL engine testbeds. Even that engine had a very provisional FADEC, and after a few test flights in 2007-08 the programme was discontinued – and the Tu-142MK re-engining project died with it.

Tu-142MM-E upgraded ASW aircraft (project)

This is apparently a revival of the Tu-142MN project, since the aircraft features a Novella-P STS and the ability

A drawing showing details of the proposed Tu-142MM-E mid-life upgrade. It includes such features as a service life extension to 30 years, carriage of eight Kh-35E ASMs in tandem pairs, and new avionics (including a weather radar).

233

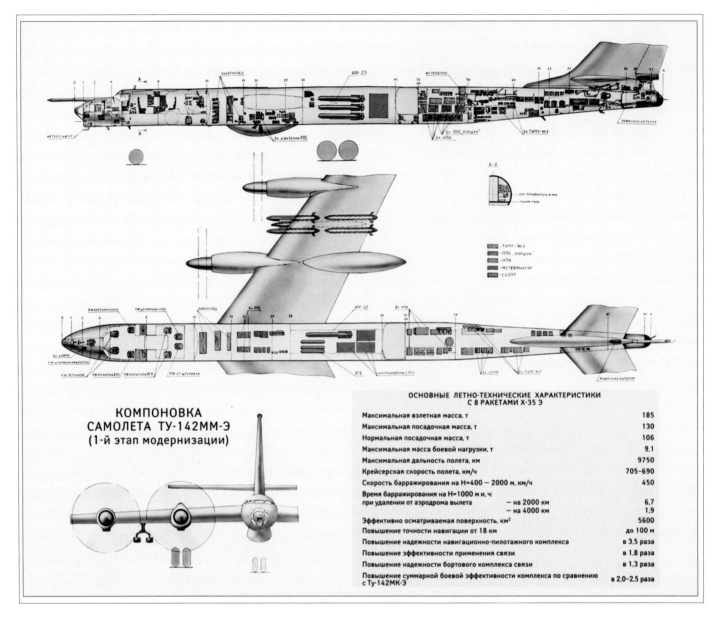

КОМПОНОВКА
САМОЛЕТА ТУ-142ММ-Э
(1-й этап модернизации)

ОСНОВНЫЕ ЛЕТНО-ТЕХНИЧЕСКИЕ ХАРАКТЕРИСТИКИ С 8 РАКЕТАМИ Х-35 Э	
Максимальная взлетная масса, т	185
Максимальная посадочная масса, т	130
Нормальная посадочная масса, т	106
Максимальная масса боевой нагрузки, т	9,1
Максимальная дальность полета, км	9750
Крейсерская скорость полета, км/ч	705–690
Скорость барражирования на Н=400 – 2000 м, км/ч	450
Время барражирования на Н=1000 м и, ч: при удалении от аэродрома вылета — на 2000 км	6,7
— на 4000 км	1,9
Эффективно осматриваемая поверхность, км²	5600
Повышение точности навигации от 18 км	до 100 м
Повышение надежности навигационно-пилотажного комплекса	в 3,5 раза
Повышение эффективности применения связи	в 1,8 раза
Повышение надежности бортового комплекса связи	в 1,3 раза
Повышение суммарной боевой эффективности комплекса по сравнению с Ту-142МК-Э	в 2,0–2,5 раза

A cutaway drawing of the Tu-142MM-E at Stage 1 of the upgrade programme showing the location of the new weapons and avionics.

to carry new weapons, including ASMs. The Novella-P comprises the following:

• a search/navigation radar, a sonobuoy system working with RGB-16/RGB-16M, RGB-41, RGB-47, RGB-48 and RGB-81 hydroacoustic buoys, RTB-91 and RTB-93 telemetric buoys (*rah*diotelemet*rich*eskiy *booy*) and special buoys for communicating with friendly subs;

• an MAD;

• a low light level TV/thermal imaging system;

• an ELINT system;

• a so-called command-tactical system recording the course of the mission for post-flight analysis.

Changes will be made to the powerplant – the Tu-142MM-E will be fitted with AV-60T propellers. In similar manner to late-production Tu-95MS missile carriers, an auxiliary power unit (APU) will be installed in the fin root fillet for engine starting and ground power supply/air conditioning, with an air intake door to

starboard and an exhaust door to port. However, the APU will be of a newer type – the NPP Aerosila TA-18-100 (rather than the TA-12).

Additionally, the aircraft is to be equipped with a new *Tsirkon* (Zircon) communications suite supplanting the Strela-142M suite, a new flight/ navigation suite, and a new BUR-3 flight data recorder system. The designers are considering deleting the tail cannon barbette (which is not much use in modern combat anyway) and replacing it with an all-round missile warning/missile protection system featuring new chaff/flare dispensers.

The range of weapons is to include Kh-35 and 3M55 anti-shipping missiles, APR-3 anti-submarine rockets, S-3V guided bombs and MDM-2 Mod. 1 and MDM-3 Mod. 1 naval mines. The aircraft is to receive a service life extension increasing the designated airframe life to 30 years.

КОМПОНОВКА
САМОЛЕТА ТУ-142ММ-Э
(2-й этап модернизации)

ОСНОВНЫЕ ЛЕТНО-ТЕХНИЧЕСКИЕ ХАРАКТЕРИСТИКИ С 8 РАКЕТАМИ Х-35 Э	
Максимальная взлетная масса, т	185
Максимальная посадочная масса, т	130
Нормальная посадочная масса, т	106
Максимальная масса боевой нагрузки, т	9,1
Максимальная дальность полета, км	9750
Крейсерская скорость полета, км/ч	705–690
Скорость барражирования на Н=400 – 2000 м, км/ч	450
Время барражирования на Н=1000 м, ч при удалении от аэродрома вылета – на 2000 км	6,7–7,6
– на 4000 км	1,9–2,2
Эффективно осматриваемая поверхность, км²	8500
Точность навигации, м	100
Освещение надводной и воздушной обстановки на дальности, км	6000
Повышение суммарной боевой эффективности комплекса по сравнению с Ту-142МК-Э	в 3–3,5 раза
Увеличение времени барражирования самолета за счет выключения одного двигателя (с зафлюгированными винтами)	на 14%

The upgrade is to proceed in two stages. Stage 1 will see some components of the Korshun STS retained but a weather radar in a chin radome and new navigation suite components in the rear fuselage avionics bay will be added, the Tip-1ZhE communications suite will be installed, and two missile pylons will be installed between the inner and outer engines, each carrying four Kh-35 ASMs in tandem pairs. At this stage navigational accuracy at ranges from 18 km (11.18 miles) upwards will be increased to 100 m (330 ft); the reliability of the flight/navigation suite and the communications suite will be improved by a factor of 3.5 and 1.3 respectively, and communications efficiency will be increased by a factor of 1.8. The overall combat efficiency of the Tu-142MM-E will be 2-2.5 times higher as compared to the Tu-142MK-E.

Stage 2 will see the Novella-P suite and the new defensive electronics suite integrated in full; in particular, Mak-UT1 (Poppy) and Sakura missile warning system sensors with a 360° field of view will be installed above and below the rear fuselage. Changes will be made to the crew workstations in the forward pressure cabin and the tail gunner's station will be eliminated, reducing the crew complement from ten to eight (one of the sonobuoy system operators will be automated away). The APU will be installed and MDM-5 Mod. 1 mines will be added to the range of compatible weapons. The aircraft will be able to scan the surface and air situation at ranges up to 6,000 km (3,730 miles). If one engine is shut down and the propellers feathered to save fuel, on-station loiter time will be increased 14%.

A similar drawing of the Tu-142MM-E at Stage 2 of the upgrade programme.

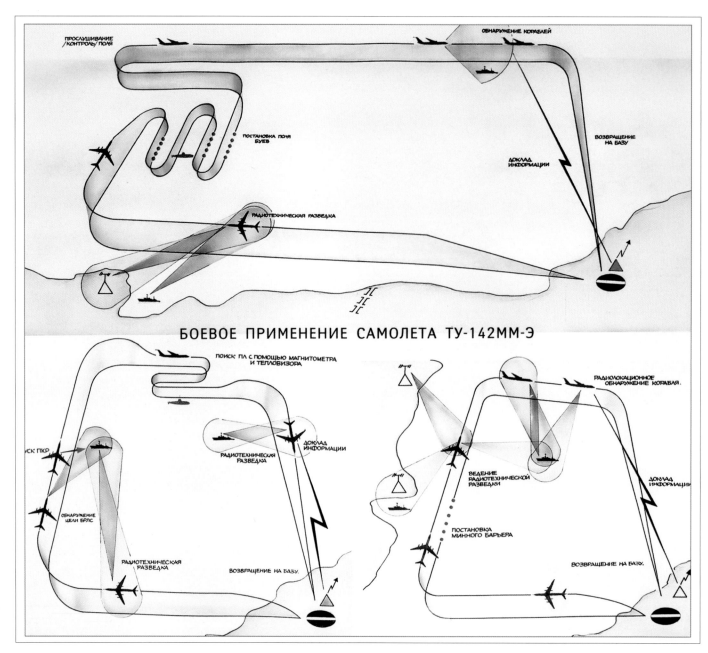

БОЕВОЕ ПРИМЕНЕНИЕ САМОЛЕТА ТУ-142ММ-Э

Basic specifications of the Tu-142MM-E		
	Stage 1	Stage 2
Maximum take-off weight, kg (lb)	185,000 (407,860)	185,000 (407,860)
Landing weight, kg (lb):		
normal	106,000 (233,690)	106,000 (233,690)
maximum	130,000 (286,600)	130,000 (286,600)
Maximum ordnance load, kg (lb)	9,100 (20,060)	9,100 (20,060)
Maximum range, km (miles)	9,750 (6,060)	9,750 (6,060)
Cruising speed, km/h (mph)	690-705 (428-437)	690-705 (428-437)
On-station loitering time at 1,000 m (3,280 ft), hours;		
2,000 km (1,242 miles) from base	6.7	6.7-7.6
4,000 km (2,490 miles) from base	1.9	1.9-2.2
Area patrolled during one sortie, km² (sq miles)	5,600 (2,162)	8,500 (3,281)
Overall combat efficiency increase versus Tu-142MK-E	x 2.0-2.5	x 3.0-3.5

Top: A diagram showing a possible mission profile of the Tu-142MM-E. Taking off and crossing the border, the aircraft conducts SIGINT of suspicious ships and shore transmitters, then flies a shuttle patterns to set up a field of sonobuoys and listens to their signals. Next, it detects suspicious ships by radar, transmits an intelligence report and returns to base.

Above left: In this case the Tu-142MM-E conducts SIGINT of a ship and, after making certain that it is hostile, detects it by radar and fires a missile. Next, it searches for a hostile submarine, using MAD and thermal imaging equipment, conducts SIGINT of suspicious ships, sends a report and returns to base.

Above: Here the Tu-142MM-E sets up a minefield on a shipping lane, then conducts SIGINT of suspicious ships and shore transmitters, detects a ship by radar, sends a report and returns to base.

CHAPTER FIVE

'Second-generation' cruise missile carriers

On 30th June 1977 US President Jimmy Carter announced that the Rockwell B-1A supersonic bomber programme would be cancelled in favour of ICBMs, SLBMs and updated Boeing B-52s armed with AGM-86B (ALCM) strategic air-launched cruise missiles. The AGM-86B, whose full-scale development began in January 1977, had a range of 2,400 km (1,500 miles), allowing it to be launched well outside the range of any Soviet air defences and penetrate at low altitude in large numbers (each B-52 was to carry 12 missiles, and the maximum number per aircraft was eventually increased to 20). The *Pacer Plank* mid-life upgrade programme to arm the B-52G and B-52H with ALCMs was indeed launched in 1977, although the up-armed bombers would not see service until 1984. Moreover, the Reagan

administration revived the B-1 programme in 1981, and the definitive B-1B Lancer also had stand-off missile capability – albeit it did not carry AGM-86Bs.

These events led the Soviet military and political leaders, as well as the nation's defence industry, to make a fundamental change to the Soviet strategic bomber programme in order to achieve parity with the USA. Like the latter, the Soviet Union pursued air-launched cruise missile programmes as a two-pronged effort. One direction of work was the creation of the Tu-160 *Blackjack* supersonic intercontinental bomber with variable-geometry wings – the Soviet answer to the B-1. The other was the decision to develop an interim cruise missile platform in the shape of an updated Tu-95.

Front view of a Tu-95MS upgraded to carry eight Kh-101 or Kh-102 cruise missiles.

Tu-242 'Shkval' missile strike aircraft (project)

The Tu-95 appeared to be an ideal launch platform for the subsonic, 'low-and-slow' Kh-55 cruise missile which, as recounted in Chapter 3, had been put through its paces on the Tu-95M-55 weapons testbed. (The Tu-160 was then being developed with 'high-and-fast' missiles in mind – the Kh-45 **Mol**niya (Lightning) long-range hypersonic missile and the Kh-15 (AS-16 *Kickback*) short-range aeroballistic missile, which were then under development at OKB-2-155 (MKB Raduga). In the long run the Tu-160 would carry neither of these weapons.) However, after considering the options on hand the Tupolev OKB designers concluded that using the 'first-generation' Tu-95 as the basis was pointless – it had no upgrade potential and the Tu-95KD/Tu-95KM had not enough service life remaining to merit such an upgrade. The more modern Tu-142, on the other hand, was a much better starting point and the Kh-55 missile carriers would have to be new-build aircraft anyway.

At the end of 1976 General Designer Aleksey A. Tupolev, who became the new head of the OKB after Andrey N. Tupolev's death in 1972, ordered the OKB's PD projects department (then headed by Grigoriy I. Zal'tsman) to prepare the project of a missile strike aircraft based on the Tu-142M's airframe and power-plant. The aircraft was to be armed with a variety of missiles – the Kh-22M, the Kh-45MS, the Kh-15 and the

Kh-55. The project was to be completed in the second quarter of 1977; Nikolay V. Kirsanov was appointed project chief.

No information is available on the Kh-45MS, except that the missile, which was also considered for the Tu-160, was rather different from the original Kh-45 *sans suffixe*, having very short strake-like wings and trapezoidal (not pentagonal) rudders set at 45° to the horizontal plane. The Kh-15 developed as a successor to the obsolete Kh-22 and KSR-5 missiles was a hypersonic weapon capable of Mach 5 flight to be used against targets with pre-programmed co-ordinates. This wingless missile had a solid-propellant rocket motor and a nuclear warhead or a conventional shaped-charge/high-explosive warhead. It was 4.78 m (15 ft 8³⁄₁₆ in) long, with a body diameter of 0.455 m (1 ft 5²⁹⁄₃₂ in) and three fins set at 120° with respect to each other, two of them being all-movable; the tail surface span was 0.92 m (3 ft 0⁷⁄₃₂ in). The Kh-15 had a launch weight of 1,200 kg (2,645 lb), including a 150-kg (330-lb) warhead, and was designed to be carried on a rotary launcher which was originally designated APU-15 but later redesignated MKU-6-1. After launch at a maximum range of 150 km (93 miles) the Kh-15 was to follow a ballistic trajectory as a means of extending range, accelerating to Mach 5 and entering the stratosphere with an apogee at up to 40 km (131,230 ft). The flight trajectory was formed by the aircraft's weapons control system (WCS) to suit the applicable launch range while the missile was still on the launcher. The missile featured an INS which guided it to the target, using pre-entered co-ordinates.)

The missile strike version was provisionally designated Tu-242, reflecting its Tu-142 origins, and the project bore the codename Shkval (Gale). Project work started in January 1977. It quickly became apparent that installing the differing pre-launch equipment for the four types of missiles would make the WCS unduly complex and add weight. Also, the CG position and CG range with the four alternative warloads would differ considerably (even though it was within acceptable limits), thereby creating an additional complication.

By June 1977, when the PD project was drawn up, a decision had been taken to proceed with a different missile strike derivative of the Tu-142M using a single missile type – the Kh-55 (see next entry). Hence the Tu-242 project was abandoned.

Tu-142MS missile strike aircraft (project)

In parallel with the Tu-242, the OKB studied another missile strike derivative of the Tu-142M/Tu-142MK which was tentatively designated Tu-142MS (*modern-izee*rovannyy, *strategich*eskiy – updated, strategic). The aircraft would be equipped with two MKU-6-5 rotary launchers to carry 12 Kh-55 cruise missiles internally in tandem weapons bays , in similar manner to the Tu-160.

A scale model of the standard Kh-55 air-launched cruise missile with the wings, tail surfaces and engine deployed.

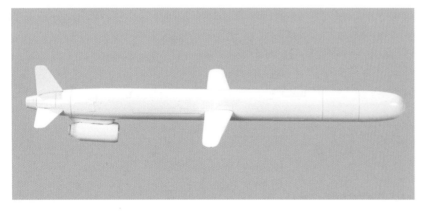

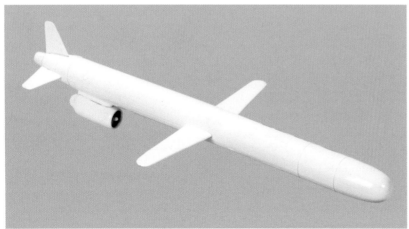

However, placing two rotary launchers in a way that ensured acceptable CG limits proved to be too difficult and the designers opted for a single rotary launcher. Thus the Tu-142MS remained unbuilt, becoming a stepping stone towards the Tu-95MS (see next entry).

Tu-95MS missile strike aircraft (Tu-342; Tu-95MS-6, *izdeliye* VP-021)

Confusingly, the first Council of Ministers directive concerning this aircraft reportedly appeared in late 1976 (at the time when the Tu-242 project was launched); a second directive on the subject, No.909-291, was issued on 10th October 1977. At the Tupolev OKB the aircraft was originally known as the Tu-342 (i.e., the third spin-off of the Tu-142) but was soon redesignated Tu-95MS, the suffix again standing for *moderni**zee**rovannyy, strate**gich**eskiy*. As already mentioned, the Tu-95M-55 testbed used for verifying the Kh-55 missile had the in-house product code *izdeliye* VM-021 – possibly as a reference to Council of Ministers directive No.1021 of 19th July 1977 which concerned the missile. For exactly the same reason the Tu-95MS received the product code *izdeliye* VP-021, which reflected the new aircraft's descent from the Tu-142 (*izdeliye* VP).

While the increased-area 'wet' wings were taken straight from the Tu-142M, the fuselage design was of necessity considerably reworked to suit the new role. The most obvious external change was a new nose configuration to accommodate a new *Ob**zor**-MS* (View, or Perspective; NATO codename *Clam Pipe*) twin-antenna target illumination/guidance radar and miscellaneous new systems associated with the Kh-55 cruise missiles. The ASW version's glazed nose was

Dmitriy A. Antonov, the third project chief of the Tu-95 who succeeded Nikolay V. Kirsanov in this capacity.

Tupolev OKB test pilot Vladimir Yu. Dobrovol'-skiy, the captain of the Tu-95MS on its maiden flight.

Tupolev OKB test pilot Valeriy V. Pavlov, the co-pilot of the Tu-95MS on its maiden flight.

replaced by a 'duck bill' radome for the search antenna (reminiscent of the Tu-95KD/Tu-95KM but much smaller and neater) and a bulged dielectric panel at the front above it below the IFR probe. The increased-headroom flight deck design introduced on the Tu-142M remained unchanged, of course. The new radar installation caused the forward fuselage to be shortened somewhat for CG reasons. (On reflection, Obzor-MS was more probably the name of the WCS, not the radar itself. Consider that the Tu-160 has a similarly named Obzor-K WCS but this is built around a different radar – the *Po**isk*** (Search, or Quest) single-antenna navigation/attack radar.)

The ventral teardrop radome below the wing centre section was deleted, as was the sonobuoy bay in the rear

The first prototype Tu-95MS at Taganrog-Yoozhnyy in late 1979.

fuselage between frames 50-58 with its clamshell doors; the length of the weapons bay between frames 28-45A was the same but the transverse partition halfway along its length was removed. Again, the locations of the manufacturing breaks between the forward pressure cabin, centre fuselage, rear fuselage and rear pressure cabin remained unchanged but the rear pressure cabin was called Section F-6.

The crew complement was reduced to seven – captain, co-pilot, navigator, Nav/Op, flight engineer, systems operator and gunner. Since the latter now had the rear pressure cabin all to himself, the lateral observation blisters which had been present up to and including the Tu-142MK were deleted and replaced with small square hatches for maintenance access to the

equipment installed at the front of the cabin. The nose gear unit had 1,140 x 350 mm (44.88 x 13.78 in) wheels and was more sharply inclined forward, while the main gear bogies were fitted with 1,450 x 450 mm (57.08 x 17.71 in) wheels.

The new weapons system included an MKU-6-5U (*izdeliye* 9A-829K2) rotary launcher mounted in the weapons bay; no provision was made for carrying free-fall bombs. The aircraft was equipped with a K-012 *Osina* (Aspen) pre-launch system. Since the six missiles carried internally were considered too few, provisions were made for carrying a further ten missiles under the wings on four pylons. New communications and ECM suites were fitted. The NK-12MV turboprops were replaced with the NK-12MP version which had the same

Front and rear views of the Tu-95MS prototype. Note the cine camera in a fairing under the starboard wingtip for recording missile launches and the original DK-12 tail turret with AM-23 cannons.

15,000-ehp take-off rating and 6,500-ehp cruise rating but featured a new constant-speed drive (CSD) for a more powerful AC generator (the P suffix probably stood for *privod [postoyannykh oborotov]* – CSD). The Tu-95MS featured a purpose-built NPK-021 navigation/flight suite (the figures refer to *izdeliye* VP-021).

The first prototype Tu-95MS was built at the Taganrog factory (TMZD) by converting a production Batch 10 Tu-142MK manufactured in 1978 (c/n 8602109, f/n 42105), using manufacturing documents prepared by MMZ Opyt. The extensive conversion was initiated in 1978 and completed in September 1979. On 18th November 1979 the uncoded aircraft made its maiden flight from Taganrog-Yoozhnyy airfield, captained by Tupolev OKB test pilot Vladimir Yu. Dobrovol'skiy; the crew also included co-pilot Valeriy V. Pavlov, flight engineers G. F. Tatarinov and Oleg N. Bobrov, navigator V. N. Sedov, Nav/Op V. L. Laïkhter, radio operator S. A. Klyuyev, electrics engineer I. Ye. Aristov, leading test engineer V. M. Khasanov and assistant test engineer G. V. Shel'menkov. In 1980 the aircraft was ferried to Zhukovskiy where manufacturer's tests continued.

The second prototype was likewise converted from a production Tu-142MK built in 1981 (c/n 1602821, f/n unknown), receiving the tactical code '31 Red'. Like the first machine, it had a cine camera in a teardrop-shaped fairing under the starboard wingtip for recording missile launches. This aircraft was involved in the state acceptance trials in Akhtoobinsk where it was flown by a GNIKI VVS crew.

Two more views of the Tu-95MS prototype in Taganrog, showing the neat 'duck bill' radome of the Obzor-MS radar and the absence of the lateral observation blisters on the rear fuselage.

After two years of flight testing and modification, the Tu-95MS entered production at TMZD in 1981. Taganrog-built production machines had 13-digit construction numbers following a system devised in 1973 and used by most Soviet aircraft factories at the time. For example, a Tu-95MS manufactured on 5th November 1982 and coded '004 Black' is c/n 6403424100004; 640 is a code for the factory, 342 is an in-house product code (obviously referring to the old designation Tu-342!), and 41 means that the aircraft was laid down in the fourth quarter of 1981. The remaining digits are again the 'famous last five' with no specific meaning, the first two of these changing independently from the final three; on Taganrog-built examples they were strictly in the 00xxx range. Only the 'famous last five' are sometimes quoted in paperwork; they are also indicated on the aircraft inside the pressure cabins. Accordingly, Tu-95MSs also have four-digit fuselage numbers; the abovementioned Tu-95MS '004 Black' is probably f/n 0103 (Batch 01, 03rd aircraft in the batch).

The initial production version with six missiles carried internally and the Osina pre-launch system was designated Tu-95MS-6. Production aircraft differed somewhat from the prototypes. In particular, antennas associated with the Sayany ECM/ESM suite were added under the nose (a triangular aerial aft of the radome), under the gunner's station (two small pylon-mounted pods) and at the trailing edge of the fin tip fairing (an egg-shaped fairing, and hemispherical faceted sensors of the Mak (Poppy) infrared missile warning sensor were added under the nose and dorsally amidships. The prototypes' PRS-1 gun-laying radar with its hemispherical radome gave place to the PRS-4 Krypton radar. The Tu-95MS's NATO reporting name was *Bear-H*.

As for the prototypes, the first machine was transferred to SibNIA for static tests after being struck off charge. The second prototype was flown to Monino airfield in the Moscow Region in February 1988,

becoming a ground instructional aircraft at the Soviet Air Force Academy named after Yuriy A. Gagarin (VVA – *Voyenno-vozdooshnaya akademiya*), right next door to the famous Soviet Air Force Museum. On learning of this, US weapons inspectors came to Monino to examine the aircraft! When the VVA was pooled with the Moscow-based Air Force Engineering Academy named after Nikolay Ye. Zhukovskiy (VVIA – *Voyenno-vozdooshnaya inzhenernaya akademiya*), becoming the Russian Air Force's Military Instructional & Scientific Centre, and transferred to Voronezh in 2012, the VVA's instructional airframes, including the Tu-95MS, were transferred to what was by then the Central Russian Air Force Museum. The latter is so far the sole Russian aviation museum to have a *Bear-H* in its collection.

Meanwhile, in March 1978 the Khar'kov Aircraft Production Association (KhAPO – *Khar'kovskoye aviatsionnoye proizvodstvennoye obyedineniye*, formerly MAP aircraft factory No.135 named after the Lenin Young Communist League) in the Ukraine started gearing up to produce the Kh-55, delivering the first production missile on 14th December 1980. As early as 25th December 1979 a decision was taken to include the missile into the Soviet Air Force inventory. The R95-300 engine entered production at MAP engine plant No.478 in Zaporozhye, the Ukraine (now called Motor Sich).

The first launch of a production Kh-55 from a Tu-95MS took place on 23rd February 1981; the event was clearly timed to Soviet Army Day, a major public holiday in the Soviet Union (now called Homeland Defenders' Day). On 3rd September that year the first production Tu-95MS (c/n 6403423100002; f/n 0101?) made a successful launch of the Kh-55 during state acceptance trials in Akhtoobinsk.

In 1983 Tu-95MS production was transferred to plant No.18 in Kuibyshev, although TMZD continued building the type until 1984. The Kuibyshev-built

Here the first prototype Tu-95MS is depicted at Zhukovskiy in 1980.

Two views of the same aircraft on the 'piano keys' of the runway at Zhukovskiy.

This three-quarters rear view of the first prototype shows the clean rear end lacking ECM aerials, the hemispherical radome of the PRS-1 gun laying radar and avionics access hatches supplanting the observation blisters.

'31 Red', a production Tu-95MS seen at Akhtoobinsk during trials. Note the ECM aerials on the nose and tail.

aircraft used the same c/n system; for example, Tu-95MS '36 Black' manufactured on 23rd October 1989 is c/n 1000213935793 – i.e., factory code 100, *izdeliye* VP-021, laid down in the third quarter of 1989, plus the famous five-digit computer number. The 'famous last five' are written on a large black metal plate on the front bulkhead of the nosewheel well. No c/n to f/n tie-ups for Kuibyshev-built examples have been made so far.

The first upgrade of the Tu-95MS was initiated by a Council of Ministers directive in June 1983. Among other things, the defensive armament was updated: the DK-12 turret with AM-23 cannons gave way to a new UKU-9K-502-II turret with two 23-mm (.90 calibre) Gryazev/Shipunov GSh-23 double-barrelled cannons

similar to that of the Tu-22M2 *Backfire-B*. The cannons were again trained by means of a PRS-4 radar. On Taganrog-built examples and early-production Kuibyshev-built aircraft this had an elongated radome tapering sharply towards the rear; later Tu-95MSs reverted to the short boxy radome which had given rise to the reporting name *Box Tail*. New ECM/ESM systems were added, the latest of which (called *Meteor*) is reputedly able to jam the extremely powerful *Zaslon* (Shield, or Barrier) WCS of the Mikoyan MiG-31 *Foxhound* heavy interceptor.

On 31st December 1983 the Tu-95MS and the Kh-55 cruise missile were officially included into the Soviet Air Force inventory. In 1986 production of the missile was

A GNIKI VVS test crew pose with Tu-95MS '31 Red' at Akhtoobinsk. A KrAZ-255B 6x6 prime mover stands by for pushback for the next test flight.

Far left: Front view of a standard Kh-55 missile on its ground handling dolly, showing the circular cross-section.

Left: Here, for comparison, is a Kh-55SM long-range missile with conformal tanks. Note that the dolly is slightly different, featuring supports for these 'jowls'.

Side views of the Kh-55 (far left) and Kh-55SM, showing how the latter's conformal tanks are shaped at the rear to fit under the wings.

Rear views of the Kh-55 (far left) and Kh-55SM. Note how the double-jointed fin and stabilators are folded.

transferred to the Kirov Machinery Factory named after the 20th Communist Part Convention (KMPO – *Kirovskoye mashinostroitel'noye proizvodstvennoye obyedineniye*) in the city of Kirov, Russia. In arms reduction talks with the West the baseline Kh-55 and the long-range Kh-55SM were referred to by the spurious designations RKV-500A and RKV-500B respectively (*raketa krylahtaya, vozdooshnovo bazeerovaniya* – cruise missile, air-launched).

Production *Bear-Hs* built from late 1986 onwards were equipped with an SKBM (Aerosila) TA-12 APU in the fin root fillet; the air intake door was on the

starboard side and the exhaust door on the port side. The exhaust door was made of heat-resistant steel, being very conspicuous even when closed, and was designed to direct the exhaust flow over the port stabiliser. The first Tu-95MS to feature the APU was '610 Black' (c/n 1000214524610), one of several 'dogships' operated by the Tupolev OKB and based at Zhukovskiy.

Following Nikolay V. Kirsanov's retirement at the end of the 1980s, Dmitriy A. Antonov was appointed Tu-95 programme chief. When he, too, retired, A. B. Kosarev took on the job; the current Tu-95 programme chief is Yevgeniy A. Deyanov.

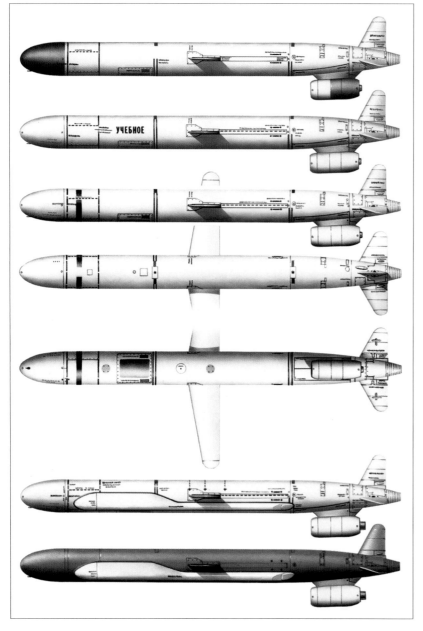

Top to bottom: An early Kh-55 cruise missile; an inert ground instructional round marked *oochebnoye*; three views of a late-production Kh-55 in standard configuration; a live Kh-55SM extended-range missile and a red-painted instrumented test round of the Kh-55SM.

Tu-95MS-16 missile strike aircraft (*izdeliye* VP-021)

The *Bear-H* was produced in two varieties. On most examples the rotary launcher was augmented by four pylons under the wings for carrying an additional ten missiles, increasing the total to 16; hence such aircraft were designated Tu-95MS-16. The inboard pylons mounted below the wing roots were each fitted with two AKU-5 ejector racks side by side, while the outboard pylons were installed between the inner and outer engines, carrying the missiles three-abreast (the centre AKU-5 rack was located much lower than the inner and outer ones). Apart from the appropriate changes to the wing structure and electric wiring in the wings, the greater number of missiles necessitated the use of a different pre-launch system called K-016 **Pikh**ta (Fir tree). The extra weight and the drag generated by the external stores entailed a reduction in performance; in particular, range was reduced by 2,000 km (1,242 miles).

One of the 'company-owned' development aircraft, Tu-95MS-16 '604 Black' (c/n 1000214424604), featured a modified NPK-021M flight/navigation suite and a modified Pikhta-M pre-launch system.

A total of 99 *Bear-Hs* had been built when production ended in 1992; 88 of these – 31 Tu-95MS-6s and 57 Tu-95MS-16s – had been delivered by early 1991. The Tu-95MS-16s, however, eventually had their wing pylons and associated wiring removed under the terms of the second Strategic Arms Limitation Treaty (SALT-2) signed on 18th June 1987 which limited the number of nuclear warheads to be carried by a single delivery vehicle. Tu-95MS production was terminated at the orders of Russia's first President Boris N. Yel'tsin, in a unilateral disarmament initiative aimed at the West which was much criticised in Russia afterwards.

The Tu-95MS was not exported. However, almost half of the Soviet DA's *Bear-H* fleet was left outside

Left: This Kh-55 has an unusually coloured yellow radome marked KTS-120 and may be a practice round.

Right and top right: Coded '31 Red', the second prototype Tu-95MS served as a ground instructional airframe at the Air Force Academy in Monino.

Above right: The second prototype's rear end with no ECM aerials below the gunner's station

Above, far right: Close-up of the second prototype's wingtip camera fairing.

GNIKI VVS test pilot V. V. Fedosov who participated in the trials of the Tu-95MS.

GNIKI VVS test pilot Col. Andrey A. Laptev who participated in the trials of the Tu-95MS.

A full frontal of a
production Tu-95MS.

Opposite page: A
production Tu-95MS-6
coded '43'. Note the
grey-painted fin leading
edge – a feature found
on quite a few *Bear-Hs*.
The hemispherical
undernose sensor of the
Mak infrared missile
warning system appears
to be missing on this
particular aircraft.

Opposite page, below:
'23 Red', another in-
service Tu-95MS in
standard silver finish.

Russia after the break-up of the Soviet Union (in Kazakhstan and the Ukraine). The Kazakh Tu-95MSs were eventually purchased by Russia but the Ukrainians chose to scrap theirs – except three examples which were sold to Russia under an agreement signed in late 1999 (see Chapter 9).

In due course Russian Air Force Tu-95MSs were upgraded to carry the Raduga Kh-555 cruise missile – a thoroughly updated derivative of the Kh-55SM. Like the latter, the missile had conformal tanks but carried a conventional high-explosive warhead, being the

Russian counterpart of the AGM-86C/D Conventional Air-Launched Cruise Missile (CALCM). The new warhead caused a shift of the missile's CG and hence a change of handling, so a pair of fixed canards were added to the Kh-555's nose to compensate for this. The missile is dimensionally identical to the Kh-55SM, having a launch weight of 1,500 kg (3,310 lb), a range of 2,000 km (1,242 miles) and a minimum flight altitude of 40 m (130 ft). The CEP is just 20 m (65 ft) – a fivefold improvement on the Kh-55. (Could *this* account for the 'extra 5' in the designation, eh?)

Rear view of a
production Tu-95MS,
showing two of the
aerials associated with
the Sayany ECM suite
and the twin GSh-23
double-barrel cannons.
Note the canvas covers
protecting the
mainwheel tyres from
the elements.

Tu-95MS '31 Blue' with stylised
'Russian knight' badge,
929th GLITs, Akhtoobinsk

Left and below left: An uncoded Tu-95MS undergoing tests at Zhukovskiy. The dielectric parts, the lower halves of the engine nacelles and some of the access panels are painted white as standard, resulting in a bit of a patchwork appearance.

Right: Three Tu-95MSs used for test work by the Russian Air Force's 929th State Flight Test Centre are pictured at Vladimirovka AB in Akhtoobinsk in the 1990s. The nearest aircraft, '31 Blue', is unusual in wearing 'Russian Knight' nose art.

Below: '25 Red', a late-production Tu-95MS, awaits the next mission. Again, the fin leading edge and fillet are painted grey.

Bottom: The same aircraft taxies for take-off. Note the open APU air intake.

Few photos are available of the Tu-95MS-16 version. The starboard inboard missile pylon is visible under the wing root.

The same aircraft coded '22 Red' is seen here from a slightly different angle, carrying a full load of Kh-55 missiles.

This rare photo shows how the Tu-95MS-16 carried ten of its 16 missiles externally. The pairs of Kh-55s on the inboard pylons and the triplets of missiles on the outboard pylons are clearly visible.

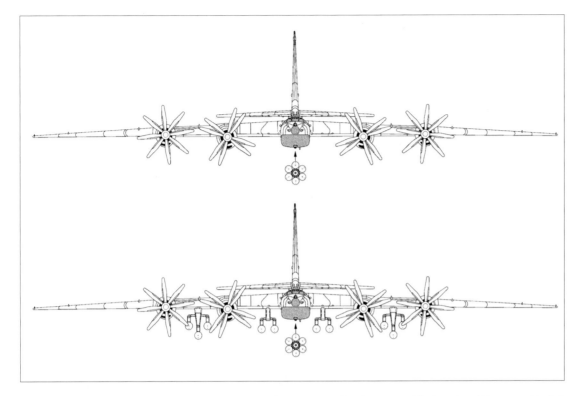

A drawing showing how the missiles were carried on the Tu-95MS-6 (above) and the Tu-95MS-16.

Together with the Tu-160, the Tu-95MS remains the primary strike asset of the Russian Air Force's Long-Range Aviation.

Tu-95MS with ELINT equipment

In the early 1990s a single Kuibyshev-built Tu-95MS coded '26 Red' (c/n 100021…732477) was modified by the Tupolev OKB for the purpose of conducting electronic eavesdropping on enemy communications in the course of the mission. The ELINT suite comprised the Shar (Ball, or Sphere), *Pastel'* and *Osen'* (Autumn) systems; the latter was an infrared line scanner. The Shar detailed SIGINT set was similar to the one used on the Mikoyan MiG-25RBF *Foxbat-B* reconnaissance aircraft. Curiously, the name Pastel' was also used for an altogether different electronic system – the L150 RHAWS used on several Soviet tactical aircraft.

The ELINT equipment was installed in the rear fuselage avionics bay, being identifiable by a large ventral dielectric fairing where the ventral cannon barbette would have been on the *Bear-A*. The aircraft was based in Zhukovskiy.

Tu-95MA development aircraft (second use of designation)

On 9th December 1976, one day after sanctioning the development of the Kh-55, the Council of Ministers let loose with another directive ordering the Central Machinery Design Bureau (TsKBM – *Tsentrahl'noye konstrooktorskoye byuro mashinostroyeniya*, formerly OKB-52) to develop a competing design – the 3M25 *Meteorit* (Meteorite) cruise missile. Actually 'competing'

is too colourless a word for it – the 3M25 was a Mach 3 supersonic missile with an advertised maximum speed of 3,000 km/h (1,863 mph), a service ceiling of 24,000 m (78,740 ft) and a range of 5,000 km (3,100 miles). The missile was developed in three versions at once – air-launched, ground-launched and sea-launched (from a submarine); these were designated 3M25A Meteorit-A (*aviatsi**on**nyy* – aviation-specific; NATO codename AS-X-19 *Koala*), 3M25N Meteorit-N (*na**zem**nyy*; NATO codename SSC-5) and P-750 Grom (Thunder), aka 3M25M Meteorit-M (*mor**skoy** – naval or maritime; NATO codename SS-N-24 *Scorpion*) respectively.

The Meteorit had a low-wing tail-first layout with small all-movable canards on the long ogival nose, cropped-delta wings and a trapezoidal ventral fin with an inset rudder. To make the missile as compact as possible the wings had a cunning triple-jointed design, the narrow root portions folding vertically down, the centre portions vertically up and the wingtips inboard over the fuselage. The main engine was a KR-23 disposable turbojet developed by the Ufa Engine Plant and breathing through a raked two-dimensional supersonic air intake positioned under the wing centre section; a solid-fuel rocket booster fitting into the sustainer nozzle was provided. Measures were taken to reduce the radar cross-section (RCS); also, the missile used an active jammer and, for the first time in Soviet practice, a towed radar decoy. An INS coupled with a radar mapping/correlation system called Kadr (Photo exposure) was used to navigate to the target.

The missile was 12.1 m (39 ft 8⅜ in) long, with a fuselage diameter of 0.78 m (2 ft 6⁴⁵⁄₆₄ in), a wing span of

Above: The one-off Tu-95MS '26 Red' fitted with ELINT equipment whose presence is indicated by the ventral dielectric fairing.

Another view of the ELINT-capable Tu-95MS on the OKB's engine test pad at Zhukoskiy.

An artist's impression of the 3M25A Meteorit-A supersonic cruise missile.

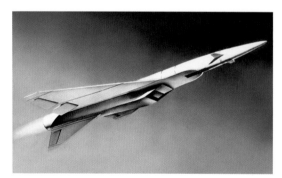

Below: A full-size mock-up of the Meteorit-A with the wings folded and the booster fitted. The slogan on the wall reads 'Glory to the heroic working class!'

5.1 m (16 ft 8²⁵⁄₃₂ in) and a wing area of 22 m² (236.81 sq ft). The launch weight was 4,500 kg (9,920 lb) less booster or 6,400 kg (14,110 lb) with booster; the thermonuclear warhead weighed 1,000 kg (2,204 lb).

In 1983 one of the first production Taganrog-built Tu-95MSs (c/n 6403424100004; f/n 0103?) was converted by TMZD into a testbed for the 3M25A missile and redesignated Tu-95MA, inheriting the designation of the nuclear-capable *Bear-A*. Coded '004 Black', the machine had two large pylons for carrying the large missiles, which were installed under the wing roots in similar fashion to the Tu-95K-22 but were of a different type. The purpose-built Lira (Lyre) pre-launch system was housed in the weapons bay.

The Tu-95MA was operated by GNIKI VVS in Akhtoobinsk (Vladimirovka AB). The first test launch of the Meteorit-A took place on 11th January 1984, ending unsuccessfully – the missile strayed off course and had to be blown up by a self-destruct radio command. It was the same story during the second launch on 24th May 1984. In one of the test launches, when the Meteorit-A was 'painted' by a ground-based air defence radar, the coded command to switch on the defensive suite was transmitted but the suite malfunctioned. As a result, when two surface-to-air missiles were fired at the Meteorit-A, the missile was shot down by the second SAM while the first one was fooled by the towed decoy.

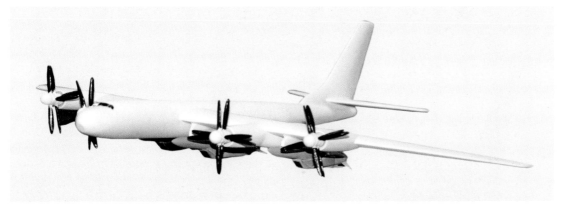

The photos on this page depict a somewhat schematic model of the Tu-95MA in a projected configuration with four Meteorit-A missiles (note the glazed nose instead of the 'duck bill' of the Obzor-MS radar).

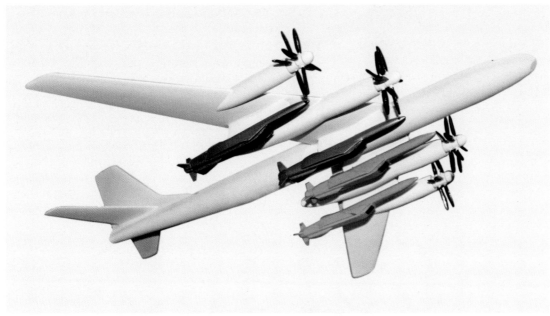

A total of 20 launches from the Tu-95MA were made in 1984-91. Yet the programme was cancelled because of the changing political situation and because the Kh-55 had entered service by then.

However, there are indications that five Tu-95MSs operated by one of the two bomber regiments in Semipalatinsk were modified to carry the Meteorit-A. These were coded '29 Red' (c/n 1000214424544), '22 Red' (c/n 1000211527615), '25 Red' (c/n 1000211528356),

'20 Red' (c/n 1000212528373) and '28 Red' (c/n 1000212528561). Apparently they were to be capable of carrying four such missiles.

Tu-95MA development aircraft (Tu-95PA?)

Later, Tu-95MA '004 Black' was reportedly used for testing an experimental hypersonic cruise missile provisionally designated Kh-90 (NATO AS-X-21); the

Tu-95MA '004 Black' comes in to land after a captive-carry test flight with one 3M25A Meteorit-A missile on the starboard pylon.

The same aircraft makes a flypast in 'clean' configuration (flaps up, gear up). Note the traditional cine camera for filming the missile launch under the starboard wingtip.

Developed by MKB Raduga, the Kh-90 was a huge and scary-looking missile having a tail-first layout and powered by a ramjet engine; the canards were carried on a distinctive 'platypus nose' above the semi-circular air intake with a semi-conical centrebody. The missile was nearly 12 m (39 ft 4 in) long, with an estimated wing span of 6.8-7 m (22 ft 3²³⁄₃₂ in to 22 ft 11¹⁹⁄₃₂ in). Since the Kh-90 was meant to be carried internally by the Tu-160, the trapezoidal wings had a double-jointed 'snap-action' design, but here the narrow root portions folded up and the rest of the wing panels vertically down; the trapezoidal fin also had a double-folding design. The Tu-95MA could only carry the Kh-90 externally, since it was too large to fit into the *Bear-H*'s weapons bay (in fact, it would be a tight squeeze even for the *Blackjack*). After the missile had been released and the wings and tail unfolded, a solid-propellant booster inside the ramjet nozzle fired to accelerate the missile until the ramjet sustainer could be ignited. The sustainer allowed the missile to reach a cruising speed of Mach 4.5 at 8,000-27,000 m (26,250-88,580 ft).

The Kh-90 project was terminated in 1992. One of the Kh-90 demonstrators was displayed at the MAKS-95 airshow in Zhukovskiy as the GELA (***ghip**erzvookovoy eksperimentahl'nyy letahtel'nyy apparaht* – Hypersonic Experimental Aerial Vehicle).

Tu-95MS weapons testbed for Kh-101 missile

In 1995 MKB Raduga began development of a new long-range air-launched cruise missile – or rather two missiles sharing the same airframe and powerplant. This time the primary version designated Kh-101 was a conventional weapon with a 400-kg (880-lb) high-explosive/fragmentation warhead; the other missile, the Kh-102, featured a thermonuclear warhead with a

designation Tu-95PA has been quoted for the aircraft in this guise. According to some sources, however, the aircraft in question was Tu-95MS '611 Black' (c/n 100021...527611) owned by the OKB and equipped with the K-032 *Yasen'* (Ash, the tree) pre-launch system.

Here the Tu-95MA is depicted with two Meteorit-A missiles.

Opposite page, left row, top to bottom: The Meteorit-A is released and the wings begin to unfold immediately.

The missile falls away from the Tu-95MA...

...until the booster ignites when the missile is at a safe distance, followed by the ramjet sustainer. Note the heavy smoke trail.

Above: Another view of the Tu-95MA in flight with one Meteorit-A missile. The ECM aerials under the nose and the rear fuselage are absent, but the aerial on the fin trailing edge is there.

Above, below and bottom: These views of Tu-95MA '004 Black' parked at Vladimirovka AB show the location and shape of the missile pylons. Note the scuffed paintwork on the radome.

Tu-95MS '01 Red' used as a testbed for the Kh-101 missile

Above: Tu-95MS '01 Red' on a test flight. The single pylon in the starboard inboard position is just visible.

Left and below left: The same aircraft on runway 12/30 in Zhukovskiy. Note the T-shaped photo calibration markings on the fuselage.

250-kiloton yield. Again, the Tu-160 and the Tu-95MS were envisaged as the missile platforms.

The Kh-101/Kh-102 differed a lot from the Kh-55, both aerodynamically and structurally. Firstly, it reverted to the low-wing layout of the Kh-55's second project version, the wings stowing beneath the fuselage and having about 15° leading-edge sweep when deployed. Secondly, in contrast to the Kh-55SM whose long-range conformal tanks were scabbed onto a circular-section fuselage, here the 'cheek tanks' were built integrally, giving the forward fuselage a quasi-triangular cross-section with prominent chines running from the tip of the radome. The airframe incorporated certain other features aimed at reducing the RCS, which is estimated to be 0.01 m² (0.11 sq ft).

Thirdly, the engine (which was mounted in a Kh-55 style pop-out nacelle) was new. While the Kh-101/

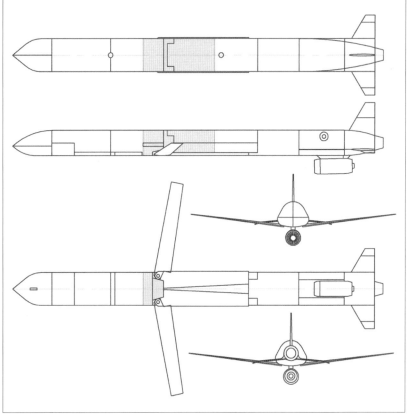

Upper view of the Kh-101 with wings stowed, plus side, front, rear and lower views in flight configuration.

A computer-generated image of a red-painted Kh-101 instrumented test round.

Port and starboard views of the Kh-101 in immediate pre-launch configuration (engine deployed, wings and tail surfaces folded) and a rather odd configuration with the tail surfaces deployed but everything else folded.

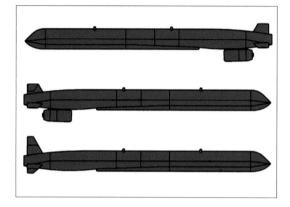

A drawing of an inboard missile pylon with a Kh-101 suspended from one of the ejector racks.

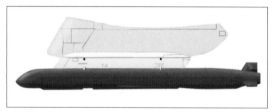

Kh-102 was initially believed to be powered by a very similar AMNTK Soyooz R95TM-300 turbofan, later reports suggested that the powerplant is a 450-kgp (990-lbst) OMKB/NPO Saturn TRDD-50A (*izdeliye* 36M; TRDD = **toor**bore'ak**tiv**nyy dvookh**kon**toornyy

*dvig*atel' – turbofan). In fact, the original *izdeliye* 36 engine had been developed by OMKB as far back as 1976 for the Kh-55 missile but had lost out to the competing R95-300. However, the sole manufacturer of the latter engine (Motor-Sich) found itself outside Russia after the break-up of the Soviet Union. When political complications rendered further deliveries of R95-300s impossible, MKB Raduga had to seek an alternative powerplant for the Kh-55 and its derivatives – and the Kh-101/Kh-102. Hence priority was again given to the OMKB design and in 2000 the suitably updated engine was put into production at the **Ryb**inskiye Mot**ory** (Rybinsk Engines) plant; this factory located in Rybinsk (Yaroslavl' Region, central Russia) is part of NPO Saturn.

The TRDD-50A is a two-spool turbofan having a single-stage axial LP compressor (fan) with wide-chord blades, a single-stage axial-diagonal HP compressor, an annular combustion chamber with a revolving fuel nozzle, single-stage axial HP and LP turbines and a fixed-area nozzle. The engine has electrohydraulic controls, a self-contained oil system and a built-in 4-kilowatt generator. SFC 0.71 kg/kgp-hr, maximum running time at full power 2 hours, diameter 0.33 m (1 ft 1 in), length 0.85 m (2 ft 9$\frac{15}{32}$ in), dry weight 82 kg (180.78 lb). The engine can be started at altitudes up to 10,000 m (32,810 ft). Fuel grades used are T-1, TS-1, T-6 or RT jet fuel (kerosene) and T-10 synthetic fuel (decilin).

Much of the information on the Kh-101/Kh-102 remains classified as of this writing. However, according to published data, the missile has a launch weight of 2,200-2,400 kg (4,850-5,290 lb), including 1,250 kg (2,760 lb) of fuel, a launch altitude of 300-11,000 m (980-36,090 ft), a cruising speed of 684-720 km/h (424-447 mph), a maximum speed of 900-972 km/h (559-

The former '01 Red' (now wearing no code) comes in to land, with the missile ejector racks barely visible beyond the nose gear unit.

The testbed comes in to land with one inert missile on the outer AKU-5M ejector rack.

621 mph) and a range of 4,500-5,500 km (2,800-3,420 miles). The missile has a variable flight profile with a maximum cruise altitude of 10,000 m and a minimum flight altitude in terrain following mode of 30 m (100 ft). The Kh-101/Kh-102 has a combined guidance system featuring an INS, with mid-course correction using the Russian GLONASS system (glo**bahl**'naya navigatsion-

naya **spoot**nikovaya sis**tem**a – global navigation satellite system), and a Sproot (Octopus) TV system for terminal guidance allowing the missile to hit moving targets as well; the CEP is just 5-6 m (16-20 ft).

The Kh-101/Kh-102 was to be carried by mid-life upgrade versions of the *Blackjack* and the *Bear-H* referred to semi-officially as the Tu-160M and

The same aircraft seen from chase plane prior to missile launch.

The Kh-101 testbed takes off at Engels with the new tactical code '101 Red'; a red-painted Kh-101 is just visible.

Below: The same aircraft in flight as '01 Red'

Below right: A drawing showing how the upgraded Tu-95MS is to carry eight Kh-101s.

Tu-95MSM respectively (see below), the (extra) M suffix standing for moderni*zee*rovannyy (updated) in both cases. However, the missile ended up being rather larger than the Kh-55, with a length of 7.45 m (24 ft 5¹⁹⁄₆₄ in), a wing span of 4.2 m (13 ft 9²³⁄₆₄ in) and a maximum fuselage width of 0.742 m (2 ft 5⁷⁄₃₂ in). Hence an immediate complication arose: the Tu-160 could carry the Kh-101/Kh-102 internally while the Tu-95MS could not – its weapons bay was too short, having been tailored for the Kh-55. (That's where the Tu-160's long weapons bays came in handy, having been designed around the aforementioned Kh-45 missile which was 9.9-10.8 m (32 ft 5⁴⁹⁄₆₄ in to 35 ft 5¹³⁄₆₄ in) long!) The only option for the Tu-95MSM was to carry the weapons externally; however, this was not too much of a problem, considering the experience gained with the Tu-95MS-16. Indeed, the missile pylons of the Tu-95MSM were installed at exactly the same locations – beneath the wing roots and between the engine nacelles; the Tu-95MS-16's existing wing hardpoints (which remained intact after the removal of the original pylons) allowed it to be upgraded fairly easily to the new

configuration. The number of Kh-101 missiles carried externally was limited to eight; hence, unlike the Tu-95MS-16, all four pylons were identical, each carrying two updated AKU-5M ejector racks side by side. The Tu-95MSM retained the standard MKU-6-5U rotary launcher and was thus capable of carrying the older Kh-55, Kh-55SM or Kh-555 cruise missiles internally, giving it operational flexibility.

Testing of the Kh-101 began in 1995, using an early production Kuibyshev-built Tu-95MS-16 coded '01 Red' (c/n 1000214215101) converted into a weapons testbed under the Tu-95MSM programme. Unlike all subsequent *Bear-Hs* equipped to carry Kh-101 missiles, this aircraft was fitted with only the starboard inboard missile pylon, and then only a single Kh-101 missile was usually carried (on the inboard AKU-5M rack). As on the Tu-95MS prototypes (and some other Tu-95 development aircraft before that), a cine camera – or, more probably, a video camera – was installed in a teardrop fairing under the starboard wingtip to record missile launches. Photo calibration markings in the shape of an inverted T were applied to the rear fuselage.

The aircraft was operated by the Russian Air Force's 929th GLITs named after Valeriy P. Chkalov (*Gosudarstvennyy lyotno-ispytahtel'nyy tsentr* – State Flight Test Centre, ex-GNIKI VVS) and based at its main facility in Akhtoobinsk (Vladimirovka AB). At some point in time the tactical code was removed, although traces of it were still visible on the nose gear doors; later, when the

testbed was given a brush-up, the code was reapplied as '101 Red' (being obviously derived from the last three digits of the c/n). The aircraft was still active in 2016.

Tu-95MS missile strike aircraft (Phase 1 upgrade)

Tu-95MS '01 Red' ('101 Red') described above was nothing more than a weapons testbed. The actual upgrade

Another view of '01 Red' about to depart Zhukovskiy's runway 12 on a routine sortie.

The Kh-555 upgraded conventional cruise missile in flight configuration.

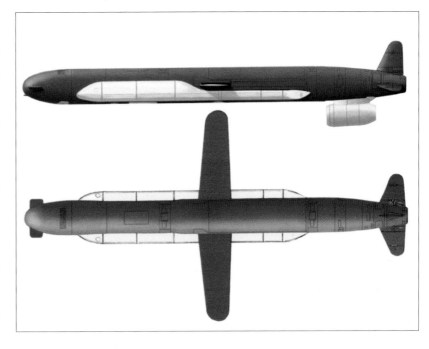

Above: Beriyev TANTK and Russian Air Force staff (and a Russian Orthodox priest) pose with a Tu-95MS named *Samara* which is on overhaul in Taganrog. The bomber received a minor upgrade (not yet Kh-101 capable).

Left: A Tu-95MS being refurbished by TANTK.

Opposite page: Gleaming with fresh paint, Tu-95MS '50 Red' was refurbished by TANTK.

Below: The same aircraft seen at Zhukovskiy where it was fitted with new avionics under the Tu-95MSM programme.

Tu-95MS '317 Red' on approach to Zhukovskiy shows off its four pylons (empty in this instance).

Below: Here the same aircraft is seen carrying eight Kh-101 missiles.

prototype with a full set of pylons was converted from Tu-95MS '317 Black' (subsequently changed to '317 Red', c/n 1000213419317), a long-serving Tupolev OKB 'dogship' which had performed at various airshows in Moscow and Zhukovskiy. Joining the test programme in 1999, this aircraft was occasionally seen at Zhukovskiy, carrying four or eight red-painted dummy Kh-101 missiles.

(A note must be made here. Since the Tu-95MSM designation has leaked out, it has become popularly associated with the *Bear-Hs* equipped to carry Kh-101 missiles and has caught on in the Russian press. However, the Tupolev PLC and the Russian Air Force prefer not to use it, referring to the machines currently in service simply as 'upgraded Tu-95MSs'. The reason is

Left: Here '317 Red' taxying at Zhukovskiy carries only one (inboard) AKU-5M ejector rack and one missile on each pylon, the outer racks having been removed for some reason.

Below left: The same aircraft carries a full set of red-painted dummy Kh-101s.

Left and above: Here, '317 Red' is caught on camera landing at Zhukovskiy with a full set of eight AKU-5Ms but only four missiles, only the inboard rack on each pylon being occupied.

that the upgrade is divided into several stages and the Tupolev PLC reserves the designation Tu-95MSM for a different upgrade (see below). Therefore the Kh-101 capable machines now in service will be referred to hereinafter as 'Tu-95MS Phase 1 upgrade'.)

The first test launches of the Kh-101 at the 929th GLITs were also made in 1999. In November 2008 the Phase 1 upgraded Tu-95MS successfully passed its state acceptance trials, the State commission recommending the new version for service.

In late December 2009 the Russian MoD signed a contract with the Tupolev Public Limited Company (as the OKB is known since the 1990s) to upgrade part of the Russian Air Force's *Bear-H* fleet to the new standard. Yet implementing the upgrade proved to be a long story because the Tu-95MSM was not all about missiles – new avionics had to be developed, tested and integrated.

In early 2011 a Russian Air Force Tu-95MS-6 coded '50 Red' and registered RF-94192 (c/n 6403423300822) was loaned to the Tupolev PLC for avionics tests under Tu-95MSM programme. This aircraft lacked wing hardpoints and could not be fitted with missile pylons. The following new items were fitted by the Beriyev TANTK factory in Taganrog, which had built this particular aircraft, under an R&D programme called 'Complex A-VP-021MS':

• a UBS module (the acronym may stand for *ooniversahl'nyy blok sopryazheniya* – versatile interface);

• an A-737 GLONASS receiver/display module developed by MKB Kompas (*Moskovskoye konstrooktorskoye byuro* – 'Compass' Moscow Design Bureau specialising in radio navigation equipment);

• a VIM-95 navigation/approach system developed by the St. Petersburg-based VNIIRA (*Vserosseeyskiy naoochno-issledovatel'skiy institoot rahdioapparatoory* – All-Russian Radio Equipment Research Institute, an establishment specialising in radio navigation systems and landing aids);

• an ARK-40 ADF developed by MKB Kompas;

• an SO-96 radar transponder developed by VNIIRA;

Above: Here Tu-95MS '317 Red' takes off with a full load of Kh-101 missiles.

Opposite page: Two fine shots of the same machine flying with four Kh-101s.

Below: Close-up of the dummy Kh-101s on the pylons, showing the folded wings.

• an RSBN-85V SHORAN developed by VNIIRA;

• a Gladiolus-PKV antenna/feeder system;

• a BMS (*bortovaya mnogofoonktsionahl'naya sistema* – on-board multi-role system, whatever that means) developed by VNIIRA;

• SD-375M distance measuring equipment (*samolyotnyy dahl'nomer* – DME);

• an AFU-M antenna/feeder device (*antenno-feedernoye oostroystvo*);

• A-053 and A-075 radio altimeters developed by the Tactical Missiles Corporation (KTRV – *Korporahtsiya "Takticheskoye raketnoye vo'oruzheniye"*);

• a system designated RTMS-4B Srs 1.

Preliminary testing of these avionics was to take place between 1st May and 30th September 2011, followed by check-up tests between 1st October and 30th November. However, the Tupolev PLC failed to

Top and top right: Tu-95MS '20/1 Red'/ RF-94122 named *Doobna* has undergone a Phase 1 upgrade at the Aviacor plant which built it. Note the mission markers.

Above: '20/1 Red' is about to be towed by a K-701 Kirovets tractor at Samara-Bezymyanka.

First things first: after a heavy snowfall in Samara, the aircraft must be cleared of snow before any other work can be done!

'10/1 Red'/RF-94128
Saratov, the first
operational Phase 1
upgraded Tu-95MS.

Left and below left: The
same aircraft in th static
display at Kubinka AB
during the Army 2015
International Military
Technical Forum.

meet the schedule; the MoD sued for liquidated damages but the suit was rejected because it turned out that the delays were caused by the aircraft being grounded for repairs.

All subsequent upgrade work to Phase 1 standard was undertaken by the Aviacor factory in Samara, starting in 2013, and the upgraded bombers are given a check by the Tupolev PLC in Zhukovskiy before being redelivered to the Air Force. Deliveries commenced in 2015. On 20th November that year, citing Aviacor's press office, the TASS News Agency wrote that *'Aviacor has handed over the first upgraded Tu-95MSM to the Russian Aerospace Force'* (sic) and that *'the aircraft has been christened "Doobna" and its adaptation to take new weapons has lasted three months; the second upgraded bomber will be redelivered before the year is out, and the third will arrive for upgrading in December'*. Yet, even such an authoritative news agency as TASS can be wrong – the Tu-95MS Phase 1 upgrade named 'Doobna' (that is, '20/1 Red'/RF-94122, c/n 1000213834496) was definitely not the first. Five months earlier, in June 2015, the Tu-95MS Phase 1 upgrade had made its public debut when an aircraft coded '10/1 Red', registered RF-94128 and named 'Saratov' (c/n 1000214835199) was in the static display at Kubinka AB during the Army-2015 International Military Technical Forum. (Speaking of which, a list of Russian Air Force Tu-95MSs with individual names is given in Chapter 7.) On 9th May 2016 three Phase 1 upgraded Tu-95MSs participated in the traditional flypast over Moscow's Red Square during the Victory Day parade for the first time.

According to the project, in addition to the missile pylons and pre-launch equipment compatible with the Kh-101/Kh-102, the Tu-95MS Phase 1 upgrade is to feature the following changes:

• the standard NK-12MP engines and AV-60K propellers are to be replaced with upgraded NK-12MPM engines driving AV-60T propellers, which will increase the bomber's range thanks to a reduced fuel consumption;

• the standard Obzor-MS radar is to be replaced with a Novella-NV1.021 radar developed by the Leninets Holding Co. – a version of the Novella suite (as fitted to the IL-38N ASW aircraft) customised for the Tu-95MS, as the '021' bit implies;

• an SOI-021 data presentation system (*sistema otobrazheniya informahtsïi*) – putting it plainly, a 'glass cockpit' replacing the traditional electromechanical flight instruments – is to be installed, the designation again indicating that it is tailored for the *Bear-H*;

• an NVS-021M navigation processor system (*navigatsionnaya vychislitel'naya sistema*) is to be installed;

• an ANS-2009 celestial navigation system (*astronavigatsionnaya sistema*) is to be fitted;

• a KSU-021 integrated flight control system (*kompleksnaya sistema oopravleniya*) is to be installed; the latter three systems are products of the Moscow Institute of Electrotechnics and Automatic Systems (MIEA – *Moskovskiy institoot elektrotekhniki i avtomahtiki*, not to be confused with MIREA – the Moscow Institute of Radio Equipment and Automatic Systems!);

• an upgraded Meteor-NM2 ECM/ESM suite is to be fitted.

As of July 2017, at least 14 Russian Air Force Tu-16MS-16s have been upgraded to carry Kh-101 missiles under Phase 1 but it remains to be seen how much of the above (including the systems tested on '50 Red') has been incorporated on these aircraft. The Tu-95MS-6s are reportedly unsuitable for such an upgrade, as incorporating the required wing hardpoints is apparently ruled out for some reason. This limits the potential Tu-95MSM fleet to 43 aircraft – the figure quoted by Lt.-Gen. Anatoliy D. Zhikharev in 2016, his final year as Commander of the Russian Air Force's strategic bomber arm.

Tu-95MSM missile strike aircraft (Phase 2 upgrade)

As mentioned earlier, the real Tu-95MSM will represent Stage 2 of the mid-life upgrade programme – an even more in-depth upgrade. Very little specific information is currently available on this version but, firstly, apart from the ability to carry Kh-101 and Kh-102 missiles, the Tu-95MSM will a considerably updated flight and mission avionics suite and updated aircraft systems. Moreover, other advanced air-to-surface weapons may be integrated in the future.

Secondly, there are now indications that Tu-95MSM conversions will not be limited to Tu-95MS-16s after all. Indeed, if Tupolev had suggested fitting Tu-142MKs (which never had wing hardpoints when new) with pylons for carrying anti-shipping missiles as part of an upgrade, there is no reason why Tu-95MS-6s with enough service life remaining cannot have their wings modified in the same way.

The upgrade also includes a service life extension. This will allow the Tu-95MSMs to remain in service until the 2040s when new-build Tu-160M2 bombers, and possibly Tupolev's next-generation strategic bomber tentatively designated PAK DA (*Perspektivnyy aviatsionnyy kompleks Dahl'ney aviahtsïi* – Future Long-Range Aviation Aircraft System), are fielded in sufficient numbers.

As of mid-2017 a Tu-95MS has been delivered to Taganrog for conversion as the prototype of the actual Tu-95MSM (the Phase 2 upgrade). However, the actual conversion work has not yet begun because the upgrade configuration and the corresponding manufacturing documents have yet to be finalised.

CHAPTER SIX

The *Bear* in detail

I. Tu-95/Tu-95M bombers, Tu-95K/Tu-95KM missile carriers and Tu-95RTs reconnaissance aircraft

The following structural description applies to the basic Tu-95 *sans suffixe* and Tu-95M. Details of other versions are given as appropriate.

Type: (Tu-95 *sans suffixe*/Tu-95M) long-range heavy bomber; (Tu-95K/Tu-95KM) long-range missile strike aircraft; (Tu-95RTs) long-range maritime reconnaissance/OTH targeting aircraft. The aircraft is designed for day and night operation in visual meteorological conditions (VMC) and instrument meteorological conditions (IMC). Depending on the version and the mission, the aircraft may have a crew of eight to eleven.

The airframe is of all-metal riveted construction and is largely made of D16 series duralumin and V95 series aluminium alloys. Other structural materials used include ML5-T4 magnesium alloy (ML = *magniy liteynyy* – magnesium optimised for casting; the T4 is a reference to the thermal treatment mode), 30KhGSA and 30KhGSNA grade steel (used for major airframe subassembly attachment fittings, certain fasteners and the crew stations' armour protection), glassfibre Textolite composite, polystyrene and Plexiglas. The materials were carefully chosen so as to ensure the best possible strength-to-weight ratio.

Fuselage: Semi-monocoque stressed-skin structure of high fineness ratio and basically circular cross-section changing to pear-

A former Tu-95MA converted to a Tu-95MU trainer but retaining the partial 'anti-flash' colours.

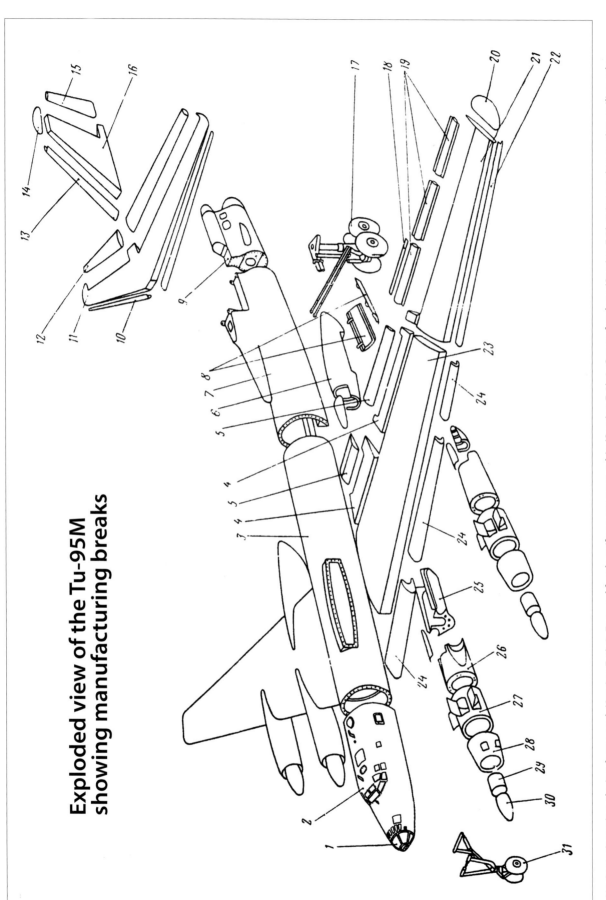

Exploded view of the Tu-95M showing manufacturing breaks

1. Navigator's station glazing framework (Section F-1); 2. Forward fuselage/front pressure cabin (Section F-1); 3. Centre fuselage (Section F-2); 3. Centre fuselage (Section F-3); 4. Inner wing section trailing-edge portion; 5. Flap (inner/outer sections); 6. Main landing gear fairing; 7. Rear fuselage (Section F-4); 8. Rear (large) mainwheel well doors; 9. Tail section/rear pressure cabin (Section F-5); 10. Detachable stabiliser leading edge; 11. Stabiliser; 12. Elevator; 13. Detachable fin leading edge; 14. Fin tip antenna fairing; 15. Rudder; 16. Fin; 17. Main gear strut; 18. Aileron trim tab/geared tab; 19. Three-section aileron; 20. Detachable wingtip fairing; 21. Outer wing section; 22. Detachable outer wing section leading edge; 23. Inner wing section; 24. Detachable inner wing section leading edge; 25. Rear portion of engine nacelle; 26. Centre portion of engine nacelle; 27. Cowling section; 28. Air intake assembly; 29. Engine reduction gearbox fairing; 30. Propeller spinner; 31. Nose gear strut.

shaped cross-section towards the rear extremity. Maximum diameter 2.9 m (9 ft 6⅛ in), cross-section area 6.6 m² (70.96 sq ft). The fuselage is of beam-and-stringer construction with smooth skin attached to the fuselage frames/bulkheads and stringers by flush rivets. The fuselage structure features more than 100 frames and bulkheads, some of which have duplicated numbers (for example, 6 and 6A); two types of frames are used – regular and reinforced (mainframes). Longerons and other local reinforcement is provided near apertures (the bomb bay, nosewheel well, access hatches etc.).

For ease of assembly the fuselage is divided by manufacturing breaks into five sections which, in line with Soviet/Russian practice, are numbered F-1 through F-5, plus the tail barbette fairing. The fuselage sections are bolted together by means of flanges.

On 'glass-nosed' versions (Tu-95 *sans suffixe*, Tu-95M, Tu-95MR and Tu-95RTs) Section F-1 is the navigator's station glazing framework (fuselage frames 0-1), which is manufactured as a one-piece casting having a modified parabolic shape. The glazing panels are attached to the cast framework made of ML5-T4 magnesium alloy by duralumin strips and screws. The lower centre pane of quasi-oval shape tapering towards the bottom is an optically flat window made of Triplex silicate glass to avoid distortions of the view during bomb-aiming. The rest of the glazing is moulded birdproof Plexiglas, with a single strongly convex crescent-shaped transparency at the tip and five panes (three trapezoidal ones and two triangular ones) in the second row.

On the Tu-95K/Tu-95KM missile carriers, Section F1 is a large structure of pear-shaped cross-section and the manufacturing break with Section F-2 is located farther aft. The metal upper half of semi-parabolic shape in side elevation accommodates an unpressurised avionics bay, featuring three pairs of detachable panels for access to the radar set and a cut-out at the front for the radar's guidance channel antenna closed by a moulded dielectric panel. It is delimited from below by a deck which carries the radar's main antenna; this deck serves as the attachment point for the dielectric radome forming most of the lower half. The detachable radome, which is wider than the upper half, is a honeycomb structure made of KAST-V glassfibre Textolite composite. On the Tu-95KM Section F-1 mounts a fixed high-set IFR probe on the centreline.

The *forward fuselage* (Section F-2, frames 1-13 on the 'glass-nosed' versions) comprises the navigator's station (frames 1-5) and the flight deck which are connected by a passage between the pilots' seats. Together with Section F-1 it forms the forward pressure cabin accommodating most of the crew members. Pressurisation is ensured by placing special sealing tape between the skin and the internal structure before riveting. The pressure cabin walls are lined with quilted

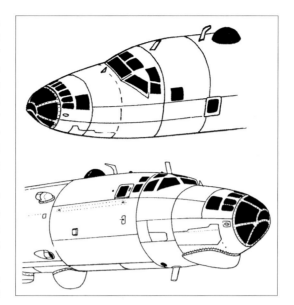

Left: The nose of the Tu-95M (above) and the one-off Tu-95MR lacking the IFR probe (note ventral fairing).

Below: The nose of Tu-95MU '67 Red', showing the standard navigator's station glazing, the radome of the Rubidiy-MM radar and the 'hockey stick' aerials of the R-808 command radio.

Bottom: The standard Tu-95MR's nose with an IFR probe; note the asymmetric glazing.

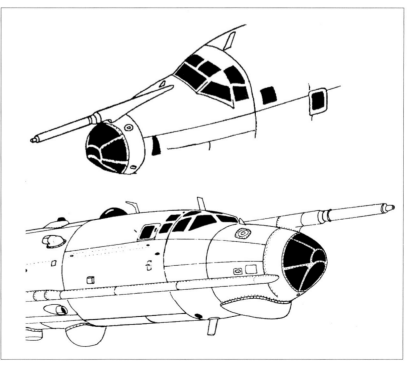

Right and far right: The nose of a Tu-95MR with a Rubin-1 radar. The IFR probe and associated fuel line to starboard required the deletion of the second row of glazing panels, save for a characteristic trapezoidal window to port. Note the new blade aerials associated with the R-832 radio.

Right and below: The nose of a retired Tu-95K with the radomes, the emergency exit covers and some access panels missing.

Far right and bottom right: The nose of an operational Tu-95K, showing the wide radome of the YaD radar's YaD1-1 search/ tracking antenna and the small radome of the YaD1-2 missile guidance antenna built into a teardrop fairing. An observation blister for the navigator is provided on the port side, with a BTs-63 star tracker above it. Note the U-shaped aerial of the Meridian SHORAN under the nose.

Right: Section F-1 of a Tu-95K's fuselage, showing the avionics bay access panels.

heat- and soundproofing mats made of ATIM-1 (*aviatsionnyy teplo'izolyatsionnyy materiahl* – aviation-specific heat insulation material) and ANZM (*aviatsionnyy nevosplamenyayemyy zvooko'izolyatsionnyy materiahl* – aviation-specific non-combustible soundproofing material). The flight controls and instruments, navigation equipment, parts of the pressurisation system, and other equipment are also located here.

On the Tu-95 *sans suffixe* and Tu-95M, the front end of Section F-2 features the remainder of the navigator's station glazing which is located asymmetrically, with eight narrow transparencies on the upper half of the nose in the third row (frames 1-2) and a single pane in the fourth row on the starboard side between frames 2-3. All of these windows are omitted on the Tu-95MR

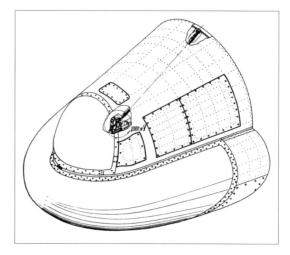

Left row, top to bottom:
The nose of a Tu-95K-22, with a single radome, an IFR probe and a metal panel carrying a thimble fairing for the SPS-141 jammer instead of the upper radome.

The port and starboard escape hatches are located asymmetrically. Note the SPS-151 jammer antennas and the retractable drogue illumination lights on the sides of the nose.

This Tu-95K-22 is being scrapped and the radome is cut open, revealing the scanner of the PNA-B radar inside. Note the fuel line conduit.

Right row, top to bottom:
The navigator's station glazing of a Tu-95RTs; the flat lower centre panel is de-iced.

The nose of a Tu-95RTs, showing the IFR probe and the chin fairing for the Oospekh-U system's missile guidance antenna.

Port and starboard views of the Tu-95K-22's forward fuselage.

panes), four side windows (the trapezoidal forward ones are aft-sliding direct vision windows) and three pairs of triangular or trapezoidal eyebrow windows. There are also two rectangular emergency exits with square windows located in a staggered arrangement at the Nav/Op's and flight engineer's workstations (the port one is further forward) and the (senior) GRO's dorsal observation/sighting blister between frames 10-13. The two windscreen panes in front of the pilots are made of Triplex silicate glass, all other panes are Plexiglas up to 10 mm (0²⁵⁄₆₄ in) thick.

The nosewheel well is located between frames 6A-11. Its roof forms part of the flight deck's pressure

and Tu-95RTs because the IFR probe and associated equipment are located on top of the nose. The navigator sits facing left. Underneath the pressure floor of his station is an unpressurised bay for the navigation/bomb-aiming radar antenna (frames 2-5), which is closed by a detachable flattened radome made of glassfibre Textolite composite; on the Tu-95RTs this is replaced by a deeper teardrop-shaped dielectric fairing for the missile guidance data link channel antenna.

The flight deck (frames 5-13) accommodates the captain on the left, the co-pilot on the right, the aft-facing navigator/operator (co-navigator) on the left, the flight engineer on the right, the ECM officer, and the gunner/radio operator (also referred to as the senior GRO), who works the dorsal cannon barbette, behind and above them. The flight deck is extensively glazed, with a framework made of duralumin profiles whose rear end is flush with the top of the fuselage. It features a three-piece windscreen (with trapezoidal optically-flat

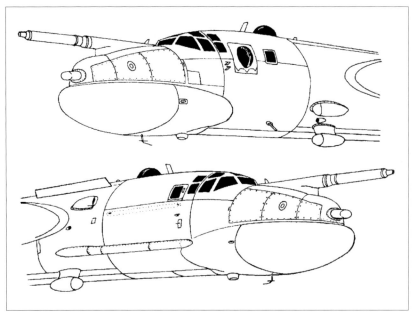

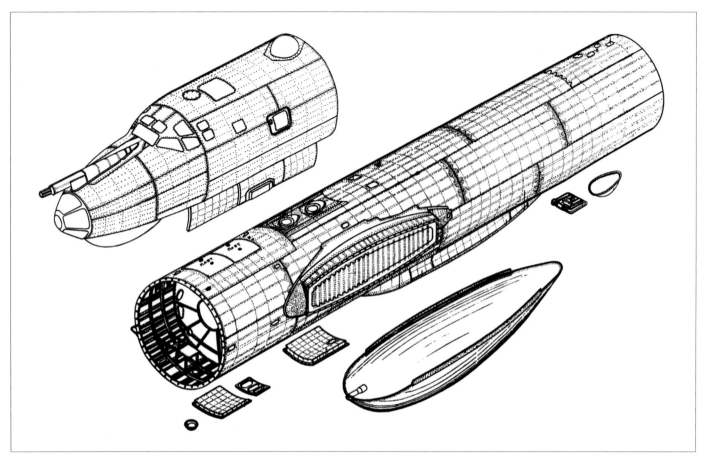

Above: The forward fuselage (Sections F-1/F-2) and centre fuselage (Section F-3) of the Tu-95RTs with the radome and ELINT antenna fairing detached. Note the forward cabin's rear pressure dome, the tandem covers of the life raft containers, the tandem BTs-63 star trackers and the faired mount for the radome.

Right: The rear fuselage (Section F-4) and tail section (rear pressure cabin, Section F-5) of the Tu-95. The flare bomb compartment doors are open.

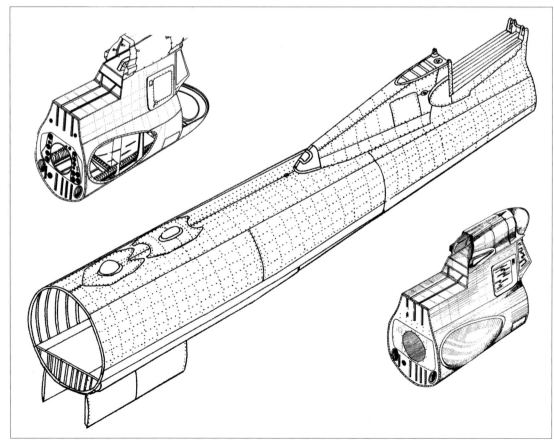

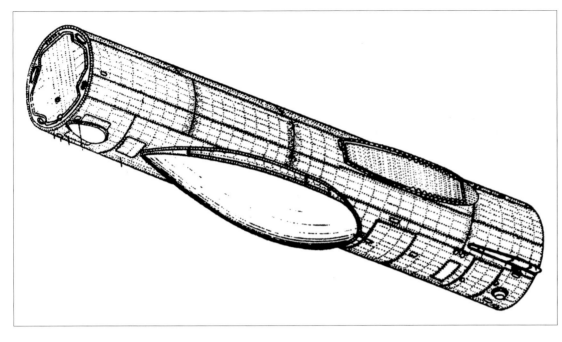

Lower rear view of the Tu-95RTs's centre fuselage with the radome and ELINT fairing fitted and the avionics bay access covers in place.

floor and incorporates the downward-opening entry hatch of the forward pressure cabin. The hatch cover (access door) is equipped with a pneumatic emergency actuator allowing the crew to bail out (if the nose gear unit is extended – see Crew protection and crew rescue system); this actuator works in concert with a valve depressurising the cabin. Section F-2 terminates in a strongly convex rear pressure dome (frame 13); the latter incorporates pressure seals allowing the control runs to exit the forward pressure cabin.

On the Tu-95K/Tu-95KM, Section F-2 is reworked, featuring a flat forward pressure bulkhead (frame 3) and cheek fairings allowing the wide radome to blend into the fuselage. Hence the navigator's workstation is relocated to a position aft of the captain's seat, featuring a large observation blister and requiring the port emergency exit to be moved aft.

The unpressurised *centre fuselage* (Section F-3, frames 13A-49) is built integrally with the wing centre section located between frames 19-28. The bomb bay is positioned amidships between frames 28-45 and closed

by hydraulically actuated clamshell doors; if the hydraulic system fails, the doors can be opened by a spring-loaded mechanism. The opening and closing of the bomb bay doors is electrically controlled by the navigator/bomb-aimer. All fuselage frames in the bomb bay area are formers, with the exception of frame 45, which is a bulkhead carrying the door actuation mechanism. The fuselage structure in this area is reinforced by two longerons acting as the bomb bay sidewalls to which the doors are hinged; the walls incorporate fittings for installing bomb cassettes. The roof of the bay features horizontal longerons which are used for installing more bomb cassettes or a beam-type bomb suspension unit for carrying the biggest bombs; the bomb suspension unit is located between frames 30-33.

A separate bay for marker or flare bombs (also closed by clamshell doors) is located aft of the bomb bay, as are fire retardant bottles. Containers housing the Nos. 1, 2, 3, 6A and 6B fuel tanks occupy most of the space in Section F-3 aft of the bomb bay. Containers

Below left: The flight deck roof of a Tu-95K-22, showing the eyebrow windows and the dorsal observation/sighting blister, with an offset aerial mast ahead of it.

Below: The top of the Tu-95K-22's centre/rear fuselage and inner wings. The dorsal cannon barbette stowed flush with the top of the fuselage is very evident, with a wire aerial mast and outlet immediately aft of it.

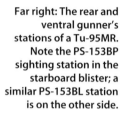

tank pressurisation, oxygen bottles, hydraulic system components and other equipment; a ventral hatch is provided for maintenance access to them. Blast plates made of heat-resistant steel are riveted to the upper and lower fuselage aft of the cannon barbettes to protect the duralumin skin from the flames of the muzzle flash. The rear end of Section F-4 incorporates a compartment for the retractable tail bumper.

The *tail section* (Section F-5, frames 87-95) is the rear pressure cabin accommodating the gunner/radio operator (working the ventral cannon barbette) and the tail gunner (defensive fire commander). The latter normally operates the tail cannon barbette and the gun ranging radar but is able to control and fire all other cannons in case of need.

Access to the rear cabin is via a ventral hatch under the tail gunner's seat with a forward-hinged cover incorporating steps; the hatch frame is made of cast ML5-T4 magnesium alloy, while the hatch cover has a cast magnesium alloy liner and duralumin armour skin. The hatch can be opened and closed in flight by a pneumatic ram if necessary. The tail gunner's port side window is an inward-opening emergency exit to be used in the event of ditching or a belly landing when the ventral hatch is unusable.

The rear cabin has two lateral sighting blisters at the GRO's station; they have a teardrop shape and are made of 10-mm (0²⁵⁄₆₄ in) Plexiglas. The glazing of the tail gunner's station comprises two side windows (with double Plexiglas panes) and three rear windows made of bulletproof Triplex silicate glass in a cast ML5-T4 magnesium alloy framework. A fairing for the gun ranging radar terminating in a hemispherical radome made of polystyrene is positioned above the cabin.

The rear pressure cabin is sealed and heat-insulated/soundproofed in the same way as the front one. Apart from frames and stringers, the structure includes a flat forward pressure bulkhead (frame 87) reinforces by vertical and horizontal beams, which is attached to longerons. Below the rear glazing is a variable-thickness armour-plated rear pressure bulkhead at frame 93 to which the tail barbette and its fairing are attached; it has apertures for the tail turret's ammunition belt sleeves.

housing two inflatable life rafts are located high on the port side between frames 14-17.

Control system cable runs and push-pull rods pass along both sides of Section F-3; some equipment items are mounted on both sides of the fuselage in the area. The bomb bay is thermally insulated and equipped with electric heating to ensure proper conditions for nuclear bombs.

On the Tu-95K/Tu-95KM the weapons bay (commencing at frame 23 and continuing into Section F-4 to frame 56) is tailored for semi-recessed carriage of a Kh-20 (Kh-20M) stand-off missile. It incorporates a BD-206 telescoping missile rack and is closed by three pairs of inward-opening pneumatically operated doors when no missile is carried. There is also a retractable semi-parabolic fairing immediately ahead of the weapons bay between frames 21-23 to close the missile's air intake until immediately before launch. A faired platform for the navigation system's star tracker is located at the front end of Section F-3, offset to port.

The Tu-95RTs has no weapons bay; instead, a recess for the search radar antenna is located amidships at the bay's former position and closed by a large teardrop radome attached to a metal fairing.

The unpressurised *rear fuselage* (Section F-4, frames 50-87) carries the tail unit; the fin root fillet located between frames 69-81 is built integrally with the rear fuselage (and houses some of the equipment accessible via lateral covers), while mainframes 81 and 87 feature attachment fittings for the fin and stabiliser spars. The rear fuselage structure includes two lower longerons which are a continuation of the centre fuselage longerons/bomb bay sidewalls. Section F-4 accommodates the Nos. 4, 5 and 5A fuel tanks, the dorsal and ventral cannon barbettes, nitrogen bottles for fuel

Wings: Cantilever mid-wing monoplane of modified trapezoidal planform. Sweepback at quarter-chord 34°59'37.3" on inner wings and 33°33'16" on outer wings, aspect ratio 8.84, taper 3.3; anhedral 2°30' from root, incidence +1° at root. To improve the aerodynamic characteristics at high subsonic speeds, the wings utilise TsAGI high-speed aerofoils which vary along the span – PR-36-10M with a 15% thickness/chord ratio at the root, PR-35-12 with a 15% T/C ratio at 40% span and PR-35-12 with a 12% T/C ratio at the tip.

The wings are of riveted two-spar stressed-skin construction with beam-type spars and 83 ribs; the main structural materials are aluminium and magnesium alloys. Structurally the wings are built in five pieces: the centre section, inner wings and outer wings, with manufacturing breaks at ribs 2 and 25/25A on each side; the sections are bolted together by means of flanges. The ribs are at right angles to the rear spar, except for the centre section ribs, which are parallel to the fuselage axis. The wing torsion box accommodates bag-type fuel

tanks; parts of the lower skin are detachable, enabling installation and removal of the tanks. The upper and lower skin panels incorporate multiple hatches for access to the control cables, fuel transfer pumps, fuel level indicators and fuel jettison valves.

The *centre section* carry-through structure is built integrally with the fuselage, the spars being attached to mainframes 19 and 28. It has five ribs forming two bays (rib 0 is on the centreline, while ribs 2L and 2R are in line with the fuselage sides); the bays house fuel tanks.

The *inner wings* (ribs 2A-25) each consist of a torsion box, a trailing-edge section riveted to the latter (built in inboard and outboard portions separated by a gap), a detachable leading edge doubling as a de-icer, and flaps (see below). Each inner wing section carries two engine nacelles of circular cross-section (see Power-plant); Heat shields made of titanium alloy are attached to the wing underside aft of the engine jetpipes to protect the skin from the heat of the engine exhaust. The wing leading edge is built in three sections divided

The starboard wing of a 'first-generation' Tu-95 showing the unevenly spaced boundary layer fences, the wing/nacelle joints and the different shades of skin along the span. Note the black paint on the main gear fairing supposed to hide the untidy exhaust stains from the inboard engine.

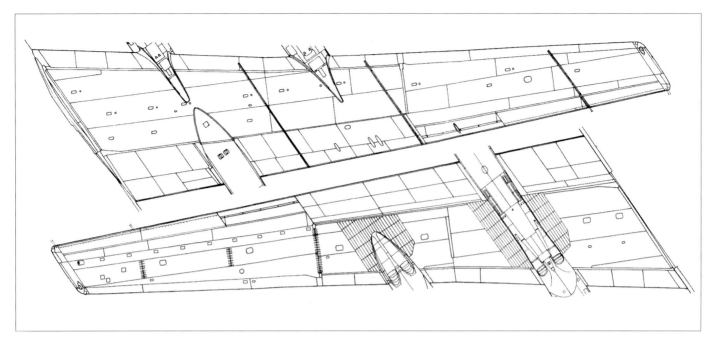

Upper and lower views of the starboard wing, showing the manufacturing break at the flap's outer end and the heat shields aft of the engine exhausts.

by the engine nacelles. The ribs on the inner wing sections are evenly spaced.

The rear ends of the inboard engine nacelles blend into large pointed main landing gear fairings extending beyond the wing trailing edge; the nacelle/fairing combination is area-ruled. The fairings have a basically rectangular cross-section with rounded corners changing to semi-circular at the front end and circular at the rear end. They are separate subassemblies of beam-and-stringer construction with upper, lower and side panels; each fairing is attached to the wing's rear spar.

Heat shields are attached to the sides of the fairings to protect the mainwheels from the heat of the engine exhaust.

The *outer wings* (ribs 25A-41) are of broadly similar design, featuring a torsion box with a trailing-edge section, a detachable leading edge, full-span ailerons (see Control system) and detachable tip fairings. Each aileron is built in three sections to prevent jamming when the wings flex; the inboard sections feature electrically operated trim tabs/servo tabs whose actuators are mounted on the rear spar.

An exploded view of the starboard inner wing panel's structure; the main gear fairing is not shown.

Opposite, top: An exploded view of the starboard outer wing panel's structure.

Opposite, centre: The port outer wing panel.

Opposite, bottom: The basic Tu-95's tail unit.

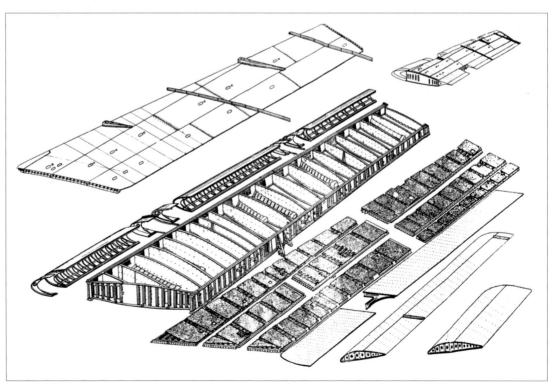

Each wing has three prominent boundary layer fences on the upper surface designed to delay tip stall (one between the engine nacelles, one just inboard of the inner/outer wing joint and one on the outer wing at the joint of the aileron's second and third sections). They are built in several portions to avoid deformation as the wings flex.

The high-lift devices consist of two-section slotted flaps located on the inner wings inboard and outboard of the main gear fairings (up to ribs 25L/25R). There are no leading-edge devices. The flaps are riveted structures made of aluminium, magnesium and steel alloys. They are electromechanically operated by an MPZ-12 electric drive (*mekhanizm privoda zakrylkov* – flap drive mechanism) with twin electric motors and common reduction gear housed in the wing centre section and transmitting torque via drive shafts and angle drives/screw jacks (two for each flap section). The flaps move on curved tracks housed entirely inside the wings; the inboard sections have two flap tracks each and the outboard ones, which are nearly twice as long, have three flap tracks each. The flaps are controlled either by the captain or the co-pilot. Flap settings are 25° for take-off and 35° for landing. In the retracted position the flaps are sealed by rubber strips attached to the wing trailing-edge structure to prevent leakage of air and reduce drag.

Tail unit: Conventional cantilever swept tail surfaces, utilising symmetrical aerofoil sections. The *vertical tail* consists of a large root fillet built integrally with the rear fuselage, a detachable fin and a one-piece rudder carried on four mounting brackets (see Control system); sweepback at quarter-chord 40°, leading-edge sweep 44°36'. The fin utilises a TsAGI S-11S-9 symmetrical aerofoil with a variable T/C ratio of 9-12%. It is a two-spar stressed-skin structure with an attachment root rib, regular and reinforced ribs, skin panels with stringers, a three-section detachable leading edge doubling as a de-icer, and a detachable tip fairing.

The rudder is a single-spar structure with a rudder post, a set of ribs, skins, and the leading edge assembly. The trailing edge features a so-called 'knife' (*nozh*) – a bendable trim tab made of magnesium alloy. A trim/balance tab and its electric drive are mounted on six supporting brackets at the base of the rudder. The rudder has 30% aerodynamic balance and a mass balance with 2% overbalancing.

The *horizontal tail* consists of two stabilisers and one-piece elevators carried on five elevator mounting brackets each (see Control system). Sweepback at quarter-chord 38° (also reported as 40°), incidence 2°30'. Originally the stabilisers were to have variable incidence but the stabiliser trim mechanism was never actually installed. Again, the TsAGI S-11S-9 aerofoil is used but the T/C ratio is 10-12%. The stabilisers are of

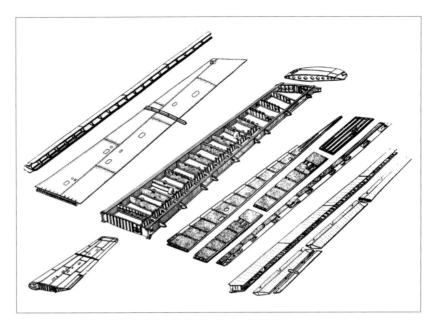

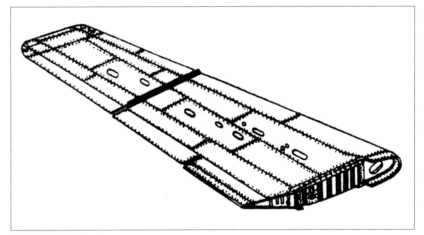

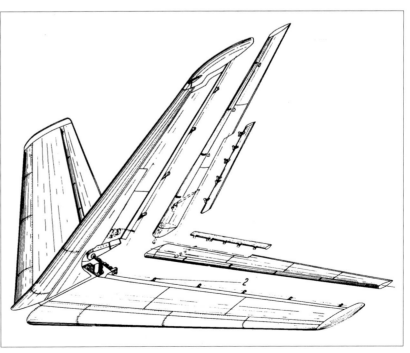

Right: The tail unit of a Tu-95RTs, with flush antennas for the RSBN-2S SHORAN system built into the fin. The large rudder trim tab is visible, as are the fairings of the Arfa antenna/feeder system at the stabiliser tips.

Far right: The tail unit of a Tu-95MU.

The tail unit of a Tu-95M with no flush antennas. Note the twin-wheel tail bumper.

Two more views of a Tu-95MU's tail surfaces. A single flush antenna on each side for a transponder has been added to the fin. The tail bumper is deleted.

nected by a shaft with a universal joint ensuring simultaneous deflection; the actuating push-pull rods are attached to the shaft assembly, which has a travel limiter. The shaft bracket serves as a sixth support point. An electrically actuated trim tab with manual back-up drive is attached on six brackets at the inboard end of each elevator.

Landing gear: Retractable tricycle type; all three units retract aft. The nose unit attached to fuselage frame 8 is hydraulically operated, with pneumatic emergency extension to allow the crew to bail out. It has a V-shaped strut (strongly inclined forward when extended) and an aft-mounted drag strut with a breaker strut. It is fitted with twin 1,100x330 mm (43.3x13.0 in) K-279 non-braking wheels. The nose unit features a twin-cylinder steering mechanism/shimmy damper. Nose gear steering is via the rudder pedals.

The main units attached to inner wing ribs 11-13 are actuated by individual MPSh-18NT twin-motor electric drives (*mekhanizm privoda shassee* – landing gear drive mechanism), with mechanical emergency extension by means of a hand-cranked winch. Each main gear strut

similar two-spar construction with a detachable leading edge doubling as a de-icer and tip fairings. They are bolted together along the fuselage centreline; each stabiliser is fastened to the fuselage by four bolt assemblies.

The elevators are single-spar structures of similar design to the rudder, again featuring 30% aerodynamic balance, a mass balance with 3% overbalancing and trailing-edge 'knives'. They are mechanically intercon-

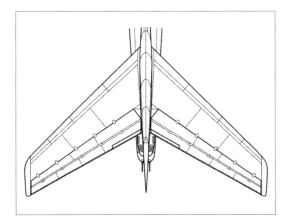

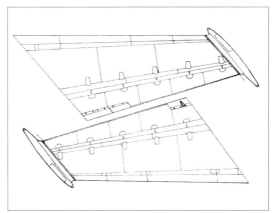

Far left: The standard Tu-95's horizontal tail.

Left: The stabilisers of the Tu-95RTs.

has twin forward-mounted drag struts, an oleo strut (inclined aft when extended) and a four-wheel bogie with 1,500x500 mm (59.0x19.68 in) KT-25 wheels (*koleso tormoznoye* – brake-equipped wheel). Each wheel is fitted with twin expander-tube brakes; an anti-skid unit is provided and the brakes are controlled automatically.

All three units have oleo-pneumatic shock absorbers and scissor links. The shock absorbers are charged with AMG-10 mineral oil-type hydraulic fluid (*aviatsionnoye mahslo ghidravlicheskoye* – 'aviation-specific hydraulic oil') and nitrogen. Nitrogen pressure is 27 kg/cm² (385.7 psi) for the nose unit and 40 kg/cm² (571.4 psi) for the main units. Tyre pressure is 9 bars (128.5 psi) for the nosewheels and 9.5 bars (135.7 psi) for the mainwheels.

When extended, all three struts are inclined forward. In no-load condition the main gear bogies assume a 4° nose-down attitude. During retraction the bogies are rotated aft through 180° by a system of linkages and oleo-pneumatic rams/rocking dampers (also charged with AMG-10 and nitrogen) to lie inverted in the abovementioned fairings forming a continuation of the inboard engine nacelles.

The nosewheel well is closed by two pairs of doors; the small forward doors are mechanically linked to the nose gear strut. Each main unit has two large main doors (bulged to accommodate the wheels), two small clamshell doors in line with the gear fulcrum (mechanically linked to the strut) and a narrow door segment attached to the drag struts. The nosewheel well doors remain open when the gear is down; the larger main gear doors open only when the gear is in transit, being operated by a special drive unit.

All three units have uplocks, downlocks and door locks. Landing gear position is indicated by pilot lights on the captain's instrument panel.

The Tu-95 *sans suffixe*/Tu-95M has a retractable tail bumper with twin 480x200 mm (18.8x97.87 in) K3-29 wheels and an oleo-pneumatic shock absorber to protect the fuselage in the event of overrotation on take-off or a tail-down landing. It is retracted/extended by an MP-250 electric drive concurrently with the

The horizontal tail of a Tu-95RTs, with the distinctive cigar-shaped fairings of the Leera data link system at the tips.

The rear fuselage and tail unit of the Tu-95RTs. Note the boxy radome of the new PRS-4 Krypton gun ranging radar.

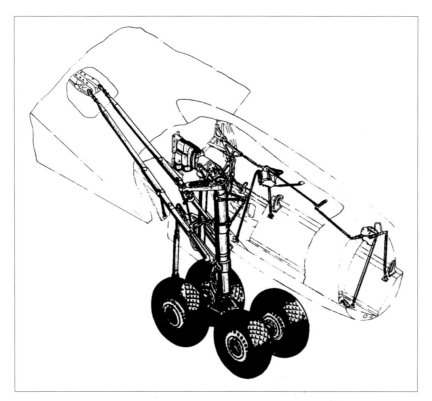

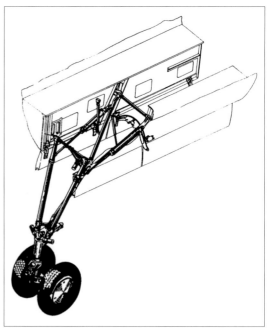

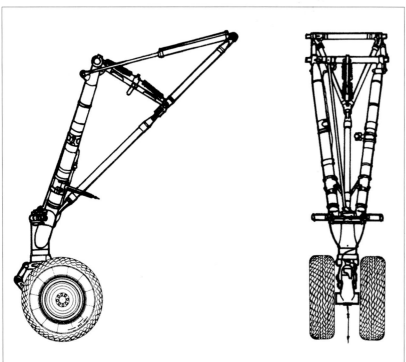

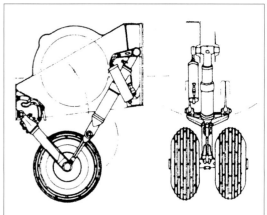

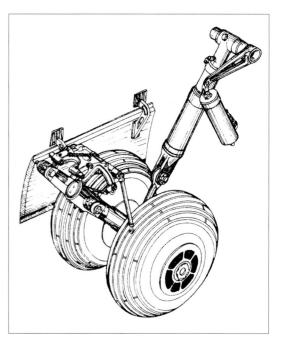

Top: The port main gear unit and the mainwheel well door actuation mechanism in the main gear fairing.

Above: The nose gear strut with breaker strut and earth connection wire.

Top right: The nose gear unit is shown here with the nosewheel well door actuating linkages.

Right and above right: The twin-wheel tail bumper and its retraction mechanism.

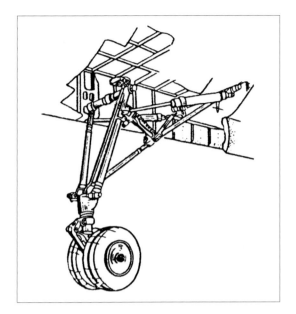

Above left: A drawing from the structural manual showing the nose gear unit and its actuation mechanism.

Above: The smaller front pair of nosewheel well doors on this retired Tu-95K is missing, giving a good view of the nose unit's breaker strut. Note the strong forward incline of the nose unit and the vertical shock absorber with a torque link.

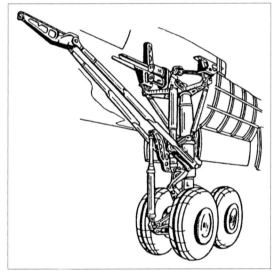

Left: A drawing from the structural manual showing one of the main gear units and its actuation mechanism with the MPSh-18NT drive ahead of the fulcrum.

Below: The main gear units and starboard main gear fairing of a Tu-95MR. Heat shields are riveted to the sides of the main gear fairings to protect the wheels from the hot exhaust.

Below left: A drawing from the structural manual showing the tail bumper and its actuation mechanism.

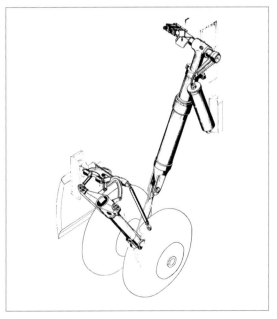

The Kuznetsov NK-12MV turboprop engine. Note the TS-12M turbine starter on the port side of the casing.

The SKBM (NPP Aerosila) AV-60K contra-rotating propellers. Note the leading edge de-icer strips.

landing gear and the bumper bay is closed by clamshell doors, which again remain open when the gear is down. The tail bumper was deleted on later versions.

Powerplant: The Tu-95 *sans suffixe* is powered by four Kuznetsov NK-12 turboprops rated at 12,500 ehp for take-off and 6,500 ehp for cruise. All subsequent variants except the Tu-95MS (see below) are powered by NK-12M or NK-12MV turboprops having a 15,000-ehp take-off rating and an identical 6,500-ehp cruise rating. The engine was manufactured by the Kuibyshev Engine Factory named after Mikhail V. Frunze (now called Motorostroitel' JSC).

The NK-12MV is a single-shaft turboprop featuring an annular air intake with the outer casing connected to the reduction gearbox housing by six radial struts, a 14-stage axial compressor with adjustable inlet guide vanes (IGVs) and air bleed valves at the 9th and 14th stages, an annular combustion chamber with 12 flame

The No.2 NK-12MV engine of a retired Tu-95K-22 with the propeller and cowling removed; note the reduction gearbox shroud and the radial struts connecting the gearbox casing to the main casing.

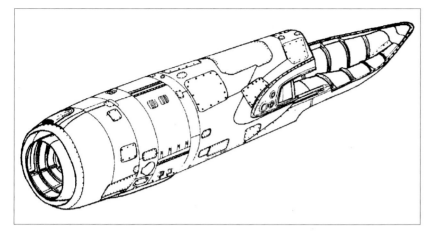

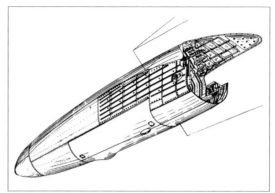

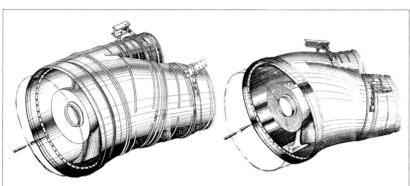

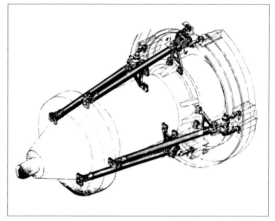

tubes, a five-stage uncooled axial turbine with cast blades and a fixed-area nozzle with an outer stressed casing and an inner liner. The combustion chamber is of welded construction and is made of heat-resistant steel. Fuel is fed through 12 fuel nozzles with two orifices each. An extension jetpipe attached to the nozzle casing bifurcates into oval-section exhaust pipes; because of the different nacelle design the jetpipes are different for the inboard and outboard engines. The NK-12 features turbine blade gap control and a vibration cancelling unit.

Two-thirds of the turbine power is used for driving the engine compressor and accessories; one-third is transmitted to the propellers (see below) via a single-stage differential planetary reduction gearbox which doubles as the accessory gearbox. The gear ratio is 0.088 (equivalent to an engine turbine speed of 8,300 rpm and a propeller shaft speed of 736 rpm). The power transfer to the propellers is not divided evenly; the front row receives 54.4% of the power and the rear row receives 45.6%. The reduction gearbox consists of three subassemblies: the rear propeller shaft casing, the front casing with drive, and the reduction gear assembly. The rear propeller shaft casing is part of the engine itself, accommodating both the propeller thrust loads and the structural loads. The reduction gearbox has its own oil cooler.

The following equipment is installed on each engine: two GSR-18000M DC generators, an SGO-30U

AC generator, an AK-150NK compressor catering for the pneumatic system, a KTA-14N integrated fuel control unit (*komahndno-top*livnyy agre*gaht* – FCU), a Model 450UK high-pressure fuel pump, a Model 1007K low-pressure fuel pump, a propeller speed governor, an oil unit, delivery and scavenge oil pumps, a Model 437F hydraulic pump, an AU-12 IGV and air bleed valve control unit (agre*gaht* oopravleniya), a centrifugal

Top left: The starboard outer engine nacelle.

Above left: The inboard (left) and outboard engines' bifurcated jetpipes

Top: The port main gear fairing.

Above: The engine bearer struts connecting the reduction gearbox housing to the engine nacelle's centre portion.

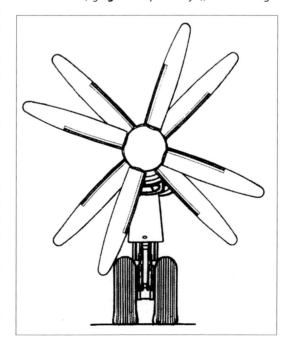

Front view of the AV-60K contraprops. The front row turns anti-clockwise, the rear row clockwise.

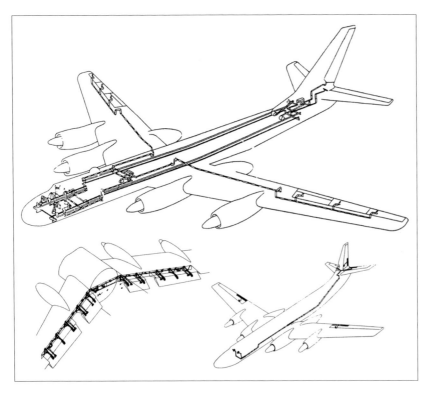

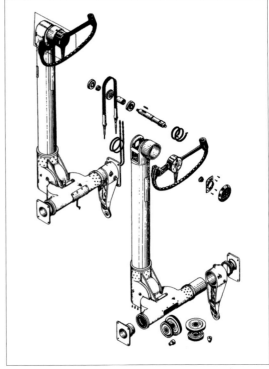

Above: The Tu-95M's flight control system linkages. The insets show the flap actuation system (left) and the trim tab controls (mechanical for the elevators and electric elsewhere).

Above right: The captain's control yoke (assembled and exploded views).

Right: As per Soviet custom, the Tu-95's control wheels had the aircraft type marked on the hub. The left spoke features radio/intercom control buttons and a rudder trim tab switch; the right spoke carries autopilot engage/ override buttons, while the centre spoke features an 'ailerons neutral' indicator arrow to be aligned with a line on the control column.

breather, and DT-2 and DT-33 rpm gauges (*dahtchik takhometra* – tachometer sensor).

Engine pressure ratio 9.5 at take-off power, mass flow at take-off power 55.9 kg/sec (123 lb/sec); turbine temperature 1,150°K. SFC (NK-12) 0.225 kg/hp-hr (0.496 lb/hp-hr) at take-off power and 0.165 kg/hp-hr (0.363 lb/hp-hr) at cruise power; (NK-12M) 0.21 kg/hp-hr (0.46 lb/hp-hr) at take-off power and 0.158 kg/hp-hr (0.34 lb/hp-hr) at cruise power. Length overall 6,000 mm (19 ft 8¼ in), maximum diameter 1,150 mm (3 ft 9¼ in); dry weight less propellers 2,900 kg (6,390 lb).

The engine is started by a TS-12M jet fuel starter (*toorbostartyor* – turbine starter) on the left side of the engine casing – a small gas turbine engine driving the spool directly via a clutch.

The engines are mounted in individual nacelles attached to the inner wing sections. Each nacelle consists of a one-piece annular forward fairing, a centre portion with hinged cowling panels and a fixed rear fairing which houses the bifurcated jetpipe; on the outer nacelles this fairing is parabolic, while the inner nacelles blend into the main gear fairings. The forward portion houses the oil tanks (three for each nacelle) positioned at the bottom and incorporates an air intake de-icer. The centre portion absorbs the structural loads and incorporates a titanium firewall; the faired oil cooler located underneath it (with air intake and rear airflow adjustment flap) is detachable. Each engine is attached to the respective nacelle's frame 0 by four tubular rods via dampers located on the forward and centre casings, and the extension jetpipe is attached to the airframe by two adjustable brackets.

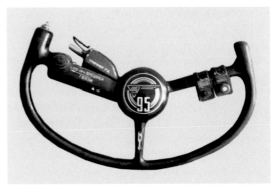

On the Tu-195 *sans suffixe* the engines drive Stoopino Machinery Design Bureau (SKBM) AV-60 eight-blade contra-rotating reversible-pitch propellers with spinners; later versions have AV-60N or AV-60K propellers. Diameter 5.6 m (18 ft 4¹⁵⁄₃₂ in), weight 1,190 kg (2,620 lb); speed at take-off power 730 rpm, thrust at take-off power 14,800 kgp (32,630 lbst). The AV-60 has four duralumin blades in each row; the front row rotates anti-clockwise and the rear propeller clockwise when seen from the front. The blades use a NACA-16 aerofoil.

The propeller is equipped with an R-60DA or R-60K speed governor (R = *regoolyator*) maintaining constant rpm; the governor automatically adjusts the propeller pitch by means of a hydromechanical drive and feathers the propeller automatically if necessary. Feathering is possible in the following ways:

• manually by means of the feathering system's oil pump when the KFL-37 button (*knopka flyughee-rovaniya s **lampoy*** – propeller feathering button with built-in [indicator] light) is pushed;

• manually by means of the speed governor's oil pump when the pneumatic emergency feathering system is activated at the push of a button;

• automatically when the electric autofeathering system sensor detects that engine torque drops below a certain limit;

• automatically (triggered by the hydraulic autofeathering system sensor).

This multiple redundancy is justified, since the propeller feathering system was one of the Tu-95's weak spots. All-mode automatic propeller feathering was introduced with the NK-12MV engine.

Engine power is controlled by throttles connected to the engines' FCUs by cable runs. The captain, the co-pilot and the flight engineer each have their own bank of throttles (using a central bank of throttles is impossible because of the passage to the navigator's station in the nose); the flight engineer controls the engine speed during take-off to ease the pilots' workload.

Control system: Conventional mechanical dual control system. The system utilises mainly rigid linkages with push-pull rods, bellcranks and levers; however, KSAN ultra-pliant steel cables (*kanaht stal'noy aviatsionnyy neraskroochivayushchiysya* – aviation-specific steel cable resistant to unravelling) are used in certain areas. Control of the aircraft is exercised via two control columns and two pairs of rudder pedals; the captain's and co-pilot's flight controls are inter-connected. Part of this is interfaced with the stability and control system. Gust locks are provided to prevent damage to the system by high winds while the aircraft is parked; they are operated by cables, with a locking handle on the captain's side console.

Directional control is provided by a one-piece rudder provided with a GU-62M reversible hydraulic actuator (*ghidro'usilitel'* – hydraulic booster); the travel limits are ±25°. The rudder features a trim tab/geared tab that is powered by an electric drive.

Pitch control is provided by one-piece manual elevators with a travel limit of 12° up/25° down. Each elevator incorporates a trim tab controlled electrically or manually by means of cables and handwheels.

Roll control is provided by three-section ailerons powered by GU-54M reversible hydraulic actuators; each section is controlled independently and the travel limits are ±25°. The inboard sections incorporate full-span trim tabs/geared tabs with electric drives.

The control system includes an AP-15 electric autopilot whose servos are hooked up to the elevator and aileron control channels in order to ease the pilot workload on long missions.

Fuel system: The fuel is carried in bag-type tanks (fuel cells) made of kerosene-proof rubber which are housed in the fuselage and the wings. The Tu-95 *sans suffixe* carries its fuel in 71 separate tanks; five of these (Nos. 1, 2, 3, 6A and 6B) are located in the centre

Fuel tank location and fuel usage sequence (Tu-95K)					
Fuel usage sequence	Engines No.1 & No.4 Fuel tank No.	Overall fuel load, kg	Fuel usage sequence	Engines No.2 & No.3 Fuel tank No.	Overall fuel load, kg
I	6	9,640	I	5-5-5A	6,960
II	7-8	7,300	II	3-4-4	6,640
III	13-16	9,300	III	2	6,640
IV	22-27	6,640	IV	17-18	5,320
V	28-32	3,980	V	9-10	8,480
VI	33-38	2,820	VI	1	4,720
VII	19-21	5,320	VII	11-12	6,640
Total		45,000			45,400

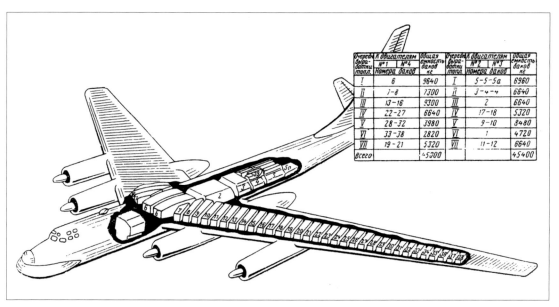

A drawing showing the Tu-95K's fuel system (except the No.39 tank which is for starting the Kh-20 missile's engine). The figures are explained in the table above.

The in-flight refuelling probe of a Tu-95KM.

For structural integrity and control reasons, fuel usage is automatically sequenced by the SETS-80A system (*soommeeruyushchiy elektricheskiy toplivomer s signalizahtsiyey* – summing electric fuel meter with a [low fuel] warning feature) to maintain the CG position within the prescribed limits and ensure the aircraft does not exceed the maximum landing weight.

The fuel tanks have a common venting system. A fuel jettison system is provided for reducing the all-up weight quickly in the event of an emergency landing; the fuel jettison pipe is located in the port wingtip fairing to minimise the risk of fire.

Fuel grades used are Soviet/Russian T-1, TS-1 or T-2 grade aviation kerosene with a specific gravity of 0.83, 0.78 and 0.775 g/cm^3 respectively. Depending on the actual grade used, the fuel load may vary.

fuselage, three (Nos. 4, 5 and 5A) in the rear fuselage, two in the wing centre section and the rest in the outer wings. The number of tanks is increased to 74 on the Tu-95M and 72 on the Tu-95MR. The fuel tanks are split into four groups, one for each engine, although the system features cross-feed valves allowing any engine to draw fuel from any group of tanks.

On the Tu-95K and Tu-95KM, the aircraft's own fuel is again carried in 74 tanks but there is also a separate fuel tank mounted between frames 45-51 to cater for the Kh-20M missile's launch requirements, allowing the engine to be started and run prior to release without wasting the missile's own fuel. This tank holds 500 kg (1,102 lb) of fuel.

On early versions, ground refuelling is by gravity; each group of tanks has a single filler cap and is filled separately. Late versions have single-point pressure refuelling. The Tu-95MR, Tu-95KM and Tu-95RTs have an in-flight refuelling system featuring a pneumatically operated telescopic IFR probe mounted atop the nose on the centreline, a fuel transfer line (with a scavenging system) running along the starboard side of the nose to the wing centre section tanks, and appropriate valves.

Oil system: Each engine has an open-type lubrication system featuring a three-section self-sealing 135-litre (29.7 Imp gal) oil tank installed in the front portion of the nacelle, a Model 242 oil cooler with an adjustable flap controlling the air flow, a delivery pump and a scavenging pump. The engines and their turbine starters use MK-8P grade mineral oil or transformer oil.

Electrics: Main 28.5 V DC power is supplied by eight GSR-18000M engine-driven generators (two on each engine). Two 12SAM-55 lead-acid batteries (55 A·h) are used as buffers and a back-up DC power source. Direct current is utilised for de-icing the propellers and the navigator's station/flight deck glazing, as well as for the communication radios and the radio navigation system.

208 V/400 Hz and 115 V/400 Hz single-phase AC is supplied by four engine-driven SGO-30U variable-frequency alternators (one on each engine). For systems requiring a stable power supply, there are two 4.5-kVA PO-4500 single-phase AC converters and three PT-70 (or PT-125) and PT-600 series three-phase AC converters. The Tu-95MR also has PT-1000TsS converters catering for the mission equipment. The Tu-95K and Tu-95KM missile carriers have an additional PO-4500 converter catering exclusively for the YaD radar, while the low-powered PT-70 and PT-125 are replaced by the PT-500Ts and PT-1000TsS (or PT-1500Ts) three-phase AC converters. Equipment requiring alternating current includes the wing and tail surface leading edge de-icers and some avionics and equipment items. Ground power receptacles are located at the rear of the nosewheel well.

The electric circuitry uses mainly BPVL and MGShV copper wire and BPVLA aluminium wire, the airframe acting as the 'earth' electrode. To reduce radio interference, part of the copper wiring is shielded BPVLE wire (*ekraneerovannyy* – shielded) or, alternatively, the wiring bundles are enclosed in a common sheath.

A schematic layout of the Tu-95's electrics showing the SGO-30U engine-driven AC generators and their wiring and controls.

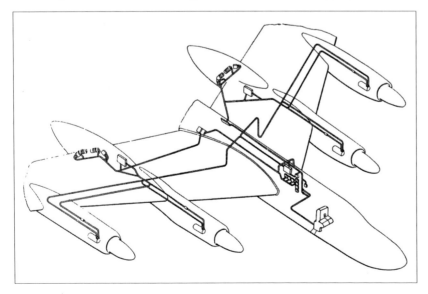

External lighting equipment includes pairs of red (port) and green (starboard) BANO-45 navigation lights (*bortovoy aeronavigatsionnyy ogon'*) above and below the wingtips in teardrop-shaped Perspex fairings and a white KhS-39 or KhS-57 tail navigation light (*khvostovoy signahl*) on the lower part of the tail turret fairing. 'Glass-nosed' versions have two retractable LFSV-45 landing/taxi lights (*lampa-fara samolyotnaya vydvizhnaya* – aircraft-type retractable sealed-beam lamp, 1945 model) or FRS-200 landing lights side by side immediately ahead of the nosewheel well between frames 5-6; on the Tu-95K/Tu-95KM the landing lights are moved slightly outward to the 'cheek fairings' behind the main radome. Some Tu-95s have OSS-61 revolving red anti-collision beacons (*ogon' svetosignahl'nyy* – signal light, 1961 model) installed in teardrop-shaped Perspex fairings on top of the centre fuselage and under the rear fuselage. Aircraft with IFR capability have two retractable FPSh-5M lights buried in the upper side of the nose, flanking the probe; they are used for illuminating the tip of probe and the tanker's drogue at night.

Interior lighting equipment comprises PS-45 and PSM-51 overhead lights (*plafon samolyotnyy* – aircraft-type lighting fixture) in the pressure cabins and the bomb bay, KLSRK-45 movable white lights, ARUFOSh-45 ultra-violet lamps (*armatoora ool'trafioletovovo osveshcheniya sharneernaya* – articulated UV lighting fixture, 1945 model) to make the instrument dials glow in the dark without revealing the aircraft's position to enemy fighter pilots, and PL-10-36 portable lamps (*perenosnaya lampa*).

Hydraulics: The Tu-95 has two independent hydraulic systems. The *high-pressure hydraulic system* has a nominal pressure of 120-150 kg/cm^2 (1,714-2,135 psi); it is powered by a Model 465A electric pump and includes hydraulic accumulators. It is responsible for normal retraction/extension of the nose landing gear strut, nosewheel steering, normal and emergency wheel braking, operation of the bomb bay doors (on the Tu-95 *sans suffixe*/Tu-95M), extension and retraction of the dorsal cannon barbette, operation of the windshield wipers and certain other items, including the flight deck escape 'conveyor belt' (see Crew rescue system).

The *low-pressure hydraulic system* with a nominal pressure of 75 kg/cm^2 (1,071 psi) is powered by two engine-driven Model 437F piston-type pumps and caters for the reversible hydraulic actuators in the aileron and rudder control circuits.

Both systems use AMG-10 hydraulic fluid. The systems feature both rigid pipelines and rubber hoses.

Pneumatic system: The pneumatic system operates the cannons' cocking mechanisms, the flare/marker bomb bay doors (on the bomber versions),

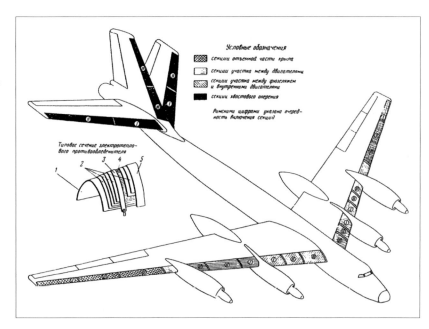

the weapons bay doors on the Tu-95K/Tu-95KM, the generator cooling airflow adjustment flaps in the engine nacelles, the fuel jettison valves, the IFR probe (on IFR-capable versions), the cabin pressurisation system valves, the rear pressure cabin's entry hatch and the inflatable perimeter seals of all entry and escape hatches. It pressurises the avionics bays housing the radar sets of the RBP-4 navigation/bomb-aiming radar and the PRS-1 gun ranging radar (or, on the Tu-95K/Tu-95KM, the YaD navigation/attack radar and the PRS-4 gun ranging radar), the RV-25A radio altimeter, the R-837 radio set and the DISS-1 Doppler speed/drift sensor, thereby preventing ingress of dust or water which may cause malfunctions. The system is also responsible for emergency extension of the nose gear unit, emergency opening of the forward pressure cabin's entry hatch and of the cabin depressurisation valves.

Compressed air is supplied by AK-150NK engine-driven compressors. Nominal pressure is 150 kg/cm^2 (2,135 psi); reduction valves are provided to reduce it where necessary.

De-icing system: The engines' air intakes, inlet guide vanes and oil coolers are de-iced by hot air bled from the 14th compressor stage. The propeller blades and spinners, the Triplex glazing panes of the flight deck/navigator's station and the star tracker window have 115 V AC electric de-icing with heating/cooling-off cycles. The heated glazing panes are provided with an AOS-81M temperature regulator (*avtomaht obogreva styokol* – automatic glazing heating controller) to prevent cracking.

The wing and tail unit leading edges, PPD-1V pitot heads (*preeyomnik polnovo davleniya*) and static ports have 28.5 V DC electric de-icing (again with

A diagram of the Tu-95's de-icing system with differently shaded zones (top to bottom: outer wings, wing leading edge between the engines, inner wings, and tail unit) and figures showing the electric heaters' operating sequence within each zone. The inset shows the design of the de-icers, with heaters sandwiched between inner and outer skins.

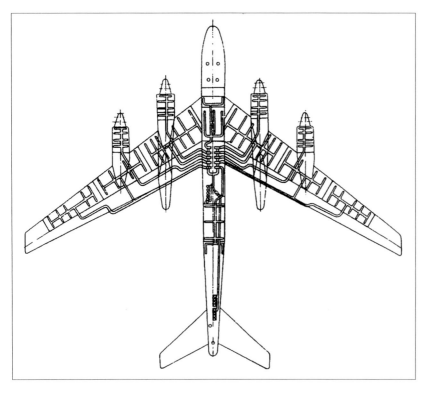

The layout of the Tu-95's fire suppression system showing the carbon dioxide distribution manifolds and the locations of the portable fire extinguishers.

heating/cooling-off cycles). Each leading edge is divided into four zones, which in turn are divided into sections; the latter are turned on and off by a mechanical sequencer.

An RIO-3 radioactive isotope icing detector (*rahdioizotopnyy indikahtor obledeneniya*) is installed on the starboard side of the nose; on the ground it is closed by a lead cover to protect ground personnel against radiation. Each engine is fitted with an SO-4A icing detector (*signalizahtor obledeneniya*).

Pressurisation and air conditioning system: To enable high-altitude operations the Tu-95 has ventilation-type pressurised cabins. Their entry hatches and windows/emergency exits have inflatable perimeter seals.

At altitudes up to 2,000 m (6,560 ft) the cockpits are ventilated by ram air (supplied by air scoops on the starboard side of the fuselage) and pressurised to a static condition – that is, the cabin pressure is equal to the ambient pressure. At higher altitude the system automatically switches to bleed air from the 9th compressor stage of the Nos. 2 and 3 (inboard) engines; in so doing, up to an altitude of 7,000 m (22,965 ft) the cabin pressure is maintained equal to 2,000 m above sea level. Above 7,000 m it decreases slowly as the aircraft climbs; a constant pressure differential of 0.4 kg/cm² (5.7 psi) is maintained by ARD-54 automatic pressure governors (*avtomaticheskiy regoolyator davleniya*), one in each cabin.

In the event that the ARD-54 is inoperative in both cabins, the pressure differential can be maintained

manually at 0.05-0.43 kg/cm² (0.71-6.14 psi), using KKD valves (*klapan kontrolya davleniya* – pressure control valve). On entering an area where anti-aircraft fire or combat with enemy fighters (and hence damage to the pressure cabins) is likely, the pressure differential is reduced to 0.2 kg/cm² (2.85 psi) – either by the ARD-54 or by the KKD valves – in order to avoid an explosive decompression at high altitude if the aircraft's skin is pierced. A depressurisation warning system is provided; in the event of bailing out the cabin pressure can be quickly reduced by emergency depressurisation valves.

Before entering the pressure cabins, the air for the front cabin is pre-cooled by an air/air heat exchanger, while the air the rear cabin is processed by a cooling turbine. The air temperature is maintained automatically by TRTVK-45 or TRTVK-45M cabin air temperature regulators (*termostaht-regoolyator temperatoory vozdukha v kabine*) within limits between +15.5° and +26.5°C (59.9-79.7°F), or set manually at between +10° and +30°C (50-86°F).

The equipment creating comfortable working conditions at high altitude also includes additional electric heating (although this is probably for the nuke, not for the crew!) and the cabins' thermal insulation.

Oxygen system: The aircraft's oxygen system consists of a KP-24M stationary breathing apparatus with a KM-32 oxygen mask (*kislorodnaya mahska*) for each crew member, KP-23 parachute oxygen sets used for bailing out, four KPZh-30 liquid oxygen converters, KAP portable oxygen equipment (*kislorodnaya apparatoora peredvizheniya* – lit. 'oxygen equipment that enables walking around') and a KAB-16 on-board oxygen fixture (*kislorodnaya armatoora bortovaya*).

Inert gas pressurisation system: The fuel tanks are pressurised with carbon dioxide (CO_2) to minimise the risk of fire and explosion if hit by incendiary rounds. The inert gas pressurisation system features eight OSU-5 spherical bottles with liquid CO_2 (*ognetooshitel' stationarnyy ooglekislotnyy* – stationary fire extinguisher charged with CO_2), a filter, reduction valves and manifolds feeding gaseous carbon dioxide into the tanks.

Fire-suppression system: The fire extinguishing equipment includes the following:
• a pressurised compartment system consisting of a OS-8M fire extinguisher charged with $114V_2$ grade chlorofluorocarbon;
• an engine fire extinguisher system;
• an SSP-2A fire warning system (*sistema signalizahtsii pozhara*);
• the abovementioned eight OSU-5 CO_2 bottles of the inert gas pressurisation system which may be used as an additional means of fire-fighting;

• five OU portable CO_2 fire extinguishers in the cabins.

Avionics and equipment

Unless otherwise indicated, the data below refers to the Tu-95 and Tu-95M after a mid-life update during the 1970s.

a) navigation and piloting equipment: The aircraft has an AP-15 autopilot; an ARK-5 (or ARK-11) automatic direction finder; an RV-UM (or RV-5) low-altitude radio altimeter and an RV-25A high-altitude radio altimeter; an SP-50 Materik ILS comprising a KRP-F localiser receiver (*koorsovoy rahdiopriyomnik*), GRP-2 glideslope beacon receiver (*glissahdnyy rahdiopriyomnik*), MRP-56P marker beacon receiver (*markernyy rahdiopriyomnik*) and SD-1 distance measuring equipment (*samolyotnyy dahl'nomer*); GPK-52 directional gyro (*gheeropolukompas*); DISS-1 Doppler ground speed and drift sensor system; A-327 formation flight equipment (showing the aircraft's position relative to other bombers in a group); an RSBN-2SV Svod SHORAN; and an ADNS-4 long-range radio navigation system with a PKTs digital co-ordinate converter (*preobrazovahtel' ko'ordinaht tsifrovoy*).

The Tu-95K and Tu-95KM missile carriers have an ARK-U2 Istok ADF and an RV-17 radio altimeter replacing the RV-25. The Put'-1B flight and navigational system was added on the Tu-95KM, providing semi-automatic control of the aircraft and easing the pilot workload. An ANU-1A automatic navigation system (*avtomaticheskoye navigatsionnoye oostroystvo*) and a KS-6D compass system are also installed.

On the Tu-95KM and Tu-95MR the ARK-U2 ADF is integrated into the radio navigation suite. Working together with the R-802 radio, it ensures rendezvous with the tanker during in-flight refuelling sessions.

b) communications equipment: The Tu-95 is equipped for long-range and short-range air-to-ground radio communication. The R-837 and R-807 radio sets are used for long-range radio communication in the high-frequency (HF) and very high-frequency (VHF) bands. An R-802 command radio with L-shaped aerials above and below the forward fuselage is provided for use in the ultra high-frequency (UHF) waveband. The Tu-95K and Tu-95KM missile carriers have an R-832M Evkalipt VHF command radio. An R-861 emergency radio is provided as a back-up.

Voice communication inside the aircraft is provided by an SPU-10G intercom (*samolyotnoye peregovornoye oostroystvo*).

For air-to-ground communication in radio silence mode (for example, in the event of a radio failure) two EKSP-39 electric flare launchers (*elektricheskaya kasseta signahl'nykh patronov*) are installed low on the starboard side of the rear fuselage. Each launcher fires four 39-mm signal flares (red, green, yellow and white).

The Rubin-1A radar on a Tu-95MR. The basic bomber has an RBP-4 Rubidiy-MM2 radar in an identical radome.

The rear end of a Tu-95K-22 with an UKhO ECM fairing housing a Siren' series jammer (SPS-151/-152/-153). Note the open entry hatch of the rear pressure cabin.

c) radar and targeting equipment: The Tu-95 *sans suffixe* and Tu-95M bombers feature an RBP-4 Rubidiy-MM-2 bomb-aiming radar in a chin radome capable of detecting large ground targets at 140 km (87 miles) range, which works in conjunction with an OPB-11RM

A different aspect of the UKhO fairing, showing the emitter antennas and cooling air scoops, as well as the absence of the gun laying radar.

Left: The weapons operator's instrument panel of a Tu-95 with two small cathode-ray tube screens.

Below left: The navigator's workstation of a Tu-95M. The navigator sits sideways, with an instrument panel and a map table to port.

Bottom left: The dorsal gunner/radio operator sits on his revolving seat beneath the observation blister, holding onto the dorsal barbette control handles.

(OPB-112) optical vector-synchronous bombsight. The sight interfaces with the autopilot and automatically calculates aircraft flight parameters and targeting data for improved bombing accuracy. The Tu-95RM has a Rubin-1D radar in the same type of radome.

The Tu-95K and Tu-95KM missile carriers have a YaD twin-antenna radar. designed for target acquisition and tracking and also for missile guidance in conjunction with the Kh-20 (Kh-20M) missile's YaR radar and YaK autopilot. The system consists of three basic parts: target acquisition and tracking equipment, guidance equipment, and control equipment. The Tu-95K-22 has a PNA-B target illumination/guidance radar with a single antenna accommodated in the existing main radome.

The Tu-95RTs has an Oospekh-U1A 360° search radar housed in a ventral teardrop radome aft of the wing centre section and an Arfa data link system for missile mid-course guidance, with receiver antennas housed in cigar-shaped fairings at the tips of the stabilisers and a transmitter antenna in a deep chin fairing replacing the ground-mapping/bomb-aiming radar of the bomber version.

A PRS-1 Argon gun ranging radar is installed above the tail gunner's station on the Tu-95 *sans suffixe*, Tu-95M and Tu-95RTs. This is replaced by the PRS-4 Krypton gun ranging radar on the Tu-95K/Tu-95KM.

d) IFF equipment: An SRZO-2M radar interrogator (*samolyotnyy rahdiolokatsionnyy zaproschik-otvetchik*) was fitted as part of an autonomous identification system for recognition of 'friendly' aircraft or ships fitted with SRO or *Fakel-MO* (Torch) transponders and for short-range radio navigation, with an operational range of 30-40 km (18.6-24-8 miles). An SRO-2P IFF transponder (*samolyotnyy rahdiolokatsionnyy otvetchik*) with an operating range of 35 km (21.75 miles) is also fitted, as is an SO-69 ATC transponder.

e) ECM and ESM equipment: The Tu-95 and Tu-95M feature SPS-1 or SPS-2 active jammers for self-protection, ASO-95 and ASO-2B chaff dispensers for passive ECM (in the bomb bay), as well as SPO-2 Sirena-2 radar warning receivers. The Tu-95K and Tu-95KM have an SPS-3 active jammer, an ASO-2B chaff dispenser (mounted on two KDS-16-23 cassettes at frames 62-63) and an SPO-3 Sirena-3 RWR. The Tu-95K-22 has a Siren' family (SPS-151K/SPS-152K/SPS-153K) active jammer in a tail fairing supplanting the tail turret, an SPS-151D/SPS-152D/SPS-153D active jammer and an SPS-141 active jammer covering the forward hemisphere, with aerials in a 'thimble' fairing on the extreme nose and in pylon-mounted pods on the lower forward fuselage.

f) cockpit instrumentation: The cockpit instrumentation includes the following flight and navigation instruments: KUS-1200 airspeed indicators (*kombineerovannyy ookazahtel' skorosti* – combined ASI); VD-20 two-needle barometric altimeter (*vysotomer dvookhstrelochnyy*); VAR-30 vertical speed indicators (*variometr* – VSI); MS-41 Mach meters; SSN-8 dynamic pressure indicator (*signalizahtor skorosnovo napora*); AGD-1 gyro horizon, UUT pitch angle indicator (*ookazahtel' oogla tangazha*); EUP-53 electric turn and bank indicators (*elektricheskiy ookazahtel' povorota*); GPK-52 gyro direction indicator; BTs-463A star tracker; KI-13 magnetic compass (*kompas indooktsionnyy*); DAK-DB-5 celestial compass (*distantsionnyy astro-kompas dahl'nevo bombardirovshchika* – remote celestial compass optimised for long-range bombers); AK-53P celestial compass, SP-1M aviation periscopic sextant; and a 13-20ChP aviation chronometer.

Ancillary instruments include the UVPD-15 cabin altitude and pressure differential indicator (*ookazahtel' vysoty i perepada davleniya*); RVU-46U airflow indicator (*raskhodomer vozdukha*); TNV-15 and TNV-45 ambient air thermometers (*termometr naroozhnovo vozdukha*); TUA-48, TV-45 and 2TUA-11 air thermometers; AM-10

Above: The co-pilot's station and centre instrument panel of a Tu-95K-22. The eight red knobs on top are the emergency engine shutdown and propeller feathering handles; the control box to the right of them is for the IFR probe and associated lights. The red button on the control wheel is the autopilot override button. The small red handle below the engine tachometers operates the conveyor belt built into the flight deck floor for bailing out. The rolled-up blind flying curtains made of blue cloth are a standard fit.

Left: The aft-facing flight engineer's workstation of the Tu-95K-22, with engine instruments in the middle, electric system controls and instruments on the right, hydraulic system and fire suppression system controls on the left, a bank of throttles (with white handles) and engine starting/shutdown levers (with brown handles). There are circuit breaker panels all over the place!

Below: A closer look at the flight engineer's instrument panel.

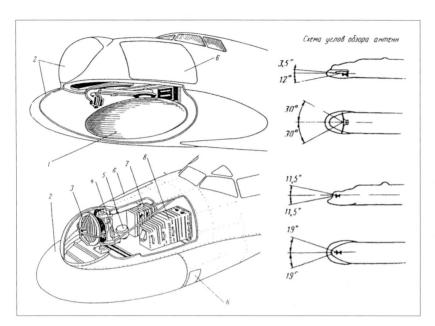

Location of the YaD radar's antennas and radar set
1. YaD1-1 search and tracking channel antenna;
2. Radomes; 3. YaD1-2 missile guidance channel antenna; 4. Guidance channel receiver's power unit;
5. Guidance channel receiver; 6. Access hatches;
7. Guidance channel transmitter; 8. Search and tracking channel transceiver.
The inset shows the radar antennas' scan sectors.

G-meter (akse*lerom*etr); VS-46 altitude warning unit (*vysot*nyy signali*zah*tor) telling the crew when it's time to don the oxygen masks; UPZ-47 flap position indicator (ooka*zah*tel' polo*zhe*niya za*kryl*kov); and AChS-1 clock with phosphorescent hands and hour marks (*aviatsion*nyye cha*sy sve*tya*shchiyesya).

The following engine instruments are fitted: 2TVG-366 exhaust gas temperature gauges (*termom*etr vykho*dyash*chikh *gah*zov); 2TUA-11 oil temperature gauges; 2EDMU-3 fuel pressure gauges (*elektrich*eskiy distantsi*on*nyy ma*nom*etr ooni*fitseer*ovannyy – electric

Location of the YaD radar's modules

1. PO-4500 AC converters; 2. K4-51 data recorder No.1; 3. K4-51 data recorder No.2;
4. Transmitter aerial of the YaD6-1 missile guidance system check equipment; 5. Receiver aerial of the YaD6-1 missile guidance system check equipment; 6. YaD5-2 heading gyro;
7. YaD5-3 vertical gyro; 8. YaD5-1 electromagnetic amplifier; 9. YaD3 avionics rack No.2;
10. YaD2 Nav/Op's avionics rack No.1; 11. Navigator's control panel; 12. YaD1-1 search and tracking channel antenna; 13. YaD1-2 missile guidance channel antenna;

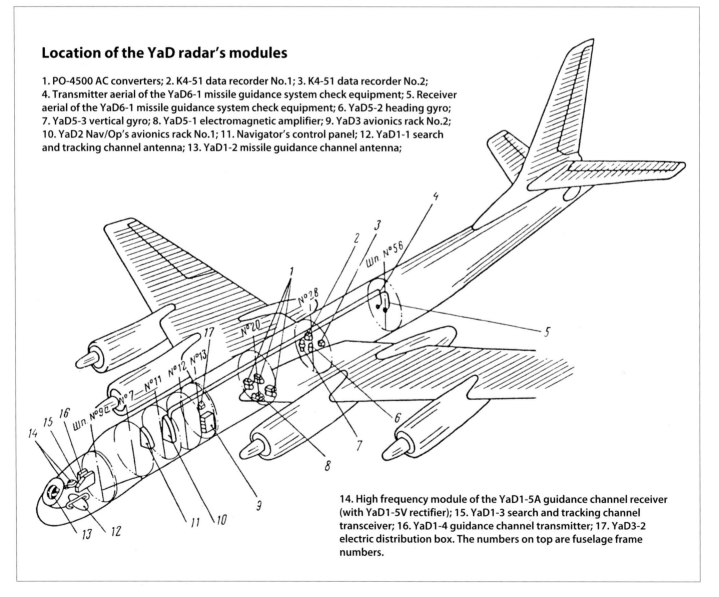

14. High frequency module of the YaD1-5A guidance channel receiver (with YaD1-5V rectifier); 15. YaD1-3 search and tracking channel transceiver; 16. YaD1-4 guidance channel transmitter; 17. YaD3-2 electric distribution box. The numbers on top are fuselage frame numbers.

remote standardised pressure gauge); 2EDMU-10 oil pressure gauges: 2TE9-1M remote-sensing rpm gauges (*ta**kho**metr elek**trich**eskiy* – electric tachometer) for the engines and TE-40 rpm gauges for the turbostarters; MT-50 thrust manometers (*ma**nom**etr **tya**gi*); UPRT-2 throttle lever position indicator (*ooka**zah**tel' polo**zhe**niya rycha**ga top**liva*); ME-95D electric remote oil contents gauges (*ma**slo**mer elek**trich**eskiy*); ICh-61 engine operating time meter; and a U-03-4 oil cooler shutter position indicator.

g) reconnaissance equipment: The bombers carry photo equipment allowing them to perform bomb damage assessment and photograph targets of opportunity. An AFA-42/100 aerial camera is installed on a stabilised platform between fuselage frames 67-69. For night sorties the aircraft carry a complement of FotAB flash bombs or SAB parachute-retarded flare bombs. A DP-3 radiation monitoring instrument (*dozime**trich**eskiy pri**bor***) is also provided to warn the crew of exposure to radiation when operating in a nuclear environment.

The Tu-95MR strategic reconnaissance aircraft has both daylight and night-time photographic capability and is equipped accordingly. A bay between frames 67-70 serves as the mounting point for the following:

Daytime photography version 1:
• two AFA-42/20 cameras on fixed mounts;
• four AFA-42/100 cameras on two dual swivelling mounts;
• an AFA-41/20 on a TAU topographic aerial camera mount;
• an AFA-42/10 on a flexible oblique installation;
• an AShchAFA-5 slit camera on a fixed mount.

Daytime photography version 2:
• two AFA-40 cameras and two AFA-42/20 cameras on fixed mounts on two trusses;
• an AFA-41/20 on a TAU topographic aerial camera mount;
• an AFA-42/10 on a tilting oblique mount;
• an AShchAFA-5 on a fixed mount.

Night version:
• two NAFA-MK-75 night cameras joint in one container on swinging photo-installation;
• AShAFA-5 on a fixed mount;
• AFA-42/100 in fixed oblique installation.

Again, flash bombs or flare bombs are carried on a cassette in a special bay in the night version.

On the Tu-95MR the bomb bay is transformed into a camera bay whose doors incorporate four camera windows to starboard for the AFA-40, AFA-42/20, AFA-42/100, and AFA-41/20 cameras with a TAU topographic mount, three camera windows to port for the AFA-40, AFA-42/20, and AFA-42/100 cameras. The camera windows are glazed with optical quality glass; when not in use they are protected by electrically actuated sliding shutters. The aft bay houses photo flare

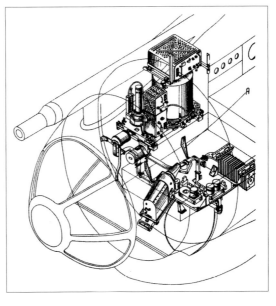

The Oospekh-1A system's avionics modules in the nose of the Tu-95RTs.

dispensers provided with a hatch-like cover similar to the sliding units provided for the photo equipment.

The Tu-95MR is equipped with the following electronic intelligence (ELINT) systems: an SRS-1 signals intelligence pack with an FRU-1 photo recording device, SRS-6 Romb-4A and SRS-7 Romb-4B SIGINT packs, and a FARM-2A photo recording attachment for the radar. Teardrop-shaped dielectric fairings for the SRS-1 are positioned on the centre fuselage underside near frames 13 and 22. The oblong dielectric fairings for the SRS-6 and SRS-7 electronic reconnaissance systems are located between frames 65-72 on both sides of the fuselage.

The Tu-95KM has an SRS-6 Romb-4 SIGINT pack.

h) data recording equipment: For mission debriefing and accident investigation the aircraft is equipped with

The Tu-95M's ECM equipment.
1. The PN receiver's power unit; 2. Heterodyne power unit; 3. POVA receiver; 4. The POVA receiver's power unit; 5. Amplification/display module; 6. The PN receiver's high frequency module; 7. The transmitter's power unit; 8. Control panel; 9. Transmitter aerial; 10. Receiver aerial; 11. ASO-2B Avtomat-2 chaff dispenser; 12. Chaff dispenser control panel.

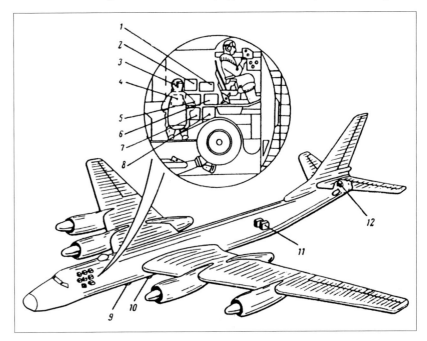

The fairing of the Oospekh-U system's transmitter antenna on the Tu-95RTs.

Far right: The Tu-95MR's lateral ELINT antenna fairing and oblique camera port.

The radome of the Oospekh-1A search radar installed on the Tu-95RTs.

Above right: The lateral antennas of the SPS-141 and SPS-153 jammers on a Tu-95K-22.

an MSRP-12-96 (MSRP-12B) primary flight data recorder (FDR; MSRP = *magnitnyy samopisets rezhimov polyota* – magnetic flight mode recorder) and a K-3-63 backup FDR. The primary FDR captures 12 parameters, including barometric altitude, indicated airspeed, roll rates, vertical and lateral G forces, control surface deflection and throttle settings, as well as gear/flap transition etc. The backup FDR records only altitude, IAS and vertical G forces.

An MS-61 cockpit voice recorder (*magnitofon samolyotnyy* – aircraft-specific tape recorder) was retrofitted in service; it uses magnetised steel wire instead of tape, making sure it won't melt in a post-crash fire. All recorders have crashworthy armoured shells.

Armament: The Tu-95 has a full set of offensive and defensive armament.

a) offensive armament: The basic Tu-95 and Tu-95M carry free-fall bombs in the bomb bay located between fuselage frames 28 and 45. Bombs of 1,500 to 9,000 kg (3,306 to 19,840 lb) calibre are normally carried in the combat configuration. When used as a trainer, bomb weights vary between 50 and 4,500 kg (110 and 9,920 lb). The normal bomb load is 5,000 kg (11,020 lb).

The following bomb suspension options are possible:
• one MBD6-95 beam-type rack with Der6-5 shackles for bombs of 5,000-9,000 kg (11,020-19,840 lb) calibre;
• Der6-4 shackles for 1,500-3,000 kg (3,306-6,612 lb); or Der6-3 shackles for bombs of 250-500 kg (551-1,102 lb) calibre;
• one BD5-95M beam-type rack with Der5-48 shackles for 5,000-kg (11,020-lb) bombs or Der5-4 shackles for 1,500-3,000 kg (3,306-6,612 lb) calibre;
• two KD4-295 bomb cassettes with Der4-49 shackles for bombs of 1,500-3,000 calibre;
• two KD3-695 bomb cassettes with Der3-48 shackles for practice bombs of 50-500 kg (110-1,102 lb) calibre.

Bomb-aiming normally is performed by means of the RBP-4 radar which is interfaced with the OPB-11RM (OPB-112) optical sight.

The Tu-95K and Tu-95KM are armed with a single Kh-20 or Kh-20M stand-off missile. The latter is carried

Far left: The PRS-1 Argon gun-laying radar.

The tail gunner's station of a Tu-95M with a DK-12 tail turret and the hemispherical radome of the PRS-1 above the glazing.

semi-recessed on a BD-206 hydraulically powered pylon with a pantographic mechanism mounted between frames 21-23. Prior to launch, the fairing closing the missile's air intake is retracted, the missile is lowered 950 mm (3 ft 1¹³⁄₃₂ in) while still attached to the pylon. Once extended into the slipstream, the missile's engine is started and run up to cruise thrust. When 'all systems are go' for launch, the missile is released for the flight to the target. The Tu-95K-22 is able to carry up to three

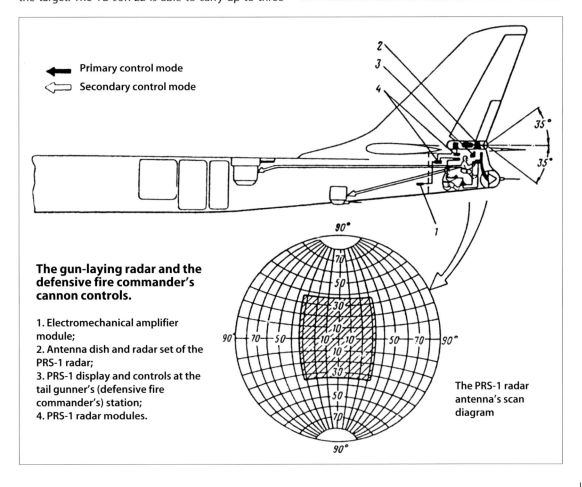

← Primary control mode
⇐ Secondary control mode

The gun-laying radar and the defensive fire commander's cannon controls.

1. Electromechanical amplifier module;
2. Antenna dish and radar set of the PRS-1 radar;
3. PRS-1 display and controls at the tail gunner's (defensive fire commander's) station;
4. PRS-1 radar modules.

The PRS-1 radar antenna's scan diagram

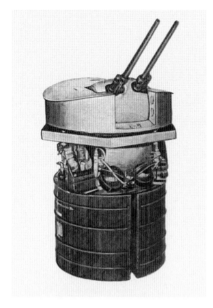 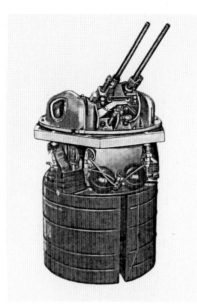 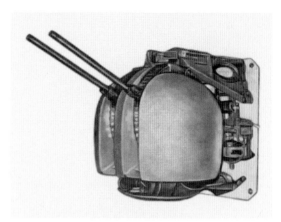

Left and far left: The DT-V12 dorsal barbette with and without fairing.

Below left and below/far left: The DT-N12S ventral barbette with and without fairing.

Above and below: The DK-12 tail turret with and without fairing

Bottom: A view of the DT-N12S ventral barbette on the Tu-95M.

Bottom left: The DT-V12 in the raised position.

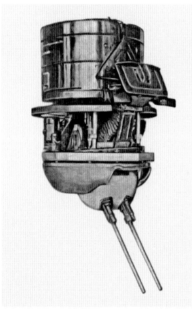 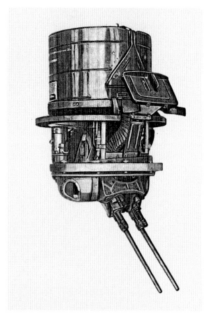 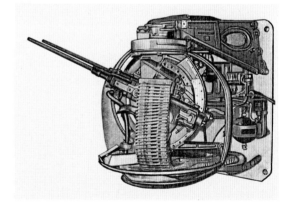

Kh-22 stand-off missiles – one on the centreline on a BD-45F hydraulically powered pylon with a pantographic mechanism (the missile is carried semi-recessed prior to launch) and two under the wing roots on BD-45K pylons.

b) defensive armament: The defensive armament comprises three electrically powered remote-controlled cannon installations – the DT-V12 dorsal barbette, the DT-N12 ventral barbette and the DK-12 tail turret; the latter is absent on the Tu-95K-22. Each of

Opposite page, left: Another view of the ventral barbette.

Opposite page, centre and right: Two views of the PS-153K tail turret sighting station.

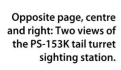 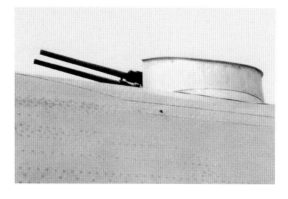 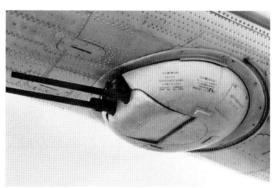

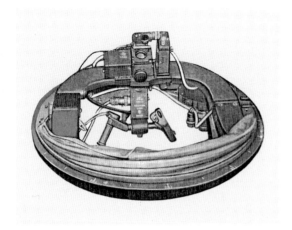

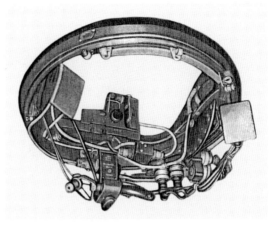

Far left: The PS-153VK dorsal turret sighting station on its mounting ring, seen from above.

Left: The PS-153VK seen from below.

Below left: The cannon controls in the forward pressure cabin.

Below: The cannons and their controls in the rear fuselage.

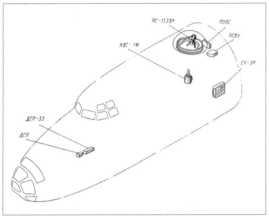

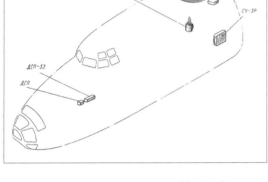

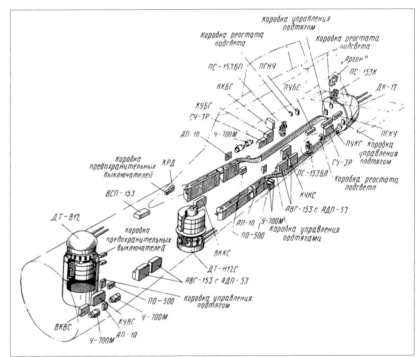

them mounts two 23-mm (.90 calibre) Afanas'yev/Makarov AM-23 cannons. The AM-23 weighs 43 kg (94.8 lb). It is belt-fed and fires 200-gram (7.05-oz) projectiles; muzzle velocity 690 m/sec (2,263 ft/sec), rate of fire 1,300 rounds per minute.

The normal ammunition complement is 2,500 rounds allocated as follows: 700 rounds for the DT-V12; 800 rounds for the DT-N12 and 1,000 rounds for the DK-12 (since the rear hemisphere is the most likely to be attacked). The dorsal barbette is retractable. It is normally flush with the top of the fuselage but can be extended into firing position at any time. The ventral barbette is semi-recessed.

The aiming equipment consists of PS-153 optical sighting stations (*pritsel'naya stahntsiya*) to which the

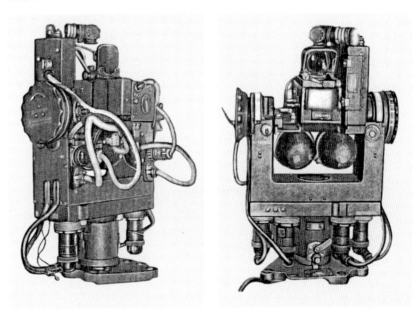

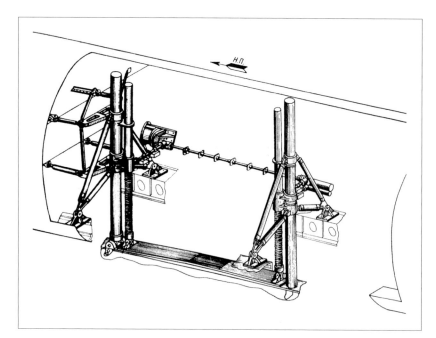

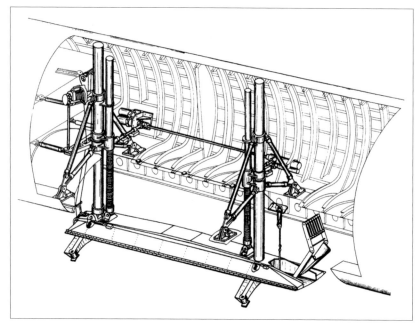

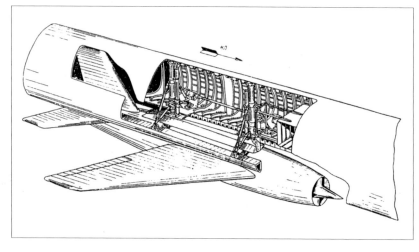

Top and above: A Kh-20 missile on a ground handling dolly.

Left and above left: The Tu-95K's BD-206 missile rack and its actuator. The arrow is marked N.P. (*napravleniye polyota* – direction of flight).

Below left: This drawing shows how the Kh-20 is carried semi-recessed on the BD-206 rack.

barbettes are slaved, a PRS-1 gun ranging radar and AVS-153 ballistic computers (*avtomaht vozdooshnoy strel'byy* – automatic air-to-air gunnery device) integrated with an ADP-153 automatic parallax compensator (*avtomaht dopolnitel'novo parallaksa*). There are four remote sighting stations for the guns: PS-153VK (*verkhnyaya koopol'naya* – for the dorsal dome), PS-153BL (*bortovaya levaya* – port lateral), PS-153BP (*bortovaya pravaya* – starboard lateral) and PS-153K (*kormovaya* – rear). This variance in suffix letters is due to the fact that the four stations have different fields of view and hence enable different fields of fire.

Above right: Two Kh-22 missiles on the BD-45K pylons of a Tu-95K-22.

Right: A Kh-22 on the Tu-95K-22's BD-45F centreline rack lowered into pre-launch position.

Far right: Three Kh-22s underneath a Tu-95K-22; the centre missile is semi-recessed for cruise flight.

A Kh-20 missile under the belly of a late-production Tu-95K (c/n 60802207). Note the fairing closing the missile's air intake until immediately before launch.

A cutaway drawing of an early-production Kh-20M missile suspended beneath the Tu-95K.

1. Supersonic pitot; 2. No.1 fuel tank (T-1 or TS-1 kerosene, 1,390 litres/305.8 Imp gal); 3. Subsonic pitot; 4. Warhead bay; 5. YaK autopilot; 6. No.2 fuel tank (2,100 litres/462 Imp gal); 7. No.4 fuel tank (2 x 250 litres/2 x 55 Imp gal); 8. Lyul'ka AL-7FK turbojet; 9. No.5 fuel tank (2 x 550 litres/ 2 x 121 Imp gal); 10. YaR command link system modules; 11. SOD-57 transponder aerial; 12. YaR system receiver aerial; 13. BD-206 missile rack lowered 950 mm (3 ft 1¹³⁄₃₂ in) before missile launch; 14. Missile rack actuating mechanism; 15. No.39 fuel tank for starting the missile's engine.

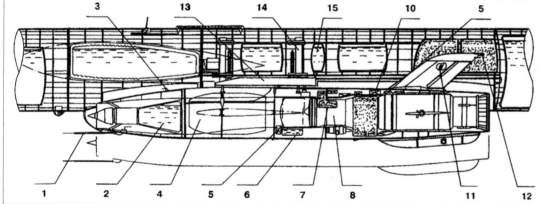

Right: The port BD-45K missile rack of a Tu-95K-22. Note the fixed sway braces.

Far right: This view of the same installation shows the curious curved shape of the Tu-95K-22's wing pylons to which the racks are attached.

A Kh-22 missile suspended on the port wing pylon.

Remote control is exercised by a transforming synchro tracking system. Mismatching between the synchro pick-up (sighting station) and the synchro receiver (cannon installation) takes place in the form of electrical signals transmitted to a SU-3R servo-amplifier (*servo'usilitel'*) and from there to a DV-1100 electric motor connected with the cannons' vertical and horizontal guidance channels.

Crew protection and crew rescue equipment: All crew stations are provided with armour protection against cannon shell fragments. Several types of armour are used: cast APBA-1L24 duralumin (*aviatsionnaya protivo'oskolochnaya bronya alyuminiyevaya* – aviation-specific aluminium armour for protection against shell fragments), cast ML5-T4 magnesium alloy and KVK-2/5Ts steel.

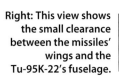

Right: This view shows the small clearance between the missiles' wings and the Tu-95K-22's fuselage.

Far right: Rear view of the same missile and pylon, showing the Kh-22's twin rocket motor nozzles. The flaps were extremely close to the missile racks when fully extended.

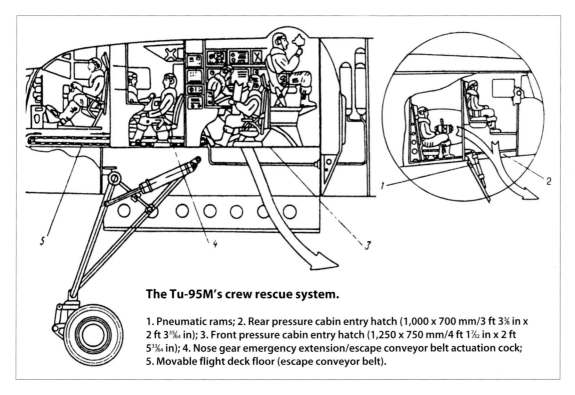

The Tu-95M's crew rescue system.

1. Pneumatic rams; 2. Rear pressure cabin entry hatch (1,000 x 700 mm/3 ft 3⅜ in x 2 ft 3³⁵⁄₆₄ in)); 3. Front pressure cabin entry hatch (1,250 x 750 mm/4 ft 1½ in x 2 ft 5³³⁄₆₄ in)); 4. Nose gear emergency extension/escape conveyor belt actuation cock; 5. Movable flight deck floor (escape conveyor belt).

In the event emergency egress is required, the following items are provided:
• a flight deck escape conveyor belt;
• special emergency opening systems for hatches at the front and rear of the flight deck;
• other emergency hatches strategically placed at various positions throughout the aircraft crew compartments;
• two LAS-5-2M five-seat inflatable rescue dinghies (**lod**ka ava**reey**no-spa**sah**tel'naya) in case of ditching.

In an emergency the crew in the forward pressure cabin bails out through the entry hatch in the nosewheel well. The sequence is initiated by opening an air cock, whereupon the nose gear unit is extended pneumatically and the entry hatch is forcibly opened by a pneumatic ram. The flight deck floor incorporates a hydraulically driven conveyor belt running all the way from the navigator's station to the entry hatch. The belt drive motor is powered by pressure from three hydraulic tanks, which allows it to run for 100 seconds even if all four engines and all electrics fail.

The gunners in the rear pressure cabin bail out via the ventral entry hatch which is opened by two pneumatic rams to serve as slipstream deflector.

Safe egress is limited to speeds up to 630 km/h (391 rnph) and an altitude of at least 200 m (660 ft). In the event of a belly landing or ditching, the crew can evacuate the forward pressure cabin via emergency exits located at the flight engineer's and Nav/Op's positions and through the pilots' sliding direct vision windows. The gunners in the rear pressure cabin can exit the aircraft through the port side emergency hatch.

II. Tu-142 ASW aircraft and its versions

Since the Tu-142 is broadly similar to the Tu-95, the relevant design differences are indicated below.

Type: Long-range ASW/maritime patrol aircraft designed for day and night operation in VMC and IMC.

One of the seats installed in the rear pressure cabin. The seat has a dished pan for a seat-type parachute.

Life raft stowage on the
Tu-95M and use of the
rescue dinghies in the
event of ditching.

1. Front pressure cabin
emergency exits;
2. LAS-5-2M rescue
dinghies; 3. Rear
pressure cabin
emergency exit;
4. CO_2 bottle;
5. Dinghy tethering
cord; 6. Rescue dinghy
container cover;
7. Bag containing
paddles; 8. Bag
containing emergency
food rations; 9. Deflated
and folded LAS-5-2M
rescue dinghy; 10. Bag
containing repair kit.

Fuselage: Basically as for the Tu-95; maximum length 46.4 m (152 ft 2⁴⁹⁄₆₄ in). Structurally the fuselage is divided into five sections in the same way as on the Tu-95 but their numbering is changed: navigator's station glazing frame (Section F-1, frames 0-1); pressurised forward fuselage (Section F-2, frames 1-13); unpressurised centre fuselage (Section F-3, frames 13A-49); unpressurised rear fuselage (Section F-5, frames 50-87) and rear pressure cabin (Section F-6,

frames 87-95). There are three avionics/equipment bays under the forward pressure cabin floor; bays 2 and 3 are pressurised.

The Tu-142 *sans suffixe* (*izdeliye* VP) had the same front pressure cabin and flight deck glazing design as most Tu-95 versions, except that the *forward fuselage* was stretched a 1.7 m (5 ft 6¹⁵⁄₁₆ in). The Tu-142M (*izdeliye* VPM, from c/n 4242 onwards) introduced an additional 0.3-m (1-ft) forward fuselage stretch and a wider flight deck with more headroom. Early Tu-142s *sans suffixe* had a chin fairing accommodating a thermal imager under the navigator's station; this was deleted from c/n 4231 onwards.

The *centre fuselage* incorporates the main weapons bay (frames 28-45) divided by a bulkhead and closed by two pairs of clamshell doors, with the No.5 fuel tank container aft of it (frames 45-49); it accommodates weapons and sonobuoys. A ventral recess is provided below the wing centre section for the revolving antenna of the search radar; it is enclosed by a teardrop-shaped glassfibre radome of honeycomb construction attached to a metal fairing. A life raft bay with tandem covers is located dorsally between frames 13A-19.

Above right and far
right: The nose of a
Tu-142 *sans suffixe*
with a Gagara-1 thermal
imager in a chin fairing,
showing the glazing
design and the fuel line
conduit from
the IFR probe.

The initial version of the
Tu-142 had the same
sloping flight deck
roof as the Tu-95.

Here, in contrast, is the nose of the Tu-142M/MK with a wide flight deck featuring a raised roof. The Gagara thermal imager is deleted.

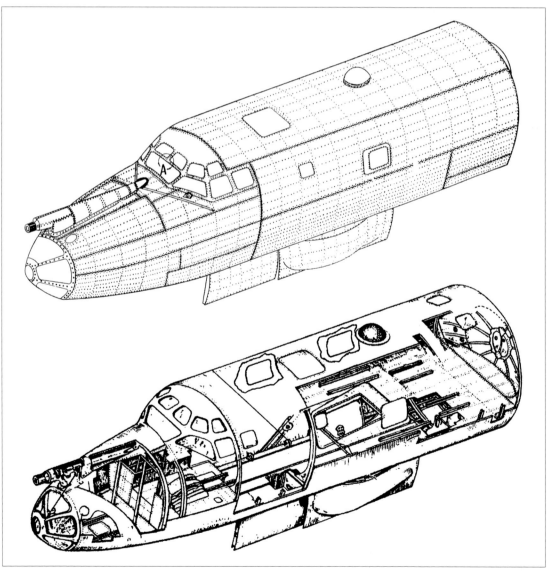

Normal and cutaway drawings of the forward fuselage from the Tu-142's structural manual.

Exploded view of the Tu-142M showing manufacturing breaks

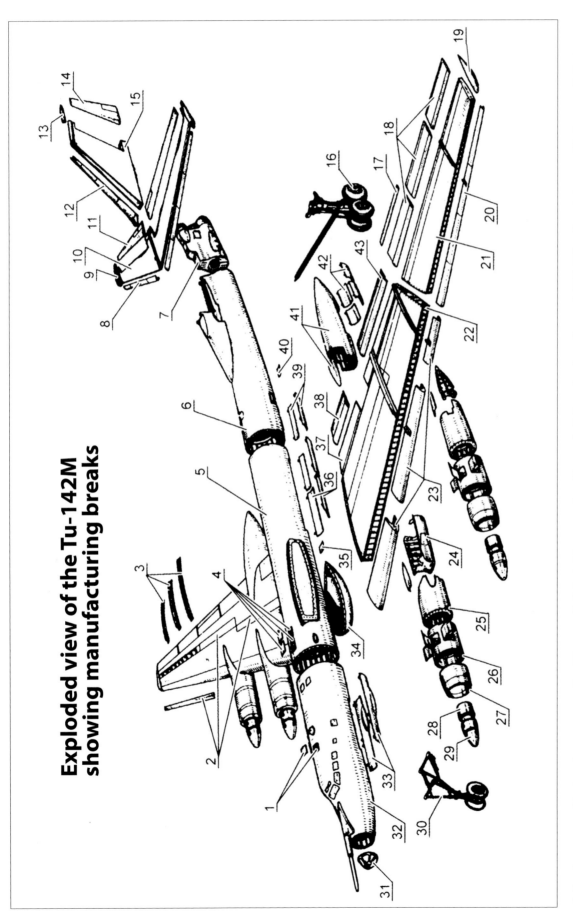

.1. Front pressure cabin dorsal emergency exit and its cover; 2. Detachable upper wing skin panels; 3. Boundary layer fences; 4. PSN-6 life raft containers and their covers; 5. Centre fuselage (Section F-3); 6. Rear fuselage (Section F-4); 7. Tail section/rear pressure cabin (Section F-5); 8. Detachable stabiliser leading edge; 9. Detachable stabiliser tip fairing; 10. Stabiliser; 11. Elevator; 12. Detachable fin leading edge; 13. Fin tip antenna fairing; 14. Rudder; 15. Fin; 16. Main gear strut; 17. Aileron trim tab/geared tab; 18. Three-section aileron; 19. Detachable wingtip fairing; 20. Detachable outer wing section leading edge; 21. Outer wing section; 22. Inner wing section; 23. Detachable inner wing section leading edge; 24. Rear portion of engine nacelle; 25. Centre portion of engine nacelle; 26. Cowling section; 27. Air intake assembly; 28. Engine reduction gearbox fairing; 29. Propeller spinner; 30. Nose gear strut; 31. Navigator's station glazing framework (Section F-1); 32. Forward fuselage/front pressure cabin (Section F-2); 33. Nosewheel well doors; 34. Radome; 35. Avionics/equipment bay access hatch cover; 36. Weapons bay doors; 37. Wing trailing-edge section; 38. Inner flap section; 39. Sonobuoy bay doors; 40. Avionics/equipment bay access hatch cover; 41. Main landing gear fairing; 42. Forward (small) and rear (large) mainwheel well doors; 43. Outer flap section.

Left row, top: The forward fuselage of the Tu-142MZ, showing the ADF strake aerial.

Left row, centre: The characteristic chin fairing of the Tu-142MZ and equally distinctive SPS-161 jammer 'thimble' antenna at the tip of the nose glazing.

Left row, below: This Tu-142MZ is equipped with a Mak-UFM missile warning system (note the undernose sensor dome).

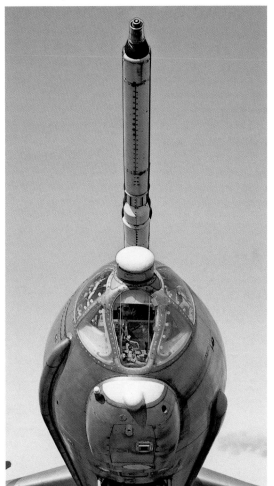

Above left: The ADF strake aerial on top of the Tu-142MZ's centre fuselage.

Left: This view shows the underside of the Tu-142MZ's chin fairing (with no MWS sensor in this case).

Far left: The Tu-142's central radome is smaller than that of the Tu-95RTs.

Left: Late versions of the Tu-142 have asymmetrically located conduits for the IFR probe's fuel line to starboard and for wiring to port; the port conduit is much longer.

Tu-142MZ cutaway drawing key

1. In-flight refuelling probe
2. Forward SPS-161 Geran' active jammer antenna
3. Arrow-shaped antenna for short-range radio navigation system
4. Navigator's station glazing
5. Navigator's workstation
6. Retractable IFR probe/drogue illumination lights (located asymetrically)
7. Antennas for electronic warfare and communication systems
8. Nose landing gear strut with KN2-4 non-braking wheels
9. Nosewheel well door
10. Flight deck entry ladder
11. Flight deck windshield
12. Captain (port position)/co-pilot (starboard position)
13. Flight engineer (port)/communications officer (starboard)
14. Dorsal emergency exit
15. Bubble window for remote astro-compass
16. Zarechye sonobuoy system operator's workstation
17. Korshun search/attack radar operator's workstation
18. Co-navigator's workstation
19. Flight deck rear pressure dome
20. ECM system waveguide cover
21. Lateral SPS-161 Geran' active jammer antenna
22. Korshun 360° search radar
23. Radar cooling intake
24. PSN-6A six-man inflatable life rafts (two)
25. Automatic direction finder strake aerial
26. Integrally built wing centre section
27. Hydraulic system equipment
28. Hydraulic fluid tank
29. Bomb/sonobuoy holders
30. AT-2 ASW torpedo
31. PLAB-250-120 depth charge
32. Main weapons bay
33. Main weapons bay doors

34. ASW weapons hoist
35. Weapons bay door actuator
36. No.5 bag-type fuel tank
37. Inner wing panel
38. Outer wing panel
39. Inboard double-slotted trailing-edge flap
40. No.1 integral fuel tank
41. Feeder tank for No.2 engine
42. No.2 integral fuel tank
43. No.3 integral fuel tank
44. Feeder tank for No.1 engine
45. No.4 integral fuel tank
46. Inert gas pressurisation system manifold
47. Outboard double-slotted trailing-edge flap
48. Engine nacelle
49. Kuznetsov NK-12MV (NK-12MP) turboprop engine
50. Aerosila AV-60K contra-rotating propellers
51. TS-12M turbine starter
52. Oil cooler

53. Bifurcated exhaust pipe
54. Engine bearer
55. Main landing gear leg with KT-106 brake wheels
56. Main landing gear fairing
57. Main landing gear bogie in retracted position
58. 50-mm chaff/flare dispensers
59. Boundary layer fence
60. Inner/outer wing panel mating joint
61. Two-section aileron
62. Trim/servo tab
63. Hot air pipe for de-icing system
64. Navigation lights
65. Static discharge wick
66. Sonobuoy bay
67. Sonobuoy bay doors
68. Avionics cooling intake

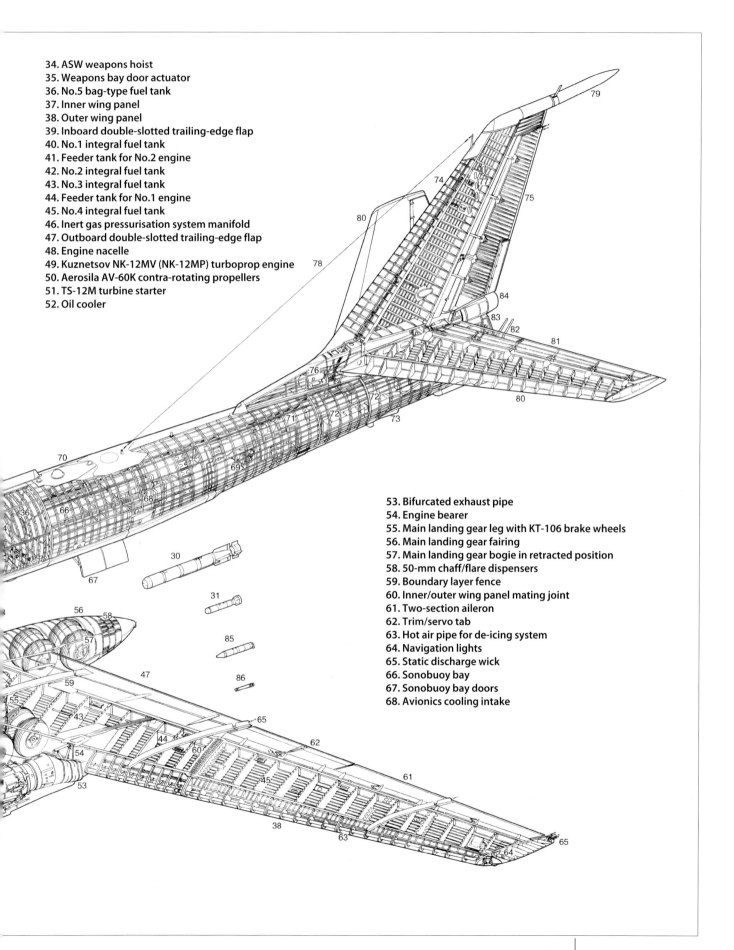

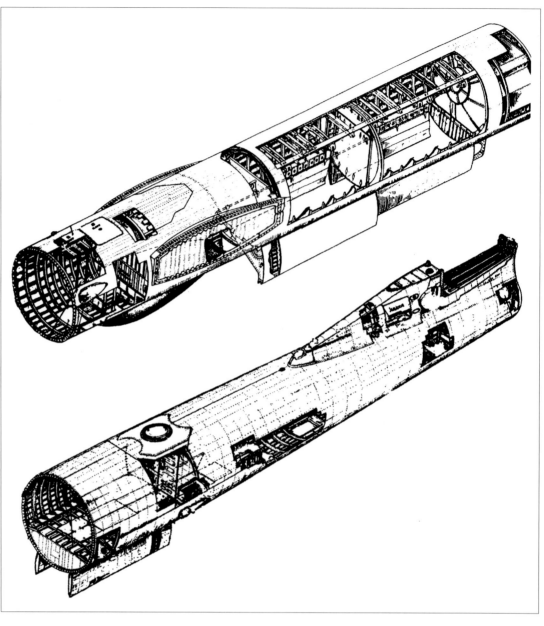

The *rear fuselage* lacks the cut-outs for the dorsal and ventral barbettes (see Armament). It incorporates the rear payoad bay closed by clamshell doors (frames 50-58), with the No.7 avionics bay above it (featuring a dorsal cutout for the star tracker window between frames 56-58) and the No.8 avionics bay (frames 58-87). On late Tu-142MKs (*izdeliye* VPMK) and the Tu-142MZ (*izdeliye* VPMZ) the lateral sighting blisters on the *tail section* are deleted and its front section accommodates avionics; the Tu-142MZ has small square hatches at the blisters' former locations for maintenance access.

Wings: Cantilever mid-wing monoplane of modified trapezoidal planform; trailing edge broken by main landing gear fairings. Sweepback at quarter-chord 33º33' on inner wings and 32º15' on outer wings, anhedral 2°15' from root, incidence +1° at root. The wing airfoils are similar to those of the Tu-95 but the leading edge is extended and drooped; this improves the lift/drag ratio and gives a sizeable fuel burn reduction; thus, the Tu-142 has a very similar fuel consumption to the basic Tu-95, despite the extra drag produced by the large ventral radome.

In common with the Tu-95, the wings are of two-spar stressed-skin construction and are manufactured in five sections: the centre section (built integrally with the centre fuselage), inner wings (carrying the engine nacelles) and outer wings. However, unlike the Tu-95, the wing torsion box accommodates integral fuel tanks housed in the inner and outer wings. The insides of the tanks are given a coat of spray-on sealant to make the manufacturing joints fuel-proof.

The wings are equipped with two-section double slotted flaps located on the inner wings (inboard and

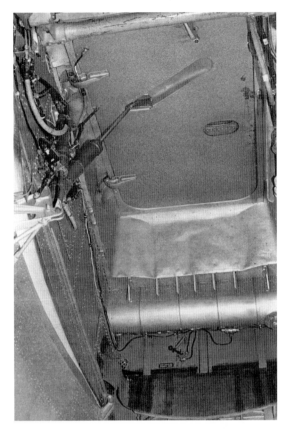

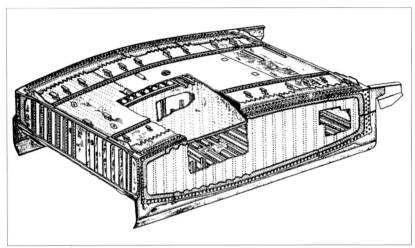

outboard of the main gear fairings) and on the outer wings. Flap area was increased from Tu-142 c/n 4232 onwards when the aircraft reverted to the original main gear design (see below). There are no leading-edge devices. Again, each wing has three boundary layer fences (one between the engine nacelles and two outboard of the outer engine).

Tail unit: Similar to that of the Tu-95 except that the stabilisers do have variable incidence (from –2°30' to

The wing centre section torsion box structure integral with the centre fuselage.

Upper and lower views of the Tu-142M's port wing from the structural manual.

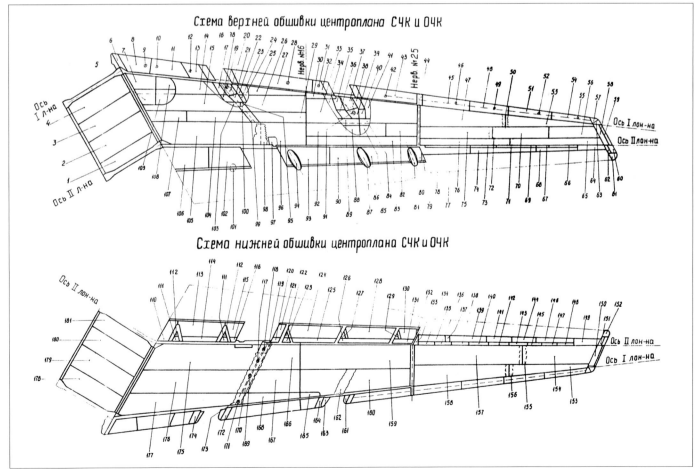

Схема верхней обшивки центроплана СЧК и ОЧК

Схема нижней обшивки центроплана СЧК и ОЧК

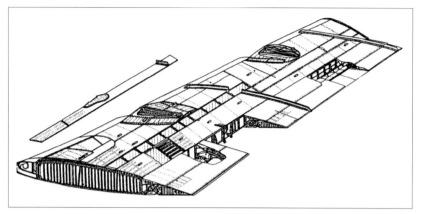

The starboard inner wing section of the Tu-142M.

The starboard outer wing section of the Tu-142M.

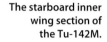

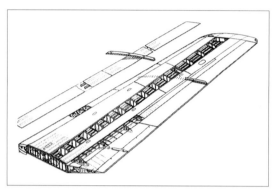

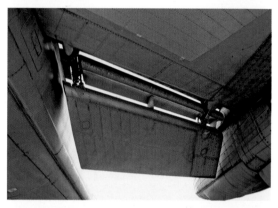

Top and centre: The inboard double-slotted flaps of a Tu-142MZ. Note the heat shields on the flap and wing skin portions adjacent to the engine nacelles.

Above: The port outboard double-slotted flap of a Tu-142MZ. The flap tracks and screwjacks are visible. Note the heat shield aft of the outer nacelle.

Opposite page, top to bottom, left row: The port stabiliser of the Tu-142 *sans suffixe* with the Lira antenna/feeder system fairing.

The rear fuselage and tail unit of the Tu-142MK (with observation blisters) and the Tu-142MZ.

Close-up of the MMS-106 Ladoga MAD sensor on the Tu-142MK and Tu-142MZ.

Right row: The tail unit of the Tu-142 *sans suffixe*.

The tail unit of the Tu-142MK/MZ and an exploded view of same.

The port outer wing of a Tu-142M. Note the static discharge wicks and the fuel jettison outlet in the tip fairing.

The port wingtip of a Tu-142MZ, showing the faired port lower navigation light and IFF aerials.

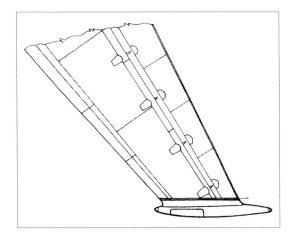

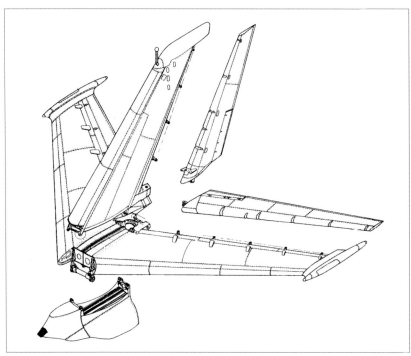

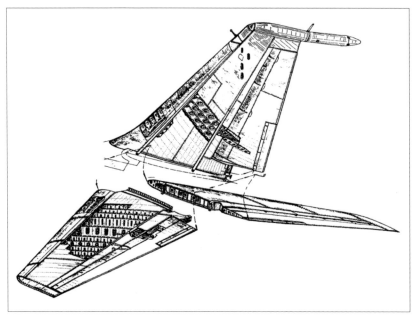

–6°30') and rudder area is increased. The Tu-142 *sans suffixe* had fairings for the Lira antenna/feeder system at the stabiliser tips which were deleted on the Tu-142M.

Landing gear: Similar to that of the Tu-95. Early production Tu-142s *sans suffixe* had main units with 12-wheel bogies featuring 1,100 x 330 mm (43.3 x 13 in) wheels in three rows of four and wider main landing gear fairings; from Tu-142 *sans suffixe* c/n 4232 onwards four-wheel main gear bogies with 1,450 x 450 mm (57.08 x 17.71 in) KT-24Sh or KT-25Sh-10 wheels, and standard main gear fairings (identical to those of the Tu-95) were reinstated. The nose gear unit has larger 1,140 x 350 mm (44.88 x 13.78 in) KN-2-4 non-braking wheels, and the nosewheel well doors are bulged accordingly. The Tu-142 *sans suffixe* had the retractable twin-wheel tail bumper which was deleted on later versions.

Above: The rear end of a production Tu-142MR with the comms aerial spike, fin- and fuselage-mounted ECM antennas.

Right and below: The 12-wheel main gear units of the early Tu-142 *sans suffixe* (*izdeliye* VP).

Below right: The nose gear unit of the Tu-142 *sans suffixe*.

Bottom right: The tail bumper of the Tu-142 *sans suffixe*.

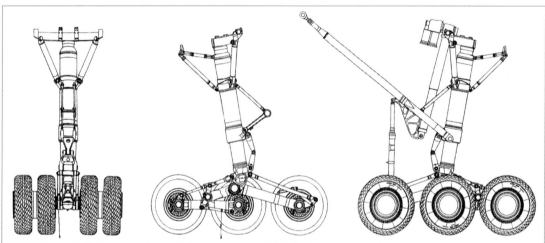

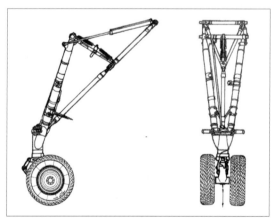

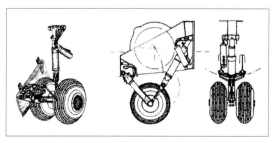

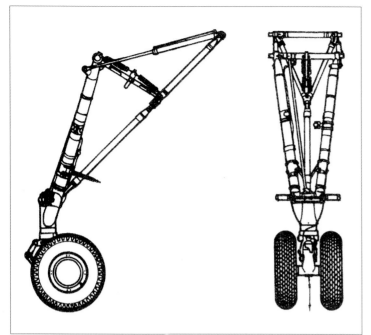

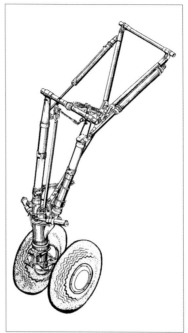

Left and far left: The nose gear unit of the Tu-142MK.

Below: Drawings of the Tu-142M's main gear units from the structural manual. Note the forward incline of the oleo strut.

Below left: The simplified main gear design of the late-production Tu-142 (*izdeliye* VP) and subsequent versions.

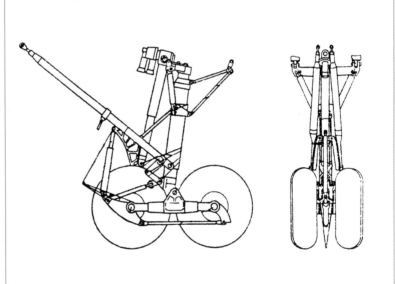

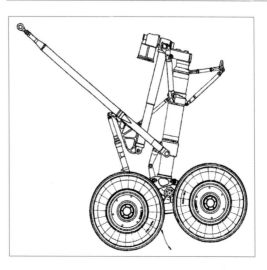

Far left: The port main gear unit of a Tu-142MZ.

Left: The main gear bogies assume a nose-down position in no-load condition.

Starboard and port views of the NK-12MP engine.

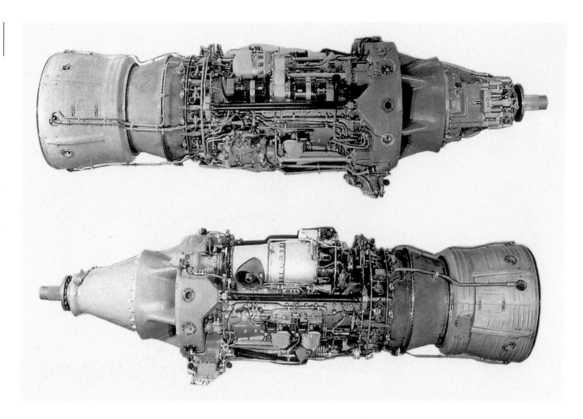

Powerplant: Four Kuznetsov NK-12MV Srs 4 or (Tu-142MZ) NK-12MP turboprops rated at 15,000 ehp for take-off driving AV-60K propellers.

Fuel system: The fuel is accommodated in eight integral wing tanks (two in each inner/outer wing panel), two bag-type tanks in the wing centre section and one more bag-type tank in the rear fuselage. The total fuel load is 91,024 kg (200,617 lb). The fuel system is split into four groups of tanks, one for each engine, but a cross-feed valve allows any engine to draw fuel from any group of tanks.

Ground refuelling takes place via four pressure refuelling connectors (two under each wing) or by gravity; the total capacity in these cases is 103,500 or 106,860 litres (22,770 or 23,5109 Imp gal) respectively. An IFR system is provided, with a telescopic refuelling probe installed on top of the fuselage nose. Anywhere from 28 to 35 tons (61,730 to 77,160 lb) can be transferred during a single refuelling session. A fuel

A drawing of the Tu-142M's starboard outer engine nacelle from the structural manual. Note the reduction gearbox shroud forming the annular air intake.

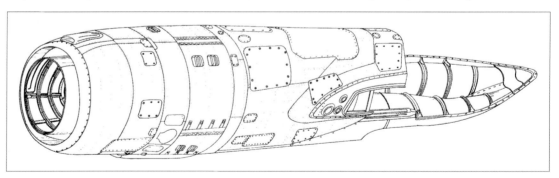

Below: A drawing of the Tu-142M's starboard inner engine nacelle and main gear fairing.

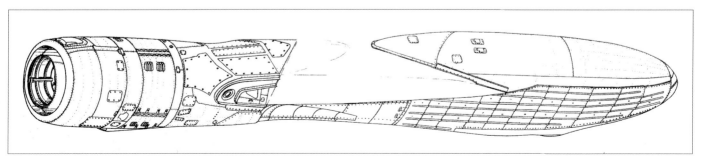

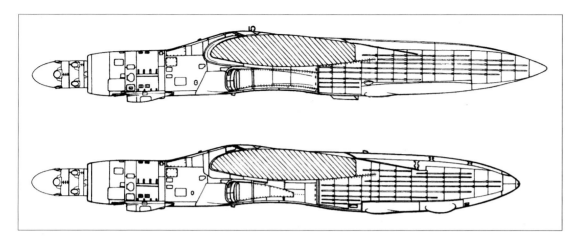

This drawing gives a comparison of the inboard engine nacelle/ main gear fairing combination of the early Tu-142 *sans suffixe* (*izdeliye* VP, above) and and the Tu-142M and subsequent versions (below). The wing is omitted for clarity.

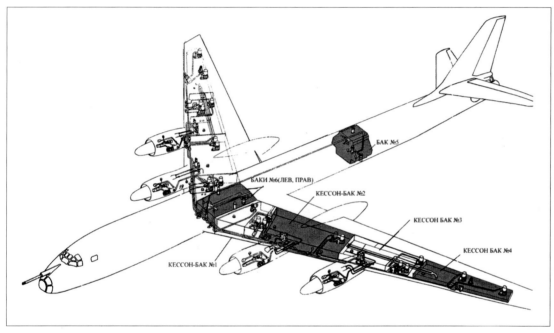

БАК №5

БАКИ №6(ЛЕВ, ПРАВ)

КЕССОН-БАК №2

КЕССОН БАК №3

КЕССОН БАК №4

КЕССОН-БАК №1

The Tu-142's fuel system (except for the IFR system), exemplified here by a picture from the Tu-142M's structural manual.

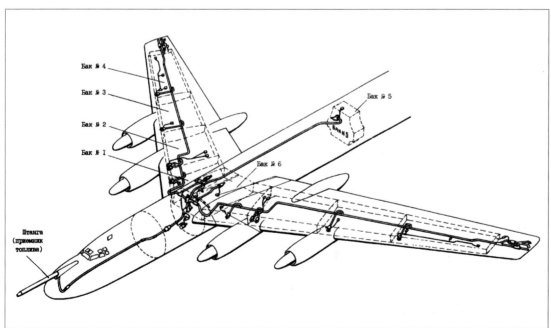

Бак № 4

Бак № 3

Бак № 2

Бак № 1

Бак № 5

Бак № 6

Штанга (приемник топлива)

The Tu-142's in-flight refuelling system.

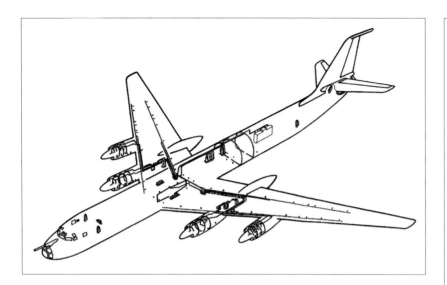

The fire suppression system of the Tu-142M.

The avionics of the Berkut-95 STS fitted to the Tu-142/Tu-142M.

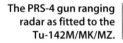

The PRS-4 gun ranging radar as fitted to the Tu-142M/MK/MZ.

Far right: The rear ventral ECM antenna of the Tu-142MZ.

The radome of the Korshun search radar on a Tu-142MZ.

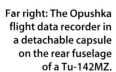

Far right: The Opushka flight data recorder in a detachable capsule on the rear fuselage of a Tu-142MZ.

The captain's control wheel of the Tu-142M

1. IFR probe emergency retraction button;
2. Autopilot override button;
3. Markers for ailerons neutral (wings level) position of the control wheel;
4. IFR probe extension button (on the reverse of the right-hand grip);
5. Radio communication selector button;
6. Intercom button (used for radio channel muting in air-to-ground communication mode);
7. Three-position elevator trim switch ('descend/neutral/ climb').

jettison system is provided, allowing the landing weight to be reduced within 25-30 minutes in an emergency.

Electrics: Similar to those of the Tu-95. The primary power sources are unchanged (main 28.5 V DC power is supplied by eight GSR-18000M engine-driven generators, with a 12SAM-55 lead-acid battery as a back-up; 208 V/400 Hz and 115 V/400 Hz single-phase

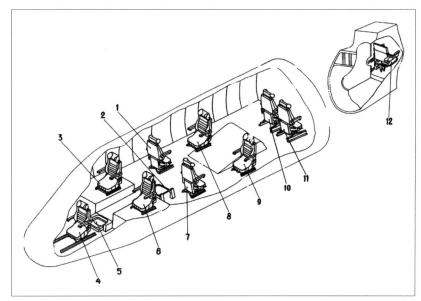

AC is supplied by four engine-driven SGO-30U alternators). However, some of the single- and three-phase AC converters are different, their parameters being selected with regard to the needs of the mission equipment (the search and targeting suite).

Avionics and equipment

a) navigation equipment and instrumentation: The Tu-142 *sans suffixe* (*izdeliye* VP) and Tu-142M (*izdeliye* VPM) feature an NPK-142 self-contained navigation/flight instrumentation suite which determines the

Above: The Tu-142M's crew workstations. 1. Chief flight engineer; 2. Instructor flight engineer (on jump seat); 3. Co-pilot; 4. Navigator; 5. Instructor navigator (on jump seat); 6. Captain; 7. Radio operator; 8. Sonar system operator No.1; 9. Sonar system operator No.2; 10. Nav/Op; 11. Combat navigator (chief navigator); 12. Tail gunner (defensive fire commander).

Top left: The Korshin radar scanner, radar set and instrument panel with radarscope.

Above left: The two operator consoles of the Kaïra-P sonar system forming part of the Korshun-K STS. Each console has two KR-4 displays, one of which shows sonobuoy data and the other displays tactical or other information at the operator's discretion.

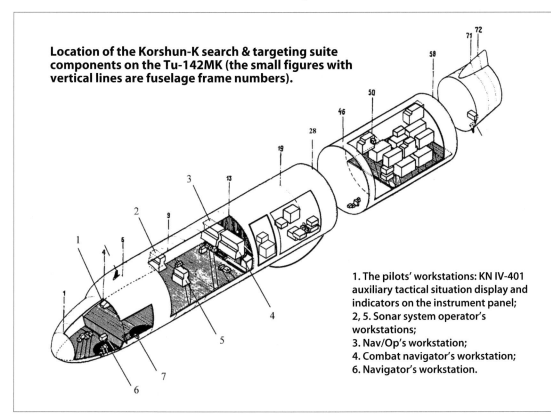

Location of the Korshun-K search & targeting suite components on the Tu-142MK (the small figures with vertical lines are fuselage frame numbers).

1. The pilots' workstations: KN IV-401 auxiliary tactical situation display and indicators on the instrument panel;
2, 5. Sonar system operator's workstations;
3. Nav/Op's workstation;
4. Combat navigator's workstation;
6. Navigator's workstation.

The Tu-142M's aft facing workstations of the Nav/Op (left) and combat navigator (right).

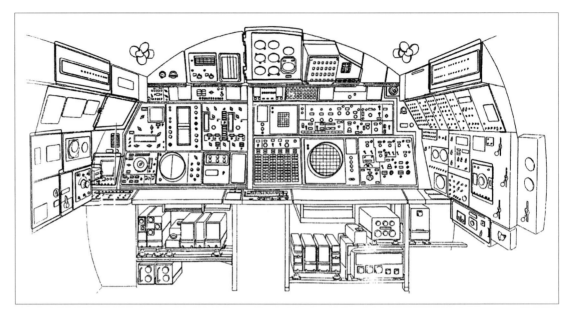

The flight deck of the Tu-142MK. The passage to the navigator's station is curtained off.

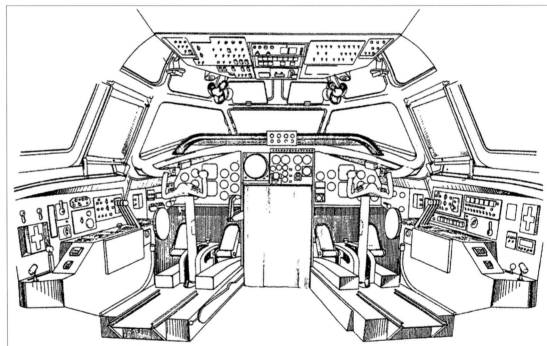

Right: The navigator's station of the Tu-142MK.

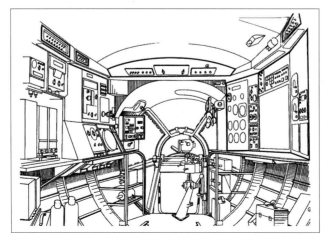

Far right: The flight engineer's workstation of the Tu-142MK and the starboard emergency exit beside it.

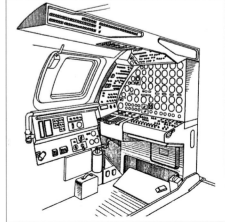

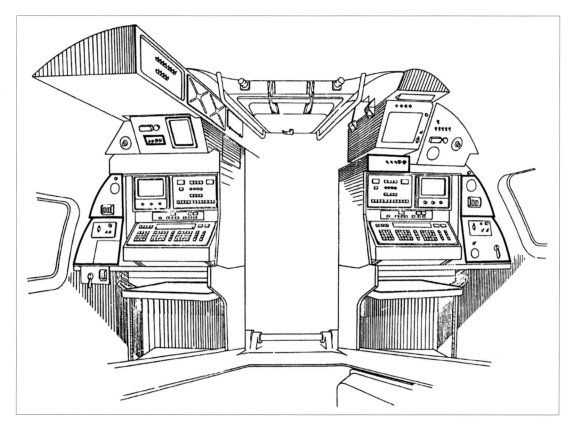

The forward-facing sonar operators' workstations (RGP-1, RGP-2) of the Tu-142M. Note the entry hatch in the floor and the port emergency exit.

aircraft's current co-ordinates, heading, speed and flight level, as well as pitch and bank angles. The suite comprises a main loop using the co-ordinates of celestial bodies and a back-up loop working with ground radio beacons. It also includes an AP-15R3 autopilot, Put'-4 and Put'-3 navigation systems.

The Tu-142MK (*izdeliye* VPMK) has an NPK-142M navigation/flight instrumentation suite. The suite offers automatic and semi-automatic flight control modes with control inputs from the navigation system and the STS. It includes the Bort-142 flight director system and the AP-15PS autopilot.

Below: The pilots' instrument panels (captain/centre/co-pilot) of the Tu-142M.

Bottom left: The navigator's instrument panels (main/starboard) of the Tu-142M.

Bottom: The flight engineer's main instrument panel of the Tu-142M.

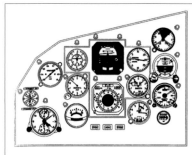
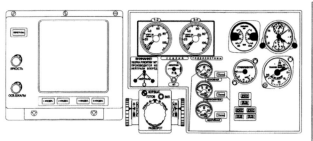
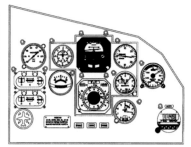

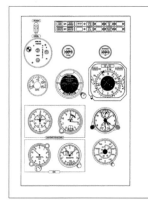

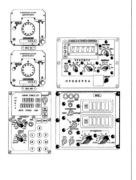
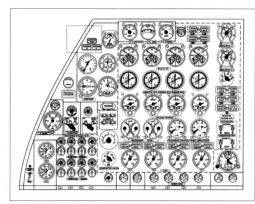

The flight deck of a 240th OSAP Tu-142MK ('93 Black'), with two banks of caution/warning lights below the instrument panel shroud. The red knobs between them are the engine fire warning lights and fire suppression system controls. The instruments are conventional (electromechanical) throughout.

The captain's and co-pilot's instrument panels and control wheels of a Tu-142MK. The control wheels feature autopilot override, intercom and pitch trim switches.

The flight engineer's workstation of Tu-142MK '93 Black', with a bank of throttles, engine instruments on the right, auxiliary flight instruments on the upper left, electrical systems controls on the lower left and on the 'tabletop', and the engine starting panel, hydraulics, de-icing and fire suppression systems controls on the sidewall.

The aft-facing ASW workstations of the navigator/operator (on the left) and the combat navigator (on the right – that is, starboard and port side respectively) on Tu-142MK '93 Black'.

Below left: The tail gunner's station and PS-153K gunsight of a Tu-142MK.

Below: The flight deck of a Tu-142MZ. The curtain is drawn, showing the navigator's station. Note the escape conveyor built into the floor.

b) communications equipment: The Tu-142M has a Strela-142M communications suite enabling two-way air-to-ground, air-to-ship and air-to-air communication over the entire range of frequencies, as well as internal communication. It also records all incoming and outgoing information transmitted via voice and data link.

c) targeting equipment: Early Tu-142s *sans suffixe* (up to c/n 4225) featured a Gagara-1 thermal imager in

The pilots' instrument panels of a Tu-142MR. Note that the captain's radarscope is of a different type than hitherto.

A wider perspective of the Tu-142MR's flight deck, showing the overhead circuit breaker panel.

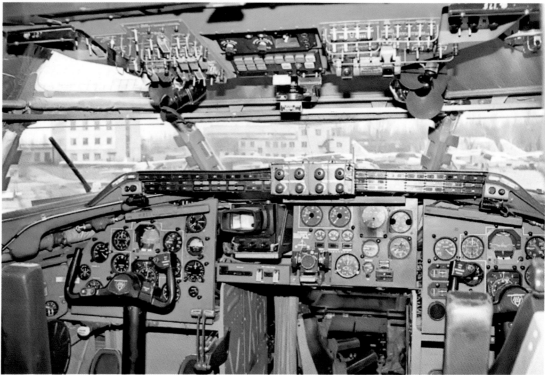

a chin fairing (which was deleted from c/n 4231 onwards and subsequently removed on earlier aircraft). This served for detecting the infrared wake of a submerged submarine, and the detected data was recorded on a strip of special electrically sensitive paper.

The Tu-142 *sans suffixe* (*izdeliye* VP) and Tu-142M (*izdeliye* VPM) are equipped with the Berkut-95 search

and targeting suite built around a Berkut 360° search radar. The STS includes the SPIU receiver/indicator processing and displaying the signals generated by the sonobuoys, the TsVM-263 digital computer, the PGK geographical co-ordinates input/display panel etc. The computer links the STS with the airspeed, heading and altitude sensors, the vertical gyro, the NPK-142

Above left: The captain's workstation of the Tu-142MR. The twin red handles are for emergency braking.

Above: The co-pilot's workstation of the Tu-142MR. Each of the pilots has his own bank of throttles and elevator trim handwheel.

Left: An aft-facing mission equipment operator's station of the Tu-142MR. Note the open escape hatch.

Far left: This view of the flight deck provides a glimpse of the navigator's station…

Below and below left: …which is extremely claustrophobic. On the radar-nosed Tu-142MR the navigator still sits in the extreme nose.

This photo gives a view of both aft-facing mission equipment operators' stations of the Tu-142MR. Note the 'unblack unbox' – the container of the MSRP-12-96 primary FDR, which is spherical in order to withstand the water pressure in the event of a crash in the sea and painted orange for higher conspicuity.

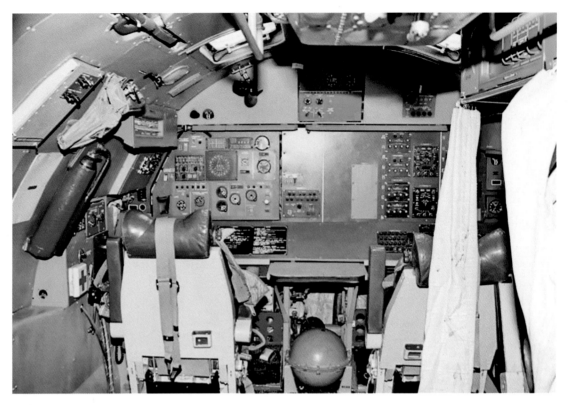

The radio operator's station of the Tu-142MR.

navigation/flight suite and the armament. The STS feeds inputs to the autopilot, the Put-4 and Put'-3 navigation systems and the weapons control panels. Together with the other mission equipment, it enables the following:

• automated flight along a predesignated route;

• tactical manoeuvring in semi-automatic mode while locating, tracking and attacking hostile submarines, or in automatic mode during fulfilment of certain other missions;

• searching for submerged submarines by means of sonobuoys;

• computation of target data and accurate weapons delivery.

The Berkut-95 STS works with RGB-1 non-directional passive sonobuoys, RGB-2 passive sonobuoys and RGB-3 active/passive sonobuoys. However, only the former two types were actually carried operationally by the Tu-142.

The Tu-142MK (*izdeliye* VPMK) has a Korshun-K STS including the Kaïra-P sonar system, an MMS-106 Ladoga magnetic anomaly detector and a sonobuoy/weapons release system. The STS works with active sonobuoys and explosive sound sources (ESS) used for detecting submarines in deep waters, making it necessary to know the speed of sound in water in the specific search area. To this end the Tu-142MK is fitted with the Nerchinsk auxiliary sonar system working with the Kaïra-P system.

The Korshun-K STS works with RGB-75 passive non-directional sonobuoys, RGB-15 passive/active non-directional buoys, RGB-25 passive directional buoys and RGB-55A active directional buoys. The first two are used for primary detection of subs and the other two for pinpointing them and monitoring their movements. The number of buoys carried is 24 RGB-75s, or 16 RGB-15s, or 10 RGB-25s, or 15 RGB-55As, depending on the mission. The RGB-15 can be used jointly with ESS in the active mode for pinpointing the target; three types of ESS are used – the MGAB-OZ, MGAB-LZ and MGAB-SZ.

The MMS-106 Ladoga MAD is a secondary source of information on underwater targets. Its sensor is mounted on a 'stinger' projecting aft from the top of the fin and enclosed by a dielectric fairing.

The Tu-142MZ (*izdeliye* VPMZ) is fitted with the Korshun-N STS which features a new Zarech'ye sonar system. The range of sonobuoys used is narrowed to the RGB-1A, RGB-2, RGB-16 and RGB-26 working with the Nashatyr'-Nefrit ASW suite.

Left row, top to bottom:
The canoe fairing housing the trailing wire aerial unit of the Tu-142MR.

Another view of the TWA unit. Note the air intake and ventral air outlet at the front for the ram air turbine driving the unit's hydraulic motor.

The perforated stabilising drogue of the trailing wire aerial.

Right row:
The cowling of the TWA unit is split down the centreline. Note the guillotine cutting the wire if rewinding the aerial is impossible for any reason.

Two views of the open cowling revealing the drum with the 8-km (5-mile) aerial and its winding mechanism making sure the aerial does not get snarled.

d) ECM/ESM equipment: The Tu-142M has an SPO-3 RHAWS, active jammers and chaff/flare dispensers. The Tu-142MZ is equipped with a Sayany defensive suite.

e) data recording equipment: MSRP-12-96 primary FDR and (Tu-142MZ) *Opushka* (Edge of a forest) secondary FDR.

Armament:

a) offensive armament: The basic Tu-142 can carry AT-1 (AT-1M) and AT-2 (AT-2M) anti-submarine torpedoes, APR-1 and APR-2 missiles (*aviatsionnaya protivolodochnaya raketa* – air-launched anti-submarine missile); on the Tu-142MZ the APR-2 is

These views show the Tu-142MZ's rear ECM antennas and rear avionics bay access hatches.

Front view of a Tu-142M, with PLAB-250 anti-submarine bombs and cassettes for those arranged in front. Note the asymmetric location of the FPSh-5M probe and drogue illumination lights caused by the fuel line on the starboard side.

A cassette loaded with RGB-75 sonobuoys with packed retarding parachutes; note that the buoys in each set are numbered.

Far right: PLAB-250 bombs (depth charges) and rgw cassettes for these.

A Tu-142MK-E with assorted sonobuoys, an AT-2 ASW torpedo and a Kh-35 anti-shipping missile (with wings deployed) arranged in front.

The main weapons bay of the Tu-142M is wide enough for weapons to be carried in three rows. Note that the doors are split into front and rear pairs which are operated independently. Here a bomb cassette is installed at the rear end; note the door actuator.

Far left: Another view of the main weapons bay, looking aft; the second weapons bay is just visible.

The second weapons bay of the Tu-142M, with a honeycomb-type cassette. The door actuator is at the front end.

augmented by the UMGT-1M Orlan homing torpedo. The aircraft can also carry naval mines (such as the MDM-3 and MDM-5 bottom mines), free-fall anti-submarine bombs (depth charges) – both conventional and nuclear ones – and, in the case of the Tu-142MZ, KAB-250PL (S-3V) guided depth charges.

The weapons system includes bomb, torpedo and sonobuoy racks, an NKBP-7 bombsight and release controls (ESBR-70 electric bomb release unit, drop sequence module, detonation depth setting module etc.), detonator controls and bomb/torpedo hoists. In an emergency, the captain or Nav/Op may dump all ordnance, setting it for detonation or non-detonation.

b) defensive armament: The defensive armament is reduced to a single DK-12 tail barbette mounting two AM-23 cannons or, on the Tu-142MZ, a UKU-9K-502 tail barbette mounting two 23-mm Gryazev/Shipunov GSh-23 twin-barrel cannons with a 2,600-rpm rate of fire. The cannons are aimed using a PS-153K optical sighting station, a PRS-4 Krypton gun ranging radar and a VB-153 ballistic computer.

Crew protection and crew equipment: Basically as for the Tu-95. There is a container with two PSN-6A inflatable life rafts near the forward pressure cabin and a container with an LAS-5M inflatable rescue dinghy in the fin root fillet near the rear pressure cabin.

Two RGB-1A sonobuoys.

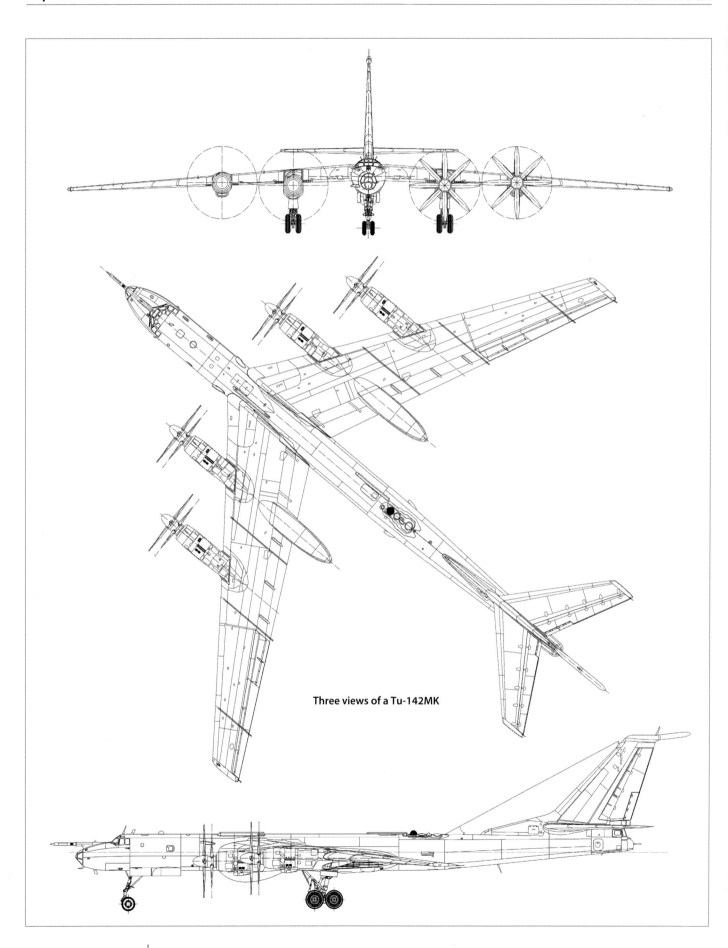

Three views of a Tu-142MK

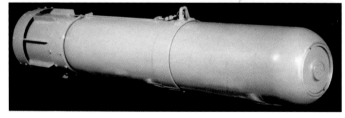

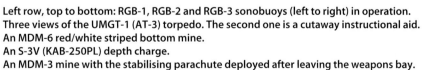

Left row, top to bottom: RGB-1, RGB-2 and RGB-3 sonobuoys (left to right) in operation.
Three views of the UMGT-1 (AT-3) torpedo. The second one is a cutaway instructional aid.
An MDM-6 red/white striped bottom mine.
An S-3V (KAB-250PL) depth charge.
An MDM-3 mine with the stabilising parachute deployed after leaving the weapons bay.

Right row, top to bottom: The APR-1 anti-submarine missile.
The APR-2 anti-submarine missile.
Two views of the APR-2E export version.
The APR-3E and APR-3ME missiles
Another view of an S-3V depth charge.

Left row, top to bottom: Front view of a production Tu-95MS. The faceted ventral dome on the centreline is the sensor of the Mak-UFM missile warning system (MWS).

The retractable landing/taxi lights, MWS sensor and icing sensors of a Tu-95MS.

On this grey-painted Tu-95MS, the MWS sensor is closed by a protective ground cover. The dark grey circle painted on around it is an anti-glare panel preventing false alarms.

Right row, top to bottom: These views illustrate the difference between the Tu-95MS prototype and production examples. The former aircraft has a metal skin panel beneath the root of the IFR probe. On production *Bear-Hs* it is substituted by a larger dielectric panel flanked by two small dielectric blisters associated with the ECM suite

The port side of the Tu-95MS prototype's nose.

The fuselage of the Tu-95MS; the lower view (with somewhat inaccurate proportions) includes cutaways of the front and rear pressure cabins.

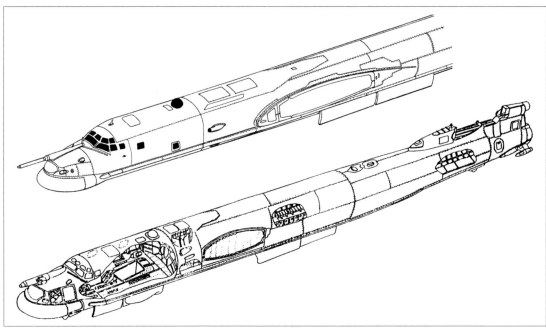

A production Tu-95MS with additional aerials under the nose and on the fuselage sides.

III. Tu-95MS missile strike aircraft

Again, only the principal differences are listed below.

Type: Long-range missile strike aircraft. The crew is reduced to seven (captain, co-pilot, navigator, Nav/Op, flight engineer, weapons systems operator and gunner).

Fuselage: Similar to that of the Tu-142M but somewhat shorter for CG reasons. Section F-1 is similar in design to that of the Tu-95KM, with twin radomes (the lower one is wider than the upper half of the nose),

The front pressure cabin's entry hatch as seen from within…

…and from outside (note the actuating ram.

Unlike western heavy bombers, the Tu-95 does not have an integral boarding ladder – it is strictly ground equipment.

The port wing
of a Tu-95MS.

Below: The starboard
wing; note that the
starboard aileron trim
tab is different.

Bottom and below left:
The Tu-95MS's main
gear units are identical
to those of the Tu-142M.

Bottom centre: Front
view of the Tu-95MS's
nose gear unit, showing
the steering actuator/
shimmy damper.

Bottom right: Rear view
of the nose gear unit.

albeit both the radome and its rear fairing are shorter (the fairing does not overlap the manufacturing break with Section F-2). Section F-2 has the Tu-142M's raised flight deck roof. Section F-3 features a weapons bay closed by hydraulically operated clamshell doors whose size is optimised for carrying six Kh-55 cruise missiles. Again, Section F-4 lacks the apertures for the dorsal and ventral cannon barbettes. Section F-5 is almost identical to that to the Tu-142MZ (with a smaller pressurised area accommodating the gunner only and equipment bay access hatches instead of the lateral sighting blisters), except that the ECM/ESM aerials are located differently.

Wings: As for the Tu-142.

Tail unit: As for the Tu-142 (with variable-incidence stabilisers).

Above and above left: The rear fuselage and tail unit of a late-production Tu-95MS equipped with an APU (note the exhaust door on the port side). The Sayany ECM suite's aerials are clearly visible.

The No.3 AV-60K propeller of a Tu-95MS with the spinner removed to show details of the front row's hub.

The Nos. 1 and 2 propellers of a Tu-95MS. The coloured spinner tips may assist in icing visualisation.

The flight deck of a standard production Tu-95MS (n slightly incomplete condition). The curtain is still there but there's no passage behind it! Note the sliding control panel which may be used by either pilot.

Two more views of the same flight deck from the captain's and co-pilot's seats.

The overhead circuit breaker panel, with the autopilot control panel in the middle.

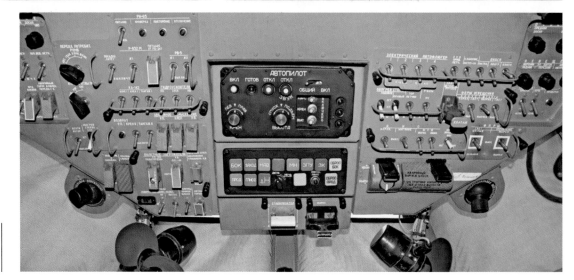

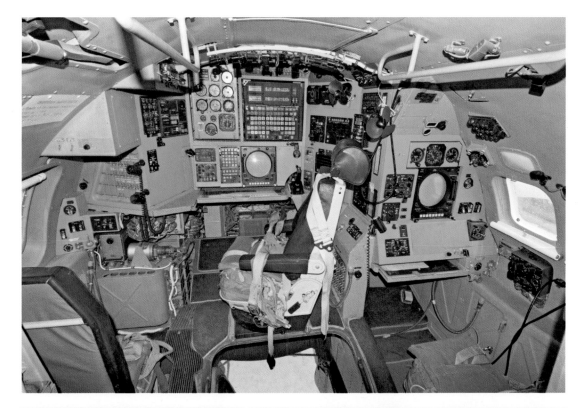

The rear end of the Tu-95MS's flight deck, with the combat navigator's workstation in the centre, the navigator's workstation on the right and a jump seat on the left.

The centre section of the Tu-95MS's flight deck, with the flight engineer's workstation on the left and the radio operator's workstation on the right.

Landing gear: As for the Tu-142M/MK.

Powerplant: Four 15,000-ehp Kuznetsov NK-12MP turboprops driving AV-60K propellers. Late-production Tu-95MSs have a Stoopino Machinery Design Bureau TA-12 APU which supplies compressed air and ground/emergency electric power. It is located in the fin root fillet, with the air intake door on the starboard side and the exhaust on the port side; the exhaust is closed by a door when the APU is not in operation. The APU can be started at altitudes below 3,000 m (9,840 ft).

Fuel system: As for the Tu-142 (eight integral tanks in the inner/outer wing panels, two bag-type tanks in the wing centre section and one more bag-type tank in the rear fuselage).

Right: The KSU-021
integrated control
system modules.

Far right: The modules
of the N-202 navigation
suite built around
the I-021 INS.

Far right, lower: The
Orbita-20 mainframe
computer.

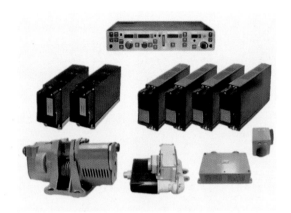

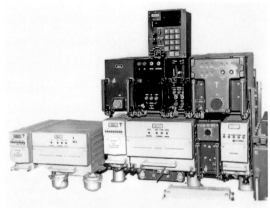

Electrics: Similar to those of the Tu-95, except that different AC converters are installed to cater for the avionics and armament. The exterior lighting includes white SI anti-collision strobe lights mounted dorsally and ventrally on the rear fuselage.

Avionics and equipment:

a) navigation and piloting equipment: The avionics suite includes an Orbita-20 digital mainframe computer responsible for flight/navigation and weapons application tasks. The aircraft has an N-202 navigation suite built around an I-21 inertial navigation system; an ANS-2009 celestial navigation system (***as**tronavigatsi**onn**aya sis**tem**a*) with a star tracker window on top of the rear fuselage, and an NVS-021 navigation

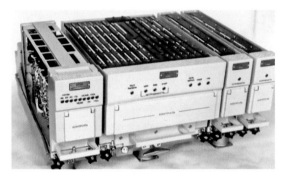

computer system re also fitted. The Tu-95MS has a KSU-021 automatic flight control system (digital autopilot).

b) communications equipment: Multi-channel digital communications suite, including an intercom for crew communication.

c) radar and targeting equipment: The targeting equipment includes an Obzor-MS twin-antenna target illumination/guidance radar in the extreme nose and a K-012 Osina (on the Tu-95MS-6) or K-016 Pikhta (on the Tu-95MS-16) missile launch control system.

d) IFF equipment: Izdeliye 023 *Parol'* (Password) IFF transponder and an SO-69 ATC transponder.

Opposite page, top left: The gunner's station of the Tu-95MS, showing the PS-153K sighting device and the front view mirrors allowing the gunner to keep an eye on the engines.

Opposite page, top right: The gunner's entry hatch with its twin actuating rams.

Opposite page, centre right: The underside of the Tu-95MS's tail section, showing the spent case outlets of the twin GSh-23 cannons.

Right: rear view of the gunner's station on the Tu-95MS, showing the PRS-4 gun-laying radar.

Far right: Close-up of the UKU-9K-502-I tail turret with its GSh-23 twin-barrel cannons.

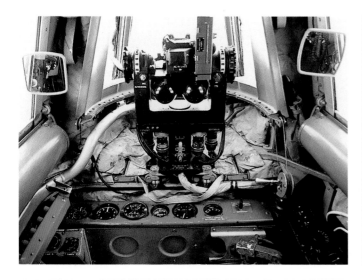

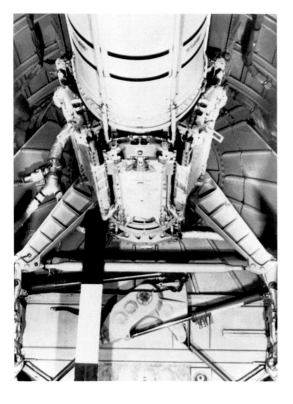

| Top: The MKU-6-5A six-round rotary launcher fitted to the Tu-95MS.

| Left: The front end of the rotary launcher installed in the weapons bay. Note the bay door actuating mechanism.

| Above: The MKU-6-5A fully loaded with six Kh-55 cruise missiles.

Right: Six Kh-55 missiles fit tightly around the rotary launcher. Note the work platform suspended from the sidewall of the bay.

Far right: Here the missiles are in a different version with a shorter nose and a grey radome. Note the dielectric panel for the altimeter.

Opposite page, top left: The open weapons bay doors of a Tu-95MS.

Opposite page, top right: A Kh-55SM long-range missile in the weapons bay of a Tu-95MS. This one has been adorned with a sharkmouth!

Opposite page, centre: A Kh-55 on a ground handling dolly. This missile has an orange radome bearing the stencil KTS-120 – possibly as a reference to the warhead.

Right: This Tu-95MS carries a mix of 'greyhead' and 'greenhead' Kh-55s.

Far right: An orange-painted Kh-555 test round with canards and conformal tanks.

Opposite page, bottom left: The Tu-95MS-16 had four pylons for an extra ten Kh-55s. The inboard pair had two AKU-5 ejector racks each.

Opposite, bottom centre and right: The outer pylons of the Tu-95MS-16 had three vertically staggered AKU-5 racks each.

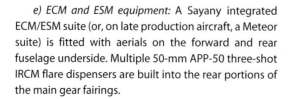

e) ECM and ESM equipment: A Sayany integrated ECM/ESM suite (or, on late production aircraft, a Meteor suite) is fitted with aerials on the forward and rear fuselage underside. Multiple 50-mm APP-50 three-shot IRCM flare dispensers are built into the rear portions of the main gear fairings.

Armament:

a) offensive armament: The Tu-95MS is designed to carry Raduga Kh-55 or longer-range Kh-55SM cruise missiles. The Tu-95MS-6 carries six Kh-55 missiles internally on an MKU-6-5 rotary launcher, while the Tu-95MS-16 had four pylons with multiple ejector racks under the wings for carrying an additional ten missiles

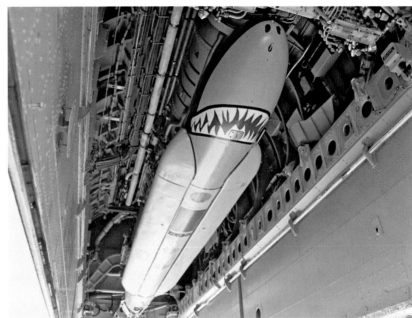

externally (two missiles side by side on each inboard pylon and three missiles abreast on each outboard pylon). The Tu-95MS-16s had their underwing missile pylons removed to comply with the START-1 treaty; however, the upgraded Tu-95MSM has had the wing pylons reinstated, and these are of a different type for carrying eight Raduga Kh-101 cruise missiles in side-by-side pairs.

b) defensive armament: Early-production Tu-95MSs had a single DK-12 tail turret with two AM-23 cannons. Later aircraft have a UKU-9K-502 tail turret with two GSh-23 cannons, which are trained by means of a PRS-4 Krypton radar.

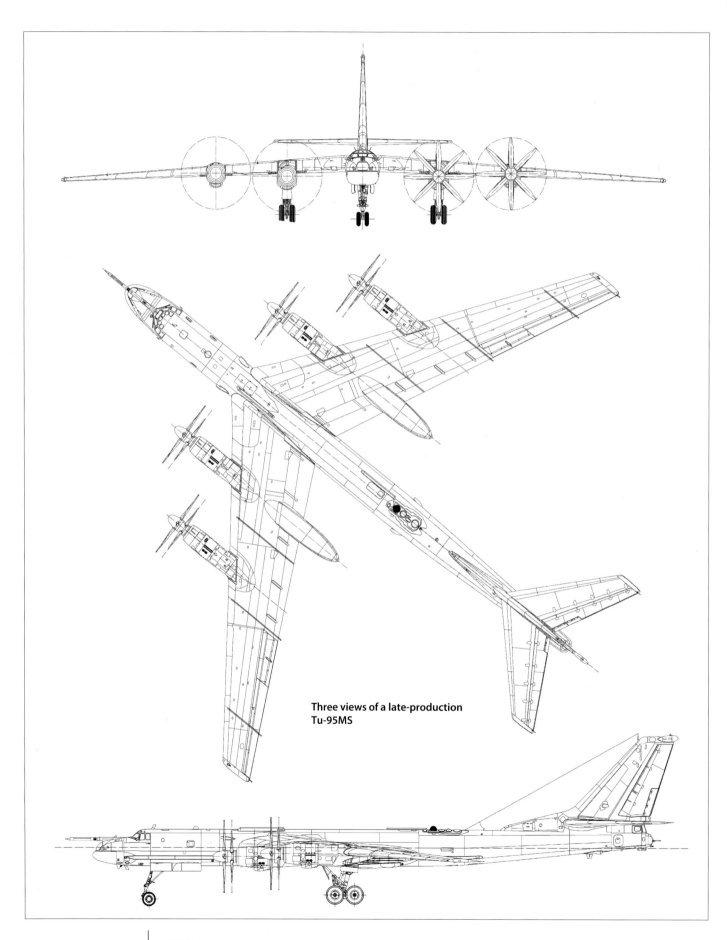

Three views of a late-production
Tu-95MS

Tu-95 family specifications

	'95/1'	'95/2'	Tu-95	Tu-95M	Tu-95MR	Tu-96
First flight	1952	1955	1955	1957	1964	1956
Powerplant (rating, shp)	4 x 2TV-2F (4 x 12,000)	4 x NK-12 (4 x 12,000)	4 x NK-12 (4 x 12,000)	4 x NK-12M (4 x 15,000)	4 x NK-12MV (4 x 15,000)	4 x TV-16 (4 x 12,500) [1]
Crew	9-11	9	9	9	9	8
Wingspan	49.8 m (163 ft 4 5/8 in)	50.04 m (164 ft 2 5/64 in)	50.04 m (164 ft 2 5/64 in)	50.04 m (164 ft 2 5/64 in)	50.04 m (164 ft 2 5/64 in)	51.4 m (168 ft 7 5/8 in)
Wing area, m² (sq ft)	283.7 (3,053)	284.9 (3,066)	283.7 (3,053)	283.7 (3,053)	283.7 (3,053)	345.5. (3,719)
Length	44.35 m (145 ft 6 1/16 in)	46.17 m (151 ft 5 23/32 in)	46.17 m (151 ft 5 23/32 in)	46.17 m (151 ft 5 23/32 in)	48.5 m (159 ft 1 29/64 in) [2]	46.2 m (151 ft 6 29/32 in)
MTOW, kg (lb)	156,000 (343,915)	167,200 (368,610)	172,000 (379,190)	182,000 (401,230)	182,000 (401,230)	n.a.
Fuel load, kg (lb)	n.a.	84,440 (186,155)	n.a.	n.a.	n.a.	n.a.
Weapons load, kg (lb)	5,000/15,000 (11,022/33,068)*	5,000/12,000 (11,022/26,455)*	5,000/12,000 (11,022/26,455)*	5,000/12,000 (11,022/26,455)*	–	5,000/12,000 (11,022/26,455) [3]
Empty weight, kg (lb)	n.a.	n.a.	83,100	84,300	n.a.	n.a.
Top speed, km/h (mph)	945 (587)	880 (546)	890 (553)	905 (562)	910 (565)	880 (546)/902 (560)
Cruising speed, km/h (mph)	n.a.	750 (466)	750 (466)	720-750 (447-466)	750 (466)	n.a.
Service ceiling, m (ft)	13,700 (44,940)	12,500 (41,010)	11,800 (38,700)	11,900 (39,030)	11,900 (39,030)	17,000 (55,760)/ 12,400 (40,670)
Range, km (miles)	15,200 (9,439)	13,900 (8,632)	12,100 (7,514)	13,200 (8,197)	13,120 (8,148)	16,200 (10,060)
Range with 1 fuel top-up, km (miles)	–	–	–	–	n.a.	–
Combat radius, km (miles)	n.a.	n.a.	n.a.	n.a.	n.a.	n.a.
Take-off run, m (ft)	1,580 (5,180)	2,300 (7,540)	2,350 (7,710)	2,730 (8,950)	1,800 (5,900)	n.a.
Landing run, m (ft)	1,370 (4,490)	n.a.	1,500 (4,920)	1,500 (4,920)	1,500 (4,920)	2,780 (9,120)
Defensive armament	6 x AM-23	6 x AM-23	6 x AM-23	6 x AM-23	6 x AM-23	n.a.

(continued)

	Tu-95K	Tu-95KM	Tu-95RTs	Tu-142	Tu-142M/MK	Tu-95MS
First flight	1956	1961	1962	1968	1975	1979
Powerplant (rating, shp)	4 x NK-12 (4 x 12,000)	4 x NK-12MV (4 x 15,000)	4 x NK-12MV (4 x 15,000)	4 x NK-12MV (4 x 15,000)	4 x NK-12MV (4 x 15,000)	4 x NK-12MP (4 x 15,000)
Crew	9	9	9	9	11	7
Wingspan	50.04 m (164 ft 2 5/64 in)	50.04 m (164 ft 2 5/64 in)	50.04 m (164 ft 2 5/64 in)	50.04 m (164 ft 2 5/64 in)	50.04 m (164 ft 2 5/64 in)	50.04 m (164 ft 2 5/64 in)
Wing area, m² (sq ft)	283.7 (3,053)	283.7 (3,053)	283.7 (3,053)	283.7 (3,053)	289.9 (3,117)	289.9 (3,117)
Length	46.9 m (153 ft 10 29/64 in)	48.7 m (159 ft 9 21/64 in) [2]	48.5 m (159 ft 1 29/64 in) [2]	49.6 m (162 ft 8 3/4 in) [2]	53.2 m (174 ft 6 31/64 in) [2]	49.13 m (161 ft 2 1/4 in) [2]
MTOW, kg (lb)	n.a.	n.a.	182,000 (401,230)	182,000 401,230)	185,000 (407,850)	185,000 (407,840)
Fuel load, kg (lb)	n.a.			n.a.	n.a.	87,000 (191,800)
Weapons load, kg (lb)	11,600-11,800 (25,573-26,014)	11,600-11,800 (25,573-26,014)	–	n.a.	n.a.	7,800/20,800 (17,195/45,855) [4]
Empty weight, kg (lb)	n.a.	n.a.	n.a.	91,200 (201,060)	n.a.	n.a.
Landing weight, kg (lb)				n.a.	n.a.	135,000 (297,619)
Top speed, km/h (mph)	860 (534)	860 (534)	885 (550)/910 (562)	n.a.	855 (531)	830 (515)
Cruising speed, km/h (mph)	750 (466)	750 (466)	680-770 (422-478)	735 (456)	735 (456)	n.a.
Service ceiling, m (ft)	11,600 (38,048)	11,600 (38,050)	10,300 (33,780)	n.a.	n.a.	10,500 (34,440)
Range, km (miles)	12,500 (7,763)	n.a.	13,460 (8,359)	12,300 (7,638)	11,800 (7,328)	10,500 (6,521)
Range with one fuel top-up, km (miles)	–	n.a.	16,350 (10,153)	n.a.	13,800 (8,570)	14,100 (8,756)
Combat radius, km (miles)	6,340 (3,937)	6,340 (3,937)	n.a.	n.a.	n.a.	n.a.
Combat radius w. one fuel top-up, km (miles)	n.a.	8,520 (5,291)	n.a.	n.a.	n.a.	n.a.
Take-off run, m (ft)	2,380 (7,810)	2,780 (9,120)	n.a.	2,380 (7,810)	2,350 (7,710)	2,540 (8,330)
Landing run, m (ft)	1,700 (5,580)	1,700 (5,580)	n.a.	n.a.	n.a.	n.a.
Defensive armament	6 x AM-23	6 x AM-23	6 x AM-23	2 x AM-23	2 x AM-23	2 x GSh-23

Notes:

1. 12,000-ehp NK-12s were actually fitted; 2. With IFR probe; 3. Normal/maximum; 4. Tu-95MS-6/Tu-95MS-16

Russian Air Force Tu-95MS '14 Red' *Voronezh* registered RF-94132 and wearing silver finish. Note the open APU intake door.

In contrast, sister ship '23/2 Red'/RF-94205 wears the new predominantly grey livery.

CHAPTER SEVEN

The Tu-95 in service: Air Force operations

The Tu-95 attained IOC as a strategic bomber in 1956. As already mentioned, deliveries of the Tu-95 *sans suffixe* to the Long-Range Aviation began in April that year, and the type's arrival heralded a major new era in the history of the DA.

The first bomber division operating the type, the 106th TBAD, had started forming as early as 1955. It comprised the newly-established 409th TBAP and 1006th TBAP, both based at Uzin AB (Chepelevka AB) in the south of the Kiev Region, central Ukraine.

The 106th TBAD was commanded by Lt.-Gen. Aleksandr I. Molodchiy, one of the most experienced commanders in the DA, who had gained two Hero of the Soviet Union titles in the Great Patriotic War. He was offered *carte blanche* when picking the personnel for his division and used it to the full – the best-trained pilots were transferred

to the 106th TBAD from Tu-16 units without delay. The situation was unusual in that new units had been set up to operate a new aircraft type. In contrast, when the Tu-4 was being introduced, it was delivered to the best but nevertheless well-established units with a long combat history and consistently high crew training levels; the scenario had been repeated when the Tu-16 entered service.

The 409th TBAP was formed at the end of 1955 under the command of Col. Nikolay N. Kharitonov, who would become the Tupolev OKB's chief test pilot two years later. The 1006th TBAP started operations in 1956 commanded by Col. Yu. P. Pavlov. The aircrews and maintenance personnel quickly mastered the new bomber. It was the 106th TBAD that received the honour of making a flypast over Moscow's Tushino airfield during the traditional Aviation Day flying display in 1956 – the

A KrAZ-260 prime mover laden with concrete slabs to increase weight and improve traction moves into position to push back a Tu-95K that has just taxied in at Dyagilevo AB, Ryazan'. Looking a bit tatty but sporting an 'Excellent aircraft' badge, '61 Red' was operated by the 43rd TsBP i PLS.

Top: Tu-95 '42 Red' escorted by two MiG-17 *sans suffixe* (*Fresco-A*) fighters took part in the 1956 Air Fleet Day flypast at Moscow-Tushino.

Top right: This view illustrates the *Bear*'s distinctive lines with a slender fuselage and high aspect ratio wings.

Centre right: Tu-95 '42 Red' and its fighter escort seen from a different angle.

Above: Another parade performance by the Tu-95. This time the lead ship in the formation is '44 Red' escorted by four MiG-17s.

Above right: At the air parades at Tushino or in Moscow's Red Square the Tu-95s appeared in large formations, flying in groups of three.

Tu-95's first public appearance. Thus, by the time the *Bear* was formally included into the inventory the DA already had a fully equipped bomber formation operating the type.

The 106th TBAD operated primarily on the northern sector. Even though the Tu-95's trials were still in progress and the unit's personnel had not yet been fully trained, division CO Molodchiy began practicing long-range flights into the High North and the Soviet Far East, including formation flying in up to regiment strength. Maj.-Gen. Vasiliy V. Reshetnikov, who succeeded

Here the same Tu-95 '42 Red' is seen at a different air event, escorted by five MiG-17s (the fifth aircraft is out of the picture).

Molodchiy as Commander of the 106th TBAD (and eventually went on to become Commander of the DA, continued this practice. This was inevitably accompanied by a deal of ostentation; in the 1960s it became common practice to send 'greetings from the North Pole' to a Communist Party convention as heavy bombers flew a mission timed to the event. Yet, such flights allowed complex mission types to be mastered.

The next unit to receive the Tu-95 was the 1023rd TBAP (often mistakenly referred to as the 1223rd TBAP) commanded by Col. Vladimir M. Bezbokov, which was established at Uzin AB in February 1956, initially flying six Tu-16s and a single Tu-95. A year later the unit was up to full strength, with Tu-95s as the principal hardware and the Tu-16s equipping Sqn 4 which was the proficiency training squadron. On 16th-30th December 1958 the 1023rd TBAP redeployed to its new home base, Chagan AB, 70 km (43.5 miles) north-west of Semipalatinsk, Kazakhstan, and came under the control of the 79th TBAD commanded by Maj.-Gen. Pavel A. Taran. This base was built in 1954-58; the location was probably chosen for reasons of proximity to the Semipalatinsk Nuclear Proving Ground; in the West this base was known under the erroneous name Dolon AB.

In 1959 the 1226th TBAP was formed at Gayok AB in Belaya Tserkov' (Kiev Region) – also starting life with Tu-16s but equipping with Tu-95s before long. In the summer of 1960 this regiment, too, redeployed to Chagan AB and was transferred to the 79th TBAD.

The division also included the 53rd OAE (*otdel'naya aviaeskadril'ya* – independent air squadron) equipped with a mixed bag of aircraft – originally piston-engined

Left: A still from a documentary movie showing a Tu-95 (apparently coded '65') performing at an air event in company with four MiG-17s.

Below: Another Tu-95 (probably from the same unit) coded '63 Red'. Such huge tactical codes on Soviet bombers were common in the 1950s and early 1960s.

A formation of *Bear-As* cruises over wispy clouds during an exercise.

73

Tu-95MA '73 Red', the 1960s

In spite of the same tactical code, '73 Red' depicted here is not the Tu-96 but an ordinary Tu-95MA (compare the style of the numerals with the photo on page 85). Here it is escorted by Convair F-102A-75-CO 56-1416 'FC-416' from the 57th Fighter Interceptor Squadron based at Keflavik, Iceland, during a sortie over the North Sea.

Lisunov Li-2 *Cab* and Ilyushin IL-14 *Crate* transports, which were later supplanted by Antonov An-26 *Curl* twin-turboprop tactical transports. However, the squadron also operated one of the two Tu-116 long-range VIP transports (CCCP-76463). Interestingly, this aircraft was erroneously believed to have taken Nikita S. Khrushchov on a visit to the USA and was therefore dubbed *kremlyovskiy* (pertaining to the Kremlin).

The 79th TBAD covered primarily the southern sector – Asia and the Indian Ocean, where the USA kept establishing new strategically important bases. In the mid-1960s the south-eastern sector was added to the division's zone of responsibility when Sino-Soviet relations became strained to the limit; China had a huge army and nuclear weapons of its own, and an armed conflict became a distinct possibility.

The Tu-95's long range made inter-theatre operations possible. Thus, the 79th TBAD could extend help on the northern theatre of operations if necessary, while the 106th TBAD could do the same in the south and the west.

The Tu-95 was intended to carry high-yield free-fall thermonuclear bombs. Originally the relatively compact 3-megaton RDS-37 bomb (*izdeliye* 37D) was regarded as the main weapon; it was loaded with a whole set of imperfections, including a limited shelf life. By the early 1960s, however, the Soviet defence industry was able to supply nukes in the 20-megaton class. Because of the limitations of the day's nuclear technology these were horrendously bulky weapons, which required the aircraft to be moved into position over a special trench for loading the bomb; the Myasishchev M-4's bicycle landing gear rendered it 'unparkable' over such trenches, limiting its usefulness until more compact H-bombs became available.

Top: Tu-95M '51 Red' is readied for a mission, using an APA-100 ground power unit on a ZiL-131 6x6 army lorry chassis and a TZ-22 articulated fuel bowser with a KrAZ-258B1 6x4 tractor unit.

Above and left: Tu-95M '71 Red' starts up the No.4 engine, using ground power from an APA-35/30-130 ground power unit on a ZiL-130 general-purpose lorry chassis.

Several FAB-3000 M46 HE bombs have been uncrated and lie on the edge of the hardstand, waiting to be loaded into Tu-95M bombers.

Seen from a sister ship, a Tu-95M flies over the Russian countryside.

Several aircraft in each unit (normally a detachment – or, in times of military crises, a whole squadron) were assigned to quick-reaction alert (QRA) duty, sitting parked over the abovesaid trenches and ready to be bombed up. However, only once (during the Cuban Missile Crisis of 1961) did Tu-95A and Tu-95MA bombers actually sit armed with nuclear bombs, never mind flying with nukes over international waters in peacetime. In contrast, USAF B-52s prowling along the Soviet borders always had nukes on board in those days.

Normally the nuclear bombs were stored in special bunkers close to the bases. Extreme security measures

were taken when handling the bombs; the bunkers were closely guarded, and only special engineering service (SES) personnel had access to the nukes. These men were dubbed 'the deaf and dumb' by the other personnel for being tight as a clam about anything that concerned their job; they even resided separately from the other personnel in the garrison to minimise unnecessary contacts and avoid security leaks. It took at least two hours to hook up the nuclear bomb, which was a major liability – the American bombers patrolled close to the Soviet borders and the USA needed less time to launch a first strike.

Additionally, the Tu-95 could carry IAB-3000 practice bombs emulating the flash and mushroom cloud of a nuclear explosion (hence IAB for *imitat-sionnaya aviabomba* – simulation bomb). These were used during exercises and for training the SES personnel in bomb loading procedures.

Later the Tu-95 was adapted to conventional warfare scenarios as well; as already mentioned, after reviewing such conflicts as the Vietnam War and the Arab-Israeli wars the Soviet military leaders concluded that a conventional warfare capability was desirable. Hence a configuration was developed permitting the carriage of up to forty-five 250-kg (551-lb) FAB-250M54 'iron' bombs. The mission in this configuration was to destroy enemy airfields and runways. However, such aircraft were few.

The Tu-95 could carry conventional 1946-model and 1954-model bombs of 1,500; 3,000; 5,000, 6,000 and 9,000 kg (3,305; 6,610; 11,020; 13,230 and 19,840 lb) calibre. The *Bear-A* normally carried 500-kg (1,102-lb) HE bombs; later the range was augmented by 250-kg (551-lb) bombs, 100-kg (220-lb) and even 50-kg (110-lb)

PB-50 and 250-kg PB-250 practice bombs (*prak-ticheskaya bomba*). The 5,000-kg (11,022-lb) UB-5000F and UBV-5 guided bombs envisaged for the *Bear* never reached the hardware stage because the R&D establishment responsible for them was assigned the task of building ballistic missiles in the mid-1950s.

The Tu-95's service introduction was not trouble-free. The initial production version of the NK-12 engine, for instance, often failed to deliver the advertised 12,000 ehp; the power output of individual engines varied and the engines had to be tuned, using the least powerful one as a reference to avoid asymmetrical thrust. As a result, range also fell short of the target figure. Moreover, the NK-12 *sans suffixe* was equipped with a manual propeller feathering system which proved inadequate. This caused one of the early Tu-95s (c/n 6800310) to crash fatally near Engels-2 AB on 24th November 1956 after an engine failure; the propeller of the affected engine could not be feathered in time, causing the aircraft to lose speed and stall. Consequently the 15,000-ehp NK-12MV engine and the improved AV-60N contraprop featuring an automatic feathering system were rapidly developed. By the end of the decade all Tu-95s were equipped with the autofeathering system, which is credited with saving many lives in emergencies. As an extra bonus, the new powerplant boasted a longer service life and higher reliability.

The very first long-range flights showed that the flight deck ergonomics left a lot to be desired, complicating operations a good deal. The cabin pressurisation and ventilation system was horrible, drawing the greatest number of complaints. At altitudes of 8,000-9,000 m (26,250-29,530 ft) or higher it was impossible to fly the aircraft without wearing oxygen masks. The crew seats were uncomfortable, causing fatigue, and the excuse for an on-board toilet fitted to the Tu-95 gave rise to the unwritten rule: 'He who useth the toilet washeth the flight deck after the mission'.

Winter operations were a separate can of worms, even in the southern regions (the Ukraine and the North Caucasus), to say nothing of the northern bases and Kazakhstan where winter temperatures could go as low as –40°C (–40°F). A peculiarity of the NK-12 turboprop was that much of the oil in the engine's capacious lubrication system was accommodated full time in the massive reduction gearbox. This oil would congeal in frosty weather; as a result, the Tu-95's combat readiness during the winter season was compromised by the need to pre-heat the engines, using mobile heaters. This was a time-consuming process which cost many a sleepless night for the ground crews, who often had to reach the hardstands three to four hours ahead of the scheduled take-off. At forward operating locations that lacked proper ground support equipment, the Tu-95s had to go through an engine run-up and warm-up cycle

Above: A Tu-95MA awaits the next mission on the taxiway of a DA base.

Below: A Tu-95MA attracts the attention of a US Air Force McDonnell Douglas F-4E-34-MC Phantom II (67-0234) from the 57th FIS at Keflavik.

Bottom: A US Navy F-4N of VF-21 embarked on USS *Coral Sea* intercepts a Tu-95M coded '75 Red'.

Above: An F-4S from CVW-5 embarked on USS *Midway* maintains a *very* close interest in a Tu-95MR (note the IFR probe and lateral ELINT blisters).

Right: A *Bear* conducts visual reconnaissance of USS *Saratoga* (CV-60).

A view of an escorting RAF BAC Lightning F.6 through the co-pilot's window of a Tu-95.

every three to six hours (depending on the ambient temperature) in order the keep the oil from congealing. After shutdown the engines had to be immediately encased in thick quilted covers to keep them warm as long as possible. Quite apart from the waste of time and human resources, such cycling of the engines created additional maintenance problems and took its toll on engine life, the early-production NK-12s' time between overhauls (TBO) being unpalatably low as it was. The problem persisted until the All-Union Petroleum Products Research Institute (VNII NP – *Vsesoyooznyy naoochno-issledovatel'skiy institoot nefteprodooktov*) developed new grades of transmission oil which retained acceptable viscosity parameters right down to –25° C (–13° F), allowing the engines to be started without preheating. Special ground support systems were also designed.

Yet, aircrew transition to the Tu-95 proved relatively smooth. By the end of the 1950s, two Long-Range Aviation regiments were fully equipped with the type. Concurrently, the Long-Range Aviation began setting up *ad hoc* tactical airfields in tundra areas of the Arctic region, which placed the bombers within practical striking distance of strategic targets in North America. These forward operating locations (FOLs) were quite tricky to use, as the runway width was only slightly greater than the aircraft's wingspan. Tu-95s and Tu-95Ms operated from such airfields during Exercise *Koopol* (Dome) with a view to training to attack the USA.

Coming back to the 79th TBAD and the 1023rd TBAP, it should be mentioned that the regiment operated the basic bomber version until 1982, when it re-equipped with the Tu-95MS. Apart from bombers, the 1023rd TBAP operated Tu-95MR long-range reconnaissance aircraft. According to some sources, the Tu-95MRs made trans-Atlantic flights on their missions, using San Antonio de los Baños AB on Cuba for a refuelling stop and crew rest.

In 1959 the 1006th TBAP in Uzin became the first unit to operate the Tu-95K missile strike version. Two years later the *Bear-B* entered service with the 1226th TBAP of the 79th TBAD at Chagan AB. Now that the missile carriers had entered service, the SES personnel handled the Kh-20 missiles' nuclear warheads.

In the early days of Tu-95K operations, mission preparation required as much as 12 hours. Later, when the units built up the numbers on the type, the preparation time was reduced to 4.5 hours.

The following is an excerpt from the recollections of Col. Vladimir V. Yegorov (Retd.), a Long-Range Aviation pilot who flew various versions of the Tu-95 for many years. Upon retirement from the Air Force he became Vice-Director of the Tupolev PLC's Training and Methodical Centre.

'Having graduated from the Tambov Military Pilot College in 1979, in December of that year I was posted

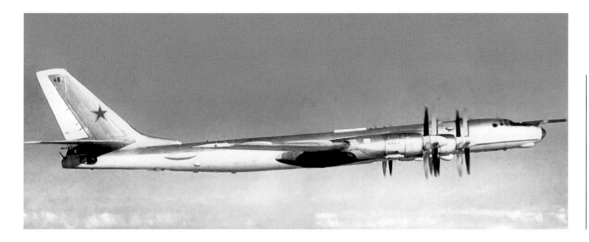

Tu-95MR '46 Red', a 1023rd TBAP aircraft, in cruise flight. The aircraft wears the same partial 'anti-flash' colour scheme as the Tu-95A and Tu-95MA bombers; the tactical code is now applied to the nose gear doors in much smaller digits and repeated on the fin.

Here a Tu-95MR (the sole example with no IFR probe) is escorted by a US Navy McDonnell Douglas F/A-18A-11-MC Hornet (BuNo 161927/ 'NK-300') from VFA-113 embarked on USS *Independence* in early 1989.

A Tu-95MR in action with all camera ports open, escorted by an F-4N.

65

Tu-95MR '65 Red', 43rd TsBP i PLS, Dyagilevo AB

with the 1223rd TBAP based near Semipalatinsk. (Sic; Yegorov consistently uses this number but the unit was actually the 1023rd TBAP! – Auth.) Soon I became a Tu-95 co-pilot in the crew captained by one of the division's most experienced pilots, detachment commander Maj. V. I. Manayev. The 1223rd TBAP was part of the 79th TBAD which, in turn, constituted part of the Long-Range Aviation Corps headquartered in Irkutsk (the 8th Independent Heavy Bomber Corps – Auth.).

In those days the regiment was equipped with Tu-95s [sans suffixe], Tu-95Ms, Tu-95MR-2s, a Tu-116 (sic; the was

Tu-116 at Chagan belonged to a different unit – Auth.) and the [one-off] Tu-95V (Tu-95-202). The latter aircraft earned the local nickname ko**bel'** (male dog – Auth.) because of the very distinctive bomb semi-recessed in the open bomb bay (and resembling a dog's genitals! – Auth.).

From the outset of my flying career with the unit, having made the required familiarisation flights, I was assigned to the third flying shift. As co-pilot I flew a 12-hour sortie, which was standard practice for the DA's Tu-95 and Tu-95M crews. On that occasion we flew to the North Pole

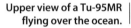

Upper view of a Tu-95MR flying over the ocean.

Below: The starboard side of the Tu-95MR's nose, showing the fuel line conduit running back from the IFR probe.

Bottom: Tu-95MR '65 Red' on the flight line at Dyagilevo AB. Note the narrow vertical window on the port side of the navigator's station instead of the usual horizontal glazing segments – a feature unique to the *Bear-E*.

and back, covering a distance of more than 9,000 km [5,590 miles]. This mission earned me my first commendation from the regiment's command – an honorary diploma "For reaching the North Pole".

This was my first flight over such a long distance, and it left a lasting impression; consider that before my assignment to that regiment I had not flown sorties lasting more than three hours (that was in the Tu-16K [missile carrier]). Even though later there would be hundreds of flights in various versions of the Tu-95, including missions over even longer distances, my first sortie in the Tu-95M was etched in my memory for life. Prior to that, on two flight shifts, I had taken a special familiarisation course involving daytime and night flights close to the base lasting 15 to 40 minutes. This had been preceded by a theoretical conversion training course which I completed in mid-January 1980.

My condition after the first long-range sortie can only be described as "bewildered"; it took me nearly 48 hours to regain my normal self. The worst bit was the constant and monotonous roar and vibrations from the powerplant that tended to lull you to oblivion, and the need to sit almost motionless for such a long time while wearing an oxygen mask. Added to this, there was the accelerated change of the time of day (as the aircraft moved against the sun – Auth.). Realising that I was still "green", the rest of the crew treated me with understanding and compassion during the mission. At any rate, knowing that I was not married yet, they kept feeding me various treats provided by their wives; this helped to cushion the impact of that first long-range flight in the Tu-95M. This first mission made me realise how close-knit the crew of a strategic aircraft is and how much depends

One of several flights of Tu-95Ks that participated in the October Revolution anniversary parade in Moscow on 7th November 1961.

Below: A Tu-95K coded '20 Red' makes a flypast at an air event in 1961; note the varying shades of the wing skin panels. The Kh-20 missile is painted red to make it more conspicuous.

Below right: Close-up of the semi-recessed missile, showing the retractable fairing closing the air intake.

on each crewmember doing his job properly during the mission. Subsequent flights took the edge off my emotions, and long-range sorties in the Tu-95 became easy to take from an emotional and psychological standpoint.

Within three months I had logged about 50 hours' total time as a Tu-95 pilot. That was when my first exercise in division strength began. 38 out of 40 Tu-95s operated by the division's two regiments were involved (the other unit – the 1226th TBAP – operated Tu-95K and Tu-95KM missile carriers). In the course of the exercise the crews of both regiments performed in-flight refuelling, practice launches of Kh-20M missiles and bombing attacks with all

compatible conventional bombs at two target ranges (in Kazakhstan and in the Far East). The missions took us over ranges in excess of 10,000 km [6,213 miles], lasting up to 14 hours. It has to be said this was the normal scenario for a division-strength exercise in the DA at the time; each regiment would put up 18-20 aircraft – that is, all available machines. This characterises the Soviet Long-Range Aviation's combat readiness and state in those days.

In addition to proficiency training and live weapons training, the crews of our division routinely flew SIGINT missions along the borders of the potential adversary (the

Another trio of Tu-95Ks performing at an air parade.

Below: A rare shot of a Tu-95KM taking off from an unpaved runway at a forward operating location.

Bottom: A Kh-20 missile is wheeled in beneath a Tu-95K, tail first. A technician prepares the BD-206 pylon for hooking up the missile.

NATO nations) and tracked the movements of US Navy carrier task forces in the Pacific, using our SIGINT, photo and radiation reconnaissance equipment. As a rule, such missions were flown by a Tu-95MR-2 accompanied by a Tu-95KM from our "brother unit", the 1226th TBAP. They included refuelling from M-4-2 or 3MS tankers (3MS-2 – Auth.) on the outbound and inbound legs; the tankers were operated by the 73rd TBAD/401st TBAP (sic; the 40th TBAP – Auth.) based at Blagoveshchensk. The reconnaissance sorties could last as long as 24-27 hours; each crew flew three or four such ultra-long missions annually.

In 1981 I started flying an IFR-equipped Tu-95MR-2 as co-pilot in the crew captained by the regiment's Deputy CO Lt.-Col. V. F. Aksyonov. With this move to the reconnaissance aircraft, the most interesting part of my flying career began, including in-flight refuelling sessions. In the spring of 1981 I made my first IFR technique familiarisation flight, flying the machine from the co-pilot's seat. My captain taught me how to maintain formation with the tanker and what to do during the contact and the fuel transfer. It should be noted that IFR was arguably the most complex kind of flight training in the DA, and proficiency in IFR procedures was the ultimate criterion of the Long-Range Aviation crews' training levels.

After making a series of familiarisation flights I began flying routine SIGINT/PHOTINT sorties in the Tu-95MR-2 along the borders of NATO nations and over the Pacific and Arctic Oceans (the Arctic missions took me further over the North Atlantic). We followed several regular routes, staying airborne for 20 hours or more.

By the end of 1983, when our regiment converted to the more modern Tu-95MS, I had flown the Tu-95M, the Tu-95MR-2 – and 'The Dog'. Within this time frame I had made six or so ultra-long-range sorties in the Tu-95MR-2.

61

A late-production Tu-95K with a PRS-4 gun-laying radar
and an 'Excellent aircraft' maintenance award badge

In each case the aircraft was painstakingly prepared by the regiment's ground personnel; as a result, no major malfunctions that could jeopardise the mission occurred during these flights.

During the sorties over the Pacific we were frequently confronted by Japanese Air Self-Defence Force aircraft and US Navy carrier-borne fighters near Alaska, the Aleutian Islands, Japan, the Philippines and Guam. When flying over the North Atlantic we had encounters with Royal Air Force, Royal Norwegian Air Force, USAF and US Navy fighters (the [BAC] Lightning, [Convair] F-106A, [McDonnell] F-4J and F-4D, [Grumman] F-14A, [Grumman] A-6 and other types). We shadowed carrier task forces led by the aircraft carriers USS Midway and USS Constellation.

The shipboard fighters tried to stop us from fulfilling our mission. Their favourite tactic was to position themselves beneath our aircraft, obstructing the cameras' field of view, or fly ahead of our aircraft or close to the propellers in an attempt to force us off the desired track during the photo run. Secondly, they would manoeuvre around our machine and display their weapons, hinting at a possible attack; this was very unnerving, considering that all we could oppose them with was AM-23 cannons, which were no match for the adversary's air-to-air missiles having a much longer "kill" range. The fighter crews took close-up pictures of our aircraft and us sitting in the cockpits; the pilots smiled and waved at us and then broke formation, returning to their base or the carrier. Occasionally, however, we ran into another kind of guys. The black pilots acted especially tough, blocking our moves with set, emotionless faces. We, too, took pictures of them with our hand-held cameras and hailed them, occasionally making gestures to make clear our request to let us do our job. Usually we reached an understanding.

The climax of the mission was the moment when the aircraft broke through the overcast after cruising for hours on end and we would suddenly find ourselves over a convoy comprising an aircraft carrier escorted by ten or twelve other warships. After this we would photograph

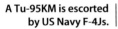

A Tu-95KM is escorted
by US Navy F-4Js.

An early Tu-95KM (note the lack of ELINT blisters on the rear fuselage)

12   9802008

the ships at low altitude, circling over the convoy for 20-30 minutes; then we climbed to 10,000 m [32,810 ft] or so and headed for the spot where we were to rendezvous with the tanker. After topping off the tanks with 35 tons [77,160 lb] of fuel we headed back to base, covering the remaining 5,000 km [3,100 miles] to Semipalatinsk almost in a straight line in autopilot mode. This was the most emotional phase of the flight – and, in a way, the most dangerous one. After all, the objective had been completed; now came the anti-climax and fatigue started to show, and there were still six to seven hours to go and the ensuing landing. This was when the risk of crew error was at its highest; the captain and I had to stay alert.

I would like to stress again that in the Long-Range Aviation a lot depended on the psychological climate within each specific crew, on how the captain got along with the rest of the crew, as well as on the training levels and crew resources management. In a way, a strategic aircraft is similar to a submarine: if each man does his job well, everybody wins; if one man screws up, everybody dies.

And even though you knew that you were sitting on a parachute and that the conveyor belt built into the flight deck floor would help you bail out through the nosewheel well in an emergency, it was better to make sure that an emergency did not happen.'

Close-up of the nose of Tu-95KM '12 Black' upgraded from a very early production Tu-95K (c/n 9802008). The photo was taken in the early 1960s when the *Bears* still displayed the c/n visibly and wore the code on the forward fuselage in huge characters.

A Tu-95KM is chased by a BAC Lightning F.6 (XR764/'AE') near the British Isles.

Tu-95K-22s often carried RR8311-100 air sampling pods for RINT duties. Here the noses of the pods can be seen peeking out from under the wing leading edge.

Low-altitude and high-altitude penetration of the potential adversary's air defences was refined during the early 1960s, using *Bear-As*. Flights of single bombers and formations were undertaken at altitudes that often did not exceed 200 m (660 ft).

In addition to the regular bomber regiments, a special independent bomber squadron operating nuclear-capable Tu-95As and Tu-95MAs was set up. It was tasked with a multitude of missions associated with nuclear testing and development of nuclear strike tactics. Most of the squadron's aircraft were assigned to it temporarily, returning to their usual regiments after one or two live nuclear missions. This was because the Tu-95 took a lot of punishment in the course of such tests due to the effects of the blast; after dropping a high-yield H-bomb entire skin panels had to be

Tu-95K-22 '35 Red' loaded with Kh-22 missiles runs up the engines at a dispersal area.

replaced. The engines, too, often had to be changed after a nuclear test mission. For the duration the aircraft seconded to the squadron were fitted out with test and recording equipment, as well as radiation measurement instruments; the lateral observation blisters in the rear pressure cabin were sometimes blanked off.

Aircraft operated by first-line units, too, occasionally dropped nukes during test missions. For instance, a 106th TBAD Tu-95 captained by Iona Bazhenov, the senior political officer in one of the two regiments at Chagan AB, dropped an H-bomb during a mission in regiment strength, and every crew experienced how it feels when a 2.5-megaton nuke goes off. Bazhenov's aircraft was subsequently relegated to the Kiev Military Aviation Engineering College (KVVAIU – *Kiyevskoye vyssheye voyennoye aviatsionnoye inzhenernoye oochilishche*) as an instructional airframe.

Tu-95s were used to drop nuclear bombs at three sites of the Semipalatinsk Proving Ground until the early 1960s. For example, in the spring of 1960 a Tu-95MA dropped a 20-megaton bomb at the Sary-Shagan test range.

The Soviet leader Nikita S. Khrushchov's 'missile itch' inevitably affected the Tu-95. As the Strategic Missile Forces (RVSN – *Raketnyye voyska strategicheskovo naznacheniya*) developed rapidly, heavy bomber units were disbanded or transferred to the new service as missile units; many in the Soviet government shared Khrushchov's views that ballistic missiles would take over all strategic strike functions. Realising the threat to the strategic bomber force, which was small as it was, Long-Range Aviation Commander Air Marshal Vladimir A. Soodets did his best to preserve it. The units equipped with Tu-95M bombers were assigned new tasks; their mission was now to attack military bases, harbours, troop concentrations and other compact

targets. The *Bear*'s weapons arsenal was expanded by adding APM and MDM anti-shipping mines and Type 45-53 torpedoes (450 mm/17⁴⁵⁄₆₄ in calibre. 1953 model); most of them were rehashed versions of pre-war weapons.

Taking advantage of the fact that the Long-Range Aviation's bombers were the only Soviet aircraft capable of patrolling remote areas of the world ocean, the Soviet Navy's Commander Adm. Sergey G. Gorshkov attempted to gain control over them. For starters the DA crews were tasked with detecting nuclear-powered

A Tu-95KM carrying no missile (that is, flying a reconnaissance sortie) is examined by a sharkmouthed Grumman F-14A from VF-111 at NAS Miramar.

Here, a Tu-95K-22 flies a practice sortie with at least one Kh-22 missile (on the centreline pylon); the missile's rear end with the folded ventral fin is just visible.

As a Tu-95K taxies to the hardstand after landing, the outer engines are shut down early to save fuel and conserve engine life.

missile submarines by means of… the Mk 1 eyeball, as the bombers had no ASW equipment whatever! Several patrol missions were flown over the Norwegian Sea, but the only 'submarine' the crews succeeded in detecting was a whale surfacing to take a breath. True, Gorshkov did demand that the *Bears* be fitted with ASW gear (at the expense of their primary bomber function), but this

was never done. The only special equipment that was fitted eventually were RR8311-100 air sampling pods carried on pylons under the outer wings; these were used for monitoring radiation levels over Soviet nuclear proving grounds and territories adjacent to foreign test ranges. (The latter means the Chinese Lop Nor Proving Ground at Malan in Xinjiang Province; for these

Opposite page, top left: The crew of a 79th TBAP Tu-95K-22 poses for a photo under the aircraft's tail at Ookraïnka AB.

Tu-95K '32 Red' was not updated to Tu-95KM standard and may be withdrawn from use in this photo, judging by the absence of the fire extinguisher that is normally placed ahead of operational DA aircraft when parked.

missions the Tu-95s were redeployed to bases in the Transbaikalian and Far Eastern Military Districts. The US, British and French test ranges in the Pacific were then out of reach.)

The need for air sampling equipment was all the more acute because occasionally two or three nuclear devices could be detonated at the same range in one day; the Novaya Zemlya proving ground was used most actively. Using ground equipment in these conditions was impossible, leaving aircraft as the sole means of observing the explosion and measuring the radioactive fallout. Interestingly, after the post-mission analysis the paper filters from the air sampling pods

Above: The crew of a Tu-95MS missile strike aircraft report mission readiness to the unit CO.

The nose of a Tu-95KM with the three landing/taxi lights deployed.

Below: Tu-95K-22 '52 Red' with RR8311-100 air sampling pods prepares for take-off.

The crew of this *Bear-G* is ready to fly but the snow-covered aircraft sure needs a bit of cleaning! Note the fire extinguisher placed in front of the bomber.

were discarded, and the personnel used them as toilet paper. One can only guess the consequences…

Given the high risk of a NATO air strike against the Soviet strategic bomber bases, the DA command, which had little faith in the Air Defence Force, attached high priority to rapidly redeploying the Tu-95 units in case of need – both in order to get closer to the targets and in order to get out of harm's way. Hence each bomber regiment had a convoy of lorries loaded with the necessary minimum support equipment and ready to move out to 'Wherever AB' at short notice. The plan was to disperse the bombers mainly to civil airports, the units' own alternate airbases and bases occupied by Tactical Aviation units.

All efforts notwithstanding, the DA's airfield network was scant. Not only that, but the bases themselves left a lot to be desired; the bombers were parked in the open (there were no revetments), the hardstands were cramped and the runways were too narrow. Trying to solve the problem, 106th TBAD CO Aleksandr I. Molodchiy set about organising the construction of a reserve base for his two regiments. Since this was almost a private venture, construction materials and equipment had to be sourced wherever possible; this was a nerve-racking job and eventually the division CO was hospitalised with a heart attack.

Some people suggested using FOLs with dirt airstrips for Tu-95 operations in case of need. The Tupolev OKB objected strongly, stating that the bomber's landing gear was not designed to take such a punishment. Yet, DA Commander Air Marshal Vladimir

A. Soodets insisted, and eventually trials began. A huge dirt runway was prepared in a field not far from an existing airbase near the Volga River. Two aircraft were involved – a Tu-16 captained by M. A. Arkatov and a Tu-95 captained by Vasiliy V. Reshetnikov. Tupolev OKB personnel and GNIKI VVS test pilots were also involved, drawing up a trials programme which envisaged taxi runs at gradually increasing speed; the engines, propellers and landing gear were to be checked for damage after each run. However, the Tu-95 lifted off immediately on the very first run involving a rotation, landing on the concrete runway at the nearby base.

In maximum take-off weight configuration the Tu-95 required a run of more than 4,000 m (13,120 ft) to take off from the dirt strip but did become airborne eventually. Encouraged by these results, the Long-Range Aviation began hurriedly constructing tactical airstrips in the tundra and bringing in supplies of most-wanted items required for bomber operations; some of these airstrips even featured control towers and other airfield infrastructure. The post of the Commander of the Arctic Sector was established in the Air Force.

The personnel's living conditions at the tundra airstrips were horrendous. Moreover, the airstrips were usable only for a few months, turning soggy when the rains set in and taking a long time to dry up again. One more problem was the added stress and strain on the aircraft structure during rough-field operations; the Tupolev OKB imposed a limit on such operations, one landing on a dirt strip equalling three landings on a paved runway. Later, the DA started using tactical runways marked on the Arctic ice with black cloth banners; the conditions at the ice airfields were even worse. The first landing on an ice runway and subsequent take-off from same were performed by 106th TBAD CO Col. Vasiliy V. Reshetnikov in 1958.

Tu-95 crews became increasingly vocal in their demands for an upgrade to the *Bear*'s avionics. The bomber's navigation system was of little help over the Arctic Ocean where there were no landmarks, the magnetic compass was useless and celestial navigation was unreliable. In the mid-1960s the Tu-95M fleet underwent a mid-life update concerning the avionics; among other things, a new Rubin-1D radar was installed, the Meridian long-range radio navigation system was replaced by a more sophisticated ADNS-4 LORAN, a DISS-1 Doppler speed and drift sensor system and an RSBN-2SV SHORAN system were added.

The Tu-95K missile carrier joined the operational inventory in late 1959. During the early 1960s, the Soviet Long-Range Aviation began tackling the task of getting the missile-carrying variants of the Tu-95 up to fully operational status. The *Bear-B* created a veritable sensation when it participated in the 7th November 1961 parade in Moscow's Red Square marking the anniversary of the October Revolution. Sixteen Tu-95Ks with missiles arrived from Uzin for the occasion; the missiles were painted red for the benefit of the spectators. Afterwards, the bomber crews were invited to a banquet in the Kremlin.

In keeping with a General Staff directive dated 12th May 1962 and a directive signed by the DA Commander

on 23rd July same year, the 182nd *Sevastopol'sko-Berlinskiy* GvTBAP (*Gvardeyskiy tyazholyy bombardirovochnyy aviapolk* – Guards Heavy Bomber Regiment), which had been disbanded just a month earlier, was re-formed at Mozdok in what was then the North Ossetian Autonomous Soviet Socialist Republic, reporting to the 106th TBAD. The unit was to fly Tu-95Ks and have a complement of 28 crews; nine of them were fully qualified for day/night operations by the time the unit was commissioned. The unit's first flying training shift was on 31st August 1962 while the unit was temporarily equipped with Tu-16s; a 182nd GvTBAP crew made the first Tu-95K sortie from Mozdok on 8th September 1962. In October three Tu-95Ms and five Tu-95Ks were operating from Mozdok.

On 14th February 1963 the 409th TBAP in Uzin took delivery of its first Tu-95KM with IFR capability and improved avionics. That same year Tu-95KMs were delivered to the 182nd GvTBAP, which commenced daytime IFR training; the unit's Deputy CO (Flight Training) Lt.-Col. A. Ya. Grigor'yev was the first to perform a refuelling session. A total of eight crews mastered the IFR procedure.

The Tu-95 units found the IFR techniques to be a major challenge. On early Soviet hose-and-drogue tankers the drogue weighed more than 200 kg (440 lb) and was rather unstable, swaying crazily in the slipstream; hence making contact with the tanker required good flying skills. The refuelling process took some 20 minutes because of the low fuel transfer rate and other reasons, and keeping formation with the

A Tu-95K-22 fitted with air sampling pods takes off on a routine sortie.

71

Tu-95U '71 Red', 43rd TsBP i PLS, Dyagilevo AB

tanker for so long took a lot of effort; the bomber pilots would lose a couple of pounds in the process!

Some serious accidents with near-disastrous consequences happened during in-flight refuelling. On at least two separate occasions (in 1973 and 1983) the tanker's hose broke and became entangled around the receiver aircraft, nearly causing it to lose control. There was a case when the drogue was ingested into the propeller of a Tu-95KM, ruining it completely; the bomber barely made it back to base. On another occasion the receiver aircraft overshot and collided with the tanker, losing part of the vertical tail and seriously damaging the tanker; luckily, both aircraft landed safely.

Yet, it was as nothing compared to the scenario when you did not make the rendezvous with the tanker for any reason; then you really were in deep trouble. In April 1978 a 1226th TBAP Tu-95KM captained by V. I. Polegayev flew a sortie to check the weather along the designated route before the entire regiment flew along the route during an exercise. Eight hours into the mission, things started to go wrong. The tanker waiting at Tiksi to refuel the Tu-95KM was unable to take off because of below-minima weather. The nearest alternate airfields shut down for the same reason, and there was not enough fuel to make the destination airfield. Yet, necessity is the mother of invention. The aircraft was carrying a Kh-20 missile; thinking fast, the crew lowered it into launch position and started the engine without release, using the missile as a fifth engine. It worked, but the problems continued snowballing: there was a heavy thunderstorm at the destination airfield. Fortunately it subsided just as the aircraft got there, landing with just 2,000 kg (4,410 lb) of fuel remaining.

Other problems unique to the missile carrier version were associated with hooking up the Kh-20 missile. When the latter was wheeled in on its ground handling dolly, the extremely limited clearance would often cause the missile's fin to strike the bomber's belly, wiping out the data link receiver antenna on the fin tip. Moreover, at the start of the Tu-95K's service career the arming procedure took 22 hours (!); in due course this was shortened to four hours.

The 182nd GvTBAP began practicing missile launches in 1963. Three crews captained by squadron commander Lt.-Col. V. P. Fisuchenko, squadron commander Maj. V. P. Kuznetsov and detachment commander Maj. A. P. Merkoolov led the way; Merkoolov was the first to make a Kh-20 launch. In the 1960s the 182nd GvTBAP launched an average of four to seven live missiles annually. Additionally, every year the unit performed 8-12 ELINT and 'carrier hunting' sorties in the Atlantic Ocean.

Of course, the Tu-95s flying close to the shores of Western Europe or approaching NATO task forces exercising in the Atlantic were detected in timely fashion by air defence radars, and fighters would scramble to see what they were up to and ward off the uninvited guests. For example, on 24th August 1966 Royal Navy de Havilland Sea Vixen fighters were launched from HMS *Ark Royal* to intercept and escort a Tu-95KM checking up on Exercise *Straitlaced* in the North Sea. In the 1970s, such intercepts were usually performed by RAF English Electic Lightnings and McDonnell Douglas F-4K Phantom IIs, or by Royal Navy British Aerospace Sea Harrier FRS.1s. In British military jargon, unidentified aircraft approaching the British Isles and being intercepted/escorted by RAF or Royal

371

Top: A Tu-95KM is refuelled by a 3MS-2 tanker.

Centre and above: These pictures show how things could go wrong if the tanker failed to maintain altitude, creating a whiplash effect and snapping the hose.

Navy fighters were known as 'trade' – and the amount of 'trade' varied from lots in certain months to none at all. Occasionally the *Bears* had similar encounters with French Navy (*Aéronavale*) Dassault Super Etendards.

During such intercepts it was a standing rule that neither aircraft may use the other as a practice target, so as to avoid incidents caused by itchy trigger fingers. Sometimes the mood was almost relaxed, the crews of the interceptor and the interceptee taking pictures of

each other's aircraft (for the fighters this was normal procedure providing photo proof of a successful intercept. Such photos came with official captions which occasionally could be rather amusing, like *'The Crusader was from the US Aircraft Carrier Independence and with other aircraft was sent up to keep tabs on the Bear, a* **four-engine piston reconnaissance plane which is a military version of the Russian Tu-114 airliner***'* (original style retained, our highlighting – *Auth.*).

In 1983 the 409th TBAP bid farewell to the *Bear*, converting to Ilyushin IL-78 *Midas-A* tanker/transports and becoming the 409th APSZ (*aviapolk samolyotov-zaprahvshchikov* – Aerial Refuelling Regiment). The Tu-95Ms phased out by this unit and by the 1023rd TBAP were transferred to the 40th TBAP of the 73rd TBAD at Ookraïnka AB in the Far East (Khabarovsk Region).

The Tu-95K and Tu-95KM were regular participants of various exercises. The most important ones were the so-called 'ministerial level' exercises (that is, the ones monitored by the Minister of Defence). The new DA Commander Vasiliy V. Reshetnikov recalled that when Marshal Rodion Ya. Malinovskiy was Minister of Defence the exercises were brief, with a dynamic scenario, albeit involving a limited the number of tasks. When Malinovskiy was succeeded by Marshal Andrey A. Grechko, such exercises were conducted on a larger scale, involving huge expanses of territory and multiple arms and services. When Marshal Dmitriy F. Ustinov became Minister of Defence, the exercises became more like a show for the benefit of the military top brass, various invited observers and the press. The exercises held under the auspices of the DA Commander ranked lower but were taken more seriously and were closer to a real-life war scenario, likewise involving interaction with other arms and services. It turned out that, unless the plan of the exercise was leaked to the opposing force by intermediaries in the headquarters, a group of Tu-95Ks had a reasonably good chance of travelling thousands of kilometres at low level in loose formation without being detected. However, the OKB imposed a limit on the number of hours to be flown at low level because the turbulence had a drastic impact on the airframe's fatigue life; one hour at low altitude equalled two hours at high altitude.

On 11th June 1969 the 182nd GvTBAP performed a first-of-a-kind mission for the Long-Range Aviation when nine Tu-95KMs flew a long-range sortie with two fuel top-ups. The first group of aircraft led by Maj. Shishkaryov headed towards the Azores Islands, staying airborne for 31 hours. Another group led by Lt.-Col. V. P. Fisuchenko skirted the shores of Greenland; the mission lasted 30 hours 13 minutes.

The *Bear-B/C* was not destined to become the main component of the Soviet nuclear triad, being overshadowed by ICBMs. Here we have to mention Soviet-US strategic arms limitation treaties. The SALT I

A Tu-95MS operated by the 43rd Training Centre in Ryazan'.

treaty signed in 1972 did not include missile carriers, which gave the USA a certain advantage because the USAF possessed a large number of B-52s carrying AGM-28 Hound Dog air-to-surface missiles. On the other hand, the treaty was never implemented. The SALT II treaty signed on 18th June 1979 did include missile carriers; ASMs with a range in excess of 600 km (372 miles) were listed as strategic. Yet the Soviet government refused to provide full details of the aircraft types in service with the Air Force and the Naval Aviation, causing complications with the identification of specific models; as a result, the USA listed all versions of the *Bear* (except the Tu-95RTs and the Tu-142) and the Myasishchev *Bison* family as strategic aircraft. A lot of wrangling ensued, but in December 1979 Soviet troops entered Afghanistan, and the outbreak of the

A Tu-95MS is refuelled by an IL-78 over heavy overcast. The curvature of the wings is a trick of the wide-angle lens.

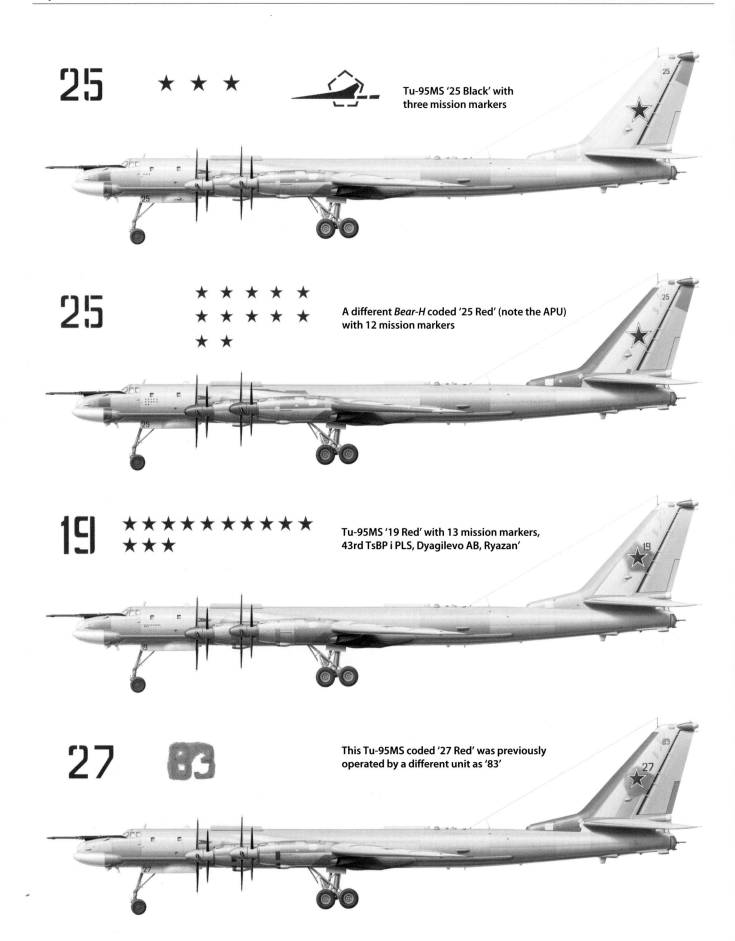

Tu-95MS '25 Black' with
three mission markers

A different *Bear-H* coded '25 Red' (note the APU)
with 12 mission markers

Tu-95MS '19 Red' with 13 mission markers,
43rd TsBP i PLS, Dyagilevo AB, Ryazan'

This Tu-95MS coded '27 Red' was previously
operated by a different unit as '83'

Afghan War rendered the issue moot – the US Congress refused to ratify the SALT II treaty.

Operational experience with the Tu-95K/KM showed that some of the weight-saving measures (the removal of certain equipment items) were unwarranted; hence the 1RSB-70 command link radio was reinstated. Various upgrades were made in service. Thus, the RSIU-4 communications radio was replaced first by the RSIU-5 and then by the more advanced R-832; the ARK-5 Amur direction finder gave way to the ARK-11 ADF. The RV-2 low-range radio altimeter was replaced by the RV-UM model, while the RV-25 high-range radio altimeter was superseded by the RV-17; a KS-6D attitude and heading reference system and a Put'-1B navigation system were added. All of this improved navigation accuracy and missile aiming accuracy perceptibly.

Another new item was the *Toocha* (Storm cloud) weather/navigation radar developed in the 1006th TBAP at Uzin; it comprised the radar set of the RBP-3 radar connected to the existing antenna of the Tu-95K's YaD target illumination radar. The modification was a bit tricky to do but worked better than predicted. In due course all *Bear-B/Cs* were retrofitted with the Toocha radar.

In the 1970s an attempt was made to make the Tu-95K/KM more versatile by giving it conventional bombing capability. Since the weapons bay was occupied by the hydraulically powered missile pylon precluding internal bomb carriage, the designers considered using two KMB bomb dispenser pods hooked up to the missile rack. A simple collimator sight would be installed in the navigator's observation blister on the port side of the forward fuselage. Such aircraft

were to attack airfields and mobile intermediate-range ballistic missiles which were considered a serious threat. According to estimates, just ninety-six RBK-500 cluster bombs (*rahzovaya **bom**bovaya kas**set**a* – disposable bomb cassette) housing 0.5-kg (1.1-lb) ShOAB-0.5 fragmentation bomblets stuffed with metal pellets (*sha**rikovaya oskol**ochnaya **a**via**bom**ba*) would be enough to wipe out a platoon of Pershing IRBMs in daylight conditions. Eventually the project did not proceed beyond the experimental stage.

To facilitate the mastering of the *Bear*, in 1983 the Long-Range Aviation's 43rd TsBP i PLS at Dyagilevo AB in Ryazan' disbanded its Tu-16 squadron and established a Tu-95 squadron instead. Designated the 2nd UTBAE (*oo**cheb**naya tya**zho**laya bombardi**rov**ochnaya **a**viaeskad**ril**'ya* – heavy bomber training

'49 Red', a typical *Bear-H* with an 'Excellent aircraft' badge.

A view of a Tu-95MS from an intercepting fighter, showing the tell-tale exhaust stains on the wing underside and main gear fairings.

A Tu-95MS coded
'05 Red' blends with the
thick cloud cover
on a bleak day.

Here, a Tu-95MS has
garnered a mixed escort
of a US Navy F-14A and
a USAF McDonnell
Douglas F-15 Eagle.

squadron), it received one Tu-95 *sans suffixe*, two Tu-95Ms and one Tu-95MR in 1984.

Later, in the 1980s, the first-generation Tu-95K/KM regiments transitioned to the upgraded Tu-95K-22. In addition to their primary role these aircraft were used for air sampling duties in the wake of nuclear tests, carrying RR8311-100 pods under the wings. Again, consideration was given to fitting the Tu-95K-22 with KMB bomb dispensers but this came to nothing.

In 1984 the 79th GvTBAP of the 73rd TBAD based at Ookraïnka AB began its conversion to the Tu-95K-22. The unit's first six *Bear-Gs* arrived on 14th September that year, flown by the airmen of Sqn 1 commanded by Lt.-Col. Yu. A. Laptev. By the end of the year nine of the unit's crews had received their Tu-95K-22 type ratings and begun practice flights, including three sorties with the objective of locating US Navy carrier task forces. Speaking of which, 'carrier hunting' was one of the 79th GvTBAP's most typical missions. Between 1982 and 1993 the unit's crews usually went searching for the carriers USS *Kitty Hawk*, USS *Abraham Lincoln*, USS *Chester W. Nimitz* and USS *Carl Vinson*.

The conversion to the *Bear-G* proceeded at a fairly rapid pace. In April 1985 a pair of Tu-95K-22s captained by Maj. Ye. A. Nikolayev and Maj. A. I. Kozlov made a landing on a tactical airstrip beyond the Arctic Circle – the first such landing which had been made by the unit. On 14th August that year six 79th GvTBAP/Sqn 2 *Bear-Gs* captained by Maj. Ye. A. Nikolayev, Maj. A. A. Taranov, Maj. M. N. Prokhorov, Maj. V. S. Kozlov, Maj. S. A. Munusov and Maj. A. A. Vetloogin flew over the North Pole.

While the Long-Range Aviation units based in the European part of the Soviet Union flew missions 'around the corner' (*za* **oo***gol* – this Soviet Air Force slang term meant rounding the Kola Peninsula and flying westward over the North Atlantic), the strategic aircraft based east of the Urals prowled along the Alaskan shores. The Americans were quick to recognise the threat; when the Tu-95K-22 made its appearance over the North Pacific, Alaska's military threat level was upgraded to that of Western Europe. Alaska was perhaps the region where the policy of nuclear deterrence and 'sabre-rattling' was used most openly. For example, in March 1987 preparations for a Soviet-US summit involving General Secretary Mikhail S. Gorbachov and President Ronald Reagan were going full steam ahead. Yet it was in March and April 1987 that the USAF's McDonnell Douglas F-15 Eagle fighters serving with the 3rd Fighter Wing (FW) stationed at Elmendorf AFB in Alaska had to intercept visiting *Bears* no fewer than 12 times, whereas only six such 'visits' had been recorded in the preceding two months. To many Americans the slang expression 'bear in the air' signifies a police helicopter (because traffic cops are known as 'bears' for their distinctive 'Smokey the Bear' hats) – but for the pilots serving with the

3rd FW this expression probably had a rather different meaning!

When ICBMs were assigned the task of destroying targets of importance in the continental United States, US Navy carrier task forces and convoys in the Atlantic and Pacific Oceans gradually became the Tu-95K-22's primary targets. The *Bear-G* proved the most suitable platform for this mission, since it was armed with three Kh-22 air-to-surface missiles. And, given proper guidance, the Kh-22 was a potent weapon; its shaped-charge conventional warhead could tear a gaping 12-m (40-foot) hole in a ship's side.

The 1980s saw the introduction of yet another missile strike version – the Tu-95MS – into the Long-Range Aviation's inventory. The *Bear-H* attained IOC in 1982; the 1023rd TBAP of the 79th TBAD was the first to receive the aircraft, taking delivery of the first two machines on 17th December 1982; these were ferried from Taganrog to Chagan AB by factory test pilot Svyatoslav N. Gordiyenko and Sqn 2 commander Maj. S. V. Ivanov. It was immediately apparent that the new missile carrier suffered from teething troubles; as Andrey N. Tupolev had once remarked, '*A new aircraft is like a baby – you don't seriously expect it to leave the maternity ward wearing a steel helmet and brandishing a submachine gun*'. An intensive debugging effort began, and in April 1983 a 1023rd TBAP crew captained by Maj. A. Ya. Doobovik made the first practice launch of a Kh-55 missile. The evaluation programme at Chagan AB was unofficially dubbed AIST; *a*ist is Russian for 'stork', but the acronym denoted, rather tautologically, *aviatsi***on***nyye ispy***tah***nita samo***lyo***ta* **Too***poleva* – 'aviation testing of Tupolev's aircraft'!

In 1984 the division's other unit, the co-located 1226th TBAP, also began converting to the *Bear-H*; the 79th TBAD eventually built up its strength to 40 aircraft. Here is another quote from the recollections of former 1023rd TBAP pilot Col. Vladimir V. Yegorov (Retd.):

'*In December 1982 our regiment took delivery of the first two Tu-95MSs and their complement of Kh-55 cruise missiles. The new aircraft were parked on a special hardstand with a barbed wire fence around it; only the command staff of the division, the regiment and its Squadron 2 (which was the first to convert to the new hardware) had access to them. Sqn 2 was commanded by S. V. Ivanov, who eventually rose to Colonel and headed the flight safety section of the DA's 43rd Combat Training & Aircrew Conversion Centre at Dyagilevo AB. He was awarded the Combat Red Banner Order and the Red Star Order for his first flights in the Tu-95MS and the first launches of the Kh-55.*

As it re-equipped with the Tu-95MS, the 1223rd TBAP (1023rd TBAP – Auth.) was tasked with training "one and a half crews" for each aircraft (in order to have replacement personnel available in case one of the regular crew members was put out of action) within six months;

20

Tu-95MS '20 Black' with a Russian flag on the nose, the early 1990s

604

Tu-95MS '604 Black', a former Tupolev OKB 'dogship', named *Ryazan'* and bearing the city crest of Ryazan', 43rd TsBP i PLS, Dyagilevo AB

20 РЯЗАНЬ

The same aircraft at a later date as '20 Red', 43rd TsBP i PLS

РЯЗАНЬ
RF-94255
ВВС РОССИИ

20

The same aircraft in later days as '20 Red'/RF-94255 with Russian Air Force titles and tri-colour insignia

each crew was to be fully qualified for day and night operations, including IFR. As if that weren't enough, the unit passed on its previous hardware to the 401st TBAP at Ookraïnka AB and hence was to assist the latter regiment in converting from the Myasishchev tankers to the Tu-95M bomber and Tu-95MR recce aircraft (including two IFR-capable Tu-95MR-2s). The command staff and personnel of the 1223rd TBAP coped admirably with this double task.

At the time I was the co-pilot in the crew of regiment CO Col. I. V. Tyurinov and was handling two tasks at once, training 401st TBAP (40th TBAP – Auth.) pilots to fly the Tu-95MR-2 even as I took my training on the Tu-95MS. This was because I had been cleared to fly in the right-hand seat with all of the regiment's pilots.

At the end of February 1983, after completing a conversion training course at the production plant in Taganrog, I made the first flight in the right-hand seat of the new version. Later, after the familiarisation programme, I carried on as a Tu-95MS co-pilot; by December 1983 I had accumulated some 100 hours on the type. In October 1985 the 1223rd TBAP participated in a routine exercise on its new mounts. 14 out of 16 aircraft were airborne on that occasion, six of them making launches of Kh-55 missiles at the weapons system's maximum combat radius. As early as the end of 1983 the unit commenced combat patrols on the Tu-95MS in the north (near the Canadian coast), east (near Alaska and the Aleutian Islands) and north-west (near Iceland). Such missions lasted more than 20 hours, involving in-flight refuelling on the way out and on the return leg. The regiment started making full-scale use of the polar airfields in Olenegorsk, Tiksi and Anadyr' for such patrol missions.

At an early stage the crews started mastering new tactics and making use of the aircraft's enhanced capabilities during flights along preset routes. This brought about a qualitative change in the crews' training levels. In particular, each sortie included at least two "tactical" (that is, simulated) missile launches, the crew completing all pre-launch operations except actually releasing the missile.

In early 1984 the 1223rd TBAP began routine patrols of its assigned areas. Now we were intercepted by [McDonnell Douglas] F-15As and F/A-18As, as well as the familiar US Navy F-14As. In the spring of 1984 a crew captained by Lt.-Col. Puzanov launched six missiles in a single sortie; this marked the successful completion of the Tu-95MS's service evaluation period. At about the same time the Kh-55's ability to penetrate real-life air defences was tested. At the time I was the co-pilot in the CO's crew and also the executive officer's assistant for combat training.

In November 1984 I was dispatched to take the Tu-95 captain training course at the 43rd TsBP i PLS. Upon completion of the course in October 1985 I was assigned

A badge marking the 79th TBAP's golden jubilee in 1998.

This simple badge marks the unit's 70th anniversary in 1998.

Starboard side view of '20 Red' in early colours

'20 Red'/RF-94255 in late colours; the name and crest are applied differently, and the spinner tips are red, not blue

Tu-95MS '12 Red' *Moskva* bearing the city crest of Moscow, 184th TBAP

The same aircraft at a later date with tri-colour insignia, *VVS Rossiï* (Russian Air Force) titles and 10 mission markers

Tu-95MS '12 Red' *Moskva* and its crew clad in VMSK-3 waterproof flight suits for an overwater mission.

Starboard side view of the same aircraft; the Gold Star Medal is due to the fact that Moscow bears the Heroic City title

to a different unit – the 182nd GvTBAP in Mozdok, serving with the squadron commanded by Lt.-Col. A. A. Vavilov, son of the regiment's wartime CO. The unit operated Tu-95K and Tu-95KM missile carriers, and I now flew a Tu-95KM from the captain's seat. Now I had to make my mark as the captain. The 182nd GvTBAP boasted the highest level of training [in the Long-Range Aviation] as regards operations from forward operating locations and adverse-weather operations; this was because the unit's base was constantly plagued by foul weather, especially in the autumn and winter when the base could be engulfed by fog within 20-30 minutes. As a result, during this period of my Air Force service I had to operate from virtually all airbases in the European part of the USSR and in Central Asia.

During each flight along a predesignated route we would make simulated launches of the Kh-20 missile; this involved starting up the missile's engine and then following the missile's anticipated flight path until the moment when it was supposed to lock onto the target for terminal guidance. Tu-95 captains averaged 150-180 flight hours per annum, allowing flight crew and ground crew proficiency to be maintained at a high level. As a rule, scheduled exercises involving maximum-range sorties by at least 18 aircraft took place twice a year.

In September 1987 this unit, too, received its first Tu-95MS. Having been promoted to detachment commander by then and having 250 hours' total time on this version, I began flying sorties in this aircraft straight away with my old crew in October. The regiment's personnel was trained at the 43rd TsBP i PLS. Due to the crisis afflicting the country the unit did not receive its sixth and final Tu-95MS until 1990.

I served on with the 182nd GvTBAP until August 1988, flying the Tu-95MS all the while. During this period there were no major hardware failures requiring the mission to be aborted.

In August 1988 I was dispatched to the Air Force Academy named after Yuriy A. Gagarin, graduating in 1991, whereupon I returned to the 1223rd TBAP as deputy squadron commander. In January 1992 I was promoted to

squadron commander; that year I started learning the IFR procedure as a Tu-95MS captain. I was fortunate in that the unit's deputy CO Lt.-Col. S. A. Shavenkov was my instructor; he coached me gently through this complex procedure. After eight daylight training flights and seven night flights I felt I was ready to perform IFR on my own. However, seven of the ten crews in my squadron did not yet have their IFR ratings, and the division command sent them to Mozdok to take their training. The group of trainees was headed by Lt.-Col. V. P. Artamokhin, and the two of us managed to train the crews within three weeks.'

During 1985 the 1006th TBAP at Uzin AB also re-equipped with the Tu-95MS – to be precise, the Tu-95MS-16 version; 25 examples were delivered to this unit. The 182nd TBAP followed suit. Concurrently with the transition to the new version these units were mastering the Kh-55 cruise missile launch technique. In mid-1985 the Tu-95MS started flying sorties with two fuel top-ups from IL-78 tankers (on the outbound and return legs) to maximise range. The first DA exercise involving Tu-95MSs (1023rd TBAP aircraft) took place in September that year. The Tu-95K-22s were then concentrated in the 79th GvTBAP at Ookraïnka AB, replacing the Myasishchev 3M bomber fleet, which was rapidly running out of service life.

During 1986, the Tu-95MSs of the Uzin regiment demonstrated their capabilities by flying around the perimeter of the Soviet Union, using in-flight refuelling. At the same time aircraft from Semipalatinsk flew from their home base across the North Pole and onward to the Canadian border. These missions proved the Bear-H's ability to deliver weapons over intercontinental ranges.

Speaking of IFR, a hair-raising episode occurred on 24th June 1986. When Tu-95MS '42 Red' captained by Maj. Aleksandr G. Firstov was being refuelled by a 3MS-2 tanker, the rotten hose broke at the drum of the HDU, whipping around the bomber. 'We're toast' – the captain thought. Flailing wildly in the slipstream, the hose repeatedly struck the elevators, making the aircraft pitch up and down; Firstov could barely keep it under

The badge of the 79th TBAP bearing the motto *Cherez nevozmozhnoye – vperyod* ('Onward through the impossible').

The badge of the 182nd TBAP with the motto *Rossii – slava, nam – chest'* ('Glory for Russia, honour for us').

Tu-95MS '20 Red' was originally named *Naukograd Doobna* ('Doobna Science City') because a nuclear physics research facility is located there. The city crest reflects both this and the name's etymology (*doob* means 'oak' in Russian), featuring the nuclear symbol and an oak tree (looking like nuclear mushroom cloud).

20 НАУКОГРАД ДУБНА

Tu-95MS '2o Red' with early *Naukograd Doobna* titles and the city crest of Doobna, 184th TBAP, Engels

20 ДУБНА

The same aircraft in later guise with the name shortened to *Doobna* and applied in stylised Old Slavic script

22 ЧЕЛЯБИНСК

Tu-95MS '22 Red' *Chelyabinsk* bearing the city crest of Chelyabinsk, 43 TsBP i PLS, Dyagilevo AB

control. All at once the seesawing subsided; the gunner reported that the end of the hose had become wedged between the cannon barrels. With all due care, the pilots brought the bomber home for a safe landing.

The introduction of the Tu-95MS led the USAF to take appropriate countermeasures. The USAF assets in Alaska were bolstered by replacing the 3rd FW's F-15As with more capable F-15Cs; these were supported by Boeing E-3A Sentry AWACS aircraft (two of which were based at Elmendorf AFB full time) and eight to ten Boeing KC-135 Stratotankers, one of which was on 24/7 hot alert. The USAF aircraft from Alaska operated in concert with US Navy 3rd Fleet ships and carrier-borne

fighters. The fighters took off with a full set of live air-to-air missiles and the pilots tried to shadow the *Bears* as long as possible to make sure the uninvited guests were leaving. A pair of F-15Cs claimed a record in this respect on 29th January 1988, shadowing a Tu-95MS for 2 hours 53 minutes.

In 1987 the 182nd GvTBAP, too, converted to the Tu-95MS-16. The first *Bear-H* arrived in Mozdok on 30th September, captained by Sqn 1 commander Lt.-Col. A. A. Vavilov, the son of the regiment's first CO. By the end of 1987 the unit had three Tu-95MSs.

On 6th May 1992 two 182nd GvTBAP Tu-95MSs coded '34 Black' (c/n 100021…935363) and '36 Black'

Starboard side view of '20 Red'; the crest reflects the name's etymology and the town's association with nuclear research

Starboard side view of '20 Red' in even later guise with tri-colour national insignia and 'Russian Air Force' titles

Starboard side view of '22 Red'; as usual, the name and city crest are carried on both sides

(c/n 1000213935793), supported by an Antonov An-124 *Ruslan* (a Russian epic hero; NATO reporting name *Condor*) four-turbofan heavy transport paid a courtesy visit to Barksdale AFB, Louisiana, which was home to the Strategic Air Command's 2nd Bomb Wing. The *Bears* were captained by deputy Commander of Sqn 1 Pilot 1st Class Maj. A. I. Pechatnyy and a detachment commander from the same squadron, Sniper Pilot (an official skill grade) Maj. Yu. I. Popel'nukha. This was a return visit for the March 1992 visit to Dyagilevo AB by two B-52s and a supporting McDonnell Douglas KC-10A Extender tanker – and the first-ever foreign visit by the Tu-95.

According to Soviet practice one or two aircraft repair plants would repair and refurbish all aircraft of a given type, regardless of where they were based (including export aircraft), though occasionally the manufacturer did the job as well. This was the case with the Tu-95. The plants handling the Air Force's *Bears* were ARZ No.148 in Belaya Tserkov' and ARZ No.360 in Ryazan' (Dyagilevo AB). The aircraft factories in Samara (Aviacor JSC) and Taganrog (Tavia) were also involved in the repair and maintenance of the type.

Post-Soviet operations: adapting to the new reality

The break-up of the Soviet Union was a severe blow to the Russian Armed Forces at large, including the Long-Range Aviation. Quite apart from the fact that much of the Soviet heavy bomber fleet found itself outside Russia (in the newly-independent Ukraine and Kazakhstan), in the mid-1990s the Russian government took the decision to 'optimise' the Armed Forces (and when the government starts talking of optimisation, this usually means cuts and closures). It took several years to realise the full magnitude of the losses and try to make them good by forming the DA anew from the remaining assets.

Until the collapse of the Soviet Union, 147 Tu-95 bombers and missile strike aircraft (84 Tu-95MSs and 63 Tu-95Ks/Tu-95K-22s) were operated by Long-Range Aviation units and various MAP divisions. These aircraft were distributed as follows: 21 Tu-95MS-16s, one Tu-95M and one Tu-95K in Uzin; 22 Tu-95MS-16s in Mozdok; 27 Tu-95MS-6s and 13 Tu-95MS-16s in Semipalatinsk; 15 Tu-95Ks and 46 Tu-95K-22s at Ookraïnka AB; and one Tu-95MS-16 at the Kuibyshev factory. This number did not include the eleven Tu-95U and Tu-95KU trainers operated by the 43rd TsBP i PLS in Ryazan' and the three or four Tu-95MSs operated by the Tupolev OKB's flight test facility in Zhukovskiy.

Speaking of the 43rd TsBP i PLS, it was reorganised again in the early 1990s. Back in 1990 the Red Banner Air Force Training Centre in Kansk, Eastern Siberia, was affiliated to the 43rd TsBP i PLS. Later, in 1992, an instructional regiment (the 49th TBAP) was set up to replace the 251st ITBAP (*instrooktorskiy tyazholyy bombardirovochnyy aviapolk* – instructional heavy bomber regiment) which had remained in the now-independent Ukraine. The Centre also came to include the training regiments based at Tambov (Tambov Region) and Orsk (Orenburg Region) which operated Tu-134UBL *Crusty-B* crew trainers. As of 1993 the Ryazan' Centre still operated eight Tu-95K-22s, eight Tu-95Ks and seven Tu-95U trainers. Yet, all of these *Bears* had been phased out by 1995, giving place to ten Tu-22M3 *Backfire-C* supersonic bombers and ten Tu-95MSs – the DA's main types at the time.

The 49th TBAP did not last long – it was disbanded in 1997. Its place at Dyagilevo AB was taken by the 203rd *Orlovskiy* GvOAPSZ (*Gvardeyskiy otdel'nyy aviapolk samolyotov-zaprahvshchikov* – Guards independent aerial refuelling regiment) operating IL-78 and IL-78M *Midas-A/B* tankers which was reorganised from the 1096th TBAP and redeployed from Engels.

Tu-95MS '01 Red' *Irkutsk* bearing the city crest
of Irkutsk, 182nd GvTBAP, Ookraïnka AB

Tu-95MS '59 Red' *Blagoveshchensk* bearing the city
crest of Blagoveshchensk, 79th TBAP, Ookraïnka AB

Tu-95MS '19 Red' *Krasnoyarsk* bearing the city crest
of Krasnoyarsk and 18 mission markers, 79th TBAP

In the 'Soviet Disunion' the disposition of the Russian strategic aviation inventory changed. The regiments in Uzin and Semipalatinsk had been taken over by the Ukraine and Kazakhstan respectively. All of the Tu-95K-22s and most of the Tu-95MS fleet, however, remained under the control of the Russian military and political powers in 'new Russia'. As of 1991, 63 *Bear-Gs* remained on the lists; yet, only 23 remained active by 1992, the rest being deactivated at the Engels-6 storage depot and progressively scrapped in compliance with arms reduction treaties.

Col. Vladimir V. Yegorov (Retd.), who had been appointed the 1023rd TBAP's Deputy CO and promoted

to Lieutenant-Colonel in 1993, reminisced: '*1993 and 1994 were a hard time for us and for all other DA units stationed outside Russia. Flight operations ground to a halt, no salary was paid, and conflicts with the government in Alma-Ata began. In late 1993 the [Kazakhstan] government set about disbanding the division; the two regiments were merged into the 1226th TBAP, which kept the Tu-95MSs, while the former 1223rd TBAP was redeployed to Khorol' AB in the Russian Far East.* (*Sic*; Yegorov probably means Ookraïnka AB, since Khorol' AB was a Naval Aviation base – *Auth.*)

In April 1994 I was appointed head of the DA's Aerial Gunnery and Tactical Training Department. The years

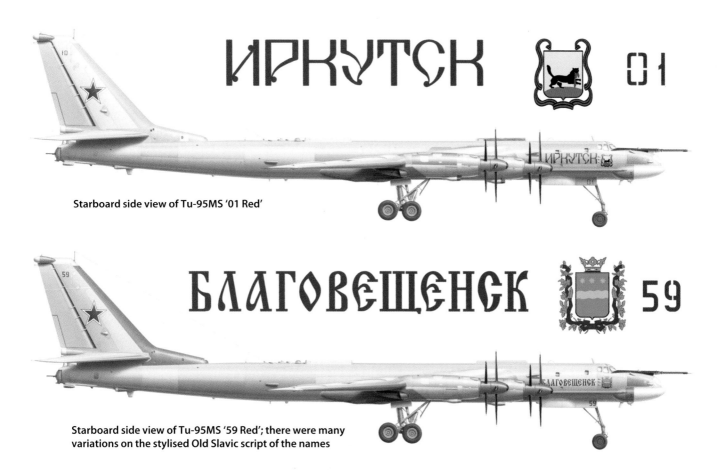

ИРКУТСК 01

Starboard side view of Tu-95MS '01 Red'

БЛАГОВЕЩЕНСК 59

Starboard side view of Tu-95MS '59 Red'; there were many
variations on the stylised Old Slavic script of the names

*1994-98 were a really tough time for the DA in general. All
Long-Range Aviation formations in the Ukraine and
Belorussia were disbanded and the aircraft disposed of,
which was a severe blow to the 37th VA's combat potential.*

*In those years I logged 80-90 flight hours per year, whereas
the average figure in the DA was a dismal 15-20 hours; in
the final three years of my Air Force service I managed to
make some 20 IFR sorties.*

'59 Red' is readied for
flight at Ookraïnka AB.
79th TBAP and 182nd
GvTBAP *Bear-Hs* have
black-tipped spinners.

The crest of Ookraïnka AB marked 'Air Force/ Long-Range Aviation'.

After 1998 the Long-Range Aviation's aircraft, including Tu-95MSs, have resumed their regular patrol missions. In this I perceive my modest contribution of a military pilot who had been flying Tu-95s for the greater part of his flying career.'

In November 1993 the Russian MoD daily **Kras**naya **zvez**da (Red Star) published an excerpt from a Russian Armed Forces' General Staff message that described a typical operational scenario for the 79th GvTBAP's Tu-95K-22s attacking US Navy ships. It ran as follows:

'On 18th July 1993, units of the US Navy Pacific Fleet ([headquartered at] San Francisco) formed a multi-purpose carrier task force (CTF) headed by the nuclear-powered aircraft carrier USS Abraham Lincoln in order to relieve the aircraft carrier USS Nimitz on combat duty in the Persian Gulf zone.

The transfer of responsibility from one carrier to the other was done under the protective umbrella of optical and electronic camouflage while maintaining complete radio silence. In order to detect the location and configuration of the carrier group, the Commander of the Russian Air Force's Long-Range Aviation decided to undertake aerial reconnaissance via a group of four Tu-95K-22 strategic aircraft.

Two pairs of missile-carriers took off from an airfield in the Far East at 18:03 GMT on 28th July. The aircraft crossed the Kurile Archipelago and, five hours later, radar signals from the CTF were intercepted at a distance of 1,400 km

[869 miles] from the shore line. Turning towards this source, the bomber crews discovered they were 220 km [137 miles] from the task force […] which consisted of six ships. As they approached the CTF, the bomber crews noted, at a distance of 3 km [1.86 miles], that four ships were moving in close formation. The carrier was 140 km [87 miles] behind.

The bombers then turned onto a heading of 190º magnetic and reduced their speed to 220 km/h [137 mph]. The first pair descended to 500 m [1,640 ft] and made their photo runs across the task force's path. A pair of F/A-18 fighters (each with two Sidewinder air-to-air missiles) was launched to intercept the bombers following their second pass. The fighters came within 200-300m [660-980 ft] of the bombers within a few minutes after take-off. Thirty minutes later, two more fighters came up from behind the bombers on the right. These approached within 100 m [330 ft]. Meanwhile, the second pair of Tu-95K-22s located their target. At the same time, they discovered and photographed a supply ship which was sailing separately from the CTF.

Thus the assignment concerning detection of this US task force at sea was successfully accomplished.'

When ethnic strife between the Ossetians and the Ingushes erupted in 1992, the 182nd GvTBAP redeployed temporarily to Engels-2 AB. This forced move, coupled with the shock therapy imposed on the emerging independent Russia by some 'wise guys' in

The following table shows the location of Tu-95 units as of late 1991.		
Unit	**Location**	**Notes**
Direct reporting units (DA Command)		
• 43rd TsBP i PLS, Dyagilevo AB, Ryazan', Russian Federation:		
49th TBAP	Dyagilevo AB	Training unit equipped with Tu-95Ks/Tu-95KUs and Tu-95Us
30th VA VGK (SN) (HQ Irkutsk, Russian Federation)		
• 79th TBAD (HQ Semipalatinsk, Kazakh SSR):		
1023rd TBAP	Chagan AB, Semipalatinsk Region	Equipped with Tu-95MSs and Tu-95Ms; sometimes referred to in error as 1223rd TBAP
1226th TBAP	Chagan AB	Equipped with Tu-95MSs
• 73rd TBAD (HQ Seryshevo, Amur Region, Russian Federation):		
40th GvTBAP	Ookraïnka AB, Amur Region	Equipped with Tu-95K-22s
79th GvTBAP	Ookraïnka AB	Equipped with Tu-95KMs and Tu-95K-22s
46th VA VGK (SN) (HQ Smolensk, Russian Federation)		
• 106th TBAD (HQ Uzin, Kiev Region, Ukrainian SSR):		
1006th TBAP	Uzin (Chepelevka) AB	Equipped with Tu-95MSs and Tu-95Ms
• 201st TBAD (HQ Engels, Saratov Region, Russian Federation):		
182nd GvTBAP	Mozdok, North Ossetian ASSR	Equipped with Tu-95MSs
Forward operating locations/auxiliary airfields		
Commandant's office	Anadyr'	
Commandant's office	Magadan	
Commandant's office	Tiksi	

A pennant of the 182nd *Sevastopol'sko-Berlinskiy* Red Banner GvTBAP. Note the unit motto 'Glory to Russia, honour to us'.

Left: Close-up of the nose of Tu-85MS '59 Red'.

Far left: A poster with the name of Ookraïnka AB, the Russian MoD crest and the Russian Air Force's 'sunburst' flag.

Tu-95MSs '01 Red' and '56 Red' at Anadyr'-Oogol'nyy airport in April 2006 during an exercise.

the government, caused the unit's flying activity to plunge dramatically. In 1993 the regiment returned to Mozdok, operating from this base for several more years.

Now we will turn our attention to the 79th GvTBAP again. The Tu-95K-22s were to be scrapped under the terms of the START II strategic arms reduction treaty. Yet the unit was not left without any aircraft, as in 1993 it began converting to the Tu-95MS. Part of the unit's new fleet had previously seen service with the 1023rd and 1226th TBAPs constituting the 79th TBAD which had remained in Kazakhstan after the collapse of the Soviet Union; the bombers were obtained in exchange

for a number of Sukhoi Su-27 *Flanker-B/C* fighters. On 25th September 1996 a crew headed by Lt.-Col. V. Ye. Shevtsov became the first 79th TBAP crew to launch a Kh-55 cruise missile.

In 1993 most of the *Bears* under Russian control were still in reasonably good condition, and renewed emphasis was made on training. Gen. A. Ivanov, head of the DA's combat training section, stated in 1993 that Tu-95 crews logged at least 70 hours annually. Missions were flown to the western borders and the shores of the Pacific Ocean. Tu-160 *Blackjack* and Tu-95MS missile carriers took part in the 1993 exercise, along with other aircraft in first-line service.

Later, Tu-160s and Tu-95MSs were deployed to tactical airfields located many thousands of kilometres from their home bases. Flying to these FOLs involved several fuel top-ups from IL-78/IL-78M tankers. The exercise demonstrated the high reliability of the Tu-95s; only minor technical problems were encountered during the deployment.

On 21st August 1994 a 182nd GvTBAP Tu-95MS made another goodwill visit to Barksdale AFB; the aircraft was captained by Lt.-Col. K. A. Yepifanovskiy.

In November 1994, one month before the outbreak of the First Chechen War, the strategic missile carriers of the 182nd GvTBAP moved to Engels again, out of harm's way. Their former base at Mozdok was now swamped

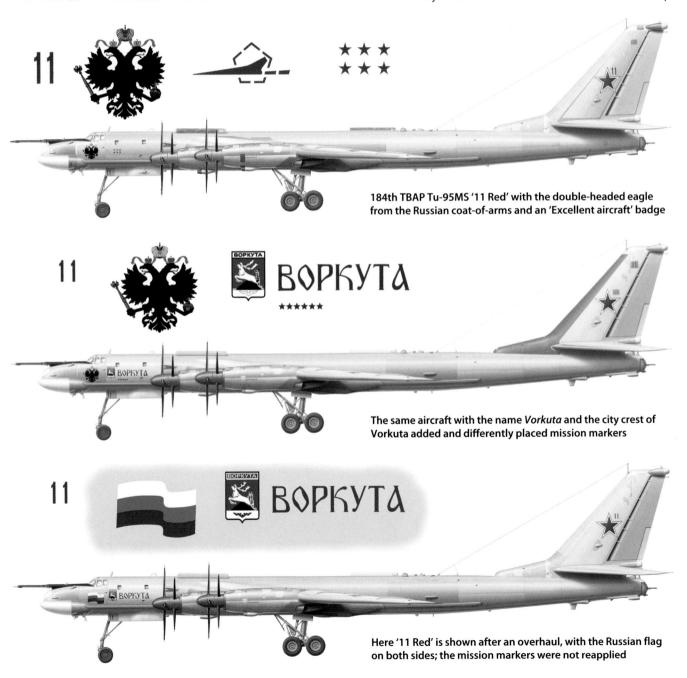

184th TBAP Tu-95MS '11 Red' with the double-headed eagle from the Russian coat-of-arms and an 'Excellent aircraft' badge

The same aircraft with the name *Vorkuta* and the city crest of Vorkuta added and differently placed mission markers

Here '11 Red' is shown after an overhaul, with the Russian flag on both sides; the mission markers were not reapplied

with Tactical Aviation strike aircraft, helicopters of the Ministry of the Interior (MoI) Troops and transport aircraft of the EMERCOM of Russia civil aid and protection agency. The ground personnel of the 182nd GvTBAP stayed at Mozdok, assisting in the maintenance of the aircraft on temporary deployment there during the military campaign.

Following the reorganisation of the formerly independent Air Force and Air Defence Force into a united air arm in April 1998 the Long-Range Aviation assets were concentrated within the 37th VA VGK (SN) (*voz**doosh**naya **ar**miya Ver**khov**novo glavnoko**mahn**dovaniya strate**gich**eskovo nazna**che**niya* – Strategic Air Army of the Supreme High Command) which now operated all surviving Air Force *Bears* (except the Naval Aviation's Tu-142s). On 8th/10th August that year the newly-organised formation held its first exercise when two 184th GvTBAP Tu-95MSs took off from Engels-2 AB and flew north. About 2,500 km (1,550 miles) from home they launched Kh-55SM cruise missiles which successfully hit their designated targets on Cape Kanin Nos. This was the first time the naval target range on Kanin Nos was used by the Air Force; the Soviet Long-Range Aviation's principal target range near Semipalatinsk was in now-independent Kazakhstan and hence unusable. This was also the first use of the KTS-15 tracking system which allowed the missiles to be tracked without using radar picket aircraft.

In accordance with a directive signed by Russia's Deputy Minister of Defence Army Gen. Anatoliy V. Kvashnin on 27th February 1999 the 182nd GvTBAP was redeployed to Ookraïnka AB in the Amur Region and merged with the resident 40th TBAP. The new unit was designated as the 40th TBAP while retaining the 182nd GvTBAP's honorary appellation and combat standard. This situation did not last long; as early as 2nd June 1999 the designation 182nd GvTBAP was reinstated.

Since the late 1990s the resumption of missions flown outside Russia's borders and demonstrative exercises involving the use of all kinds of weapons'

Above: The nose of Tu-95MS '11 Red' originally featured a 'double eagle' and six mission markers.

Opposite page: Tu-95MS '11 Red' *Vorkuta* was the only 184th TBAP aircraft to carry a Russian flag on the nose.

Starboard side view of Tu-95MS '11 Red' in pre-overhaul colours with the the Russian flag to starboard only

The same aircraft' in current colours as '11 Red'/RF-94127 with tri-colour insignia and Russian Air Force titles

Russian Air Force Tu-95MS '22 Red'/ RF-94120 *Kozel'sk* flies over the ocean.

Another version of the 182nd GvTBAP's crest.

A fine perspective of a Russian Air Force Tu-95MS as it approaches the tanker.

became a routine in the life of Long-Range Aviation crews. Plagued as it was in the 1990s by the dearth of fuel which lead to a drastic fall in the number of yearly flying hours per pilot, the Russian Air Force nevertheless managed to cope with the most acute problems and confirm its ability to maintain an adequate level of proficiency for DA crews. For example, in 1997 a 182nd GvTBAP Tu-95MS captained by Sqn 2 Deputy Commander Maj. V. S. Zemnukhov successfully made a live practice launch of a Kh-55 cruise missile in the course of Exercise *Re**doot-9**7* (Redoubt, or Fort).

The NATO offensive against (former) Yugoslavia in 1999 (Operation *Allied Force*) was a powerful impetus to the development of the Russian Long-Range Aviation. Having seen the real capabilities of air power applied to a modern conventional war, the Russian political and military leaders decided to take all necessary steps to 'rehabilitate' strategic aviation and its ability to 'project power' within the shortest possible time. The message sent to Russia by Operation *Allied Force* was loud and clear – 'you may be next', and the Russian leaders were determined to do whatever it takes to discourage any potential aggressor.

In a flashback of the Cold War confrontation, in the summer and autumn of 1999 Tu-160 and Tu-95MS strategic missile carriers participating in a series of exercises flew sorties towards the North American continent. This was meant to demonstrate 'Russia's response' to the Allied bombing of the Balkans and to NATO's eastward expansion, both of which caused much concern and consternation in Russia. Part of the scenario involved flights to within a short distance of the North American continent. These exercises aroused considerable interest – not least because the Long-Range Aviation's activities were unmistakably linked to the more hard-line military-political course pursued by the Russian government. In particular, as early as in the mid-1990s, the DA's missile carriers had practiced – for the first time – simulated nuclear strikes against unpopulated regions of the country and over international waters as the strategy of an all-out nuclear war was revisited.

For example, the strategic command/staff exercise **Zapad-99** (West-99), which commenced on the night of 25th/26th June 1999, included significant participation by DA aircraft. A pair of Tu-160s and a pair of Tu-95MSs took off from Engels-2 AB and headed northwards. Having reached their designated waypoint over the Arctic Ocean, they turned southwest. On reaching the Norwegian coast, the bombers parted. The pair of Tu-160s passed down the entire coastline of Norway and carried out a simulated launch of their Kh-55SM long-range cruise missiles. Next, one of the Tu-160s set course for the Ashuluk weapons training range in southern Russia where a missile was actually launched.

Russian Air Force Tu-95MS '28 Red' is depicted on a practice sortie.

17th September 1999 saw a routine 'combat readiness check' for the USAF's 3rd FW at Elmendorf AFB. As Exercise *Vostok-99* (East-99) unfolded, two 326th TBAD *Bear-Hs* captained by Lt.-Col. S. P. Danilenko and Maj. A. P. Smurygin took off from the FOL in Anadyr' on the Chukotka coast, heading east over the international waters of the Pacific. Two more *Bear-Hs* took off from the Arctic FOL at Tiksi and set course for the Canadian coast, overflying the North Pole. They were under the control of an Ilyushin IL-22 *Coot-B* airborne command post based on the IL-18D airliner which orbited near the Kamchatka Peninsula. The exercise co-ordinators had ordered the crews to communicate in clear code so as not to alarm the American neighbours. Nevertheless, in the USA the threat was taken seriously, and 20 minutes after the Tu-95MSs had taken of from Anadyr', USAF fighters scrambled to intercept. They did not close on the Russian aircraft, and visual contact was not established. However, the fighters did 'paint' the *Bears* with their radars; ESM used by the Tu-95 crews identified three or four 'attacks' carried out by the F-15s and F-16s. Having completed their objective, which was evidently to simulate the launch of Kh-55SM ALCMs from a notional waypoint over the ocean, the Russian bombers returned to their base.

During the 1990s a large proportion of Russia's heavy bombers, including the Myasishchev 3M family and older versions of the Tu-95, was scrapped at the Engels-6 AB military aircraft storage and disposal centre, and the Russian Air Force suddenly found itself short of bombers. Consequently efforts were made to reclaim the Tu-95s left outside Russia after the break-up of the Soviet Union. While the *Bear-Hs* stationed in Kazakhstan

A badge issued to celebrate the 79th TBAP's 60th birthday in 1998.

Above: A Russian Air Force Tu-95MS cruises at high altitude at sunset.

Left: Tu-95MS '59 Red' Blagoveshchensk is intercepted by a 3rd FW Lockheed Martin F-22A Raptor on 29th November 2007.

Opposite page, top: Tu-95MS '10 Red' Saratov takes off at Engels-2 AB for a late-evening sortie. Note the IL-78 tanker and some of the aircraft in the DA Museum (including an IL-62 staff transport) in the background.

Far left: A pair of Bear-Hs taxies out at Engels-2 in the fading light.

were returned without any trouble, getting back those that were based at Uzin AB proved to be a Herculean task because Russia and the Ukraine were at odds over the Black Sea Fleet and other issues. The Ukrainian Air Force (UAF) had no use for these aircraft, as they did not fit into the republic's official non-nuclear status, but the Ukraine was determined not to give them away for free. Negotiations with Russia on the purchase of the bombers dragged on and on, both parties haggling for more favourable terms.

Meanwhile, the Ukrainian government began considering the option of scrapping the bombers in keeping with its non-nuclear status, especially since the USA was offering to finance the operation. At first, this prospect was not taken too seriously in Russia, the authorities regarding this as a ploy to 'make us buy the bombers while they're still there'. However, when two Tu-160s, one of which was a very low-time aircraft, were scrapped at Priluki AB, the Russian government realised the Ukrainians meant business and was no longer in a mood to tolerate such an awful waste.

In October 1999 a deal was finally signed for the delivery of eight ex-UAF Tu-160s and three Tu-95MSs, along with several hundred Kh-55 cruise missiles, to offset the Ukraine's outstanding debt for Russian natural gas deliveries. The deal was worth US$285 million, or roughly US$25.9 million per aircraft – a nice result, considering the Ukraine's original demands of US$75 million per aircraft. The bombers arrived at

Above left: 184th TBAP Tu-95MS '14 Red' *Krasnoyarsk* taxies out for take-off at Engels-2, with a 121st TBAP Tu-160 hot on its heels.

Left: Tu-95MS '12 Red' *Moskva* approaches an IL-78 tanker over a winter landscape. The hose and drogue from the centre UPAZ-1 HDU are already deployed.

Above: An air-to-air of Tu-95MS '11 Red' *Vorkuta* in post-overhaul colours with the Russian flag on the nose.

Below: A Kh-55SM with the engine and tail surfaces deployed is catapulted from the weapons bay of a Tu-95MS during an exercise; the wings will unfold in a moment.

Above: Several Russian Air Force Tu-95MSs sported this 'double eagle' motif from the Russian coat-of-arms until the higher powers demanded its removal.

Below: Tu-95MS '10 Red' *Saratov* on the flight line at Engels-2 AB. Note the location of the 'Excellent aircraft' badge.

Engels AB in November 1999; this was a most welcome boost for the Russian Air Force's depleted strategic aircraft inventory.

Thus, in 2000 the 37th VA VGK (SN) included three units of Tu-95MSs organised into two bomber divisions – the 22nd GvTBAD's 121st GvTBAP at Engels-2 AB in European Russia and the 326th TBAD's 40th GvTBAP and 79th GvTBAP, both at Ookraïnka AB in the Far East.

The 121st TBAP had operated a mix of Tu-160s (Sqn 1) and Tu-95MSs (Sqns 2 and 3) since 1998. Now, the arrival of the ex-UAF aircraft made it possible to transform this regiment into an all-*Blackjack* unit. The two *Bear-H* squadrons were used to establish a new

regiment, the co-located 184th TBAP; its personnel included many pilots and technicians who had previously served with the 182nd GvTBAP at Ookraïnka AB. (The new regiment had no connection with the former 184th TBAP at Priluki in the Ukraine, a Tu-160 unit which was disbanded when the Ukraine disposed of its *Blackjacks*.) By July 2001 the Russian Air Force had 63 Tu-95MSs on strength, with a stockpile of 504 Kh-55 missiles reserved for them.

On 18th-21st April 2000 a further series of exercises was held by the 37th Air Army to wrap up the winter period of training for 1999-2000. Within the framework of these exercises conducted in the middle and lower reaches of the Volga River and over the Caspian and Black Seas, a number of tasks were carried out which had never been conducted in these areas before. The bombers acquired from the Ukraine took part in this exercise; both Tu-160s and Tu-95MSs carried out launches of Kh-55SM ALCMs. The principal objective was to test the combat readiness of aircraft and equipment which had sat idle for a considerable time (particularly the aircraft recovered from the Ukraine), as well as to polish the combat skills of the participants. The scenario also involved co-operation between the DA and Tactical Aviation to disrupt the notional enemy's air defence system, employing ECM.

Combat training for DA crews continued in the summer of 2000, with the Tu-95MSs from Engels participating in a further command and staff exercise involving the launch of long-range ALCMs at targets on northern and southern practice ranges. All the missiles destroyed their designated targets and the crews demonstrated a high level of training and combat proficiency, achieving 'excellent' scores.

In September 2000 two pairs of Russian Air Force bombers operated from airfields in the Republic of Belarus during an exercise, demonstrating the close defence union between the two nations. In particular, on 7th September a pair of Tu-95MSs (one of them captained by Lt.-Col. S. P. Danilenko) landed at Machoolishchi AB just south of Minsk. This was the *Bear-H*'s first visit to Machoolishchi since 1994.

On 19th December 2000 two Tu-95MSs ('01 Red' *Irkutsk* and '08 Red' *Smolensk*, captained by Maj. I. V. Boyarintsev and Lt.-Col. S. Ye. Zhookov respectively) made the first flight over the North Pole after a ten-year break. The mission included a stopover at a tactical airfield in Tiksi. On 24th August 2002 the crews of Lt.-Col. I. V. Boyarintsev and Maj. S. A. Ovsyannikov performed successful practice launches of Kh-55 missiles at a northern target range.

From 2001 onwards the 184th TBAP participated in almost all major command and staff exercises, becoming one of the most active units in the Russian Air Force's Long-Range Aviation. The first such exercise was staged in February 2001, the crews led by Lt.-Col.

A fine study of Tu-95MS '10 Red' *Saratov* on final approach. Note the open APU air intake in the fin root fillet.

Tu-95MS '23 Red' *Tambov* is pictured at Dyagilevo AB making a check flight after being refurbished by the 360th Aircraft Repair Plant. Note the red-tipped spinners and the unusual dark grey colour of the avionics bay access panels on the nose.

15 КАЛУГА

Tu-95MS '15 Red' *Kaluga* bearing the city crest of Kaluga, 184th TBAP, Engels-2 AB

10 САРАТОВ

Tu-95MS '10 Red' *Saratov* bearing the city crest of Saratov, 184th TBAP

08 СМОЛЕНСК

Tu-95MS '08 Red' *Smolensk* bearing the city crest of Smolensk, 182nd GvTBAP, Ookraïnka AB

23 ТАМБОВ

Tu-95MS '23 Red' *Tambov* bearing the city crest of Tambov

Starboard side view of Tu-95MS '15 Red'

Starboard side view of '10 Red'; note that the
'Excellent aircraft' badge is applied on both sides

Starboard side view of Tu-95MS '08 Red'

Starboard side view of '23 Red'; note the variance
in the name typeface and tactical code style

Tu-95MS '21 Red' *Samara* bearing the city crest of Samara, 184th TBAP

The same aircraft after an overhaul with the name in a different typeface, tri-colour insignia and the registration RF-94121

A. M. Pechatnov and Maj. V. A. Kostikov making practice launches of Kh-55 cruise missiles. That year the unit twice participated in festive events involving a display of military hardware.

In 2002 the 184th TBAP's Tu-95MSs operated from tactical airfields (FOLs) and were used to check the combat readiness of the Russian air defence system in an active ECM environment during an exercise. Again, two practice missile launches were made. In 2003 the *Bear-Hs* and *Blackjacks* from Engels caused quite a stir by heading south to the Sea of Arabia instead of following the usual route over the North Sea. The bombers were captained by Lt.-Col. V. N. Kuznetsov, Lt.-Col. I. V. Gorlov, Lt.-Col. Ye. I. Dmitriyev and Lt.-Col. V. S. Zemnukhov. In July 2003 a pair of 184th TBAP *Bear-Hs* posed as intruders, 'harassing' Russian air defences during an exercise. A month later two Tu-95MSs from the same unit played the same part during a Commonwealth of Independent States (CIS) joint air defence exercise.

In 2003, for the first time in Russia's modern history, Tu-95MS strategic missile carriers performed an ultra-long-range flight and simulated launches of cruise missiles in the Indian Ocean area. The exercises were held in two stages in Russia's airspace and in the strategically important sea areas of the Arctic Ocean and the Pacific. In the course of Exercise *Zapad-2003*, for the

first time in the entire post-Soviet period, Tu-160, Tu-95MS and Tu-22M3 bombers of the DA took off almost simultaneously from several bases and set off to carry out their assigned combat training tasks in different areas, some of which lay far beyond the Russian borders. After a flight of many hours' duration along the designated routes the bombers performed live and simulated launches of ALCMs and dropped bomb loads on target ranges in northern and southern Russia. Between 11th and 16th May more than 30 Long-Range Aviation aircraft were involved in the exercise, and its key episode, in the light of the war in Iraq, had a clearly anti-Western flavour. In the Indian Ocean area Tu-95MSs launched two Kh-55SM ALCMs against a 'maritime target', while Tu-160s simulated a launch of Kh-55SMs against the US Navy base on Diego Garcia from a distance of 2,500 km (1,554 miles).

In June 2004 a Russian Air Force Tu-95MS coded '12 Red' and christened *Moskva* (Moscow) was due to make a heritage flight from Russia to the USA via the North Pole along the route taken by the legendary Soviet test pilot Valeriy P. Chkalov. Regrettably the flight never materialised because of a disagreement at the top level. The aircraft was ready to take off at short notice but the US government insisted that an American navigator should be on board, and the Russian military adamantly said no.

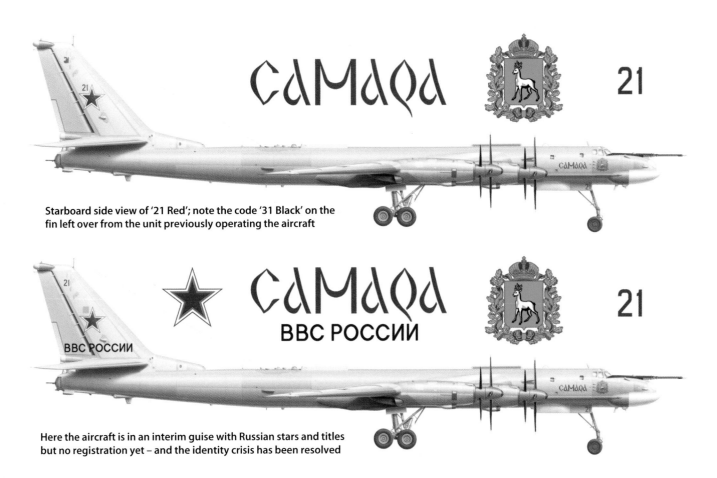

Starboard side view of '21 Red'; note the code '31 Black' on the fin left over from the unit previously operating the aircraft

Here the aircraft is in an interim guise with Russian stars and titles but no registration yet – and the identity crisis has been resolved

In February 2004, during a strategic command and staff exercise of Russia's Armed Forces, the crews of Tu-160 and Tu-95MS strategic missile carriers made nearly 20 sorties; during two days alone the crews of these aircraft logged a total of some 130-140 hours. In particular, the crews of two 184th TBAP *Bear-Hs* carried out live launches of Kh-55SM ALCMs and successfully hit their practice targets on the Novaya Zemlya archipelago. The flight from Engels-2 AB to the Barents Sea area and back lasted more than nine hours and proceeded in adverse weather conditions. Despite this, the crews fully coped with the assigned tasks.

Tu-95MS bombers supported by IL-78M tankers were also involved in Exercise *Peace Mission-2005* – the first Sino-Russian joint exercise under the auspices of the Shanghai Co-operation Organisation (SCO). The exercise took place on 18th-25th August 2005 in Vladovostok and on the Shandong Peninsula in China. Among other things, it involved the Pacific Fleet's Type 775 (NATO *Ropucha-M* class) landing ship RNS *Peresvet* (BDK-11); this elicited a nervous reaction from Taiwan, which claimed that China was 'rehearsing an invasion'.

Between 26th and 30th September 2006 the 37th Strategic Air Army again conducted a command and staff exercise. In the course of this exercise 93 sorties were flown; four regiments dropped bombs at target ranges with which they had no previous experience,

three actual launches of long-range ALCMs were made, complemented by 48 simulated missile launches. in particular, on 29th September 54 assorted Long-Range Aviation aircraft (Tu-160s, Tu-95MSs, Tu-22M3s and IL-78Ms) were airborne simultaneously in the northern, southern, western and eastern parts of Russia. During

The nose of Tu-95MS '21 Red' *Samara*. Note the ground cover on the lower sensor of the Mak missile warning system.

Tu-95MS '02 Red' *Mozdok* bearing the city crest of Mozdok, 182nd GvTBAP, Ookraïnka AB

Tu-95MS '16 Red' *Velikiy Novgorod* bearing the city crest of Velikiy Novgorod

Tu-95MS '16 Red' *Velikiy Novgorod* is seen here on final approach. The open exhaust door shows that the APU is still running.

this exercise the Tu-95MSs which flew missions to the Atlantic Ocean and Caspian Sea areas had several in-flight refuelling sessions, receiving a total of 40 tons (88,180 lb) of fuel.

In April 2006, a command/staff exercise and readiness check of the 326th TBAD commanded by Maj.-Gen. Aleksandr I. Afinogentov was successfully held in the Russian Far East and Siberia; Lt.-Gen. Igor' I.

Khvorov, the Commander of the 37th Strategic Air Army, was in control of the exercise. For starters, the division was placed on ready alert. Four 182nd TBAP Tu-95MSs ('01 Red' *Irkutsk*, '05 Red', '56 Red' and '59 Red' *Blagoveshchensk*) redeployed from Ookraïnka AB to the polar airstrip at Anadyr'. The flight lasting many hours passed in difficult weather conditions over international waters of the Pacific Ocean. It is worth noting that the

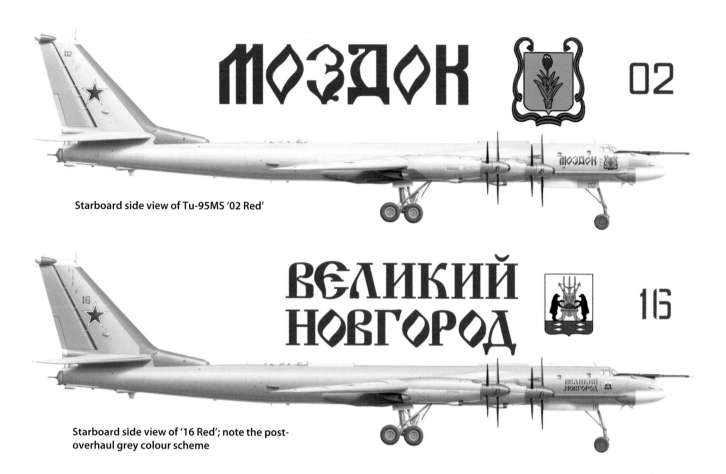

МОЗДОК 02

Starboard side view of Tu-95MS '02 Red'

ВЕЛИКИЙ НОВГОРОД 16

Starboard side view of '16 Red'; note the post-overhaul grey colour scheme

mission was carried out by aircraft captains in their first and second year of training; this was the first time they participated in an operation involving such a high degree of responsibility. For the first time in many years, young crews were allowed to participate in the exercise. This was made possible by preliminary training sessions held in the division. Over a three-month period the 182nd TBAD was able to prepare 38 crews which, after

due analysis of their training results, were cleared for the exercise.

Maj. Denis Pustobayev, the captain of '59 Red', told the journalists after the flight that such long missions had not been flown in the division for a long time – the outbound leg of the flight alone had taken 12 hours non-stop. The only thing that caused some 'disappointment' on the part of the pilots was that the

Tu-95MSs '20 Red' *Doobna* and '22 Red' *Kozel'sk* make a formation flypast at an air parade.

Above left: *Bear* meets Raptor: the first encounter between a Tu-95MS ('59 Red' *Blagoveshchensk*) and an F-22A on 29th November 2007.

Above and below: Royal Canadian Air Force/4th Wing CF-188s (F/A-18As) intercepted Russian Tu-95MSs on several occasions.

Bottom: 3rd FW/19th FS F-15C-39-MC 85-0104/AK escorts 182nd GvTBAP Tu-95MS '02 Red' *Mozdok* away from Alaskan shores.

bombers were not intercepted by foreign fighters when flying over international waters. This was probably caused by adverse weather. Nevertheless, the Russian missile carriers slipped through the NORAD radar coverage zone near Canadian shores unhindered.

Meanwhile, a further two Tu-95MSs – this time from the 79th TBAP at Ookraïnka AB – and a pair of Tu-22M3 bombers from the 444th TBAP based at Vozdvizhenka AB – took off to fly a practice sortie over the Sea of Japan and the Pacific. The crews acquainted themselves with the peculiarities of prolonged flight over the ocean at a considerable distance from the shore while practicing the use of cruise missiles. The *Bears* were forced to return to base earlier than planned after encountering severe turbulence caused by a storm front.

As they crossed the border and headed into international waters near Japan, the Tu-95MSs were intercepted by two Japanese Air Self-Defence Force (JASDF) fighters which shadowed them for more than two hours, with a Boeing KC-767 tanker tagging along some way behind. A radio exchange took place between the sides. One of the Tu-95MS captains, Maj. Aleksandr Shmit'ko, said that the crew used a set of standard phrases to communicate with the Japanese pilots. *'There were no provocations on our part* – he said. *– We were calmly doing our job while they did theirs.'*

The events described above took place in Siberia and in the Russian Far East; yet the exercise also involved aircraft from European Russia – the missile carriers of the 22nd TBAD from Engels-2 AB. Two 121st TBAP Tu-160s and two 184th TBAP Tu-95MSs launched their Kh-55 cruise missiles at a northern target range, operating in concert with the Tu-22M3s of the 326th TBAD. All designated targets were destroyed by this united group of aircraft which converged on the target range from bases located thousands of kilometres apart. This was excellent work, especially given that the launch had occurred in adverse weather.

In August 2007, due to the deterioration of the military-political situation in the world (in particular, a series of steps of military character taken by the USA), on instructions from Vladimir V. Putin, the then President of the Russian Federation, the aircraft of the 37th Strategic Air Army of the Supreme High Command resumed

A pennant of the 184th TBAP (military unit 24755) bearing the unit's motto *Vera, masterstvo, otvaga* (Faith, Skill, Courage).

A pennant of the 182nd TBAP issued to celebrate the unit's 60th birthday, with the legend 'Guarding the Homeland frontiers'.

Left and above left: Two more views of Tu-95MS '59 Red' being escorted by a 3rd FW F-22A off the Aleutian Islands on 29th November 2007.

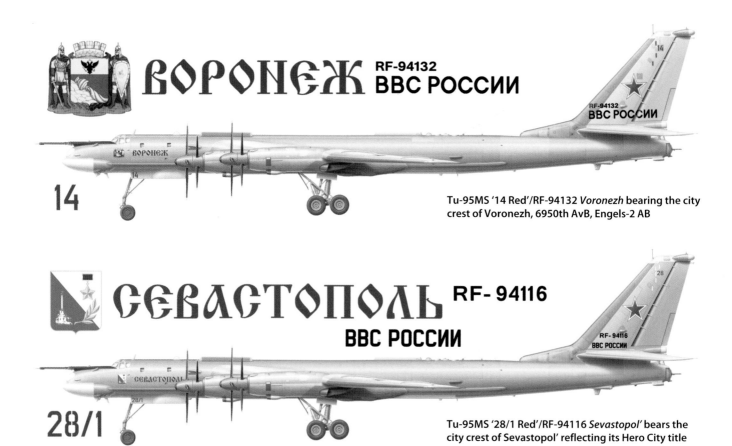

ВОРОНЕЖ RF-94132
ВВС РОССИИ

14

Tu-95MS '14 Red'/RF-94132 *Voronezh* bearing the city crest of Voronezh, 6950th AvB, Engels-2 AB

СЕВАСТОПОЛЬ RF- 94116
ВВС РОССИИ

28/1

Tu-95MS '28/1 Red'/RF-94116 *Sevastopol'* bears the city crest of Sevastopol' reflecting its Hero City title

ИЗБОРСК RF-94117 ВВС РОССИИ

27/1

Tu-95MS '27/1 Red'/RF-94117 *Izborsk* bears the city crest of Izborsk – and the emblem of the Izborsk Club business club

КОЗЕЛЬСК ВВС РОССИИ

22

Tu-95MS 22 Red' *Kozel'sk* bearing the city crest of Kozel'sk

patrol flights outside the territory of the Russian Federation and regular flights over the Pacific and Atlantic Oceans which had not been conducted since 1992. From 0 hours on 17th August 2007, in furtherance of the President's instructions, some two dozen 37th Air Army aircraft – Tu-160s, Tu-95MSs, Tu-22M3s and IL-78s,

supported in some cases by Mikoyan MiG-31 *Foxhound* interceptors and Ilyushin/Beriyev A-50 *Mainstay-A/B* AWACS aircraft, flew 50 sorties over international waters, operating from FOLs at Olenegorsk, Vorkuta, Monchegorsk, Tiksi, Anadyr', Engels and Shaikovka. The Tu-160s and Tu-95MSs remained airborne for an

Opposite page: Tu-95MS '28/1 Red'/RF-94116 *Sevastopol'* becomes airborne at Engels-2 AB, with three sister ships parked in the background.

Left: '27/1 Red' *Izborsk* is registered RF-94117 but the registration is obviously altered from RF-94177, which had been applied in error and was already assigned to a different Tu-95MS at the time!

409

Tu-95MS '21 Red' *Samara* departs on a routine practice sortie on a glorious sunny day.

average of 13 hours. In the course of these flights 21 NATO fighters were observed to approach the Russian aircraft, shadowing them for a total of five hours. According to a news item in *The Times*, the UK military command had to scramble two Panavia Tornado F.3s which escorted the Russian aircraft for 20 minutes.

On 6th-7th September 2007, Long-Range Aviation aircraft took off from airfields at Engels, Anadyr', Vorkuta and Tiksi to carry out yet another routine patrol in distant geographical areas. According to Deputy Commander of the 37th Air Army Maj.-Gen. Anatoliy D. Zhikharev, the Tu-160s and Tu-95s flew their missions without nuclear munitions on board.

A ground crewman touches up the paintwork on the nose of a Russian Air Force Tu-95MS.

29th November 2007 was the first case when a Tu-95MS was intercepted by a Lockheed Martin F-22A Raptor. As an unexpected 'greeting' on Thanksgiving Day, the US air defence radars on Alaska detected several *Bear-Hs* over international; waters, and the one which came closest to the Aleutian Islands ('59 Red' *Blagoveshchensk*) was escorted for several minutes by a pair of Raptors until it made for home.

During the first Long-Range Aviation exercise held in 2008 (in February) more than 70 sorties were flown. More than 30 Tu-95MS missile-carriers, Tu-22M3 bombers and IL-78 tankers were involved in a two-day tactical flight training exercise of the DA. In one of the sorties a pair of *Bear-Hs* approached a US Navy carrier task force in the Pacific Ocean; one of the bombers passed over the force's flagship, the aircraft carrier USS *Nimitz*, at an altitude of 610 m (2,000 ft). USAF and JASDF fighters were scrambled to intercept the Russian bombers.

The Pentagon and NATO voiced their concern over the bombers' increased activity, stating that the Russian Long-Range Aviation's pattern of actions resembles the one practiced during the Cold War period. Commander of the 37th Air Army Major General Pavel Androsov commented this as follows: *'We have flown, are flying and **will** fly to whatever areas that we deem necessary for the training of our pilots'*.

On 9th June 2008 a pair of 184th TBAP Tu-95MSs flying a routine long-range practice sortie over the Arctic Ocean and the North Atlantic were detected by a NATO radar in Iceland. Two French Air Force (Armée de l'Air) Dassault Mirage 2000 fighters scrambled from Keflavik AB, intercepting the *Bears* and escorting them at a safe distance for about 90 minutes. The Mirages were on a four-month temporary duty (TDY) in Iceland as part of Operation Air Islande. A month later, four *Bear-Hs* from

184th TBAP Tu-95MSs (with '10 Red' *Saratov* nearest to camera) await the next mission at Engels on a winter day. A ZiL-131 lorry tows a train of dollies laden with inert Kh-55 missiles under tarpaulins marked *oochebnaya* (practice round).

Ookraïnka AB flew a 14-hour sortie over the Arctic Ocean and the North Atlantic. A similar mission was flown on 20h July by two 184th GvTBAP Tu-95MSs which took off from FOLs in the High North to fly over the Norwegian Sea, landing at the home base at Engels.

Times of reform

On 5th-8th August 2008 Russia conducted a brief military intervention in Georgia, responding to the latter's aggression against South Ossetia. This operation, whose reasons and course are outside the scope of this book, was officially announced by the then President Dmitriy A. Medvedev as an 'operation for compelling Georgia to peace'. However, it is more commonly known as the Russo-Georgian War – or by the unofficial name of 'the Five-Day War' (by analogy with the Six-Day War between Israel and the Arab nations in 1967). The Tu-95MS was not involved in this operation because there were no targets that warranted its use. However, the operation was an eye-opener, showing that command and control of the Russian forces involved was poor; as a result, the objective had been attained, but with excessively high combat losses which could have been avoided.

Tu-95MS '20 Red' *Doobna* vacates the runway after coming back from a training sortie.

A pennant marking the 65th birthday of the 79th TBAP awarded the Red Banner Order and Red Star Order. Again, the pennant features the unit motto *Onward through the impossible.*

A different pennant celebrating the same unit's 70th birthday and featuring the same 'Mission Impossible' motto.

This triggered a large-scale military reform in 2009-2010 which, among other things, changed the Russian Air Force's order of battle completely; it is widely known as 'the Serdyukov reform' after the then Minister of Defence Anatoliy E. Serdyukov. The traditional Soviet/Russian organisation dating back to the 1930s (air army – air division – air regiment – air squadron) was scrapped; the entire order of battle was reshuffled to form Aviation Bases (AvB) and their constituent Aviation Groups (AvGr) – oddly resembling the OrBat of some NATO nations. In so doing, almost every single unit was redeployed and/or merged with other units.

The 37th Strategic Air Army was no exception. The 184th TBAP was pooled with the other bomber unit resident at Engels-2 AB – the 121st GvTBAP – to become the 1st AvGr of the 6950th *Donbasskaya* GvAvB (*Gvardeyskaya aviatsionnaya bahza* – Guards Aviation Base) of the 1st Category. It inherited the honorary appellation and other awards of the disbanded 22nd GvTBAD, the honorary appellation *Donbasskaya* having been given to one of its constituent units for its part in the liberation of the Donetsk coal-mining area (Donbass, or Donetsk Basin) in the Ukraine during the Great Patriotic War. The aircraft complement for 2010 was 16 Tu-160s in Sqn 1 and 18 (?) Tu-95MSs in Sqn 2.

In the Far East, the former 79th TBAP and 182nd GvTBAP were similarly pooled to form the 6952nd *Ternopol'skaya* AvB of the 1st Category; the honorary appellation had been given to one of its constituent units for participating in the liberation of the Ukrainian city of Ternopol' during the Great Patriotic War. The aircraft complement for 2009 was 36 Tu-95MSs.

The supporting 203rd GvOAPSZ was not left out either, becoming the 6954th AvB. However, it was soon formally incorporated into the 43rd TsBP i PLS, as it was deemed expedient to streamline the command structure by forming a single unit.

Another consequence of the 2009 military reform was the introduction of quasi-civil registrations prefixed RF- ('Russian Federation') on military aircraft, as opposed to RA- ('Russian Aviation') for truly civil aircraft. This had nothing to do with the war – the RF- prefix signifies the government aviation register which is not limited to military aircraft; rather, the registrations served the same purpose as the serials on western military aircraft, allowing positive identification (unlike the tactical codes, which are still used in parallel). The Russian MoD did this to enable checks of aircraft fleet strength for the purpose of checking Russia's compliance with arms reduction treaties. Thus, operational Tu-95MSs were registered in the same RF-94*** block as the other strategic bombers.

Despite the problems associated with the changing order of battle and the relocation of units, the DA kept up the flight training and participates in exercises on a regular basis. For example, in June 2009 two Tu-95MSs

from Engels flew a routine practice mission (or, as the Russian Air Force puts it, patrol mission) over the Arctic Ocean. In September 2009 two Tu-95MS crews from Ookraïnka AB practiced navigation over featureless terrain during a patrol mission over the Arctic Ocean and the international waters of the Pacific. As usual, at some points of the mission the *Bears* were escorted by a pair of US Air Force F-15 fighters from Alaska to see what the Russians were up to. The mission lasted more than ten hours and involved several fuel top-ups from IL-78s.

On 21st October 2009 two *Bear-Hs* and two Tu-160s from Engels flew similar missions. More long-range practice missions were flown by pairs of Tu-95MSs on 18th-19th November and 24th-25th November; their routes took them over the Arctic Ocean and out to the international waters of the Atlantic Ocean.

More 'patrol' missions were flown on 18th December 2009, in January, February and April 2010. On 28th December 2009 two Tu-95MSs from Ookraïnka AB flew a routine training mission over the Sea of Japan and the international waters of the Pacific; the crews practiced navigation over featureless terrain and in-flight refuelling from IL-78 tankers. That year Tu-95MS strategic bombers also participated in Exercise *Zapad-2009* held jointly with Belorussia.

In March, April and August 2010 the Long-Range Aviation undertook a series of exercises. One more mission over the Sea of Japan and the Pacific was flown by a pair of *Bear-Hs* on 24th June 2010. On 16th July two 6952nd AvB Tu-95MSs made live launches of Kh-55 cruise missiles in the course of a tactical exercise.

The Long-Range Aviation's operations in 2010-11 were quite intensive, too. Thus, on 20th May 2010 a pair of Tu-95MSs flew yet another long-range training sortie that took them over the Arctic Ocean and near the Aleutian Islands. This time it was F-22A fighters that scrambled from Alaska to escort the uninvited guests. The mission time exceeded 15 hours, and of course in-flight refuelling from IL-78 tankers was involved.

As mentioned in Chapter 5, Russian Air Force Tu-95MSs are currently undergoing a multi-stage upgrade programme. The current Phase 1 upgrade aircraft are able to carry eight Kh-101 conventional cruise missiles or Kh-102 nuclear-tipped cruise missiles on paired wing pylons while retaining the ability to carry six Kh-55SMs or Kh-555s internally. The second phase, designated Tu-95MSM, will see new avionics integrated, expanding the aircraft's capabilities further – possibly including new-generation strategic cruise missiles carried externally or internally. For a while, some observers believed that the Kh-101 would not necessarily join the inventory, being used as a 'joker' in Russia's 'deck of cards' during the next round of strategic arms reduction talks with the USA. They have now been proven wrong – the Kh-101 has made its mark in the Syrian War (see below).

With a supporting IL-78 tanker in the background, '11 Red' *Vorkuta* taxies out for a night flight.

Silhouetted against the setting sun, a Tu-95MS climbs away on a late evening sortie.

Right and below right: Tu-95MS '12 Red'/ RF-94126 *Moskva* in seen here in Phase 1 upgraded form, showing off the four pairs of AKU-5M missile ejector racks under the wings.

Opposite page, top: Phase 1 upgraded Tu-95MS '16 Red' *Velikiy Novgorod* flies with four Kh-101 missiles on the inboard rail of each pylon.

Opposite page, bottom: Phase 1 upgraded Tu-95MS '10/1 Red'/ RF-94128 *Saratov* is pushed back by a BAZ-6306 prime mover at Engels-2 AB, with four Kh-101s on the pylons. For security reasons the live missiles are always kept under wraps when on the ground.

Syrian War: Russia joins in

In December 2011 – February 2012 a wave of protests and revolutions swept the Arab nations of northern Africa and the Middle East, becoming known as the Arab Spring. Starting in Tunisia, it spread to Algeria, Libya, Jordan, Mauretania, Sudan, Oman, Yemen, Saudi Arabia, Egypt, Syria, Morocco, Djibouti, Somalia, Bahrain, Iraq, Kuwait, Western Sahara and Lebanon, in that order. The scenario was usually the same: what started as peaceful civic protests (caused by economic reasons) quickly turned into political rebellion and often into armed insurrection; the slogan was usually 'the people want to bring down the regime'. In some countries this was limited to minor or major protests (in the case of Jordan, Oman, Morocco, Kuwait and Lebanon there were governmental changes caused by the protesters' demands, while in Algeria a 19-year state of national emergency was lifted). Elsewhere, however (in Tunisia, Egypt and Yemen), governments were overthrown and the ex-leaders forced into exile or prosecuted. In Libya, the protests encouraged by the western world escalated into a full-blown civil war and NATO intervention with the purpose of toppling the strongly anti-Western leader Col. Muammar Abu al-Qaddafi (who was eventually captured and lynched by the rebels in October 2011 as he attempted to flee the country).

A fine study of Tu-95MS '24 Red'/RF-94130. Note the exhaust stain on the fin caused by running the APU in flight.

A Phase 1 upgraded Tu-95MS prepares to top off its fuel tanks from an IL-78.

For many of the countries caught in the Arab Spring, the downfall of the government did not mean a change for the better – the situation degenerated into chaos as the various opposition groups began fighting over the scraps. This was the case in Libya (the Second Libyan Civil War) and Iraq, where there is an ongoing civil war since ex-President Saddam Hussein was overthrown in December 2003 and executed three years later. Worst of all, the Arab Spring has caused a resurgence of all manner of Islamist and terrorist organisations which are sworn enemies of the western world.

On 26th January 2012 unrest broke out in Syria. At first, the Libyan scenario looked set to be repeated: what started as civic protests (for much the same reason as in Libya) quickly turned into armed insurgency goaded and financed by the western powers and Saudi Arabia in a drive to remove President Bashar al-Assad. On 27th September Syrian government forces had their first

major clash with the Free Syrian Army (FSA) guerrillas in the city of Rastan, Homs Governorate (= province), which had been under opposition control for a couple of weeks. The FSA was just one of several insurgent groups controlling large parts of Syria, some of these groups having affiliations with the al-Qaeda terrorist network.

A shaky ceasefire was concluded in the spring of 2012 but collapsed on 1st June, the rebels beginning a new nationwide offensive against the government troops. The pretext was what had been described as the Houla massacre by the rebels, who accused the government troops of killing innocent civilians, while the government argued that the victims had been armed guerrillas and President Assad vowed to crush the uprising.

Up to then, the western powers masterminding 'colour revolutions' had succeeded; in Syria, they failed. Firstly, the Syrian regime turned out to be far more resilient than the West had expected. This was partly due to continuing Russian political and military aid, as Syria is Russia's last remaining ally in the Middle East. Bashar Assad is aware of what happened to Hussein and Qaddafi, and he knows all too well that if his regime is overthrown he will probably have a similar fate. Secondly, an overt military intervention with the purpose of overthrowing Assad (in the manner of the NATO operations in Iraq and Libya) is not possible – not at the moment, at least.

Thirdly, a new complication arose – a complication which has changed the world for ever. A new Islamist militant group had sprung up in 1999, joining al-Qaeda in 2004. In October 2006 it declared an Islamic state in war-torn Iraq, challenging the authority of the post-Saddam Hussein government; in April 2013 it claimed territory in the Levant (a historical geographical term referring to a large area in the eastern Mediterranean) and declared a caliphate, originally styling itself as the Islamic State of Iraq and the Levant (ISIL), or the Islamic State of Iraq and Syria (ISIS). In 2014 the group split off from al-Qaeda, which was 'not radical enough', and shortened its name to Islamic State (IS), thereby declaring its aim to extend its influence beyond just Iraq and Syria. And indeed, it 'exports' Islamic fundamentalism to other parts of the world, seeking to establish a worldwide caliphate, and is responsible for a number of terrorist attacks in Europe and the USA.

The so-called Islamic State has become infamous for human rights abuses and war crimes (massacres of civilians, the taking and cruel killing of hostages – including Muslims!) and for destruction of cultural heritage sites. The group has been designated a terrorist organisation by the United Nations, the European Union member nations, the USA, Russia, India, Indonesia, Israel, Turkey, Saudi Arabia, Syria, Iran and other countries. In December 2014 the US-led Global Coalition to Counter the Islamic State of Iraq and the Levant, composed of NATO nations and Co-operation Council for the Arab States of the Gulf (CCASG) member nations, was established launching Operation *Inherent Resolve* – a US-led military intervention against IS and Syrian al-Qaeda affiliates. Thus, the conflict in Syria became more than just a civil war.

In Russia, Islamic State is a banned organisation – among other things, because in June 2015 it laid claim to Russia's constituent republics in the North Caucasus, which have a largely Muslim population.

In the summer of 2015 President Bashar Assad addressed his Russian colleague Vladimir V. Putin, requesting military assistance for the government troops fighting IS and another Islamist terrorist group, Jabhat an-Nusrah (JaN, or al-Nusra Front), which is likewise banned in Russia. (JaN originated as the Syrian offshoot of what was then the Islamic State of Iraq but split from it in 2013, purporting to be a 'less radical' group. It now calls itself Jabhat Fateh al-Sham, 'Front for the Conquest of the Levant' – but, as a Russian saying goes, 'a snake may change its skin but not what is within'.) On 30th September 2015 Putin received authorisation from the Federation Council (the upper house of the Russian Parliament) to use Russian military forces in Syria in response to Assad's request. With that, Russia sent an expeditionary force which consisted largely of an Air Force component, plus military advisers; Russia stated explicitly that it would not use ground troops in Syria.

For the Russian Aerospace Force (VKS – *Voz**doosh**no-kos**mich**eskiye **seel**y*), as the former VVS is known since 1st August 2015, the Syrian campaign became the first 'hot' war – the first serious viability test of the reformed air arm. It is an operation of paramount importance, giving the VKS its first taste of a large-scale offensive campaign involving interaction between various branches of aviation and co-ordination of their actions with those of the ground forces (albeit allied ones, specifically Syrian government troops). It also provides the Russian Armed Forces with one-of-a-kind experience of deploying and supporting a tactical expeditionary force far away from home ground.

In this book, the authors have chosen not to discuss the political aspects of Russia's military intervention in the Syrian War, concentrating on the aviation aspect. Still, Russia's main motives for this intervention are not only the fight against IS, as a global threat, but also the desire to support the pro-Russian government of Syria and President Assad, as well as the desire to prevent the spread of Islamic fundamentalism into Russia, where much of the population is Muslim. On the other hand, it is highly important for Russia to avoid becoming involved in a prolonged war, to minimise own losses, to choose the targets for air strikes carefully and flexibly, to avoid a military confrontation with the western

Above and above right: armourers prepare a Kh-555 cruise missile for loading into a Tu-95MS during the first Russian strikes against IS in 2015. Note the work platform suspended from the weapons bay wall.

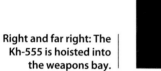

Right and far right: The Kh-555 is hoisted into the weapons bay.

Right: The first Kh-555 has been hooked up to the rotary launcher, and more are to follow.

Far right: An action cam shot showing a Kh-555 being released by a Tu-95MS during the Syrian War.

Below: A Tu-95MS launches a Kh-555 against an IS target in Syria in late 2005.

coalition waging war against IS and, finally, to pull out of the Syrian campaign at the right time.

Up to then, Russia had no airbases in Syria, but on 26th August 2015 the two nations signed an agreement allowing the future Russian task force in Syria to use Bassel al-Assad International Airport located 25 km (15.5 miles) south of Latakia, the capital of the eponymous governorate in eastern Syria. The airport is also a military base, and militarily it is known by its pre-1994 name, Khmeimim AB. The first four Russian Air Force jets – Su-30SM *Flanker-H* two-seat fighters – arrived on 18th September 2015. Within the next few days they were joined on TDY by Su-24M *Fencer-D* tactical bombers and Su-25/Su-25UB *Frogfoot-A/B* attack aircraft, and shortly afterwards by Su-34 *Fullback* tactical bombers. Mil' Mi-24P *Hind-F* attack helicopters and

Mi-8AMTSh-V *Hip-H* transport/assault helicopters were also deployed; all the aircraft were likewise seconded from first-line units and flown by ordinary service pilots.

The composition of the Russian task force left no doubts as to its intended mission: to annihilate the terrorists' battle positions and ground infrastructure. Targets included gun and rocket launcher emplacements, command posts, workshops where makeshift rockets and improvised explosive devices (IEDs) were manufactured, petrol, oil and lubricant (POL) dumps, weapons and materiel dumps, concealed bases and training camps. The task force was also to strike at the terrorists' convoys (trafficking in stolen crude oil was an important source of revenue for IS) and, if necessary, bridges and other targets.

On 30th September 2015 the Russian task force in Syria drew first blood when its tactical aircraft flew the first missions against IS, JaN and other militant groups opposing the Syrian government. According to a Russian Ministry of Defence press release, some 20 sorties were flown on the first day of active operations, with bomb and rocket strikes delivered against ammunition and POL dumps, combat vehicle concentrations and command posts. During the first week of active operations Russian Air Force aircraft hit 112 designated targets in Syria.

Operations were initially conducted on a fairly small scale with tactical aircraft only. On 31st October 2015, however, an Airbus Industrie A321-231 airliner registered EI-ETJ (c/n 663) and operated by the now-defunct Russian charter carrier MetroJet crashed about 50 km (31 miles) south-east of Hasna, North Sinai Governorate (Egypt), while en route from the Red Sea resort of Sharm el Sheikh to St. Petersburg, Russia, as flight 7K9268. All 224 on board were killed, making it Russia's worst-ever commercial aviation accident. Suspicions of a terrorist attack were quickly confirmed when Investigation of the crash showed that the aircraft had been blown out of the sky by an IED planted in the bulk cargo compartment. IS later claimed responsibility for the attack, which reinforced the Russian resolve to take up arms against it; President Vladimir V. Putin demanded that the strikes against the terrorists operating in Syria be stepped up.

17th November 2015 was a notable day as far as the Russian operation in Syria is concerned – for two reasons. Firstly, Russia used air-launched and sea-launched cruise missiles in combat for the first time ever – and, for the first time since the beginning of the operation in Syria, the Russian Aerospace Force used long-range bombers and strategic missile strike aircraft against the IS. Tu-95MSs from Engels AB were involved, along with Tu-160s from the same base and Tu-22M3s from Mozdok. The latter aircraft were the first to go into battle; 12 *Backfire-Cs* actually flew over Syria, delivering free-fall HE bombs on targets in Raqqah Governorate

Above: A Tu-95MS takes off at Engels on a missile strike mission in Syria.

Left: The combat navigator of a Tu-95MS at work during a sortie against Islamic State targets in Syria.

Another Kh-555 launch against terrorist targets in Syria. The missile's wings will deploy in a second.

with between 0500 hrs and 0530 hrs Moscow time. Shortly afterwards the *Blackjacks* and *Bear-Hs* joined the action; between 0900 hrs and 0940 hrs Tu-160Ms launched 16 Kh-101 cruise missiles, while Tu-95MSs launched eight Kh-555 CALCMs. They launched their weapons from outside Syrian airspace; nevertheless, like the *Backfires*, they were provided with fighter escort in the form of Su-27SM3 *Flanker-B Mod 3s*. They were supported by IL-78M tankers loitering over the Caspian Sea, ready to top off the bombers' tanks on the way home. On this first mission against IS the *Blackjacks* and *Bear-Hs* were airborne for 8 hours 20 minutes.

A still from a Russian Ministry of Defence video filmed from an escorting Su-30SM, showing a Phase 1 upgraded Tu-95MS making the type's first live Kh-101 launch against an IS target on 5th August 2017.

This was a truly historic day for the Russian Armed Forces. Whereas the Tu-22M3 was already a battle-proven type that had fought in Afghanistan and Chechnya, the Tu-160 and Tu-95MS strategic missile carriers had never been used in anger; thus both types received their baptism of fire in the Syrian War. Undoubtedly, the use of cruise missiles against targets in Syria was not caused by pressing military need – it was a check of the missiles' performance in a real-life scenario, but also a military-political gesture demonstrating the potential of the Russian Armed Forces.

Secondly, on the same day (17th November) the Russian Aerospace Force contingent deployed at Khmeimim AB was renamed the Special Mission Air

Another view of the missile as it falls away from the aircraft. The Tu-95MS's weapons bay doors stay closed, indicating this is a Kh-101 all right, since the Kh-101 is not carried internally by the *Bear*.

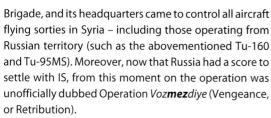

Above: A Tu-95MS is escorted by a Su-35S en route to the launch area for a strike against terrorists in Syria.

Above left: A Phase 1 upgraded Tu-95MS launches another Kh-101 in combat.

Left: Here, in contrast, is a stock *Bear-H* launching a Kh-555 at Syria.

Below and bottom: Bull's eye! Images from a Russian reconnaissance UAV showing a Kh-101 missile (marked with an arrow) as it hits the designated target.

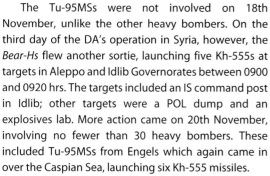

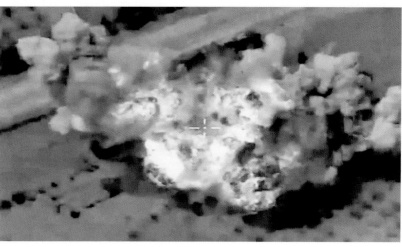

Brigade, and its headquarters came to control all aircraft flying sorties in Syria – including those operating from Russian territory (such as the abovementioned Tu-160 and Tu-95MS). Moreover, now that Russia had a score to settle with IS, from this moment on the operation was unofficially dubbed Operation *Vozmezdiye* (Vengeance, or Retribution).

The Tu-95MSs were not involved on 18th November, unlike the other heavy bombers. On the third day of the DA's operation in Syria, however, the *Bear-Hs* flew another sortie, launching five Kh-555s at targets in Aleppo and Idlib Governorates between 0900 and 0920 hrs. The targets included an IS command post in Idlib; other targets were a POL dump and an explosives lab. More action came on 20th November, involving no fewer than 30 heavy bombers. These included Tu-95MSs from Engels which again came in over the Caspian Sea, launching six Kh-555 missiles.

Another notable episode occurred in July 2017 – 20 months after the Tu-95's combat debut. Up to then, launching the latest Kh-101 cruise missiles in actual combat had been a privilege of the Tu-160M. On 5th July 2017, however, a pair of upgraded Tu-95MSs (including '11 Red'/RF-94127) flew the first real combat sortie, taking off from Engels-2 AB to launch four Kh-101s at IS targets on the borderline between Hama and Homs Governorates in Syria from about 1,000 km

Not only aircraft sport nose art – occasionally, so do missiles. This Kh-55SM has been adorned with pirate-themed artwork (the portrait of the recipient, eh?).

'Bat outa Hell' – another colourful Kh-55SM ready for loading into a Tu-95MS.

(621 miles) away. Over the Caspian Sea the *Bear* was escorted to and from the launch zone by Su-30SM and Su-35S *Flanker-E+* fighters on TDY at Khmeimim AB, the back-seaters of the *Flanker-Hs* filming the launches on video. Post-attack reconnaissance confirmed that all four designated targets – three materiel dumps and a terrorist command centre near the town of Aqayrbat (Hama Governorate) – had been destroyed.

What's in a name?

Together with the formation of the Russian Air Force's first Tu-160 squadron a long-forgotten tradition was revived. Nose art was generally frowned upon in the Soviet Air Force (and later the Russian Air Force), being broadly regarded as characteristic of the potential

adversary and hence unbecoming for the Soviet airmen – except in times of war when it helped keep up the fighting spirit. (In fairness, it should be said that USAF-style frivolous pin-up artwork was never encountered on Soviet/Russian military aircraft.) Soon, however, the Russian Air Force command conceded that naughty drawings painted on without as much as a by your leave by the unit personnel are one thing and officially christening an aircraft is another. Hence in the late 1990s the Russian Air Force began naming individual aircraft – mostly heavy bombers and transports, although quite a few tactical aircraft have also received individual names.

In the Long-Range Aviation this naming tradition follows a fairly distinctive pattern. While operational Tu-160s are christened to honour specific persons – mostly Soviet Air Force (Long-Range Aviation) airmen who had fought with gallantry in the Great Patriotic War but also men who were associated with the development of the *Blackjack*, some of the Russian Air Force Tu-95MSs are named after Russian cities. The names are bestowed by the Military Council of the 37th Air Army, and many of them have some connection with the Long-Range Aviation. Each aircraft wears the city crest on both sides of the nose together with the name, and the latter is usually applied in stylised Old Slavic script (whose rendering varies a lot from aircraft to aircraft). Curiously, the christening ceremonies included consecration by a Russian Orthodox priest (to enlist 'God's support' for safe operations perhaps?).

At least 20 Tu-95MSs sported individual names (the name *Ryazan'* was seen on at least two different aircraft at different times). Details are given in the table on page 423.

Showtime

As already mentioned, the Tu-95's public debut took place on 3rd July 1955 during the Aviation Day display at Moscow-Tushino. The type also participated in these displays in later years – albeit not annually.

On 1st May 1956 a trio of production Tu-95s participated in a parade in Moscow's Red Square for the first time. The lead aircraft was captained by test pilot Aleksey P. Yakimov, the right-hand wingman by GK NII VVS test pilot Viktor D. Sergeyev and the left-hand wingman by Maj.-Gen. Aleksandr I. Molodchiy.

On 9th July 1961, after a four-year break, Tushino hosted the biggest air parade held there hitherto. The participating aircraft included a formation of 19 Tu-95Ks from the 409th TBAP; the lead aircraft escorted by seven Mikoyan/Gurevich MiG-17 *Fresco* fighters was captained by 106th TBAD CO Gen. Aleksey A. Plokhov.

In 1992 Kubinka AB, the 'showcase base' that had been off limits to the general public until then, started holding 'open houses', allowing hundreds of aviation enthusiasts to see current operational Russian Air Force

A Tu-95MS escorted by four MiG-29s from Kubinka (two of them in the old colours of the Strizhi display team) follows IL-78M '36 Blue' during a rehearsal of the V-Day parade in 1995 when the 50th anniversary of the victory over Nazi Germany was celebrated.

aircraft up close and personal. The first such event took place on 11th April 1992. The weather literally watered down the festivities a bit, with brief but frequent blizzards leading to annoying interruptions in the flying display. Yet the public did have a chance to see a Tu-95MS in a simulated refuelling formation with IL-78 *sans suffixe* '34 Blue'; another *Bear-H* was parked in front of the display base hangar for close inspection.

In 1993 a 182nd GvTBAP Tu-95MS ('20 Black', c/n 1000211834108) captained by Maj. V. S. Zemnukhov represented the Russian Air Force at the Royal International Air Tattoo '93 at RAF Fairford. The scenario was repeated at the Farnborough International '94 airshow in July 1994 when the same unit put up Tu-95MS '23 Black' (c/n 1000212834379), again captained by Zemnukhov. The *Bear* was one of the stars

Known Russian Air Force Tu-95MSs with individual names		
Tactical code/registration	**Name**	**Notes**
01 Red/RF-94185	Irkutsk	Christened 1-11-2000. 6952nd AvB
02 Red/RF-94184	Mozdok	6952nd AvB
04 Red/RF-94182	Kurgan	Christened 6-10-2009. 6952nd AvB
08 Red	Smolensk	Christened 19-5-1999 (also reported as 5-6-1999). Became, see next line
29/2 Red/RF-94178	Smolensk	6952nd AvB
10/1 Red/RF-94128	Saratov	Christened 12-6-1999. 6950th AvB, Phase 1 upgrade to carry Kh-101/Kh-102 missiles
11 Red/RF-94127	Vorkuta	Christened 24-11-2001. 6950th AvB
12 Red/RF-94126	Moskva	121st TBAP, later 6950th AvB, Phase 1 upgrade to carry Kh-101/Kh-102 missiles
14 Red/RF-94132	Voronezh	Christened 29-5-2014. 182nd TBAP, to 121st GvTBAP; Phase 1 upgrade to carry Kh-101/Kh-102 missiles
15 Red/RF-94125	Kaluga	Christened 4-10-1999
16 Red/RF-94124	Velikiy Novgorod	Christened 23-6-2007. 6950th AvB, Phase 1 upgrade to carry Kh-101/Kh-102 missiles
19 Red/RF-94123	Krasnoyarsk	Christened 28-8-2010. 6950th AvB
20/1 Red/RF-94122	Doobna	Christened 5-7-2008. 6950th AvB, Phase 1 upgrade to carry Kh-101/Kh-102 missiles
21/2 Red/RF-94121	Samara	Christened 8-8-2008. 6950th AvB. Damaged beyond repair by fire Ryazan'-Dyagilevo 26-2-2013
22 Red	Chelyabinsk	Christened 29-9-2001
22/1 Red/RF-94120	Kozel'sk	Christened 15-4-2010. 6950th AvB
23/1 Red/RF-94129	Tambov	Christened 8-7-2000. 6950th AvB, Phase 1 upgrade to carry Kh-101/Kh-102 missiles
27/1 Red/RF-94117	Izborsk	Christened 12-8-2014. 6950th AvB, Phase 1 upgrade to carry Kh-101/Kh-102 missiles
28/1 Red/RF-94116	Sevastopol'	6950th AvB, Phase 1 upgrade to carry Kh-101/Kh-102 missiles
47 Red	Ryazan'	6952nd AvB. Name not reapplied after overhaul and repaint in grey c/s
59 Red/RF-94206	Blagoveshchensk	Christened 23-6-1999. 6952nd AvB. Named after a border city in the Far East
604 Black	Ryazan'	Christened 20-12-1999. Became, see next line!
20 Red	Ryazan'	

Tu-95MS '28 Red' escorted by two very colourful MiG-29s from the Tactical Aviation's 4th TsBP i PLS in Lipetsk, makes a flypast over Monino during the air parade on 12th August 2007 to celebrate the Russian Air Force's 95th birthday.

of the show on both occasions. Too bad that such visits are no longer possible in the current political climate…

On 14th May 1994 another 'open house' was held at Kubinka. This time the weather was fine; the static display did not feature any heavy bombers, but the flying programme included a *Bear-H*, a *Backfire-C* and a *Blackjack*.

On 21st August 1994 a 182nd GvTBAP Tu-95MS and a supporting IL-78 tanker visited Barksdale AFB again; the aircraft was captained by Lt.-Col. K. A. Yepifanovskiy. As a USAF serviceman who witnessed these events put it, *'they (the Russian airmen – Auth.) spent about a week here each time, and they absolutely HATED to leave – and to be honest, we really hated to see them go. They're just like us in many ways. The Barksdale and Bossier*

City/Shreveport communities really rolled out the red carpet for the Bear and An-124 (1992), and IL-76 (1994) crews both times.' There were a lot of informal contacts between the Russian and US pilots – right down to swapping items of flight clothing as souvenirs!

On 9th May 1995 a tremendous military parade was held in Moscow to celebrate the 50th anniversary of the Soviet victory in the Great Patriotic War against Nazi Germany. In a departure from tradition, the parade was held at Poklonnaya Gora in the western-central part of the city, not in Red Square. Hence the participating aircraft approached the city from the west, flying along the Mozhaisk Highway and Kutuzovskiy Prospekt (Kutuzov Avenue). For the first time in many years the V-Day parade included a large Air Force component

Here we have a somewhat unusual parade formation – Tu-95MS '16 Red' *Velikiy Novgorod* and IL-78M '36 Blue' are each escorted by a pair of MiG-29s from Lipetsk.

A Tu95MS escorted by Su-27s follows an IL-78M tanker en route to Moscow for a parade flypast.

(79 fixed-wing and rotary-wing aircraft). The Long-Range Aviation was also represented, putting up one Tu-95MS (plus one more in hot reserve), along with one Tu-160 and three Tu-22M3s. The *Bear-H* and *Blackjack* flew in line astern formation with IL-78M tankers to simulate the in-flight refuelling procedure. A day earlier,

the same formation had passed over the city during the dress rehearsal of the parade. Thus, the V-Day air parade tradition (weather permitting) was restored.

Surprisingly enough, it was not until 2001 that the Tu-95 became a participant in the biennial MAKS airshows at the LII airfield in Zhukovskiy. The static park

A scene from the V-Day parade in Moscow on 9th May 2010 as Tu-95MS '15 Red' *Kaluga* passes over Red Square in company with MiG-29SMTs from Lipetsk.

Tu-95MS '12 Red'/
RF-94126 *Moskva* in
the static park of the
MAKS-2013 airshow.

of MAKS-2001 (14th-19th August) included a 'company-owned' Tu-95MS coded '604 Black'.

On the opening day of the MAKS-2005 airshow (16th-21st August), the flying display was opened by five Tupolev machines – four company-owned aircraft (a Tu-95MS, a Tu-160, a Tu-204-100C freighter and the Tu-334 short-haul airliner prototype) and one Long-Range Aviation aircraft (Tu-22M3 '28 Red' of the 52nd GvTBAP from Shaikovka AB). The five aircraft passed over the runway in V formation, fanning out spectacularly at the end.

The MAKS-2007 airshow (21st-26th August) introduced a welcome change – the Russian Air Force started putting up operational heavy bombers. The static display at included Tu-95MS '16 Red' *Velikiy Novgorod* representing the 184th TBAP from Engels.

A few days before the show, on 12th August 2007, a major air event took place in Monino to celebrate the 95th birthday of the Russian Air Force. The grass airfield adjacent to the Russian Air Force museum and to the Air Force Academy compound was turned into a spectator area, and the public was allowed access to the

A Phase 1 upgraded
Tu-95MS, '10/1 Red'/
RF-94128 *Saratov*, is
shown in the static park
at the MAKS-2017
airshow in July 2017.

Tu-95MS '16 Red'/ RF-94124 *Velikiy Novgorod* follows IL-78M '81 Blue'/ RF-94285 in a simulated refuelling formation on 9th May 2015 during the V-Day parade.

A Tu-95MS trailing an IL-78 tanker flies over Sevastopol' Bay on 9th May 2014 during the V-Day celebrations.

Here, '10/1 Red'/ RF-94128 *Saratov* is depicted at Kubinka AB in July 2015 during the Army 2015 Military Technical Forum. This was the Phase 1 upgrade's public debut.

Tu-95MS '04 Red'/ RF-94182 *Kurgan* flies over St. Petersburg on 9th May 2015.

A scene from Kubinka AB as three Phase 1 upgraded Tu-95MSs pass in V formation on 5th August 2017 during a rehearsal of the Russian Air Force 105th anniversary parade.

Three upgraded *Bear-Hs* pass over Red Square on 4th May 2017 during a rehearsal of the V-Day flypast; '10/1 Red' *Saratov* leads '27/1 Red' *Izborsk* (left) and '26/1 Red' *Sevastopol'* (right). Eventually the flypast on 9th May had to be cancelled because of poor weather.

Academy's instructional flight line. The centrepiece of the event was a grand air parade involving most of the types currently in Russian Air Force service – including the DA types. First, a Tu-95MS coded '28 Red' passed over the field, escorted by two MiG-29 *Fulcrum-C* fighters of the Air Force's 4th TsBP i PLS in Lipetsk. Next came a pair of Tu-22M3s ('16 Red' and '60 Red') in echelon starboard formation with the wings at minimum sweep. They were followed by Tu-160 '11 Red' *Vasiliy Sen'ko*, again with fighter escort from the Lipetsk Centre – this time a Su-27SM *Flanker-B* single-seater and a Su-27UB *Flanker-C* trainer. Then, after a brief pause, came IL-78M '35 Blue' leading another Tu-95MS ('28 Red') in a simulated in-flight refuelling formation.

On 9th May 2008 a Tu-95MS from Engels participated in the V-Day parade, which now took place at the usual location – in Red Square. Accordingly the participating aircraft approached the city from the north, flying along Leningradskiy Prospekt (Leningrad Avenue) and Tverskaya Street. The *Bear* was following an IL-78M in a simulated refuelling formation escorted by two MiG-29s of the 4th TsBP i PLS from Lipetsk.

In March 2009 Kubinka AB became the scene for a grand display of military hardware (primarily aircraft and aviation weapons, including the latest ones). It's no secret that after the Five-Day War with Georgia in August 2008 the Russian political leaders, who were dissatisfied with the 'quality' of the operation and excessive losses suffered by the Russian Air Force, demanded that the Russian MoD should immediately take measures not only to increase the command and control efficiency but also to speed up the introduction of the latest combat hardware. The then President of Russia Dmitriy A. Medvedev, being the Supreme Commander-in-Chief, promised to keep a tab personally on the reforming and re-equipment of the Armed Forces. Six months after the war he decided to check personally how his order was being carried out. By the end of March two dozen aircraft and helicopters – both production models in first-line service and new models then under test – had flown in to Kubinka AB; these included three Long-Range Aviation aircraft – Tu-95MS '15 Red' *Kaluga* and Tu-160 '08 Red' *Vitaliy Kopylov* from Engels-2 AB, plus Tu-22M3 '15 Red' from Shaikovka AB. The *Bear's* weapons bay housed a Kh-55SM cruise missile; a closed hangar at the display base, which was off limits to the reporters who had arrived for the event, contained the latest types of aircraft weapons, including the new Kh-555 and Kh-101 cruise missiles, which were shown to the President and his retinue.

The V-Day parade over Red Square on 9th May 2009 traditionally included an IL-78M/Tu-95MS combo ('36 Blue' and '21 Red' *Samara* respectively) which was escorted by four MiG-29 *Fulcrum-C* fighters (two plain grey examples from Kursk and two in blue display colours from the 4th TsBP i PLS in Lipetsk). Just over three months later, on 18th-23rd August, the same

Tu-95MS '21 Red' *Samara* was in the static display of the MAKS-2009 international airshow in Zhukovsky. Two years later this very aircraft was again displayed at the MAKS-2011 show (16th-21st August) – now with '21/1 Red' on the port nose gear door and registered RF-94121. The MAKS-2013 airshow (27th August – 1st September) featured a different *Bear-H* for a change – '12 Red'/RF-94126 *Moskva*. Tu-95MS '16 Red' *Velikiy Novgorod* (by then registered RF-94124) was on display at MAKS-2015, which was held on 25th-30th August.

The Long-Range Aviation was heavily involved in the V-Day parade in Red Square on 9th May 2010 which involved 127 assorted aircraft. These included 14 missile carriers, three IL-78M tankers ('31 Blue', '35 Blue' and '51 Blue') and several more aircraft in hot reserve. The DA's aircraft converged on Moscow from two bases – Engels and Shaikovka. For the first time in the history of flypasts over Red Square, the parade included a trio of Tu-95MSs ('21 Red' *Samara*, '20 Red' *Doobna* and '22 Red' *Kozel'sk*), plus a further *Bear-H* ('15 Red' *Kaluga*) in simulated refuelling formation. Like most of the participating aircraft, the bombers and tankers wore new-style Russian Air Force pentastars (with a blue outline added inside the usual red/white outline to symbolise the Russian flag) and bold 'VVS ROSSII' (RUSSIAN AIR FORCE) titles on the tail.

As mentioned in Chapter 5, in June 2015 the Phase 1 upgraded Tu-95MS capable of carrying Kh-101 missiles made its public debut at the Army-2015 International Military Technical Forum when an aircraft coded '10/1 Red', registered RF-94128 and named *Saratov* was in the static display at Kubinka AB. A year later, however, visitors at the Army-2016 International Military Technical Forum had to make do with a perfectly standard *Bear-H* ('29/2 Red'/RF-94178 *Smolensk*).

On 9th May 2016 three Phase 1 upgraded Tu-95MSs participated for the first time in the traditional flypast over Red Square during the V-Day parade, flying in V formation. In 2017, however, the spectators watching the parade were in for a disappointment. The rehearsal flypasts on 2nd May and 7th May (involving three upgraded Tu-95MSs) went without a hitch, but on 9th May the entire flypast was cancelled because of appalling weather, with a cloudbase not exceeding 50 m (164 ft). The rule 'safety first' always applies – and no one would be able to see the aircraft anyway, with clouds that low.

In a break with established tradition, MAKS-2017 was held a month earlier than usual on 18th-23rd July 2017. This was the first time a Phase 1 upgraded Tu-95MS (the abovementioned '10/1 Red'/RF-94128) was displayed at Zhukovskiy.

The latest show performance by the Tu-95MS was on 12th August 2017 when a huge armada of assorted military aircraft flew over Patriot Park in Kubinka on occasion of the Russian Air Force's 105th birthday.

CHAPTER EIGHT

Bears over the oceans: Navy versions in action

The Soviet Naval Aviation (AVMF) introduced the *Bear* almost a decade later than the Air Force. The type saw service with two of the Soviet Navy's four fleets – the North Fleet and the Pacific Fleet.

The first naval unit to operate the Tu-95 was the North Fleet Air Arm's 392nd ODRAP (ot**del'**nyy **dahl'**niy raz**ved**yvatel'nyy **avia**polk – independent, i.e., direct reporting long-range reconnaissance air regiment), the first unit of the kind in the AVMF. The unit was established at Severomorsk-1 AB (Naval Air Station Severomorsk-1) in the Murmansk Region on 1st September 1963, with Lt.-Col. Aleksandr S. Fedotov as its first CO. The instructors and command personnel for the 392nd ODRAP was hand-picked in all four fleets among top-notch pilots, navigators and technicians with experience in the AVMF and the DA. For a year the regiment operated ordinary Tu-95M bombers on loan from the DA for the purpose of 'building up the numbers' on the

type and maintaining proficiency. It was not until 5th November 1964 that the 392nd ODRAP took delivery of the first operational Tu-95RTs long-range maritime reconnaissance/OTH target designator aircraft; when enough *Bear-Ds* had been delivered to commence normal operations, the *Bear-As* were returned to the Air Force. Incidentally, the Tu-95RTs prototype was also delivered to the 392nd ODRAP after being operated by GK NII VVS for a while. In the unit this particular aircraft was dubbed *komolyy* (hornless) because, unlike the other *Bear-Ds*, it lacked the IFR probe.

However, from the outset Severomorsk-1 was seen only as a temporary base. As early as 1963, construction of a brand-new airbase specifically for the 392nd ODRAP had started near Kipelovo railway station 50 km (31.5 miles) west of the city of Vologda in the north of central Russia. On 29th December 1964 the unit received orders from

A 392nd ODRAP Tu-95RTs prepares to taxi out from its snow-covered hardstand at Kipelovo AB.

The early days of 392nd ODRAP operations. A Tu-95M bomber (note the smooth belly lacking the search radar's huge radome) is pictured at Severomorsk-1 AB in September 1964.

Another view of the same scene; the bomber is undergoing routine maintenance, with an APA-2 GPU on a ZiL-164 chassis in attendance. The unit's maintenance chiefs (left to right: Sqn 1 Chief Engineer A. K. Plotnikov, Sqn 2 Chief Engineer S. T. Yevstigneyev and the regiment's Chief Engineer V. Kh. Roonets) are walking away from the aircraft, satisfied that everything is OK.

Convair F-106A-90-CO 57-2494, a Massachusetts Air National Guard (102nd FIW/101st FIS) aircraft from Otis ANGB, escorts a 392nd ODRAP Tu-95RTs off Cape Cod on 15th April 1982. Note the open oblique camera port under the Bear-D's ELINT blister.

the North Fleet Commander Fleet Adm. Semyon M. Lobov to move to the newly-completed Kipelovo AB (NAS Kipelovo). By early 1965 the unit's first two crews were cleared to fly solo in the type Tu-95RTs. On 27th May that year a crew captained by unit CO Lt.-Col. Aleksandr S. Fedotov flew the first maximum-range sortie, with Deputy CO Lt.-Col. Ivan F. Gladkov acting as instructor. On 31st August 1965 the 392nd ODRAP completed its relocation to Kipelovo AB.

Speaking of conversion training, Tu-95RTs crews converted to the type at the AVMF's 33rd Training Centre stationed at Kul'bakino AB on the east side of Nikolayev in southern Ukraine on the Black Sea. In 1967 the outfit was redesignated as the 33rd TsBP i PLS named after Yevgeniy N. Preobrazhenskiy, who had been AVMF Commander from 1950 to 1962. The Centre included several instructional units, including the 316th OPLAE (*ot**del'**naya protivo**lod**ochnaya **a**viaeskad**ril'**ya –* Independent ASW Air Squadron) at Kul'bakino AB. In due course the 'hornless' Tu-95RTs prototype was transferred to this unit from the 392nd ODRAP.

Unfortunately, on 23rd January 1966 an Antonov An-8 *Camp* twin-turboprop transport of the North Fleet's 912th OTAP (*ot**del'**nyy **trahns**portnyy **avia**polk –* independent airlift regiment) carrying the 392nd ODRAP's entire command staff to a North Fleet Air Arm command conference crashed on approach to Lakhta AB near Arkhangel'sk due to severe icing. The crew of five headed by Capt. V. A. Kropanyov and the 20 passengers, including Aleksandr S. Fedotov (by then promoted to Colonel), were killed. On 12th February 1966 the Vologda Region administration passed a decision bestowing the name Fedotovo on the garrison at Kipelovo AB to commemorate the unit's first CO.

Still, life goes on, and the 392nd ODRAP continued building up its aircraft fleet and practicing, with Lt.-Col. Ivan F. Gladkov appointed as the new CO. By September 1966 the unit had ten Tu-95RTs reconnaissance aircraft on strength and ten fully qualified crews, and more were coming. Thus on 15th September 1966 the regiment went on active duty in accordance with a directive signed by the North Fleet Commander. The crews began preparing for routine sorties.

Until 1969 the 392nd ODRAP's aircraft were coded sequentially from '01 Black' upwards, odd-numbered aircraft being assigned to Sqn 1 and even-numbered ones to Sqn 2. Later, when a third squadron was activated, each of the squadrons received its own tactical code sequence, the first digit denoting the squadron number.

Gradually the crews polished their skills – with occasional inevitable spills. The Tu-95RTs underwent a constant modification and upgrading process in the course of their service, which meant the modified equipment had to be mastered again; yet the crews managed to do it, training systematically in providing

Top: A North Fleet Tu-95RTs is intercepted over the North Atlantic by a McDonnell F-4B from CVW-8 embarked on USS *Forrestal*.

Above: Escorted by F-4J-34-MC BuNo 155773, a 392nd ODRAP *Bear-D* shadows the carrier USS *Chester W. Nimitz* (CVN-68).

Below: F-4J-42-MC BuNo 157283/'AA-104' from VF-74 checks out a visiting Tu-95RTs. Note the black-painted main gear fairings and the exhaust stains on the wings.

target information to ships in harbours and in training areas on the high seas. By August 1966 the unit was capable of transmitting target data simultaneously to three missile submarines in the Barents Sea.

Almost concurrently the Tu-95RTs was fielded with the Pacific Fleet. On 4th September 1965 the 867th ODRAP was established at Khorol' AB (NAS Khorol') in the south of the Primor'ye Territory, sharing the base with the resident 169th MRAP (*morskoy raketonosnyy aviapolk* – Maritime Missile Strike Air Regiment) flying Tu-16K-10s. The unit's first Tu-95RTs (c/n 65MRTs105) had arrived in April 1965. By the end of the year the 867th ODRAP had completed its conversion training course, taking delivery of 22 such aircraft by 1969. On 20th July 1966 a pair of *Bear-Ds* captained by the regiment's CO Col. Smirnov and deputy CO Lt.-Col. Yoorchikov flew the first reconnaissance mission to locate the amphibious assault ship USS *Iwo Jima* (LPH-2) in the middle of the Pacific Ocean.

From the mid-1960s onwards, the Tu-95RTs became a familiar sight in the ocean areas used by the Western navies, as these aircraft constantly monitored NATO naval operations in the Arctic, Atlantic and Indian oceans during the Cold War era. They prowled over the Bay of Biscay and the Persian Gulf, the Azores and the Cape Verde Islands, the Cape of Good Hope and the Falklands. A single Tu-95RTs could monitor an area of 8-10 million square kilometres (3,088,800-3,864,000 square miles) in a single sortie and classify the targets it

Opposite, top: No fewer than three Tomcats from VF-143 'Pukin' Dogs' based aboard USS *Dwight Eisenhower* – F-14A-140-GR BuNo 162692/'AG-101', F-14B-145-GR BuNo 162921/'AG-102' and F-14B-150-GR BuNo 163220/'AG-100' – are tailing a single *Bear-D*.

Opposite, centre: This *Bear-D* shadowing USS *Midway* is intercepted by F-4J-45-MC BuNo 158349/'NF-207' from VF-151.

Opposite, bottom: Another Tu-95RTs flies a routine mission in 1989.

Left: F-14A-95-GR BuNo 160393/'AC-110' from VF-11 escorts a high-flying Tu-95RTs.

detected. A regiment of *Bear-Ds* could survey more than 90 million square kilometres (34,749,000 square miles) and shadow two or three CTFs without let-up for 15-20 days. The intensity of Tu-95RTs operations was such that the Western military bestowed a nickname on the type – 'the Eastern Express'. In the Soviet Navy the Tu-95RTs was jocularly called 'the eyes and ears of the fleet' (well, actually this sobriquet applied to the reconnaissance element of the AVMF as a whole).

In the course of operations the crews studied the geographical and climatic peculiarities of the region which had to be taken into account in order to accomplish the mission and return home safely. The North Fleet crews had to deal with inclement weather – the prevalent conditions over the Norwegian Sea and the North Atlantic were cloudy, with fog and rain (or snow, depending on the season) on most days. There were rough seas (sea state 4 or 5 on the Beaufort scale)

A badge commemorating the 70th birthday of the Pacific Fleet's 304th GvODRAP.

F-4E-32-MC 66-0328 wearing the markings of the 57th FIS stationed at Keflavik, Iceland, inspects a Tu-95RTs passing through the Greenland Gap.

Top: A 392nd ODRAP Tu-95RTs is refuelled by a 3MS-2 from Engels-2 AB.

Above: The first intercept of a Tu-95RTs by a Royal Navy BAe Sea Harrier FRS.1 (XZ495/'N-005' from No.801 Sqn) during Exercise *Ocean Venture* in August 1981.

Below: Grumman EA-6B-85-GR Prowler BuNo 161247/'NF-407' from CVW-5 embarked on USS *Midway* maintains an interest in a *Bear-D*.

for 20-30% of the year in those parts. The climatic and weather conditions on the Pacific theatre of operations were more varied. Lots of cloud were encountered over the Sea of Okhotsk and the Sea of Japan; in the summer the cloud cover was heavier than in the winter (6-7 oktas versus 4-5 oktas) and cumulus clouds stretching vertically up to 13,000 m (42,650 ft) were encountered.

On 18th February 1967 two *Bear-Ds* from the 392nd ODRAP overflew the carrier USS *America* (CVA-66) near the Strait of Gibraltar, causing two McDonnell Douglas F-4B Phantom IIs to scramble and escort them away. The carrier was making her second trans-Atlantic cruise from Norfolk, Virginia, to the Mediterranean.

On 16th April 1967 a pair of 392nd ODRAP Tu-95RTs aircraft captained by Lt.-Col. Ivan F. Gladkov and Lt.-Col. V. I. Khayarov flew the first reconnaissance sortie involving in-flight refuelling. Having no hose-and-drogue tankers of its own, the AVMF co-operated with the Air Force – the reconnaissance aircraft were topped up by the Long-Range Aviation's Myasishchev M-4-2 tankers (and subsequently 3MS-2 tankers) based at Engels. Probe-and-drogue IFR turned out to be no easier than the wing-to-wing techniques used by the Tu-16. By June 1968 ten 392nd ODRAP crews had received their IFR procedure ratings.

In September 1968 a group of four 392nd ODRAP *Bear-Ds* participated in an inter-fleet exercise with Pacific Fleet, redeploying temporarily to the Soviet Far East for the purpose of practicing reconnaissance on the Far Eastern theatre of operations.

On 8th March 1968 a Soviet Navy Type 629A (NATO *Golf II* class) diesel-electric ballistic missile submarine – the Pacific Fleet submarine K-129 (hull number 722) – went missing in the Pacific Ocean during a routine combat patrol with three R-21 (NATO SS-N-5 *Serb*) nuclear-tipped SLBMs aboard. A massive search and rescue effort involving ships and aircraft was launched; surprisingly enough, the Tu-95RTs crews from the North Fleet (392nd ODRAP), not the Pacific Fleet (867th ODRAP), were involved. The operation conti-nued throughout March and into early April but in vain – the submarine and her crew of 98 were not found. In fact, there weren't any survivors – the K-129 was lost with all hands, sinking in 4,900 m (16,000 ft) of water about 1,560 nautical miles (2,890 km) northwest of Oahu, Hawaii, when two of the missiles exploded in their launch tubes. (In August 1968 the Americans located the wreckage and clandestinely retrieved part of it in 1974, and a Pacific Fleet/304th GvODRAP Tu-95RTs shadowed the CIA's purpose-built salvage ship *Hughes Glomar Explorer* which lifted the submarine – in both the literal meaning of the word and the slang meaning; but that's another story.)

On 26th June 1968 a pair of Royal Canadian Air Force (416 Sqn) McDonnell CF-101 Voodoo fighters from RCAFB Chatham intercepted a Tu-95RTs for the first

Above: A Tu-95RTs prepares to photograph a US Navy aircraft carrier moving on a reciprocal heading.

Below: This shot shows how the shadowing fighters would take pictures of the *Bears* from every possible angle.

437

Left row, top to bottom: USS *Independence* (CV-62) seen from a 392nd ODRAP Tu-95RTs captained by Maj. Tyurkov.

The same carrier pictured in 1977.

This picture of USS *Midway* (CV-41) was taken from 5 km (3.1 miles) range by a 392nd ODRAP Tu-95RTs captained by Maj. Natal'yin, flying at 300 m (980 ft).

A photo of USS *Independence* taken on 17th November 1975 by a North Fleet Tu-95RTs captained by Maj. Rykov.

Here, the *Midway* was photographed by a Pacific Fleet/304th ODRAP *Bear-D*.

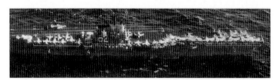

Bottom: USS *Midway* and a *Knox* class destroyer being replenished on the high seas.

Right row, top: A photo taken by a Tu-95RTs showing HMS *Hermes* (R12), partly obstructed by one of her F-4Ks, with a replenishment vessel.

Centre: The *Hermes* being refuelled off St. Helena Island in 1982 during the Falklands War.

Opposite page, left row: A US Navy carrier seen from a *Bear-D*.

Right row, top: HMS *Invincible* (R05) with Sea Harriers on deck.

Centre: Another view of the same carrier

Bottom: The container ship S/S *Atlantic Conveyor* used as an auxiliary carrier with Harriers and Westland Wessex helicopters seen from a Tu-95RTs en route to the Falklands war zone.

438

An enamel badge issued in 1983 to mark the 20th birthday of the 392nd ODRAP.

A 25th anniversary badge of the same unit showing its appellation 'named after the 70th anniversary of the Great October Socialist Revolution'.

A badge marking the 30th birthday of the 392nd ODRAP in 1993.

time. On 17th July that year a 392nd ODRAP Tu-95RTs overflew and photographed the carrier USS *Saratoga* (CV-3) near the Azores Islands; several of the carrier's fighters scrambled to intercept.

In addition to its primary mission, the Tu-95RTs was used to support the Soviet space programme. 392nd ODRAP *Bear-Ds* were called upon to locate Soviet military space vehicles which splashed down in the Indian Ocean after re-entry, transmitting their coordinates to Soviet Navy ships; it was imperative that the latter reached the space capsules and retrieved them before the Americans did. Such missions were codenamed **El***lips* (ellipse). The extreme range and duration of these missions over the Indian Ocean necessitated in-flight refuelling. For demonstration purposes, on 1st August 1968 two *Bear-Ds* captained by 392nd ODRAP CO Ivan F. Gladkov (by then promoted to Colonel) and squadron commander Maj. A. I. Startsev flew a 20-hour reconnaissance mission over the Indian Ocean, refuelling over Iranian territory. Occasionally, however, the *Bears* would make refuelling stops at forward bases in 'friendly nations' rather than 'hit the tanker'.

The first Ellips mission took place on 21st September 1968 and was led by Col. Ivan F. Gladkov; the vehicle to be detected was a Soviet lunar probe. Eight *Bears* took off from Mozdok in pairs at one-hour intervals; a 3MS-2 tanker would take off first, followed two minutes later by a Tu-95RTs. Knowing the space probe's estimated time of arrival (that is, the planned recovery parachute deployment time), the first pair's departure was scheduled so that the *Bear* would be on location at the southernmost point of the search area, which was about ten hours' flight time away from Mozdok. After take-off each pair headed for Tbilisi, Georgia; thence the aircraft proceeded to Djul'fa, a town on the Iranian border, where the international airway exiting Soviet airspace began. Next, the pair made a port turn and headed for Tehran and then via Mashhad, Birjand and Zahedan to the coast of the Indian Ocean. The refuelling procedure began over the coast; by then the Tu-95RTs had used up about 20 tons (44,090 lb) of fuel – the maximum amount which the tanker could transfer and still make it back to base. The procedure took 10-12 minutes, then the tanker turned back while the *Bear* continued its flight all alone over the endless ocean – first in darkness, then in daylight and then again in darkness. No long-range radio navigation (LORAN) systems existed yet, so the crew had to rely entirely on the course plotted on the chart by means of navigation instruments until the aircraft passed over the northernmost ship of the Soviet Navy's search task force.

During this first Ellips mission the crew of Ivan F. Gladkov (with V. Doodin as navigator) witnessed an unforgettable sight – the probe streaked earthwards, leaving a long purple wake during re-entry. Shortly

afterwards the crew heard the signals of the spacecraft's beacon which they knew from the training sessions prior to the mission; zeroing in on the source of the signal, the aircraft passed over the floating space capsule and transmitted its co-ordinates to the nearest space tracking station. All in all, 392nd ODRAP crews flew more than ten such missions from Mozdok in support of the Soviet lunar research programme.

Valentin I. Votyakov, a former Tu-95RTs co-pilot who served in the 392nd ODRAP in 1969-77, recalled this first mission as follows. *'In October 1970 we redeployed to Engels AB (sic! – Auth.) to fly missions under the Ellips programme. Our task was to find the re-entry capsule of the Lunar probe and guide our ships towards it if anything went haywire. We were to refuel over Iran on the outbound leg and head for the Indian Ocean. Maj. D'yachenko's crew flew first for a weather check and Ivan Fyodorovich Gladkov led the main group. The refuelling was to take place between Mashhad and Zahedan. I was in the crew captained by Maj. Korobkin; Sqn 1 Chief Political Officer G. Plaksin was the Nav/Op.*

Well, our captain and I messed up the IFR procedure, not managing to take on fuel. At the group leader's instructions we reached the point where the group assembled on the way back and flew home, bringing up the rear. Night fell, the captain and navigator Vsevolod Mal'tsev went to take a nap; I took over the controls and the Chief Political Officer took care of the navigation. A while later the SHORAN indicator needles started showing that the leader was straying off course and "running away" from us. The Nav/Op told me everything was OK. When SHORAN contact with the leader was lost I woke the navigator. "Look at the lights of Ashkhabad below us", I told him. He replied: "This is Zahedan. Those lights over there, that's Mashhad. Now, see that little light on the horizon? That's Ashkhabad." The long and short of it is that we made it back to Engels all right.'

The 392nd ODRAP was also tasked with ice reconnaissance in the interests of civilian agencies as a secondary role. Some crews were on ready alert for search and rescue duties. The first such mission was the fruitless search for K-129 mentioned above. Another SAR mission in which the unit was involved was the search for a Soviet Air Force An-22 registered CCCP-09303 (c/n 00340207) which went missing on 17th June 1970 while en route from Keflavik to Halifax, Nova Scotia; the transport was on an earthquake relief flight, carrying medical supplies to Peru. During the active phase of the search, six *Bear-Ds* were airborne at a time – two aircraft circled over the assumed crash site, two were heading to the area to relieve them and two more were going home. This time the search operation turned up pieces of wreckage floating off the coast of Greenland, indicating that the An-22 had crashed into the Atlantic Ocean; none of the aircraft's 22 occupants were found alive.

392nd ODRAP CO Col. Ivan F. Gladkov in the flight deck of a Tu-95RTs.

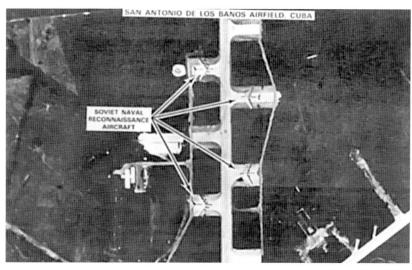

In 1969 the 392nd ODRAP provided OTH targeting for Soviet missile submarines in the Atlantic Ocean and for North Fleet surface ships participating in live firing exercises in the Norwegian Sea. That same year the unit began routine reconnaissance sorties over the Atlantic Ocean involving in-flight refuelling. The performance of the Tu-95RTs unparalleled by any other aircraft in Soviet Navy service allowed it to reach areas whose climatic and weather conditions had to be taken into account if the mission was to be completed safely (as already mentioned, the weather over the Norwegian Sea and the North Atlantic was often adverse).

The 392nd ODRAP's golden hour came in 1970 when the unit performed very impressively during Exercise *Okean-70* (Ocean-70, pronounced *okiahn*), a strategic exercise involving all four Soviet Navy fleets. Eight *Bear-Ds* captained by Ivan F. Gladkov, V. I. Khayarov, A. I. Startsev, Vladimir S. Melennyy, Bandorin et al. followed several routes fanning out over the Norwegian Sea and the North Atlantic, detecting all surface ships all the way to Nova Scotia and the Canary Islands. The sorties involved IFR and lasted 22 hours. At the closing stage of the exercise, on 18th-21st April 1970, two aircraft captained by Gladkov and Startsev made a trans-Atlantic flight to Cuba, landing at Havana's José Martí International airport. Thus started the type's operations from foreign bases (of which more will be discussed later).

The Pacific Fleet's 867th ODRAP also participated in Exercise *Okean-70*. The *Bear-Ds* from Khorol' flew reconnaissance missions over the Philippine Sea and the central part of the Pacific Ocean, supplying target data to Pacific Fleet cruise missile submarines.

On 15th July 1971 the 867th ODRAP was redesignated, becoming the 304th Red Banner GvODRAP (*Gvardeyskiy otdel'nyy dahl'niy razvedyvatel'nyy aviapolk* – Guards independent long-range reconnaissance air regiment). Shortly afterwards the unit started flying missions over the Indian Ocean.

The intensive combat training and high mission rate made for a high professional level among the *Bear-D*'s flight and ground crews. Yet, the aircraft and men were subjected to considerable strain, and the frequent and demanding missions took their toll. The first operational loss of a Tu-95RTs occurred in January 1971 when a 392nd ODRAP aircraft captained by Lt.-Col. Aleksey G. Rastyapin caught fire in mid-air and plunged into the Barents Sea, killing all on board. Valentin I. Votyakov recalled that Rastyapin, an old-timer in the unit, *'used to say: "I'm old and experienced; I'll never get killed in an accident". Make no mistake, he was experienced – but apparently he ended up in a situation when all that experience could not help. Another favourite saying of his was "The Navy pilot has an advantage: no-one will be able to shit on his grave". This turned out to be very true. For a year afterwards, on our way back to base from missions*

Above: US aerial reconnaissance imagery of San Antonio de los Baños AB shows four *Bear-Ds* in the dispersal area.

Below: Two 392nd ODRAP *Bear-Ds* at Havana-José Martí airport, which served as one of the two Cuban bases for Tu-95RTs operations.

Bottom: Another view of the same apron, with a quasi-civil North Fleet Tu-114 airliner and a Cubana Il'yushin IL-14P in the background.

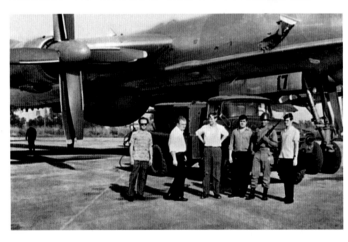

Top: The crew of Tu-95RTs '11 Black' captained by G. N. Simachov receives congratulations upon arrival to Cuba.

Top right: A *Bear-D* crew headed by V. A. Rykov, with instructor pilot Leonid M. Balyukov, in Havana.

Centre left: Tu-95RTs '19 Black' and the crew of R. N. Mannanov at Havana-José Marti in September 1980.

Centre right: Soviet airmen from the 392nd ODRAP communicate with Cuban servicemen at a Cuban base.

Above and above right: Wearing civilian clothes for a leave to the city, Soviet airmen pose with an armed guard at a Cuban base beside Tu-95RTs '17 Black' and an APA-35-2MU ground power unit on a ZiL-130 chassis.

over the Atlantic we would pass over Gremikha Bight (the site of Rastyapin's crash – Auth.) *and salute him with signal flares.'*

On 3rd September 1971 the 392nd ODRAP lost its second commander in a flying accident when Col. Ivan F. Gladkov's aircraft crashed on landing at Kipelovo AB in thick fog. This was a sore blow for the regiment because Gladkov was a competent and respected commander who flew complex missions as much as his subordinates. After this, the post of the unit's CO was taken up by Lt.-Col. Vladimir I. Dubinskiy who was transferred from a co-located ASW unit flying Tu-142s (see below).

On 3rd January 1973 the 392nd ODRAP's Deputy CO Lt.-Col. Grigoriy Ye. Filonenko made a series of post-repair check flights in a Tu-95RTs which had been damaged in a crash landing at Havana-José Martí International airport in November 1972. First the aircraft was flown with limited fuel, then in maximum TOW configuration. These flights turned up numerous malfunctions which could not be eliminated on site, and it was decided to ferry the *Bear* back to Kipelovo AB for more repairs; Filonenko was aware of the mission's complexity and high risk but agreed to fly. The standard operational procedure for flight to and from Cuba over the Arctic and Atlantic Oceans was to fly in pairs; this time Filonenko was ordered to fly alone.

On 4th January at 0600 hrs local time the Tu-95RTs departed Havana and headed east. Over the Bermudas part of the radio navigation equipment went unserviceable; knowing that high navigation accuracy was required in the area of the Faeroe Islands and the British Isles so as not to stray off the airway into foreign airspace, the navigator suggested returning to Cuba. Still, the engines were running normally, the gyro magnetic compass was functioning, and the captain decided to carry on. The aircraft was travelling against the sun, and five hours after take-off the darkness began to fall. At 0500 hrs Moscow time the following day the heavy aircraft touched down at Kipelovo AB after the long journey that took it across two oceans. Shutting down the engines on the main taxiway, the crew climbed out – and saw that the aircraft had 'cast a shadow': the concrete underneath was soaking wet with jet fuel that seeped from every crevice in the airframe, forming an outline of the aircraft. A technician opened the access door of the rear avionics/equipment bay and was immediately doused with fuel. Only by the

392 ODRAP Tu-95RTs '35 Black' on the hardstand at San Antonio de los Baños AB with tropical scenery as a backdrop.

purest of luck had a fire been avoided. The 392nd ODRAP's chief engineer G. A. Sosnovskiy took one look at the 'bleeding' aircraft and uttered: *'I've seen lots of things in aviation, but I've never seen anyone fly an aircraft like this!'*

On 4th August 1976 a Tu-95RTs operating out of Cuba crashed in the Sargasso Sea on the way home after completing a mission near US shores, killing the crew led by Maj. Arkadiy I. Krasnosel'skikh. In January 1984, another Tu-95RTs piloted by Maj. V. K. Vymyatnin crashed on take-off at Olen'ya AB (Murmansk Region) which was used as a staging point. The aircraft had a full fuel load – almost 90 tons (198,400 lb), and the resulting explosion produced a tremendous fireball that could be seen for miles. Throughout its service the 392nd ODRAP lost four aircraft and 61 crewmen.

A medal awarded to Soviet servicemen for deployments to Cuba.

Tu-95RTs '02 Black' wearing an 'Excellent aircraft' badge shares the hardstand with two sister ships and an APA-80. The scenery indicates this is a Soviet base, not an overseas location.

A Certificate of Honour awarded to the 392nd ODRAP for high results in combat training and political training achieved in the so-called 'socialist competition' among military units in 1978/1979.

In February-March 1979, when China invaded Vietnam, 304th GvODRAP Tu-95RTs aircraft flew a number of reconnaissance missions over the South China Sea. That year the unit's aircraft occasionally redeployed to Tashkent, the capital of the Uzbek SSR, from where they flew missions over the Indian Ocean, entering the area via Pakistan and Iran.

Of course, visiting *Bear-Ds* were intercepted and escorted whenever possible by NATO fighters scrambling both from aircraft carriers and from shore bases. At least two fighters were always involved, their crews photographing each other's aircraft with the Tu-95RTs as a backdrop to obtain photo proof of a successful intercept. All sorts of fighters flew such sorties. On 16th March 1979 Grumman F-14A Tomcats and LTV A-7 Corsair IIs from the carrier USS *America* intercepted a pair of North Fleet Tu-95RTs aircraft near the Bermudas; the *Bears* were heading for the Cuban airbase at San Antonio de los Baños. Interestingly, 'the real McCoy' appeared the very next day after a US Navy exercise where fighter pilots practiced intercept techniques, with a Lockheed P-3A Orion ASW aircraft based on the Bermudas posing as a *Bear-D*.

In August 1981 a Tu-95RTs was intercepted by a Royal Navy BAe Sea Harrier FRS.1 for the first time during Exercise *Ocean Venture*. The fighter (XZ498/'N-005') was piloted by Lt. Hugh Slade from No.801 Sqn who intercepted the *Bear* over the Greenland Gap, about 1,130 km (700 miles) from Greenland.

In late January 1982 two 392nd ODRAP *Bear-Ds* captained by Maj. R. Mannanov (leader) and Maj.

K. Zakharov were scrambled from San Antonio de los Baños AB to detect and photograph the then-latest US Navy aircraft carrier USS *Carl Vinson* (CVN-70). The carrier, which was undergoing sea trials with no aircraft on deck except a single SAR helicopter, was detected almost on the borderline of the USA's territorial waters.

On 19th March 1983 a pair of F-14As from the US Navy's 142nd Shipboard Fighter Squadron (VF-142) intercepted a solitary North Fleet Tu-95RTs monitoring a US Navy exercise in the Caribbean. After the intercept the *Bear* returned to Cuba from where it had flown the mission.

Incidentally, the Tu-95's NATO reporting name proved oddly appropriate from an acoustic standpoint. NATO pilots reported that the deep-throated roar of the *Bear*'s mighty contra-rotating propellers could be heard from more than a mile away over the roar of their own engines!

Occasionally the atmosphere during such intercepts was almost relaxed. On 8th July 1977 the British newspaper *Aviation News* published a picture taken by the back-seater of a RAF No.111 Sqn F-4M from RAF Leuchars, showing the gunner of a Tu-95RTs cheerily demonstrating a bottle of Pepsi Cola to the British pilots! The caption was that '...such decadence should never be allowed!'

Moreover, sometimes the western fighter pilots acted in a *quid pro quo* fashion. Valentin I. Votyakov recalled flying a sortie to locate two aircraft carriers. *'In 1973 three US Navy aircraft carriers were exercising in the Norwegian Sea and near the Black Sea Straits. The crews of our regiment kept a tab on them. The exercise was unexpectedly cut short – one of the carriers suffered damage to her top deck and headed for harbour in order to be repaired, accompanied by another carrier. A while later both carriers disappeared from view, slipping undetected past our ships. My wingman Maj. Grook and I took off to try and find them; we believed they were making a beeline to the States for more extensive repairs. A blip appeared on the radarscope and we headed towards it. Ensign Yefimov, my ELINT officer, told me that a Phantom was being vectored towards us from the carrier. The interceptor approached and the pilot made a gesture to show that the carrier was below us. I gave him signs to tell him "I need the other carrier". Then he came up in front of our aircraft, guided us to the other carrier, did a series of ascending barrel rolls, said goodbye and headed back.'* It was like 'look guys, we're all professionals, so we'll let you do your job if you let us do ours'.

Crews flying sorties over the West and South Atlantic deserved combat pay (even if there was no such thing in the USSR): the missions were often risky. Some of the intercepting pilots were 'cowboys' with combat experience and a devil-may-care attitude; they thought nothing of coming up between two of the *Bear*'s engines in order to obstruct the oblique cameras' field of view. Occasionally the '*Bear* drivers' answered in kind, flying low over the carrier and trying (unsuccessfully) to blow the SAR helicopters off the deck! Sometimes, if an armed conflict was on, there was considerable danger of being fired upon. However, the results were worth the effort. For instance, during the Falklands War in 1982 the 392nd ODRAP monitored the Royal Navy deployment closely all the way, from the moment the task force started assembling in the Bay of Biscay to its arrival in the war zone – all British security measures notwithstanding.

Gradually the Soviet Navy lost interest in the Tu-95RTs. For one thing, the P-500 *Bazal't* (Basalt, NATO SS-N-12 *Sandbox*), P-700 *Granit* (Granite, NATO SS-N-19 *Shipwreck*) and P-1000 *Vulkan* (Volcano, NATO SS-N-12 Mod. 2 *Sandbox*) anti-shipping missile systems fielded in the 1980s relied on the *Kasatka-B* (Orca) targeting system based on surveillance satellites. For another, in the 1980s Soviet Navy ships rarely ventured far afield. Finally, the *Bear-Ds* were starting to show their age; from March 1985 onwards they were being grounded increasingly often due to fatigue cracks.

In 1985-88 the 304th GvODRAP temporarily redeployed to Vladivostok-Knevichi airport while Khorol' AB was under reconstruction. The reason was that the base had been designated as an alternate airfield for the ill-starred Soviet space shuttle *izdeliye* 11F35 Buran (Snowstorm, pronounced *boorahn*) as Spaceport *Vostochnyy* (Eastern). (This is not to be confused with the current Vostochnyy Space Centre which is located in the Amur Region.) Accordingly the existing 3,000 x 60 m (9,840 x 196 ft) concrete runway had to be enlarged to 3,700 x 70 m (12,140 x 230 ft) and resurfaced, and the special *Vympel* (Pennant) approach system for the shuttle had to be installed; new hardstands were also built. (However the Buran was never to use this base, its one and only space mission on 15th November 1988 starting and ending at the Baikonur Space Centre.)

In 1989 the 392nd ODRAP left Kipelovo AB, moving to Ostrov-5 AB (aka Veret'ye AB; *ostrov* is Russian for 'island') near Pskov in north-western Russia. This naval air station was mostly used by the Baltic Fleet but occasionally shared by the North Fleet.

A medal from the North Fleet Air Arm's Political Department awarded to celebrate the 392nd ODRAP's 20th birthday.

A map illustrating the actions of the 392nd ODRAP during Exercise *Okean-70*, showing Olen'ya AB, Kipelovo AB, the IFR zone, and areas the Tu-95RTs reached with one fuel top-up.

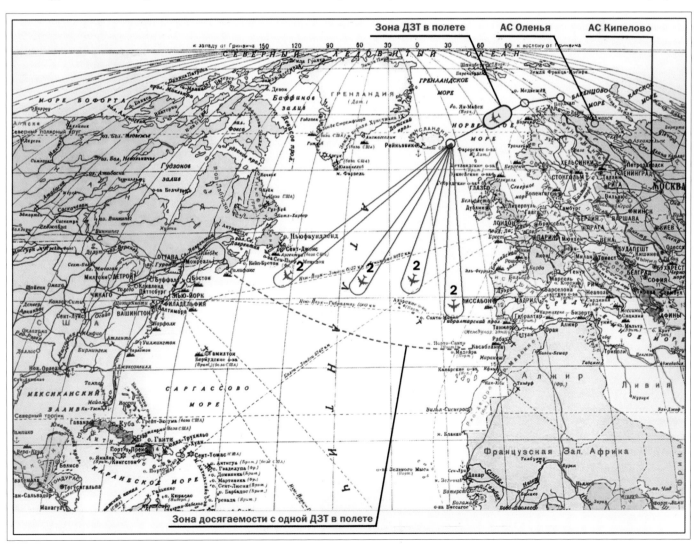

A fine study of a cruising *Bear-D*. The camera port is open, although heavy overcast seemingly rules out photography of surface targets!

The gunner of a Tu-95RTs gives the victory sign to the crew of an intercepting NATO fighter.

Sub hunting

The Tu-142 was utilised by the AVMF no less intensively than the Tu-95RTs. On 22nd June 1969 the North Fleet Air Arm began picking personnel for a long-range ASW air regiment to be equipped with Tu-142s; this unit would handle ocean ASW patrol duties in regions which were beyond the reach of the IL-38 and the Be-12.

The *Bear-F*'s service history officially began on 22nd July 1969 when the Soviet Navy Main Staff issued directive No.701/2/27008 establishing the 76th OPLAP DD (*otdel'nyy protivolodochnyy aviapolk dahl'nevo deystviya* – Independent Long-Range ASW Air Regiment), with Lt.-Col. Vladimir I. Dubinskiy as its first CO. This was followed by an North Fleet HQ order on 15th August 1969 and by order No.0014/4 to the same effect signed ten days later by North Fleet Air Arm Commander Fleet Adm. Semyon M. Lobov.

The new unit took up residence at Kipelovo AB (which, as we remember, already hosted the 392nd ODRAP). The regiment's first two sub-units – Sqn 1 commanded by Lt.-Col. Vasiliy A. Shamanskiy and the maintenance department – were formed in December 1969. The first group of naval pilots and ground personnel started conversion training for the Tu-142 on 4th March 1970 at the Kuibyshev aircraft factory; they completed the course in about three months. On 15th April 1970, Lt.-Col. Dubinskiy's crew made their first solo flight in a Tu-142 at Kuibyshev-Bezymyanka. However, the second group of airmen and technicians did not begin training until December 1971, so it was a long time before the 76th OPLAP DD was ready for action. Later, conversion training for the *Bear-F* took place at the AVMF's 33rd TsBP i PLS – specifically, in the 316th OPLAE in Nikolayev (Kul'bakino AB).

The 76th OPLAP DD was equipped with brand-new Tu-142s *sans suffixe* – early-production Kuibyshev-built aircraft with the famous 12-wheel main gear bogies (the so-called 'centipedes'). The first two aircraft (coded

'40 Black' and '41 Black') arrived at Kipelovo AB on 21st May and 25th May 1970. A few days later, on 5th June, Lt.-Col. Vladimir I. Dubinskiy flew the first practice sortie from Kipelovo. The first weapons training sortie involving torpedo launches and bomb drops at a practice range followed on 26th June. On 7th July the first real 'sub hunt' training sortie was flown by a crew captained by Lt.-Col. Shamanskiy, with Lt.-Col. Dubinskiy as instructor. Other crews followed suit at the end of July, and night flights started in September. In the course of the following year the Tu-142 became fully operational. By then the 76th OPLAP DD had a new CO, Lt.-Col. Leonid I. Sreznikov, who was appointed in the autumn of 1971 after Col. Dubinskiy's transfer to the 392nd ODRAP.

When getting to grips with the Tu-142's Berkut-95 search and targeting suite the unit's personnel received assistance from the navigators/sonar operators of the North Fleet's 24th OPLAP, who had become familiar with the suite on their IL-38s. However, there were significant differences between the two types as regards the STS's performance. Back at the development (mathematical analysis) and flight test phase it became apparent that the lumbering Tu-142 would be inferior to the lighter and more manoeuvrable IL-38 as regards certain temporal characteristics, despite having almost identical mission equipment. Thus, the Tu-142's crew needed 19-27 minutes to detect

and engage a submarine, using two strings of RGB-1 sonobuoys to determine its course and speed; in the same circumstances the crew of the IL-38 required 12-17 minutes. Time performance with RGB-2 sonobuoys was likewise worse; the *Bear-F*'s sonar operator needed six to eight minutes to begin loading data into the digital processor after receiving a 'submarine detected' signal from the buoy – twice as long as on the *May*.

Computer simulation showed that an average of 35-65 sonobuoys per hour were required to track a

The colour of the dielectric parts on individual *Bear-Ds* varied. This one has a white fin cap.

F-14A-100-GR BuNo 160687/'NL-113' of VF-51 from USS *Kitty Hawk* intercepts a Tu-95RTs.

'There will be a slight technical delay, folks…' This publicity photo shows naval airmen studying a map in front of a Tu-142M *Bear-F Mod 2* which is jacked up and is having its propellers worked on.

submarine travelling at 6-8 kts; this, together with the cost of fuel (the Tu-142's fuel burn was higher than the IL-38's), meant that the hourly operating costs in search mode were much higher as compared with the IL-38. Later, early operational experience with the *Bear-F*, in particular as regards mission preparation of the STS and especially the sonobuoys and weapons, made it possible to give a realistic assessment of the time required to prepare a single Tu-142, a tactical group or an entire regiment for a scramble. Hooking up the sonobuoys was a major headache. In the early years of Tu-142 operations another constant source of problems

Crewmen wearing white-topped Navy caps prepare for a sortie in an early Tu-142 'centipede'.

was the torpedoes' DC batteries which took anywhere between 12 and 24 hours to charge; the introduction of disposable ampoule-type batteries took care of the problem.

Thus, the Tu-142's initial service period gave little reason for optimism – mission preparation time in search configuration was seven to eight hours; it was not until much later that this time was drastically cut. Of the 20 assorted payload configurations that could be carried, the most effective by far was the search/strike weapons fit comprising 176 RGB-1 sonobuoys, ten RGB-2 buoys, three RGB-3 buoys and three AT-1M ASW torpedoes (later replaced by AT-2s and AT-2Ms) or APR-1 anti-submarine missiles.

The number of sonobuoys carried in pure search (maritime patrol) configuration varied widely, depending on the mission. The Tu-142 came complete with 20 cassettes holding 22 buoys each; thus, in theory the aircraft could carry a maximum of 440 buoys. However,

this configuration was completely unnecessary from a tactical standpoint; only 'chairborne' top brass with little knowledge of the Tu-142's real-life missions could be delighted by this monstrous figure.

The **Bereg-38** (Shore-38) land-based simulation system set up at the North Fleet Air Arm's Loombovka practice range on the White Sea coast (Murmansk Region) proved to be a great help when Tu-142 crews were gaining experience with the Berkut-95 STS, including live weapons training. As the designation suggests, the simulation system had been originally developed for the IL-38. Practice bombs were used instead of ASW torpedoes, but otherwise the targeting procedure was unchanged. Weapons training at Loombovka occasionally included incidents that did not result in major damage or loss of life only by sheer luck. On one occasion the navigator of a Tu-142 decided that the aircraft had strayed from the desired track during the target run. After the aircraft's course had been

A Tu-142 *sans suffixe* from the first two production batches as originally built (with the Gagara-1 thermal imager in a chin fairing).

The very pointed main gear fairings show this is still a 'centipede' (not a *Bear-F Mod 1*) but with the unsatisfactory thermal imager removed.

Armourers prepare RGB-1 (upper row) and RGB-2 sonobuoys for loading into a Tu-142 *sans suffixe*. This view illustrates the flattened rear ends of the Centipede's wide main gear fairings.

Two AT-2 torpedoes are about to be hoisted into a Tu-142's main weapons bay; the radome of the Berkut-95 radar is visible in the foreground.

Another significant event in the unit's history took place on 15th February 1971 when the 76th OPLAP DD received its Combat Standard; the banner was handed over on the runway of Kipelovo AB with the unit's entire personnel in attendance.

Another maximum-range sortie over the Norwegian Sea – the first active duty sortie – was flown on 27th July 1971; the pair of Tu-142s was captained by Dubinskiy and Lt.-Col. V. A. Shamanskiy, staying airborne for 13 hours 50 minutes. Since sonobuoys were in short supply, only the radar was used during these and the next few flights, making it possible to detect only surface ships. On 23rd-24th August that year six of the unit's aircraft made their first ASW torpedo launches, operating from Severomorsk-1 AB near Murmansk.

The 76th OPLAP's Sqn 2 was formed in February 1972 under Lt.-Col. Igor' A Yefimov. On 3rd April 1972 four of the unit's Tu-142s captained by Lt.-Col. Leonid I. Sreznikov, Maj. V. N. Gabalov, Maj. V. N. Bulgakov and Maj. A. I. Khamzin flew a sortie in the area between the Faeroe Islands and the British Isles; a US Navy F-4 Phantom II put in an appearance but did not prevent the crews from completing their mission. Three days later the regiment took part in its first North Fleet exercise which involved practicing methods of tracking down and destroying hostile submarines.

Some time later the 76th OPLAP DD was included into the North Fleet's constant duty forces. By October 1972 ten of the regiment's crews had received their all-weather, day/night operations ratings. From 15th November 1972 onwards the unit routinely patrolled the Soviet Union's northern borders By 1974 all of its 14 crews were fully qualified to seek and destroy hostile missile subs anytime, anyplace. That year the AVMF started taking delivery of the Tu-142M *Bear-F Mod 2* featuring a more spacious flight deck and other revisions; ignoring this fact, the Navy continued referring to the new model simply as the Tu-142.

Gradually the long-range naval aviation made its mark. Indeed, the success of certain search operations was wholly attributable to the participation of long-range ASW aircraft. One notable mission involving the tracking down and shadowing of a foreign submarine which had intruded into Soviet waters took place in the Barents Sea on 19th/22nd August 1974. Four Tu-142s captained by Maj. V. N. Morozov, Maj. V. I. Pavlov, Maj. A. A. Karpinchik and Lt.-Col. I. A. Yefimov participated in the operation, mainly for the sake of training. Maj. Morozov's crew kept tailing the submarine for 2 hrs 55 min before passing it on to ASW ships. In the course of time such missions became fairly frequent.

On 11th July 1974 Maj. V. N. Bulgakov's crew completed a first-of-a-kind mission for the Soviet Navy, successfully launching two APR-1 anti-submarine missiles from a Tu-142. A month later, the airmen's skill was put to the test when 76th OPLAP DD Tu-142s

'corrected', the STS delivered the bombs squarely onto the range operations team's barracks, demolishing the firearms locker room.

Practical training of aircrews in ASW techniques was constantly hampered by stringent limits for the expenditure of sonobuoys, as the latter were expensive.

On 11th December 1970 a 76th OPLAP DD crew under Lt.-Col. Vladimir I. Dubinskiy flew the first maximum-range sortie. On the way back the Tu-142 had to divert to Ostrov AB because Kipelovo AB had shut down due to below-minima weather; the flight lasted 12 hours 36 minutes. The following day, when the weather improved, the aircraft made a short hop back to its home base.

To mark the centenary of Vladimir I. Lenin, the founder of the Soviet state (1870-1924), in 1970 thirty-two of the 76th OPLAP's officers were awarded the Combat Valour Medal for their distinguished service.

shadowed a foreign submarine, operating jointly with IL-38s from another unit. That year the AVMF command instructed the fleets to use sonobuoys more rationally (that is, sparingly) by increasing the distance between individual buoys to 8-10 times the buoy's detection range. This reduced the probability of detecting the target from the usual 70-80% to 20-30% but increased the area to be monitored fourfold to sixfold.

In the early 1970s the Soviet Armed Forces began practicing inter-theatre operations during which strike aircraft groups of varying composition would be deployed to other theatres of operations. ASW exercises involving aviation assets were held in all fleets from time to time. In April 1975 the 76th OPLAP DD took part in Exercise *Okean-75*. During the exercise two crews captained by Maj. V. N. Gabalov and Maj. N. S. Ostapenko detected a 'hostile' submarine on 17th April and shadowed it for 1 hr 7 min before passing it on to another pair of Tu-142s piloted by Maj. V. I. Pavlov and Maj. A. A. Karpinchik. They stayed on the submarine's tail for another 3 hrs 16 min.

In May 1976 the unit participated in Exercise *Akvatoriya-76* which involved penetrating the notional adversary's air defences on the north-western TO. The Tu-142s performed an auxiliary 'show of force' function. No encounters with NATO fighters took place this time.

On several occasions aircraft from Kipelovo AB were detached to the Pacific Fleet to participate in various operations. For example, on 29th June 1976 seven of the unit's aircraft redeployed to Khorol' AB to take part in Operation *Rezonans*. Operating from another Far Eastern airbase, Kamennyy Ruchey AB ('Stone Brook')

Armourers hook up a practice bomb to a Tu-142.

near Mongokhto township in the Khabarovsk Territory, they flew 14 ASW search sorties before returning home on 17th July. The first mission failed dismally because the fuel load had been calculated incorrectly and the *Bears* had to abort the mission; moreover, the pilots headed to Khorol' AB instead of Kamennyy Ruchey and had to circle the base for a while, burning off fuel in order to reduce the landing weight.

On 20th September 1976, Lt.-Col. Vladimir G. Deyneka was appointed as the new CO of the 76th OPLAP DD (he went on to become AVMF Commander in March 1994.). That year the unit logged a total of

A mysterious enamel badge obviously showing a *Bear* over the sea but stating the years as 1962-72 (whereas the Navy's first *Bear* unit was formed in 1963!).

A North Fleet Tu-142M coded '09 Black' and an F-14A from VF-51 (modex NL-103) pass over USS *Kitty Hawk* (CV-63).

2,156 flight hours, including 940 hours of night operations and 387 hours of combat sorties.

Up to then, the 76th OPLAP DD had been unique by Soviet Navy standards. On 1st October 1976, however, the Pacific Fleet established its own 'Bear den' – the 310th OPLAP DD. The unit was set up at Khorol' AB, drawing personnel from the resident 304th GvODRAP. In August-September 1976 the first group of airmen and technicians took theoretical training for the Tu-142 in Nikolayev; the second group followed in June-August 1977, while the 310th OPLAP's command staff took conversion training *in situ* at Khorol'. When the training had been completed, on 27th October 1978 the new

regiment moved to Kamennyy Ruchey AB because 'two is company and three is a crowd' – Khorol' AB had become too congested. Ironically, Kamennyy Ruchey AB also had two resident units by then (the 568th and 570th MRAPs flying Tu-16s) but was being expanded with new hardstands, making sure there was enough room for everyone. Now that the Tu-142M was being fielded, in 1978 the AVMF command took the decision to transfer all remaining Tu-142s *sans suffixe* to the

Pacific Fleet, and by the year's end the 310th OPLAP DD had increased its strength to 14 aircraft.

In April 1977 the 76th OPLAP DD participated in Exercise ***Sever-77*** (North-77), flying 14 ASW search sorties over the North Sea and the Norwegian Sea. The exercise included practicing submarine search/tracking techniques and techniques of classifying the target's parameters, based on the information supplied by RGB-2 sonobuoys. The techniques of penetrating the

Not a routine intercept; here, Russian Navy Tu-142MK '93 Black' is escorted by RAF Tornado F.3s en route to RAF Fairford for the 1994 Royal International Air Tattoo.

Opposite page, top: AVMF personnel propel a trolley laden with filters past a Tu-142M. The bike saved a lot of legwork when moving around the base – but not in this case.

Opposite page, centre: Tu-142MK '93 Black' taxies out for a training sortie at Ostrov past a pair of sister ships and two IL-38 ASW aircraft.

Left and opposite page, bottom: '66 Black', another Tu-142MK, on final approach to Nikolayev-Kul'bakino AB.

80

Tu-142MK '80 Black', North Fleet,
76th OPLAP DD, Kipelovo AB

NATO's continental air defences, particularly the Faeroes/Iceland line of defence, were tried out. On 10th October 1977 five of the unit's aircraft on TDY to Khorol' AB flew four sorties against US Navy submarines in the Philippine Sea. In one of these sorties, Lt.-Col. Vladimir G. Deyneka's crew located a submarine and tracked it for 4 hrs 5 min.

In November-December 1977 the 76th OPLAP DD expanded when a third squadron was added. The personnel of Sqn 3 took their training at Taganrog (where Tu-142 production had been transferred in the meantime) and at the 33rd TsBP i PLS in Nikolayev. The new squadron was equipped with the then-latest version of the *Bear-F* – the Tu-142MK equipped with the new Korshun-K STS (it was commonly known in the AVMF as the Tu-142M). The first four *Bear-F Mod 3s* were formally accepted and ferried to Kipelovo AB as early as September 1978.

On 6th April 1978, 76th OPLAP DD Tu-142s flew the first joint patrol mission in the North-East Atlantic; operating in concert with surface ships, they located and shadowed a Western missile submarine (presumably a US Navy *Lafayette* class sub). Conversion training to the Tu-142MK proceeded in parallel; on 1st January 1979 a crew under Lt.-Col. V. A. Kibal'nik flew the first solo circuit of Kipelovo AB in a *Bear-F Mod 3*, followed on 20th February by Maj. Pavlov's crew. On 19th March Kibal'nik made the first flight along a designated route, knocking out a practice target with bombs after pinpointing it with the Korshun radar. On 17th April, a crew headed by Lt.-Col. V. V. Groozin scored another 'first' for the unit, dropping an inert AT-2 torpedo after locating the practice target with the Korshun-K STS. Twelve days later a crew under Lt.-Col. Kibal'nik flew the first operational sortie in which the Korshun-K STS was used, locating a Western submarine

Tu-142MK '50 Black' sporting the 'Excellent aircraft' badge is seen on short finals to Kipelovo AB.

and shadowing it for 1 hr 10 min. Initially Tu-142MKs used old sonobuoys associated with the Berkut-95 STS. Originally the North Fleet's Tu-142s *sans suffixe* and Tu-142Ms soldiered on alongside the new version. Yet, as mentioned earlier, in 1978 they were transferred to the Pacific Fleet. The first Tu-142 departed to the Far East as early as August 1978; the final aircraft was ferried in December 1980.

Gradually Tu-142MK missions over the North Atlantic became more frequent. Usually the *Bear-Fs* operated from Severomorsk-1 AB. Tu-142s cruising at 8,000-10,000 m (26,250-32,810 ft) were usually intercepted by NATO fighters off the Faeroes and Iceland; however, descending to 400-600 m (1,310-1,970 ft) in timely fashion made it possible to escape detection.

The missions did not always go as planned because the shadowing NATO aircraft could be a real nuisance. For example, on 25th May 1979 a Tu-142 had hardly dropped a string of sonobuoys in the Norwegian Sea when a Lockheed P-3 intervened, dropping white-coloured ECM buoys near the last six sonobuoys; for the next 90 minutes, all the *Bear*'s sonar operators could hear was a lot of static. Generally attempts to detect NATO submarines in the Atlantic Ocean were less productive than expected; this was because the search was undertaken only sporadically, and then in areas of just a few thousand square kilometres, while NATO missile submarines prowled in areas measuring millions of square kilometres.

In 1979 the 76th OPLAP DD crews flew 64 combat sorties, detecting ten western submarines and accumulating 2,900 hrs total time. That year the unit made a joint effort with the co-located 392nd ODRAP to evaluate the chances of air defence penetration near the Faeroe Islands and Iceland, considering that the potential adversary would employ Boeing E-3A Sentry AWACS aircraft. On 15th October 1979 Lt.-Col. V. V. Groozin became the 76th Regiment's new CO.

Also in 1979, the Pacific Fleet's 310th OPLAP DD started flying missions over the Indian Ocean with a refuelling stop in Tashkent. Taking off from Tashkent-Vostochnyy (= Eastern), the factory airfield of MAP aircraft factory No.84, the Tu-142s proceeded to the designated patrol area over Iran and Pakistan.

In March 1980, 76th OPLAP DD Tu-142MKs participated in Operation *Svet* (Light) mounted by the Northern Fleet, the crews of Maj. Usol'tsev, Maj. Marakoolin and Maj. Kosyakov flying ten sorties and searching for a North Fleet submarine posing as the adversary. Two actual western subs were also detected and tracked in the process. On 28th June 1980 the unit participated in Exercise *Atlantika-80*, two groups of aircraft flying six sorties to set up minefields amid tight security measures. The following year the unit, which by then had been completely re-equipped with

Tu-142MKs, joined the ready alert forces within the Soviet Armed Forces structure.

In 1982 the 76th OPLAP DD flew 90 combat sorties, detecting 18 submarines and accumulating 4,520 hrs total time. The following year it took part in Exercise *Razbeg-83* ('Running Start').

In February-June 1983 the 76th OPLAP DD practiced dispersing its aircraft to remote bases, temporarily moving part of the fleet to Kazan'-Borisoglebskoye (the factory airfield of plant No.22). In November that year the regiment became part of the newly formed 35th PLAD DD (*protivolodochnaya aviadiveeziya dahl'nevo deystviya* – Long-Range ASW Air Division) headquartered at Kipelovo AB – a one-of-a-kind formation in the AVMF. Since the regiment was no longer a direct reporting unit, the 'O' disappeared from its designation, which was now 76th PLAP DD. The division's other unit was the co-located 135th PLAP DD, which was established at the same time as a two-squadron regiment and also operated Tu-142s.

In the 1980s the Soviet Navy's aviation stepped up its ASW activities. In 1981 the North Fleet air arm commenced combat duty operations with the Tu-142MK. For starters, the crews mastered flights over a combat radius of up to 4,200 km (2,610 miles). In this case, however, on-station loiter time had to be reduced because Engels-2 AB, a strategic bomber base designated as the alternate airfield in case Kipelovo AB shut down due to weather minima, was a long way from the coast. When planning trans-Atlantic missions, allowance had to be made for the Tu-142's higher hourly fuel consumption due to the worse aero-dynamics and higher weight as compared to the Tu-95RTs. Therefore, on flights to Cuba the Tu-142MK was preceded by a pair of *Bear-Ds*, even though their navigation equipment was less sophisticated. In order to cut fuel burn per mile the mission was flown 'hugging the ceiling' – that is, at the maximum possible altitude for the momentary all-up weight, using a special technique.

The late 1970s and 1980s were characterised by an alarming trend: in spite of the agreements concerning military aircraft flights over international waters, NATO fighters were becoming increasingly aggressive when intercepting Soviet aircraft. The fighters would often use the Soviet aircraft as practice targets, 'painting' them with their fire control radars and disrupting the operation of navigation systems, which was a flagrant breach of generally accepted rules. Tu-142s were often intercepted off Iceland when en route to the Atlantic.

By the end of 1983 the 76th PLAP DD had flown 93 combat duty sorties, detecting 31 western submarines. In 1984 it was 79 combat sorties, 19 detected submarines and 4.171 hrs total time. On 20th January that year a new technique was used for the first time in the Norwegian Sea: the Tu-142Ms dropped

A badge with the legend 'Naval Aviation – Kipelovo – Tu-142' depicting a Tu-142MK.

This badge depicting a Tu-142MK was issued to celebrate the 30th birthday of the 76th OPLAP DD in 1999.

An almost identical badge of Kamennyy Ruchey AB.

Above: RAF 12 Sqn Panavia Tornado F.3 ZE808/'FA' escorts a North Fleet Tu-42MK.

Right: A *Bear-F Mod 3* flies over the Russian Navy's sole aircraft carrier, RNS *Fleet Admiral Kuznetsov*, during an exercise. The carrier's deck is empty, except for a solitary Kamov Ka-27PS *Helix-C* search and rescue helicopter.

Below right: The same aircraft makes a gentle turn over the coastline.

Below: Birds of a feather flock together? Lockheed P-3C-155-LO Orion BuNo 159319 of VP-45 'Pelicans' escorts a Tu-142MK heading for Cuba off the coast of Florida on 6th March 1986.

RGB-55A sonobuoys and UPLAB-50 practice bombs to scare off unfriendly subs.

On 23rd-27th August 1984 the 76th PLAP's Tu-142MKs were involved in Operation *Nasest* (Hen Perch) with the task of detecting and tracking foreign submarines. In 1985 the unit flew 64 combat sorties and detected 14 submarines; in 1986 it was 84 sorties and seven submarines.

The Tu-142MK seemed to be growing increasingly effective in the Atlantic Ocean and the Norwegian Sea. The mission success figures exceeded all reasonable estimates, so gradually the AVMF command grew suspicious – and with good reason. The only possible explanation was that the crews either mistook some 'innocent' signals for submarines (which was quite possible, since the Korshun-K STS was notorious for giving false alarms) or deliberately embellished their scores. The latter was also possible, since the data recorders used for debriefing were rather inadequate at the time. Hence a series of test flights was made in 1984 and a mission equipment upgrade plan was drawn up.

Quite apart from this, the Tu-142 suffered from reliability issues with both the airframe and the equipment, which caused operations to be suspended repeatedly. In particular, numerous cases of fatigue cracking in the wings were detected from March 1985 onwards. The main gear fairings were found to crack all

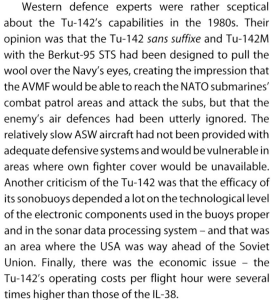

Western defence experts were rather sceptical about the Tu-142's capabilities in the 1980s. Their opinion was that the Tu-142 *sans suffixe* and Tu-142M with the Berkut-95 STS had been designed to pull the wool over the Navy's eyes, creating the impression that the AVMF would be able to reach the NATO submarines' combat patrol areas and attack the subs, but that the enemy's air defences had been utterly ignored. The relatively slow ASW aircraft had not been provided with adequate defensive systems and would be vulnerable in areas where own fighter cover would be unavailable. Another criticism of the Tu-142 was that the efficacy of its sonobuoys depended a lot on the technological level of the electronic components used in the buoys proper and in the sonar data processing system – and that was an area where the USA was way ahead of the Soviet Union. Finally, there was the economic issue – the Tu-142's operating costs per flight hour were several times higher than those of the IL-38.

A ground crewman checks the trailing wire antenna of a Tu-142MR.

A badge marking the 25th birthday of the 837th Aircraft Maintenance Base (military unit 53043) at Kipelovo AB.

This badge commemorates 45 years of Fedotovo garrison.

Russian Navy Tu-142MR '26 Red, a Pacific Fleet/ 568th GvOMSAP aircraft.

over the place, causing 35 *Bear-Fs* built in 1978-86 to be grounded for repairs in 1986; initial attempts to reinforce the fairings gave no results, and it was not until April 1989 that an acceptable solution was found. In 1985-89 the Navy had to address the VPK three times and lodge 12 complaints with MAP. In 1989 the AVMF began retiring the Tu-142s *en masse* as their designated service life in terms of years drew to an end (early aircraft had a 22-year designated service life, which was extended to 25 years on later *Bear-Fs* with a redesigned and reinforced wing structure). On the other hand, the Tu-142/Tu-142M/Tu-142MK had a fairly good flight safety record, the accident rate being only 3.5 per 100,000 flight hours.

In May 1985 the 76th PLAP DD began conversion training for the Tu-142MR communications relay aircraft; the first two *Bear-Js* arrived at Kipelovo on 1st August. On 24th December 1985 the Soviet Navy C-in-C signed an order establishing a special TACAMO detachment within the regiment to operate the Tu-142MRs. As early as January 1986 three crews captained by Maj. S. S. Kichigin, Maj. I. P. Serebryakov and A. V. Pryanikov started practicing, and in June 1986 the detachment became operational, joining the North Fleet's ready alert forces in early September. Later, as more Tu-142MRs were delivered, the detachment was upgraded to a TACAMO squadron within the regiment.

Also in 1986, a similar squadron of Tu-142MRs was established in the 310th OPLAP DD.

Overseas deployments

The reform of the Soviet Armed Forces initiated by Nikita S. Khrushchov in the 1950s had a devastating effect on the Navy and the Air Force, many military programmes being scrapped and many units being disbanded. Pretty soon, however, the Soviet leaders were in for a sobering experience: the outbreak of the Cuban Missile Crisis in 1962 showed clearly that certain situations cannot be resolved without involving the Navy and long-range reconnaissance aviation assets. After the crisis the confrontation between the East and the West eased up a little, but still political tensions remained strong. The Soviet military top brass got the notion that in this situation the fleet of Tu-95RTs aircraft could keep them informed of the situation in vast areas of the world ocean. The *Bear-D*'s reach could be extended appreciably by deploying the aircraft in 'friendly nations'.

As already mentioned, the first deployment of the Tu-95RTs to Cuba took place on 18th-21st April 1970 in the course of Exercise *Okean-70*. After this, 392nd ODRAP Tu-95RTs aircraft were detached to Cuba on a regular basis right up to the demise of the Soviet Union, making 25-35 flights annually. These missions had a few peculiarities. Between 36°N and 55°N the westbound aircraft had to fight their way through jetstreams whose speed at flight levels of 5,000-10,000 m (16,400-32,810 ft) could be as high as 200-300 km/h (124-186 mph), increasing the flight time by 2.5-3 hours. Occasionally the headwind was so strong that reaching Havana became impossible. Between 30°N and 60°N, storm fronts and single heavy cumulus clouds could be encountered at 9,000-10,000 m (29,530-32,810 ft) over stretches 800-1,500 km (496-931 miles) long and up to 150 km (93 miles) wide; in that case the aircraft had to make diversions from the intended track up to 200 km (124 miles) to circumnavigate them.

Another complication arose because the ambient air temperature south of 40°N was 10-15°C (18-27°F) above the international standard atmosphere (ISA) value, which caused an increase in fuel consumption. In maximum range flights, the hourly fuel consumption at 710 km/h (441-460 mph) could go as high as 4,910 kg (10,820 lb) and the fuel burn per mile reached 7.5 kg/km (26.62 lb/mile), which was 12-14% higher than anticipated. As if that wasn't enough, the fairly heavy commercial traffic on the trans-Atlantic international airways had to be taken into account. The Tu-95RTs pilots chose flight levels in between those normally used by civil aircraft in order to avoid near-misses or collisions; this was possible in the days before reduced vertical separation minima (RVSM) were implemented. Finally, the crews had to be physically fit and

psychologically trained to cope with the demanding long missions and able to use the aircraft's navigation and communications suites effectively.

As the flights to Cuba became a routine matter, the 'Bearonauts' gained professionalism and grew more confident. On Cuba the Soviet airmen were treated like close friends, or even like family. To this day, many in the Russian military believe that the decision to withdraw the Soviet military contingent from Cuba was an awful waste. Also, for the North Fleet airmen, who were unaccustomed to warm climes, the luxury of even a brief stay on sunny Cuba was a very welcome break.

The possibility to operate from overseas bases in 'friendly nations' improved the capabilities of the Soviet Navy's aerial reconnaissance element no end. In September 1972, two *Bear-Ds* stationed on Cuba made it possible to detect in timely fashion two NATO carrier task forces led by the carriers USS *Forrestal* (CV-59) and USS *Enterprise* (CVN-65) in the West Atlantic as they set sail from American shores to the Norwegian Sea to participate in Exercise *Strong Express* – the biggest NATO exercise up to then. For two days the *Bears* operating from Cuban bases shadowed both CTFs before turning their charges over to other North Fleet reconnaissance aircraft operating from Soviet territory. In those Cold War years the successful operations of naval reconnaissance aircraft imbued the Soviet government with confidence that hostile aircraft carriers would not approach Soviet borders undetected.

Assessing the results of Tu-95RTs deployments to Cuba, the AVMF top command gradually decided that Tu-142M crews had to master transatlantic flights as well, especially considering the fact that the *Bear-F*'s navigation suite was far better than the *Bear-D*'s. On

The obverse and reverse of an AVMF medal saying, respectively, Naval Aviation – for valour in the sky' and 'To a naval airman – a veteran of the Cold War on the seas'.

View over the IFR probe of a Tu-142 overflying a US Navy aircraft carrier.

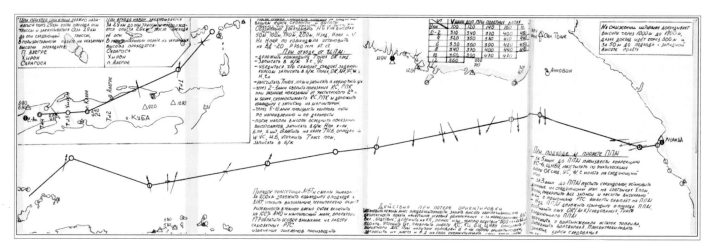

A navigational chart for a flight from Havana to Luanda, with instructions on passing waypoints and what to do in case of disorientation.

21st March 1983 two 76th OPLAP DD Tu-142MKs captained by Maj. N. N. Karpus' and Maj. V. M. Bychkov made the type's first deployment to San Antonio de los Baños AB, marking the beginning of a ten-year period of Tu-142 operations from Cuba. Subsequently *Bear-Fs* undertook combat sorties over the Atlantic from there, making it harder for the US Navy to deploy covertly to the central part of the Atlantic Ocean.

The first Tu-142MK deployment to Cuba was on 14th March 1983. Operating from Havana-José Marti airport, a pair of North Fleet *Bear-F* Mod 3s flew ten submarine hunt sorties over the Sargasso Sea, dropping a series of sonobuoys. The crews reported contacts with six submarines, tracking them for a total time of 11

hours 40 minutes. Trans-Atlantic flights by pairs of Tu-142MKs to Cuban bases (Havana and San Antonio de los Baños) were quite frequent – two to four per month; as a rule, when the aircraft landed there would be only five to seven tons (11,020-15,430 lb) of fuel remaining.

At San Antonio de los Baños the Cubans built a special hardstand for the Tu-142s, which was big enough for eight aircraft, and a maintenance hangar. The hardstand was equipped with a centralised pressure refuelling system obviating the need for tanker lorries; it was never made operational, however, due to changes in the situation. The hangar, on the other hand, was used quite a lot because the turbine blades of the *Bears'* NK-12MV turboprops often failed, necessitating engine removal.

After carefully analysing the 'submarine noises' recorded by the Tu-142MK crews by means of sonobuoys the experts at the acoustics laboratory voiced doubts as to whether these were really submarines. Other 'bugs' of the aircraft surfaced as well. In order to deal with them the number of Cuban deployments was significantly reduced; then, in 1985 the Tu-142's trans-Atlantic flights were stopped altogether – ostensibly due to the need to debug the search and targeting suite, but actually for political reasons. In the second half of the 1980s the Tu-142M and Tu-142MK appeared over international waters extremely rarely, and then only in remote areas of the world ocean which were of interest to the Soviet Navy.

Deployments to Angola and Guinea began soon after the first Cuban missions. In 1971 the Soviet Union set up a naval base at Conakry at the request of the Guinean government; a detachment of Soviet Navy ships was deployed there full time. Shortly afterwards, in February 1972, a Soviet-Guinean agreement was signed to set up an airbase with an aircraft maintenance facility at Conakry's Gbessia airport; Tu-95RTs aircraft were allowed to use it twice a month, staying there for five or six days at a time for maintenance and crew rest. The first such visit was on 27th July 1973 when two aircraft captained by Maj. V. A. Rykov and Maj. Leonid M.

A Tu-95RTs navigator's chart showing the landing approach details at Luanda airport.

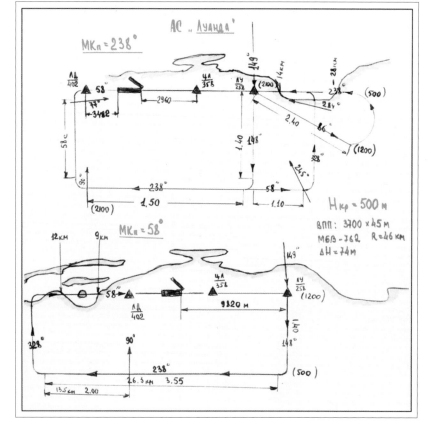

Balyukov made a stopover at Conakry; the group was commanded by Lt.-Col. Vladimir S. Melennyy. On 6th April 1974 Commander of the Guinean People's Army (Minister of Defence) Toumani Sangaré visited Conakry-Gbessia, where a Tu-95RTs and an Antonov An-12 *Cub* transport were staying at the time. In his brief speech at the base, he said: *'I have come here specifically to welcome the Soviet airmen on the soil of free Guinea and to thank them on behalf of the President of Guinea, our people and our Armed Forces for always extending help in our struggle for independence when things get difficult'*. A total of 112 Tu-95RTs sorties were flown from Conakry.

When Angola gained independence from Portugal in 1975 after 15 years of fighting, the Soviet Union supported the winning Popular Movement for the Liberation of Angola (MPLA – *Movimento Popular por la Libertação de Angola*) led by Agostinho Neto. In the ensuing First Angolan Civil War that began in 1975, the Soviet Union extended military aid to the Angolan government, supplying arms and sending military advisors to help build up the Angolan armed forces. Another Soviet Navy forward base was established at Luanda, the Angolan capital, to cater for operations in the East Atlantic, while 392nd ODRAP *Bear-Ds* operated from Luanda-Quatro de Fevereiro airport (the name refers to 4th February 1961 – the date of the MPLA-led uprising against Portuguese colonial rule) from time to time. The first mission to Angola was flown by a pair which departed Olen'ya AB on 27th January 1977; the aircraft were captained by Maj. V. K. Kolobov and Maj. Yu. P. Kornilov, with Col. Vladimir S. Melennyy and Lt.-Col. Leonid M. Balyukov respectively as instructor pilots. After a two-day stopover in Conakry the *Bears* arrived at Luanda on 29th January. On 9th February the crews flew a reconnaissance sortie over the South Atlantic; on 15th February they staged through Conakry again, departing for Severomorsk the following day. After this, the flights of 392nd ODRAP *Bear-Ds* to Angola became a matter of routine; as a rule, each aircraft flew several reconnaissance sorties over the Central and South Atlantic during each deployment. Over the ensuing 13 years (1977-1990) the *Bears* made more than 300 sorties from Luanda alone; also, in 1978-79 they flew a total of 450 sorties from Havana, Conakry and Luanda.

The operating conditions in Africa, especially western Africa, were rather unusual. Since Luanda is located on the ocean coast, tropical circulations of air with small temperature variances between night and day are present there any time of the year. Since the coast is washed by the Benguela Current, hot and dry winds with speeds of 15-20 m/sec (30-40 kts) are frequent there; this had to be taken into account when planning flight operations.

A new stage in Naval Aviation operations began in 1973 when groups of Tu-95RTs reconnaissance aircraft began making reciprocal flights from Cuba to Guinea

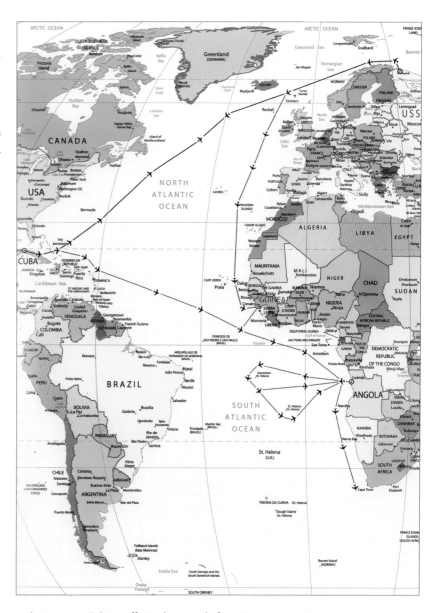

and vice versa. Taking off simultaneously from Havana and Conakry, the groups followed different routes, documenting ship movements over much of the Atlantic Ocean. Later, such shuttle missions were flown between Cuba and Angola. The missions involved considerable difficulties – over the ocean the *Bear-Ds* usually had to cross tropical storm fronts. The latter were up to 2,000 km (1,242 miles) long, with a cloud top as high as 14,000-15,000 m (45,930-49,210 ft), which was in excess of the aircraft's service ceiling. In addition to that, heavy cumulus clouds (again with a top at 15,000 m) were encountered along the entire route. Again, the ambient air temperatures were 10-15°C (18-27°F) above the ISA value, with an attendant increase in fuel burn; the probability of this was 70% in the western half of the route, dropping to 40% in the eastern half.

In spite of all these complications, the North Fleet aviators usually coped with the task, demonstrating a high training standard and the ability to adapt quickly to

This map shows the routes taken by 392nd ODRAP crews from Kipelovo to Angola via Cuba and Guinea and the routes of aerial reconnaissance sorties over the South Atlantic.

an unfamiliar situation. The reminiscences of Col. (Retd.) Yevgeniy V. Kalinin, a former 392nd ODRAP pilot who flew such trans-Atlantic missions more than once, illustrate the point:

'On 31st May 1977 – which happens to be my birthday – I was high up in the sky, flying a mission to Guinea. At the time I was still a co-pilot in the crew captained by S. I. Kiriyenko – an experienced captain, despite his young age. Our aircraft was the leader of the pair because we had an instructor pilot aboard, the regiment's Deputy CO O. N. Kharitonov. The wingman was captained by detachment commander A. I. Yeriomin, a seasoned pilot. We took off from Kipelovo, our home base. As we approached Guinea, we encountered a mighty tropical storm front over the ocean. That was probably when I realised for the first time how dangerous the elements can get. The storm front was too long to dodge and too high to "jump" over it; we had no choice but to press on and go

Top: Tu-95RTs '23 Black' at Luanda-Cuatro de Fevereiro airport in December 1978.

Above: Soviet and Angolan representatives welcome the Tu-95RTs crew of Yu. P. Kornilov at Luanda airport on 29th January 1977.

Above right: The Angolan friends are given a guided tour of the aircraft.

Tu-95RTs '22 Black' is manoeuvred into position by a KrAZ-255B prime mover at Luanda airport.

right through it. The wingman got separated from us; we could only rely on the radar and the entire crew's skill. I don't know if it was the radar that started acting up or it was the young radar operator who lost his wits and messed things up, but fact is that we went smack into the worst of the weather. The aircraft was shaking, heaving and rolling so hard that its strength was put to the test. The flight deck was alternately lashed by rain or pelted by hailstones, and it was so dark you could think night had fallen. The two pilots had trouble keeping the aircraft under control. The ordeal lasted only a few minutes, but it seemed like an eternity. Eventually we literally dropped out of the clouds into a clear blue sky. The African coastline was in front of us, perfectly visible, and Conakry airport was straight ahead. Our wingman was more lucky – he did not wander about in the clouds but went straight through the front; in fact, he landed at Conakry ahead of us. After a couple of days' rest, on 3rd June we made the nine-hour flight to Luanda – a short flight, by our standards. Thus I crossed the Equator for the first time, an occasion which we celebrated by opening the tinfoil tubes of cherry juice that went with the on-board rations. This was my first flight to Angola.

The flights to Havana and Luanda were a harrowing experience. The abrupt change of climate, the temperature fluctuations and jet lag (or should we say 'turboprop lag'? – Auth.) took their toll on the men and the hardware alike. Because of the daytime heat virtually all flights were performed at night. In each flight we almost invariably crossed through tropical storm fronts, encountered jetstreams, flew for lengthy periods in the clouds above the ocean, with no landmarks and no usable alternate airfields. The navigators and pilots worked wonders in these circumstances, and the crews at large displayed notable restraint and bravery. Take-offs were performed almost invariably at night and at maximum take-off weight, which was one of the most complex flight stages for our aircraft type. One of the fatal crashes in our regiment occurred in such circumstances, when the aircraft was taking off from Olen'ya AB with maximum fuel and crashed in full view of the air traffic control group and a second crew waiting their turn to take off (Kalinin is referring to Maj. Vymyatnin's crash – Auth.). Both crews were due for a tour of duty abroad…

In 1987, when detachment commander V. I. Mar'yasov and I flew to Luanda for a fortnight's tour of duty, we got stuck there for a long time, being unable to make the flight to Cuba because of unfavourable winds over the Atlantic Ocean. There were strong headwinds along the entire route, and a full fuel load (the required amount was calculated daily by the HQs in Moscow and Severomorsk) would be barely enough to reach the destination. On the first try we had to turn back at the point of safe return, as our estimates showed we did not have enough fuel to make "Freedom Island" (an oft-used cliché for Cuba in Soviet times – Auth.). We landed at Luanda with bingo fuel remaining. Each day we would watch the weather

situation along the route, calculate the route. The results were disheartening. This dragged on for quite a while. We had no choice but to organise a night flying training shift, making additional flights from Luanda. Someone suggested staging through Guinea, with a refuelling stop at Conakry, but unfortunately we did not have navigation charts for that area; neither did the crews of the other Soviet aircraft then at Luanda. At length a selection of navigation charts was delivered from Moscow, and we began preparing for the homeward flight via Conakry. Well, prepare we did, but something did not click in the diplomatic machinery. There were rumours that the Americans, who were strongly opposed to our landing at Conakry, had thrown a spanner in the works. At that time the Guineans were on better terms with the Americans than with us.

We started preparing for the flight to Cuba once again. Taking off and passing the point of safe return, we managed to reach Holguín (the nearest alternate airfield on Cuba) and land there. We could have taken a chance and pressed on for San Antonio [de los Baños], which was the destination, but that would have been an unwarranted risk. Our arrival at Holguín came as a complete surprise, but I had never received a more heartfelt welcome – before or afterwards. After refuelling the aircraft, 24 hours later we made a positioning flight to San Antonio and, after a short rest, we were on our way home across the Atlantic. On this tour we set a record, roaming across the North-East, West and South Atlantic for two and a half months; usually such tours of duty lasted two or three weeks.'

In August 1977 two 392nd ODRAP crews headed by the aforementioned Maj. V. K. Kolobov and Maj. Yu. P. Kornilov were preparing for a shuttle sortie from Cuba to Angola – the unit's first sortie of the kind. The plan was that, having flown a number of sorties from Angola, the *Bears* would shuttle back to Cuba and thence fly home to the Soviet Union. In addition to the usual reconnaissance en route, the crews were ordered to practice contacts with Soviet submarines on combat patrol in the Central Atlantic, and the subs were some way off the planned route. Of course, this detour meant an additional expenditure of fuel, so Conakry was designated as an alternate airfield in case of a fuel emergency; after landing there the aircraft were to refuel and head for Luanda straight away. It has to be said that, even then, the Guinean government was less than overjoyed about Soviet aircraft operating from Conakry.

Departing Havana-José Martí International on 6th August, the crews went ahead with the mission. Finding and contacting the submarines took about two hours, and of course, as a result, the *Bears* did not have enough fuel left to make Luanda. Requesting a diversion, the crews received permission to land at Conakry. However, Murphy's Law worketh: Kolobov's aircraft suffered some minor damage on landing and was grounded. While the crew was repairing it, the other crew had a short rest and departed for Luanda the next day. However, the misadventures did not end at that: Kornilov's aircraft had to land at night and the runway was much narrower than the one at home. During the first approach the runway lights were off and Kornilov had to make a go-around, landing safely on the second try when the lights were switched on.

Having flown a reconnaissance sortie over the South Atlantic, Kornilov's crew began preparing for the return flight to Cuba. The Soviet Navy Main Staff took the decision that Kornilov should fly alone, without waiting for the other Tu-95RTs to be fixed and rejoin him at Luanda. Halfway across the Atlantic Ocean he was to rendezvous with another pair of 392nd ODRAP *Bear-Ds* captained by Maj. Fedotov and Maj. G. N. Simachov, which were on Cuba at the time. The three aircraft took off from Luanda and Havana right on schedule on 19th August. Having skirted the Antilles Archipelago and recorded radar contact with it for the last time, the 'Cuban' pair headed for the rendezvous point with Kornilov's aircraft. Yet, as the saying goes, if you have bad luck in the morning it will be with you all day; three hours into the mission the solitary westbound Tu-95RTs suffered a failure of the Doppler ground speed/drift sensor system – the all-important instrument allowing the navigator to check if the aircraft is on the desired track during flights over the sea where there are no landmarks. Kornilov's navigator V. N. Borodayev had to rely on a weather map with the wind speeds/directions marked on it and recall all his knowledge of navigation theory and methods of determining the drift angle by means of back-up instruments. With five hours' mission time over the ocean to go, it was one-on-one with the elements. Throughout the mission the crews gave hourly situation reports to the ground command posts and maintained long-range radio communication with each other – and reconnoitred military and commercial shipping all the while.

Three hours before the planned rendezvous the crews determined the estimated time of arrival at the rendezvous point; Kornilov's aircraft and the 'Cuban' pair were then about 4,500 km (2,800 miles) apart. When the distance had diminished to some 500 km (310 miles), all radio navigation systems ensuring the rendezvous were switched on. The SHORAN system came into play at 300 km (186 miles) range; at last the crews were able to see their relative position and communicate on the VHF radio. When the distance was down to 80 km (49 miles) the pair did a U-turn and assumed line astern formation with the oncoming single Tu-95RTs, staying 25 km (15.5 miles) behind; reporting the rendezvous to ground command centres, the entire formation set course for Cuba. A while later the three *Bears* landed safely, completing the unit's first non-stop Luanda-to-Havana mission. After the crews

had had a short rest, all three aircraft made an uneventful flight to Kipelovo AB; Maj. Kolobov's aircraft, which had been stranded in Conakry, also returned home after the damage had been repaired. The unit's first Havana-to-Luanda shuttle mission to go entirely as planned was flown shortly afterwards, on 6th October 1977, by a pair of *Bear-Ds* captained by A. I. Yeriomin and S. I. Kiriyenko. After this, the 392nd ODRAP flew its missions to Angola strictly via Cuba, the use of Conakry as a staging point being discontinued.

The Soviet Navy's Main Staff was well pleased with the results of these shuttle missions, which gave a good idea of the nature and intensity of the shipping in this part of the world ocean. The Soviet military had not enjoyed such capabilities before. There was one more rewarding aspect to it – the sight and sound of the mighty *Bears* passing overhead was most welcome for the crews of Soviet Navy ships on combat patrol in the South Atlantic, and it boosted the morale of the seamen who were fed up with seeing only US Navy P-3s circling overhead.

Another foothold for the Soviet military in Africa was the Somali Republic, which was on friendly terms with the Soviet Union in the 1960s and 1970s. A Soviet-Somalian Friendship Treaty was signed on 11th July 1974, enabling use of three Somalian seaports (including Berbera) by Soviet Navy ships. Additionally, in 1976 the 304th GvODRAP's *Bear-Ds* began operating from forward bases in Somalia (at Dafet in the south and Hargeisa in the north, in what is now Somaliland). That year the crews of Lt.-Col. Grechko and Maj. Kulikov scored a 'first' for the Soviet Navy by flying a reconnaissance mission over the US Navy base at Diego Garcia. In return, the Soviet Union supplied large amounts of military hardware and sent military advisors to Somalia. In July 1977, however, the Somalian dictator Gen. Siad Barré invaded Ethiopia without declaring war, attempting to wrest the Ogaden Province from it. In the ensuing brief conflict known as the Ogaden War, the Soviet Union sided with Ethiopia. Infuriated by this, Barré unilaterally terminated the Soviet-Somalian Friendship Treaty in November 1977 and further Soviet deployments to Somalia became impossible; much of the materiel accumulated at the bases (fuel, spares etc.) was abandoned when the Soviet contingent evacuated.

During the 1970s and 1980s, the Pacific Fleet's 304th GvODRAP constantly flew TDY missions to Vietnam, from where patrols were undertaken in and around South-East Asia. The first two *Bear-Ds* to land on Vietnamese soil were captained by Lt.-Col. Viktor D. Lopasov and Maj. Yuriy A. Lavrook. Initially the Tu-95RTs used the former American military base at Da Nang in Quáng Nam Province of central Vietnam. A detachment of four such aircraft operated from Da Nang in April-September 1979 and January-April 1980. The living conditions for the Soviet personnel at Da Nang were horrendous, but the numerous complaints of the aircrews and ground crews hardly ever brought about a change for the better. A different base at Cam Ranh in south-eastern Vietnam (Khánh Hòa Province) was used by the 304th GvODRAP from April 1980.

While originally confining their activities to the Sea of Okhotsk and the Sea of Japan, Pacific Fleet Tu-142s soon began venturing farther afield over the Pacific and South-East Asia. In 1980 the 310th OPLAP DD, too, started deploying its Tu-142MKs to Da Nang AB, operating from this base until 1982. In 1982 the aforementioned 169th MRAP of the Pacific Fleet was reorganised as the 169th GvSAP (*Gvardeyskiy smeshannyy aviapolk* – Guards composite air regiment), redeploying from Khorol' AB to Cam Ranh AB

Right: A Tu-95RTs on the apron at Conakry-Gbessia airport.

Below right: '38 Black' at Conakry-Gbessia. An APA-80 supplies ground power, with all cowlings open to keep the generator drive engine from running hot.

Bottom right and below: Pre-flight maintenance at Conakry. The tech staff had to work stripped to the waist in the sweltering heat. The man in civvies is V. I. Soorkov, one of the Soviet specialists.

Reconnaissance imagery of Cam Ranh AB, Vietnam, on 9th February 1987, with three Tu-95RTs or Tu-142s and at least sixteen Tu-16s present.

The apron at Cam Ranh AB with a Tu-95RTs, a quasi-civil Tu-154M airliner in Aeroflot colours and a pair of Tu-142s.

A Tu-95RTs seconded to the 169th GvSAP starts its engines at Cam Ranh.

under an agreement with the Vietnamese government. In addition to the four *Bear-Ds*, four *Bear-Fs* and two Antonov An-26 *Curl* tactical transports operated by Sqn 2, it included Sqn 1 with Tu-16K-10-26 *Badger-C Mod* missile carriers, Tu-16SPS *Badger-J* ECM aircraft and Tu-16Z tankers, plus a rotary-wing detachment with Mil' Mi-14PL *Haze-A* ASW helicopters. A third squadron with 14 Mikoyan MiG-23MLD *Flogger-K* fighters seconded from the Air Force was added in 1984 to provide protection. This was the only case since 1955 (the year when the Soviet fighter units deployed in China during the Korean War returned home) when a full AVMF regiment, complete with support units, was stationed abroad. The regiment was originally part of the 25th MRAD (*morskaya raketonosnaya aviadiveeziya* – Maritime Missile Strike Air Division) but soon became a direct reporting unit – the 169th GvOSAP.

The route to Cam Ranh lay over the Tsushima Strait or east of Japan, the flight lasting 9 or 10.5 hours respectively. The Tu-142s carried a complement of 268 RGB-1 sonobuoys and ten RGB-2s. The limited runway length and strength at Cam Ranh – the runway was 3,050 m (10,000 ft) long and suitable for aircraft with a take-off weight of 165,000 kg (363,760 lb) – imposed restrictions on the Tu-142 whose maximum TOW was 180,500 kg (397,930 lb); the fuel load had to be reduced from 84 to 70 tons (from 185,185 to 154,320 lb) – just enough for ten hours' flight. From Cam Ranh the *Bears* flew sorties over the south part of the Philippine Sea; yet the expedience of these missions was open to question, and quite often the planned number of sorties was reduced.

By the end of the decade the 169th GvOSAP had flown some 400 sorties from Cam Ranh, including 130 over the Philippine Sea; the Tu-142s also inspected the Aleutian Islands from time to time. The schedule of combat sorties and training sorties was drafted on site but subject to approval by the Pacific Fleet Air Arm HQ in Vladivostok.

The late 1980s saw a change in the Soviet political situation which had its impact on Tu-95/Tu-142 operations. From 1989 onwards the number of sorties began to decline due to political turmoil and the onset of fuel shortages (the latter would become notorious in the 1990s). For example, in 1992 the 76th PLAP DD flew only six sorties and accumulated only 1,054 hours versus 32 and 2,138 respectively in 1991. Considering all of this, the Naval Aviation HQ addressed the Navy's Main Staff, requesting that the number of planned sorties be reduced. Deployments of Tu-142MKs to Cuba were stopped in 1992 for political reasons (or, officially, suspended until the more sophisticated RGB-16 sonobuoys had been fully mastered), but the Tu-142s stationed in Vietnam remained there for some time yet. On 28th August 1989 Minister of Defence Marshal Dmitriy T. Yazov signed an order downsizing the 169th GvOSAP to an independent composite squadron – the 362nd GvOSAE (*Gvardeyskaya otdel'naya smeshannaya aviaeskadril'ya*) with a complement of four Tu-142MKs, four Tu-95RTs reconnaissance/OTH targeting aircraft and two An-26 transports.

It may be mentioned that in 1992 the 76th PLAP DD dispatched a group of instructors on a special assignment to Indian Navy Air Station Dabolim near Goa (the capital of the eponymous state) where they helped Indian crews master their newly acquired Tu-142MK-Es.

Post-Soviet operations

The break-up of the Soviet Union appeared to have little immediate effect on the naval *Bears* because, unlike the Air Force's Tu-95s, almost all of them were stationed in Russia – except those operated by the 33rd TsBP i PLS in

Overleaf: A Tu-95RTs with green radomes cruises at high altitude.

An excellent upper view of the same aircraft illustrating the wing planform and showing variations in the skin panels' colour.

Page 469: A port side view of Tu-95RTs performing high-altitude photo reconnaissance.

Lower view of a Tu-95RTs with grey radomes showing the heat shields aft of the engine exhausts and the tell-tale exhaust stains on the wing underside. The black tactical code shows it to be a North Fleet/392nd ODRAP machine.

Soviet Naval Aviation Tu-95/Tu-142 units in early 1992		
Unit	**Base**	**Aircraft (quantity)**
North Fleet (HQ Severomorsk, Murmansk Region)		
a) Direct reporting units		
392nd ODRAP	Kipelovo AB, Vologda Region, Russian Federation	Tu-95RTs
b) 35th PLAD (HQ Fedotovo, Vologda Region)		
135th PLAP DD	Kipelovo AB	Tu-142MK (20), Tu-142MR (4)
76th PLAP DD	Kipelovo AB	Tu-142MK (25?)
Pacific Fleet (HQ Vladivostok, Primor'ye Territory)		
a) Direct reporting units		
310th OPLAP	Kamennyy Ruchey AB, Mongokhto, Primor'ye Territory, Russian Federation	Tu-142, Tu-142MZ, Tu-142MR
312th OPLAP	Pushchino AB, Russian Federation	Tu-142 (12)
304th GvODRAP	Khorol' AB, Primor'ye Territory, Russian Federation	Tu-95RTs
b) 25th MRAD (HQ Vladivostok, Primor'ye Territory)		
169th GvSAP	Khorol' AB/Cam Ranh AB, Vietnam	Tu-95RTs, Tu-142

Opposite, top: The personnel of the 392nd ODRAP/Sqn 1 with one of the squadron's aircraft, '19 Black'.

Opposite, bottom: The 392nd ODRAP's command staff with the same Tu-95RTs in June 1993; the aircraft now wears an 'Excellent aircraft' badge.

A badge marking the 40th birthday of the 392nd ODRAP (not stating the unit number, but the reference to the North Fleet is good enough).

Top: A photo inscribed by US Navy Atlantic Fleet C-in-C Adm. Paul David Miller ('Having another look – All the best') and Kent Walker Ewing, the CO of VF-102 embarked on USS *America* ('Thanks for the visit! 8 November 1991) as a present to North Fleet air arm Commander Maj.-Gen. Viktor P. Potapov (mis-spelled as 'Potatov').

A self-explanatory inscription by VF-102 CO Cdr. Kent W. Ewing on a photo depicting an intercept of a Tu-95RTs during Exercise *North Star 1991*.

Crew readiness levels in the 76th OPLAP DD				
	1990	**1991**	**1992**	**1993**
Planned number of flight crews:				
Tu-142MK	27	27	30	30
Tu-142MR	4	7	10	10
Actual number of complete crews:				
Tu-142MK	26	27	22	20
Tu-142MR	4	7	6	5
Crews cleared to fly in daytime:				
Tu-142MK	26	24	21	18
Tu-142MR	4	6	6	5
Crews cleared to fly at night:				
Tu-142MK	22	16	18	15
Tu-142MR	4	6	6	5

Nikolayev. Soon enough, however, the impact of the political and economic chaos of the 1990s in the post-Soviet nations was felt. Active use of the *Bear-Ds* tapered off gradually. In May 1993 the 392nd ODRAP at Ostrov AB expanded its fleet, receiving sixteen Tu-16K-10-26 missile carriers from the Baltic Fleet's recently disbanded 240th *Sevastopol'sko-Berlinskiy* GvMRAP (*Gvardeyskiy morskoy raketonosnyy aviapolk* – Guards Maritime Missile Strike Air Regiment). On 29th May 1993 two Tu-95RTs crews captained by Lt.-Col. Ye. V. Kalinin and Maj. D. A. Proshkevich flew the type's final mission in the North Fleet. The last flight of a Pacific Fleet Tu-95RTs from Khorol' AB took place just a month later, on 24th June.

In 1993 the Tu-95RTs was phased out, the North Fleet's 392nd ODRAP and the Pacific Fleet's 304th GvODRAP

Aircraft serviceability rates in the 76th OPLAP DD							
	1987	**1988**	**1989**	**1990**	**1991**	**1992**	**1993**
Planned fleet:							
Tu-142MK	20	20	20	20	20	20	20
Tu-142MR	7	7	7	7	7	7	7
Actual fleet:							
Tu-142MK	15	14	14	16	18	19	20
Tu-142MR	5	6	5	5	6	6	8
Serviceable aircraft:							
Tu-142MK	12	14	11	10	7	6	3
Tu-142MR	3	5	4	3	3	3	3

Opposite: The flight line at Kipelovo AB in August 2013, showing 73rd OAE Tu-142MKs. Some of the aircraft have individual names.

A Pacific Fleet Tu-142MR makes a low flypast, showing the large ventral fairing of the trailing wire aerial drum and the tandem pairs of strake aerials aft of it.

both disbanding on 1st December 1993. This left the Russian Navy without OTH targeting capability because no successor to the *Bear-D* was fielded. Within a short time the *Bear-Ds* were thoughtlessly scrapped – the North Fleet machines at Kipelovo AB and Ostrov AB, the Pacific Fleet machines at the 3273rd Aircraft Storage Depot in Khorol'. Sadly, not a single Tu-95RTs has been preserved for posterity; in Russia, the 1990s were a time of wild and woolly capitalism when profit was king and historic traditions were brushed aside.

Pacific Fleet Tu-142MZs, including '63 Red', sit parked among piles of snow at Kanemmyy Ruchey AB. Bears like these are not supposed to hibernate!

Tu-142MK '97 Black' *Vologda* with the city crest of Vologda, North Fleet, 73rd OAE, Kipelovo AB

Tu-142MK '50 Black' *Fedotovo* with the emblem of Fedotovo garrison, 73rd OAE

Tu-142MK '95 Black' *Cherepovets* with the city crest of Cherepovets, 73rd OAE

Tu-142MR '11 Black' *Belo'ozero* with the crest of the Vologda Region's Belozerskiy District, 73rd OAE

Tu-142MZ '53 Red' *Vanino* with the town crest of Vanino, Pacific Fleet, 568th GvOSAP, Kamennyy Ruchey AB

Looking immaculate in post-overhaul colours, Tu-142MK '95 Black' *Cherepovets* returns to Kipelovo AB after a practice sortie.

In contrast, Tu-142MZ '53 Red' *Vanino* seen parked at Kamennyy Ruchey AB sure could use a fresh coat of paint. The red colour of the national insignia has almost vanished. Still, in spite of the weathered finish, the aircraft was fully operational when this picture was taken.

Left: A dramatic shot of the same Tu-142MZ '53 Red' on short finals to Kamennyy Ruchey AB.

Below: '11 Black' *Belo'ozero*, the only Tu-142MR with a glazed nose, on final approach to Kipelovo AB.

Opposite page: In a probably unique occurrence, Pacific Fleet/7061st Guards Aviation Base Tu-142MZ '54 Red' wore the logo of the local telecommunications company TTK Dal'niy Vostok (TransTeleCom Far East) by way of a name. Here it is seen operating from Kamennyy Ruchey AB.

Tu-142MK '66 Black' *Ivan Borzov (HSU)* bearing the crest of the Vologda Region's Vashkino District, 73rd OAE, Kipelovo AB

Tu-142MK '94 Black' *Yevgeniy Preobrazhenskiy (HSU)* bearing the crest of the of the Vologda Region's Kirillovo District, 73rd OAE

Tu-142MK '51 Black'/RF-34059 *Yuriy Malinin* wearing tri-colour national insignia and VMF Rossiï (Russian Navy) titles, 73rd OAE

Tu-142MK '56 Black' *Aleksandr Mozhaiskiy* bearing the crest of the Vologda Region's Vologda District, 73rd OAE

Tu-142MZ '58 Red' with *Rossiya* (Russia) titles and the Russian
Navy flag, Pacific Fleet, 568th GvOMSAP, Kamennyy Ruchey AB

That same day, on 1st December 1993, the 362nd
GvOSAE at Cam Ranh AB was also disbanded, leaving
only a military commandant's office to maintain the
base in working order. Pacific Fleet Air Arm operations
from Cam Ranh AB were finally discontinued in 2001
when the Russian government chose not to renew the
agreement with Vietnam. In the spring of 2014 Russian

military aircraft started using the base again after a long
pause but these are not naval operations any more –
Cam Ranh AB occasionally hosts IL-78 tankers supporting the operations of Russian Air Force Tu-95MSs.

Moreover, the 33rd TsBP i PLS in Nikolayev had been
'privatised' by the newly-independent Ukraine, leaving
the Russian Naval Aviation without an aircrew training

Tu-142MK '51 Black'/
RF-34059 *Yuriy Malinin*
is the latest *Bear-F* to be
christened.

Here, Tu-142MK '56 Black' is seen in current guise with
Russian Navy titles and the registration RF-34063 added

479

Here '51 Black'/
RF-34059 *Yuriy Malinin* is
depicted on final app-
roach to Kipelovo AB.

Tu-142MR *Velikiy Ustyug*
in post-overhaul colours
as '17 Red'/RF-34063.

A Tu-142MZ is on display during an 'open house' at a Russian Naval Aviation base, with weapons and sonobuoys arranged alongside.

Here, Tu-142MR RF-34105 is escorted by a Russian Air Force Su-30SM ('17 Red'). Unfortunately the *Bear*'s tactical code is not readable, being stencilled on the nose gear doors only.

23

Tu-142MR '23 Red', 568th GvOMSAP, Kamennyy Ruchey AB; the badge reads 'Pacific Fleet Air Force & Air Defence Force, Russia'

12 ВЫТЕГРА

Tu-142MR '12 Black' *Vytegra* bearing the crest of the Vologda Region's Vytegra District, North Fleet, 73rd OAE

15 ТАГАНРОГ

Tu-142MR '15 Black' *Taganrog* bearing the city crest of Taganrog, 73rd OAE

17 Великий Устюг МА ВМФ РОССИИ RF-34073

Tu-142MR *Velikiy Ustyug* in post-overhaul grey colours as '17 Red'/RF-34073 with 'Russian Naval Aviation' titles

| Above: Tu-142MR '24 Red'/RF-34113 prepares to taxi at Kipelovo AB on 23rd July 2017.

| Tu-142MR '17 Red'/RF-34073 *Velikiy Ustyug* takes off at Kipelovo AB for a flypast at the Navy Day parade in St. Petersburg on 28th July 2017.

The same Tu-142MR in old natural metal colours as
'17 Black' with the city crest of Velikiy Ustyug, 73rd OAE

centre. This was an insupportable situation, and on 1st September 1994 the Russian Naval Aviation's new 444th TsBP i PLS was established at Ostrov-5 AB. By an order of the Naval Aviation Commander Col.-Gen. Viktor P. Potapov the former 392nd ODRAP and 240th GvMRAP were pooled to form the 240th GvIIOSAP (*Gvardeyskiy issledovatel'sko-instrooktorskiy otdel'nyy smeshannyy aviapolk* – Guards Research & Instructional Independent Composite Air Regiment). The regiment, which inherited the missile strike unit's number, Guards title and honorary appellation, became part of the 444th TsBP i PLS, operating a mixed bag of aircraft – including two Tu-142MKs transferred from the 76th PLAP DD.

Flight hours continued to go downhill as the fuel shortages got worse and aircraft serviceability declined. The 76th PLAP DD logged only 1,176 hours in eight sorties in 1993 and only 362 (!) hours in 1994.

In the course of a reform of the Russian Armed Forces, on 15th December 1994 the 35th PLAD and the 135th PLAP DD were disbanded. As a result, the 76th PLAP became a direct reporting unit (76th OPLAP DD) once more, comprising two squadrons of Tu-142MK ASW aircraft, a squadron of Tu-142MR communications relay aircraft and a maintenance unit. The unit carried on with its combat activities. For example, on 31st March 1995 the crew of Lt.-Col. Kudashkin detected and tracked a NATO submarine. On 13th-20th March 1996 the 76th OPLAP took part in a North Fleet command and staff exercise; in so doing the crews led by Col. I. A. Vyazmetinov, Lt.-Col. P. A. Mozheyko and Maj. A. F. Boodkeyev detected three Russian submarines and three western ones.

By mid-1996 the AVMF nominally had 15 Tu-142Ms, 39 Tu-142MKs and 14 Tu-142MZs on strength. Yet more than half of this number was officially 'in reserve' – putting it plainly, grounded and unlikely to fly again. In October 1996 the Russian Navy command decided to retire 14 high-time *Bears* operated by the 76th OPLAP; the aircraft were scrapped at Kipelovo AB.

On 11th-14th May 2001 some of the 76th OPLAP's aircrews had an opportunity to participate in a joint Long-Range Aviation/Naval Aviation exercise – the first in a long, long while. This was a welcome event; in the course of the exercise a detachment of Tu-142s from Kipelovo AB headed out over the Atlantic Ocean, while the DA's Tu-95MSs and Tu-160s from Engels-2 AB headed south and crossed Iranian airspace to interact

Several 73rd OPLAE DD (73rd OAE) aircraft have individual names, including Tu-142MK '50 Black' *Fedotovo* (named after the garrison at Kipelovo AB)…

…Tu-142MR '11 Black' *Belo'ozero* (named after a town which is a district centre in the Vologda Region)…

…and Tu-142MK '50 Black' *Vologda* named after the region's administrative centre.

with Russian Navy/Black Sea Fleet and Pacific Fleet ships in the Arabian Sea. The Russian ships were there for a joint exercise with the Indian Navy.

On 1st November 2001 the Russian Navy's Main Staff issued a directive downsizing the 76th OPLAP DD to the 73rd OPLAE DD (ot**del**'naya protivo**lod**ochnaya **a**viaeskad**ril**'ya **dahl**'nevo **dey**stviya – independent long-range ASW air squadron). In so doing the unit's command element was eliminated almost entirely and part of the flying personnel discharged from military service. In spite of its name, the squadron operated not only ASW aircraft but also Tu-142MR aircraft intended for maintaining communications between shore command centres and nuclear missile submarines in the event of war. Hence some sources referred to the unit simply as the 73rd OAE (ot**del**'naya **a**viaeskad**ril**'ya – Independent Air Squadron) without specifically mentioning its role.

In the Pacific Fleet, the 310th OPLAP DD was merged with the 568th GvMRAP in 2002 to form the 568th GvOMSAP (Gvar**dey**skiy ot**del**'nyy mor**skoy** smesh**annyy a**via**polk** – Guards Independent Maritime Composite Air Regiment). Its Sqn 3 operated the former ASW unit's Tu-142MZ *Bear-F* Mod 4 ASW aircraft and Tu-142MR communications relay aircraft, the other two squadrons operating Tu-22M3 bombers/missile carriers.

In July 2008, North Fleet Tu-142MKs and upgraded IL-38Ns flew a number of operational evaluation missions over the Barents Sea and the Norwegian Sea. The Russian Navy C-in-C's aide Captain 1st Rank Igor' V. Dygalo stated at a press briefing on 24th July that *'new avionics and weapons control systems were tested during [these] flights, which showed them to be highly effective'.* He also said that the Russian Navy aircraft were escorted by NATO aircraft at certain stages of the mission and stated that the flights of the Russian aircraft had proceeded in strict compliance with international law. Dygalo went on to say that long-range sorties flown by Russian Navy aircraft in the Arctic are becoming normal practice and are in the interests of the nation. (Captain 1st Rank (kapi**tan per**vovo **ran**ga) is a Soviet/Russian Navy rank equivalent to Colonel in the Army and Air Force and to the Captain (OF-5) rank in NATO navies.)

More changes came after the Five-Day War with Georgia – the Naval Aviation, too, was subjected to the controversial 'Serdyukov reform' introducing the new

Tu-142MK '95 Black' *Cherepovets* is also named after a town which is a district centre in the Vologda Region.

Another 73rd OAE Tu-142MK, '66 Black', is named after Ivan I. Borzov (HSU), a Baltic Fleet bomber unit commander, and bears the crest of the Vashkino District of the Vologda Region where he was born.

In contrast, Tu-142MR '15 Black' *Taganrog* is named after its birthplace.

64

Tu-142MZ '64 Red', Pacific Fleet,
568th GvOMSAP, Kamennyy Ruchey AB

54

ТТК - Дальний Восток
КОМПАНИЯ ТТК

Tu-142MZ '54 Red' with TransTeleCom Far East advertising,
568th GvOMSAP

RF-34099

ВМФ РОССИИ

RF-34099
ВМФ РОССИИ

Tu-142MZ '65 Red'/RF-34099 with new-style insignia and Russian
Navy titles, Pacific Fleet, 7062nd AvB, Kamennyy Ruchey AB

Opposite page, top left: The flight deck of this Tu-142MZ shows evidence of an upgrade (note the multi-function display in front of the captain).

Opposite page, top right: Tu-142M '94 Black', a 7050th AvB/Kipelovo Aviation Group aircraft, is named after Lt.-Gen. Yevgeniy N. Preobrazhenskiy (HSU) and bears the crest of the Vologda Region's Kirillovo District where he was born.

Opposite page, centre: Tu-142MR '17 Black' *Velikiy Ustyug* is named after a town in northern European Russia. The aircraft belongs to the same unit.

Far right: Tu-142MZ '62 Red' operated by the 7061st GvAvB (formerly 568th GvOMSAP) wears the badge of the Pacific Fleet's Air Force & Air Defence Force and the legend *Rossiya* (Russia).

Right: Tu-142MZ '62 Red' of the same 7061st GvAvB wears the same badge.

order of battle. In line with this 'new order', in 2010 the North Fleet's 924th MRAP operating Tu-22M3s at Olen'ya AB near Olenegorsk (Murmansk Region), the 73rd OPLAE DD at Kipelovo AB, the 837th Aircraft Maintenance Base and three other support units were fashioned together into the 7051st Aviation Base (AvB). The bombers at Olen'ya AB were operated by the 1st Aviation Group (AvGr), while the *Bears* belonged to the 2nd AvGr. In 2011, however, a new reorganisation occurred – the *Backfire-Cs* were transferred to the Air Force and came under the control of the 6950th AvB. Hence the 7051st AvB was disbanded and the unit at Kipelovo AB became an Aviation Group of the

7050th AvB, continuing to operate Tu-142MK/ Tu-142MZ ASW aircraft and Tu-142MR TACAMO aircraft.

It was much the same story in the Pacific Fleet, where the 568th GvOMSAP at Kamennyy Ruchey AB became the 7061st GvAvB in 2010. A year later, however, its Tu-22M3s were transferred to the Air Force and the unit ceased to exits as such, being downsized to a squadron and becoming an Aviation Group of the 7062nd AvB headquartered at Nikolayevka AB (Khabarovsk Territory). Once again, however, this did not involve a change of base – the *Bears* still operate from Kamennyy Ruchey AB.

Additionally, the 444th TsBP i PLS at Ostrov-5 AB was disbanded on 1st December 2009; after more than three years of inactivity the base was transferred to the Army Aviation and currently hosts attack helicopters. Instead, a new Russian Naval Aviation combat training and aircrew conversion centre, the 859th TsBP i PLS, was formed at Yeisk (Krasnodar Territory) on the Sea of Azov – or rather reformed from a smaller training centre with the same number which had hitherto specialised in helicopter crew training. Part of the 444th Centre's hardware was transferred to the new unit, but not the Tu-142MKs.

Above left: Tu-142MK '56 Black'/RF-34063 on the flight line at Kipelovo AB.

Left: Tu-142MK '65 Red'/RF-34099 departs Kipelovo AB for the Navy Day parade in St. Petersburg on 28th July 2017.

Below left: Tu-142MR '24 Red'/RF-34113 is caught by the camera just as it becomes airborne

Above: Tu-142MK '50 Black' *Fedotovo* makes a low flypast. The name, which is applied in fairly small type and in blue, is not very conspicuous – unlike the other named aircraft at Kipelovo AB.

Overleaf: A fine view of Tu-142MZ '53 Red' *Vanino* on final approach.

Below: A full frontal of a Tu-142MR running its engines in front of a concrete blast deflector.

A list of named Russian Navy Tu-142s			
Tactical code/ registration	Type	Name	Notes
11 Black	Tu-142MR	Belo'ozero	North Fleet/73rd OAE. Christened 16-7-2006; named after an ancient Russian city (known since 1777 as Belozersk) in the current Vologda Region of Russia
12 Black	Tu-142MR	Vytegra	North Fleet/73rd OAE. Christened 18-8-2007; named after a town (district administrative centre) in the Vologda Region
15 Black	Tu-142MR	Taganrog	North Fleet/73rd OAE. Christened 26-12-2007; named after the city in the Rostov Region of Russia where the Tu-142 was produced
17 Black	Tu-142MR	Velikiy Ustyug	North Fleet/73rd OAE. Christened 17-10-2008; named after a town ('Great Ustyug') in the Vologda Region known, among other things, as the residence of Ded Moroz ('Grandfather Frost' – the Russian counterpart of Santa Claus)
50 Black	Tu-142MK	Fedotovo	North Fleet/73rd OAE. Christened 31-8-2013; named after the garrison at Kipelovo AB
51 Black/RF-34059	Tu-142MK	Yuriy Malinin	North Fleet/73rd OAE. Named after Yuriy Aleksandrovich Malinin (1934-2010) who was the 76th OPLAP DD's Chief of Staff in 1972-84. 50th Tu-95/Tu-142 refurbished by Beriyev TANTK, redelivered 12-8-2016
56 Black/RF-34063	Tu-142MK	Aleksandr Mozhaiskiy	North Fleet/73rd OAE. Christened 11-8-2012; named after Aleksandr Fyodorovich Mozhaiskiy (1825-1890), a Russian aviation pioneer who built the first Russian aircraft (unflown) in 1882
66 Black	Tu-142MK	Ivan Borzov	North Fleet/73rd OAE. Christened 17-10-2008; named after Air Marshal Ivan Ivanovich Borzov, Hero of the Soviet Union (1915-1974) who commanded the North Fleet air arm in 1953-55
94 Black	Tu-142MK	Yevgeniy Preobrazhenskiy	North Fleet/73rd OAE. Christened 17-10-2008; named after Col.-Gen. Yevgeniy Nikolayevich Preobrazhenskiy, Hero of the Soviet Union (1909-1963), a Baltic Fleet torpedo-bomber unit CO who led a mission to bomb Berlin on 7th August 1941 and was AVMF Commander in 1950-62
95 Black	Tu-142MK	Cherepovets	North Fleet/73rd OAE. Christened 23-5-2004; named after a city in the Vologda Region
97 Black	Tu-142MK	Vologda	North Fleet/73rd OAE. Christened 16-10-2004
53 Red	Tu-142MZ	Vanino	Pacific Fleet/7061st AvB. Christened 16-7-2006; named after a town and seaport in the Primor'ye Territory
54 Red	Tu-142MZ	TTK 'Dal'niy Vostok'	Pacific Fleet/7061st AvB. Christened (or rather advertisement unveiled) 17-8-2008; the name means TransTeleCom – Far East

Tu-142MR '17 Red'/ RF-34073 tails IL-78M '35 Blue' over Palace Square in St Petersburg during the 28th July 2017 parade.

Left: A landing study of Tu-142MK '95 Black' *Cherepovets*.

A badge showing all Naval Aviation units which have been resident at Kipelovo AB since 1963 – the 392nd ODRAP, 76th OPLAP DD, 35th PLAD DD, and 24th OPLAP (the latter unit operated IL-38s).

A Pacific Fleet Tu-142MZ basks in the sunshine at Kamennyy Ruchey AB, with impressive snow-capped mountains as a backdrop.

A high-flying Tu-142MK contrailing across the sky is seen over the Nos. 3 and 4 engines of a sister ship, the leader of the pair.

April 2011 was a period of intensive training for Pacific Fleet airmen. In the course of a tactical exercise the Tu-142MZ and Tu-142MR crews from Kamennyy Ruchey AB flew numerous sorties. One of the sorties took two *Bear-F Mod 3s* over international waters in the Sea of Okhotsk and the Bering Sea, the crews practicing navigation over featureless terrain in daytime and at night. During the 14-hour mission the Russian aircraft were occasionally escorted by US Air Force Lockheed Martin F-22A Raptor fighters.

An incident involving a North Fleet/7050th AvB Tu-142MZ captained by Guards Maj. Polyakov occurred on 12th April 2011. As the aircraft came in to land at Kipelovo AB after a training sortie, the starboard main landing gear unit jammed halfway through extension. At 1710 hrs Moscow time the crew sent out a distress call, requesting an emergency landing. For 90 minutes the aircraft circled the airfield, burning off fuel to reduce the landing weight and minimise the potential damage. Meanwhile, the runway was covered with foam (a common procedure preventing a fire in the event of a wheels-up landing). Thankfully this proved to be unnecessary; when the aircraft touched down on the port main gear bogie, the jolt dislodged the starboard strut, which extended and locked into position, whereupon the aircraft landed safely at 1840 hrs. This

was the fourth gear-related incident in the years of Tu-95/Tu-142 operations at Kipelovo.

In the first decade of the 21st century the Russian Naval Aviation, too, started giving individual names to its aircraft (see table on page 490). Actually what one of the Pacific Fleet Tu-142MZs sported was not a name but the logo of the TTK **Dal'***niy Vos****tok*** (TransTeleCom – Far East) company, one of Russia's mobile networks and Internet services providers (of all things!). Have you ever heard of combat aircraft carrying advertising for a private enterprise, and not in the 'wild and woolly 1990s' of nascent Russian capitalism but in the 2000s?

Showtime

The Tu-142 has largely been neglected when it comes to airshows and similar events. One may recall an uncoded brand-new Tu-142MZ (c/n 2605426) in the static park at MosAeroShow '92 (11th-16th August 1992) – the first full-fledged international airshow at Zhukovskiy – and a similarly uncoded sister ship (c/n 9604012) at the MAKS-93 airshow (31st August/5th September 1993). In July 1994 a 240th GvOSAP Tu-142MK coded '93 Black' (c/n 1603062) made a surprise appearance at that year's Royal International Air Tattoo at RAF Fairford.

Two years later, a 76th OPLAP DD Tu-142MK took part in a flypast at the parade in St. Petersburg on 28th July 1996 to celebrate the Russian Navy's 300th birthday (a second aircraft was in hot reserve). The crews of Lt.-Col. P. A. Mozheyko and Lt.-Col. Metelin were entrusted with the mission; a ground crew team under Lt.-Col. Voronovich prepared the *Bears* for the flypast. Escorted by two MiG-29 fighters, the Tu-142MK headed the succession of aircraft that passed over the city along the Neva River on that festive occasion.

On 31st August 2013 an 'open house' was held at Kipelovo AB on occasion of the former 392nd ODRAP's golden jubilee. On that day one of the resident squadron's Tu-142MKs ('50 Black') was christened *Fe****do****tovo* after the local garrison and the public was allowed to examine seven of the unit's aircraft at close range; apart from '50 Black', these included Tu-142MKs '95 Black' *Chere***po***vets* and '97 Black' **Vo***logda*, Tu-142MZ '56 Black' *Aleksandr Mozhaiskiy* and Tu-142MR '15 Black' *Tagan****rog***.

On 9th May 2015 Tu-142MR '17 Red'/RF-34073 *Velikiy Ustyug* took part in the V-Day parade in Severomorsk. The most recent airshow appearance by the Tu-142 was on 30th July 2017 when three *Bears* took part in the Navy Day parade, first passing over St. Petersburg and then proceeding west to pass over Kronshtadt (Leningrad Region). First, Tu-142MR '17 Red'/RF-34073 *Velikiy Ustyug* flew with IL-78M '35 Blue'/RF-94273 in a simulated refuelling formation. It was followed in short order by Tu-142MKs '51 Black' /RF-34059 *Yuriy Malinin* and '56 Black'/RF-34063 *Akeksandr Mozhaiskiy* in echelon starboard formation.

CHAPTER NINE

Tu-95 and Tu-142 operators

The Tu-95/Tu-142 family was not built with exports in mind, and India was the only true export customer. After the break-up of the Soviet Union, however, the *Bears* ended up in three of the 12 CIS republics. Only one of these – the Russian Federation – still operates the type.

Soviet Union/Russia

The **Soviet Air Force** (Long-Range Aviation) units that have operated the Tu-95 have been listed in Chapter 7. About half of them were inherited by the **Russian Air Force** (VVS), namely the 182nd *Sevastopol'sko-Berlinskiy* GvTBAP at Mozdok in Ingushetia with Tu-95MSs, the 40th TBAP and 79th GvTBAP at Ookraïnka AB near Belogorsk in the Far East (both with Tu-95K-22s), and an instructional

regiment of the 43rd TsBP i PLS at Dyagilevo AB in Ryazan' with assorted versions. When the Tu-95K-22s were withdrawn and scrapped under the terms of the SALT II treaty, in 1993 the 79th GvTBAP re-equipped with the Tu-95MS, which was made possible by the transfer of 33 *Bear-Hs* from Kazakhstan. After the 1997 reorganisation of the formerly independent Air Force and Air Defence Force into a united air arm, in April 1998 the Long-Range Aviation was transformed into the 37th VA VGK (SN), or 37th Strategic Air Army of the Supreme Command.

The 182nd GvTBAP redeployed to Engels-2 AB in November 1994, subsequently moving to Ookraïnka AB in 1999 and absorbing the resident 40th TBAP. The 'new' 121st GvTBAP based at Engels (the

A Russian Air Force Tu-95MS upgraded to carry Kh-101 missiles prepares for a practice sortie from Engels.

**Right and below: Still
wearing Soviet-era
markings without
Russian Air Force
titles or registration,
Tu-95MS '14 Red' cruises
over heavy clouds.**

former 1096th TBAP reformed in December 1994 as a
successor of the Soviet-era 'old' 121st GvTBAP) had
operated a mix of Tu-160s (Sqn 1) and Tu-95MSs (Sqns 2
and 3) since 1998. When three more Tu-95MSs were
procured from the Ukraine in 1998, the two *Bear-H*
squadrons were transformed into a separate co-located

regiment, the 'new' 184th TBAP (which inherited the
number of a disbanded Tu-160 unit in the Ukraine),
while the 121st Regiment received more Tu-160s and
became an all-*Blackjack* unit. By July 2001 the Russian
Air Force had 63 Tu-95MSs on strength, with a stockpile
of 504 Kh-55 missiles reserved for them.

As already mentioned, the sweeping reform of the Russian Armed Forces begun in 2009 in the wake of the Five-Day War with Georgia changed the Russian Air Force's order of battle completely. The traditional Soviet/Russian structure (air army – air division – air regiment – air squadron) was scrapped and replaced by Aviation Bases (AvB). The 37th VA VGK (SN) was transformed into the Long-Range Aviation Command. The two units at Engels-2 AB – the 121st GvTBAP and the 184th TBAP – were merged into the 6950th *Donbasskaya* GvAvB, the Tu-95MSs of the former 184th TBAP equipping Sqn 2; the aircraft complement for 2010 was 16 Tu-160s in Sqn 1 and 14 (some sources say 18) Tu-95MSs in Sqn 2. At Ookraïnka AB, the 6952nd AvB was formed by pooling the 182nd GvTBAP and 79th TBAP, with 36 Tu-95MSs in two squadrons; a further four Tu-95MSs remained in the 43rd TsBP i PLS at Dyagilevo AB. The *Bears* were supported by the 18 IL-78 *Midas-A* tanker/transports and IL-78M *Midas-B* dedicated tankers of the 6954th AvB (formerly 203rd *Orlovskiy* GvOAPSZ, *Gvardeyskiy otdel'nyy aviapolk samolyotov-zaprahvshchikov* – Guards independent aerial refuelling regiment) which moved from Engels to Dyagilevo.

However, when the hugely unpopular civilian Minister of Defence Anatoliy E. Serdyukov was fired from his post inNovember 2012 and replaced by one of Putin's closest aides Army Gen. (i.e., four-star general) Sergey K. Shoigu, the latter reversed some of his predecessor's decisions, starting a trend which has been jocularly called 'de-Serdyukovisation'. Among other things, the Russian Air Force's tri-colour insignia (red pentastars edged in white, blue and red), which had caused much controversy when introduced in March 2010 but had gradually gained acceptance, reverted to the Soviet-style version with a plain white/red surround on 25th January 2015 and are being applied as such to new-build aircraft. Moreover, within each VVS/PVO Army the aviation bases and their constituent aviation groups (AvGr) are to be reorganised back into air regiments and air divisions; apparently the MoD top brass has decided that the aviation base/aviation group system used for the last five years was not so efficient after all. This process began in December 2013, and many of the former air regiments have already regained their original numbers; the Tu-95 units may also do so in due course.

On 1st August 2015 the Russian Air Force was merged with the Aerospace Defence Force by Presidential decree to form the **Russian Aerospace Force** (VKS). Yet, the formation of this new service did not cause a change in the Cyrillic 'VVS Rossiï' (Russian Air Force) titles, mockingly called 'BBC of Russia' by some observers, which were introduced in the course of the 'Serdyukov reform' and worn by the Long-Range Aviation aircraft along with the others.

As of 2010 the VVS had a total of 64 Tu-95MSs, although three *Bear-Hs* have been lost in accidents since then. The ones that are in good shape and with enough

Tu-142MZ '17 Red'/ RF-34073 *Velikiy Ustyug* cruises over broken cloud en route from Kipelovo AB to St. Petersburg for the Navy Day parade on 28th July 2017.

service life remaining are being progressively upgraded to carry Kh-101/Kh-102 missiles. Still, the bombers were mostly manufactured in the 1980s and will be due for retirement as time-expired in ten years or so from now. Also, the stock of spare engines for both of the DA's strategic bombers is almost depleted, since the NK-12MV turboprop is long since out of production.

More or less positively identified Soviet and Russian Air Force Tu-95s are listed in the following table (aircraft operated by other CIS republics are not included if identified as such). Unfortunately, relatively few Tu-95s have been identified by their construction numbers. In the early days of Tu-95 operations the c/n was writ large on the nose and tail, but this practice was abandoned in the 1960s for security reasons. As already mentioned, some development aircraft carried four-digit numbers

in the same positions but these had nothing to do with the c/n. Some aircraft whose c/ns are unknown have been included because their details, such as the quasi-civil registrations prefixed RF-, can serve as a reasonable identification in view of the limited quantity built or operated. Some Russian Air Force Tu-95MSs currently wear curious 'fractional' tactical codes on the nose gear doors (usually on the port one only; elsewhere the code is applied conventionally). This is due to the fact that some aircraft in the two units now operating the type have the same code but different registrations. Since the latter are regarded as the primary identifier for arms limitation treaty purposes, the 'fractions' serve as an additional identifier to convince inspectors that the registration has not been altered and Russia is not trying to exceed the limit on strategic air strike systems.

Known Soviet and Russian Air Force Tu-95s				
C/n	**F/n**	**Version**	**Tactical code/ registration**	**Notes**
?		Tu-95	none	First prototype ('95/1'), Tupolev OKB. F/F 12-11-1952. Crashed near Noginsk 11-5-1953
?		Tu-95	none	Second prototype ('95/2'), Tupolev OKB. F/F 16-2-1955. Converted to, see next line
		Tu-95LL	?	Engine testbed, LII. Scrapped Zhukovskiy
4800001		Tu-95	?	First pre-production aircraft. Converted to, see next line
		Tu-95K	?	First prototype, Tupolev OKB, later GK NII VVS. To Chelyabinsk Military Navigators' School as GIA
4800002		Tu-95	?	Second pre-production aircraft. Damaged Kuibyshev-Bezymyanka 4-4-1955 and ?-4-1956 but repaired. To 1023rd TBAP
580001		Tu-95	?	409th TBAP
580002		Tu-95	77 Red	1023rd TBAP, Semipalatinsk
580003		Tu-95	5 Black	GK NII VVS, state acceptance trials. Became, see next line
			56 Red	Crashed into Black Sea 25-8-1965, crew killed
5800101		Tu-95	6 Black	First production aircraft. GK NII VVS, state acceptance trials. Converted/recoded to, see next line
		Tu-95M	46 Red/'4807'	Prototype, Tupolev OKB, state acceptance trials. Converted to, see next line
		Tu-95N	46 Red/'4807'	Test aircraft, Tupolev OKB. Preserved Central Russian Air Force Museum, Monino, as 4807 Black
5800102		Tu-95	44 Red	409th TBAP, Uzin AB; also reported as 1023rd TBAP
5800103		Tu-95	?	1023rd TBAP
5800104		Tu-95	?	409th TBAP
5800105		Tu-95	?	409th TBAP
5800201		Tu-95	?	409th TBAP
5800202		Tu-95	?	1023rd TBAP
5800203		Tu-95	?	1023rd TBAP
5800204		Tu-95	?	1023rd TBAP
5800205		Tu-95	?	1023rd TBAP. Crashed 5-10-1976, crew killed
5800301		Tu-95	?	1023rd TBAP; later used for repeat static tests
5800302		Tu-95	?	1023rd TBAP. Converted to, see next line
		Tu-95V	?	Development aircraft, Tupolev OKB. To 409th TBAP; later to 1023rd TBAP, scrapped Chagan AB
6800304		Tu-95	?	1023rd TBAP
6800305		Tu-95	?	409th TBAP? Crashed near Belaya Tserkov' 20-9-1959
6800306		Tu-95	?	1023rd TBAP, later to 43rd TsBP i PLS. Crashed near Alma-Ata 5-10-1976, crew killed
6800307		Tu-95	none	1023rd TBAP
6800308		Tu-95	?	1023rd TBAP
6800309		Tu-95	?	1023rd TBAP
6800310		Tu-95	?	GK NII VVS. Crashed near Engels 24-11-1956, crew killed (accident date also reported as 24-12-1956 or 16-3-1957)
6800401		Tu-95	?	409th TBAP
6800403		Tu-95	?	409th TBAP

6800404	Tu-95	?	Converted to, see next line	
	Tu-95K	?	Second prototype, Tupolev OKB. To 1006th TBAP, Uzin AB; to 182nd TBAP, Mozdok. Converted to, see next line	
	Tu-95KM			
7800405	Tu-95	?	1023rd TBAP	
7800406	Tu-95	?	1023rd TBAP	
7800407	Tu-95M	?	409th TBAP	
7800408	Tu-95M	?	Converted to, see next line	
	Tu-95LAL	51 Red	Test aircraft, Tupolev OKB. To Irkutsk Military Aviation Technical School as GIA; scrapped Irkutsk	
7800410	Tu-95M	?	GK NII VVS, check-up tests; to 409th TBAP. Converted, see next line	
	Tu-95MR	?	Prototype; also reported as Tu-95MR-2. Converted to, see next line	
	Tu-95U	68 Red	43rd TsBP i PLS. Scrapped Ul'yanovsk	
7800501	Tu-95M	?	1023rd TBAP. Converted to, see next line	
	Tu-95MR	?		
7800502	Tu-95M	?	1023rd TBAP. Converted to, see next line	
	Tu-95MR	?		
7800503	Tu-95M	51 Red	409th TBAP	
7800504	Tu-95M	?	GK NII VVS. Crashed 25-8-1965, crew killed	
7800505	Tu-95M	?	409th TBAP, later to 182nd TBAP	
7800506	Tu-95M	?	409th TBAP. Converted to, see next line	
	Tu-95MR	66 Red	No IFR probe. To 43rd TsBP i PLS, Dyagilevo AB	
7800507	Tu-95M	?	409th TBAP	
8800508	Tu-95M	?	1023rd TBAP	
8800509	Tu-95M	?	409th TBAP; to 43rd TsBP i PLS	
8800510	Tu-95M	60 Red?	409th TBAP. Converted to Tu-95RTs prototype (see next table)	
8800601	Tu-95M	?	409th TBAP. Converted to, see next line	
	Tu-95M-5	none	Weapons testbed, Tupolev OKB. Converted to, see next line	
	Tu-95M-55	none	Weapons testbed, Tupolev OKB. Crashed Zhukovskiy 28-1-1982, crew killed	
8800602	Tu-95M	?	1023rd TBAP	
8800603	Tu-95M	?	409th TBAP	
8800604	Tu-95M	?	409th TBAP	
8800605	Tu-95M	57 Red	409th TBAP	
?	Tu-95M	71 Red	Converted to, see next line	
	Tu-95U		43rd TsBP i PLS	
?	Tu-95MA	55 Red		
?	Tu-95MA	75 Red		
?	Tu-95MR	46 Red	C/n 7800410, 7800501 or 7800502	
?	Tu-95MR	65 Red	C/n 7800410, 7800501 or 7800502. To 43rd TsBP i PLS; scrapped at Engels-6 AB (storage and disposal facility)	
?	Tu-95MR	69 Red	C/n 7800410, 7800501 or 7800502	
?	Tu-96	73 Black/'5836'	Development aircraft, Tupolev OKB; scrapped	
6800402	Tu-116	7801 Blue	Converted Tu-95M, f/f 23-4-1957. Also reported as '7802 Red'! 1023rd TBAP; became, see next line	
		CCCP-76462	1023rd TBAP. SOC 1980, preserved Civil Air Fleet Museum, Ul'yanovsk	
7800409	Tu-116	7802 Blue	Converted Tu-95M, f/f 3-6-1957. Also reported as '7801 Red'! 409th TBAP; became, see next line	
		CCCP-76463	409th TBAP; scrapped Uzin AB	
8802004	Tu-95K	58 Red?	First production Tu-95K. GNIKI VVS, state acceptance trials. Crashed 5-1-1963	
8802005	Tu-95K	?	182nd TBAP, Mozdok; later to Engels. Converted to, see next line	
	Tu-95KM		Converted to, see next line	
	Tu-95K-22			
8802006	Tu-95K	?	1006th TBAP, Uzin AB; later to Engels. Converted to, see next line	
	Tu-95KM		Converted to, see next line	
	Tu-95K-22			

9802007	Tu-95K	?	1006th TBAP	
9802008	Tu-95K	12 Black	1006th TBAP, later to Engels. Converted to, see next line	
	Tu-95KM		Converted to, see next line	
	Tu-95K-22			
9802009	Tu-95K	?	182nd TBAP	
9802010	Tu-95K	66 Red	182nd TBAP (also reported as 1006th TBAP). Crashed 26-8-1977 (mid-air collision with Tu-95K c/n 60802301), crew killed	
9802101	Tu-95K	?	182nd TBAP. Converted to, see next line	
	Tu-95KM		Converted to, see next line	
	Tu-95K-22			
9802102	Tu-95K	?	182nd TBAP	
9802103	Tu-95K	?	1006th TBAP, later to Engels. Converted to, see next line	
	Tu-95KD		Prototype, Tupolev OKB; to GNIKI VVS, state acceptance trials. Converted to, see next line	
	Tu-95KM		Converted to, see next line	
	Tu-95K-22		Stored Engels-6 AB/scrapped?	
9802104	Tu-95K	?	182nd TBAP. Converted to, see next line	
	Tu-95KM		Converted to, see next line	
	Tu-95K-22		Stored Engels-6 AB/scrapped?	
9802105	Tu-95K	?	182nd TBAP	
9802106	Tu-95K	?	182nd TBAP	
9802107	Tu-95K	?	1006th TBAP, later to Engels. Converted to, see next line	
	Tu-95KM		Converted to, see next line	
	Tu-95K-22		Stored Engels/scrapped?	
9802108	Tu-95K	?	1226th TBAP, Semipalatinsk. Converted to, see next line	
	Tu-95KM		Converted to, see next line	
	Tu-95K-22			
9802109	Tu-95K	?	1006th TBAP. Converted to, see next line	
	Tu-95KM		Converted to, see next line	
	Tu-95K-22			
9802110	Tu-95K	?	182nd TBAP, later to Engels. Converted to, see next line	
	Tu-95KM		Converted to, see next line	
	Tu-95K-22		Stored Engels/scrapped?	
9802201	Tu-95K	?	1006th TBAP	
9802202	Tu-95K	?	1226th TBAP. Converted to, see next line	
	Tu-95KM		Converted to, see next line	
	Tu-95K-22			
9802203	Tu-95K	?	1006th TBAP, later to 1226th TBAP. Converted to, see next line	
	Tu-95KM		Converted to, see next line	
	Tu-95K-22			
60802205	Tu-95K	?	1226th TBAP. Converted to, see next line	
	Tu-95KM		Converted to, see next line	
	Tu-95K-22			
60802206	Tu-95K	?	1006th TBAP, Uzin AB. Converted to, see next line	
	Tu-95KM		Converted to, see next line	
	Tu-95K-22			
60802207	Tu-95KM	?	Prototype. 182nd TBAP. Converted to, see next line	
	Tu-95K-22			
60802208	Tu-95K	?	182nd TBAP. Converted to, see next line	
	Tu-95KM		Converted to, see next line	
	Tu-95K-22		Stored Engels-6 AB/scrapped?	
60802209	Tu-95K	?	182nd TBAP. Crashed 24-12-1987	
60802210	Tu-95K	?	182nd TBAP. Converted to, see next line	
	Tu-95KM		Converted to, see next line	
	Tu-95K-22		Stored Engels/scrapped?	
60802301	Tu-95K	68 Red	182nd TBAP (also reported as 1006th TBAP). Modified for RINT duties. Crashed 26-8-1977 (mid-air collision with Tu-95K c/n 9802010), crew killed	

60802302	Tu-95K	?	1226th TBAP. Converted to, see next line	
	Tu-95KM		Converted to, see next line	
	Tu-95K-22		Stored Engels-6 AB/scrapped?	
60802303	Tu-95K	?	1006th TBAP. Converted to, see next line	
	Tu-95KM		Converted to, see next line	
	Tu-95K-22		Stored Engels-6 AB/scrapped?	
60802304	Tu-95K	?	182nd TBAP	
60802305	Tu-95K	?	1226th TBAP; later to Engels. Converted to, see next line	
	Tu-95KM		Converted to, see next line	
	Tu-95K-22		Stored Engels-6 AB/scrapped?	
60802306	Tu-95K	?	182nd TBAP	
60802307	Tu-95K	35 Red	182nd TBAP; to 43rd TsBP i PLS, preserved Ryazan'-Dyagilevo AB base museum	
60802308	Tu-95K	?	1226th TBAP	
60802309	Tu-95K	?	1226th TBAP. Converted to, see next line	
	Tu-95KM		Converted to, see next line	
	Tu-95K-22			
60802310	Tu-95K	40 Black?	1226th TBAP	
60802401	Tu-95K	?	1226th TBAP. Converted to, see next line	
	Tu-95KM		Converted to, see next line	
	Tu-95K-22			
61802402	Tu-95K	?	182nd TBAP. Converted to, see next line	
	Tu-95KM		Converted to, see next line	
	Tu-95K-22			
61802403	Tu-95K	?	1006th TBAP. Converted to, see next line	
	Tu-95KM		Converted to, see next line	
	Tu-95K-22		Stored Engels-6 AB/scrapped?	
61802404	Tu-95K	?	1226th TBAP. Converted to, see next line	
	Tu-95KM		Converted to, see next line	
	Tu-95K-22			
61802405	Tu-95K	36 Red	1006th TBAP. Scrapped Ul'yanovsk 1992	
61802406	Tu-95K	?	1226th TBAP. Converted to, see next line	
	Tu-95KM		Converted to, see next line	
	Tu-95K-22		Damaged beyond repair in heavy landing	
61802407	Tu-95K	?	1226th TBAP	
61802408	Tu-95K	?	1226th TBAP	
61802409	Tu-95K	?	1226th TBAP	
61802410	Tu-95K	?	1006th TBAP	
61802501	Tu-95K	?	1226th TBAP	
?	Tu-95K	11 Red	1006th TBAP?	
?	Tu-95K	32 Red	43rd TsBP i PLS	
?	Tu-95KU	33 Red	43rd TsBP i PLS	
?	Tu-95K	34 Red	43rd TsBP i PLS	
?	Tu-95K	61 Red	43rd TsBP i PLS	
62M52502	Tu-95KM	?	First production aircraft. 1226th TBAP; modified for RINT duties	
62M52503	Tu-95KM	?	1226th TBAP. Modified for RINT duties. Converted to, see next line	
	Tu-95K-22	02 Red	Scrapped 148th ARZ, Bila Tserkva (the Ukraine)	
62M52504	Tu-95KM	?	1006th TBAP. Modified for RINT duties. Converted to, see next line	
	Tu-95K-22		Stored Engels/scrapped?	
62M52505	Tu-95KM	?	1226th TBAP. Converted to, see next line	
	Tu-95K-22			
62M52506	Tu-95KM	02 Red	1006th TBAP. Modified for RINT duties. Converted to, see next line	
	Tu-95K-22		Stored Engels/scrapped?	
62M52507	Tu-95KM	?	1226th TBAP. Modified for RINT duties. Converted to, see next line	
	Tu-95K-22			

62M52508	Tu-95KM	?	1006th TBAP. Converted to, see next line
	Tu-95K-22		
62M52509	Tu-95KM	?	1226th TBAP. Modified for RINT duties. Converted to, see next line
	Tu-95K-22		
62M52510	Tu-95KM	?	1006th TBAP. Converted to, see next line
	Tu-95K-22		
62M52601	Tu-95KM	?	1226th TBAP. Modified for RINT duties. Converted to, see next line
	Tu-95K-22		
63M52602	Tu-95KM	20 Red	1226th TBAP, to 1006th TBAP. Converted to, see next line
	Tu-95K-22	05 Red	Scrapped at 148th ARZ, Bila Tserkva (the Ukraine)
63M52603	Tu-95KM	?	182nd TBAP. Converted to, see next line
	Tu-95K-22		
63M52604	Tu-95KM	?	182nd TBAP. Converted to, see next line
	Tu-95K-22		
63M52605	Tu-95KM	?	182nd TBAP. Modified for RINT duties. Converted to, see next line
	Tu-95K-22		
63M52606	Tu-95KM	?	1006th TBAP. Converted to, see next line
	Tu-95K-22		
63M52607	Tu-95KM	?	LII, Zhukovskiy; later GNIKI VVS. Converted to 'mother ship' for Mikoyan '105.11' experimental aircraft; scrapped
63M52608	Tu-95KM	?	1006th TBAP. Converted to, see next line
	Tu-95K-22		First aircraft upgraded
63M52609	Tu-95KM	?	182nd TBAP, to 1006th TBAP. Converted to, see next line
	Tu-95K-22		
63M52610	Tu-95KM	?	182nd TBAP, to 1006th TBAP. Converted to, see next line
	Tu-95K-22	53 Red	Preserved DA Museum, Engels-2 AB
64M52701	Tu-95KM	?	1006th TBAP. Converted to, see next line
	Tu-95K-22		
64M52702	Tu-95KM	?	1226th TBAP. Converted to, see next line
	Tu-95K-22		
64M52703	Tu-95KM	?	182nd TBAP. Converted to, see next line
	Tu-95K-22		
64M52704	Tu-95KM	?	182nd TBAP. Converted to, see next line
	Tu-95K-22	57 Red	
?	Tu-95KM	08 Red	
?	Tu-95KM	12 Red	Possibly 1006th TBAP, named *Svetlana*
?	Tu-95K-22	01 Red	
?	Tu-95K-22	02 Red	
?	Tu-95K-22	04 Red	Scrapped Engels-6 AB
?	Tu-95K-22	05 Red	
?	Tu-95K-22	09 Red	Modified for RINT duties
?	Tu-95K-22	20 Red	
?	Tu-95K-22	24 Red	
?	Tu-95K-22	25 Red	Scrapped Engels-6 AB
?	Tu-95K-22	26 Red	
?	Tu-95K-22	27 Red	Scrapped Engels-6 AB
?	Tu-95K-22	30 Red	
?	Tu-95K-22	31 Red	
?	Tu-95K-22	32 Red	Scrapped Engels-6 AB
?	Tu-95K-22	35 Red	
?	Tu-95K-22	38 Red	
?	Tu-95K-22	42 Black	
?	Tu-95K-22	44 Red	Scrapped Engels-6 AB
?	Tu-95K-22	47 Red	
?	Tu-95K-22	43 Red	
?	Tu-95K-22	52 Red	Modified for RINT duties

?		Tu-95K-22	55 Red	Derelict
?		Tu-95K-22	56 Red	Modified for RINT duties
?		Tu-95K-22	64 Black	
?		Tu-95K-22	66 Red	Scrapped Engels-6 AB
?		Tu-95K-22	67 Red	
?		Tu-95K-22	68 Red	Scrapped Engels-6 AB
?		Tu-95K-22	91 Red	Modified for RINT duties
8602109	42105	Tu-95MS	no code	Taganrog-built, converted Tu-142MK (c/n is the original Tu-142 c/n). First prototype, Tupolev OKB. SOC 1990, to SibNIA for static tests
1602821	42...	Tu-95MS	31 Red	Taganrog-built, converted Tu-142MK (c/n is the original Tu-142 c/n). Natural metal finish. Second prototype, GNIKI VVS; later GIA Air Force Academy (Monino), now preserved Central Russian Air Force Museum. See next line
6403423100002	0101?	Tu-95MS	?	This c/n reported for the above aircraft!
6403424100003	0102?	Tu-95MS	52 Red*	Taganrog-built (new production)
6403424100004	0103?	Tu-95MS	004 Black	GNIKI VVS, Akhtoobinsk. Converted to, see next line
		Tu-95MA		Weapons testbed, 929th GLITs, Akhtoobinsk. Natural metal finish.
6403423200201	?	Tu-95MS	58	1023rd TBAP, Semipalatinsk; to 79th TBAP, Ookraïnka AB
6403424200402	?	Tu-95MS	24	1023rd TBAP, Semipalatinsk; to 43rd TsBP i PLS
6403424200603	?	Tu-95MS	21/2 Red	Grey c/s. DBR by fire Ryazan'-Dyagilevo 26-2-2013
6403424300804	?	Tu-95MS	?	Weapons testbed for Meteor-N missile
6403422300811	?	Tu-95MS	62	1023rd TBAP, to 79th TBAP
6403423300822	?	Tu-95MS	50 Red	1023rd TBAP, to 79th TBAP; used for avionics tests under Tu-95MSM programme. Became, see next line
			50 Red/RF-94192	6952nd AvB, grey c/s
6403424300843	?	Tu-95MS	23 Red*	1023rd TBAP; to 79th TBAP, then to 43rd TsBP i PLS; see c/n 6403421400875!
6403424300854	?	Tu-95MS	77 Red*	Based Ookraïnka AB. Converted to, see next line
		Tu-95MS upg†	77 Red/RF-94204	6952nd AvB. Crashed near Ivankovtsy village (Khabarovsk Territory) 14-7-2015
6403421400875	?	Tu-95MS	23/2 Red/RF-94205	1023rd TBAP, to 79th TBAP; code reused after transfer of Tu-95MS c/n 6403424300843 to the 43rd TsBP i PLS. Grey c/s
6403422400903	?	Tu-95MS	22 Red	1023rd TBAP; to 79th TBAP, then to 43rd TsBP i PLS
6403422400905	?	Tu-95MS	20 Red/RF-94255	43rd TsBP i PLS
100021**10317	?	Tu-95MS	12 Red	Kuibyshev-built. 326th TBAD, Ookraïnka AB
1000214215101	?	Tu-95MS	01 Red	Tupolev OKB, weapons testbed under Tu-95MSM programme. Became, see next line
			no code	929th GLITs. Became, see next line
			101 Red	929th GLITs. Still in same testbed configuration
1000213316202	?	Tu-95MS	47 Red	6952nd AvB, natural metal finish, named *Ryazan'*. Became, see next line
			47 Red/RF-94201	Grey c/s, no name
1000214319215	?	Tu-95MS	60	1023rd TBAP, to 79th TBAP
1000213419317	?	Tu-95MS	317 Black	Tupolev OKB, weapons testbed. Converted to, see next line
		Tu-95MS upg	317 Red	Prototype, based Zhukovskiy, natural metal finish
1000211419421	?	Tu-95MS	53 Red	1023rd TBAP, to 79th TBAP, natural metal finish. Became, see next line
			53 Red/RF-94195	6952nd AvB, grey c/s
1000211419429	?	Tu-95MS	49 Red/RF-94191	6952nd AvB, grey c/s
1000212419743	?	Tu-95MS	48 Red*	1023rd TBAP, to 79th TBAP, to 6952nd AvB
1000212421802	?	Tu-95MS	56 Red*	1023rd TBAP, to 79th TBAP; became, see next line
			56 Red/RF-94198	6952nd AvB
1000212421906	?	Tu-95MS	54 Red/RF-94196	6952nd AvB
1000213421914	?	Tu-95MS	55 Red/RF-94197	6952nd AvB
1000213423103	?	Tu-95MS	43 Red*	1023rd TBAP, to 79th TBAP, to 6952nd AvB
1000213423107	?	Tu-95MS	41 Red/RF-94186	6952nd AvB
1000214423419	?	Tu-95MS	57 Red *	1023rd TBAP, to 79th TBAP; became, see next line
			57 Red/RF-94199	6952nd AvB
1000214424530	?	Tu-95MS	42 Red	DBR by fire at Ookraïnka AB, date unknown
1000214424532	?	Tu-95MS	51 Red/RF-94193	6952nd AvB
1000214424544	?	Tu-95MS	29 Red*	1023rd TBAP, to 79th TBAP; was equipped to carry Meteorit missile
1000214424604	?	Tu-95MS	604 Black	Development aircraft, Tupolev OKB, based Zhukovskiy. Natural metal finish. To 79th TBAP, named *Ryazan'*. Became, see next line
			20 Red	Named *Ryazan'*; eventually scrapped Ryazan'-Dyagilevo AB

100021*524608	?	Tu-95MS	608 Black	Development aircraft, Tupolev OKB, based Zhukovskiy. Natural metal finish
1000214524610	?	Tu-95MS	610 Black	Development aircraft, Tupolev OKB, based Zhukovskiy. Natural metal finish. To 929th GLITs, Akhtoobinsk; later to 6950th AvB and probably recoded
100021*527611		Tu-95MS	611 Black	Development aircraft, Tupolev OKB. Natural metal finish. Stored Zhukovskiy, scrapped 1998
1000211527615		Tu-95MS	22 Red*	1023rd TBAP, to 79th TBAP; was equipped to carry Meteorit missile. Became, see next line
			22 Red/RF-94176	6952nd AvB
1000211528356		Tu-95MS	25 Red*	1023rd TBAP, to 79th TBAP; was equipped to carry Meteorit missile
1000212528373		Tu-95MS	20 Red*	1023rd TBAP, to 79th TBAP; was equipped to carry Meteorit missile
1000212528382	?	Tu-95MS	24 Red*	1023rd TBAP, to 79th TBAP
1000212528561	?	Tu-95MS	28 Red*	1023rd TBAP, to 79th TBAP; was equipped to carry Meteorit missile. Became, see next line
			28 Red/RF-94170	6952nd AvB. Tactical code probably '28/2 Red'
1000212528575	?	Tu-95MS	26 Red*	1023rd TBAP, to 79th TBAP
1000213528593	?	Tu-95MS	21 Red*	1023rd TBAP, to 79th TBAP. Became, see next line
			21 Red/RF-94207	6952nd AvB
1000213529526	?	Tu-95MS	23 Red*	1023rd TBAP, to 79th TBAP
1000213529608	?	Tu-95MS	27 Red*	1023rd TBAP, to 79th TBAP
100021*732477	?	Tu-95MS	26 Red*	Development aircraft equipped with ELINT suite, Tupolev OKB, based Zhukovskiy
1000212733111	?	Tu-95MS	59 Red	182nd TBAP, Mozdok, later Ookraïnka AB. Became, see next line
			59 Red/RF-94206	6952nd AvB, named *Blagoveshchensk*
1000213733255	?	Tu-95MS	10 Red*	1023rd TBAP, to 79th TBAP
1000213733299	?	Tu-95MS	12 Red*	121st TBAP, Engels. Named *Moskva* (Moscow), natural metal finish. Converted to, see next line
		Tu-95MS upg	12 Red/RF-94126	6950th AvB, named *Moskva*
1000213733322	?	Tu-95MS	18 Red*	182nd TBAP, to 184th TBAP. Converted to, see next line
		Tu-95MS upg	18 Red/RF-94131	6950th AvB, natural metal finish; c/n also reported as 100021**33622
1000214733412	?	Tu-95MS	14 Red*	182nd TBAP, to 184th TBAP, named *Voronezh*. Converted to, see next line
		Tu-95MS upg	14 Red/RF-94132	6950th AvB, named *Voronezh*
1000214733447	?	Tu-95MS	17 Black*	182nd TBAP, to 121st TBAP. Converted to, see next line
		Tu-95MS upg	17 Red/RF-94259	6950th AvB
100021**33567	?	Tu-95MS	?	182nd TBAP. SOC 23-10-1998, scrapped
1000211834108	?	Tu-95MS	20 Black*	Converted to, see next line
		Tu-95MS upg	20 Red/RF-94177	This c/n also reported for '15 Red'/RF-94125! See comment for c/n 1000212937345
1000211834135	?	Tu-95MS	16 Red*	182nd TBAP, to 121st GvTBAP, named *Velikiy Novgorod*. Converted to, see next line
		Tu-95MS upg	16 Red/RF-94124	6950th AvB, named *Velikiy Novgorod*
1000212834278	?	Tu-95MS	22/1 Red/RF-94120	6950th AvB, named *Kozel'sk*
1000212834379	?	Tu-95MS	23 Black*	121st GvTBAP. Converted to, see next line
		Tu-95MS upg	23/1 Red/RF-94129	6950th AvB, named *Tambov*, natural metal finish
1000213834415	?	Tu-95MS	24/1 Red/RF-94130	6950th AvB; c/n also reported as [10002147]33415
1000213834444	?	Tu-95MS	25/1 Red/RF-94119	6950th AvB
1000213834496	?	Tu-95MS	20 Red*	184th TBAP, named *Naukograd Doobna*, later simply *Doobna*. Converted to, see next line
		Tu-95MS upg	20/1 Red/RF-94122	6950th AvB, grey c/s, named *Doobna*; first in-service Tu-95MSM delivered to the Russian AF
1000214834666	?	Tu-95MS	31 Black	182nd TBAP, Mozdok. Became, see next line
			21 Red	184th TBAP, named *Samara*; still carried '31 Black' on tail in addition to '21 Red'! Became, see next line
			21/1 Red/RF-94121	6950th AvB, named *Samara*
1000214834757	?	Tu-95MS	11 Red/RF-94127	6950th AvB, named *Vorkuta*
1000214835199	?	Tu-95MS	38 Black	182nd TBAP. Became, see next line
			10/1 Red*	184th TBAP, grey c/s, named *Saratov*. Converted to, see next line
		Tu-95MS upg	10/1 Red/RF-94128	6950th AvB, named *Saratov*
1000211935249	?	Tu-95MS	26 Red/RF-94172	6952nd AvB
100021*935363	?	Tu-95MS	34 Black*	182nd TBAP
1000212935367	?	Tu-95MS	04 Black*	182nd TBAP, Mozdok, later Ookraïnka AB. Became, see next line
			04 Red/RF-94182	6952nd AvB, named *Kurgan*
1000213935765	?	Tu-95MS	05 Red/RF-94181	6952nd AvB. Crashed Ookraïnka AB 8-6-2015
1000213935793	?	Tu-95MS	36 Black*	182nd TBAP. Became, see next line
			01 Red/RF-94185	6952nd AvB, named *Irkutsk*

1000214936177	?	Tu-95MS-16	19 Red*	Ex-Ukrainian AF '10 Red', bought 1998. 148th TBAP. Became, see next line
		Tu-95MS	19 Red/RF-94123	6950th AvB, natural metal finish, named *Krasnoyarsk*
1000214936487	?	Tu-95MS	02 Red/RF-94184	6952nd AvB, named *Mozdok*
1000211036785	?	Tu-95MS	06 Red*	182nd TBAP, Mozdok, later Ookraïnka AB. Became, see next line
			06 Red/RF-94180	6952nd AvB
1000212936853	?	Tu-95MS	07 Red/RF-94179	6952nd AvB
1000213037098	?	Tu-95MS	03 Red*	182nd TBAP, Mozdok, later Ookraïnka AB. Became, see next line
			03 Red/RF-94183	6952nd AvB
1000214037187	?	Tu-95MS-16	28 Red*	Ex-Ukrainian AF '96 Red', bought 1998. 121st TBAP. Became, see next line
		Tu-95MS upg	28/1 Red/RF-94116	6950th AvB, natural metal finish, named *Sevastopol'*
1000212937345	?	Tu-95MS	27 Red	Ex-Ukrainian AF '08 Red', bought 1998. 121st TBAP. Became, see next line
			27/1 Red/RF-94177	6950th AvB. Registration applied in error; see c/n 1000211834108! Became, see next line
		Tu-95MS upg	27/1 Red/RF-94117	6950th AvB, now with its proper registration, named *Izborsk*
1000214137566	?	Tu-95MS	08 Red	Named *Smolensk*. Became, see next line
			29/2 Red/RF-94178	43rd TsBP i PLS, named *Smolensk*
?	?	Tu-95MS	13 Black*	121st TBAP, 1997; later recoded?
?	?	Tu-95MS	15 Red*	121st TBAP. Converted to, see next line
		Tu-95MS upg	15 Red/RF-94125	Named 'Kaluga'. C/n reported as [10002118]34108 (see above)
?	?	Tu-95MS	25 Black*	121st TBAP; to '25 Red' after overhaul
?	?	Tu-95MS	31 Black*	Development aircraft, 929th GLITs, Akhtoobinsk
?	?	Tu-95MS	33 Black/RF-94118	6950th AvB
?	?	Tu-95MS	45 Red*	Converted to, see next line
?	?	Tu-95MS upg	45 Red/RF-94189	
?	?	Tu-95MS	49 Red*	121st TBAP
?	?	Tu-95MS	52 Red/RF-94194	6952nd AvB
?	?	Tu-95MS	55 Red*	121st TBAP
?	?	Tu-95MS	56 Red*	121st TBAP
?	?	Tu-95MS	58 Red/RF-94200	43rd TsBP i PLS
?	?	Tu-95MS	60 Red/RF-94202	43rd TsBP i PLS
?	?	Tu-95MS	95 Red*	
?	?	Tu-95MS	100 Red	182nd TBAP?

* Russian Air Force
† Tu-95MS Phase 1 upgrade to carry Kh-101/Kh-102 missiles (often referred to as Tu-95MSM, see comment in Chapter 5)

In the **Soviet Naval Aviation**, and subsequently in the **Russian Naval Aviation** (AVMF), the Tu-95RTs and various versions of the Tu-142 saw service with the North Fleet and the Pacific Fleet. In the North Fleet the 392nd ODRAP (originally stationed at Severomorsk-1 AB near Murmansk but then redeployed to Kipelovo AB and then to Ostrov AB) was stood down in 1993 when the Tu-95RTs maritime reconnaissance/OTH targeting aircraft were retired and the envisaged Tu-142MRTs successor failed to achieve production. The 76th OPLAP DD ASW regiment, also at Kipelovo AB, was 'demoted' to an independent squadron (the 73rd OAE) and subsequently reorganised as the 7051st AvB and then the 7050th AvB/2nd AvGr during the 'Serdyukov reform' of 2009. It currently operates a mix of Tu-142MK/Tu-142MZ ASW aircraft and Tu-142MR communications relay aircraft.

It was much the same story in the Pacific Fleet where the 304th ODRAP at Mongokhto (Kamennyy Ruchey AB) near Sovetskaya Gavan' was disbanded when its *Bear-D*s ran out of service life, while the co-located 310th OPLAP

DD was transformed into the 568th GvOMSAP (*Gvardeyskiy otdel'nyy morskoy smeshannyy aviapolk* – Guards Independent Maritime Composite Air Regiment) with a mix of types, subsequently becoming the 7061st GvAvB; the unit's Sqn 3 operates the *Bear-F* Mod 4 and *Bear-J*. Two of the Tu-142MZs have individual names. '54 Red' is named *Vanino* after a seaport providing a ferry connection with Sakhalin Island (to the port of Kholmsk), while '55 Red' is named *TTK 'Dal'niy Vostok'* (TransTeleCom – Far East), of all things! Have you ever heard of combat aircraft carrying advertising for private enterprises?

A few Tu-142s served for crew training with the 240th OSAP which was part of the AVMF's 444th Combat Training & Aircrew Conversion Centre at Ostrov AB near Pskov. When the 444th TsBP i PLS was disbanded on 1st December 2009, the base was transferred to the Army Aviation, hosting helicopters. Instead, a new naval conversion training centre – the 859th TsBP i PLS – was established in Yeysk on the Sea of Azov, but this unit does not have any Tu-142s.

			Known Soviet and Russian Navy Tu-95s and Tu-142s	
C/n	F/n	Version	Tactical code/ registration	Notes
8800510		Tu-95RTs	60 Red	Converted Tu-95M, no IFR probe. Prototype, Tupolev OKB, later GNIKI VVS. Became, see next line
			15 Black	North Fleet/392nd ODRAP, Severomorsk-1 AB. Became, see next line
			16 Black	North Fleet/392nd ODRAP/Sqn 1, Kipelovo AB, recoded in 1969. Transferred to 33rd TsBP i PLS, Nikolayev-Kul'bakino AB
63MRTs 001		Tu-95RTs	01 Black?	North Fleet/392nd ODRAP/Sqn 3, Severomorsk-1 AB. Became, see next line
			30 Black*	North Fleet/392nd ODRAP/Sqn 3, Kipelovo AB. Scrapped Kipelovo AB early 1990s
63MRTs 002		Tu-95RTs	02 Black?	North Fleet/392nd ODRAP/Sqn 2, Severomorsk-1 AB. Became, see next line
			20 Black*	North Fleet/392nd ODRAP/Sqn 2, Kipelovo AB. Scrapped Kipelovo AB early 1990s
63MRTs 003		Tu-95RTs	03 Black?	North Fleet/392nd ODRAP, Severomorsk-1 AB. Became, see next line
			?	North Fleet/392nd ODRAP, Kipelovo AB. Crashed 1 km from Kipelovo AB 3-9-1971
63MRTs 101		Tu-95RTs	21 Black*	North Fleet/392nd ODRAP/Sqn 2, Severomorsk-1 AB, later Kipelovo AB. Scrapped Kipelovo AB early 1990s
64MRTs 102		Tu-95RTs	39 Black*	North Fleet/392nd ODRAP/Sqn 3, Severomorsk-1 AB, later Kipelovo AB. Scrapped Kipelovo AB early 1990s
64MRTs 103		Tu-95RTs	32 Black*	North Fleet/392nd ODRAP/Sqn 3, Severomorsk-1 AB, later Kipelovo AB. Scrapped Kipelovo AB early 1990s
64MRTs 104		Tu-95RTs	22 Black*	North Fleet/392nd ODRAP/Sqn 2, Severomorsk-1 AB, later Kipelovo AB. Scrapped Kipelovo AB early 1990s
65MRTs 105		Tu-95RTs	?	Pacific Fleet/867th ODRAP (304th GvODRAP), Khorol' AB
65MRTs 106		Tu-95RTs	?	Pacific Fleet/867th ODRAP (304th GvODRAP). Crashed into Pacific Ocean 10-4-1978, crew killed
65MRTs 107		Tu-95RTs	25 Black*	North Fleet/392nd ODRAP/Sqn 2, Kipelovo AB. Scrapped Kipelovo AB early 1990s
65MRTs 201		Tu-95RTs	14 Black*	North Fleet/392nd ODRAP/Sqn 1, Kipelovo AB. Scrapped Kipelovo AB early 1990s
65MRTs 202		Tu-95RTs	13 Black	North Fleet/392nd ODRAP/Sqn 3, Kipelovo AB. Became, see next line
			34 Black*	Recoded in 1969. Scrapped Kipelovo AB early 1990s
65MRTs 203		Tu-95RTs	23 Black*	North Fleet/392nd ODRAP/Sqn 2, Kipelovo AB. Scrapped Kipelovo AB early 1990s
65MRTs 204		Tu-95RTs	?	Pacific Fleet/867th ODRAP (304th GvODRAP). Crashed 20-7-1967
65MRTs 205		Tu-95RTs	?	Pacific Fleet/867th ODRAP (304th GvODRAP)
65MRTs 206		Tu-95RTs	?	Pacific Fleet/867th ODRAP (304th GvODRAP)
65MRTs 207		Tu-95RTs	?	Pacific Fleet/867th ODRAP (304th GvODRAP)
66MRTs 208		Tu-95RTs	?	Pacific Fleet/867th ODRAP (304th GvODRAP)
66MRTs 209		Tu-95RTs	11 Black	North Fleet/392nd ODRAP/Sqn 1, Kipelovo AB. Became, see next line
			15 Black*	Recoded in 1969
66MRTs 210		Tu-95RTs	26 Black*	North Fleet/392nd ODRAP/Sqn 2, Kipelovo AB. Scrapped Ostrov AB early 1990s
66MRTs 301		Tu-95RTs	?	Pacific Fleet/867th ODRAP (304th GvODRAP)
66MRTs 302		Tu-95RTs	?	Pacific Fleet/867th ODRAP (304th GvODRAP)
66MRTs 303		Tu-95RTs	?	Pacific Fleet/867th ODRAP (304th GvODRAP)
66MRTs 304		Tu-95RTs	37 Black	North Fleet/392nd ODRAP/Sqn 3. Crashed into Atlantic Ocean 4-8-1976, crew killed
66MRTs 305		Tu-95RTs	10 Black*	North Fleet/392nd ODRAP/Sqn 1. Scrapped Kipelovo AB early 1990s
66MRTs 306		Tu-95RTs	11 Black*	North Fleet/392nd ODRAP/Sqn 1. Scrapped Kipelovo AB early 1990s
66MRTs 307		Tu-95RTs	12 Black	North Fleet/392nd ODRAP/Sqn 1. DBR Kipelovo AB 15-4-1985, crew OK. Scrapped Kipelovo AB
67MRTs 308		Tu-95RTs	?	Pacific Fleet/867th ODRAP (304th GvODRAP)
67MRTs 309		Tu-95RTs	?	Pacific Fleet/867th ODRAP (304th GvODRAP)
67MRTs 310		Tu-95RTs	33 Black*	North Fleet/392nd ODRAP/Sqn 3. Scrapped Ostrov AB early 1990s
67MRTs 401		Tu-95RTs	31 Black	North Fleet/392nd ODRAP. Equipped with rear ECM fairing instead of tail turret. Crashed into Barents Sea 15-1-1971, crew killed
67MRTs 402		Tu-95RTs	?	Pacific Fleet/867th ODRAP (304th GvODRAP)
67MRTs 403		Tu-95RTs	?	Pacific Fleet/867th ODRAP (304th GvODRAP)
67MRTs 404		Tu-95RTs	?	Pacific Fleet/867th ODRAP (304th GvODRAP)
67MRTs 405		Tu-95RTs	?	Pacific Fleet/867th ODRAP (304th GvODRAP)
67MRTs 406		Tu-95RTs	35 Black*	North Fleet/392nd ODRAP/Sqn 3, Kipelovo AB. Scrapped Ostrov AB early 1990s
67MRTs 407		Tu-95RTs	?	Pacific Fleet/867th ODRAP (304th GvODRAP)
68MRTs 408		Tu-95RTs	28 Black*	North Fleet/392nd ODRAP/Sqn 2. Scrapped Ostrov AB early 1990s
68MRTs 409		Tu-95RTs	17 Black*	North Fleet/392nd ODRAP/Sqn 1. Scrapped Ostrov AB early 1990s
68MRTs 410		Tu-95RTs	?	Pacific Fleet/867th ODRAP (304th GvODRAP)
68MRTs 501		Tu-95RTs	?	Pacific Fleet/867th ODRAP (304th GvODRAP)
68MRTs 502		Tu-95RTs	?	Pacific Fleet/867th ODRAP (304th GvODRAP)

68MRTs 503		Tu-95RTs	?	Pacific Fleet/867th ODRAP (304th GvODRAP)
68MRTs 504		Tu-95RTs	36 Black*	North Fleet/392nd ODRAP/Sqn 3. Scrapped Ostrov AB early 1990s
68MRTs 505		Tu-95RTs	?	North Fleet/392nd ODRAP
68MRTs 506		Tu-95RTs	24 Black*	North Fleet/392nd ODRAP/Sqn 2. Scrapped Ostrov AB early 1990s
68MRTs 507		Tu-95RTs	18 Black*	North Fleet/392nd ODRAP/Sqn 1. Scrapped Ostrov AB early 1990s
69MRTs 508		Tu-95RTs	?	Pacific Fleet/867th ODRAP (304th GvODRAP)
69MRTs 509		Tu-95RTs	?	Pacific Fleet/867th ODRAP (304th GvODRAP)
69MRTs 510		Tu-95RTs	?	Pacific Fleet/867th ODRAP (304th GvODRAP)
69MRTs 601		Tu-95RTs	38 Black*	North Fleet/392nd ODRAP/Sqn 3. Scrapped Ostrov AB early 1990s
69MRTs 602		Tu-95RTs	19 Black*	North Fleet/392nd ODRAP/Sqn 1. Scrapped Ostrov AB early 1990s
?		Tu-95RTs	06 Black	North Fleet/392nd ODRAP; D/D 5-11-1964. Last flight from Severomorsk-1 AB to Kipelovo AB in 1965, to AVMF Junior Tech School in Vyborg as GIA, later scrapped
?		Tu-95RTs	10 Black	North Fleet/392nd ODRAP
?		Tu-95RTs	17 Black	North Fleet/392nd ODRAP
?		Tu-95RTs	22 Black	North Fleet/392nd ODRAP
?		Tu-95RTs	27 Black	North Fleet/392nd ODRAP. Crashed at Olen'ya AB 25-1-1984, crew killed
?		Tu-95RTs	28 Black	North Fleet/392nd ODRAP
?		Tu-95RTs	31 Black	North Fleet/392nd ODRAP
?		Tu-95RTs	32 Black	North Fleet/392nd ODRAP
?		Tu-95RTs	37 Black	North Fleet/392nd ODRAP
?		Tu-95RTs	38 Black	North Fleet/392nd ODRAP
?		Tu-95RTs	39 Black	North Fleet/392nd ODRAP
4200		Tu-142 (early)	no code?	First prototype, Tupolev OKB. Converted to, see next line
		Tu-142LL	?	Engine testbed, LII
4201		Tu-142 (early)	no code	Second prototype, Tupolev OKB; became an avionmics testbed with APM-106 Ladoga MAD
4202		Tu-142 (early)	?	Third prototype, Tupolev OKB
4211		Tu-142 (early)	?	Tupolev OKB
4212		Tu-142 (early)	?	
4213		Tu-142 (early)	?	North Fleet/76th OPLAP DD, Kipelovo AB
4221		Tu-142 (early)	?	North Fleet/76th OPLAP DD
4222		Tu-142 (early)	?	North Fleet/76th OPLAP DD
4223		Tu-142 (early)	?	
4224		Tu-142 (early)	?	
4225		Tu-142 (early)	?	Last Tu-142 *sans suffixe* with 12-wheel main gear bogies
4231		Tu-142 (late)	?	Tupolev OKB; first Tu-142 *sans suffixe* with four-wheel main gear bogies. To North Fleet/76th OPLAP DD
4232		Tu-142 (late)	?	North Fleet/76th OPLAP DD
4233		Tu-142 (late)	?	
4234		Tu-142 (late)	?	
4235		Tu-142 (late)	?	
4241		Tu-142 (late)	?	
?		Tu-142	12 Red	Pacific Fleet/310th OPLAP DD
?		Tu-142	23 Red	Pacific Fleet/310th OPLAP DD
?		Tu-142	27 Red	Pacific Fleet/310th OPLAP DD
?		Tu-142	44 Red	Pacific Fleet/310th OPLAP DD
?	?	Tu-142?	51 Black	Could be Tu-142M; North Fleet/76th OPLAP DD
?	?	Tu-142?	52 Black	Could be Tu-142M; North Fleet/76th OPLAP DD
4242		Tu-142M	?	Prototype/last Kuibyshev-built example
?	4243	Tu-142M	?	Built 1974. First Taganrog-built example. Immediately converted to, see next line
?		Tu-142MK		First prototype, Tupolev OKB. Converted to, see next line
?		Tu-142LL	043 Black	Engine testbed, LII; WFU Zhukovskiy
3600405	4244	Tu-142M	16 Red*	Immediately converted to, see next line
?		Tu-142MK	?	Second prototype, Tupolev OKB; later to Pacific Fleet/310th OPLAP DD, Kamennyy Ruchey AB. Scrapped Kamennyy Ruchey

3600501	4245	Tu-142M	17 Red*	First production example. Pacific Fleet/310th OPLAP DD. Scrapped Kamennyy Ruchey
4600502	4246?	Tu-142M	06 Red*	Pacific Fleet/310th OPLAP DD. Scrapped Kamennyy Ruchey
4600617	4247?	Tu-142M	04 Red*	Pacific Fleet/310th OPLAP DD. Scrapped Kamennyy Ruchey
5600635	4248?	Tu-142M	18 Red*	Pacific Fleet/310th OPLAP DD. Scrapped Kamennyy Ruchey
5600801	4249?	Tu-142M	15 Red*	Pacific Fleet/310th OPLAP DD. Scrapped Kamennyy Ruchey
6600980	4250?	Tu-142M	14 Red*	Pacific Fleet/310th OPLAP DD. Scrapped Kamennyy Ruchey
6601101	4251	Tu-142M	01 Red*	Pacific Fleet/310th OPLAP DD. Used for fatigue testing by Beriyev OKB in 2005
6601318	4252	Tu-142M	02 Red*	Pacific Fleet/310th OPLAP DD. Scrapped Kamennyy Ruchey
6601332	4253	Tu-142M	08 Red*	Pacific Fleet/310th OPLAP DD. Scrapped Kamennyy Ruchey
6601347	4254	Tu-142M	03 Red*	Pacific Fleet/310th OPLAP DD. Scrapped Kamennyy Ruchey
6601366	4255	Tu-142M	10 Red*	Pacific Fleet/310th OPLAP DD. Scrapped Kamennyy Ruchey
7601401	4256?	Tu-142M	05 Red*	Pacific Fleet/310th OPLAP DD. Scrapped Kamennyy Ruchey
7601505	4257?	Tu-142M	09 Red*	Pacific Fleet/310th OPLAP DD. Scrapped Kamennyy Ruchey
?	4261	Tu-142M		
?	4262	Tu-142M	?	Converted to, see next line
?		Tu-142MP		Test aircraft, Tupolev OKB
?	4263	Tu-142M	?	Converted to, see next line
?		Tu-142MR		Prototype, Tupolev OKB
?	4264	Tu-142M	?	Converted to, see next line
?		Tu-142MK		Third prototype, Tupolev OKB
?	4265	Tu-142M	?	
?	4271	Tu-142M	?	
?	4272	Tu-142M	?	
?	4273	Tu-142M	?	
?	4274	Tu-142M	?	
?	4275	Tu-142M	?	
?	4281	Tu-142M	?	
?	4282	Tu-142M	?	
?	4283	Tu-142M	?	
?	4284	Tu-142M	?	
8601801	?	Tu-142MK	62 Red*	Transferred to NARP repair plant (Nikolayev, the Ukraine) as debt payment
8602025	?	Tu-142MK	66 Black*	North Fleet/76th OPLAP DD (73rd OAE), named *Ivan Borzov*
9602280	?	Tu-142MK	71 Black*	North Fleet/76th OPLAP DD (73rd OAE)
9602363	?	Tu-142MK	73 Black*	North Fleet/76th OPLAP DD (73rd OAE)
0602446	?	Tu-142MK	98 Black*	North Fleet/76th OPLAP DD
1602821	42105	Tu-142MK	?	Converted to Tu-95MS prototype, which see
1602904	?	Tu-142MK	87 Black*	North Fleet/76th OPLAP DD (73rd OAE)
1602946	?	Tu-142MK	90 Black*	240th OSAP, Ostrov AB
1602987	?	Tu-142MK	91 Black*	North Fleet/76th OPLAP DD (73rd OAE)
1603021	?	Tu-142MK	92 Black*	North Fleet/76th OPLAP DD (73rd OAE)
1603062	?	Tu-142MK	93 Black*	North Fleet/76th OPLAP DD (73rd OAE)
2603187	?	Tu-142MK	94 Black*	North Fleet/76th OPLAP DD (73rd OAE), named *Yevgeniy Preobrazhenskiy*
2603222	?	Tu-142MK	95 Black*	North Fleet/76th OPLAP DD (73rd OAE), named *Cherepovets*
2603305	?	Tu-142MK	97 Black*	North Fleet/76th OPLAP DD (73rd OAE), named *Vologda*
3603388	?	Tu-142MK	50 Black*	North Fleet/76th OPLAP DD (73rd OAE), named *Fedotovo*
3603472	?	Tu-142MK	51 Black*	North Fleet/76th OPLAP DD (73rd OAE). Became, see next line
			51 Black/RF-34059	73rd OAE; named *Yuriy Malinin*
3603556	?	Tu-142MK	52 Black	
5603763	?	Tu-142MK	53 Black*	North Fleet/76th OPLAP DD (73rd OAE)
5603846	?	Tu-142MK	54 Black*	North Fleet/76th OPLAP DD (73rd OAE)
5603887	?	Tu-142MK	55 Black*	North Fleet/76th OPLAP DD (73rd OAE)
6603930	?		56 Black*	North Fleet/76th OPLAP DD; looks like a Tu-142MZ but does not have the Zarechye system (hence c/n in the Tu-142MK series). Became, see next line
			56 Black/RF-34063	Named *Aleksandr Mozhaiskiy*

?	?	Tu-142MK	80 Black*	North Fleet/76th OPLAP DD (73rd OAE)
?	4285	Tu-142MK	?	
?	4291	Tu-142MK	?	
?	4292	Tu-142MK	?	
?	4293	Tu-142MK	?	
?	4294	Tu-142MK	?	
?	4295	Tu-142MK	?	
?	42101	Tu-142MK	?	
?	42102	Tu-142MK	?	
?	42103	Tu-142MK	?	
?	42104	Tu-142MK	?	
9603970	?	Tu-142MZ	53 Red	Pacific Fleet/568th GvOMSAP, Kamennyy Ruchey AB, named *Vanino*
9604012	42185	Tu-142MZ	no code	Displayed at MAKS-93 airshow, Zhukovskiy
9604133	?	Tu-142MZ	54 Red/RF-34106	Pacific Fleet/568th GvOMSAP, named *TTK Dal'niy Vostok*
0604175	?	Tu-142MZ	55 Red	Pacific Fleet/568th GvOMSAP. Crashed in the Strait of Tartary 6-11-2009, crew killed
0604215	?	Tu-142MZ	56 Red/RF-34109	Pacific Fleet/568th GvOMSAP; upgraded by TANTK Beriyev
0604255	?	Tu-142MZ	57 Red*	Pacific Fleet/568th GvOMSAP
0604295	?	Tu-142MZ	58 Red*	Pacific Fleet/568th GvOMSAP
0604336	?	Tu-142MZ	59 Red/RF-34108	Pacific Fleet/568th GvOMSAP
0604362?	?	Tu-142MZ	?	
0604387	?	Tu-142MZ		Converted to, see next line
		Tu-142MRTs		Tupolev OKB, prototype; scrapped
1604440?	?	Tu-142MZ	60 Red*	Pacific Fleet/568th GvOMSAP; c/n was reported as 1609440 but this seems to be an error
1604491	?	Tu-142MZ	61 Red*	Pacific Fleet/568th GvOMSAP
1604543	?	Tu-142MZ	62 Red*	Pacific Fleet/568th GvOMSAP
1604595	?	Tu-142MZ	63 Black/RF-34097	North Fleet/76th OPLAP DD (73rd OAE); also reported as a Pacific Fleet/568th GvOMSAP aircraft coded 63 Red!
1605386	?	Tu-142MZ	64 Red	Pacific Fleet/568th GvOMSAP
2605426	?	Tu-142MZ	no code	Displayed at MosAeroShow'92, Zhukovskiy. Became, see next line
			65 Red/RF-34099	Pacific Fleet/568th GvOMSAP
*60****	?	Tu-142MZ	?? /RF-34105	Probably Pacific Fleet/568th GvOMSAP
8058014301002	?	Tu-142MR	27 Black	
8058014401005	4263?	Tu-142MR	11 Black	Prototype? 'Glass nose'. North Fleet/76th OPLAP DD (73rd OAE), named *Belo'ozero*. WFU/stored Kipelovo AB by 2009
8058014402007	?	Tu-142MR	18 Black	North Fleet/76th OPLAP DD (73rd OAE), natural metal. C/n also reported as 80580102007 (without quarter and year of manufacture). WFU/stored Kipelovo AB by 2009
8058014502009	?	Tu-142MR	28 Black	North Fleet/76th OPLAP DD (73rd OAE)
8058014602017	?	Tu-142MR	23 Black	North Fleet/76th OPLAP DD (73rd OAE). Probably became, see next line
			23 Red/RF-34105	Pacific Fleet/568th GvOMSAP; also reported as a Tu-142MZ with this registration!
8058013702019	?	Tu-142MR	14 Black	North Fleet/76th OPLAP DD (73rd OAE)
8058013702021	?	Tu-142MR	15 Black	North Fleet/76th OPLAP DD (73rd OAE), named *Taganrog*
8058014702023	?	Tu-142MR	16 Black	North Fleet/76th OPLAP DD (73rd OAE)
8058013802025	?	Tu-142MR	24 Black	North Fleet/76th OPLAP DD (73rd OAE). Became, see next line
			24 Red/RF-34113	Pacific Fleet/568th GvOMSAP
8058014802026	?	Tu-142MR	25 Black	North Fleet/76th OPLAP DD (73rd OAE)
8058014802027	?	Tu-142MR	26 Black	North Fleet/76th OPLAP DD (73rd OAE). Probably became, see next line
			26 Red	Pacific Fleet/568th GvOMSAP
8058014902030	?	Tu-142MR	17 Black	North Fleet/76th OPLAP DD (73rd OAE), named *Velikiy Ustyug*. Became, see next line
			17 Red/RF-34073	Named *Velikiy Ustyug*
8058014902038	?	Tu-142MR	19 Black	North Fleet/76th OPLAP DD (73rd OAE).C/n also reported as 80580102038 (without quarter and year of manufacture). WFU/stored Kipelovo AB by 2009
8058014503011	?	Tu-142MR	22 Black	North Fleet/76th OPLAP DD (73rd OAE)
8058013603015	?	Tu-142MR	12 Black	North Fleet/76th OPLAP DD (73rd OAE), natural metal; named *Vytegra*

* Russian Navy

Note: In the case of the Tu-142's ASW versions, manufacturer's designations are used in the table, not service designations which are 'one step behind' and thus misleading.

Kazakhstan

With the dissolution of the Soviet Union, the materiel of the former Soviet Armed Forces was up for grabs, and the CIS republics took possession of whatever military assets were located in their territory. The 27 Tu-95MS-6s and 13 Tu-95MS-16s of the 79th TBAD (1023rd TBAP and 1226th TBAP), all based at Chagan AB 70 km (43.5 miles) from Semipalatinsk (the city is now called Semey), were taken over by the **Kazakhstan Air Defence Force** (*Auye korganysy kushteri*) along with 370 Kh-55 cruise missiles. However, Kazakhstan had no real use for them; in 1992 it declared a non-nuclear status, which rendered the 40 *Bear-Hs* unnecessary. In 1993 the bomber division was disbanded and the aircraft were placed in storage; the base and the nearby Chagan Military Town subsequently fell into disuse.

Of course, Russia did not want to let such a valuable strategic asset be wasted. An inter-government agreement was reached, whereby the Kazakh Tu-95MSs were transferred to Russia together with the missiles in February 1994 in exchange for a number of Mikoyan MiG-29 *Fulcrum* light fighters and Sukhoi Su-27 *Flanker* heavy fighters. To be precise, 33 of the 40 bombers were transferred, the other seven remaining at Chagan AB; these seven aircraft were deemed not worth repairing and had been cannibalised for spares. On 23rd March 1995 an international expert group under James M. Fowler visiting Kazakhstan on an inspection trip discovered the seven hulks still sitting in the hangar at Chagan AB and perceived this as a contravention of international arms reduction treaties. The seven dead bombers were eventually scrapped.

(It may be mentioned that one source claims that Russia resorted to an underhand trick to get the bombers stationed at Chagan AB. In Soviet times it was common for strategic bombers to redeploy between remote bases during practice sorties, especially during exercises. It is alleged that the Russian Air Force devised

a plan whereby the Tu-95MSs piloted by specially instructed crews took off from Chagan AB in full strength and flew to Ookraïnka AB in the Russian Far East, while a similar number of Tu-95K-22s from that base took off and flew in the opposite direction. Halfway along the route the groups of bombers switched radio callsigns (in case someone was eavesdropping) and the Tu-95K-22s landed at Chagan. Thus Russia cunningly substituted the new *Bear-Hs* for old *Bear-Gs* which were due for retirement anyway (and were ultimately scrapped at Chagan). The 'Bear swap' mission was allegedly led by Col. Valeriy Artamokhin of the Russian Air Force.

No Kazakh Tu-95MSs have been identified by their tactical codes or construction numbers.

The Ukraine

• The Ukraine, which became an independent state on 24th August 1991, claimed the resident units of the Long-Range Aviation's 24th and 46th Air Armies along with other military aviation assets stationed on Ukrainian soil. The units that were integrated into the nascent **Ukrainian Air Force** (UAF, or VPS – *Viys'kovo-povitryani syly*) included the 1006th TBAP at Uzin AB (aka Chepelevka AB) south of Kiev, which also hosted another bomber unit – the 251st TBAP equipped with Tu-16s. The 1006th TBAP operated 23 to 25 Tu-95MSs built in 1987-91 – that is, about 30% of the Soviet *Bear-H* fleet.

Additionally, the UAF took over the co-located 409th APSZ equipped with 21 IL-78 tanker/transports supporting the operations of the 1006th TBAP. This was a sore blow to the Russian Air Force, which thus lost a sizeable share of the DA's Soviet-era tanker fleet.

UAF Tu-95s retained the standard natural metal finish with grey or white skin panels here and there, but very few wore the new national insignia – an elongated blue shield with the stylised yellow trident of St. Volodimir on the tail and yellow roundels with a blue centre on the wings. In most cases the old Soviet star insignia were simply painted out (rather untidily) and the UAF insignia never applied. Additionally, a Tu-95M preserved at Uzin AB as a memory of the days when the 409th APSZ was still a bomber unit (the 409th TBAP) was painted in UAF insignia, but this is purely symbolic as the aircraft had been decommissioned much earlier.

When in the spring of 1992 the Ukrainian government began administering the oath of allegiance to the military units stationed in the republic, some of the Air Force personnel refused to swear allegiance to the new state, and an exodus of personnel ensued. Besides, the heavy bombers were the ones most difficult and expensive to maintain; according to the Ukrainian Air Force command, the maintenance costs of the strategic bomber fleet (this included 19 Tu-160s operated by the 184th GvTBAP at Priluki AB, but possibly the non-

'08 Red', one of the few Tu-95MSs to wear full Ukrainian Air Force insignia.

A Ukrainian Tu-95MS with the Soviet star insignia crudely painted out (and, strangely enough, not even a tactical code) taxies after landing at Uzin (Cheplevka AB).

strategic Tu-22M2/Tu-22M3 *Backfire-B/C* bombers as well) amounted to US$ 1.4 million per year. Combat training had to be curtailed at once; the Ukraine had no target ranges of its own that were adequate for strategic bombers, and plans to establish a combat and conversion training centre for the Ukrainian heavy bomber crews never materialised.

Furthermore, ANTK Tupolev and the factories which had built the bombers were no longer providing product support. Fuel and spares shortages, coupled with the shortage of qualified cadre, quickly grounded part of the Ukrainian *Bear* fleet. The severance of traditional ties within the former Soviet Union was a prime cause but there were also political difficulties into the bargain; the relationship between post-Soviet Russia and the Ukraine became pretty rocky right away. With no new spares forthcoming, the maintenance department of the 1006th TBAP was forced to cannibalise some of the aircraft to keep the others flyable.

Moreover, the strategic bombers absolutely did not fit into the nation's defensive doctrine, since the Ukraine had declared a non-nuclear status; on 23rd May 1992 the Ukraine had signed the Lisbon Protocol, a supplement to the START I treaty, as one of the successor nations of the Soviet Union which had been a signatory of the said treaty. In March 1993 V. Zakharchenko, the advisor of the Ukrainian military attaché in Moscow, stated that *'the Ukrainian Armed Forces have no missions which these aircraft could fulfil'.* Even keeping the bombers in storage was both expensive and pointless. Therefore soon enough Kiev began to reflect on how to get rid of them. There wasn't much of a choice: the bombers could be either transferred to Russia (following the example of Kazakhstan) or scrapped.

Of course, Russia tried to recover the Tu-160s at Priluki and the Tu-95MSs at Uzin. The first negotiations about the purchase of the strategic aircraft and air-launched cruise missiles remaining in the Ukraine began as early as 1993. These failed to yield any results: the price of US$ 25 million apiece offered by Moscow was dismissed as ridiculous by Kiev, which demanded US$ 75 million for each bomber. Next, Russia proposed exchanging the bombers for tactical aircraft and spares for same, but the Ukraine showed no interest.

The negotiations continued in 1995; over the years the sale of the bombers was brought into discussion more than 20 times but the parties could not agree on the price. Meanwhile, the condition of the bombers slowly deteriorated. Given the tensions between Moscow and Kiev, many people in Russia believed that the Ukraine was intentionally dragging out the deal and would sooner let the bombers rot away than let the Russians have them!

Another anonymous Ukrainian Tu-95MS seen immediately after landing, as the fully deployed flaps indicate.

01

Ukrainian Air Force Tu-95MS '01 Red' 251st TBAP, Uzin AB

This Tu-95MS coded '01 Red' is preserved in the UAF Museum at the decommissioned airbase in Poltava. Note some of the other exhibits (a Tu-16 and a Sukhoi Su-15UM fighter trainer) in the background.

While Russia needed these aircraft badly (having only six Tu-160s in service at Engels while most of the *Blackjack* fleet remained in the Ukraine), the prospect of such a sale absolutely did not suit the USA, which would much rather see the bombers destroyed than have them fall into Russian hands. Hence, riding hard upon the anti-Russian sentiment that existed in parts of the Ukrainian society, the US State Department started putting pressure on Kiev, demanding that the Ukraine comply with the START-2 treaty which required the Soviet Union to dismantle its strategic bombers not later than 4th December 2001.

After the first round of negotiations failed, on 17th April 1998 the Ukrainian National Security and Defence Council took the decision to dispose of the Tu-95MS and Tu-160 strategic aviation/missile systems. The appropriate weapons reduction programme was endorsed by the then President of the Ukraine Leonid D. Kuchma on 14th May 1998. The carnage was funded by the USA under the Co-operative Threat Reduction Program (also called the Nunn-Lugar Program after Senators Samuel Nunn and Richard Lugar who got it through Congress). The US Congress officially allocated funds – variously reported as US$ 8 million or US$

13 million – for the destruction of the heavy bombers and cruise missiles remaining on Ukrainian soil; a US-Ukrainian agreement to this effect had been signed as early as 25th November 1993 (according to some reports, 25th October 1993), and an appropriate contract was signed with the Raytheon Technical Services Co. on 12th June 1998. Once the bombers had been scrapped the Ukraine would have the right to sell the metal. On 5th December 1998 the Ukrainian Ministry of Defence and the US Department of Defense formally signed an agreement on the destruction of 44 Ukrainian heavy bombers and 1,068 Kh-55 cruise missiles which the US military were so worried about. The Ukrainians were so eager to please their American partners that the first Tu-95MS was scrapped on 16th November 1998, before the contract was even signed.

Faced with the prospect of losing the bombers, the Russian government began a new round of negotiations. In April-May 1999 Moscow and Kiev discussed the possibility of exchanging eight Tu-160s and three Tu-95MSs for Antonov An-22 and An-124 *Rus**lan** (a Russian epic hero; NATO *Condor*) heavy transports from Russian Air Force stocks. The Ukrainians were in a hurry to strike a deal on favourable terms because of the 4th December 2001 deadline. The USA attempted to throw a spanner in the works, trying by all means to prevent Russia from bolstering its strategic power, and insistently urged the Ukraine to scrap the bombers, promising to finance the disposal.

Nevertheless, the American plans were foiled. In early August 1999 Russia and the Ukraine finally drafted an inter-government agreement on the transfer of eight fully serviceable Tu-160s, three Tu-95MSs and 575 Kh-55, Kh-55SM and Kh-22NA cruise missiles (the latter type was carried by the Tu-22M3), plus ground support equipment for same. This was to offset the Ukraine's US$ 275 million outstanding debt for Russian natural gas deliveries; having no money to settle the debt, the Ukraine had to agree. The total worth of the bombers was approximately US$ 285 million.

On 6th September 1999 Vladimir V. Putin, the then Prime Minister of Russia, signed a directive in Yalta formally approving this draft agreement. The directive also ordered the creation of a Russian inter-department work group which would finalise the agreement before it was signed by the governments of the Russian Federation and the Ukraine. The work group was headed by Aleksey L. Koodrin, who was then Russia's First Vice-Minister of Finance. The Russian MoD was represented by first Vice-Minister of Defence Nikolay V. Mikhailov (deputy head and permanent secretary), the Air Force Commander-in-Chief Army General Anatoliy M. Kornukov and Maj.-Gen. Pyotr D. Kazazayev. The latter was then Deputy Commander (Engineering Aviation Service) of the 37th VA, but since a certain

government official level was required for executing government directives, he was listed as the C-in-C's reviewer. Additionally, the work group included representatives from the Foreign Ministry, the Ministry of Taxes and Duties, the Ministry of State Property, the Ministry of Economics, the Gazprom natural gas company, the Russian Aerospace Agency and the government of the Russian Federation. The group was to define the nomenclature, quantity and cost of the property to be transferred from Ukraine to Russia and the transfer procedures.

The appropriate Ukrainian work group was headed by Vice-Minister of Economics V. A. Choomakov. The two groups held two sessions, and the joint draft agreement was approved on 30th September 1999. On 8th October 1999 the Agreement between the Government of the Russian Federation and the Ukrainian Cabinet of Ministers on the transfer of the strategic missile carriers, cruise missiles and support equipment was finally signed at a meeting of the government delegations in Yalta.

On 20th October 1999 a 65-man group of 37th VA technical staff led by Maj.-Gen. Kazazayev flew to the Ukraine aboard a Russian Air Force IL-78 tanker to take charge of the newly-acquired bombers. Upon landing at Uzin AB the *Midas* disgorged a small part of the group tasked with accepting and ferrying the three Tu-95MSs; the following morning it departed for Priluki AB, carrying the rest of the group (including Kazazayev) which was to work with the Tu-160s. The group worked at the two bases until 9th November, preparing the bombers for the flight to their new home at Engels-2 AB.

As for the other *Bears*, a single Tu-95MS was donated to the Ukrainian Air Force Museum in Poltava. The rest were destroyed under the Nunn-Lugar Program; the last of these was scrapped at Uzin on 17th May 2001. By May 2001 the Ukraine had scrapped 27 Tu-95s, 11 Tu-160s and 483 Kh-55 missiles. These included three other Tu-95MSs and two older *Bears* (a Tu-95K and a Tu-95KM) which had been nominally transferred to Russia back in 1992; the five aircraft had been languishing at the 148th ARZ at Gayok AB in Belaya Tserkov' (or Bila Tserkva in Ukrainian) were but never actually handed over because the Ukraine demanded US$ 14 million for their repair, which Russia did not pay. The scrapping took place in Uzin, Belaya Tserkov' and Kul'bakino AB on the outskirts of the city of Nikolayev where several Tu-95s had been flown apparently for overhaul at the Nikolayev Aircraft Repair Plant (NARP).

A separate item of the 14th May 1998 programme envisaged converting two demilitarised *Bear-Hs* into ecological monitoring aircraft; appropriate design documents were to be developed and US$1.6 million were allocated for this. However, in 2011 the two aircraft were included into the surplus military stocks list and sold off to private owners (!) under a shady scheme which caused the Attorney General's Office to take up the matter; at least one of them was eventually scrapped.

According to some reports, the UAF intended to convert the above two *Bear-Hs* into monitoring aircraft under the Open Skies treaty (this had been announced by the UAF's new Commander-in-Chief Col.-Gen. Viktor I. Strel'nikov). However, the plans came to naught, forcing the UAF to stick with Antonov An-30B *Clank* photo survey aircraft for Open Skies monitoring flights.

• The aviation component of the **Ukrainian Navy** (VMS – *Viys'kovo-mors'ki syly*) took over a handful of Tu-142 ASW aircraft at the break-up of the Soviet Union – obviously the ones operated by the AVMF's 33rd TsBP

i PLS at Nikolayev-Kul'bakino AB, since the Black Sea Fleet did not operate the type. The *Bear-Fs* were not operated by the Ukrainian Navy, though, and two machines ended up as museum exhibits.

One Russian Navy Tu-142MK was reportedly transferred to NARP as debt payment when this aircraft was repaired by the plant along with four Tu-142MRs under a 1998 contract (the *Bear-Js* were eventually paid for and flown to Russia). This aircraft became the subject of a dispute between the plant and the Ukrainian Customs Service which demanded that the aircraft be either re-exported or cleared through customs (i.e., import duties be paid) by 1st June 2010. This Tu-142MK was probably scrapped in late 2013.

Version	C/n	F/n	Tactical code	Notes
	**Known Ukrainian Air Force Tu-95s and Ukrainian Navy Tu-142s**
Tu-95M	7800503		51 Red	Ex-409th TBAP aircraft, preserved Uzin AB, painted in UAF insignia. Current status unknown (may be damaged or scrapped)
Tu-95K-22	62M52503		02 Red	Wfu Bila Tserkva; formally transferred to Russia in 1992 but scrapped 7-12-2000
Tu-95K-22	63M52602		05 Red	Wfu Bila Tserkva; formally transferred to Russia in 1992 but scrapped 7-12-2000
Tu-95MS	6403423400909	?	34 Red	Taganrog-built. Wfu Bila Tserkva; formally transferred to Russia in 1992 but scrapped 1/2-12-2000
Tu-95MS-16	100021*315119	?	24 Red	Kuibyshev-built; full c/n probably 1000211315119. Wfu Bila Tserkva; formally transferred to Russia in 1992 but scrapped 21-10/7-11-1999
Tu-95MS	100021*316204	?	15 Red	Full c/n probably 1000213316204. Wfu Bila Tserkva; formally transferred to Russia in 1992 but scrapped 4-12-2000
Tu-95MS-16	1000212421744	?	41 Red	Wfu Bila Tserkva by 3-1997; scrapped 7-11-1999
Tu-95MS	100021**24550	?	25 Red	Full c/n probably 1000214424550. Wfu Bila Tserkva; formally transferred to Russia in 1992 but scrapped 28/29-11-2000
Tu-95MS-16	1000213529561	?	02 Red	Wfu Bila Tserkva by 3-1997; scrapped 11-12-1999
Tu-95MS-16	100021**29732	?	03 Red	Wfu Uzin by 5-1998; scrapped 24/26-3-2000
Tu-95MS-16	100021**29843	?	04 Red	Wfu Uzin by 5-1998; scrapped 17/18-4-2000
Tu-95MS-16	100021**30108	?	05 Red	Wfu Uzin by 5-1998; scrapped 25/27-5-2000
Tu-95MS-16	100021**30183	?	06 Red	Wfu Uzin by 5-1998; scrapped 29/30-6-2000
Tu-95MS-16	100021**30203	?	07 Red	Wfu Bila Tserkva by 3-1997; scrapped 1-12-1999
Tu-95MS-16	100021**30235	?	20 Red	Wfu Uzin by 5-1998; scrapped 25/26-8-2000
Tu-95MS-16	100021**30306	?	21 Red	Wfu Uzin by 5-1998; scrapped 27/28-8-2000
Tu-95MS-16	100021**30309	?	22 Red	Wfu Uzin by 5-1998; scrapped 4/6-10-2000
Tu-95MS-16	100021**30419	?	23 Red	Wfu Uzin by 5-1998; scrapped 31-1-1999
Tu-95MS-16	100021**31135	?	24 Red	Wfu Uzin by 5-1998; scrapped 6/7-11-2000
Tu-95MS-16	100021**31198	?	25 Red	Wfu Uzin by 5-1998; scrapped 15/16-12-2000
Tu-95MS-16	100021**31249	?	90 Red	Wfu Uzin by 5-1998; scrapped 15/16-1-2001
Tu-95MS-16	100021**31370	?	91 Red	Wfu Uzin by 5-1998; scrapped 12-3-2001
Tu-95MS-16	100021**31483	?	92 Red	Wfu Uzin by 5-1998; scrapped 26/27-3-2001
Tu-95MS-16	100021**31509	?	93 Red	Wfu Uzin by 5-1998; scrapped 16/17-4-2001
Tu-95MS-16	100021**32179	?	94 Red	Wfu Uzin by 5-1998; scrapped 07/17-5-2001
Tu-95MS-16	1000211732191	?	01 Red	SOC 6-11-2000; preserved UAF Museum, Poltava
Tu-95MS-16	1000211732386	?	95 Red	SOC 28-11-2000; stored Nikolayev since at least 10-2005, earmarked for conversion as an ecological survey aircraft; scrapped by 4-2014
Tu-95MS	100021*732644	?	52 Red	Full c/n either 1000211732644 or 1000212732644. Reported as Ukrainian AF but not in official list, fate unknown
Tu-95MS-16	1000212733144	?	31 Red	SOC 28-11-2000; stored Nikolayev since at least 10-2005, earmarked for conversion as an ecological survey aircraft; up for sale 3-2014
Tu-95MS	100021**33757	?	61 Red	Reported as Ukrainian AF but not in official list, fate unknown
Tu-95MS-16	1000214936177	?	10 Red	Listed in a Ukrainian list as '100 Red'. Wfu Uzin by 5-1998; sold to Russia in 1999, became Russian AF '19 Red'
Tu-95MS-16	1000214037187	?	96 Red	Wfu Uzin by 5-1998; sold to Russia in 1999, became Russian AF '28 Red'
Tu-95MS-16	1000212937345	?	08 Red	Wfu Uzin by 5-1998; sold to Russia in 1999, became Russian AF '27 Red'
Tu-142	4201		no code	Pre-production aircraft. Opb 33rd TsBP i PLS? Preserved in museum at Lugansk-Ostraya Mogila AB
Tu-142M?	*60****	42...	86 Black	Probably Tu-142MK. Scrapped 2005

Tu-142MK	8601801	42...	62 Red	Transferred from Russian Navy to NARP repair plant (Nikolayev, the Ukraine) as debt payment; scrapped Kul'bakino AB
Tu-142MZ	8601903	42...	85 Black	Preserved State Aviation Museum, Kiev-Zhulyany; composite airframe, see next line
Tu-142MZ	8601986	42...		Scrapped, rear fuselage section fitted to the above aircraft
Tu-142MZ	*60****	42...	10 Red	Scrapped 2005
Tu-142MZ	*60****	42...	52 Red	Scrapped 2005
Tu-142MZ	*60****	42...	53 Red	Scrapped 2005

India

In the mid-1980s, alarmed by the increased naval activities of its arch-enemy Pakistan, India decided to bolster its ASW capability urgently in order to oppose Pakistan Navy submarines which were roaming the Indian Ocean. Hence the **Indian Navy** (*Bharatiya Nau Sena*) started sizing up the Tu-142MK-E *Bear-F Mod 3*, which was quite a modern ASW aircraft by the day's standards. At the time its ASW aviation component was limited to five second-hand IL-38s transferred from the Soviet Navy in 1977 and 1983, which was clearly not enough. On the other hand, the Tu-142MK-E could use the same models of sonobuoys, which facilitated operation and logistics.

In late 1985 the Indian Navy ordered eight Tu-142MK-Es. In May 1987 the first four Indian crews went to the Soviet Union to take conversion training for the type, with Indian Navy Commander V. C. Pandey as project leader. Maj. V. N. Ushakov, one of the instructors, recalled: *'In the spring of 1987 I had the privilege of participating in the training of Indian aircrews to fly a new type, the Tu-142ME (sic – Auth.) To this end an ad hoc conversion training centre was established in one of the Baltic Fleet's garrisons near Riga. The place was in a beautiful setting and conveniently placed, with just a 40 minutes' ride from Riga and at a similar distance from Jurmala (pronounced **Yoor**mala, a popular Baltic Sea resort – Auth.) The Indians were staying at a brand-new hotel, while we were accommodated in an older one but the place had been decently cleaned up for us. Col. N. N. Karpus', a North Fleet Air Arm instructor pilot, was put in charge of the conversion training centre. Stage One (theoretical training) involved mostly officers from the AVMF's [33rd] Combat Training & Aircrew Conversion Centre in Nikolayev, as well as personnel from an ASW air unit. Here it should be noted that our instructors were extremely competent and that the Indian trainees were well motivated to master the new hardware.*

Stage Two involving practice flights began in August. The crews of Lt.-Col. Tsvetkov and Lt.-Col. Shaforostov came into the picture at this stage, which lasted almost a full year. Finally, in May-June 1988 the Indian crews flew their new mounts home. It was an unforgettable sight as the aeroplanes rolled past us, taxying for take-off, and the crews waved goodbye from each workstation. The relations during the training course had been quite good, with friendships forming.

Stage Three was in the spring of 1989 when the Indian Navy sent a telegram, asking us to send a navigator and an ASW equipment operator to help the Indians master certain techniques of sub hunting which, for various reasons, had not been taught in full in the Soviet Union. Col. Nemolochnov and Col. Ushakov were sent to India to cope with the task. You have to give the Indians credit for creating proper conditions for the training process – from issues like accommodation and food to the actual training. On the other hand, they burdened us with a lot of work; in the first few weeks we would fly five sorties a week, each lasting eight or nine hours, each time with a new crew – and keep in mind that we had to work at temperatures above 30°C [86°F] and in high air humidity. Still, it should be noted that the Indians treated us with great respect; the squadron CO used to say "The Russian instructor is God". The bottom line is that, having flown 19 sorties in 40 days, we managed to work the crews up to an adequate skill level as far as ASW techniques are concerned.'

Unlike the IL-38s, the Tu-142MK-Es were delivered new. The first three aircraft arrived on 30th (some sources say 29th) March 1988, flying non-stop from Simferopol' (Zavodskoye airport) in the Ukraine to Indian Navy Station (INS) Hansa near the town of Dabolim in Goa, India's smallest state. The 9.5-hour flight took them across six nations over Ankara, Larnaca, Cairo, Jeddah, Aden and Bombay (now called Mumbai), covering a distance of 7,000 km (4,350 miles). Over the sea they were shadowed by Grumman F-14A Tomcat fighters launching from US Navy aircraft carriers. Two more *Bear-F Mod 3s* followed on 13th April 1988, allowing Indian Naval Air Squadron (INAS) 312 'Albatross' to be reactivated three days later under the command of Cdr Pandey. This unit had been established at INS Hansa on 18th November 1972 but was deactivated in 1983 when its five ex-Air India Lockheed L-1049G Super Constellation airliners modified for the ASW role were retired, leaving it with no aircraft at all.

The final three Tu-142MK-Es were delivered between August and October 1988, bringing the squadron up to full strength. The aircraft wore albatross nose art from the squadron badge and, according to some sources, were affectionately dubbed 'Albatross' by their crews.

Originally the unit operated from INS Hansa in Dabolim on the west coast, sharing the base with INAS 315 'Winged Stallions' – a maritime reconnais-

Indian Navy Tu-142MK-E IN314 as delivered
INAS 312 'Albatross', NAS Rajali, Arakkonam

The albatross/windrose emblem of INAS 312 applied to the Indian *Bears*.

The nose of Tu-142MK-E IN314, showing the badge of the INAS 312 'Albatross' squadron.

Here, IN314 is depicted at Taganrog in company with a Russian Air Force Tu-95MS, undergoing heavy maintenance.

sance/ASW squadron which operated the IL-38s. Like the US Air Force, the Indian Navy often uses tailcodes to denote the unit's location, and the Tu-142MK-Es wore the tailcode DAB. In the spring of 1992 INAS 312 moved to the newly commissioned INS Rajali located at Arakkonam on the east coast, 90 km (55.9 miles) from Chennai (formerly Madras) in Tamil Nadu, and the tailcode was changed to ARK. The first Tu-142MK-E landed at Rajali on 7th March 1992 and the transition was completed in April. Occasionally, however, the *Bears* still operated from INS Hansa where a major maintenance facility for the type had been set up.

India reportedly negotiated with Rosoboronexport (the Russian Defence Export Agency) to purchase six to eight more Tu-142MKs from Russian Navy storage stocks. However, when two of the Indian Navy's original five IL-38s were lost in a mid-air collision on 1st October 2002, the priorities shifted to making up the loss and upgrading the *Mays* to IL-38SD configuration with the Sea Dragon multi-mission avionics suite. Hence the plans to buy additional Tu-142s were shelved.

The aircraft were used for long-range maritime patrol and surveillance duties. For example, they

Tu-142ME IN317 with modifications; note that the Navy titles to starboard are in Sanskrit

Indian Navy Tu-142ME IN314 makes a low flypast at a military parade; the aircraft is still in its original guise.

The tail unit of Tu-142ME IN314. The ARK tailcode stands for Arakkonam, the place where this aircraft is based. Note the lack of the rear observation blisters.

routinely conducted reconnaissance of the Palk Bay and the Gulf of Mannar – the stretches of the Indian Ocean closest to Sri Lanka. The reason was the ongoing guerrilla war waged by the Sri Lankan separatist movement Liberation Tigers of Tamil Eelam (LTTE), causing a steady influx of Tamil refugees from Jaffna to the Tamil Nadu coast.

In November 1988 the Tu-142MK-Es participated in Operation *Cactus* – the Indian military intervention in Maldives to foil an attempted *coup d'état* against President Maumoon Abdul Gayoom led by Abdullah Luthufi and assisted by armed mercenaries of the Sri Lankan secessionist organisation People's Liberation Organisation of Tamil Eelam (PLOTE, an offshoot of the LTTE). When in response to President Gayoom's appeal Indian Army paratroopers of the 50th Independent Parachute Brigade had regained control of the Maldivian capital Malé, the *Bears* helped to locate and

Tu-142MK-E IN314 on the hardstand at INS Hansa, Dabolim.

Above: The personnel of INAS 312 'Albatross' stand to attention in front of one of the unit's 142MK-Es

track a freighter which had been hijacked by the fleeing mercenaries.

Strangely enough, the Tu-142MK-Es were reportedly used in Operation *Vijay* ('Victory' in Hindi) – in other words, the Kargil War, an armed conflict between India and Pakistan that took place between May and July 1999 in the Kargil district of Kashmir. The Kargil War was waged in the mountains, far from the sea, and it is hard to imagine how maritime patrol aircraft could have been involved.

Also in 1999, the Indian *Bears* acted in concert with Israel Aircraft Industries (IAI) Searcher unmanned aerial

vehicles to detect and shadow a brand-new destroyer intended for the People's Liberation Army Navy (PLAN) of China, with which India was not exactly on friendly terms. The Russian-built Type 956EM (NATO reporting name *Sovremenny* class) guided missile destroyer was on her delivery voyage via the Mediterranean, the Red Sea and the Arabian Sea. A Tu-142MK-E spotted the Chinese destroyer and an accompanying replenishment ship off Yemen's Socotra Island, almost 2,300 km (1,430 miles) away from the Indian mainland.

In 2002 the Indian *Bears* took part in Operation *Parakram* ('Valor' in Sanskrit) – a large-scale mobilisation of the Indian Armed Forces during the 2001-02 India-Pakistan standoff. Although this mostly involved massing of troops on either side of the border and along the Line of Control (LoC) in the region of Kashmir, the Tu-142MK-Es were to watch for possible moves by the Pakistan Navy in the event of hostilities.

At the turn of the century the Tu-142MK-E's mission equipment became obsolescent. Hence in November 2003 the Indian Navy approached Rosoboronexport with a request to upgrade the *Bear* fleet so as to enable submarine detection at 150 km (93 miles) range. The refitted aircraft was also to provide a linkage between India's nuclear command centre and the Indian Navy's

The Indian Navy Tu-142MK-Es				
Serial	Version	C/n	F/n	Notes
IN311	Tu-142MK-E	6609646	?	Upgraded with undernose sensor. Wfu INS Rajali by 10-2014; preserved INS Rajali 29-3-2017
IN312	Tu-142MK-E	7609686	?	Upgraded with undernose sensor
IN313	Tu-142MK-E	7609726	?	Upgraded with undernose sensor
IN314	Tu-142MK-E	7609766	?	Upgraded with undernose sensor
IN315	Tu-142MK-E	76098806?	?	Upgraded with undernose sensor. Wfu INS Rajali by 10-2014
IN316	Tu-142MK-E	8609846	?	Wfu INS Rajali by 10-2014
IN317	Tu-142MK-E	8609886?	?	Upgraded with undernose sensor
IN318	Tu-142MK-E	8609925	?	Upgraded with undernose sensor. Wfu INS Rajali by 10-2014

Left and below left: An upgraded Tu-142ME (IN316) starts up its engines at INS Rajali. A crash rescue tender stands by – just in case.

The shoulder patch worn by Indian Navy Tu-142 crews.

The squadron badge of INAS 312 'Albatross'.

Another view of IN316 running its engines. The chin-mounted weather radar is clearly visible.

nuclear submarine, performing the same functions as the Tu-142MR into the bargain. Finally, the Tu-142MK-E was to carry anti-shipping missiles. The Russian 3M54AE *Kalibr* (Calibre; aka Klub) subsonic missile developed by the Novator design bureau and an air-launched version of the co-developed Russian/Indian SK-310 BrahMos missile were under consideration, as was the well-known Russian Zvezda Kh-31A supersonic anti-shipping missile.

The original equipment manufacturer (the Tupolev PLC) offered the Tu-142ME project envisaging installation of the same Sea Dragon suite (see Chapter 4); the modification work was to be performed by the TMZD plant in Taganrog, with all eight aircraft to be upgraded within around two and a half years. However, Rosoboronexport charged a price of US$ 888.9 million, which India considered exorbitant, being prepared to spend no more than US$ 555.5 million. (Some sources say this was a case of gazumping; the original contract price had been US$ 555.5 million but then Rosoboronexport chose to revise the work schedule and install the Sea Dragon suite, which was not in the original contract, raising the price to US$ 888.9 million, whereupon the Indians said no.) Also, the Indian Navy was not satisfied with the performance of the Sea Dragon suite which was fitted to the IL-38SDs. Hence the Indian government put the contract on hold with the intention of renegotiating the price. In January 2004 a team of Indian Navy pilots visited Russia to evaluate a Tu-142 demonstrator fitted with the Sea Dragon suite – and reportedly found it inadequate. Also, the Sea Dragon programme was running behind schedule.

In February 2004 the Indian Navy approached Rosoboronexport again, proposing that Israeli firms be allowed to participate in shaping the upgraded Tu-142MK-E's mission avionics suite. Rosoboronexport refused, insisting that the upgrade would have to be wholly Russian and based on the Sea Dragon suite. Unabashed, the Indian Navy turned directly to Elbit Systems, a division of IAI, with a request to develop a state-of-the-art maritime reconnaissance and electronic warfare suite. This was to enable the Tu-142MK-E to detect and intercept surface vessels and submarines within a range of 150 km (93 miles), detect mines and carry out long-range and long-endurance surveillance.

In 2004 the clouds began to gather over the Tu-142MK-Es. The *Times of India* reported that the *Bears* were being retired following the collapse of negotiations with Russia and Israel to upgrade them; instead, the Indian Navy was to acquire western types. Yet this statement proved to be premature – the likely timeline for long-range replacement aircraft from Boeing or Airbus warranted keeping the type in service for a while longer, and the Israeli upgrade did go ahead. Tu-142MK-E IN 315 was the first to be modified in early 2004; it was reportedly refitted with the Elta

EL/M-2022A (V3) radar replacing the Korshun radar, plus a comprehensive ELINT/ECM/SATNAV package. Some sources, though, identify the radar as the AN/M-2202A – the same as used in Spain's Lockheed P-3C Orion upgrades. Outwardly the upgraded aircraft was readily identifiable by the large chin fairing with a dielectric front end housing VHF/UHF antennas and by a ventral P-band antenna farm. At least six of the eight aircraft were thus upgraded.

The Russian news agency ITAR-TASS reported that four Indian Tu-142MK-Es were being upgraded to carry Kh-31A missiles in St. Petersburg. Two Tu-142MK-Es were being outfitted for testing the BrahMos-A missile, whose integration and testing was expected to be completed by 2010. There were also reports that improved NK-12MPT engines and AV-60T propellers were to be refitted to the fleet under a contract signed in 2005.

Starting in 2011, the Tu-142MK-Es took on a new task, participating in anti-piracy operations around the Horn of Africa where the notorious Somalian pirates were in action. However, the upgrade would no longer save the day. On 4th January 2009 the Indian Ministry of Defence placed a US$ 2.1 billion order with Boeing for the delivery of eight P-8I Poseidon twin-turbofan maritime patrol/ASW aircraft based on the Boeing 737-800ERX airliner. As far as range is concerned, the P-8 is somewhere in between the IL-38 and the Tu-142MK, having a 2,500-km (1,552-mile) combat radius with 2,500 kg (11,020 lb) of ordnance versus 6,400 km (3,980 miles) and up to 11,340 kg (25,000 lb) for the Tu-142MK. On the other hand, the P-8 has more advanced mission avionics and more fuel-efficient engines. India selected the P-8 over the P-3C Orion and the proposed EADS MPA319CJ based on the Airbus A319CJ business jet, becoming first export customer for the type; this was also Boeing's first military sale to India. In July 2016 it was confirmed India had ordered another four P-8Is due for delivery by 2020.

This spelled the end of the road for the *Bears*; by October 2014 half of India's Tu-142 fleet had been withdrawn from use due to advanced age and serviceability issues. On 13th November 2016 the P-8I (known as the Neptune in Indian Navy service) was inducted, entering service with the new INAS 312-A squadron at INS Rajali. On 29th March 2017 the Tu-142MK-E was officially phased out by the Indian Navy. The farewell ceremony at INS Rajali was attended by the Chief of the Naval Staff Admiral Sunil Lanba, Cdr (Retd) V. C. Pandey and Cdr Yogender Mair, the squadron's last CO of the 'Bear Age', who formally handed over the command of the squadron to Cdr Venkateshwaran Ranganathan. At the ceremony Tu-142MK-E IN312 – one of the three remaining flyable examples – was flanked on the hardstand by P-8Is IN326 and IN327 to symbolise 'the changing of the guard';

another *Bear*, IN317, took part in the farewell flypast which included an IL-38SD, a P-8I, HAL-Dornier 228 maritime patrol aircraft, HAL Chetak helicopters and British Aerospace Hawk Mk 132 jet trainers.

One of the Tu-142MK-Es was preserved at INS Rajali on the same day; another was flown to INAS Dega at Vishakapatnam, Andhra Pradesh, for preservation and a third example will become an exhibit at the Indian Naval Academy (INA) at Ezhimala in the south-western state of Kerala. The fate of the other five aircraft was still undecided as of this writing. It has to be said that the retirement of the Tu-142MK-E was by no means a 'good riddance' ceremony; the aircraft had served its country well.

Above and below: Upgraded Tu-142ME IN317 performs at the Aero India 2009 airshow at Yelahanka AB, Bangalore.

Left: Close-up of the nose showing the Israeli weather radar under the nose.

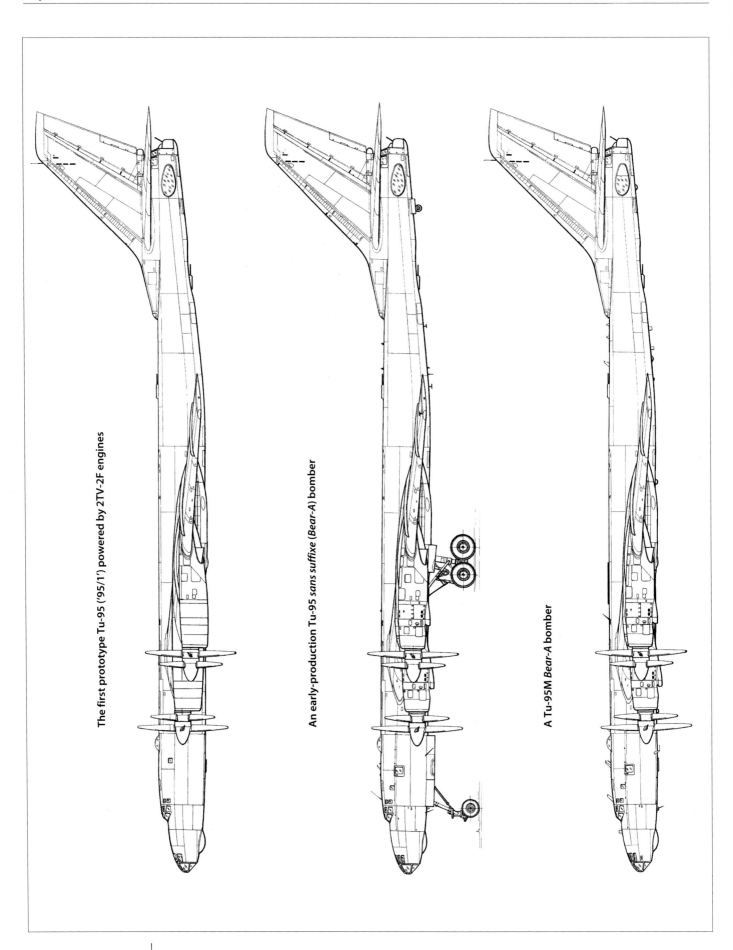

The first prototype Tu-95 ('95/1') powered by 2TV-2F engines

An early-production Tu-95 sans suffixe (*Bear-A*) bomber

A Tu-95M *Bear-A* bomber

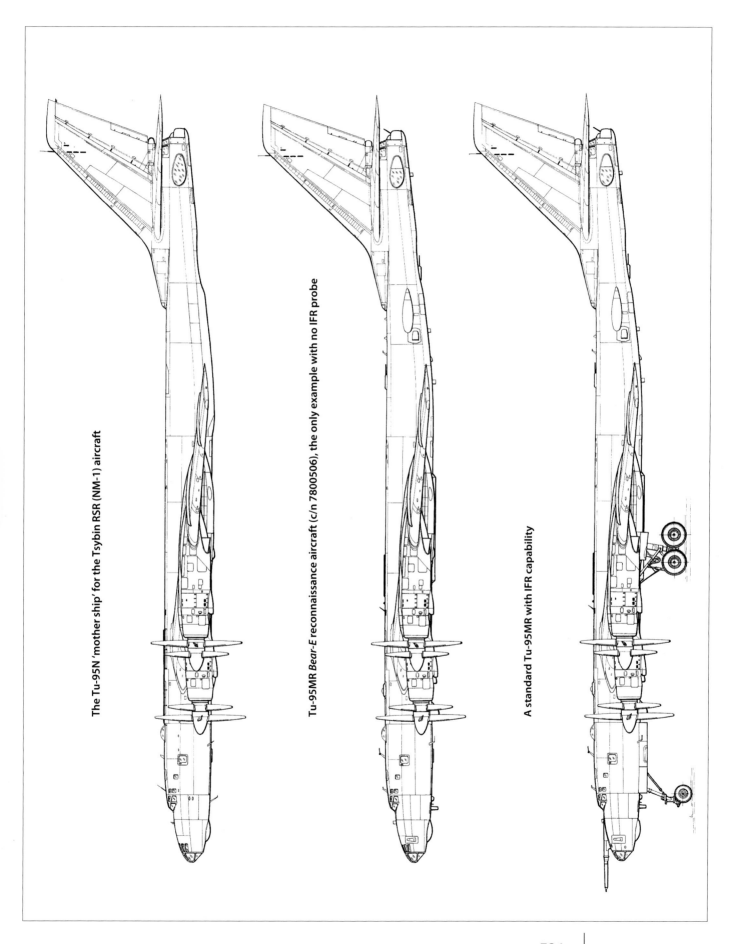

The Tu-95N 'mother ship' for the Tsybin RSR (NM-1) aircraft

Tu-95MR *Bear-E* reconnaissance aircraft (c/n 7800506), the only example with no IFR probe

A standard Tu-95MR with IFR capability

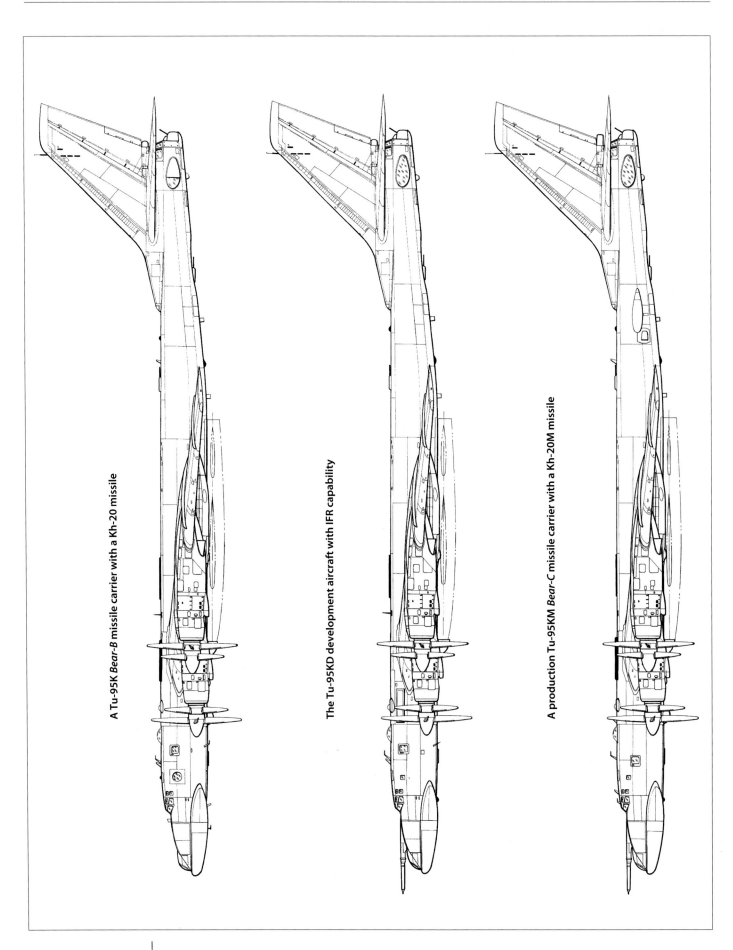

A Tu-95K *Bear-B* missile carrier with a Kh-20 missile

The Tu-95KD development aircraft with IFR capability

A production Tu-95KM *Bear-C* missile carrier with a Kh-20M missile

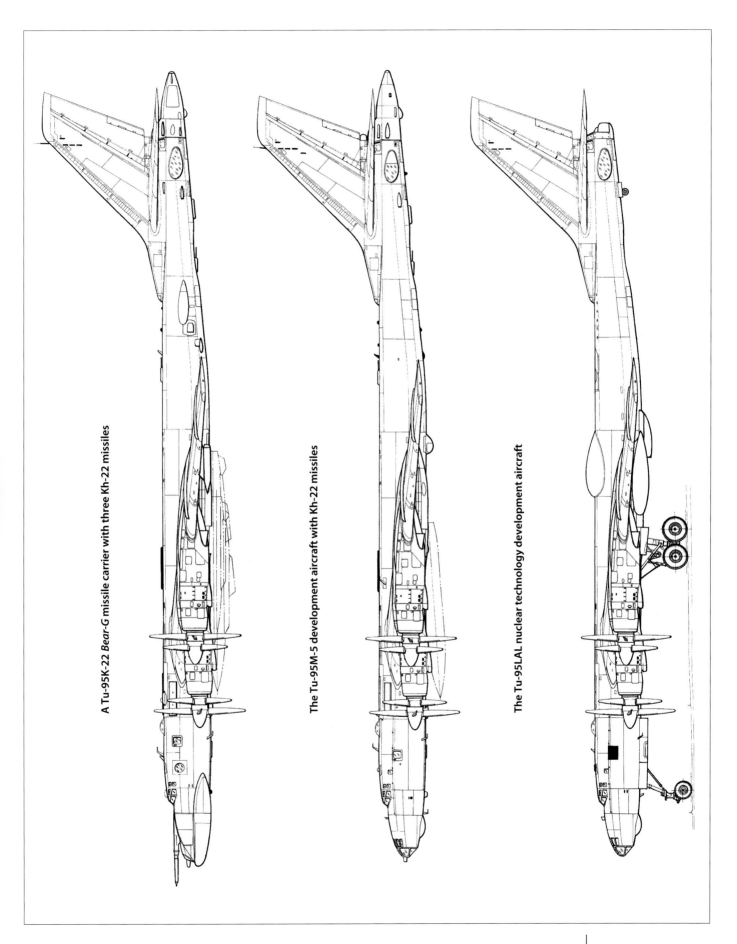

A Tu-95K-22 *Bear-G* missile carrier with three Kh-22 missiles

The Tu-95M-5 development aircraft with Kh-22 missiles

The Tu-95LAL nuclear technology development aircraft

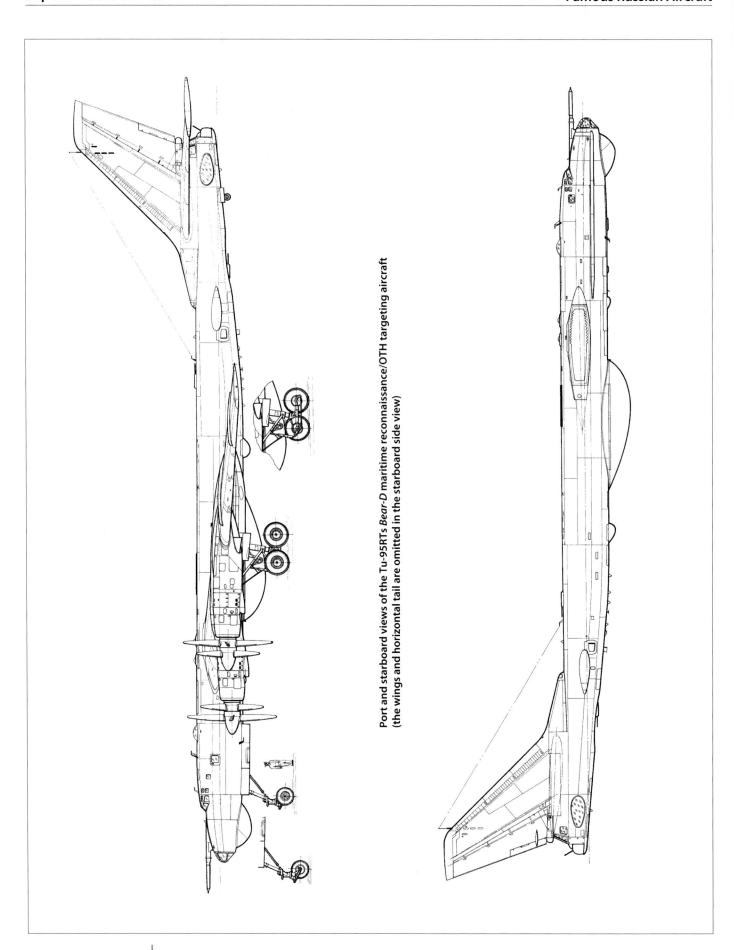

Port and starboard views of the Tu-95RTs *Bear-D* maritime reconnaissance/OTH targeting aircraft (the wings and horizontal tail are omitted in the starboard side view)

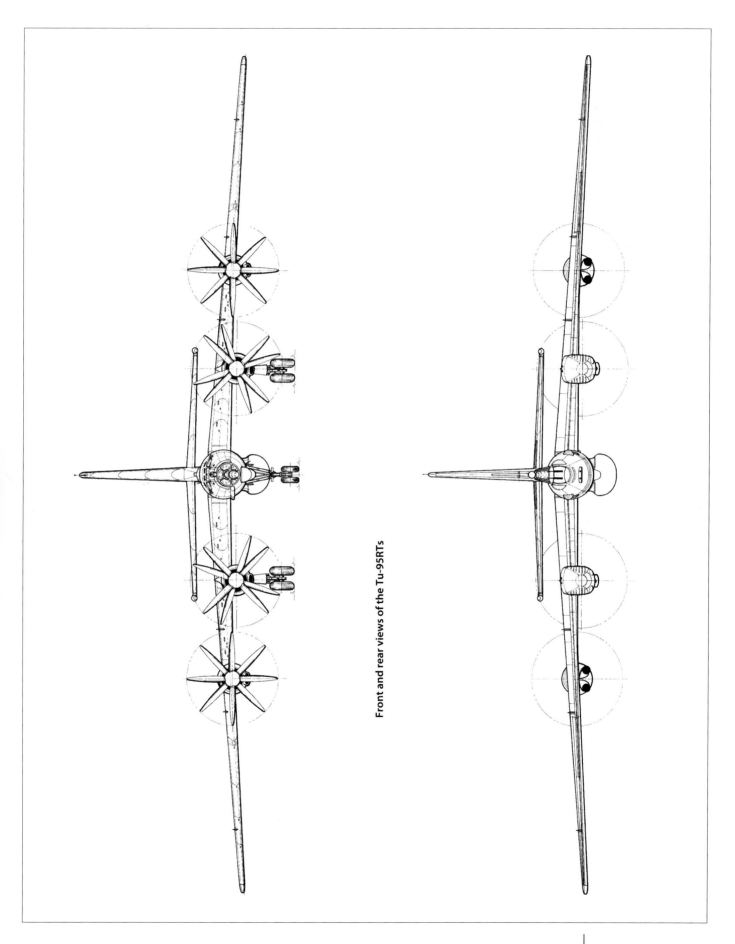

Front and rear views of the Tu-95RTs

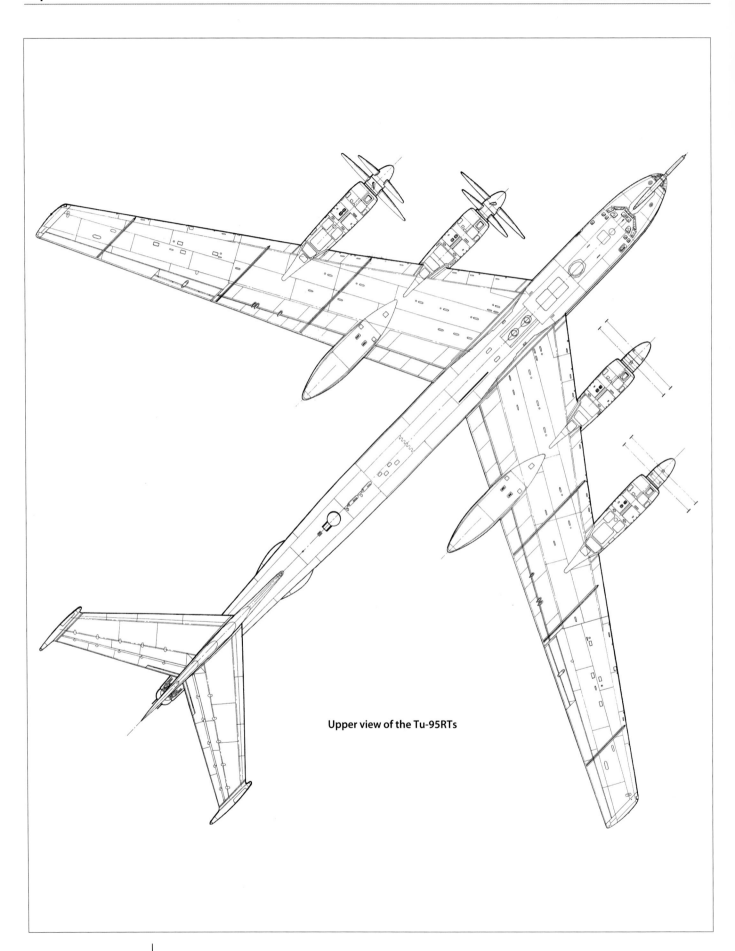

Upper view of the Tu-95RTs

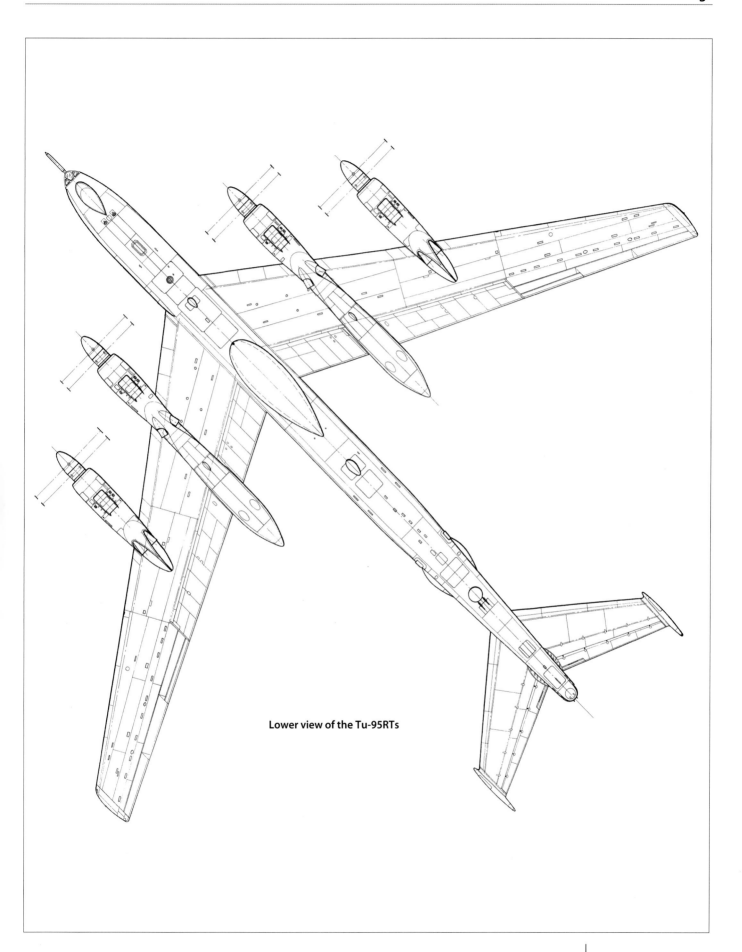

Lower view of the Tu-95RTs

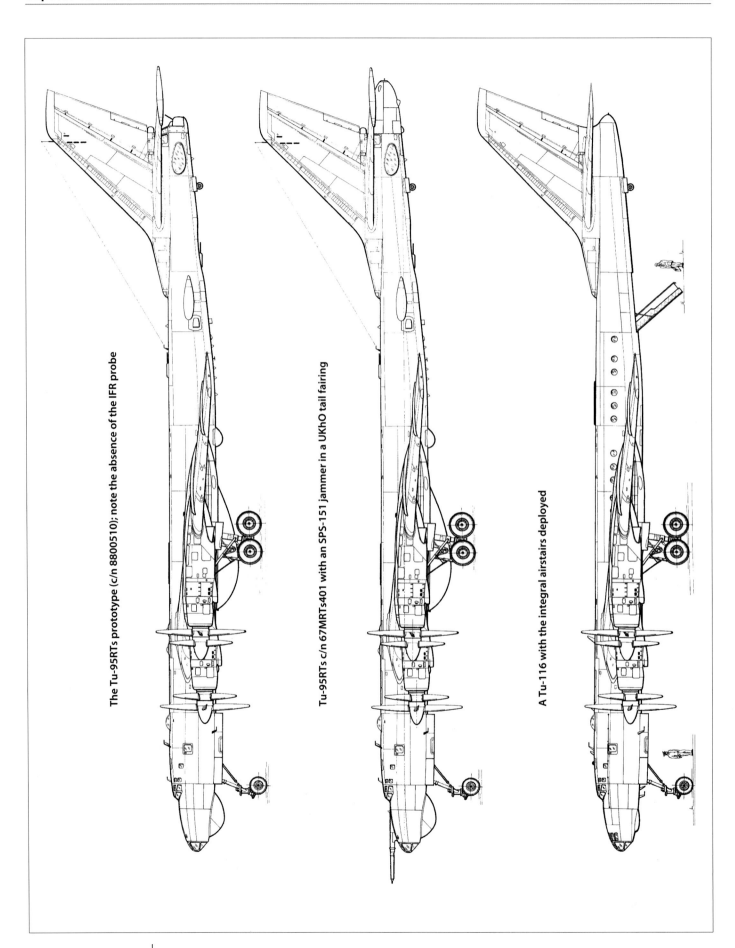

The Tu-95RTs prototype (c/n 8800510); note the absence of the IFR probe

Tu-95RTs c/n 67MRTs401 with an SPS-151 jammer in a UKhO tail fairing

A Tu-116 with the integral airstairs deployed

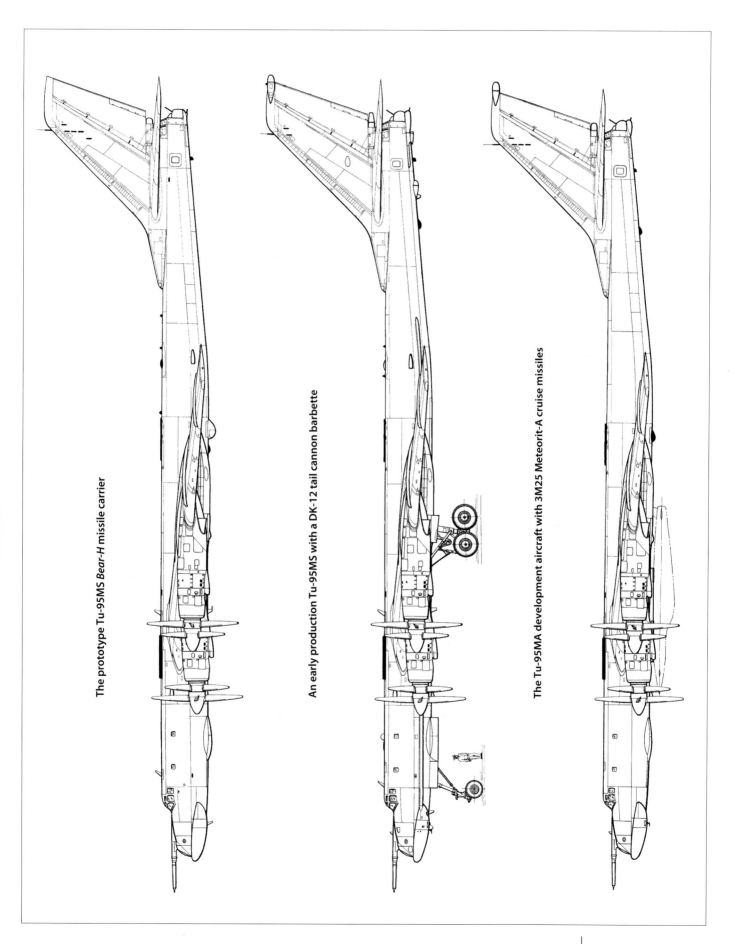

The prototype Tu-95MS *Bear-H* missile carrier

An early production Tu-95MS with a DK-12 tail cannon barbette

The Tu-95MA development aircraft with 3M25 Meteorit-A cruise missiles

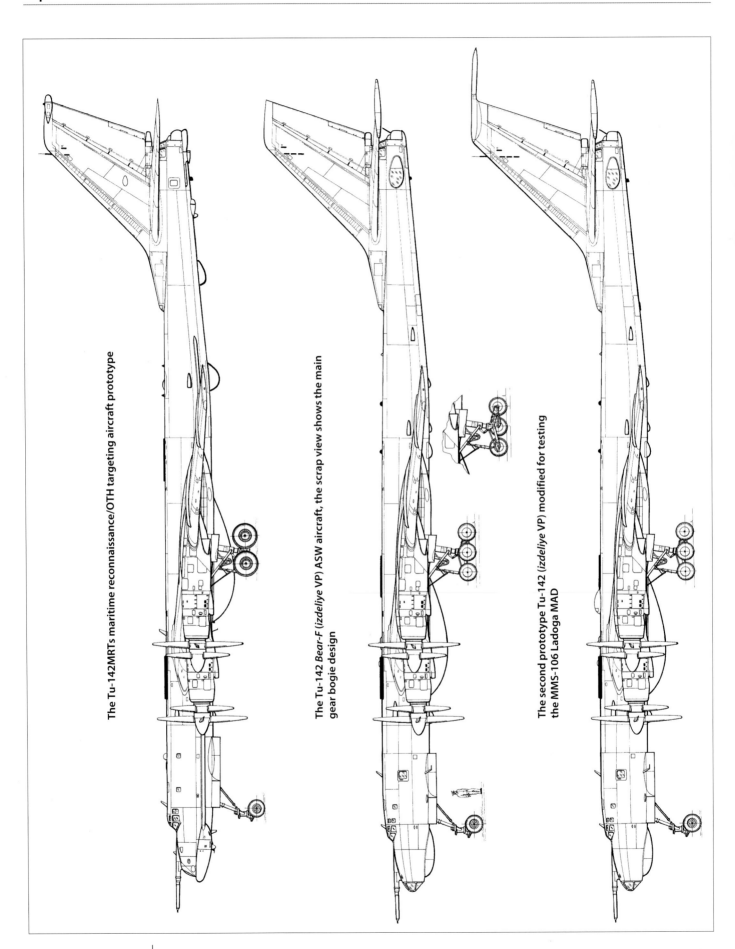

The Tu-142MRTs maritime reconnaissance/OTH targeting aircraft prototype

The Tu-142 *Bear-F* (*izdeliye VP*) ASW aircraft, the scrap view shows the main gear bogie design

The second prototype Tu-142 (*izdeliye VP*) modified for testing the MMS-106 Ladoga MAD

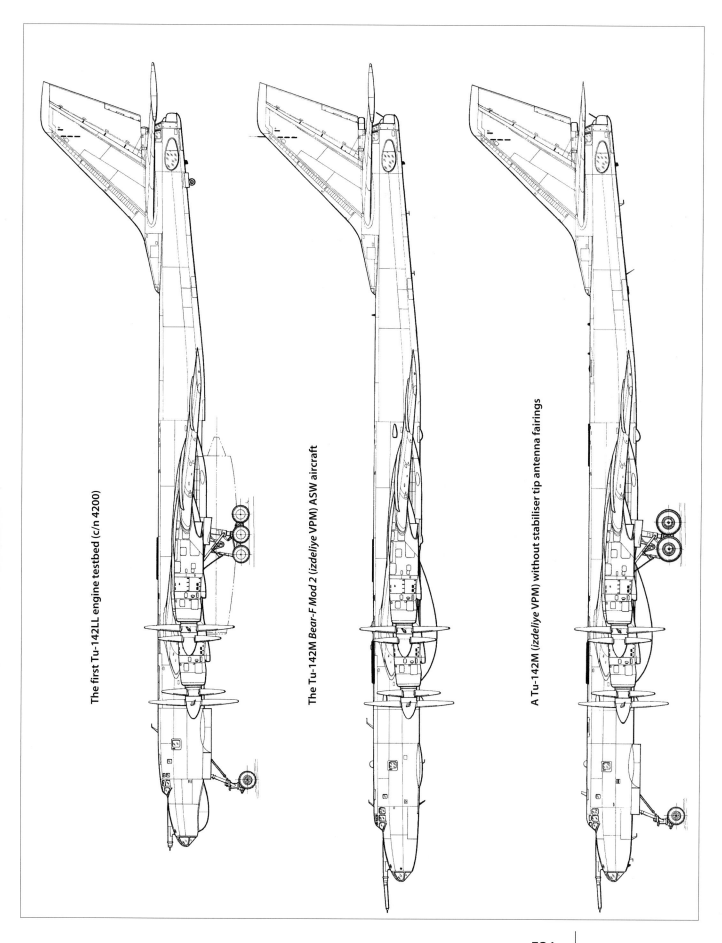

The first Tu-142LL engine testbed (c/n 4200)

The Tu-142M *Bear-F Mod 2 (izdeliye VPM)* ASW aircraft

A Tu-142M *(izdeliye VPM)* without stabiliser tip antenna fairings

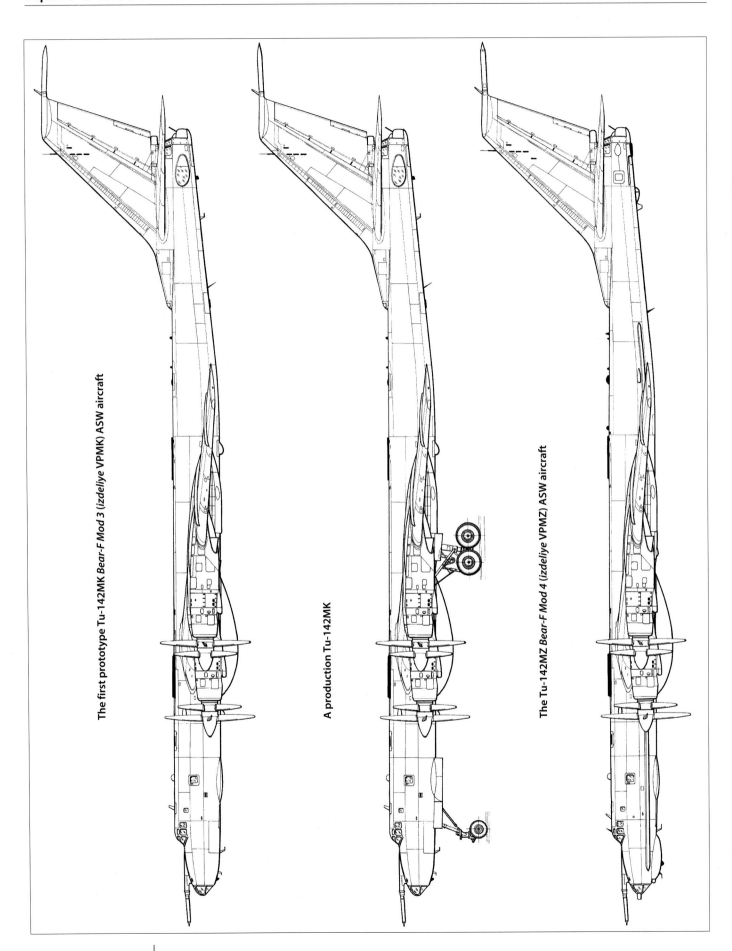

The first prototype Tu-142MK *Bear-F Mod 3 (izdeliye VPMK) ASW aircraft*

A production Tu-142MK

The Tu-142MZ *Bear-F Mod 4 (izdeliye VPMZ) ASW aircraft*

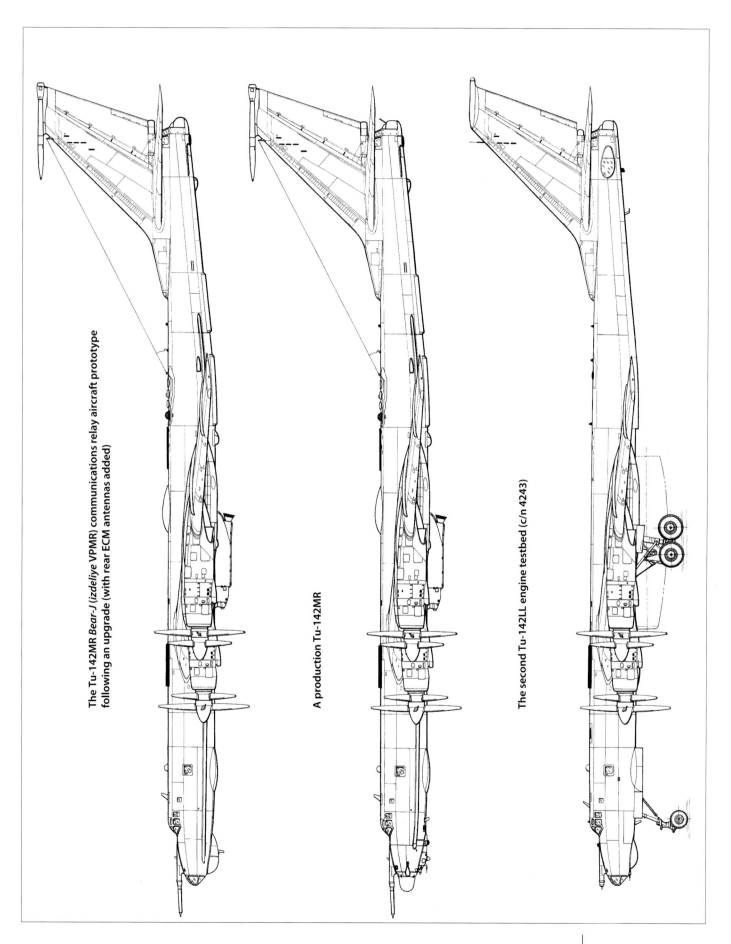

The Tu-142MR *Bear-J* (*izdeliye* VPMR) communications relay aircraft prototype following an upgrade (with rear ECM antennas added)

A production Tu-142MR

The second Tu-142LL engine testbed (c/n 4243)

Appendix 1

Tu-95/Tu-142 production list

The *Bear* family's production run amounted to nearly 400 aircraft – two Moscow-built Tu-95 prototypes (plus a static test airframe) and Kuibyshev-built and Taganrog-built production aircraft – 30 Tu-95s *sans suffixe*, 19 Tu-95Ms, two Tu-116s, 48 new-build Tu-95Ks, 23 new-build Tu-95KMs, 52 new-build Tu-95RTs's, 99 Tu-95MSs and 107 Tu-142s in various versions, including 19 Tu-142s *sans suffixe* (13 *Bear-F Mod-1s* and six *Bear-F Mod 2s*), eight Tu-142MK-Es, 15 Tu-142MRs and one Tu-142MRTs. Known aircraft are listed in construction number order. If one or more digits in a c/n to are not known, these are substituted with asterisks. Crashed or destroyed examples are indicated by 'RIP crosses' where known, with the date of the accident. The variance in manufacture dates is caused by different sources quoting different dates from the aircraft's record card.

C/n	F/n	Version	Serial/tactical code/registration/name	Manufacture date
1. MMZ No.156, Moscow				
?		Tu-95 ('95/1')	no serial † 11-5-1953	
?		Tu-95 (static test)	no serial	
?		Tu-95 ('95/2')	no serial	
		Tu-95LL		
2. Kuibyshev aircraft factory No.18 (Aviacor Joint-Stock Co., Samara)				
System 1: 5.8.001.05 = year of manufacture 1955, plant No.18, Batch 001, 05th aircraft in the batch				
4800001		Tu-95	?	31-10-1955
		Tu-95K (prototype)		
4800002		Tu-95	no code	31-7-1956
580001		Tu-95	?	23-6-1956
580002		Tu-95	Soviet AF 77 Red	18-2-1956
580003		Tu-95	Soviet AF 5 Black	31-8-1955
			Soviet AF 56 Red † 25-8-1965	
5800101		Tu-95	Soviet AF 6 Black	31-8-1955
		Tu-95M (prototype)	Soviet AF 46 Red/'4807'	
		Tu-95N	Soviet AF 46 Red/'4807', no code	
5800102		Tu-95	Soviet AF 44 Red	30-12-1955
5800103		Tu-95	?	29-2-1956
5800104		Tu-95	?	31-3-1956
5800105		Tu-95	?	13-3-1956 (13-4-1956?)
5800201		Tu-95	?	28-3-1956
5800202		Tu-95	?	31-3-1956 (31-4-1956?)
5800203		Tu-95	?	26-4-1956 (16-4-1956?)
5800204		Tu-95	?	20-4-1956
5800205		Tu-95	**? † 5-10-1976**	31-4-1956
5800301		Tu-95	?	28-3-1956 (31-3-1956?)
5800302		Tu-95	?	25-4-1956 (23-2-1956?)
		Tu-95V		
6800303		Tu-95	no code (static test airframe)	?-4-1956
6800304		Tu-95	?	25-4-1956
6800305		Tu-95	**? † 20-9-1959 (or 2-9-1959?)**	?-5-1956
6800306		Tu-95	**? † 5-10-1976**	25-7-1956 (5-7-1956?)
6800307		Tu-95	? (originally no code)	30-9-1956
6800308		Tu-95	?	30-9-1956
6800309		Tu-95	?	30-12-1956
6800310		Tu-95	**? † 24-12-1956 (or 16-3-1957?)**	30-11-1956
6800401		Tu-95	?	30-11-1956
6800402		Tu-116 (Tu-114D)	Soviet AF 7801 Blue, CCCP-76462	31-5-1957
6800403		Tu-95	?	30-4-1957
6800404		Tu-95	no code	?-10-1956
		Tu-95K (prototype)	no code	
		Tu-95KM	?	
7800405		Tu-95	?	30-4-1957

7800406	Tu-95	?	31-5-1957
7800407	Tu-95M	?	31-10-1957
7800408	Tu-95M	?	?-9-1957
	Tu-95LAL	Soviet AF 51 Red	
7800409	Tu-116 (Tu-114D)	Soviet AF 7802 Blue, CCCP-76463	?-9-1957
7800410	Tu-95M	?	31-12-1957
	Tu-95MR (prototype)	?	
	Tu-95U	Soviet AF 68 Red	
7800411	Tu-95M	no code (repeat static test airframe)	?-?-1957
7800501	Tu-95M	?	31-12-1957
	Tu-95MR	?	
7800502	Tu-95M	?	30-12-1957? (30-4-1958?)
	Tu-95MR	?	
7800503	Tu-95M	Soviet AF 51 Red	28-2-1958
7800504	Tu-95M	? † **25-8-1965**	?-12-1957
7800505	Tu-95M	?	21-5-1958
7800506	Tu-95M	?	?-12-1957? (6-2-1958?)
	Tu-95MR	Soviet AF 66 Red	
7800507	Tu-95M	?	31-5-1958
8800508	Tu-95M	?	30-7-1958
8800509	Tu-95M	?	30-4-1958
8800510	Tu-95M	Soviet AF 60 Red	
	Tu-95RTs (prototype)	Soviet Navy 60 Red, 15 Black, 16 Black	?-5-1958
8800601	Tu-95M	?	?-6-1958
	Tu-95M-5	no code	
	Tu-95M-55	no code? † **28-1-1982**	
8800602	Tu-95M	?	17-6-1958
8800603	Tu-95M	?	1-9-1958
8800604	Tu-95M	?	30-9-1958
8800605	Tu-95M	Soviet AF 57 Red	31-12-1958
8802004	Tu-95K	Soviet AF 58 Red? † **5-1-1963**	?-8-1959
8802005	Tu-95K	?	31-7-1959
	Tu-95KM	?	
	Tu-95K-22	?	
8802006	Tu-95K	?	31-7-1959
	Tu-95KM	?	
	Tu-95K-22	?	
9802007	Tu-95K	?	30-9-1959
9802008	Tu-95K	?	31-8-1959
	Tu-95KM	?	
	Tu-95K-22	Soviet AF 12 Black	
9802009	Tu-95K	?	30-1-1960
9802010	Tu-95K	Soviet AF 66 Red † **26-8-1977**	?-7-1959
9802101	Tu-95K	?	31-8-1959
	Tu-95KM	?	
	Tu-95K-22	?	
9802102	Tu-95K	?	30-9-1959
9802103	Tu-95K	?	26-9-1959
	Tu-95KD	?	
	Tu-95KM	?	
	Tu-95K-22	?	
9802104	Tu-95K	?	30-9-1959
	Tu-95KM	?	
	Tu-95K-22	?	
9802105	Tu-95K	?	31-8-1959 (31-10-1959?)
9802106	Tu-95K	?	31-10-1959
9802107	Tu-95K	?	31-8-1959 (31-10-1959?)
	Tu-95KM	?	
	Tu-95K-22	?	

9802108	Tu-95K	?	30-11-1959 (31-11-1959?)
	Tu-95KM	?	
	Tu-95K-22	?	
9802109	Tu-95K	?	30-12-1959
	Tu-95KM	?	
	Tu-95K-22	?	
9802110	Tu-95K	?	30-12-1959
	Tu-95KM	?	
	Tu-95K-22	?	
9802201	Tu-95K	?	31-12-1959
9802202	Tu-95K	?	31-12-1959
	Tu-95KM	?	
	Tu-95K-22	?	
9802203	Tu-95K	?	30-1-1960
	Tu-95KM	?	
	Tu-95K-22	?	
9802204	Tu-95K	no code (static test airframe)	?-?-1960
60802205	Tu-95K	?	29-2-1960
	Tu-95KM	?	
	Tu-95K-22	?	
60802206	Tu-95K	?	31-3-1960
	Tu-95KM	?	
	Tu-95K-22	?	
60802207	Tu-95K	?	8-3-1960
	Tu-95KM (prototype)	?	
	Tu-95K-22	?	
60802208	Tu-95K	?	24-10-1960
	Tu-95KM	?	
	Tu-95K-22	?	
60802209	Tu-95K	? † **24-12-1987**	30-9-1960
60802210	Tu-95K	?	31-10-1960
	Tu-95KM	?	
	Tu-95K-22	?	
60802301	Tu-95K	Soviet AF 68 Red † **26-8-1977**	?-9-1960
60802302	Tu-95K	?	30-9-1960
	Tu-95KM	?	
	Tu-95K-22	?	
60802303	Tu-95K	?	30-9-1960
	Tu-95KM	?	
	Tu-95K-22	?	
60802304	Tu-95K	?	30-10-1960
60802305	Tu-95K	?	18-11-1960
	Tu-95KM	?	
	Tu-95K-22	?	
60802306	Tu-95K	?	12-12-1960
60802307	Tu-95K	Soviet AF 35 Red	12-12-1960
60802308	Tu-95K	?	?-12-1960
60802309	Tu-95K	?	30-11-1960
	Tu-95KM	?	
	Tu-95K-22	?	
60802310	Tu-95K	Soviet AF 40 Black?	30-11-1960
60802401	Tu-95K	?	30-11-1960
	Tu-95KM	?	
	Tu-95K-22	?	
61802402	Tu-95K	?	31-5-1961
	Tu-95KM	?	
	Tu-95K-22	?	

61802403		Tu-95K	?	31-5-1961
		Tu-95KM	?	
		Tu-95K-22	?	
61802404		Tu-95K	?	31-5-1961
		Tu-95KM	?	
		Tu-95K-22	?	
61802405		Tu-95K	Soviet AF 36 Red	?-6-1961
61802406		Tu-95K	?	30-9-1961
		Tu-95KM	?	
		Tu-95K-22	?	
61802407		Tu-95K	?	30-9-1961
61802408		Tu-95K	?	30-9-1961
61802409		Tu-95K	?	31-10-1961
61802410		Tu-95K	?	30-11-1961
61802501		Tu-95K	?	30-12-1961

System 2: 62.M5.25.05 = year of manufacture 1962, Tu-95KM (product code M5), Batch 25, 05th aircraft in the batch

62M52502		Tu-95KM	?	?-?-1962
62M52503		Tu-95KM	?	30-11-1962
		Tu-95K-22	Soviet AF 02 Red	
62M52504		Tu-95KM	?	30-6-1962
		Tu-95K-22	?	
62M52505		Tu-95KM	?	30-6-1962
		Tu-95K-22	?	
62M52506		Tu-95KM	Soviet AF 02 Red	26-6-1962
		Tu-95K-22	?	
62M52507		Tu-95KM	?	24-9-1962 (24-4-1962?)
		Tu-95K-22	?	
62M52508		Tu-95KM	?	31-8-1962
		Tu-95K-22	?	
62M52509		Tu-95KM	?	29-9-1962
		Tu-95K-22	?	
62M52510		Tu-95KM	?	30-12-1962
		Tu-95K-22	?	
62M52601		Tu-95KM	?	30-12-1962
		Tu-95K-22	?	
63M52602		Tu-95KM	Soviet AF 20 Red	28-2-1963
		Tu-95K-22	Soviet AF 05 Red	
63M52603		Tu-95KM	?	31-3-1963
		Tu-95K-22	?	
63M52604		Tu-95KM	?	30-4-1963
		Tu-95K-22	?	
63M52605		Tu-95KM	?	29-6-1963
		Tu-95K-22	?	
63M52606		Tu-95KM	?	31-8-1963
		Tu-95K-22	?	
63M52607		Tu-95KM	?	?-?-1963
63M52608		Tu-95KM	?	30-12-1963
		Tu-95K-22	?	
63M52609		Tu-95KM	?	30-12-1963
		Tu-95K-22	?	
63M52610		Tu-95KM	?	20-10-1964
		Tu-95K-22	Soviet AF 53 Red	
64M52701		Tu-95KM	?	25-11-1964
		Tu-95K-22	?	
64M52702		Tu-95KM	?	30-12-1964
		Tu-95K-22	?	

64M52703		Tu-95KM	?	28-9-1965 (28-3-1965?)
		Tu-95K-22	?	
64M52704		Tu-95KM	?	2-7-1965
		Tu-95K-22	57 Red	

System 3: 63.MRTs.0.03 = year of manufacture 1963, Tu-95RTs, Batch 0, 03rd aircraft in the batch

63MRTs 001		Tu-95RTs	Soviet Navy 01 Black?, Soviet/Russian Navy 30 Black	?-?-1963
63MRTs 002		Tu-95RTs	Soviet Navy 02 Black?, Soviet/Russian Navy 20 Black	?-?-1963
63MRTs 003		Tu-95RTs	Soviet Navy 03 Black?, ?? Black † **3-9-1971**	?-?-1963
63MRTs 101		Tu-95RTs	Soviet/Russian Navy 21 Black	?-?-1964
64MRTs 102		Tu-95RTs	Soviet/Russian Navy 39 Black	?-?-1964
64MRTs 103		Tu-95RTs	Soviet/Russian Navy 32 Black	?-?-1964
64MRTs 104		Tu-95RTs	Soviet/Russian Navy 22 Black	?-?-1964
65MRTs 105		Tu-95RTs	Soviet Navy ?? Red	?-4-1965
65MRTs 106		Tu-95RTs	Soviet Navy ?? Black † **10-4-1978**	?-4-1965
65MRTs 107		Tu-95RTs	Soviet/Russian Navy 25 Black	?-?-1965
65MRTs 201		Tu-95RTs	Soviet/Russian Navy 14 Black	?-?-1965
65MRTs 202		Tu-95RTs	Soviet Navy 13 Black, Soviet/Russian Navy 34 Black	?-?-1965
65MRTs 203		Tu-95RTs	Soviet/Russian Navy 23 Black	?-9-1965
65MRTs 204		Tu-95RTs	Soviet Navy ?? Black † **20-7-1967**	?-10-1965
65MRTs 205		Tu-95RTs	Soviet Navy ?? Red	?-11-1965
65MRTs 206		Tu-95RTs	Soviet Navy ?? Red	?-?-1965
65MRTs 207		Tu-95RTs	Soviet Navy ?? Red	?-?-1965
66MRTs 208		Tu-95RTs	Soviet Navy ?? Red	?-2-1966
66MRTs 209		Tu-95RTs	Soviet Navy 11 Black, Soviet/Russian Navy 15 Black	?-4-1966
66MRTs 210		Tu-95RTs	Soviet/Russian Navy 26 Black	?-4-1966
66MRTs 301		Tu-95RTs	Soviet Navy ?? Red	?-5-1966
66MRTs 302		Tu-95RTs	Soviet Navy ?? Red	?-6-1966
66MRTs 303		Tu-95RTs	Soviet Navy ?? Red	?-7-1966
66MRTs 304		Tu-95RTs	Soviet Navy 37 Black † **4-8-1976**	?-8-1966
66MRTs 305		Tu-95RTs	Soviet/Russian Navy 10 Black	?-9-1966
66MRTs 306		Tu-95RTs	Soviet/Russian Navy 11 Black	?-11-1966
66MRTs 307		Tu-95RTs	Soviet Navy 12 Black † **15-4-1985**	?-12-1966
67MRTs 308		Tu-95RTs	Soviet Navy ?? Red	?-?-1967
67MRTs 309		Tu-95RTs	Soviet Navy ?? Red	?-?-1967
67MRTs 310		Tu-95RTs	Soviet/Russian Navy 33 Black	?-?-1967
67MRTs 401		Tu-95RTs	Soviet Navy 31 Black † **15-1-1971**	?-?-1967
67MRTs 402		Tu-95RTs	Soviet Navy ?? Red	?-?-1967
67MRTs 403		Tu-95RTs	Soviet Navy ?? Red	?-?-1967
67MRTs 404		Tu-95RTs	Soviet Navy ?? Red	?-?-1967
67MRTs 405		Tu-95RTs	Soviet Navy ?? Red	?-?-1967
67MRTs 406		Tu-95RTs	Soviet/Russian Navy 35 Black	?-?-1967
67MRTs 407		Tu-95RTs	Soviet Navy ?? Red	?-?-1967
68MRTs 408		Tu-95RTs	Soviet/Russian Navy 28 Black	?-?-1968
68MRTs 409		Tu-95RTs	Soviet/Russian Navy 17 Black	?-?-1968
68MRTs 410		Tu-95RTs	Soviet Navy ?? Red	?-?-1968
68MRTs 501		Tu-95RTs	Soviet Navy ?? Red	?-?-1968
68MRTs 502		Tu-95RTs	Soviet Navy ?? Red	?-?-1968
68MRTs 503		Tu-95RTs	Soviet Navy ?? Red	?-?-1968
68MRTs 504		Tu-95RTs	Soviet/Russian Navy 36 Black	?-?-1968
68MRTs 505		Tu-95RTs	Soviet Navy ?? Red	?-?-1968
68MRTs 506		Tu-95RTs	Soviet/Russian Navy 24 Black	?-?-1968
68MRTs 507		Tu-95RTs	Soviet/Russian Navy 18 Black	?-?-1968
69MRTs 508		Tu-95RTs	Soviet Navy ?? Red	?-?-1969
69MRTs 509		Tu-95RTs	Soviet Navy ?? Red	?-?-1969
69MRTs 510		Tu-95RTs	Soviet Navy ?? Red	?-?-1969
69MRTs 601		Tu-95RTs	Soviet/Russian Navy 38 Black	?-?-1969
69MRTs 602		Tu-95RTs	Soviet/Russian Navy 19 Black	?-?-1969

System 4: 42.3.5 = Tu-142, Batch 3, 5th aircraft in the batch

4200		Tu-142 *Bear-F*	no code	1968
		Tu-142LL	no code	
4201		Tu-142 *Bear-F*	no code	1968
4202		Tu-142 *Bear-F*	?	1969
4211		Tu-142 *Bear-F*	?	1969
4212		Tu-142 *Bear-F*	?	1969
4213		Tu-142 *Bear-F*	?	1969
4221		Tu-142 *Bear-F*	?	1969
4222		Tu-142 *Bear-F*	?	1970
4223		Tu-142 *Bear-F*	?	1970
4224		Tu-142 *Bear-F*	?	1970
4225		Tu-142 *Bear-F*	?	1970
4231		Tu-142 *Bear-F Mod 1*	?	1970
4232		Tu-142 *Bear-F Mod 1*	?	1971
4233		Tu-142 *Bear-F Mod 1*	?	1971
4234		Tu-142 *Bear-F Mod 1*	?	1971
4235		Tu-142 *Bear-F Mod 1*	?	1971
4241		Tu-142 *Bear-F Mod 1*	?	1971
4242		Tu-142M (prototype)	?	1972

System 5: 100.021.4.7.33412= plant No.18 (code 100), *izdeliye* VP-021 (Tu-95MS), 4th quarter of 1987, plus the five-digit computer number meaning nothing

100021**10317	?	Tu-95MS	?, Russian AF 12 Red	
1000214215101	?	Tu-95MS-16	no code (Soviet AF), Russian AF 01 Red, no code, Russian AF 101 Red	18-5-1984
1000211315105	?	Tu-95MS	?, Russian AF 45 Red/RF-94189	31-8-1983
100021*315119	?	Tu-95MS-16	Soviet/Russian AF 24 Red	20-12-1983
1000213316202	?	Tu-95MS	Russian AF 47 Red *Ryazan'*, 47 Red/RF-94201	24-12-1983
100021*316204	?	Tu-95MS	Soviet/Russian AF 15 Red	17-1-1984
1000214319215	?	Tu-95MS	Soviet/Russian AF 60	29-2-1984
1000213419317	?	Tu-95MS-16	?	19-4-1985!
		Tu-95MS (upgrade)*	Soviet AF 317 Black, Russian AF 317 Red	
1000211419421	?	Tu-95MS	Soviet/Russian AF 53 Red, 53 Red/RF-94195	23-4-1984
1000211419429	?	Tu-95MS	?, Russian AF 49 Red/RF-94191	23-4-1984
1000212419743	?	Tu-95MS	Soviet/Russian AF 48 Red	30-7-1984
1000212421744	?	Tu-95MS-16	Soviet/Ukrainian AF 41 Red	28-7-1984
1000212421802	?	Tu-95MS	Soviet/Russian AF 56 Red, 56 Red/RF-94198	31-8-1984
1000212421906	?	Tu-95MS	?, Russian AF 54 Red/RF-94196	31-8-1984
1000213421914	?	Tu-95MS	?, Russian AF 55 Red/RF-94197	12-11-1984
1000213423103	?	Tu-95MS	Soviet/Russian AF 43 Red	30-10-1984
1000213423107	?	Tu-95MS	?, Russian AF 41 Red/RF-94186	31-10-1984
1000214423419	?	Tu-95MS	Soviet/Russian AF 57 Red, 57 Red/RF-94199	25-12-1984
1000214424530	?	Tu-95MS	Soviet/Russian AF 42 Red †	30-6-1985
1000214424532	?	Tu-95MS	?, Russian AF 51 Red/RF-94193	24-7-1985
1000214424544	?	Tu-95MS-16	Soviet/Russian AF 29 Red	30-7-1985
		Tu-95MA		
1000214424550	?	Tu-95MS	Soviet/Ukrainian AF 25 Red	
1000214424604	?	Tu-95MS	?, Russian AF 604 Black (*Ryazan'*), Russian AF 20 Red *Ryazan'*	15-1-1987!
100021*524608	?	Tu-95MS	?, Russian AF 608 Black	
1000214524610	?	Tu-95MS	?, Russian AF 610 Black, Russian AF ?? Red?	22-3-1986!
100021*527611	?	Tu-95MS	?, Russian AF 611 Black	31-12-1984
1000211527615	?	Tu-95MS-16	Soviet/Russian AF 22 Red, 22 Red/RF-94176	8-8-1985
		Tu-95MA		
1000211528356	?	Tu-95MS-16	Soviet/Russian AF 25 Red	5-8-1985
		Tu-95MA		
1000212528373	?	Tu-95MS-16	Soviet/Russian AF 20 Red	5-9-1985
		Tu-95MA		
1000212528382	?	Tu-95MS	Soviet/Russian AF 24 Red	6-8-1985

1000212528561	?	Tu-95MS-16	Soviet/Russian AF 28 Red, 28 Red/RF-94170	15-11-1985
		Tu-95MA		
1000212528575	?	Tu-95MS	Soviet/Russian AF 26 Red	5-11-1985
1000213528593	?	Tu-95MS	Soviet/Russian AF 21 Red, 21 Red/RF-94207	4-11-1985
1000213529526	?	Tu-95MS	Soviet/Russian AF 23 Red	5-11-1985
1000213529561	?	Tu-95MS-16	Soviet/Ukrainian AF 02 Red	5-11-1985
1000213529608	?	Tu-95MS	Soviet/Russian AF 27 Red	30-5-1986
100021**29732	?	Tu-95MS-16	Soviet/Ukrainian AF 03 Red	
100021**29843	?	Tu-95MS-16	Soviet/Ukrainian AF 04 Red	
100021**30108	?	Tu-95MS-16	Soviet/Ukrainian AF 05 Red	
100021**30183	?	Tu-95MS-16	Soviet/Ukrainian AF 06 Red	
100021**30203	?	Tu-95MS-16	Soviet/Ukrainian AF 07 Red	
100021**30235	?	Tu-95MS-16	Soviet/Ukrainian AF 20 Red	
100021**30306	?	Tu-95MS-16	Soviet/Ukrainian AF 21 Red	
100021**30309	?	Tu-95MS-16	Soviet/Ukrainian AF 22 Red	
100021**30419	?	Tu-95MS-16	Soviet/Ukrainian AF 23 Red	
100021**31135	?	Tu-95MS-16	Soviet/Ukrainian AF 24 Red	
100021**31198	?	Tu-95MS-16	Soviet/Ukrainian AF 25 Red	
100021**31249	?	Tu-95MS-16	Soviet/Ukrainian AF 90 Red	20-1-1987
100021**31370	?	Tu-95MS-16	Soviet/Ukrainian AF 91 Red	20-1-1987
100021**31483	?	Tu-95MS-16	Soviet/Ukrainian AF 92 Red	21-1-1987
100021**31509	?	Tu-95MS-16	Soviet/Ukrainian AF 93 Red	21-1-1987
100021**32179	?	Tu-95MS-16	Soviet/Ukrainian AF 94 Red	24-4-1987
1000211732191	?	Tu-95MS-16	Soviet/Ukrainian AF 01 Red	22-7-1987
1000211732386	?	Tu-95MS-16	Soviet/Ukrainian AF 95 Red	23-7-1987
100021*732477	?	Tu-95MS	Soviet/Russian AF 26 Red	23-7-1987
100021*732644	?	Tu-95MS	Soviet/Ukrainian AF 52 Red	
1000212733111	?	Tu-95MS	Soviet/Russian AF 59 Red, 59 Red/RF-94206 *Blagoveshchensk*	28-9-1987
1000212733144	?	Tu-95MS-16	Soviet/Ukrainian AF 31 Red	31-8-1987
1000213733255	?	Tu-95MS	Soviet/Russian AF 10 Red	26-10-1987
1000213733299	?	Tu-95MS-16	Soviet/Russian AF 12 Red *Moskva*	26-10-1987
		Tu-95MS (upgrade)*	12 Red/RF-94126 *Moskva*	
1000213733322	?	Tu-95MS-16	Soviet/Russian AF 18 Red	9-2-1988
		Tu-95MS (upgrade)*	18 Red/RF-94131	
1000214733412	?	Tu-95MS-16	Soviet/Russian AF 14 Red *Voronezh*	9-2-1988
		Tu-95MS (upgrade)*	14 Red/RF-94132 *Voronezh*	
1000214733447	?	Tu-95MS-16	Soviet/Russian AF 17 Black	3-3-1988
		Tu-95MS (upgrade)*	17 Red/RF-94259	
100021**33567	?	Tu-95MS	? (Russian AF)	30-9-1987
100021**33757	?	Tu-95MS	Soviet/Ukrainian AF 61 Red	
1000211834108	?	Tu-95MS-16	Soviet/Russian AF 20 Black	5-5-1988
		Tu-95MS (upgrade)*	20 Red/RF-94177	
1000211834135	?	Tu-95MS-16	Soviet/Russian AF 16 Red *Velikiy Novgorod*	2-6-1988
		Tu-95MS (upgrade)*	16 Red/RF-94124 *Velikiy Novgorod*	
1000212834278	?	Tu-95MS	?, Russian AF 22 Red, 22/1 Red/RF-94120 *Kozel'sk*	29-7-1988
1000212834379	?	Tu-95MS-16	Soviet/Russian AF 23 Black	29-7-1988
		Tu-95MS (upgrade)*	23/1 Red/RF-94129 *Tambov*	
1000213834415	?	Tu-95MS	?, Russian AF 24 Red, 24/1 Red/RF-94130	22-10-1988
1000213834444	?	Tu-95MS	?, Russian AF 25 Red, 25/1 Red/RF-94119	22-10-1988
1000213834496	?	Tu-95MS-16	Soviet/Russian AF 20 Red (*Naookograd Doobna*, later *Doobna*)	19-11-1988
		Tu-95MS (upgrade)*	20/1 Red/RF-94122 *Doobna*	
1000214834666	?	Tu-95MS	Soviet/Russian AF 31 Black, 21 Red, 21/1 Red/RF-94121 *Samara*	21-1-1989
1000214834757	?	Tu-95MS	11 Red/RF-94127 *Vorkuta*	21-1-1989
1000214835199	?	Tu-95MS	Soviet/Russian AF 38 Black, 10/1 Red *Saratov*	29-5-1992!
		Tu-95MS (upgrade)*	10/1 Red/RF-94128 *Saratov*	
1000211935249	?	Tu-95MS	?, Russian AF 26 Red/RF-94172	20-7-1989
100021*935363	?	Tu-95MS	Soviet/Russian AF 34 Black	
1000212935367	?	Tu-95MS	Soviet/Russian AF 04 Black, 04 Red/RF-94182 *Kurgan*	20-7-1989
1000213935765	?	Tu-95MS	?, Russian AF 05 Red/RF-94181 † **8-6-2015**	20-10-1989

1000213935793	?	Tu-95MS	Soviet/Russian AF 36 Black, 01 Red/RF-94185 *Irkutsk*	23-10-1989
1000214936177	?	Tu-95MS-16	Soviet/Ukrainian AF '10 Red',	22-1-1990
			Russian AF 19 Red, 19 Red/RF-94123 *Krasnoyarsk*	
1000214936487	?	Tu-95MS	?, Russian AF 02 Red/RF-94184 *Mozdok*	27-4-1990
1000211036785	?	Tu-95MS	Soviet/Russian AF 06 Red, 06 Red/RF-94180	14-6-1990
1000212936853	?	Tu-95MS	?, Russian AF 07 Red/RF-94179	15-8-1990
1000213037098	?	Tu-95MS	Soviet/Russian AF 03 Red, 03 Red/RF-94183	16-1-1991
1000214037187	?	Tu-95MS-16	Soviet/Ukrainian AF '96 Red', Russian AF 28 Red	26-3-1991
		Tu-95MS (upgrade)*	28/1 Red/RF-94116 *Sevastopol'*	
1000212937345	?	Tu-95MS	Soviet/Ukrainian AF '08 Red', Russian AF 27 Red	3-10-1991
		Tu-95MS (upgrade)*	27/1 Red/RF-94177 (incorrect registration), 27/1 Red/RF-94117 *Izborsk*	
1000214137566	?	Tu-95MS	Soviet/Russian AF 08 Red *Smolensk*, 29/2 Red/RF-94178 *Smolensk*	20-8-1992

3. Taganrog aircraft factory No.86 (TMZD, later Tavia)
System 1: 4.6.00502 = year of manufacture 1974, plant No.86, plus the five-digit computer number meaning nothing

3600***	4243	Tu-142M	no code	1974
		Tu-142MK (prototype)	no code	
		Tu-142LL	(Soviet/Russian AF 043 Black)	
3600405	4244	Tu-142M	?	1974
		Tu-142MK (prototype)	Soviet/Russian Navy 16 Red	
3600501	4245	Tu-142M	Soviet/Russian Navy 17 Red	1975
4600502	4246	Tu-142M	Soviet/Russian Navy 06 Red	1975
4600617	4247	Tu-142M	Soviet/Russian Navy 04 Red	1975
5600635	4248	Tu-142M	Soviet/Russian Navy 18 Red	1975
5600801	4249	Tu-142M	Soviet/Russian Navy 15 Red	1975
6600980	4250	Tu-142M	Soviet/Russian Navy 14 Red	1976
6601101	4251	Tu-142M	Soviet/Russian Navy 01 Red	1976
6601318	4252	Tu-142M	Soviet/Russian Navy 02 Red	1976
6601332	4253	Tu-142M	Soviet/Russian Navy 08 Red	1976
6601347	4254	Tu-142M	Soviet/Russian Navy 03 Red	1976
6601366	4255	Tu-142M	Soviet/Russian Navy 10 Red	1976
7601401	4256	Tu-142M	Soviet/Russian Navy 05 Red	1977
7601505	4257	Tu-142M	Soviet/Russian Navy 09 Red	1977
?	4261	Tu-142M	?	
?	4262	Tu-142M		
		Tu-142MP (prototype)	?	
?	4263	Tu-142M		
		Tu-142MR prototype?	?	
?	4264	Tu-142M		
		Tu-142MK (prototype)	?	
?	4265	Tu-142M	?	
?	4271	Tu-142M	?	
?	4272	Tu-142M	?	
?	4273	Tu-142M	?	
?	4274	Tu-142M	?	
?	4275	Tu-142M	?	
?	4281	Tu-142M	?	
?	4282	Tu-142M	?	
?	4283	Tu-142M	?	
?	4284	Tu-142M	?	
8601801	?	Tu-142MK	Soviet/Russian Navy 62 Red	1978
8602025	?	Tu-142MK	Soviet/Russian Navy 66 Black Ivan Borzov	1978
8602109	42105	Tu-142MK	no code	1978
		Tu-95MS (prototype)	no code (Soviet AF)	1980
9602280	?	Tu-142MK	Soviet/Russian Navy 71 Black	1979
9602363	?	Tu-142MK	Soviet/Russian Navy 73 Black	1979

* Tu-95MS upgraded to carry Kh-101/Kh-102 missiles

0602446	?	Tu-142MK	Soviet/Russian Navy 98 Black	1980
1602821	?	Tu-142MK	?	1981
		Tu-95MS (prototype)	Soviet AF 31 Red	
1602904	?	Tu-142MK	Soviet/Russian Navy 87 Black	1981
1602946	?	Tu-142MK	Soviet/Russian Navy 90 Black	1981
1602987	?	Tu-142MK	Soviet/Russian Navy 91 Black	1981
1603021	?	Tu-142MK	Soviet/Russian Navy 92 Black	1981
1603062	?	Tu-142MK	Soviet/Russian Navy 93 Black	1981
2603187	?	Tu-142MK	Soviet/Russian Navy 94 Black *Yevgeniy Preobrazhenskiy*	1981
2603222	?	Tu-142MK	Soviet/Russian Navy 95 Black *Cherepovets*	1982
2603305	?	Tu-142MK	Soviet/Russian Navy 97 Black *Vologda*	1982
3603388	?	Tu-142MK	Soviet/Russian Navy 50 Black *Fedotovo*	1983
3603472	?	Tu-142MK	Soviet/Russian Navy 51 Black, 51 Black/RF-34059 *Yuriy Malinin*	1983
3603556	?	Tu-142MK	Soviet/Russian Navy 52 Black	1983
5603763	?	Tu-142MK	Soviet/Russian Navy 53 Black	1985
5603846	?	Tu-142MK	Soviet/Russian Navy 54 Black	1985
5603887	?	Tu-142MK	Soviet/Russian Navy 55 Black	1985
6603930	?	Tu-142MK	Soviet/Russian Navy 56 Black, 56 Black/RF-34063 *Aleksandr Mozhaiskiy*	1986
6609646	?	Tu-142MK-E	Indian Navy IN311	20-2-1987
7609686	?	Tu-142MK-E	Indian Navy IN312	1987
7609726	?	Tu-142MK-E	Indian Navy IN313	1987
7609766	?	Tu-142MK-E	Indian Navy IN314	1987
7609806?	?	Tu-142MK-E	Indian Navy IN315	
8609846	?	Tu-142MK-E	Indian Navy IN316	1988
8609886?	?	Tu-142MK-E	Indian Navy IN317	1988
8609925	?	Tu-142MK-E	Indian Navy IN318	1988
?	4285	Tu-142MK	?	1978
?	4291	Tu-142MK	?	1978
?	4292	Tu-142MK	?	1978
?	4293	Tu-142MK	?	1978
?	4294	Tu-142MK	?	1978
?	4295	Tu-142MK	?	1978
?	42101	Tu-142MK	?	1978
?	42102	Tu-142MK	?	1978
?	42103	Tu-142MK	?	1979
?	42104	Tu-142MK	?	1979
8601903	?	Tu-142MZ	Soviet/Ukrainian Navy 85 Black	1988
8601986	?	Tu-142MZ	? (Soviet/Ukrainian Navy)	1988
9603970	?	Tu-142MZ	Soviet/Russian Navy 53 Red *Vanino*	1989
9604012	42185	Tu-142MZ	no code	4-5-1989
9604133	?	Tu-142MZ	Soviet/Russian Navy 54 Red/RF-34106 *Dal'nevostochnaya TTK*	1989
0604175	?	Tu-142MZ	Soviet/Russian Navy 55 Red † **6-11-2009**	1990
0604215	?	Tu-142MZ	Soviet/Russian Navy 56 Red/RF-34109	1990
0604255	?	Tu-142MZ	Soviet/Russian Navy 57 Red	1990
0604295	?	Tu-142MZ	Soviet/Russian Navy 58 Red	1990
0604336	?	Tu-142MZ	Soviet/Russian Navy 59 Red/RF-34108	1990
0604362?	?	Tu-142MZ	?	1990
0604387	?	Tu-142MRTs	no code	1990
1604440?	?	Tu-142MZ	Soviet/Russian Navy 60 Red	1991
1604491	?	Tu-142MZ	Soviet/Russian Navy 61 Red	1991
1604543	?	Tu-142MZ	Soviet/Russian Navy 62 Red	1991
1604595	?	Tu-142MZ	Soviet/Russian Navy 63 Black/RF-34097	1991
1605386	?	Tu-142MZ	Soviet/Russian Navy 64 Red	1991
2605426	?	Tu-142MZ	no code, Russian Navy 65 Red/RF-34099	1992
?	42135	Tu-142MZ	?	
?	42141	Tu-142MZ	?	
?	42142	Tu-142MZ	?	
?	42143	Tu-142MZ	?	

?	42144	Tu-142MZ	?	
?	42145	Tu-142MZ	?	
?	42151	Tu-142MZ	?	
?	42152	Tu-142MZ	?	
?	42153	Tu-142MZ	?	
?	42144	Tu-142MZ	?	
?	42155	Tu-142MZ	?	
?	42161	Tu-142MZ	?	
?	42162	Tu-142MZ	?	
?	42163	Tu-142MZ	?	
?	42164	Tu-142MZ	?	
?	42165	Tu-142MZ	?	
?	42171	Tu-142MZ	?	
?	42172	Tu-142MZ	?	
?	42173	Tu-142MZ	?	
?	42174	Tu-142MZ	?	
?	42175	Tu-142MZ	?	
?	42181	Tu-142MZ	?	
?	42182	Tu-142MZ	?	
?	42183	Tu-142MZ	?	
?	42184	Tu-142MZ	?	
?	42191	Tu-142MZ	?	
?	42192	Tu-142MZ	?	
?	42193	Tu-142MZ	?	

System 2: 640.342.1.4.00875 = TMZD (code 640), Tu-95MS (*izdeliye* 342), 1st quarter of 1984, plus the five-digit computer number meaning nothing

6403423100002	0101?	Tu-95MS	? (Soviet AF)	28-10-1981
6403424100003	0102?	Tu-95MS	Soviet/Russian AF 52 Red	31-8-1982
6403424100004	0103?	Tu-95MS	?	5-11-1982
		Tu-95MA	Soviet/Russian AF 004 Black	
6403423200201	?	Tu-95MS	Soviet/Russian AF 58	30-9-1982
6403424200402	?	Tu-95MS	Soviet/Russian AF 24	30-11-1982
6403424200603	?	Tu-95MS	?, Russian AF 21/2 Red † **26-2-2013**	29-12-1982
6403424300804	?	Tu-95MS	?	?-?-1983
6403422300811	?	Tu-95MS	Soviet/Russian AF 62	29-3-1983
6403423300822	?	Tu-95MS	Soviet/Russian AF 50 Red, 50 Red/RF-94192	28-10-1983
6403424300843	?	Tu-95MS	Soviet/Russian AF 23 Red	26-12-1983
6403424300854	?	Tu-95MS	Soviet/Russian AF 77 Red, 77 Red/RF-94204 † **14-7-2015**	7-4-1984
6403421400875	?	Tu-95MS	Russian AF 23/2 Red/RF-94205	13-4-1984
6403422400903	?	Tu-95MS	Soviet/Russian AF 22 Red	30-6-1984
6403422400905	?	Tu-95MS	Russian AF 20 Red/RF-94255	30-6-1984
6403423400909	?	Tu-95MS	Soviet/Russian AF 34 Red	13-9-1984

System 3: 805.801.4.6.02017 = TMZD (code 805), Tu-142MR (*izdeliye* 801), 4th quarter of 1986, plus the five-digit computer number meaning nothing

8058014301002	4263?	Tu-142MR (prototype)	Soviet/Russian Navy 27 Black	
8058014401005	?	Tu-142MR	Soviet/Russian Navy 11 Black *Belo'ozero*	
8058014402007	?	Tu-142MR	Soviet/Russian Navy 18 Black	
8058014502009	?	Tu-142MR	Soviet/Russian Navy 28 Black	
8058014602017	?	Tu-142MR	Soviet/Russian Navy 23 Black; 23 Red/RF-34105?	
8058013702019	?	Tu-142MR	Soviet/Russian Navy 14 Black	
8058013702021	?	Tu-142MR	Soviet/Russian Navy 15 Black *Taganrog*	
8058014702023	?	Tu-142MR	Soviet/Russian Navy 16 Black	
8058013802025	?	Tu-142MR	Soviet/Russian Navy 24 Black, 24 Red/RF-34113	
8058014802026	?	Tu-142MR	Soviet/Russian Navy 25 Black	
8058014802027	?	Tu-142MR	Soviet/Russian Navy 26 Black	
8058014902030	?	Tu-142MR	Soviet/Russian Navy 17 Black *Velikiy Ustyug*, 17 Red/RF-34073 *Velikiy Ustyug*	
8058014902038	?	Tu-142MR	Soviet/Russian Navy 19 Black	
8058014503011	?	Tu-142MR	Soviet/Russian Navy 22 Black	
8058013603015	?	Tu-142MR	Soviet/Russian Navy 12 Black *Vytegra*	

Appendix 2

Accident attrition

As of July 2017, 31 aircraft of the Tu-95/Tu-142 family had been lost in accidents, claiming the lives of 209 crewmen. All known fatal and non-fatal accidents (both total and partial hull losses), as well as flight incidents (events not serious enough to qualify as a non-fatal accidents), are listed here in chronological order. Aircraft operated by the Air Force and the Navy are listed separately.

Tu-95 accidents and incidents in the Air Force are listed first.

• As already mentioned, the first accident involving a Tu-95 was the loss of the first prototype ('95/1') in its 17th flight on 11th May 1953. When the aircraft was returning to Zhukovskiy, a fire broke out in the No.3 2TV-2F engine due to uncontained failure of the reduction gearbox. The fire spread to the starboard wing, causing the aircraft to lose control and crash near the town of Noginsk (Moscow Region). Four of the 11 crewmembers (captain Aleksey D. Perelyot, navigator S. S. Kirichenko, flight engineer Aleksandr F. Chernov and test equipment technician A. M. Bol'shakov) lost their lives; the other seven (co-pilot Vyacheslav P. Marunov, radio operator Nikolay F. Mayorov, lead engineer Nikolay V. Lashkevich, assistant lead engineer A. M. Ter-Akopyan, flight electrics engineer I. Ye. Komissarov, flight engineer L. I. Borzenkov and test engineer K. I. Vaiman) parachuted to safety.

• On 4th April 1955 the second pre-production Tu-95 (no tactical code, c/n 4800002) came to grief at the end of its third test flight. When landing at Kuibyshev-Bezymyanka in a stiff crosswind the aircraft's captain Lt. (SG) Mikhail I. Mikhaïlov, a factory test pilot of plant No.18, could not keep the bomber on the runway centreline; the aircraft swung and ran off the runway onto the left shoulder, collapsing the port main gear unit and suffering damage to the Nos. 1 and 2 propellers and the port outer wing. The propeller of the No.1 engine was feathered at the time of the accident, suggesting there was a problem beyond just strong crosswind. Mikhaïlov was no rookie pilot, having flown more than 60 sorties as a transport aircraft captain in the Great Patriotic War and then worked as a test pilot at the co-located plant No.1, but he had no prior experience with the Tu-95. The aircraft was repaired.

• In July 1955 an early-production Tu-95 captained by factory test pilot Konstantin K. Rykov suffered a leak in the No.3 engine's fuel line during a pre-delivery test flight from Kuibyshev-Bezymyanka. Luckily the gunner watching through the lateral blisters was quick to notice the fuel streaming from the starboard inboard nacelle and alert the pilots; the affected engine was promptly shut down, averting a fire.

• In April 1956 Tu-95 c/n 4800002 suffered an almost identical mishap at the same location during another test flight. As the bomber took off from Kuibyshev-Bezymyanka and the aircraft's captain Lt. Yuriy A. Dobrovol'skiy, another factory test pilot, selected gear up, the port main gear unit jammed halfway through retraction. Moreover, when the crew attempted to dump the fuel in order to lighten the aircraft before an emergency landing, the fuel jettison valve in the starboard wing would not open and the fuel was dumped asymmetrically; the bomber tended to bank, requiring a lot of effort to keep the wings level. As the aircraft touched down, the augmented load on the port side proved too much for the damaged port main gear unit, which collapsed; the port wing touched the runway, sending the aircraft skidding onto the runway shoulder. The aircraft was again repaired and eventually delivered to the 1023rd TBAP.

• As already mentioned, the first loss of an in-service Tu-95 occurred on 24th December 1956 when Tu-95 *sans suffixe* c/n 6800310 operated by GK NII VVS (tactical code unknown) suffered a turbine failure in one of its NK-12 turboprops. The propeller of the affected engine could not be feathered; the resulting drag caused the aircraft to lose speed and stall, entering a spin. The bomber crashed near Engels-2 AB, killing the entire crew. (It should be noted that the accident date of Tu-95 c/n 6800310 is also reported as 16th March 1957 – or even 24th November 1956, which is impossible because the aircraft was manufactured on 30th November 1956.)

• On 20th September 1959 Tu-95 c/n 6800305 (possibly a 409th TBAP aircraft from Uzin AB) crashed fatally near Belaya Tserkov' in the Ukraine.

The tail unit of Lt.-Col. Gershunenko's Tu-95KM after a mid-air collision with an M-4-2 tanker on 27th June 1966. The starboard observation blister is shattered.

• On 5th January 1963 Tu-95K c/n 8802004 crashed fatally while undergoing trials at GNIKI VVS.

• On 25th August 1965 two 409th TBAP *Bear-As* – a Tu-95 *sans suffixe* (c/n 580003) captained by Maj. Ivanov and a Tu-95M (c/n 7800504) captained by Col. Tropynin – crashed independently for the same reason during formation flying over the Black Sea. When the dorsal cannons were fired to repel a simulated fighter attack, vibration caused the rear fuselage tanks' filler caps to pop open and the escaping fuel vapours ignited, causing a massive fire. Ivanov's aircraft fell into the sea; the other bomber made it to the coast but crashed 10 km (6.2 miles) from the nearest airfield. All 14 crew members on the two aircraft lost their lives.

• On 27th May 1966 a 1006th TBAP Tu-95KM captained by Lt.-Col. Gershunenko and an M-4-2 tanker from the 1096th TBAP captained by Maj. Vasil'yev were flying a mission involving two refuellings and four 'dry' contacts. After this, the *Bear* was to pass the tanker on the right with a horizontal and vertical separation of 300 m (990 ft) for the purpose of photographing it. Yet, Gershunenko, considering himself to be a top-class pilot, deliberately ignored instructions and overtook the tanker with a much smaller separation. After assuming line abreast formation he stopped observing the tanker and concentrated on the flight deck equipment (which was actually the co-pilot's responsibility). Neither did the other crew members keep an eye on the M-4, believing the captain was doing this.

Losing concentration briefly, Gershunenko inadvertently banked the aircraft slightly to port with a gentle climb. As a result, the Tu-95KM drifted towards the tanker, striking the latter's forward fuselage underside with its tail unit. The M-4's crew, too, had not been watching the Tu-95 closely enough and was late in reacting – the collision came as a total surprise for everyone. As a result, the *Bear* lost part of the fin, half the rudder and part of the starboard tailplane; the tanker suffered damage to two of the four engines, the nose gear doors and the fuel system. Luckily both aircraft landed safely at Engels-2 AB.

• On 14th September 1974 a 1006th (?) TBAP Tu-95K captained by Capt. Maksimov was flying a mission when smoke poured from the dorsal gunner/radio operator's circuit breaker panel. Dorsal gunner/radio operator Ens. Piskoon switched off all electric power on his panel and rotated his revolving seat into a different position; the smoke vanished, and the flight was completed without further incident. It turned out that the loose end of a control cable linking the seat and the sighting station had caused a short circuit.

• On 19th February 1976 a 1006th (?) TBAP Tu-95K captained by Maj. Tsybin was climbing away from Uzin AB when it turned out that the rear pressure cabin would not pressurise properly. The cause was that the tail gunner Pvt. Surtsukov had failed to close the entry hatch properly.

• On 8th April 1976 a 1023rd TBAP Tu-95K captained by Lt. (SG) V. K. Gubanov was participating in an exercise. When the captain called the rear gunners over the intercom for a routine check 3 hours 20 minutes after take-off, there was no response. Aborting the mission, the crew descended from 8,700 to 3,900 m (from 28,540 to 12,800 ft) and made an emergency landing at the nearest suitable airfield. To everyone's dismay, gunner Pvt. A. D. Mastryakov was dead and defensive fire commander Sgt. A. M. Bogachov was missing. The entry hatch had been improperly closed; the tail gunner had attempted to fix it and the hatch had burst open at 8,700 m. The luckless sergeant had fallen out, whereupon the private, who was not wearing his oxygen mask, had died of hypoxia.

• On 5th October 1976 a 1023rd TBAP Tu-95 *sans suffixe* (c/n 6800306) captained by Pilot 1st Class Maj. V. V. Mal'tsev was flying a night sortie. At the end of the mission the weather at the destination airfield deteriorated below minima and the aircraft together with eight other Tu-95s was diverted to Alma-Ata which was the alternate airfield. When the group got there the weather at Alma-Ata was below minima as well, with heavy rain and a horizontal visibility of 2-3 km (1.24-1.86 miles); still, there was no choice but to land.

After entering the circuit at Alma-Ata airport the crew followed the instructions of the circuit air traffic controller. The crew had to use the visual approach slope indicators (VASI) because the ground part of the ILS was out of order. When the bomber was 12 km (7.45 miles) out, the controller informed the crew that the machine was on the glideslope; the crew set the flaps 20° and began the descent from 500 m (1,640 ft). Shortly afterwards, while making a turn onto a heading of 270° as commanded by the controller, the aircraft descended and collided with trees and a power line located 111 m (364 ft) above the runway level. The aircraft crashed and burned 7,800 m (4.84 miles) from the runway threshold and 3,650 m (2.26 miles) to the left of the runway centreline, killing the crew of seven. The other eight bombers landed safely.

• Another 1023rd TBAP Tu-95 *sans suffixe* (c/n 5800205) is also reported as having crashed that same day.

• On 3rd February 1977 a 409th (?) TBAP Tu-95 captained by Lt. (SG) V. N. Zhogolev was climbing at the beginning of a sortie when the pressurisation system malfunctioned – the pressure differential would not increase above 0.2 kg/cm^2 (2.85 psi) from 4,300 m (14,110 ft). The captain instructed gunner Ens. Denisenko to check the closure of the entry hatch and the operation of the ARD-54 cabin pressure regulator. The ensign used his oxygen equipment improperly, fainting when the aircraft climbed to 11,000 m (36,090 ft), at which point the cabin altitude was 6,800 m (22,310 ft). The co-navigator came to his aid and the mission was aborted.

• On 26th August 1977 the 182nd GvTBAP was performing an exercise in full strength; the Tu-95Ks were flying in groups of three, maintaining a V formation. Three of the aircraft involved were coded '66 Red' (c/n 9802010), '67 Red' and '68 Red' (c/n 60802301) captained by Pilots 3rd Class Lt. (SG) A. V. Bibishev, Capt. Yu. V. Pyl'nev and Capt. P. F. Popov respectively. Pyl'nev was the flight leader; Popov's aircraft was 6 km (3.73 miles) to port and 26 km (16.16 miles) behind, while the other wingman was 6 km to starboard and 36 km (22.37 miles) behind.

The sortie was to last four hours, and halfway through the mission the bomber flights were to execute a U-turn over the Aral Sea. As he completed the turn, Pyl'nev suddenly lost radio contact with his wingmen. Contacting ground control, he requested permission to return for a look-see, but just then the leader of the next flight reported two fires on the ground. It came to light that the wingmen had come dangerously close to each other during the turn, Popov commencing the manoeuvre 1 minute 26 seconds after the leader and Bibishev following suit 47 seconds later. One of the wingmen should have climbed and the other descended to provide adequate vertical separation, but for reasons unknown neither crew took corrective action. As a result, 2 hours 6 minutes after take-off (at 18:10.20 Moscow time) the Tu-95Ks collided in broad daylight at 9,600 m (31,500 ft); '66 Red' disintegrated and exploded immediately, killing the entire crew of seven. '68 Red' became uncontrollable and flicked into a spin; only the ECM officer and the tail gunner managed to bail out, the other five crew members perishing when the aircraft hit the ground.

The accident investigation panel placed the blame with the pilots. As a result of this accident, LNPO Leninets was tasked with developing a collision avoidance system optimised for close formation flying specifically for the *Bear*. This emerged in the late 1970s as the A-326 *Rogovitsa* (Cornea) and was fitted to the Tu-95KM; however, the system proved unsatisfactory.

• On 3rd September 1978 a 1006th (?) TBAP Tu-95K captained by Maj. Kitrar' was making a positioning flight back to Uzin AB. As the bomber climbed to 4,000 m (13,120 ft), the tail gunner reported that the rear cabin failed to pressurise properly. The captain reduced the flight level to 3,000 m (9,840 ft); 2 hours 15 minutes later the pressurisation system revived. The investigation showed that the tail gunner had inadvertently opened the emergency depressurisation valve before take-off.

545

• On 25th December 1978 a 1023rd TBAP Tu-95K captained by Maj. Nekrasov was making a training flight. As the aircraft was warming up the engines before take-off, gunner Pvt. Kochetkov lit a cigarette and then passed it to tail gunner PFC Gorbatkov when the latter asked him to share a smoke. Gorbatkov dropped the cigarette, setting the heat- and soundproofing blankets in the rear pressure cabin alight. Using a fire extinguisher and his flying jacket, the tail gunner managed to put out the fire. Yet he did not notify the captain immediately, doing so (and faking the fire-fighting procedures) only during the landing run after the aircraft had made four circuits of the airfield.

• In 1979 (the exact date is unknown) two Long-Range Aviation Tu-95s crashed into the Black Sea during live gunnery exercises. The scenario was identical: a leak had developed in the oxygen system when the cannons were fired (presumably due to vibrations), causing an in-flight fire and loss of control. The entire crew of seven was lost in both cases.

• As already mentioned, on 28th January 1982 the Tu-95M-55 weapons testbed operated by the Tupolev OKB (no tactical code, c/n 8800601) crashed on take-off at Zhukovskiy, killing the crew of ten – captain Nikolay Ye. Kool'chitskiy, co-pilot Viktor I. Shkatov, navigator Aleksandr S. Shevtsov, Nav/Op Aleksandr I. Nikolaïchev, radio operator Igor' N. Gorstkin, flight engineer Aleksandr A. Zhilin, test engineer Valeriy E. Serman, electrics engineer Vitaliy Ya. Ampleyev, flight technician Khaidar I. Sungatulin and flight technician Konstantin P. Makarov. The cause was a combination of icing, serious overloading and a too-far-aft CG.

• On 10th February 1982 a 1023rd TBAP Tu-95K captained by Maj. Pasookhin was climbing at the beginning of a mission when tail gunner Pvt. Tokmakov reported that the rear cabin would not pressurise as there was no bleed air supply. Remedial action by the crew gave no result. It was discovered later that the tail gunner had applied excessive force to the pressure adjustment cock, causing a control cable to come off the roller.

• Nine days later another Tu-95K from the same unit captained by Maj. Bankovskiy was due to take off. Acting on the captain's instructions, gunner Ens. Ryabonenko switched on various electrically powered systems, including the low-altitude cabin ventilation system. After take-off Ryabonenko reported a cabin pressurisation failure. The problem was due to his faulty actions and the pressurisation system's operation was quickly restored when the proper switches were flipped.

• On 16th April 1982 yet another 1023rd TBAP Tu-95K was making a check-up flight with Maj. Bychkov as captain. At an altitude of 4,200 m (13,780 ft) tail gunner Ens. Simatov inexplicably removed the seal from the entry hatch emergency opening handle and moved it to 'open'. Realising his mistake, he promptly moved the handle back into the initial position, but too late – the hatch opened. The mission was aborted without any dramatic consequences.

• On 7th January 1984 a 40th TBAP Tu-95K captained by Maj. Zabegalov took off from Ookraïnka AB. As the aircraft climbed to 4,000 m (13,120 ft) the tail gunner reported that the pressure differential would not increase past 0.1 km/cm² (1.42 psi) and the mission was aborted. The problem was traced to a faulty valve.

• On 23rd March 1984 a 1023rd TBAP Tu-95KM captained by Maj. Bachev was topping up its fuel tanks en route. When the operation had been completed, tail gunner Ens. Fil'kovskiy reported that the fire extinguisher in the rear pressure cabin had 'fired'. The bomber descended to 4,200 m (13,780 ft) and the crew temporarily depressurised the rear cabin in order to ventilate it, whereupon the flight continued normally. The culprit was the tail gunner who had accidentally pushed the fire extinguisher actuating lever.

• On 28th September 1984 a 1226th TBAP Tu-95K captained by Pilot 1st Class Maj. V. A. Polozhiy was making a late night diversion to Zhana-Semey, its designated alternate airfield in Kazakhstan; its home base in Semipalatinsk had shut down due to below-minima weather. On final approach the aircraft dropped below the glideslope, the crew mistaking the bright lights at the side of a railway line for the runway lights; this error was corrected at the tower's commands but then the captain misjudged the flareout altitude and touched down too fast, nosewheels first with a vertical acceleration of 1.9 Gs. Due to the pilots' improper control inputs the landing was so rough that the aircraft bounced thrice and the fuselage snapped ahead of the wings after the third touchdown, the flight deck section separating; rearing up, the rest of the airframe became briefly airborne again before crashing to the left of the runway and bursting into flames. The two gunners in the rear pressure cabin were killed in the crash.

• On 16th April 1984 a 182nd TBAP Tu-95KM captained by Pilot 1st Class Maj. A. P. Boogayev was flying a training mission (a circuit of the airfield) at night. At the end of the downwind leg of the circuit a fire broke out in the rear pressure cabin. After trying unsuccessfully to tackle the blaze with portable fire extinguishers, tail gunner Ens. V. P. Filippov and commander of the ventral/dorsal gun positions Ens. N. N. Filovchenko bailed out at 400 m (1,310 ft) without notifying the captain, using a single parachute (!). Tragically, they let go of the harness when the parachute opened, falling to their death. Meanwhile, unaware of the fire, the pilots executed a normal landing. The crash rescue team put out the fire, and the aircraft returned to service after the charred rear pressure cabin had been replaced with a new one. The fire was probably caused by a short circuit – or by one of the gunners smoking in flight, in violation of the rules.

Tu-95K-22 '02 Red' collapsed its landing gear after veering off the runway at Ookraïnka AB on 16th November 1988. The aircraft was declared a write-off. Two AA-60(7310)-160.01 airfield crash tenders stand beside.

• On 18th January 1985 a 409th (?) TBAP Tu-95 captained by Maj. Belyayev was taking off on a formation flying practice mission when the rear cabin's entry hatch opened at 500 m (1,640 ft) two minutes after take-off. Investigation showed that the gunner (Ens. Sokolyuk) had opened the hatch on purpose in order to extract a strap which had become jammed by the hatch cover.

• On 28th February 1985 a 43rd TsBP i PLS Tu-95 (version unknown) captained by Pilot 2nd Class Capt. V. V. Klimov was returning to base after a training sortie. The inexperienced aircraft captain made a series of errors, touching down 30 km/h (18.6 mph) too fast and 14 m (46 ft) to the right of the centreline with a vertical acceleration of 1.6. After this the aircraft bounced twice, making contact with a vertical acceleration of 1.85 and 1.7 respectively. During the third touchdown the port main gear unit collapsed and the aircraft scraped the runway with the port wing, groundlooping through 120° and coming to rest on the runway shoulder. The port outer wing and Nos. 1 and 2 propellers were also damaged; the crew suffered no harm. Even though the pilot had obviously handled the machine roughly, it turned out that the main gear strut was defective, cracking along a welded joint. The aircraft was repaired.

• On 12th April 1985 a 1023rd TBAP Tu-95K captained by Maj. Koozin was following its designated route. 47 minutes after take-off tail gunner Ens. Abel'dinov reported in a sleepy voice that he was 'feeling all right'; his subsequent responses to queries over the intercom were jumbled. Descending to 4,000 m (13,120 ft), the captain aborted the mission. It turned out that the gunner had not fastened his oxygen mask properly; wishing to cool down the rear cabin a bit, he reduced the air flow and... fell asleep, feeling unwell when he woke up.

• Three days later a Tu-95K captained by Sniper Pilot Lt.-Col. I. P. Mal'tsev was landing at Ozyornoye AB after an exercise. It was a rainy night with a cloudbase at 500 m (1,640 ft) and a horizontal visibility of 4 km (2.5 miles). Even though the crew applied reverse thrust and brakes, the bomber overran the wet runway, collapsing the nose gear and suffering damage to all four propellers. The captain was held responsible.

• In early August 1985 a 182nd TBAP Tu-95K was flying a practice sortie involving a so-called tactical (simulated) launch of a Kh-20 missile over the Caspian Sea. When the Nav/Op completed the pre-launch sequence and pushed the simulated launch button, the aircraft was suddenly shaken by a heavy blow but remained controllable. Reporting a collision with an unidentified object, the crew proceeded to make a safe landing back at Mozdok – and only then was it seen that the missile was gone. It turned out that a technician performing maintenance on the Nav/Op's instrument panel had accidentally torn off the wiring to the launch buttons. To cover up his blunder, he soldered the wires back on – cross-wiring the simulated and live launch wires to the wrong buttons. The operation of the electric circuit was not checked befpre the flight. As a result, the missile was released inadvertently, pitching up and striking the aircraft's fuselage and No.2 propellers before crashing into the sea.

• On 12th October 1985 a 79th TBAP Tu-95K captained by Pilot 1st Class Maj. V. A. Sharnin was following its designated route at 8,350 m (27,400 ft) and 750 km/h (466 mph). It was a cloudy night, with a cloudbase at 1,000 m (3,280 ft) and a cloud top at 2.500 m (8,200 ft); horizontal visibility was 10 km (6.2 miles). 38 minutes after take-off from Ookraïnka AB, the navigator reported seeing a flash on one of the port engines. In fact, all four engines were running stably; yet, reacting to the navigator's hasty and erroneous report, the crew shut down the No.2 engine, followed ten seconds later by the No.1 engine, and feathered their propellers. Next, the captain began a descent in an effort to keep the aircraft from losing speed; as the altitude became too low for comfort he initiated a climb and pulled the machine up into a stalled position. As the aircraft 'fell through', the navigator bailed out, parachuting to safety; the other six crew members were killed when the Tu-95 hit the ground. Poor crew resources management was cited as the cause.

• On 4th February 1986 a 40th TBAP Tu-95K captained by Maj. Volodin was taking off on a training mission to check the piloting technique at maximum altitude. As the aircraft climbed to 80 m (260 ft) tail gunner Ens. Vasyuchenko reported that the rear cabin entry hatch had opened spontaneously. It turned out that the pressure in the pneumatic rams operating the hatch was too low; in spite of the tail gunner's report to this effect, the hatch had been shut but had failed to lock properly.

• On 13th February 1986 a 182nd TBAP Tu-95K captained by Capt. Tolmachov was flying a 'hi-lo-hi' mission. After descending to 1,500 m (4,920 ft) the crew depressurised the cabins; moreover, tail gunner Pvt. Yeskenin activated the low-altitude ram air ventilation system and forgot to deactivate it when the aircraft climbed again. He realised his mistake only when the aircraft had climbed to 8,000 m (26,250 ft); the mission had to be aborted.

• On 4th April 1986 a 79th TBAP Tu-95K captained by Maj. Avdeykin took off on a training mission. At 3,000 m (9,840 ft) tail gunner Pvt. Kaliyev reported that the rear cabin pressurisation system was totally out of order, with a zero pressure differential. At the captain's instructions the gunner switched on his pure oxygen supply, but as the machine reached 3,600 m (11,810 ft) he reported feeling unwell and the aircraft returned to base. As the machine descended, the gunner started feeling better; it transpired that he had forgotten to deactivate the low-altitude ram air ventilation system.

• On 17th June 1986 another Tu-95K from the same unit captained by Capt. Tool'skiy had to abort a mission when the pressurisation system failed. A defective shutoff valve was the cause this time.

• On 20th January 1987 one more 79th TBAP Tu-95K captained by Capt. Kondrat'yev was making a circuit of the airfield when tail gunner Pvt. Dyugai heard an unfamiliar sound and saw that the entry hatch had opened partially, with a gap of 20-30 cm (7⅞ to 11¹³⁄₁₆ in). Acting on the captain's instructions, the gunner shut off the air supply and re-closed the hatch which had not been locked properly before the mission.

• On 24th March 1987 a 40th TBAP Tu-95K captained by Maj. Chebykin was flying a mission. At 4,200 m (13,780 ft) the crew checked the operation of the emergency cabin depressurisation system; in so doing an air duct in the system came undone. Reporting this to the captain, the tail gunner reactivated the pressurisation system; the captain, however, did not advise ATC of the malfunction and carried on with the mission. As a result, the port side observation blister in the rear cabin cracked at 8,100 m (26,530 ft). The blame rested with the captain in this case.

• On 14th August 1987 a 79th TBAP Tu-95K captained by Maj. Potapov was flying a mission when tail gunner Pvt. Aleksandrov reported a failure of the cabin pressurisation system at 4,000 m (13,120 ft). Again, he had simply neglected to deactivate the low-altitude ram air ventilation system.

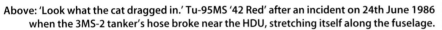

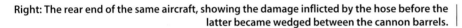

Above: 'Look what the cat dragged in.' Tu-95MS '42 Red' after an incident on 24th June 1986 when the 3MS-2 tanker's hose broke near the HDU, stretching itself along the fuselage.

Above right: A different incident of the same sort; this time the hose broke off from the drogue, which the bomber brought home without suffering any damage.

Right: The rear end of the same aircraft, showing the damage inflicted by the hose before the latter became wedged between the cannon barrels.

• On 15th September 1987 another Tu-95K from the same unit captained by Lt.-Col. Korelov had just climbed to 2,000 m (6,560 ft) when the rear cabin pressurisation system failed and the mission was aborted. In this case a valve had stuck in the closed position, putting the system out of action.

• On 24th December 1987 a 182nd TBAP Tu-95K (c/n 60802209) captained by the aforementioned Maj. A. P. Boogayev was flying an instrument flight rules training mission from Mozdok at night. The cloudbase was 220 m (720 ft) and horizontal visibility was 3 km (1.86 miles). Again, the mission was simply to make a circuit of the airfield. When the aircraft attained holding pattern altitude (400 m/1,310 ft), on the downwind leg of the circuit the flight engineer reported an icing warning and switched on the engine and propeller de-icing system at the captain's instructions. Too late – seconds later, the Nos. 3, 2 and 4 engines flamed out in quick succession after ingesting ice, their propellers feathering automatically. Reporting this to the tower, the captain ordered the crew to bail out; five of the crew followed his orders, parachuting to safety. Flying on one engine, the aircraft struggled on; extending the undercarriage and switching on the landing lights, the pilots attempted an off-field emergency landing. However, the attempt was unsuccessful; touching down in a ploughed field, the aircraft broke up, killing both pilots and the navigator.

• On 4th March 1988 a 409th (?) TBAP Tu-95 captained by Lt.-Col. Grechikhin had just taken off when, 15 minutes into the mission, the tail gunner reported that the rear cabin entry hatch had opened spontaneously. A check showed that the pressure in the actuating rams had dropped to zero and the mission was aborted. The blame rested with the gunner who had not closed the hatch properly.

• On 16th November 1988 a 79th TBAP Tu-95KM captained by Capt. Vikhrov was flying a 'hi-lo-hi' mission with an instructor running a proficiency check. During the initial climb the captain had ordered the crew to activate the pressurisation system; tail gunner Sgt (JG) Fabyanchuk twice reported his compliance. After climbing to 8,990 m (29,490 ft) the crew discovered that the MS-61 cockpit voice recorder had failed. Since the CVR was in the rear cabin, the captain ordered the tail gunner to check it and try to fix it, but there was no response. Yet, not until 2 hours 10 minutes later did the captain and the instructor realise the need to descend. When the aircraft landed at an alternate airfield, the gunner was already dead; his oxygen mask was off and the oxygen cock shut. There was evidence that the gunner had been smoking in flight and had deliberately shut off the oxygen supply in order to avoid a fire.

• On 16th November 1988 a 79th TBAP Tu-95KM captained by Pilot 1st Class Maj. A. A. Lopatkin was making a night landing after an 11-hour mission in the course of an exercise. Due to pilot error the aircraft deviated to the left from the runway centreline during the landing roll. In order to correct this the captain applied full right rudder and, thinking this was not enough, revved up the two port side engines, which ran counter to the flight manual. He overdid it; the aircraft yawed strongly to the right, crossing the runway centreline, and looked set to run off the runway. Now Lopatkin throttled back the port engines to ground idle and revved up the starboard engines instead. That only made matters worse; the Tu-95KM yawed to the left, slewing onto the runway shoulder, and slithered sideways, collapsing the starboard and nose gear units. No one was hurt but the aircraft was declared a write-off.

• On 26th February 2013 a Tu-95MS coded '21/2 Red' (c/n 64034200603), which was operated by the Russian Air Force's 43rd TsBP i PLS, was preparing to take off for a training sortie from Dyagilevo AB when a fire broke out in the forward pressure cabin. The crew promptly shut down the engines and evacuated the aircraft without injury. Fire-fighters were quick to arrive on the scene and extinguish the blaze, but not before it had burned a hole in the starboard side of the forward fuselage aft of the emergency exit. The investigation established that the fire had been caused by a short circuit in an electric distribution panel which had resulted from incorrect installation of the wiring during a recent scheduled overhaul. The latter, which was performed by the manufacturer (the Beriyev TANTK in Taganrog), had been completed on 28th December 2012 and the aircraft had logged only 24 flight hours since then.

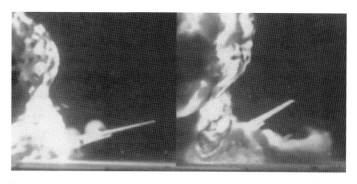

Stills from a video showing the fatal crash of Tu-95MS '05 Red'/ RF-94181 at Ookraïnka AB on 8th June 2015.

Upon careful examination and calculation of the costs the bomber was declared beyond economical repair, even though it had received a service life extension with 2,004 flight hours remaining that would have allowed it to remain operational for maybe another ten years. (By then this aircraft, which was manufactured in 1982, would have been 40 years old.) The investigation panel ordered that a fleetwide check of the electric distribution panel and the wiring in general be made on Russian Air Force Tu-95MSs (and apparently Russian Navy Tu-142s as well).

• On 8th June 2015 a Russian Air Force/6952nd AvB Tu-95MS ('05 Red'/RF-94181, c/n 1000213935765) was flying practice sorties from Ookraïnka AB with no missiles on board. At approximately 2300 hrs local time (1700 hrs Moscow time), when the aircraft was accelerating down runway 16 for another take-off, two explosions occurred in quick succession – a small explosion low down near the port main gear unit, followed a split second later by a powerful explosion in the port wing. The port main gear immediately collapsed; the aircraft banked, scraping the port wing along the runway, then groundlooped and burst into flames. WSO Aleksey Fedoseyev was killed instantly; the other six crewmembers scrambled from the wreckage but the aircraft's captain Maj. Sergey Gorshnev suffered severe burns over 75% of his body when an explosion doused him with burning fuel. After initial treatment at the local hospital in Belogorsk he was rushed to St. Petersburg in an ambulance aircraft for further treatment at the Military Medical Academy named after Semyon M. Kirov; still, despite all efforts so save his life, Gorshnev succumbed to his injuries on 4th August.

In the absence of official information from the Ministry of Defence, rumours as to the cause of the accident were circulated on the grapevine and in the media. Many cited an engine explosion as the most likely cause – probably without having seen the video of the crash which was filmed by a ground crewman, although a few crackpot conspiracy-mongers asserted that the bomber had been sabotaged by enemy agents (!). Not until a year later did the MoD disclose the real reason – improper maintenance. The port main gear bogie's oleo-pneumatic rocking damper had been charged incorrectly – apparently topped up with compressed air instead of pure nitrogen. During the last take-off the damper was excessively hot because only some 20 minutes had elapsed after the bomber's previous flight. When the Tu-95MS accelerated to 220-230 km/h (136-142 mph), the combination of high temperature and a high oxygen content caused the oil-air mixture to detonate, sending a fragment of the damper like a rocket through the lower panel of the No.2 fuel tank and triggering the second explosion.

• Of course Tu-95MS operations had been suspended after the 8th June accident pending investigation. Yet, no sooner had the grounding order been lifted than on 14th July 2015 the 6952nd AvB lost another Tu-95MS ('77 Red'/RF-94204, c/n 64034200854). The aircraft was flying a routine practice sortie at the Litovko target range – a specialised bomber and attack aviation practice range 60 km (37.2 miles) north of Khabarovsk – when three of the four engines (or, according to some reports, all four engines) quit unexpectedly. The captain sent a mayday call and ordered the crew to bail out; five of the seven crewmembers parachuted to safety but the captain and the co-pilot were killed when the Tu-95MS crashed in woodland near Ivankovtsy village in the Khabarovsk Territory at 1550 hrs local time (0950 hrs Moscow time). Analysis of the wreckage showed that the crash was caused by faulty valves in the fuel system which had closed of their own accord, cutting off the fuel supply.

Accidents and incidents involving naval *Bears* are listed below.

• On 20th July 1967 a Pacific Fleet/867th ODRAP Tu-95RTs (c/n 65MRTs 204) captained by Capt. Fakhtaurov (the wingman in a pair) suffered a failure of the No.4 engine during climb. The bewildered captain cound not control the situation and the aircraft stalled and crashed, killing the crew of seven. The captain of the lead aircraft, Maj. A. I. Igrevskiy, was held responsible for not giving the wingman proper instructions and removed from his post as squadron commander.

• On 5th (some sources say 15th) November 1969 a North Fleet/392nd ODRAP Tu-95RTs coded '24 Black' captained by Maj. N. N. Stepanenko had a flight incident, stalling on take-off and recovering at the last moment.

• On 15th January 1971 a sister ship from the same unit (c/n 67MRTs 401) crashed into the Barents Sea during a training sortie; again, all 12 occupants (captain Lt.-Col. Aleksey G. Rastyapin, co-pilot Capt. Pyotr A. D'yachko, navigator Maj. Ivan I. Babkin, co-navigator Lt. (SG) Rafkhat M. Yamalutdinov, Nav/Op Lt. Aleksey A. Osipov, flight engineer Capt. Yevgeniy A. Mikhaïlov, radio operator Capt. Leonid I. Kirichenko, ELINT operators Capt. Ghennadiy A. Shatalov and Lt. Pyotr R. Fyodorov, operator MSgt Nikolay I. Pilyugin, gunner MSgt Vladimir A. Pinchuk and defensive fire commander tail gunner Capt. Vladislav A. Pichoogin) were killed. Engine fire was suspected as the cause of the crash. Aleksey G. Rastyapin was a saeasoned pilot, but apparently he ended up in a situation when all his experience could not help.

The charred interior of the flight deck of Tu-95MS '21/2 Red' after the fire. The aircraft was declared a write-off.

The charred interior of the flight deck of Tu-95MS '21/2 Red' after the fire. The aircraft was declared a write-off.

• On 3rd September 1971 another 392nd ODRAP *Bear-D* (c/n 63MRTs 003) captained by the regiment's CO Col. Ivan F. Gladkov crashed at its home base, Kipelovo AB, in near-zero visibility. The crew had been involved in an unexpected special mission. At 1500 hrs local time, when the day's flying shift was drawing to a close, the unit unexpectedly received orders from the North Fleet Air Arm Commander to find a clearing in the pack ice near the North Pole where a Soviet nuclear-powered submarine could surface. According to the flight operations manual, in these conditions the crew could not fly without an eight-hour rest. Yet this was a highly important mission and orders had to be obeyed. Gladkov decided he would fly this mission.

The objective was completed, and when the aircraft was coming home at around 0400 hrs the airbase was wrapped in thick fog. The base's ATC shift supervisor Vladimir S. Melennyy (the unit's Deputy CO/Flight Training) informed the crew of this, instructing Gladkov to divert to Migalovo AB (a Military Transport Aviation base in Kalinin, now Tver') which was the alternate airfield. However, Gladkov requested permission to pass over the runway; the ATC shift supervisor gave the go-ahead but neglected to check the aircraft's position on the radarscope. Descending to 25-30 m (80-100 ft), the crew failed to spot the runway and began a go-around but as the aircraft commenced a turn at low altitude the starboard wing struck treetops and the No.4 engine flamed out. Moments later, the Tu-95RTs struck the ground and disintegrated, killing the crew – Gladkov, co-pilot Lt. Yuriy V. Domashnev, navigator Lt.-Col. Vitaliy I. Krooglov, Nav/Op Lt (SG) Vasiliy D. Pen'kovskiy, flight engineer Capt. Valentin I. Dodonov, instructor flight engineer Capt. Ivan S. Galayko, ELINT operators Lt (SG) Yuriy N. Khazov and Lt (SG) Stanislav M. Grigor'yev, GRO MSgt Valentin A. Karev, gunner MSgt Ivan F. Kritskiy and defensive fire commander SSgt Andrey A. Sorokin.

• In November 1972 one more 392nd ODRAP Tu-95RTs crash-landed at Havana-José Martí International airport (aka Rancho Bueros). As usual, a pair of *Bear-Ds* had been flying a reconnaissance mission over the Atlantic Ocean, outbound from Olen'ya AB; the lead aircraft was captained by Maj. Vladimir I. Doobinskiy, with Maj. A. Z. Khadartsev as his wingman. 17 hours later the pair approached Havana in the middle of a thunderstorm; to make matters worse, the navaids at Rancho Bueros were sorely inadequate, with only a VOR beacon (and on the wrong side of the runway at that). Doobinskiy landed safely but Khadartsev was late in spotting the runway; seeing that he was off course, he nevertheless continued the descent, making an S-turn at low altitude. In so doing the *Bear* struck the ground with the starboard wingtip and No.4 propeller, destroying both; fragments of the propeller blades punctured the fuselage. The local crash rescue team reacted quickly and the aircraft was saved from total destruction. Embarrassingly, the accident took place in full view of the passengers awaiting their flights from Havana.

• On 4th August 1976 one more 392nd ODRAP Tu-95RTs ('17 Black', c/n 66MRTs 304) captained by Pilot 2nd Class Maj. Arkadiy I. Krasnosel'skikh was redeploying from Havana to Olen'ya AB on the Kola Peninsula. At 2015 hrs Havana time, 6 hours 20 minutes after departure, the aircraft crashed into the Sargasso Sea 333-425 km (180-230 nm) from Newfoundland, killing the crew of seven (Maj. Arkadiy I. Krasnosel'skikh, co-pilot Capt. Fyodor Ye. Garynychev, navigator Capt.

The charred interior of the flight deck of Tu-95MS '21/2 Red' after the fire. The aircraft was declared a write-off.

The crash of the 392nd ODRAP Tu-95RTs captained by Col. Ivan F. Gladkov at Kipelovo AB on 3rd September 1971. The furrow in the ground and the pieces of fuselage skin visible in the top left photo show the direction of the aircraft's travel.

The burning remains of Gladkov's aircraft. Fire-fighters are working on the blaze.

Aleksandr F. Bychkov, flight engineer Capt. L. I. Skorokhodov, Lt. (SG) V. A. Poznyak, Lt. (SG) N. F. Vasil'yev, Lt. (SG) Ye. N. Lebedev, WO M. N. Trifonov, WO V. I. Gribalyov, WO A. I. Taranenko and cadet V. M. Kolibabchuk). A Soviet Navy task force despatched to the scene (the rescue vessels SNS *Aldan* and SNS *Vladimir Trefolev*, the tug SB-28, the tanker SNS *Doobna* and the passenger ship M/V *Adjaria*) managed to recover some body fragments, parts of the wreckage, including the MSRP-12 flight data recorder, and the 'ship's papers' from a depth of 43 m (141 ft). The crew was given a burial at sea with full military honours. The accident investigation panel established that the aircraft had stalled and entered a spin while climbing from 8,700 to 9,000 m (from 28,540 to 29,530 ft). The FDR readouts showed that the crew had tried to parry some external influence and that the aircraft had stalled when the vertical G load reached 1.8; subsequent attempts to recover from the spin were to no avail and the high G loads had negated any chance of bailing out. The most likely cause was that the aircraft had hit wake turbulence from an airliner cruising along an international airway some time earlier. However, some sources intimated that the Tu-95RTs may have been shot down by the Americans.

• Also on 4th August 1976 a 392nd ODRAP Tu-9RTs captained by Maj. Kolobov was damaged in a hard landing at Kipelovo AB but soon repaired.

Left: Photographed from an RCAF Canadair Argus, a Soviet Navy rescue vessel uses a diving bell to locate the wreckage of a Nort Fleet Tu-95RTs which crashed south-east of Newfoundland on 4th August 1976. Right: A fragment of the wing structure is lifted from the seabed.

• Two days later a North Fleet/76th OPLAP DD Tu-142 took off from Severomorsk-1 AB on a training mission involving a circuit of the airfield. Trainee pilot Lt. Vladimir M. Khazagerov was the pilot in command, with instructor Pilot 1st Class Maj. Vladimir P. Morozov in the right-hand seat; the crew included Capt. M. A. Basimov, Capt. Vladimir P. Popov, Capt. Pyotr V. Khavkunov, Lt. Ivan I. Pidroochnyy and Ens. Sirotin. A malfunction occurred in the course of the flight and the crew decided to abort the mission. Landing 30-40 km/h (18.6-24.8 mph) too fast, the aircraft suddenly veered to starboard 740 m (2,430 ft) from the touchdown point at 280 km/h (174 mph). After travelling another 540 m (1,770 ft) along the runway verge the Tu-142 went into a huge bomb crater that had been there since World War II and came apart. The crater was filled with water and the forward fuselage sank. Khavkunov and Pidroochnyy drowned, failing to extricate themselves from the wreckage in time; Popov, Basimov and Sirotin were killed by the impact.

• On 10th April 1978 (some sources say 10th January 1978!) a pair of Pacific Fleet/304th ODRAP Tu-95RTs aircraft took off from Khorol' AB on a night mission in support of a spacecraft launch. The lead aircraft was captained by Lt.-Col. A. A. Grechko, the other *Bear-D* (c/n 65MRTs 106) by Pilot 1st Class Maj. G. P. Veyshnarovich. The weather was poor; at 8,400 m (27,560 ft), having encountered a storm front over the Pacific Ocean with a cloud top at 8,500 m (27,890 ft), Grechko decided to climb and instructed Veyshnarovich to follow suit. Five minutes later, however, radio contact with the wingman was lost. A search and rescue effort turned up nothing more than an empty MLAS-1 one-man life raft. None of the ten occupants of the aircraft was ever found.

• In the autumn of 1983 a pair of North Fleet/135th PLAP Tu-142Ms were damaged in a ground collision at Kipelovo AB when a taxying aircraft ran into another due to faulty brakes.

• On 25th January 1984 a North Fleet/392nd ODRAP Tu-95RTs coded '27 Black' and captained by Maj. V. K. Vymyatnin crashed immediately after take-off from Olen'ya AB on the Kola Peninsula, bound for Cuba. It was a cloudy day, with an ambient temperature of −17°C (+1.4°F). 1 minute 55 seconds after lift-off the crew prematurely retracted the landing gear and flaps at 346 km/h (215 mph) and an altitude of 350 m (1,150 ft). The aircraft's CG was too far aft at 24.55% MAC (the maximum permitted aft position was 24.5%); gear retraction caused it to shift further aft and the

The half-submerged wreckage of Vladimir Khazagerov's Tu-142 (76th OPLAP) in a flooded bomb crater at Kipelovo AB on 6th August 1976; the severed rear fuselage is lying on the edge of the crater.

angle of attack began increasing to a critical value. Not recognising the danger of the situation, the pilots took no corrective action and eventually the *Bear* stalled and spun into the ground, falling like a leaf with alternating bank angles up to 60° and a vertical speed of 25 m/sec (82 ft/sec) at the moment of impact. The crew of ten (V. K. Vymyatnin, Yu. M. Filippov, A. P. Krivonos, Ye. V. Zotikov, Yu. K. Pigalitsyn, V. P. Vasil'yev, R. A. Kuznetsov, F. F. Khalyapov, A. G. Lysakov and V. N. Kopylov) was killed outright.

• Three months later, on 20th April 1984, a pair of Pacific Fleet/310th OPLAP DD Tu-142s took off from Kamennyy Ruchey AB on a maximum-range training flight over a remote ocean area. 1 hour 15 minutes into the mission, when the pair was cruising over the Sea of Okhotsk at 7,200 m (23,620 ft) and 730 km/h (453 mph), an emergency developed. One of the *Bear-Fs* captained by Pilot 1st Class Col. V. I. Zoobkov started losing altitude, trailing black smoke and a pall of white mist from the starboard wing. One minute later, flames erupted and the stricken aircraft entered a descending spiral to the right with bank angles up to 60-70°, crashing into the sea and exploding. None of the nine crew members (Col. V. I. Zoobkov, Lt. (SG) V. I. Taran, Lt.-Col. A. V. Kootya, Capt. V. N. Loskutov, Lt. V. A. Bochanov, Capt. S. N. Borovkov, Capt. A. Ya. Latsis, WO I. T. Bobrovskiy and Maj. V. V. Gridnev) managed to bail out, presumably because the aircraft was pulling negative G at the time. The 'black boxes' rested in deep water and were not found, making it impossible to determine the cause of the crash. Catastrophic failure and fire of the No.3 engine was cited as the most probable cause.

• On 13th February 1985 a pair of Pacific Fleet/169th SAP *Bear-Ds* took off from Cam Ranh AB (Vietnam) on a night sortie that took them along the coast of the South China Sea. The weather was poor. Just over six hours after take-off Pilot 1st Class Maj. Sergey D. Krivenko, the captain of the lead Tu-95RTs, radioed to his wingman that he was aborting the mission and taking a short cut back to Cam Ranh – without explaining why. 50 minutes later, cruising 15 km (9.3 miles) behind and 300 m (990 ft) above the lead aircraft, the crew of the wingman watched the other machine move vigorously to starboard and start descending; next, they heard a garbled radio transmission: *'We're going down! We're going down! Anybody hear us? We're go…'* Nobody saw the actual moment of the crash because the stricken aircraft dived into thick overcast with a cloud top at 2,000 m (6,560 ft). The crew of nine (Maj. Sergey D. Krivenko, Capt. V. V. Komarov, Capt. V. M. Ivanov, Lt. (SG) V. S. Serebryakov, Capt. A. M. Abuhadjiyev, WO V. V. Kantsevan, WO A. I. Below, WO A. A. Zakharov and WO V. M. Sidorkin) did not attempt to bail out and perished. The crash was most probably caused by an engine failure and attendant failure of the propeller feathering system, the strong drag causing the aircraft to lose control.

• On 15th April 1985 a North Fleet/392nd ODRAP Tu-95RTs ('12 Black', c/n unknown) captained by Maj. A. M. Bobrov was returning to Kipelovo AB from a mission over the Atlantic Ocean. The aircraft was 15 km (9.3 miles) out when the Nos. 4 and 3 engines failed with an interval of six or seven seconds on final approach to runway 17. Dipping 100 m (330 ft) below the glide path, the aircraft yawed to starboard, finding itself 1,000 m (3,280 ft) off the desired track, and made a go-around. On the second try, landing at higher-than-usual speed (as required by the flight manual in such cases), the Tu-95 bounced twice, then veered off the runway onto the left shoulder, collapsing the nose gear, and came to a halt with the nose amid a belt of trees. The crew, which included co-pilot V. Stepanov and navigator V. N. Borodayev, escaped unhurt but the aircraft was declared a total loss.

The port wing of a Tu-142MK damaged in a collision in the autumn of 1983.

Below and bottom: Three views of the crash site of 392nd ODRAP Tu-95RTs '27 Black' which stalled after take-off from Olen'ya AB on 25th January 1984.

Top left: 392nd ODRAP Tu-95RTs '12 Black' captained by Maj. A. M. Bobrov after overrunning at Kipelovo on 15th April 1985.

Above left: The bent Nos. 1 and 2 propellers on Bobrov's aircraft.

Top: The nose of Tu-95RTs '12 Black' snapped off when the nose gear collapsed.

Above: The severed extreme nose of Bobrov's Tu-95RTs recovered from the crash site; part of the flight deck roof with eyebrow windows is seen on the left.

Headless bear – the same aircraft after evacuation from the crash site; the extent of the damage is evident and repair was out of the question. Note the inner wing leading edge panels hinged open for access to the piping and wiring inside.

• On 25th August 1986 one more Pacific Fleet/304th ODRAP Tu-95RTs (identity unknown) captained by Maj. S. A. Stolyarov was taking off from Vladivostok-Knevichi airport, which is also a military base. 2 minutes 47 seconds after the aircraft became airborne a control system failure occurred at an altitude of 500 m (1,640 ft) and a speed of 470 km/h (292 mph). An uncommanded rudder hardover to port caused by a faulty trim tab actuator led the aircraft to bank to port with an increasing roll rate, losing altitude as it did. The pilots applied opposite aileron input and hauled back on the control columns but to no avail. The *Bear-D* impacted 10 km (6.2 miles) beyond the runway threshold in a 70° nose-down attitude with 80° left bank and exploded. ECM equipment operator Ens. Zvyagintsev managed to bail out at 200-250 m (650-820 ft) and survived; he 'abandoned ship' of his own accord because the captain had not had time to order the crew to bail out – the emergency developed all too fast. The other ten occupants were killed.

• On 13th October 1987 a Pacific Fleet/310th OPLAP DD Tu-142 captained by Capt. Razumov could not rotate on take-off due to a worn-out push-pull rod in the control system. The take-off was aborted but the aircraft overran 375 m (1,230 ft) into a ravine, collapsing the nose gear. The aircraft was declared to be a write-off.

• On 18th January 1989 a North Fleet/135th PLAP DD Tu-142M ('81 Black') captained by Maj. Anatoliy A. Zoobkov was damaged when a faulty de-icing system caused fuel vapours in an empty port outer wing tank to explode in flight, blowing a hole in the wing skin. The aircraft rolled and yawed strongly to port; luckily the pilots managed to regain control, bringing the aircraft back to Kipelovo AB for a safe landing. For their bravery and good airmanship the crew was duly rewarded: Zoobkov was awarded the Red Banner Order, while co-pilot Capt. Yevgeniy M. Kornev, flight engineer Capt. Aimatdin S. Islamov and navigator Lt. (SG) Vladimir A. Mikhaïlov received the Combat Service Medal. The port outer wing was removed and taken to Taganrog for repairs in an An-22 transport, after which it was reinstalled and the aircraft returned to service.

Damage to the No.3 propeller of a 392nd ODRAP Tu-95RTs caused by ingesting the tanker's drogue during a refuelling session.

• In February 1989 a North Fleet/135th PLAP Tu-142M captained by Lt.-Col. Mel'nikov suffered a landing gear malfunction on approach to Kipelovo AB – the starboard main unit would not extend. Landing at night on a slippery runway, the pilots tried a touch and go – and succeeded in shaking the main gear strut loose, landing normally.

• In May 1993 a pair of Russian Navy 135th PLAP Tu-142Ms captained by Galiullin and Komarov were due to fly a mission from Kipelovo AB. Galiullin took off normally but Komarov aborted the take-off when a back-up artificial horizon failed at the line-up point. Requesting permission to vacate the runway at taxiway 1 and forgetting that the inboard engines were running at 36% power, the pilots revved up the outer engines to the same setting and released the brakes. The aircraft picked up speed rapidly, reaching 216 km/h (134 mph) halfway down the runway, and the navigator shouted in alarm, realising the speed was way too high. The pilots throttled back the inboard engines (forgetting the outer engines) and slammed on the brakes, trying to negotiate the intersection with the taxiway. Luckily the co-pilot had forgotten to set the nose gear steering switch back from 'take-off/landing' to 'taxi' setting and the machine went off the runway and sank into the soggy ground, sustaining only minor damage. Had the nose gear been set to large steering angles, the fully fuelled aircraft would have gone smack into a concrete building – with obvious results.

• On 6th November 2009 a Russian Navy (Pacific Fleet/568th GvOSAP) Tu-142MZ coded '55 Red' (c/n 0604175, f/n unknown) took off from Kamennyy Ruchey AB on a routine practice sortie over the Sea of Japan. The aircraft was captained by Maj. Vadim Ye. Kapkin; the crew of 11 also included co-pilot Capt. Aleksey S. Timofeyev, navigator Lt. (SG) Pavel N. Cholak, the ASW Squadron's Chief Navigator Maj. Aleksey Ye. Ablonskiy, WSO Lt. Artyom V. Blank, systems operators Warrant Officer Senior Grade Valeriy V. Voronkov and WO (SG) Andrey V. Fefilov, chief flight technician Capt. Konstantin A. Sholokhov, flight engineer Capt. Sergey

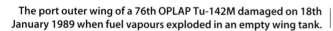

The port outer wing of a 76th OPLAP Tu-142M damaged on 18th January 1989 when fuel vapours exploded in an empty wing tank.

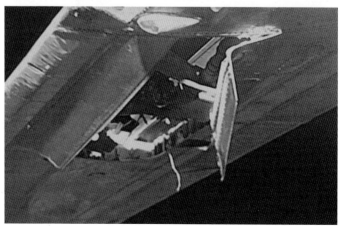

A 135th PLAP Tu-142MK after running off the runway at Kipelovo onto soggy ground during an aborted take-off in May 1993. Note the damage to the No.2 propeller spinner.

A. Goolyayev, gunner WO (SG) Nikolay S. Palamar and maintenance technician Lt. Yevgeniy V. Dolgov. At 1417 hrs Moscow time (2117 hrs local time), when the aircraft was coming in to land, the crew requested permission to turn onto the base leg of the landing pattern, whereupon radio contact was lost and the aircraft's blip vanished from the radarscopes of air defence and air traffic control radars. At that time '55 Red' was 24 km (14.91 miles) out, flying over the Strait of Tartary at 1,200 m (3,940 ft).

(It should be noted that one account of the crash, citing the RIA Novosti news agency as a source, says that radio contact was lost at 1700 hrs Moscow time (which equals midnight in Khabarovsk). In that case 1417 hrs may have been the time of departure – a three-hour sortie seems plausible.)

A large-scale search and rescue operation was mounted immediately, initially using tugboats from the seaport of Vanino and the rail ferries M/V *Sakhalin-9* and M/V *Sakhalin-10* plying the Vanno-Kholmsk line to Sakhalin Island, in the hope that the Tu-142MZ had ditched and the crew had used the rescue dinghy. Aviation joined the action in the morning, including a Mil' Mi-8 helicopter from Kamennyy Ruchey AB, an IL-38 from the 568th GvOSAP's ASW Squadron and a Beriyev Be-200ChS amphibian from the Far Eastern Regional Centre of the Russian Ministry for Civil Aid and Protection (EMERCOM of Russia) based at Khabarovsk-Tsentral'nyy AB. So did the Pacific Fleet's Type 537 rescue vessel RNS *Alagöz* equipped with the underwater drones 'Tiger' and 'Obzor'. Flotsam and jetsam pertaining to the missing aircraft, including fragments of bodies, were first discovered on 9th November and taken to Kamennyy Ruchey AB. Large pieces of wreckage were detected on the seabed on 25th December; the Tu-142MZ had crashed in the Strait of Tartary off Point Sading, some 15-20 km (9.3-12.4 miles) from the shore, with no survivors.

Foul weather and heavy seas caused an interruption in the search and recovery effort, which resumed in the spring of 2010; among other things, the 'black boxes' were retrieved in reasonably good condition and sent to Moscow for decoding. Various causes of the crash were considered, including hardware failure and birdstrike, but the final report released in the spring of 2011 placed the blame with the crew, citing the human factor as the main cause.

• A case is on record (the date of the accident is unknown) when a North Fleet/76th OPLAP DD Tu-142M captained by Maj. Bulgakov made a crash landing after the port main gear unit failed to lock down and all attempts to extend it proved fruitless. As the speed bled off, the aircraft banked to port, scraping the runway with the port wing and catching fire. Unbelievably, the base's crash rescue team was totally unprepared – the foam tenders did not even have water in their tanks. The crew jumped to safety and then attacked the blaze with portable fire extinguishers and earth; more personnel came to the aid and the fire was extinguished. After a lengthy investigation the aircraft was eventually deemed repairable. The port wing was sourced from the first prototype Tu-142 which was flown to Kipelovo for the occasion, and the repair effort took a full year.

• The history of the North Fleet's 392nd ODRAP included an unusual episode involving a Tu-95RTs captained by the aforementioned Vladimir S. Melennyy (unfortunately the source does not specify the date). The aircraft was making a positioning flight from Olen'ya AB, where it had made a refuelling stop after a sortie over the Atlantic Ocean, to Kipelovo AB when the dorsal observation/sighting blister cracked and popped off at 7,000 m (22,965 ft) and 700 km/h (435 mph). The forward pressure cabin decompressed instantly and dorsal gunner/radio operator Vyacheslav Arsen'yev, who sat under the blister, was nearly sucked out of the aircraft; he was saved by his seat harness which snagged his foot. WSO Lev A. Frolkin jumped from his seat and grabbed hold of the gunner's legs, but that was all he could do – he could not overpower the slipstream tugging at the hapless man. Realising what had happened, Melennyy ordered the co-pilot to take the controls, ran over and pulled Arsen'yev back in with a single jerk. Flying to Kipelovo AB was out of the question and the Tu-95RTs made an emergency landing at Severomorsk-1 AB. The gunner had been stripped to the waist by the slipstream and had suffered a severe frostbite – the ambient temperature was –50°C (–58°F). Nevertheless, after lengthy hospital treatment in Leningrad he returned to active duty.

World records held by the Tu-95/Tu-142					
Date	Aircraft	FAI class/group	Crew	Description	Result
26-9-1989	Tu-95MS	C-1q, Group 2	Lev V. Kozlov Sergey S. Popov G. P. Mal'tsev Pyotr P. Merzlyakov	Speed with payload (0/1,000/2,000/5,000/10,000/15,000/20,000/25,000/30,000 kg; 0/2,204/4,409/11,023/22,045/33,068/44,091/55,114/66,137 lb) over a 1,000-km (621-mile) closed circuit	816.25 km/h (506.98 mph; 441.21 kts)
26-9-1989	Tu-95MS	C-1p, Group 2	Vladimir Ye. Mosolov Ivan A. Chalov Yaroslav I. Koshitskiy Aleksandr G. Bezhenaru	as above	807.37 km/h (501.47 mph; 436.41 kts)
27-9-1989	Tu-95MS	C-1q, Group 2	Vyacheslav N. Gorelov Mikhail I. Pozdnyakov V. N. Neretin P. I. Petrov	Speed with payload (0/1,000/2,000/5,000/10,000/15,000/20,000/25,000/30,000 kg; 0/2,204/4,409/11,023/22,045/33,068/44,091/55,114/66,137 lb) over a 2,000-km (1,242-mile) closed circuit	813.13 km/h (505.049 mph; 439.52 kts)
28-9-1989	Tu-95MS	C-1p, Group 2	Viktor D. Naïmooshin Sergey D. Osipov F. A. Ivlev V. A. Zolotaryov	as above	834.82 km/h (518.52 mph; 451.25 kts)
5-10-1989	Tu-95MS	C-1q, Group 2	Yuriy M. Kabanov V. V. Alfyorov	Altitude with payload (0/1,000/2,000/5,000 kg; 0/2,204/4,409/11,023 lb)	10,823 m (35,508 ft)
5-10-1989	Tu-8895MS	C-1p, Group 2	Igor' G. Malyshev Mikhail M. Bashkirov V. Ye. Yegorov	as above	12,265 m (40,239 ft)
10-10-1989	Tu-95MS	C-1q, Group 2	Konstantin I. Pripooskov Vitaliy D. Baskakov	Speed with payload (0/1,000/2,000/5,000/10,000/15,000/20,000 kg; 0/2,204/4,409/11,023/22,045/33,068/44,091 lb) over a 5,000-km (3,105-mile) closed circuit	785.3 km/h (487.65 mph; 424.48 kts)
11-10-1989	Tu-95MS	C-1p, Group 2	Valeriy R. Smelov Igor' G. Malyshev	Speed with payload (0/1,000/2,000/5,000 kg; 0/2,204/4,409/11,023 lb) over a 5,000-km (3,105.5-mile) closed circuit	786.1 km/h (488.26 mph; 424.92 kts)
31-10-1989/ 1-11-1989	Tu-95MS	C-1q, Group 2	Vladimir I. Pavlov Naïl' Sh. Sattarov A. S. Tsarakhov A. A. Oschchepkov	Speed with payload (0/1,000/2,000 kg; 0/2,204/4,409 lb) over a 10,000-km (621-mile) closed circuit	647.89 km/h (402.41 mph; 350.21 kts)
3-5-1990	Tu-142LL	C-1p	Aleksandr A. Artyukhin Valeriy F. Van'shin V. N. Sedov V. M. Donskov	a) Time to height (6,000/9,000 m; 19,685/29,527 ft) b) Sustained altitude	4 min 23 sec/ 6 min 3.5 sec 12,520 m (41,076 ft)
16-11-1990	Tu-142M	C-1q, Group 2	V. K. Nikolayev Ye. S. Kobyakov A. G. Tsiberkin	Altitude with payload (25,000/30,000 kg; 55,114/66,137 lb)	10,110 m (33,169 ft)
23-11-1990	Tu-142M	C-1p, Group 2	Mikhail M. Bashkirov V. V. Samorodov E. A. Looshnikov	as above	11,410 m (37,434 ft)
23-11-1990	Tu-142M	C-1p, Group 2	V. V. Alfyorov V. K. Nikolayev N. V. Vydrin	Altitude with payload (10,000/15,000/20,000 kg; 22,045/33,068/44,091 lb)	12,240 m (40,157 ft)
28-11-1990	Tu-142M	C-1q Group 2	Viktor A. Bobylyov Yu. P. Makarov A. A. Shishka	as above	11,100 m (36,417 ft)

Index